To my wife Glyn with all my love

DS
26.02.08

Employment Law

Sixth Edition

Tom Harrison

BA (Hons), Grad Cert Ed, LLM (London)

Senior Lecturer in Law New College Durham
Visiting Tutor in Employment Law at Durham University

Business Education Publishers Limited

ISBN 1 901888 47 9
ISBN 978 1 901888 47 8

Cover Design Murphy Creative Ltd

First Published 1990
  Reprinted 1992
Second Edition 1995
Third Edition 1997
Fourth Edition 2000
Fifth Edition 2003
Sixth Edition 2006

Published in Great Britain by
Business Education Publishers Limited
The Teleport
Doxford International
Sunderland
Tyne & Wear
SR3 3XD

Tel: 0191 5252410
Fax: 0191 5201815

British Cataloguing-in-Publications Data
A catalogue record for this book is available from the British Library

Printed in Great Britain by Athenaeum Press, Gateshead

Table of Contents

Chapter 3   Employment Relationships

Chapter 4   Establishing the Contract of Employment

Chapter 5   Changing Contractual Arrangements

Chapter 6   Equal Opportunity Law

Chapter 7   Work/Life Balance

Chapter 8   Health and Safety at Work

Chapter 9 Statutory Employment Rights and Continuity of Employment

Chapter 10 The Termination of Employment

Chapter 11 Unfair Dismissal

Chapter 12 Redundancy

Preface

The primary aim of the text remains to produce a text book which gives a thorough treatment of the subject in a readable and accessible style for individuals responsible for human resource functions and students of employment law in higher education. Now in its sixth edition, I have attempted to structure the book in such a way that the subject is a manageable unit of study over a full academic year or a single semester. In my experience of teaching students who are law business and management undergraduates, the breadth of employment law necessarily requires the teacher to make decisions about the input and the degree of emphasis of material from each of the 12 chapters.

The task of explaining this complex and dynamic subject is a challenging one and while I do occasionally comment on my view of the law, in the main I have left it to the law teacher to set the subject in context. There is inevitably a growing body of text and reluctantly I have decided to omit some case-law in favour of more recent authorities. Once again the text does rely heavily on case-law, and hopefully I have chosen wisely. I am aware of the fact that many students do not have access to source material and consequently I have included numerous cases and statutory provisions with supporting explanations. It should be a fundamental aim of an employment law course to encourage students to approach source material with confidence and recognise how it is applied in the resolution of conflict. As the sole author I must take responsibility for any errors. The fact that Monty no longer appears on the back cover of the book in his father's favourite shirt is solely due to the fact that the publisher is based in Sunderland.

For ease of expression the book adopts the practice of using 'he' for 'he or she' and 'his' for 'his and hers'.

Acknowledgement

I would like to thank Moira Page for her patience and skill in designing and typesetting this book.

The law is stated as at 1 March 2006

TH
Durham
April 2006

Table of Cases

B

C

D

E

F

G

H

I

J

K

L

M

Q

R

S

T

U

V

W

X

Y

Z

Table of Statutes, Statutory Instruments and Treaties

Chapter 1

Sources of Employment Law

Any introduction to the subject of employment law must necessarily include a consideration of where the law comes from and the legal institutions where it is applied and interpreted. Consequently there are two introductory chapters before we consider rules of substantive employment law. Chapter 1 is devoted to the various sources of employment law and Chapter 2 to the role of courts and tribunals and other agencies involved in the administration of employment law. These Chapters are particularly important if you are new to the study of law and legal institutions.

Chapter 1 then will include an exploration of the various sources of employment law, both National and European, and a consideration of the legal framework in which the law is applied. Here an attempt is made to identify the modern sources of employment law with particular emphasis on the increasing impact of European legislation. The fundamental aim of the book is to explore rights and responsibilities in relation to individual employment law, and exclude the collective position relating to trade unions which is now regarded as a distinct legal subject. The impact of collective bargaining by trade unions and health and safety law[1] has direct impact on the individual worker and are appropriate topics for inclusion in this book.

Modern Sources of Employment Law

A major source of UK law is of course statute, and in the field of employment law there has been an increasing tendency for contemporary governments to legislate. A serious student of employment law must be prepared to recognise that many of the legal rules are to be found within numerous statutory provisions of relatively recent origin. The most significant is still a consolidating Act passed in relation to individual employment rights, the Employment Rights Act 1996. This Act has of course been substantially amended, in particular by the Employment Relation Act 1999 and the Employment Act 2002[2]. In addition there is

---

1. See Chapter 8
2. Also The Work and Families Bill 2006

widespread legislation on equal opportunity law including sex, race, disability, sexuality and religious belief discrimination and from October 2006 age discrimination.

The table below identifies some of the main statutory rights, their statutory source and the individuals protected including employees, workers, and contractors.

Table of Key Statutory Employment Rights		
Statutory Right	**Statutory Source**	**Individuals Protected**
Not to suffer discrimination in recruitment and employment on the grounds of race, sex, disability religion, sexuality and in 2006, age.	Sex Discrimination Act 1975. Race Relations Act 1976. Equal Treatment Directive. Disability Discrimination Act 1995. Employment Equality (Age) (Sexuality) (Religious Belief) Regulations.	Full-time and part-time employees. Contractors providing personal services. Individuals attempting to secure employment.
To be provided with a safe working environment.	The Health and Safety at Work Act 1974. The Health and Safety (Work Place) Regulations 1992.	Full-time and part-time employees. Contractors providing personal services.
To have a written statement of employment terms. To have an itemised pay statement. Not to suffer unlawful deductions. To receive maternity, paternity, parental and adoption leave and to request flexible working where appropriate. To be given time off for union activities, public duties, dependents, antenatal care etc.	The Employment Rights Act 1996 as amended by Employment Relations Act 1999 and the Employment Act 2002.	Full-time and part-time employees.
To have preferential status against an insolvent employer.	Insolvency Act 1986.	Full-time and part-time employees.
Not to suffer discrimination in recruitment and employment on the grounds of Trade Union Membership or activities.	The Trade Union and Labour Relations (Consolidation) Act 1992.	Full-time and part-time employees.
To be paid a minimum wage and to work a limited number of hours with paid annual leave.	The National Minimum Wage Act 1998. The Working Time Regulations 1998.	Workers.
Not to be unfairly dismissed. To be paid a redundancy payment where appropriate. To notice on the termination of employment. To receive a written statement of the reasons for dismissal where appropriate.	The Employment Rights Act 1996 as amended by the Employment Relations Act 1999 and Employment Act 2002. Employment Act 2002 (Dispute Resolution) Regulations 2004.	Full-time and part-time employees who have one years continuous service with the same employer (subject to exceptions).
Not to suffer a detriment or be dismissed for revealing a protected disclosure.	Public Interest (Disclosure) Act 1998.	Workers.
Not to be subjected to degrading treatment, to have freedom of association and respect for private life.	Human Rights Act 1998	Employees, contractors and workers.

Delegated legislation

While primary legislation is a major source of employment law, many Statutes contemplate further law making by means of delegated legislation. Numerous Statutory Instruments contain a multitude of Regulations which have the force of law, and provide a convenient means of amending previous statutory provisions. Significant changes to the law may be introduced by Regulation.

Originally the Disability Discrimination Act 1995[3] applied only to employers with twenty or more employees. Now following the Disability Discrimination Act (Amendment) Regulations 2003 from 1 October 2004 all employers are covered by the legislation.

Under the Unfair Dismissal and Statement of Reasons for Dismissal (Variation of Qualifying Period) Order 1999 the qualifying period for unfair dismissal rights was lowered from two years to one year's continuous employment.[4] As a consequence from June 1999 the number of employees who qualify for unfair dismissal rights was dramatically increased.

The National Minimum Wage Regulations 1999 put the meat on the bone of the National Minimum Wage Act 1998.[5] The Part-Time Workers (Prevention of Less Favourable Treatment) Regulations 2000 confers significant rights on part-time workers in relation to pay, maternity, pensions and time off.[6]

It has become an increasingly popular though disconcerting practice for our legislators to pass primary legislation which does little more than provide regulatory powers to the Secretary of State to incorporate the law in Regulations. The Employment Relations Act 1999 is an excellent example of an amending statute which provides that regulation will constitute the primary form of enactment. Even at this point in the text you may appreciate some of the changes introduced by the 1999 Act in particular the raising of the maximum compensatory award for unfair dismissal and the removal of the ability for employers to require employees on fixed term contracts to opt out of unfair dismissal rights. The Employment Act 2002 significantly amends the law relating to maternity leave and introduces a number of new rights such as paternity , adoption leave, and the right to request flexible working. Again however this statute is supported by numerous Regulations which contain the detail of these rights.[7]

Later in the chapter we will focus on how Statutory Instruments may be used to incorporate European Community legislation into the domestic law of the United Kingdom. The Transfer of Undertaking (Protection of Employment) Regulations 2006 are intended to give effect to obligations which arose under EC Acquired Rights Directive 2001. Also the Equal Pay (Amendment) Regulations 1983 amended the Equal Pay Act of 1970 to bring it into line with Article 119 of the Treaty of Rome and the Equal Pay Directive of 1975. The Working Time Regulations 1999 were enacted to give effect to the Working Time Directive.

---

3. See Chapter 6
4. Increased from one year to two years 1985
5. See Chapter 9 Statutory Rights
6. See Chapter 7 Worklife Balance
7. See Chapter 7

Codes of Practice

Statutes and Statutory Instruments are only enacted of course after undergoing a strict parliamentary process. It should not be necessary in a book of this nature to examine the Parliamentary process for the passage of legislation. It would however be a useful exercise to briefly describe the process involved in the passage of European Community law and its legal status, with which you may be less familiar. In addition, draft Codes of Practice require the approval of both Houses of Parliament and only come into effect on such date as the Secretary of State appoints

Codes of Practice have an increasingly important role in the regulation of employment relationships and industrial relations generally. Their primary function is to provide guidance to employers, employers' associations, workers, and trade unions with the aim of improving industrial relations. While a failure to observe the provision of a code of practice does not of itself make a person liable to legal proceedings before a court or tribunal, compliance or non compliance with a code is admissible in evidence. Codes of Practice may emanate from the Secretary of State for Employment who has produced codes on picketing, closed shop agreements, and trade union industrial action balloting. In addition, other agencies have authority to issue codes, including the Advisory, Conciliation and Arbitration Service, (ACAS) the Commission for Racial Equality, the Equal Opportunities Commission and the Health and Safety Commission.[8]

A good example of a significant code of practice is the ACAS Code on Disciplinary Practices and Procedures 2000. An employment tribunal is entitled to use the code as a bench mark when considering the fairness of the employer's conduct in reaching the conclusion to dismiss someone. The Employment Appeal Tribunal held in *Lock v. Cardiff Rail Co. Ltd.* 1998 that a train conductor had been unfairly dismissed when his employer relied on a one-off error of judgment. Such a decision to dismiss did not accord with the code of practice which provides for warnings and counselling in such circumstances and was as a consequence found to be unfair.

The Common Law and Statutory Interpretation

While it would be tempting to believe that a broad knowledge of the numerous statutory provisions in relation to employment law is all that is needed to acquire a sound understanding of the subject, such a notion is far from the truth. Many areas of employment law are governed by common law principles embodied within judicial precedent. In the following chapters you will discover that the nature and content of the primary legal instrument that regulates employment relationship, the contract of employment, is determined by applying principles of common law developed and refined in case law. The termination of employment is also largely governed by common law principles as is civil redress in relation to health and safety at work. The common law is continually developed and refined by the courts. The law of contract is embodied within the common law and so it is only by applying common law principles in relation to the implication of terms into contracts that the precise nature of a contract of employment can be appreciated.[9]

---

8. See later in the chapter
9. See Chapter 4 Establishing of the Contract of Employment

Contract law

A recent interpretation of contract law in the Court of Appeal will serve as an example of the relevance of the common law. It is a fundamental element of the law of contract that verbal promises that are intended to have legal consequences will have contractual effect. There is also a common law inference that promises made in a business context are presumed to have been intended to be legally binding. The difficulty facing the Court of Appeal in *Judge v. Crown Leisure* 2005 was determining the legal impact of a promise made by a senior manager to the claimant at a Christmas party, a junior operations manager. The promise related to salary increases within the organisation, in particular the intention to bring the salaries of all operational managers, including the claimant, in line. Subsequent letters by the senior manager referred to the verbal promise that he had made and when two years later full parity had not been achieved, the claimant resigned claiming unfair constructive dismissal. The Employment Appeal Tribunal had agreed with the Employment Tribunal that the letters written by the senior manager were not an acknowledgement of an existing contractual commitment but rather confirming an intention to act. The Court of Appeal agreed and held that for there to be an enforceable contractual commitment there must be certainty otherwise a promise amounts to nothing more than a statement of intention. The words used at the Christmas party did not carry an intention to create legal relations but only a general intention to move towards parity of salary at some point. There was therefore no fundamental breach of contract for the purposes of constructive dismissal.

It is the role of the judiciary to declare the common law but more significantly, in employment law, the courts and tribunals are called upon to apply and interpret statutory provisions. It is through the process of establishing binding and persuasive precedents in court and tribunal judgments that statutory provisions are given meaning. A student of employment law should appreciate therefore that a thorough understanding of the rules of employment law embodied within statutory provisions can only be achieved by carrying out a study of case-law where the provisions are applied.

Harassment

A highly controversial development which is potentially of concern to employers is the extent to which they are potentially liable under statute for the bullying and harassment of employees under their control.[10] If the claim is for psychiatric injury caused by a fellow employee, can a claimant maintain an action for damages against an employer relying on vicarious liability for breach of the Protection from Harassment Act 1997. The prevalent view was that this particular statute was designed to deal with the evil of stalking by creating a new criminal offence rather than have any application in employment law. Nevertheless the thorny issue faced by the Court of Appeal in *Majrowski v. Guy's and St. Thomas's NHS Trust* 2005 was the extent to which a victim of bullying at work could rely on the Protection of Harassment Act 1997. Here the claimant was employed by the Trust as a clinical audit coordinator. He alleged that, whilst working in that post, he was bullied, intimidated and harassed by his departmental manager, acting in the course of her employment by the Trust. The bullying took the form of excessive criticism, ostracism, abusive conduct and the setting of unreasonable targets. His claim was brought against the Trust under s.3 of the Protection from Harassment Act which provides a civil remedy where the manager's conduct amounted to harassment in breach of s.1 of the Act for which the Trust, as her employers, were vicariously liable.

---

10. See Chapter 6 Discrimination

The claim was originally rejected by the county court on the grounds that the Act does not permit the imposition of vicarious liability for breach of its provisions. On appeal the Court of Appeal held that employers may be vicariously liable under s.3 of the Protection from Harassment Act for their employees' acts of harassment of third parties, including fellow employees, committed in the course of employment.

This decision thus provides an alternative potential remedy against the employer for employees who claim to have been bullied at the workplace and is considered in Chapter 8.

Statutory Time Limits

In the Employment Rights Act 1996 you will discover that there are numerous provisions which confer rights on employees. In particular if a qualified employee believes that he has been dismissed without good reason he may under section 111 present a complaint of unfair dismissal against his employer before an employment tribunal.[11] The Act provides however that there are strict time limits to be complied with, otherwise the right to present a complaint will be lost.

Section 111(2) of the Act states that ... *'an employment tribunal shall not consider a complaint under this section unless it is presented to the tribunal before the end of the period of three months beginning with the effective date of termination or within such further period as the tribunal considers reasonable in a case where it is satisfied that it was not reasonably practicable for the complaint to be presented before the end of the period of three months'.*

The legal rule is stating therefore, in relatively straightforward terms, that if a dismissed employee wants to complain of unfair dismissal before an employment tribunal he must start the proceedings within three months, but if he fails to do so the tribunal still has a discretion to hear the case if it was not reasonably practicable for him to present it within the time limit. If a legal dispute arises over whether an unfair dismissal claim has been presented within the time limits it is the function of the courts and tribunals to attempt to resolve the conflict by applying the exact wording of s.111(2) to the factual situation before it. The subsection requires the employment tribunal therefore to ask itself one or possibly two questions:

(1) Has the complaint been brought within the three months time limit prescribed in the section?

(2) If not, was it reasonably practicable to present the complaint within the time limit?

If the answer to the first question is no and the answer to the second question is yes then the tribunal should not proceed to hear the complaint of unfair dismissal. If the reverse is true however and either the complaint is within the time limits or it was not reasonably practicable to present it in time then the tribunal does have jurisdiction to proceed.

There are many case decisions which over the years have provided guidance to employment tribunals as to the approach to be adopted in addressing these questions. To determine the relevant time period it is necessary to know *'the effective date of termination'* which may be difficult to decide particularly if the complainant is dismissed without being given the notice to which he is entitled.

11. See Chapter 11 Unfair Dismissal

The specific wording of the section was analysed in *University of Cambridge v. Murray* 1993 where a tribunal held that the phrase 'beginning with' meant that that date forms part of the time period. If the words '*from*' or '*after*' had been used then the three months would be calculated to the corresponding date of the relevant later month or if no corresponding date the last day of the month. As the expression '*beginning with*' is used in the section however the starting date is a day earlier and so ends with the day before the corresponding date of the later relevant month. If the effective date of termination is the 30th of April therefore the time period expires on the last moment of the 29th July. This case is therefore of great assistance in interpreting the section and provides guidance to future tribunals who are required to apply it.

If a tribunal decides that the complaint was not presented within the time period it would still proceed to hear it if it was not *reasonably practicable* to present the complaint in time. Parliament has left it to the courts and tribunals therefore to determine the issue of reasonable practicability in any given case. Reasons for late claims brought before tribunals have included postal delays, bad advice from lawyers or civil servants, and obstructive employers. Case decisions made in relation to these reasons provide guidance and in some cases lay down precedents for future cases.[12] In *Marks & Spencer v. Williams* 2005 The Court of Appeal ruled that time limit provisions should be interpreted liberally in favour of employees particularly when they receive advice which is misleading and insufficient.

To summarise therefore it is possible to say that the law on time limits for presenting a complaint of unfair dismissal is most certainly contained within s.111(2) of the Employment Rights Act 1996 but also as interpreted in the numerous decisions of our courts and tribunals.

Conflicting statutes

Finally you should also appreciate that sometimes the courts and tribunals are required to rule upon the primacy of what seem to be irreconcilable statutory provisions. *Lane group v. Farmiloe* 2004 provides an interesting illustration of the relationship between disability discrimination law and health and safety law. Here the Personal Protective Equipment Regulations could not be complied with in relation to a warehouseman due to his disability, a skin disorder. The EAT felt that an employer should not be required to balance the risk of injury to the applicant against the detriment of a potential dismissal. If the only safe route was dismissal in the absence of alternative employment, then the health and safety regulations would prevent the dismissal from being discriminatory and would also undermine a separate unfair dismissal complaint.

European Community Law

As a Member State of the European Union since 1 January 1973 the United Kingdom is bound by Community Law. In the field of business this is of enormous significance. This is because the European Union is essentially economic in nature and the community objective of the completion of a single European market is based upon the actual harmonisation of laws relating to business and trade between Member States. Examples can be seen in the fields of:

---

12. See Chapter 11 Unfair Dismissal

- company law harmonisation;
- consumer rights and consumer protection;
- data protection;
- environmental protection;
- intellectual property rights;
- employment law.

In each of these fields European law has been active in amending and adding to existing UK law, as well as requiring the introduction of new law. For example in employment law the Community has been active in the following areas:

- pregnancy dismissals, maternity leave and parental leave;
- statutory rights for part-time workers and fixed term contract workers;
- collective redundancy procedures;
- dismissals and detrimental conduct relating to health and safety;
- acquired rights on a business transfer;
- health and safety at work;
- equal opportunity law.

The framework of Community law is set out in the Treaty of Rome 1957 as amended by the Single European Act of 1986, the Treaty on European Union signed at Maastricht in 1992 and the Treaty of Amsterdam 1999. The institutions of the European Union must operate within and give effect to these Treaties.

The Treaty on European Union and the Amsterdam Treaty

The Treaty on European Union which was negotiated in Maastricht in November 1991 came into effect at the beginning of November 1993, after completing the difficult process of ratification in each of the member states. The Treaty creates a European Union which has three main elements, often described as *pillars*. The first is the European Community itself, the powers and decision making procedures of which are extended and modified. The second element relates to foreign and security policy, and the third to justice and home affairs. The second and third pillars operate outside of the formal institutional framework of the EC and are based on new inter-governmental arrangements between the member states. As such their decisions do not form part of the body of EC law, which is created by the Council of Ministers acting with the Commission and European Parliament, and are not subject to the jurisdiction of the Court of Justice.

In the present context we are concerned only with the first pillar of the Treaty which provides for closer European integration within the framework of Community law. This part of the Treaty expands the areas of Community activity. Under the Treaty the task of the European Community will be to promote a harmonious and balanced development of economic activities, sustainable and non-inflationary growth respecting the environment, a high degree of convergence of economic performance, a high level of employment and of social protection, the raising of the standard of living and quality of life, and economic and social cohesion and solidarity.

The UK, however originally negotiated to opt out of two important parts of the Treaty, the *Social Chapter* and the third stage of economic and monetary union which is the adoption of a single currency. The remainder of the Treaty applies with full effect to the UK. The present government has now fully adopted the social chapter.

The consequence of adopting the Social Chapter is that the UK government became immediately subject to the European Directives which were previously not binding due to the opt out under the Maarstricht Treaty. A good example is the EU Parental Leave Directive which the UK government has since implemented. The rules in relation to parental leave are found in schedule 4 to the Employment Relations Act 1999 which adds a new s.76-80 to the Employment Rights Act 1996 and supported by the Maternity and Parental Leave Regulations 1999.[13]

The European Commission has more room to manoeuvre in proposing legislation under the new Social Chapter in fields such as working conditions information, consolidation of workers and equal pay. Importantly decision making is by qualified majority vote for a number of issues. A new Article 13 allows the Council on the European Union to take appropriate action to combat discrimination based on 'sex, racial or ethnic origin, religion or belief, disability, age or sexual orientation. The appropriate actions would include encouraging legislation at national level on equal opportunities.

It is clear from an examination of the major EC treaties that the Community has power to legislate over a very broad range of issues which embrace the entire area of employment law. It is in practice by far the most important source of new law in some spheres such as health and safety, maternity rights and equal opportunities. The European Union achieve most of its objectives through the use of legal mechanisms, notably in the field of employment law by directives. Occasionally this has led to direct and well published conflict between the UK government and the European Union.

Primacy of Community Law

It is a central feature of Community Law that it takes precedence over any conflicting provisions in the national law of member states. This feature has been strongly developed by the Court of Justice in a series of cases as the issue of priority is not addressed directly in the Treaty of Rome. In *VanGend en Loos v. Nederlands Administratie der Belastingen* 1963 the Court of Justice described the relationship between Community law and domestic law in the following way: *'By creating a community of unlimited duration, having its own institutions, its own personality, its own legal capacity and capacity of representation on the international plain and, more particularly, real powers stemming from a limitation of sovereignty or a transfer of powers from the states to the community, the member states have limited their sovereign rights albeit within limited fields, and have thus created a body of law which binds both their nationals and themselves.'*

The principle of supremacy of Community law was clearly affirmed by the Court of Justice in the case of *Costa v. ENEL* 1964 in which it held that a provision in the EC Treaty took precedence over a rule in a subsequent Italian statute. The Court relied on the statement in Van Gend en Loos, together with the duty imposed by Article 5 on each member state to ensure that their obligations under the Treaty are fulfilled, and stated *'The law stemming from the Treaty, an independent source of law, could not, because of its special and original*

---

13. See Chapter 7 Worklife Balance

nature, be over-ridden by domestic legal provisions, however framed, without being deprived of its character as Community Law and without the legal basis of the Community itself being called into question.'

The pervasive nature of Community law was described by Lord Denning MR in *Bulmer Ltd. v. Bolinger SA* 1974 in a famous passage. *'When we come to matters with a European element, the Treaty is like an incoming tide. It flows into the estuaries and up the rivers. It cannot be held back. Parliament has decreed that the Treaty is henceforward to be part of our law. It is equal in force to any statute.'*

> In *Internationale Handelsgesellachaft mbH* 1970, the Court of Justice, in a case which involved a conflict between an EC regulation and the provisions of the German constitution, decided that the EC rule took precedence. *'The validity of a community instrument or its effect within a member State cannot be affected by allegations that it strikes at either the fundamental rights as formulated in that State's constitution or the principles of a national constitutional structure.'*

The significance of these decisions in UK law is underlined by s.3(1) of the European Communities Act 1972, which provides *'For the purposes of all legal proceedings any questions as to the meaning or effect of any of the Treaties, or as to the validity meaning or effect of any community instrument, shall be treated as a question of law and, if not referred to the European Court, be for determination as such in accordance with the principles laid down by and any relevant decision of the European Court.'*

This section represents the acceptance by the UK government in the 1972 Act of the principles developed by the Court of Justice in its decisions, including those relating to the supremacy of Community law.

The position of EC law within the English legal system is established by the European Communities Act 1972 which, in s.2(1), gives legal effect to the Community law within the UK. It states *'All such rights, powers, liabilities, obligations and restrictions from time to time created or arising by or under the Treaties, and all such remedies and procedures from time to time provided for by or under the Treaties, as in accordance with the Treaties are without further enactment to be given legal effect or used in the United Kingdom shall be recognised and available in law, and be enforced, allowed and followed accordingly, and the expression "enforceable community right" and similar expressions shall be read as referring to one to which this subsection applies.'*

This gives legal force to those provisions in the Treaties and in secondary legislation which are directly applicable. This occurs automatically without the need for further UK legislation. The words from time to time make it clear that future as well as existing Community laws are within the scope of s.2(1). In relation to those Community measures which do not have direct applicability, s.2(2) gives power to make delegated legislation for the purpose of giving them effect within the UK. This power is often used to make Statutory Instruments in order to implement Community directives. The Employment Protection (Part-time Employees) Regulations 1995 were made under s.2(2) to bring the legal position of part-time workers in the UK in line with Europe.

The 1972 Act states that where there is a conflict between domestic law and Community law, the latter will take priority. This is laid down in s.2(4) which provides *'... any enactment passed or to be passed shall be construed and have effect subject to the foregoing provisions of this section'.*

An example of the primacy of community law is provided by the important decision of the House of Lords in *R v. Secretary of State for Employment ex parte Equal Opportunities Commission* 1994. Here their Lordships ruled by a majority of four to one that UK legislation that gives part-time workers (most of whom are women) less protection in relation to unfair dismissal and redundancy than full-time workers (most of whom are men) is indirectly discriminatory and therefore incompatible with European Union Law as to equality between employees.

Types of Community Law

The major sources of Community law are *primary* legislation found in the treaties establishing and developing the EC; *secondary* legislation made on an ongoing basis by the Community institutions; judgments of the Court of Justice and unwritten general principles of law. In relation to treaty provisions and secondary legislation it is useful to distinguish between the concepts of *direct applicability* and *direct effect*.

A Community law is said to be directly applicable when it is of a type which is directly incorporated in its entirety into the laws of the members states without the need for further legislative or administrative action on the part of the member state or the Community institutions. Such rules create immediate rights and obligations as between individuals and or organisations and as against member states. These rights or obligations are directly enforceable in the ordinary courts within the member states. Article 189 states that EC regulations are directly applicable. Certain provisions of the treaties have been held to be directly applicable, although they only come within this category where they are:

- clear and unambiguous;
- unconditional;
- precise;
- self-contained.[14]

Directly applicable Community laws will automatically take effect within the UK by virtue of s.2(1) of the 1972 Act.

A Community law which is not directly applicable may nonetheless have direct effects in terms of conferring rights upon individuals which may be enforced in the domestic courts. Such provisions usually will not have direct applicability because they are not self-contained, in the sense that they require some action, usually by the member state, in order to implement them. Typically this will apply where directives have not been implemented in full or at all, and the deadline for implementation has passed. In these circumstances the directive may produce direct effects provided it is sufficiently clear, unconditional and precise. One significant limitation on the doctrine of direct effects is that directives are only directly effective as against the state. This is known as *vertical direct effect* and is examined below in the context of the defective implementation of directives.

It may be seen that whilst all directly applicable provisions will have direct effects, the reverse will not be true so that a rule may be directly effective without being directly applicable. Not surprisingly, the two are often confused and even the courts tend to use them interchangeably.

---

14. Requiring no further action to put into effect

The Treaties

The primary legislation of the EC consists of the European Treaties and associated documents, agreements and protocols. These include the Treaty of Rome, the Single European Act 1986, the Treaty on European Union 1992 and the Treaty of Amsterdam.

Under the UK constitution each new treaty requires an Act of Parliament to give it effect within the national legal system. This was achieved by the European Communities Act in 1972 in relation to the treaties which pre-dated it. Separate legislation has been introduced for each subsequent treaty so that, for example, the European Communities (Amendment) Act 1993 gives effect to the Treaty on European Union. The European Treaties set out the framework of Community law, create the institutions and lay down the procedures for making secondary legislation on an ongoing basis.

Whilst certain provisions in the treaties lay down broad policies which need to be fleshed out in secondary legislation, the Court of Justice has held that others can be directly applicable. Article 119 of the Treaty of Rome, (now Article 141 following the Treaty of Amsterdam) provides that *'Each member state shall ... maintain the application of the principle that men and women receive equal pay for equal work'.* In *Defrenne v. Sabena* 1976 the Court of Justice held that Article 141 imposed on member states *'A duty to bring about a specific result to be mandatorally achieved'* and that it could be relied on in an action between an individual and her employer. Defrenne, an air hostess, claimed to be entitled to the same pay as a male steward whose duties were identical to hers. It was held that she could rely on Article 141 even though it was addressed to the member state and was not framed as a rule giving rights to individuals. In so far as it relates to direct discrimination and equal work it was held to be directly applicable. The case of *Macarthys v. Smith* 1979, is a further example of a direct application of Article 141.

> In *Barber v. Guardian Royal Exchange* 1990 the Court of Justice applied Article 141 in its decision that occupational pension schemes, as opposed to state retirement pension, and the benefits conferred under them on employees, are pay for the purpose of Article 141. It is therefore unlawful to discriminate between men and women in relation to them. Mr. Barber claimed to be entitled to benefit under his company pension scheme on the same basis as female employees and objected to the fact that he could not receive benefits under the scheme until he reached the age of 65 whereas his female counterparts could benefit at 60. The Court of Justice's decision in his favour caused major changes in many occupational pension schemes to give effect to the equalisation of pension ages and benefits as between men and women.

Secondary legislation

The Treaties confer significant law making powers on the Institutions of the Community. These powers are limited in that they extend only to areas where the Community has competence to legislate. There are some areas which remain within the exclusive domain of the national sovereignty of the member states. As we have seen, however, the Community's law making competence extents to virtually all aspects of employment law.

Article 189 of the Treaty of Rome states *'In order to carry out their task the Council and the Commission shall, in accordance with the provisions of this Treaty, make regulations, issue directives, take decisions, make recommendations or deliver opinions.'* The Article goes on to define each of them.

A *Regulation* has general application. It is binding in its entirety and directly applicable in all member states. Regulations are the equivalent of UK statutes on a community scale. They apply to all member states and there is no requirement for action at a national level to bring them into effect. This occurs on the 20th day following their publication in the Official Journal where no other date is specified in them.

A *Directive* is binding, as to the result to be achieved, upon each member state to which it is addressed but leaves it to the national authorities the choice of form and methods of implementation. Directives are the major instrument for achieving the harmonisation of national laws as between the member states and they occur frequently in UK employment law. They operate by setting out the objectives which the proposed new laws must achieve, giving a time limit within which member state governments must achieve them. In order to comply with the European Community Framework Directive 2000 legislation had to be prohibiting discrimination on the grounds of sexual orientation and religion by 2 December 2003.[15] The resulting law is in the form of a domestic law within the member state. In the UK directives are implemented either by a new Act of Parliament or by delegated legislation using the enabling powers in s.2(2) of the 1972 Act. The Treaty gives some discretion as to the manner of implementation, provided that the result is achieved. This allows for a certain degree of flexibility, for example, in relation to the consequences for breach of a particular rules which need not be identical in each member state. Breach of the same substantive rule may, for example, give rise to criminal liability in the UK and civil liability in France. There are many examples of directives in the field of employment law in particular in relation to health and safety, equal opportunities, business transfers and redundancy procedures.

A *Decision* is binding in its entirety upon those to whom it is addressed. They may be addressed to a member state, a business or other organisation or an individual. There is no discretion as to the manner of implementation, and decisions take effect upon notification.

Recommendations and *Opinions* are not legally binding or enforceable. They are often addressed to member states and may give a view on a particular matter or set out guidelines to be followed in relation to an issue, sometimes with the implication that if they are not followed proposals for a stronger type of Community law may be made at a later date.

Failure to implement

Where a member state has failed to implement a directive within the specified time period, or where implementation has taken place in part only, there are a number of possible consequences:

Infringement proceedings may be taken by the Commission against the member state. This process is outlined above and ultimately results in a ruling against the member state by the Court of Justice. One problem with this process had been the lack of any power to enforce the judgment of the Court of Justice. Since the coming into effect of the Treaty on European Union however, as we have seen, the Court of Justice has power to fine a member state which fails to comply with a judgment against it.

---

15. The Equality (Religion or Belief) Regulations 2003

A directive may have direct effects in a case involving the state as defendant. By definition a directive cannot be directly applicable as it requires some action on the part of the member state to give it effect in national law. Where the member state fails to do this, either in whole or in part, the principle of *vertical direct effect* may come into play. This will prevent the member state from using its own wrongful act of failing properly to implement the directive as a defence to a legal action taken by someone who wishes to enforce the rights contained in the directive against it. In order to be directly effective, the rights set out in the directive must be clear, unambiguous, unconditional and precise.

> In *Marshall v. Southampton and South West Hampshire Area Health Authority (Teaching)* 1986, the Health Authority operated a retirement policy for employees under which the normal retirement age was 60 for women and 65 for men. This was consistent with s.6(4) of the Sex Discrimination Act 1975, and in line with state retirement pension ages. An employee's retirement could be postponed by mutual agreement and Miss Marshall continued to work until she was dismissed at age 62. The sole reason given for her dismissal was that she had passed the normal retirement age. She claimed that her dismissal was an unlawful discrimination because men could not be dismissed on grounds of retirement at that age. Her claim was based upon the following Articles of the Equal Treatment Directive:
>
> *'1(1). The purpose of this directive is to put into effect in the member states the principle of equal treatment for men and women as regards access to employment, including promotion, and to vocational training and as regards working conditions...*
>
> *2(1). The principle of equal treatment shall mean that there shall be no discrimination whatsoever on grounds of sex either directly, or indirectly by reference in particular to marital or family status.*
>
> *5(1). Application of the principle of equal treatment with regard to working conditions, including those governing dismissal, means that men and women shall be guaranteed the same conditions without discrimination on grounds of sex.'*

The Court of Appeal sought a preliminary ruling from the Court of Justice as to whether the retirement policy of the Health Authority constituted discrimination on grounds of sex contrary to the directive; and if so, whether Article 5(1) could be relied upon as against a state authority acting in its capacity as employer, in order to avoid the application of s.6(4) of the Sex Discrimination Act 1975. The Court of Justice ruled that the difference in compulsory retirement ages as between men and women was discriminatory and that Article 5(1) was clear, unconditional and sufficiently precise to be directly effective. As the date for implementation had passed, it could be relied upon so as to avoid the application of s.6(4) as against the Health Authority, a public sector organisation *'Where a person involved in legal proceedings is able to rely upon a directive as against the state, he may do so regardless of the capacity in which the latter is acting, whether employer or public authority. In either case it is necessary to prevent the state from taking advantage of its own failure to comply with Community Law.'*

An excellent contemporary example of the failure to fully implement a directive is provided by the introduction of the right to paid holidays under the Working Time Regulations.[16] Originally the government decided to introduce a qualifying period of 13 weeks for a

---

16. See Chapter 9 Statutory Rights

worker to become entitled to annual leave. This rule was the subject of a successful legal challenge in *R v. Secretary of State for Trade & Industry ex* parte *BECTU* 2001 and as a consequence the government has amended the Regulations to include a right to take one twelfth of the annual leave entitlement for each month worked.

So the provisions of a directive are capable of direct enforcement against an emanation of the State if there has been a failure to implement the directive into domestic law and it has been written with sufficient precision. The directive will of course have primacy in the event that its provisions conflict with contractual terms.

A good example of contractual conflict and direct enforceability is provided by *Gibson v. East Riding of Yorkshire Council* 2000 a complaint about the failure to enact Article 7(1) of the Working Time Directive providing that workers are entitled to four weeks annual leave. The EAT had held that during the period the directive had not been implemented it had direct effect and an employee of an emanation of the State was able to take advantage of its protection. The directive was clear and precise with no conditions and *'although it as argued that the complainant expressly contracted on the basis that she would receive no paid annual leave her contractual rights were varied by the directive'*. Parties are not entitled to contract out of the entitlement conferred upon them by European Directives, save to the extent that the directive may permit. The Court of Appeal disagreed with the EAT however and held that the right to paid annual leave is not sufficiently defined in Article 7 to be directly enforceable by an individual in national courts or tribunals. As Article 7 leaves key questions unanswered, such as a precise definition of 'working time' it is not possible to decide which workers are entitled to annual leave.

Member state courts have a duty to interpret national law in the light of the wording and purpose of a relevant directive, not only where the national law in question was introduced in order to give effect to the directive, but also where it pre-dates the directive if no further implementing measure has been introduced and the date for implementation has passed.

A member state may be liable in damages to an individual for any loss suffered as a result of the state's failure to implement a directive. This important principle was established by the Court of Justice in the case of *Francovich v. Italian State and Bonifaci* 1992. Liability will arise as against a member state which has failed to implement a directive where the following conditions are met:

(a)   the result to be achieved by the directive includes the creation of rights in favour of individuals;

(b)   the content of those rights are sufficiently defined in the directive; and

(c)   the individual's loss is caused by the failure of the state to implement the directive.

In the *Francovich* case, the Italian government had failed to implement directive 80/987 on the protection of employees in the event of the insolvency of their employer. Under the directive it had been required to ensure that a guarantee institution was in place from which employees could claim payments which could not be met by insolvent employers. *Francovich* was owed 6 million lire which he was unable to recover from his insolvent employer. He sued the Italian government for damages for its failure to comply with the directive and the Court of Justice gave a preliminary ruling on an Article 177 reference that the government was liable in damages for its failure to set up the guarantee institution.

The development of the rule that a member state may be liable to pay damages where it has failed properly to implement a directive is significant in a number of ways. Firstly because the rule of vertical direct effect established in the Marshall case does not provide a remedy against a private sector defendant. As a result of the *Francovich* decision, a plaintiff who is unable to sue such a defendant may now be able to sue his government for its failure to legislate. On a broader front the decision is significant because it demonstrates the ability and willingness of the Court of Justice to develop creatively the principles of Community law and new mechanisms for ensuring its effectiveness in areas where the Treaties provide little or no guidance.

The principle established in the *Francovich* case has now been extended to cover the situation where an individual or organisation suffers loss as a result of national legislation which is contrary to EC law, for example because it is incompatible with a provision of the Treaty of Rome. The member state will be liable in damages where the following conditions are met:

(a) the provision in community law was intended to create rights in favour of individuals;

(b) the breach of community law is a serious breach; and

(c) the loss is directly caused by the member states breach of EC law.

The European Convention on Human Rights and Fundamental Freedoms

The above Convention has emerged as a further significant source of UK employment law. The Human Rights Act 1998 incorporated the European Convention on Human Rights into UK law from October 2000. As a result the UK courts are obliged to interpret domestic employment law in accordance with the European convention on Human Rights.

It should be stressed from the outset that the Human Rights Act only directly binds public bodies and it is clearly drafted in terms that do not bind the private sector. There is however case-law to suggest that there is a 'potential line of enquiry' regarding the extent to which the provisions of the Act apply to the private sector. It does seem to overly complicate matters to apply principles of employment law differently depending on the public or private status of the employer. Under Section 3(1) of the Act *'So far as it is possible to do so, primary legislation and subordinate legislation must be read and given effect in a way which is compatible with the Convention rights.'*

In *X v. Y* 2003 Lord Justice Mummery in the Court of Appeal provided guidance as to the approach to be adopted when Human Rights Act points are raised in unfair dismissal cases in the private sector. He said an employment tribunal should properly consider their relevance, dealing with them in a structured way, even if it is ultimately decided that they do not affect the outcome of the unfair dismissal claim. Usually the State will not have a positive obligation to secure enjoyment of the relevant Convention right between private persons so it is unlikely to affect the outcome of an unfair dismissal claim against a private employer.

However the Human Rights Act is directly enforceable against public bodies and as employers they should be concerned about any policies that they have which could offend the Articles of the Convention. While the Act does not directly extend to private employers, the courts and tribunals are obliged to act compatibly with the Convention so that a dismissal on the grounds of sexual orientation such as *Saunders v. Scottish National Camps Association* 1980[17] should almost certainly be regarded as unfair.

There are a number of Articles in the Convention which will have impact on employment rights such as:

- Article 8, the respect for private life;
- Article 6, the right to a fair hearing;
- Article 10, freedom of expression;
- Article 3, subjecting an individual to degrading treatment; and
- Article 11, freedom of assembly and association.

An infringement of Article 6, the right to a fair hearing 'within a reasonable time' was upheld by the European Court of Human Rights in *Somjee v. United Kingdom* 2002. The applicant had brought a race discrimination, victimisation and unfair dismissal complaints and it had taken eight years for the complaint to be dealt with by the Employment Tribunal and the Employment Appeal Tribunal. While acknowledging that the proceedings were factually and legally complex the court found that the UK was in violation of Article 6 as a significant proportion of the blame for the delay lay with the tribunal and the EAT.

Recently *McGowan v. Scottish Water* 2005 raised the issue as to the means by which an employer can acquire evidence of fraudulent conduct by an employer. Here the claimant was employed at a water treatment plant and lived in a tied house nearby. Suspecting that he was falsifying his time sheet, the employer decided to employ private investigators to carry out a surveillance of his working week. For this purpose the investigation filmed the claimant's house and their evidence eventually led to the applicant's dismissal. The claimant argued that his dismissal was unfair as an infringement of his Article 8 rights of respect for his private and family life. Both the Tribunal and the EAT disagreed concluding that there had been no breach of Article 8. The conduct of the employer, bearing in mind the gravity of the offence investigated, was entirely reasonable and proportionate.[18]

An infringement of Article I which provides that '*every person is entitled to peaceful enjoyment of his possessions*' was alleged in *Nerva v. United Kingdom* 2002 . The claim was brought by waiters who claimed that tips left as additions to credit cards or cheques belonged to them, and so when distributed by the employer, should not count towards their wages for the purpose of statutory minimum wage legislation. Unfortunately the court ruled that tips left in this manner were the legal property of the employer and if distributed appropriately the employees could not maintain that they had a legal right to them and a separate right to a minimum wage without reference to the tips.

Goodwin v. United Kingdom 2002 arose out of the then lack of recognition under UK law of gender changes. The European Court of Human Rights ruled that the lack of recognition of a transsexual's new gender identity was a breach of Article 8 of respect for private life and Article 12 the right to marry. Freedom of Association under Article 11 of the Convention is a right ultimately enforceable in the European Court of Human Rights and *Wilson v. United Kingdom* 2002 was the first case where the court has upheld a claim relating to trade union rights under Article 11.

---

17. See Chapter 11 Unfair Dismissal
18. See Chapter 11 Unfair Dismissal

The UK ban on homosexuals in the armed forces has been held to contravene the right to private life under the convention. The European Court of Human Rights also ruled in *Smith and Grady v. United Kingdom* 1999 that the investigation into the applicants homosexuality and subsequent discharge from the armed forces were clear breaches of Articles 3 and 8 of the Convention. Evidence from the UK Government that the presence of homosexuals in the armed forces would have a substantial and negative effect on morale and operational effectiveness was found by the court to be unconvincing. '*These negative attitudes cannot of themselves be considered by the court to amount to sufficient justification, for the interferences with the applicants rights outlined above any more than similar negative attitudes toward those of a different race, origin or colour.*'

The following case provides helpful guidance on the approach to be adopted when an infringement of the Human Rights Act is raised in an unfair dismissal case brought against a public sector employer.

In *Pay v. Lancashire Probation Service* 2004 a probation officer working with sex offenders was dismissed after his employers, a public body, discovered that he was involved in activities including the merchandising of products connected with bondage, domination and sado-masochism and that he performed shows in hedonist and fetish clubs. Photographs of him involved in acts of bondage, domination and sado-masochism were available on the internet. The employers took the view that these activities were incompatible with his role and responsibilities as a probation officer. Mr. Pay complained that his dismissal was unfair in that it entailed an infringement of the Human Rights Act, in particular his right to respect for his private life under Article 8 and to freedom of expression under Article 10.

Article 8 provides that:

1. Everyone has the right to respect for his private and family life, his home and his correspondence.

Under Article 10:

1. Everyone has the right to freedom of expression. This right shall include freedom to hold opinions and to receive and impart information and ideas without interference by public authority and regardless of frontiers.

The claim was dismissed by the tribunal which felt that the dismissal fell within the range of responses of a reasonable employer and that the procedure adopted by the employers was not flawed. In addition since the claimants activities had been publicised on the internet and he promoted them in public places, they were in the public domain and, therefore, could not be termed part of his private life. On appeal the EAT held that the employment tribunal had not erred in holding that dismissal of the applicant did not constitute an infringement of his rights under the Human Rights Act to respect for his private life and to freedom of expression. The employment tribunal was entitled to find that the applicant's right to respect for his private life under Article 8 was not engaged because his activities were publicised on the internet and promoted in public places. The tribunal was also entitled to find that, whilst the right to freedom of expression under Article 10 was engaged, balancing the competing interests of the employers' concern to protect their reputation and maintain public confidence there was no unjustified interference with that of the reputation or rights of others.

We shall return to this case in Chapter 11 on Unfair Dismissal.

Conclusion

To sum up, a student of employment law should be aware that the courts will apply law from various sources both national and European in the resolution of conflict. It should also be appreciated that a constructive analysis of an employment dispute will often require an application of employment law from a number of areas of the subject. While it is convenient in a text of this nature to divide the subject into a number of topics dealt with in distinct chapters unfortunately conflict does not usually fall neatly into one topic area and will normally involve a number of legal issues. The case below provides an example.

> In *Bass Leisure Ltd. v. Thomas* 1994 the complainant was employed as a collector for the defendants for ten years working from their Coventry depot. Her job involved travelling to a number of public houses to empty fruit machines. In 1991 the defendants decided to close the Coventry depot and the complainant was offered relocation in Erdington, some twenty miles away. The complainant tried the new work location but it soon became obvious that the more onerous travelling made the alternative employment unrealistic and she terminated her employment claiming a redundancy payment. The defendants disputed her claim relying on an express term of her contract which provided that *'the company reserves the right to transfer any employee either temporarily or permanently to a suitable alternative place of work and to change the terms and conditions of employment to meet the needs of the business. Domestic circumstances will be taken into account in reaching a decision if relocation is involved'*. As the parties were unable to resolve the conflict a complaint was made to the employment tribunal and from the tribunal's decision an appeal heard by the Employment Appeal Tribunal. In reaching a decision the tribunal had to analyse the express terms of the contract of employment to determine whether the employer was authorised in requiring the employee to move. Both the tribunal and the EAT thought that in applying the relocation term the employer had not taken account of domestic circumstances or judged objectively offered a suitable alternative place of work. Having decided that the employer was in breach of contract the next issue was whether the breach of contract was so fundamental that it justified the employee leaving and claiming constructive dismissal by reason of redundancy. This was a constructive dismissal and as it was by reason of redundancy under the definition in the above Act, then the applicant was entitled to a redundancy payment.

In reaching its decision in the above case the tribunal found it necessary to apply a number of legal principles to the conflict. In the text you will find principles of law relating to job relocation and terms of employment in Chapters 4 and 5, constructive dismissal in Chapter 10 and redundancy in Chapter 12.

Further Reading

Ewing, KD *The Human Rights Act and Labour Law* (1998) 27 ILJ 275.

Morris, Gillian *Fundamental Rights Exclusion by Agreement?* (2001) 30 ILJ 49.

Vickers, Lucy *Unfair Dismissal and Human Rights* (2004) 33 ILJ 52.

Chapter 2

Institutions of Employment Law

Having considered the various sources of employment law, to complete the introduction to the subject it is also necessary to describe those bodies, judicial and otherwise, which have jurisdiction to interpret the law and have a part to play in the resolution of employment law conflict. Today there is much less reluctance to litigate and prospective litigants, more aware of their legal rights and no doubt encouraged by lawyers earning conditional fees, are much more likely to pursue a compensation claim against an employer. The lifting of caps on compensation, particularly in relation to discrimination claims is also a contributory factor. The marked increase in the number of tribunal complaints and the consequential cost, has led this government to adopt policies, which are designed to promote alternative forms of dispute resolution. The introduction of statutory disciplinary and grievance procedures in 2004 and the ACAS arbitration procedure for unfair dismissal in 2001, are examples of this trend. Comparisons with tribunal claims in member states are instructive and in 2002 there were 38,000 unfair dismissal claims in the UK, 296,000 in Germany and 170,000 in France.

Employment Tribunals

Under the Employment Rights (Disputes Resolutions) Act 1998 industrial tribunals were renamed as employment tribunals. The vast majority of individual employment law rights and duties are legally enforceable by means of presenting a complaint before an employment tribunal. Originating in 1964[1] with only a minimal function, the employment tribunal is now the focus for dealing with all statutory employment law conflict.

Jurisdiction

The jurisdiction of employment tribunals include claims for unfair dismissal, redundancy, trade union rights, wage deductions, discrimination, and many other employment rights

---

1. The Industrial Training Act 1964

and obligations considered throughout the book. Their original aim remains to *provide 'an easily accessible, speedy, informal and inexpensive procedure'* for the settlement of disputes.

One significant employment law limitation on the jurisdiction of tribunals was the fact that claims based on breach of contract were matters to be dealt with in the ordinary courts rather than tribunals. There was a change in this practice in 1994[2] and now employment tribunals are given jurisdiction over breach of contract claims with certain exceptions, the ordinary courts retaining concurrent jurisdiction. Employees may not make a breach of contract claim in a tribunal until their employment has ended[3] but they do not have to make a concurrent statutory claim. They have three months from the end of employment to commence proceedings for a cause of action, which could have arisen in the last six years. Certain claims are excluded including personal injury actions, claims about providing living accommodation, intellectual property, confidentiality and restraint of trade. The maximum award which a tribunal could order in respect of a contract claim is £25,000[4]. In *Sarker v. South Tees Acute Hospitals NHS Trust* 1997 the EAT held that the tribunal had jurisdiction to hear a claim for damages for breach of contract where a contract of employment was terminated by the employer before the employee commenced work.

It should be stressed that an employment tribunal as a body which discharges judicial functions and forms part of the judicial system should be regarded as a 'court' rather than an administrative organ of the state. The Divisional Court of the Queen's Bench Division of the High Court held in *Peach Grey & Co. v. Sommers* 1995 that an employment tribunal is an *'inferior court'* and consequently the Divisional Court has power to make an order for committal *'where contempt of court … is committed in connection with … proceedings in an inferior court'*. Here the complainant was sentenced to one month's imprisonment as he had attempted to pervert the course of justice by interfering with a witness in employment tribunal proceedings and, therefore, he was guilty of contempt of court.

Constitution

The constitution of an employment tribunal is laid down in the Industrial Tribunals Act 1996[5] which provides that a tribunal is composed of three members, a legally qualified chairman and two lay members, one of whom is usually a nominee of an employer's organisation, and the other the nominee of a trade union. With the parties consent a tribunal could be composed of a chairman and one other member. Also for a number of proceedings a tribunal could be validly constituted by the chairman sitting alone. Following the Employment Rights (Disputes Resolutions) Act 1998 the Chairman has a discretion to sit alone in matters including the determination of rights on the employer's insolvency, redundancy payments, statements of employment particulars and cases where the parties agree in writing to the chairman sitting alone.

From the outset it is crucial to appreciate the role of the employment tribunal in the resolution of conflict in employment law. It has often been said that the tribunal panel is an *'industrial jury'* and as such is the final arbiter on questions of fact. The Court of Appeal in *Wilson v. Post Office* 2000 when considering the role of the employment tribunal emphasised

---

2. Employment Tribunals (Extensions of Jurisdiction) (England and Wales) Order 1994
3. Wrongful Dismissal
4. The County Court limit
5. Now cited as the Employment Tribunals Act 1996

its authority to make judgments on findings of fact *'An employment tribunal is not merely a fact-finding body, it is an industrial jury. This is not merely a phrase but a concept which is to be taken seriously'.* Recently in *Voith Turbo Ltd. v. Stowe* 2005 the Employment Appeal Tribunal said that *'The goal of good industrial practice has long survived the demise of the Industrial Relations Act and its unfair industrial practices. It is the job of the specialist tribunals, in applying the law, to shape good employment relations practice.'*

There are many occasions, particularly in relation to unfair dismissal, that the tribunal is called on to determine whether in the circumstances of the case the decision taken by the employer is a reasonable one. In making this determination the tribunal must examine the employers decision from a background of sound industrial experience and practice and then decide whether the decision falls within a band of reasonable responses from an employer in similar circumstances. This determination is a core function of the tribunal and should not be disturbed by an appeal court or tribunal other than in exceptional circumstances.[6]

In *Borders Regional Council v. Maule* 1993 the EAT considered the role of the employment tribunal in decision-making. The EAT said that *'In order to show that they have performed their statutory function it is necessary for the tribunal to explain what considerations have been taken into account and make some attempt to explain how these considerations have been balanced before reaching the conclusion that the employer acted unreasonably.'*

Submitting the claim

To present a claim it is usual to complete and submit an Employment Tribunal 1 (ET1) form to the Regional Office of Employment Tribunals. Previously the use of that particular form was not a statutory requirement and another form of writing would suffice. From 1 October 2005 the new ET1 forms on which employment tribunal claims are made became mandatory. A claim or response to an Employment Tribunal will not be accepted if it is not on an approved form provided by the Employment Tribunal Service. Paper copies of the approved form are available from tribunals and job centres and are also available online.[7] The Regional office acknowledges receipt of the ET1 by sending the claimant a form which confirms that copies of the complaint have been sent to the employer and passed on to the Advisory Conciliation and Arbitration Services (ACAS).

It is a requirement that the ET1 should be completed in accordance with new Employment Tribunals (Constitution and Rules of Procedure) Regulations 2004. The Regulations introduced a new 'pre acceptance procedure' under which the legal chairman can decide not to accept either the ET1 claim or the ET3 response. The circumstance include:

1.   If the claim or response is not on the prescribed form or do not contain all the prescribed information.

2.   If the tribunal does not have jurisdiction or

3.   If the statutory grievance procedure has not been complied with.[8]

The legal chairman must inform the parties in writing.

---

6. See later Employment Appeal Tribunal
7. From the Employment Tribunal Service
8. See below

While it is a requirement that the ET1 should be completed in accordance with new Employment Tribunals (Constitution and Rules of Procedure) Regulations 2004, recently the EAT has ruled that priority should be given to ensuring that individuals have access to the employment tribunal system.

In *Grimmer v. KLM Cityhopper* 2005 the tribunal refused to admit a claim on grounds that the claimant did not provide 'details of the claim' as required by the new rules.[9] She put 'flexible working' on her claim form and gave as details of her claim that: 'The company's business argument for refusing my application is based upon their assumption that, if they concede to my request, others would be requesting similar/same working arrangements. The EAT disagreed and held that it is '*a vital principle' that 'the Rules of Procedure cannot cut down on an employment tribunal's jurisdiction to entertain a complaint which the primary legislation providing an employment right empowers it to determine. If there is a conflict, the Rules must give way.' That principle accords with the interests of justice and 'those responsible for introducing these Rules do not appear to have had proper regard.'* The EAT ruled that in determining whether a claim form contains the required details of the claim, the test is '*whether it can be discerned from the claim as presented that the claimant is complaining of an alleged breach of an employment right which falls within the jurisdiction of the employment tribunal'*.

Claims to an employment tribunal can now be made online by use of a claim form on the Employment Tribunals Service website. The Employment Tribunals Service now advertises that it is prepared to accept claims presented via the internet and this service is offered through its own website. In fact no mention is made of the fact that the service is not operated directly by the tribunals but is hosted by a commercial email service. The online applications are received by the host which should then transfer them to the Employment Tribunals Service where they are received both in a central mailbox and in the mailbox of the relevant regional office.

In *Tyne and Wear Autistic Society v. Smith* 2005 the EAT has held that an application is 'presented' to the tribunal for time limit purposes once it is successfully submitted online to the Employment Tribunal Service website, rather than when it is received by the email service which hosts the ETS website, or when it is forwarded on to a tribunal office. The EAT agreed with the tribunal in holding that the claimant's online application claiming unfair dismissal was presented to the tribunal when it was received by the email service which hosts the Employment Tribunals Service website, and that since the application had reached the host within the statutory period, it had been presented in time even though it had never in fact reached the tribunal.

Obviously it makes sense for employers and employees to resolve any conflicts they may have informally without resorting to tribunal claims. If there is an issue relating to an employee's poor performance or bad behaviour, then an informal discussion pointing out the required standards of performance and behaviour may be sufficient to resolve the issue. If however there is no resolution, or the matter is a serious one, then it may be appropriate to call a formal meeting where both sides are heard and represented. The decision at such a meeting could be an oral or written warning for the employee. If the situation still does not improve then the statutory procedures should be implemented with a view of dismissal.

---

9. Rule 1(4)

The Employment Act 2002 and the Employment Act (Dispute Resolution) Regulations 2004 haves introduced new dispute resolution procedures which apply to all employers and employees. The procedures are designed to encourage parties to avoid litigation by resolving differences through proper internal procedures and imposing sanctions if they do not. The aim is to encourage employers and employees to discuss problems openly before resorting to a claim before a tribunal. They came into effect in October 2004 requiring employers to have procedures for dealing with disciplinary matters and employee grievances.

The main aim is to discourage tribunal claims where the parties have not implemented the dispute resolution regulations. Under the Act a complaint may not be made to a tribunal in relation to a matter to which the statutory grievance procedure applies unless the employee has complied with step one of the grievance procedure or 28 days have not expired since the employee did so. Failure to complete the grievance procedure due to the employee's fault will entitle the tribunal to reduce any compensation award by between 10 and 50%.[10]

In *Commotion Ltd. v. Butty* 2006 the EAT confirmed that a claimant's request to work flexibly under s.80F[11] could also constitute the presentation of a grievance for the purposes of the Dispute Resolution Regulations 2004. Whether a document constitutes the presentation of a grievance is a question of fact and it is possible for a document to fulfil more than on one function.[12]

Responding to the claim

The ET1 form also informs the employee (claimant) that notice of the hearing will be sent at a future date. The employer (respondent), having received a copy of the ET1 and also a formal notice that the application has been made, has then 28 days to respond by filling in and returning the ET3 response form. Again the response can be made on-line. It is at this stage that the respondent should attempt to clarify the legal position, consider the evidence. If necessary, the respondent may apply to the Regional office for an extension of time before responding to the claim. If he requires further clarification of the claimant's grounds for the claim he can make a request for further particulars. A further ground for an extension would be the unavailability of an important witness. A Chairman will decide whether or not to grant an extension.

If, in the response notice, the respondent fails to provide sufficient particulars of his ground for resisting the claim, he can be required to do so by the tribunal. It is important to note that if the response is not on the approved form, not returned or out of time, then the tribunal will issue a default judgment allowing a tribunal chairman to give a decision without the need for a hearing.

If the response is accepted a copy will be sent to the claimant and to ACAS, the independent conciliation service which will try to help the parties to reach an agreed settlement. The Regional office then sets a date for the hearing but a postponement can be applied for in writing and is normally granted when requested. It may be that the respondent disputes that the applicant is qualified to bring the claim, perhaps on the ground that the employee has insufficient continuous employment for the purposes of a complaint of unfair dismissal. In these circumstances it is usual to request a preliminary hearing to determine the issue.

---

10. See Chapter 11
11. Employment Rights Act 1996
12. See Chapter 7

Case management

While the aim of conferring jurisdiction on tribunals is to encourage decision-making which is both inexpensive and speedy, the reality is that there has been increasing legal complexity introduced into tribunal proceedings. A number of changes have been introduced[13] in particular an increase in the power of the Chairman to conduct the preliminary proceedings prior to the hearing. There is a case management period where a chairman can give directions or make orders which the parties must follow. During this period the tribunal has more of an inquisitorial role in that it can order the discovery and inspection of documents and the attendance of witnesses on its own initiative. The applicant or respondent can be ordered to answer questions before the hearing to clarify issues or assist in the process of the trial. This enables information to be gathered in advance of the hearing. This is particularly useful where the respondent is a large organisation and it is easy for individuals to deny responsibility.

The rules that to govern the procedure of tribunals are the Employment Tribunals (Constitution and Rules of Procedures) Regulations 2004 made under the Employment Act 2002. There is an overriding objective provision designed to enable tribunals to deal with cases justly. This includes ensuring in so far as is practicable:

- that the parties are on equal footing;
- that expense is saved;
- that cases are dealt with in ways which are proportionate to the complexity of the issues;
- that cases are dealt with expeditiously and fairly.

The aim is that tribunals should give effect to this overriding objective when exercising their powers and interpreting the Regulations. Under the Regulations referred to later are the increase in the amount that can be ordered to be paid as a deposit on pre hearing review from £150 to £500 and the increase of a costs order from £500 to £10,000. The 2004 Regulations are presently under review.

Time limits

It is of crucial importance that an applicant to an employment tribunal presents the claim within the appropriate time limits. The law relating to time limits and the discretion of a tribunal to hear a complaint presented out of time was mentioned in Chapter 1 and is covered in Chapter 6 in relation to discrimination and Chapter 11 in relation to unfair dismissal. One fundamental principle should be stressed from the outset however. Unlike the ordinary courts the traditionally short time limits in tribunals are jurisdictional. This means that a tribunal is bound to consider the issue of whether or not this is raised by the respondent and the point cannot be waived. The civil courts will only consider whether a claim is presented in time (e.g. three years for personal injuries) if it is raised as a defence by the defendant.

Under s.111(2) of the Employment Rights Act ... *'an employment tribunal shall not consider a complaint under this section unless it is presented to the tribunal before the end of the period of three months beginning with the effective date of termination or within such further period*

---

13. Under the 2004 Rules

as the tribunal considers reasonable in a case where it is satisfied that it was not reasonably practicable for the complaint to be presented before the end of the period of three months'.

In Chapter 1 we said that the three month time period begins on the date that the employment ended and terminates on the day before the corresponding date of the subsequent month. For a termination of employment on 10 June the last day to submit a claim is 9 September. Time limits will be extended by a further 3 months in non dismissal cases if the employee raises a grievance with the employer within the time limit. You will also see in Chapter 11 that if it is the claimant's fault that grievance or disciplinary proceedings are not completed before the complaint is presented, then the tribunal has authority to reduce the amount of any compensation awarded.

For statutory employment claims the rules on time limits are quite strict and ignorance of the law will not normally apply. However in *Marks & Spencer v. Williams-Ryan* 2005 the tribunal held that the claimant's lack of knowledge of the three month rule in an unfair dismissal complaint meant that it was not reasonably practicable for her to present the claim within the time limits. By the time that she had exhausted the internal appeal process she was out of time and presented her application with a covering letter one month late. Other factors included the misleading advice that she had received from the Citizens Advice Bureau and her employer which together with her lack of knowledge convinced the tribunal to exercise it's discretion in her favour. The Court of Appeal felt that the tribunal had reached a conclusion open to it on the facts and that s.111(2) of the Employment Rights Act, should be given a liberal interpretation in favour of the employee. While there would be a different outcome if the delay was due to a solicitors negligence it could not be held that fault on the part of an adviser such as the CAB falls to be treated as fault on the part of the employee.

Initial Electronic Security v. Avdic 2005 provides an example of a tribunal application being presented by email. Here the application was transmitted 8 hours before the expiration of the time limit but despite appearing in the sent message folder it was not received. When this was discovered a week later the application was made in writing and hand delivered. The employment tribunal found that it was reasonable for the claimant to assume that her email would be received on the day it was sent and she had no reason to suspect or believe that the message and claim form had not been sent. In the circumstances, it was not reasonably practicable to present her complaint before the three-month time limit expired. The EAT agreed applying the principle that the reasonable expectation of the sender of a claim form by post is that it will be received by the tribunal in the ordinary course of post, the reasonable expectation of the sender of an electronic mail communication is that, in the absence of any indication to the contrary, it will be delivered and will arrive within a very short time after transmission, normally 30 or 60 minutes. The EAT also confirmed that it is always of relevance as to why the claimant waited until the last moment to present a complaint.

You will see later[14] that to qualify to present a claim of unfair dismissal the claimant must have been continuously employed by the respondent for not less than one year. There are however a number of exceptions to that rule for instance if the claimant was dismissed for joining a trade union. In this case the claim must be made within 7 days of the dismissal.

---

14. See Chapter 11

Conciliation

One of the functions of ACAS[15] is in relation to conciliation whenever a complaint is presented alleging that a statutory right has been infringed. The role of a conciliation officer in an unfair dismissal claim is to endeavour to promote a settlement of the complaint without the dispute having to go to an employment tribunal. Since 10 October 2005 the tribunal can inform ACAS that the claim has been given a fixed period for conciliation. The length of this period will depend upon the nature of the complaint and its complexity. In standard cases the period is 13 weeks but this can be extended by a further 2 weeks if a settlement seems likely. At the end of the period ACAS has no duty to conciliate but has a power to do so. In claims of discrimination and whistleblowing there is no fixed period and ACAS has a continuing duty to conciliate. If a settlement is not reached then the claim can be heard by the tribunal as soon as possible after the period has ended.

The role of the conciliation officer is to promote a settlement if requested to do so by either party or if he feels that he could act with a reasonable prospect of success. For this purpose an officer could seek to promote the reinstatement or re-engagement of a dismissed employee on equitable terms or if this is not practicable, attempt to persuade the employer to agree to make the employee a compensation payment. His function is not to negotiate with the parties but rather to act as a channel of communication through which the parties do their bargaining. The conciliation officer will have vast experience of this type of conflict of course, and if asked to do so, he can draw on his experience to give an impartial opinion on the legal position. If a settlement is needed, and this happens in over fifty percent of cases, it is usual for it to be arranged through the conciliation officer. Such a settlement would be enforceable in the same way as an award from an employment tribunal, if necessary by action in the county court. The parties can also settle without the assistance of ACAS.

Compromise agreements

It is an important feature of employment law that an employee cannot opt out of his statutory rights so that if a private settlement is reached, which is not approved by an ACAS conciliation officer, either party could still present a complaint to an employment tribunal. Any sum of money agreed as compensation in a private settlement would however be taken account of in determining a tribunal award. The relevant statutory provision is contained in s.203(1) of the Employment Rights Act 1996.

> Under s.203(1) 'Any provision in an agreement (whether a contract of employment or not) shall be void in so far as it purports:
>
> (a) to exclude or limit the operation of any provision of this Act; or
>
> (b) to preclude any person from presenting a complaint to, or bringing any proceedings under this Act before, an employment tribunal.'

While it would be prudent to call in a conciliation officer to give his stamp of approval to any private settlement it is now possible for the parties to agree not to institute tribunal proceedings without the need to involve ACAS. The agreement will be valid if it satisfies certain criteria and constitutes under s.203(3) a compromise agreement. The criteria are that the agreement must:

---

15. See later in the chapter

- be in writing;
- relate to a specific complaint;
- be reached after the complainant has received independent legal advice from a qualified lawyer as to its terms and effect;
- identify the adviser who is covered by a policy of insurance.

Under s.9 of the Employment Rights (Disputes Resolution) Act 1998 a compromise agreement will be valid if advice has been received from *a 'relevant independent advisor'* rather than a qualified lawyer. Such advisors would of course include lawyers but also trade union officials and advice workers.

There is no reason why a compromise agreement should not contain detailed information in order to prevent further conflict and costly litigation. *Cox v. Sun Alliance Life Ltd.* 2001 is a case which focuses on the content of a reference where an employee had resigned while under investigation. Lord Justice Mummery in the Court of Appeal said *'in a case where the terms of an agreed resignation or the compromise of an unfair dismissal claim make provision for the supply of a reference, the parties should ensure as far as possible that the exact wording of a fair and accurate reference is fully discussed, clearly agreed and carefully recorded in writing at the same time as other severance terms'.*

Recently in *Hinton v. University of East London* 2005, the Court of Appeal has adopted a strict interpretation of the requirements for a valid compromise agreement and reversed the more liberal interpretation of the EAT. To be valid and effective the compromise agreement must specifically identify a statutory complaint in order to prevent a claimant bringing that complaint in future proceedings. Here a complaint in relation to a specific statutory provision[16] had been raised by the claimant and to compromise any potential claim the Court of Appeal ruled that the agreement needed to specifically mention the particular s.47(B) complaint. In relation to claims that were not yet subject to proceedings it was *'good practice for the particulars of the nature of the allegations and of the statute under which they are made or the common law basis of the alleged claim to be inserted in the compromise agreement in the form of a brief factual and legal description'.*

If an opinion is reached that a party's case is particularly weak then the tribunal can issue a warning that if the party concerned proceeds to a full trial, an order for costs may be made against him. While the tribunal rarely awards costs, it has a discretion to do so where a party, in bringing the proceedings, has acted frivolously, vexatiously or otherwise unreasonably. By proceeding with a claim after a pre-trial review has decided that it is particularly weak, a party would be regarded as acting unreasonably. An employee who brings a claim without any substance with the aim of harassing the employer, acts frivolously or vexatiously and could have costs awarded against him of up to £10,000 under the 2004 Regulations.

Under the Employment Tribunals Act 1996 the EAT has power to make a restriction order against a vexatious litigant to bar him from bringing any further proceedings without the leave of the EAT. In *Attorney General v. Wheen* 2000 such an order was made against the applicant who had instituted 13 separate discrimination proceedings against various employers all of which were unsuccessful and some of which were regarded as frivolous or vexatious. The aim of this power is to protect respondents from the cost of anxiety of

---

16. S.47(B) Employment Rights Act 1996

vexatious claims and ensure that the tribunal time is devoted to proceedings where the applicant has a reasonable prospect of success.

Pre-hearing review

In 1980 a screening process of pre-hearing assessments was introduced under which either party would apply to the tribunal to examine the papers and rule on the merits of the case and the defence. The system of pre-hearing assessments has now been replaced by the pre-hearing review. Under this procedure either party to the proceedings can apply to the tribunal to order a pre-hearing review. This can be carried out by a single person[17] or the full tribunal and significantly, at the review, a party to the proceedings may be required to pay a deposit of up to £500 if he wishes to continue to participate in the proceedings. The aim of course is obvious, to discourage unmeritorious or ill founded claims.

The pre-hearing reviews replace the pre-hearing assessment where the present possible warning as to costs, if the tribunal decides that a party has no reasonable prospect of success, has been of limited success in weeding out ill founded complaints. The danger of introducing a system of deposit which may not be returnable and possibly paid over to another party is that it may have the effect of discouraging applicants of limited means from approaching a tribunal at all. It has been called 'a tax on justice'. The availability of a sum such as £500 to a claimant who has just lost his/her job should not be assumed. Bear in mind also that legal aid does not extend to representation before an employment tribunal.

The Hearing

An employment tribunal hearing is not conducted with the same degree of formality as a trial in a court of law and the Rules of Procedure makes it clear that a tribunal may conduct a hearing in a manner most suitable to clarify the issues, without the need to comply strictly to the normal rules relating to the admissibility of evidence. This makes it possible for lay representation, often by a trade union official.

> In *Bache v. Essex County Council* 2000 the Court of Appeal considered the statutory right of an applicant to be represented by the person of their choice and ruled that even if the tribunal believes that the representation is incompetent it cannot take away the applicants choice of representation. The tribunal does have power to regulate the conduct of the representative in the performance of his task.
>
> In tribunal proceedings oral evidence is adduced through the process of witness examination, cross examination and re-examination similar to court proceedings. Tribunals do have power however to control this process and the EAT held in *Zurich Insurance Co. v. Gibson* 1998 that a party does not have an absolute right to cross examination and the tribunal could take the view that it would not be assisted by a particular line of enquiry and so prevent a cross examination. The tribunal may feel that an issue has been sufficiently considered without hearing further evidence.

Legal aid is not available for legal representation which may put the claimant under a disadvantage, particularly if the employer is legally represented. In an attempt to speed up

---

17. The legal chairman

the tribunal proceedings there is no longer a requirement to provide full reasons for a decision except in cases involving discrimination. The reasons must be recorded in a written document signed by the chairman but they could be recorded in a 'full' or 'summary' form. The EAT considered this in *Speciality Care v. Pachela* 1996 and indicated that the mandatory requirement for a tribunal to give reasons for its decision, means that there should be sufficient reasons to show the parties why they won or lost. This particular complaint involved an allegation of dismissal by reason of trade union membership. The EAT stated that *'in practice where a complaint of dismissal by reason of union membership is made, as in this case, it will be for the tribunal to find as a fact whether or not the reason or principal reason for dismissal related to the applicant's trade union membership not only by reference to whether he or she had simply joined a union, but also by reference to whether the introduction of union representation into the employment relationship has led the employer to dismiss the employee. Tribunals should answer that question robustly, based on their findings as to what really caused the dismissal in the mind of the employer'.*

In relation to summary reasons, Lord Donaldson MR in the Court of Appeal hearing of *William Hill Organisation Ltd. v. Gavas* 1990 said that *'It is the practice for employment tribunals to give summary reasons and then, if asked, to amplify them as full reasons. It may be convenient to say that, certainly in my experience...we are getting into the position...in which summary reasons have grown and grown until they are scarcely distinguishable from full reasons.'* He went on to suggest that guidance should be given by the EAT to get tribunals *'back to first principles'* so that the applicant and respondent are given no more than in essence what is the reason for the decision when summary reasons are given.

As a general rule a tribunal must not award costs or expenses against a party unless it considers that the party has acted frivolously, vexatiously or otherwise unreasonably in bringing or conducting the case.

> In *Port of London Authority v. Payne (No2)* 1993 it was held that an order for costs is appropriate where one of the parties has been deliberately untruthful in the presentation of the case. Here the employer had been deliberately untruthful in giving reasons for dismissal and was ordered to pay 40% of the claimant's costs.

If a tribunal postpones or adjourns a hearing at the request of a party it can order that party to pay costs or expenses incurred.

In *Cooper and Edwards v. Weatherwise (Roofing & Walling) Ltd.* 1993 a late application for the adjournment of an unfair dismissal claim by the complainant was rejected by the tribunal. Nevertheless, given the complainants non appearance at the hearing, an adjournment was granted and an order made that the complainant should pay the defendant's costs, £4,000, otherwise the application would not proceed. The EAT held that the tribunal had exceeded its powers in granting costs incurred as a result of the adjournment and specifying that the application could only proceed on their payment.

While tribunals will always endeavour to reach unanimous decisions they have authority to reach majority verdicts, exceptionally the lay members disagreeing with the legal chairman.

In *Anglian Home Improvements v. Kelly* 2004 Lord Justice Mummery in the Court of Appeal said that *'It is undesirable, on the whole, for tribunals to reach split decisions. In some cases that will be inevitable but it is preferable, if it is possible to do so, for all efforts to be made to reach a unanimous decision. Unanimity is more likely if time is given after an initial disagreement for everybody to consider the position. If at the conclusion of the hearing, members are unable to agree on what the result of the complaint should be, it is preferable for the chairman to reserve the decision so that he can write it up and circulate it to the other members. If it is the two lay members who are in the majority and are disagreeing with the chairman, it is preferable to give the two lay members not only an opportunity to see that their views are correctly expressed in the decision document drafted by the chairman, but also an opportunity to reflect on the grounds on which they are disagreeing with the chairman about the outcome of the hearing.'*

The various remedies that are available to a tribunal will depend upon the nature of the claim but they range from compensation awards to orders requiring a course of action such as reinstatement, declarations and recommendations. An employment tribunal has no power to enforce its own remedies so that if a mandatory order such as reinstatement is not complied with, it can be reduced to a compensation award and if necessary enforced in the county court. If a party wishes to lodge an appeal against a tribunal decision they must do so within 42 days of the document recording the decision being sent to the parties.

The Employment Appeal Tribunal (EAT)

An appeal from an employment tribunal in England, Wales and Scotland on a question of law or a mixed question of law and fact will lie to the Employment Appeal Tribunal. The major part of the case-law referred to throughout this text will be references to judgments of the EAT. First established in 1975, the EAT is regulated by the Employment Tribunals Act 1996. The President of the EAT will be a High Court judge or a Lord Justice of Appeal who will normally sit with two lay members drawn from a panel of persons who have proven industrial relations experience. The procedure of the EAT is regulated by the Employment Appeal Tribunal Rules 1993. The time limit for submitting an appeal from a tribunal decision is 42 days and this involves submitting a notice of appeal together with the reasons for it and a copy of the tribunal decision. Even without the full reasons the EAT can authorise an appeal if it considers that it would lead to the *'more expeditious or economic disposal of any proceedings or would otherwise be desirable in the interests of justice'.* Appeal from the decision of the EAT lies to the ordinary courts, namely the Court of Appeal and from there, in rare cases, an appeal lies to the House of Lords.

We have already said that the tribunal is the final arbiter on questions of fact so you should appreciate that the EAT has only limited jurisdiction to interfere with its decision-making.

> In *East Berkshire Health Authority v. Matadeen* 1992, a case which we will consider in relation to unfair dismissal, the Employment Appeal Tribunal, after examining previous case law, stated its own view of its authority to reverse the decision of an employment tribunal. The EAT identified three situations where it can allow an appeal against the decision of a tribunal, if, *'first, there is an error of law on the face of the decision, a misdirection or misapplication of the law; secondly, if there is a material finding of fact relied on by the tribunal in the decision which was unsupported by any evidence or contrary to the evidence before them; and thirdly, if there is a finding of perversity'.* An incorrect application of the law or a misinterpretation of the evidence could justify an intervention by the EAT as could more controversially a finding of perversity. To conclude that a decision is perverse the EAT must decide that in the light of their own experience the decision reached is not a permissible option. A perverse decision is one which is *'a conclusion which offends reason or is one to which no reasonable employment tribunal could come'* or *'so very clearly wrong that it just cannot stand'.* The EAT stressed that *'the occasion upon which the EAT can interfere with the decision of*

an employment tribunal on the grounds of perversity is likely to be very rare. EAT members should caution themselves against so doing and in particular be careful not merely to substitute their own views for those of the tribunal. They cannot interfere merely because they disagree. They cannot interfere even if they feel strongly that the result is unjust. However, in that latter case, it may be that on careful analysis the decision flies in the face of properly informed logic'.

Perversity then is only a limited ground for interfering with the discretion of the tribunal in relation to questions of fact.

In *Clancy v. Cannock Chase Technical College* 2001 the employment tribunal upheld a complaint of unfair dismissal brought by a college lecturer who was dismissed by reason of redundancy, mainly because of the many serious procedural shortcomings in the way he was selected. The tribunal declined however to make an order for his re-engagement on the grounds that it would not be reasonably practicable having regard to the worsening redundancy situation at the college. The applicant appealed against the tribunal's finding that it was not practicable to make an order for re-engagement claiming that the decision was perverse. The appeal was rejected by the EAT which stressed the limited nature of a plea of perversity *'where an employment tribunal directs itself correctly on the law and hears and accepts evidence as to impracticability and then sets out its reasoning clearly and fully, a plea that the tribunal's refusal to order re-employment was perverse is virtually impossible. The task of an appellant raising the plea of perversity, never easy, is, if anything, more difficult in this area. Of all the subjects properly to be left to the exclusive province of an employment tribunal as an 'industrial jury', few can be more obviously their territory than the issue of 'practicability' with the Employment Rights Act'.*[18]

If an appellate body decides that the tribunal has reached its decision by relying on findings of fact not supported by the evidence then it is entitled to overturn the decision. There are few examples of cases where the EAT has clearly relied on the misinterpretation of the evidence as a ground for interfering with a tribunal's decision

An early example is provided by *City of Edinburgh District Council v. Stephen* 1977. Here the evidence suggested that a night watchman had absented himself from his duties and falsified the signing off book. The tribunal felt that the decision to dismiss him was an unduly harsh penalty and upheld the complaint of unfair dismissal. On appeal however the EAT held that the finding of fact that the employee should have been given the benefit of the doubt when he claimed that his absence was due to illness was contradictory to the evidence. *'The question was whether the employers could reasonably conclude on the material available to than … that the employee was not ill … and that was the only reasonable conclusion they could have reached.'* The finding of fact, relied on by the tribunal was not supported by the evidence so the decision would be reversed. In addition in finding that dismissal was an unduly harsh penalty for an employee of the applicant's age and experience, the tribunal had applied the wrong test by substituting its own views rather than asking whether the employer acted reasonably in dismissing the applicant.

If a decision of the EAT conflicts with a higher court then an employment tribunal is bound to follow the higher court's decision. If two EAT decisions conflict then the tribunal has a choice as to which decision to follow. The EAT is not bound to follow its own decisions, which are persuasive, but the EAT will normally try to be consistent. In Chapter

---

18. See Chapter 11

11 on Unfair Dismissal there is a consideration of the *'band of reasonable response, test'* which is applied to determine the fairness or otherwise of an employer's decision to dismiss an employee Despite the fact that this test was approved by the Court of Appeal, the EAT in *Haddon v. Van Den Bergh Foods* 1999 held that it should no longer be applied. In March 2000 a differently constituted EAT held in *Maddon v. Midland Bank* 2000 that the EAT has no authority to disregard a test from the Court of Appeal and that the test should be applied until the Court of Appeal decides otherwise. *'In the light of the doctrine of precedent no court short of the Court of Appeal can disregard the band of reasonable response test as the determinative test in considering whether dismissal was reasonable in the circumstances.'*

Subsequently the Court of Appeal ruled in *Post Office v. Foley* 2000 that the EAT had indeed departed from previous authorities and reaffirmed the band of reasonable response test.[19]

The Ordinary Courts

In addition to the important appellate jurisdiction of the Court of Appeal and the House of Lords, the ordinary courts of first instance, both civil (the county court and the High Court) and criminal (the Magistrates Court and the Crown Court) have a role to play in the resolution of conflict in employment disputes. In the early chapters of the book the nature of the contract of employment will be explored and like any other contract the mutual obligations of the parties to it are enforceable by legal action in the ordinary courts. An action for breach of contract in the county court or the High Court seeking damages, a declaration or an injunction, as a remedy, will be at the suit of the employer or employee in the event of non-performance or partial performance of contractual obligations. Generally the High Court will hear claims where the damages claimed exceed £50,000.

Previously we stated employment tribunals now have concurrent jurisdiction over breach of contract claims of up to £25,000, when the contract of employment has terminated. There are some important differences between bringing a claim before a court or a tribunal. In the courts the claimant can represent himself or more usually employ legal representation. In the tribunal however an applicant can be represented by the person of their choice, often a trade union official. Even if the tribunal feels that the representative is unsuitable the applicant has the final discretion as to representation. Representation in courts may be legally aided and costs awarded at the discretion of the court, usually against the unsuccessful party. There is no provision for legally aided representation in tribunals and costs are awarded only in exceptional cases.

In Chapters 4 and 5 you will see that a court order such as a declaration or an injunction may be sought usually in the High Court, where an employer alleges that industrial action is in breach of contract. When we consider health and safety at work[20], you will see that a civil action based on the tort of negligence may be brought against employers in the county court or the High Court alleging primary or vicarious liability. Also breaches of the Health and Safety at Work Act 1974 could lead to criminal prosecutions brought by the Health and Safety Executive in the Magistrates Court or in serious cases, on indictment in the Crown Court. In Chapter 2 the significant role of the European Court of Justice in interpreting Community law was considered. Following the adoption of the European

---

19. See Chapter 11
20. See Chapter 8

Convention on Human Rights in October 2000 the European Court of Human Rights has a role to play in the development of employment law.

The European Court of Justice

The Court of Justice sits in Luxembourg and is composed of 15 judges who are appointed by the mutual agreement of the member states for renewable periods of six years. They must be persons of absolute independence who are qualified to hold the highest judicial office in their own country or who are legal experts of recognised competence. The court is assisted by nine Advocates-General, who must hold similar qualifications to the judges and are appointed on the same basis. It is the duty of the Advocate-General, acting with complete impartiality and independence, to make reasoned submissions in open court as to the application of Community law to the questions posed in the case before the court. The opinion of the Advocate-General is not binding on the court, which may decide the case in a different way, although this is unusual. There is no equivalent to the Advocate-General within the English legal system.

The Court of Justice has power to hear the following types of case:

- *Actions against member states* Where it appears that a member state has failed to fulfil an obligation under Community law the Commission may take infringement proceedings under Article 169. Other member states are also able to bring this type of case, under Article 170, provided that they first bring the matter to the attention of the Commission. Prior to the Treaty on European Union the powers of the Court of Justice in such cases were limited to making a declaration requiring the defaulting member state to take the necessary measures to comply with its judgment. There was no effective sanction, other than political pressure, to enforce compliance. Under the new Treaty, however, a member state may ultimately be fined if it fails to comply with the court's ruling.

- *Actions against community institutions* The Court of Justice has power to review the legality of acts of Community Institutions, or their failure to act. The court may declare void any illegal action, award damages and review decisions.

- *Employment disputes between the Community and its employees* The Court of Justice acts as an employment tribunal for the employees of Community institutions. Cases of this type account for just under a quarter of its case load.

- *Preliminary rulings under Article 177* Any court or tribunal in a member state may request a preliminary ruling from the Court of Justice as to the meaning or interpretation of an aspect of Community law. Such a request may be made where the ruling is required to enable that court or tribunal to give judgment in a case before it. Where there is no appeal from its decision, the court or tribunal must request a preliminary ruling if it considers this necessary to enable it to give judgment. This procedure provides an important bridge between the legal systems of member states and that of the Community. It is designed to ensure that Community law is applied and interpreted in a uniform manner throughout all member states. The function of the Court of Justice is simply to rule on the interpretation of Community law, in the light of which the domestic court or tribunal will decide the case before it.

As stated the request for a preliminary ruling as to the meaning of Community Law may come from any Member State. This means the Community Law is interpreted and applied by the European Court of Justice through case-law from France, Germany, Italy etc. and those decisions are reported in the UK to assist our understanding of the law. The Equal Treatment Directive 1976 is a good example of a measure which has been subject to case-law interpretation.

In *Mahlburg v. Lond Mecklenburg-Vorpommem* 2000 a Regional Labour Court in Germany referred a number of questions to the European Court of Justice for a ruling. In the case before it a nurse employed under a fixed term contract at Rostock University became pregnant and applied for a theatre nurse post on an indefinite contract. The employers had rejected her application on the grounds that the German law on the protection of working mothers prohibited employers from employing pregnant women in areas where they would be exposed to harmful substances. The nurse claimed that the decision to reject her under this law infringed the Equal Treatment Directive and constituted sex discrimination. This issue was the subject of the request for a preliminary ruling. The European Court ruled in favour of the nurse and held that it is contrary to the Equal Treatment Directive for an employer to refuse to appoint a pregnant woman to a post of an unlimited duration because of a statutory prohibition relating to pregnancy. The potential financial loss suffered by the employer caused by the fact that she could not work in the post for the duration of her pregnancy was not a justification to refuse to employ her.

You should appreciate that although the above case originated in Germany it is reported in the UK law reports because it provides a useful authority when considering the extent to which the European Treatment Directive may override UK statutory provisions.

Advisory Conciliation and Arbitration Service (ACAS)

ACAS has a crucial role to play in the resolution of conflict in employment law both at the individual level between employer and employee and the collective level between the trade union and the employer or employer's organisation. It is charged under s.209 of the Trade Union and Labour Relations (Consolidation) Act 1992 with the general duty of *'promoting the improvement of industrial relations'*. Under the Trade Union Reform and Employment Rights Act 1993 the previous duty of ACAS to encourage the extension of collective bargaining was removed as from the 30 August 1993. Based in London with offices in regional centres, ACAS is managed by a Council consisting of a full-time chairman and nine other members. Its many functions are now contained in the Trade Union and Labour Relations (Consolidation) Act 1992, ranging from conciliation, arbitration, advice, inquiry and the production of Codes of Practice. In relation to collective employment law the range of matters where ACAS can give advice are contained in s.213.

- *The organisation of workers or employers for the purpose of collective bargaining.*
- *The recognition of trade unions by employers.*
- *Machinery for the negotiation of terms and conditions of employment and for joint consultation.*
- *Procedure for avoiding and settling disputes and workers' grievances.*
- *Questions relating to communication between employee and workers.*
- *Facilities for officials of trade unions.*

- *Procedures relating to the termination of employment.*
- *Disciplinary matters.*
- *Manpower planning, labour turnover and absenteeism.*
- *Recruitment, retention, promotion and vocational training of workers.*
- *Payment systems, including job evaluations and equal pay.*

In addition ACAS may if it thinks fit, inquire into any question relating to industrial relations generally or in relation to a particular industry or a particular undertaking. If it appears desirable the findings of the inquiry may be published. Also, the service has power to issue Codes of Practice containing practical guidance for the purpose of promoting the improvement of industrial relations. Furthermore the service is required to issue Codes of Practice providing practical guidance on the disclosure of information for collective bargaining purposes and time off for trade union officials and members.

For the purpose of this text, concentrating on individual employment law, we are more concerned with the role of ACAS in conciliating in individual conflict rather than industrial action. We have already mentioned the significant role played by ACAS in promoting the settlement of tribunal cases and the high rate of success. A further significant development will be the Arbitration scheme for Unfair Dismissal, drawn up by ACAS, which is aimed at easing the burden on tribunals.

Alternative dispute resolution

On the 21 May 2001 a system of voluntary binding arbitration administered by ACAS was introduced for 'straightforward' unfair dismissal complaints. The aim is to ease the case-load of Employment Tribunals by offering a system of dispute resolution which is confidential, relatively fast and cost efficient. Procedures under the scheme are intended to be non legislative and flexible offering an alternative approach to conflict resolution by applying general principles of fairness and good employment conduct to the complaint relying on ACAS Codes of Practice rather than strict legal rules. The scheme was introduced under s.212A(1) of the Trade Union and Labour Relations (Consolidation) Act 1992 and applies only to cases of unfair dismissal which are categorised as straightforward because they do not involve jurisdictional or complex legal issues or raise points of EC law. A jurisdictional issue in an unfair dismissal complaint could involve questions such as:

- is the applicant qualified as an employee?
- does the applicant have the necessary continuous service?
- has the claim been brought within the time limits?

As the scheme is entirely voluntary both parties must agree to refer an existing complaint. This means that the employer could not rely on an automatic reference claim in a contract of employment. The written agreement to use the scheme must have arisen through ACAS consultation or a compromise agreement. The agreement must be accompanied by a separate waiver of rights of appeal completed by both parties. Such a waiver however would not affect the operation of the Human Rights Act 1998 in so far as it is relevant and applicable.

In agreeing to arbitration the parties must have agreed that a dismissal has taken place but as you will see in Chapter 10 an allegation of constructive dismissal is sometimes the core of the conflict. Cases of alleged constructive dismissal will only be accepted for arbitration on the issue of fairness alone, a highly unlikely scenario. To save costs the location of the private hearing would be the workplace or the ACAS office. Evidence is presented informally and while there is no power to make witness orders failure to cooperate can count against parties when decisions are reached. As yet, alternative dispute resolution has not provided a popular alternative to tribunal proceedings and only a handful of cases have been dealt with using this process. In 2003 only seven cases were dealt with by this process.

Commission for Equality and Human Rights

You will see in Chapter 6 that the law on discrimination in employment is contained in various Statutes and Regulations. There is a strong feeling among employment lawyers that there should be a single and comprehensive Equality Act. The government is committed to implement the creation of a Commission for Equality and Human Rights, which will eventually take over from the Equal Opportunities Commission, the Commission for Racial Equality and the Disability Rights Commission, as well as being responsible for Human Rights. The new Commission will be required to conduct a review of the law with the aim of producing a single Act to deal with all forms of discrimination. For the moment we have a number of Commissions dealing with discrimination.

The Commission for Racial Equality

The Commission for Racial Equality was established under the Race Relations Act 1976 and is charged with the following duties:

- to work towards the elimination of discrimination;
- to promote equality of opportunity and good relations between persons of different racial groups generally; and
- to help keep under review the working of the Act and when required to do so by the Secretary of State, draw up and submit proposals for amendments.

Power is also conferred on the Commission to grant financial assistance to organisations which appear to be concerned with the promotion of racial harmony and also undertake or assist in research on educational activities for this purpose. Every year the Commission must submit an annual report to the Secretary of State to be laid before Parliament.

The law relating to racial discrimination is examined later in the text (see Chapter 6). It is found in the Race Relations Act 1976 and its interpretation in numerous reported case-law decisions.

A major role of the Commission is to review the working of the legislation, report and make recommendations. Under its Code of Practice for the elimination of racial discrimination and the promotion of equal opportunity in employment the Commission recommends that employers should monitor the effects of selection decisions and personal practices. The legal status of the Code is that it is admissible in evidence in tribunal proceedings and *'if any provision of such a code appears to be relevant to any question arising in the proceedings it shall be taken into account on determining that question'.*

The present power to conduct formal investigations is that they may be instigated for any purpose in connection with the Commission's duties. On completion of an investigation, the Commission must prepare a report within which it can make recommendations for changes in policies or procedures to individuals or organisations, and recommendations for changes in the law to the Secretary of State. Only the Commission may bring proceedings before the county court in respect of certain unlawful acts, namely discriminatory advertising, unlawful instructions to discriminate and unlawful inducements to discriminate.

As an agency upon which statutory power has been conferred, the Commission is obliged to ensure that it does not misinterpret those powers, otherwise its actions may be declared unlawful.

> In *Commission for Racial Equality v. Prestige Group* 1984 the House of Lords considered the power of the Commission to conduct an investigation of a named person, in this case the respondent company. The court held that before such an investigation can commence the Commission must have formed the opinion that an act of unlawful discrimination had occurred (albeit on tenuous evidence). Here the investigation had started without such a belief, or without firstly having given the company an opportunity to make representations. The investigation was therefore unlawful and the non-discrimination notice issued as a result of it was ultra-vires and void.

The Equal Opportunities Commission

In relation to sex discrimination, the Sex Discrimination Act 1975 established the Equal Opportunities Commission charging it with similar duties to those imposed on the Commission for Racial Equality. They include:

- to work towards the elimination of discrimination;
- to promote equality of opportunity between men and women;
- to keep under review the legislation.

The EOC is also obliged to produce and submit an annual report to be laid before Parliament by the Secretary of State. Similar powers are also conferred on the EOC to finance research and educational activities and issue Codes of Practice. The EOC is empowered to conduct formal investigations in which persons may be required to furnish information or give evidence. The EOC must then report and make recommendations in the light of any of their findings. If in the course of an investigation the EOC is satisfied that discriminatory acts or practices have occurred, then it may issue a non-discrimination notice. Proceedings in respect of discriminatory advertising, discriminatory instructions or inducements can only be brought by the EOC. Both the CRA and EOC have a role to play in assisting an individual who is an actual or prospective complainant. This assistance may be granted if the case in question raises an issue of principle or because of its complexity, it is unreasonable to expect the complainant to deal with it unaided or by reason of any other special considerations. The assistance which both Commissions may offer extends to giving advice, procuring a settlement of the dispute, arranging for legal advice and/or representation and any other appropriate assistance.

When we explore the law relating to gender discrimination you will recognise that there are many areas of conflict between domestic law and European Community Law. The House of Lords has confirmed that part of the role of the EOC, and presumably other similar agencies, is to challenge UK legislation in the courts where there is perceived to be a conflict with EC law. In the momentous decision in *R v. Secretary of State for Employment ex parte EOC* 1994 the House of Lords struck out national limitations on redundancy and unfair dismissal rights for part-time workers as contrary to Article 119 of the Treaty of

Rome.[21] Their lordships ruled that in considering the statutory duties of the EOC, in particular to work towards the elimination of discrimination, it was perfectly proper for the EOC to work towards securing amendments to legislation and to attempt to achieve this by means of an application for judicial review in the High Court.

Disability Rights Commission

The Disability Rights Commission Act 1999 established the Disability Rights Commission and from April 2000 it took over the role of the National Disability Council. The Commission was given powers which mirror the EOC and the CRE but in relation to the Disability Discrimination Act 1995:

- to promote opportunities for disabled people;
- to monitor the Act and eliminate discrimination;
- to inform and assist individuals in bringing claims under the Act;
- to inform and advise employers;
- to conciliate in certain disputes;
- to conduct formal investigations and publish the outcome;
- to issue the code of practice;
- to issue a non discrimination notice when it believes a person is committing or has committed an unlawful act or apply for an injunction.

Disability discrimination law is dealt with in Chapter 6.

Health and Safety Commission/Executive

A further example of where agencies have been created by statute to monitor and enforce an area of employment law is the Health and Safety at Work Act.[22] By this Act the Health and Safety Commission and the Health and Safety Executive were created. The Commission consists of a chairman and a number of commissioners and performs its functions under the direction of the Secretary of State for Employment. Its wide ranging duties include:

- arranging for research and promoting training in health and safety at work;
- submitting proposals for regulation and issuing Codes of Practice;
- assisting and encouraging the furtherance of the objectives of the 1974 Act;
- acting as an information and advisory service.

The Executive took over the role of the Factory Inspectorate and its essential function is to enforce health and safety law. To this end the Executive through its inspectorate carries out inspections of work places, suggests improvements and has power to issue improvement and prohibition notices and, if necessary, bring prosecutions. The law on health and safety is the subject of Chapter 8.

The Working Time Regulations limit the number of hours that a worker can work in a week. The Regulations make the Health and Safety Executive responsible for enforcing certain requirements including the requirement on an employer under Regulation 4(2) to

---

21. Now Article 141
22. See Chapter 8

take all reasonable steps to ensure compliance with the 48 hour limit, with the possibility of criminal proceedings if an employer fails to comply.

An example of a health and safety prosecution by the Health and Safety Executive, and the imposition of a fine is provided by *R v. Rollco Screw and Rivet Co. Ltd.* 1999. The case concerned the inadequate precautions taken when carrying out shipping of asbestos. Factory staff and public were put in danger when work was carried out without proper precautions. The prosecution was brought against the company and its two directors who had contracted out the work to a firm and who had in turn sub contracted the work. A severe fine was imposed on the company and its directors. On appeal it was argued that the sum the company was ordered to pay was grossly excessive amounting to over seventy thousand pounds payable over six years. The period of repayment was excessive and was reduced by a year and sum payable for the costs element was reduced by £10,000. In assessing fines in health and safety law the Court of Appeal held that two questions should be posed *first, what financial penalty does the offence merit? Second, what financial penalty can a dependent (whether corporate or personal) reasonably be ordered to meet? That second question invariably raises the question of the time period over which any sum is payable.'*

Further Reading

Collins and Freedland *Finding the Right Direction for the 'Industrial Jury'* (2000) 29 ILJ 288.

Dolder, Cheryl *The Contribution of Mediation to Workplace Justice* (2004) ILJ 320.

Earnshaw and Hardy *Assessing an Arbitral Route for Unfair Dismissal* (2001) 30 ILJ 215.

Macmillan, John *Employment Tribunals Philosophies and Practicabilities* (1999) 28 ILJ 33.

Philips and Bowers *Restricting Reporting Orders in the Employment Tribunal* (1999) 28 ILJ 85.

Points of Procedure (2004) 735,749 IRLB 3.

Chapter 3

Employment Relationships

An employment relationship exists where one person, an employer, who may be an individual, partnership, or corporate body, employs another person or persons to perform some work. The relationship could be one of employed status as an employer and employee under a contract of service. Alternatively it could be that of self-employed status as an employer and contractor under a contract for services. Status as an employed or self-employed person can have numerous legal and economic consequences.

There is in addition a further legal relationship recognised by statute, that of employer and worker.[1] This would normally include an individual who provides personal service for an employer either as an employee or as a contractor other than through a business. Both employees and workers are defined under statute and we will examine these definitions and how they have been interpreted. A difficult but further important issue to address is the legal status of agency workers which will be considered at the end of the Chapter.

There are an infinite variety of terms and conditions under which one person may do work for another. The requirements of employers will range from the need to engage full-time employees where a long standing indefinite relationship with their staff is envisaged, characterised by mutual trust and confidence between the parties, to the use of atypical temporary workers engaged to complete a particular task employed through an agency or for a fixed term. It may be that the temporary worker, such as an accountant, plumber or solicitor, provides a specialist skill which is required by the employer only on an intermittent basis. Alternatively temporary and casual employment only may be offered, because of economic necessity or the expansion or contraction of the size of the workforce in line with demand. There is evidence to suggest that some employers use casual staff merely as a device to avoid inconvenient statutory rights and costs. These economically dependent workers, often at the bottom of the employment ladder, are surely deserving of the protection of employment law.

---

1. Numerous statutory rights apply to workers

Independent contractors (or self-employed workers) are now well established as a substantial proportion of the workforce of some industries, for instance, the media, catering and construction. There are many skilled workers in the UK who see the flexibility and independence of self-employed status as a beneficial and entirely appropriate employment relationship. Of the million or so construction workers in the UK well over half a million are self-employed. This form of employment can have many advantages for both sides to the contract. The employer 'gets the job done' and the self-employed contractor has the freedom to accept or refuse work and is normally well paid in return. A criticism of the system is that it can be used by employers to deny basic employment rights to casual workers who may be classified as self-employed. Our first task is to examine the traditional employment relationship in the UK, that of employer and employee under a contract of employment.

Employees and Employers

You should appreciate that the process of identifying a contract of employment has been an employment law issue for many decades to which distinguished labour lawyers have applied their minds. Many years ago the eminent labour lawyer Otto Kahn-Freund said that the contract of employment *'is the cornerstone of a modern system of labour law and we should be able to recognise it'*. Lord Wedderburn of Charlton likened the contract to an elephant when he said that it was *'an animal easy to recognise when you see it but too difficult to define'*.

The definition of an employee is contained in s.230 of the Employment Rights Act 1996.

Under s.230(1) *an employee means an individual who has entered into or works under (or worked under) a contract of employment.*

Under s.230(2) *a contract of employment means a contract of service or apprenticeship whether express or implied and if express oral or in writing.*

The definition tells us that to achieve the status of an employee it is necessary to have agreed a contract of employment. Furthermore such a contract could be expressly agreed or implied from the conduct of the parties. An express contract may also be orally agreed and could even consist of written and oral terms. We will examine the law relating to the formation of a contract of employment in Chapter 4.

In *Hewlett Packard Ltd. v. O'Murphy* 2002 the EAT emphasised an obvious but nonetheless significant fact. To fall within the statutory definition under s.230 the individual concerned must at least have a contract with the alleged employer. *'If an individual fails to satisfy the tribunal that there was a contract of some kind, that is the end of the claim based on the assertion that he has entered into or worked under a contract of employment within the meaning of s.230 of the Employment Rights Act.'* Here the individual had supplied his services through a service company to an agency who placed him with the client. Despite a long relationship with the client, as there was no contract between the respective parties there could be no contract of employment.[2]

Certainly it would be difficult for a volunteer worker to claim the status of employee without establishing the existence of a contractual relationship.

---

2. Contracts can of course be implied

Recently in *Melhuish v. Redbridge CAB* 2005 the EAT agreed with the Tribunal that a volunteer advice worker, working one or two days a week, could not establish his status as an employee under s.230 of the Employment Rights Act and without a contract of employment could not bring a complaint of unfair dismissal. In addition the lack of any mutuality of obligation and the absence of a wage meant that there was no consideration for the purposes of any contractual relationship.[3]

It should be stressed however that an implied contract of employment under s.230 may be found by the courts or tribunals having examined all of the circumstances of the particular case.

Helpful guidance was provided by the Court of Appeal in *Franks v. Reuters* 2003 when deciding the relationship between an agency worker and the Agency's client.[4] The court held that in determining status the tribunal is not limited to the documentation but should take account of all the relevant evidence about the dynamics of the work relationship between the parties and then make findings of fact. While a person cannot become an employee because of long service, dealings between the parties over a number of years as distinct from weeks or months, typical of temporary or casual work, are capable of generating an implied contractual relationship. *'An employment tribunal should not conclude that an individual is not an 'employee' in terms of s.230 of the Employment Rights Act without first determining as a fact whether, on a consideration of all the relevant evidence, including what was said and done, as well as any relevant documents, there was an implied contract of service between the relevant parties. Drawing a line between those who are employees, and so have statutory employment rights, and those who are not entitled to statutory employment protection has become more difficult as work relations in and away from the workplace have become more complex and more diverse. This development makes it all the more important that the employment tribunal, as the tribunal of fact, should consider all the relevant evidence about the dynamics of the work relationship between the person claiming to be an employee and the putative employer. Before characterising the relationship, the tribunal must make clear and comprehensive findings of fact on the relevant evidence, including not only any documentation, but also the circumstances surrounding it, the subsequent conduct of the parties, and the way in which the parties operated and understood the situation. Unless and until the tribunal has conducted this exercise and obtained an overall picture of the work relationships between the parties, it is impossible in many cases for it to reach an informed and sound conclusion on whether there is mutuality of obligation in the form of an express or implied contract of service.'*

The Court of Appeal in *Franks* above is emphasising the difficulty of recognising a contract of employment and stressing the fact that the tribunal must examine all of the evidence including documentation, the parties intention and their conduct.

Unfortunately section 230 is circular and provides no guidance as to how a contract of employment may be distinguished from other contractual arrangements where individuals are engaged to perform work as self-employed contractors. It is to the common law that we must turn to provide us with the tools to tackle the issue of contractual status and this necessarily involves an analysis of the relevant case-law.[5]

---

3. See also *Sheffield CAB v. Grayson* 2005
4. See later in the chapter
5. See later in the chapter

You should also appreciate that the statutory definition of employee may vary with different statutory regimes. For instance the definition of employee for the purposes of the Race Relations Act 1976 is contained in s.78 and includes 'employment under a contract of service or of apprenticeship or a contract personally to execute any work or labour.' The issue faced by the Court of Appeal in *Mingeley v. Pennock and Ivory* 2004 was whether a taxi driver who owned his own vehicle and paid a taxi firm a weekly sum of £75 to operate under its radio and computer system fell within the definition. While the driver decided his own hours of work, when he did so he was required to wear the taxi firm's uniform and adhere to its scale of charges. The court held that the driver was not employed under a contract *'personally to execute work or labour'* in circumstances in which there was no mutual obligation to offer or accept work. While this meant that the tribunal had no jurisdiction to hear a complaint of race discrimination the court did comment as to whether it was truly the intention of Parliament to exclude such working relationships from the legislation.

Alternatively in *Percy v. Church of Scotland Board of National Mission* 2006 the House of Lords in a majority decision held that an associate minister's relationship with his employer, the Church of Scotland, constituted employment under the Sex Discrimination Act. She was employed under a contract to personally execute work and was entitled to bring her sex discrimination claim before a tribunal. The finding was not inconsistent with the fact that her status also constituted an eccliastical office.

Particular employees

Some employees, for instance civil servants, the police, prison officers and health services employees, are regarded as special categories and their legal position tends to differ from employees generally. Also while an apprentice is not regarded strictly as an employee, in practice both the common law and statutory rights available to such a person are very similar to those of any full-time worker under a contract of service. Expiration of the apprenticeship contract however does not carry with it a right to a redundancy payment or the right to claim unfair dismissal in the case where there is no offer of full time employment.

In *Wallace v. C A Roofing Services Ltd.* 1996 the plaintiff was employed as an 'apprentice sheet metal worker' for four years and in his statutory statement it provided that 'at the end of your apprenticeship your employer will terminate unless there is a suitable vacancy that we can offer you at the time'. When the plaintiff was dismissed prematurely by reason of redundancy he claimed that his apprenticeship contract could not be terminated on that ground and he sued for damages. The High Court held that the oral agreement entered into was a contract of apprenticeship rather than a contract of employment and it could not be terminated by redundancy other than closure of the business or a fundamental change in the character of the work. The plaintiff was therefore entitled to damages for breach of his apprenticeship contract. *'Although modern legislation has assimilated apprenticeships to contract of employment the contract of apprenticeship remain a distinct entity at common law. Its first purpose is training, the execution of work for the employer is secondary. In such a relationship, the ordinary law as to dismissal does not apply. The contract is for a fixed term and is not terminable at will as a contract of employment is at common law.'*

A company director is regarded as an office holder rather than as someone having an employment relationship with the company. Increasingly, however, company directors have executive positions in their companies and in such circumstances a contract is likely to be drawn up, which will specify their management role. It is then that an employment relationship will arise under which the director could be regarded as an employee of the company, or in some cases an independent contractor.

It is a fundamental principle of company law that a company is a distinct legal entity with its own legal personality. This principle is supported by case-law such as *Lee v. Lees Air Farming* 1961 which recognise the distinction between a company and its membership even where the sole majority shareholder and director is in unrestricted control of the company. The issue in *Buchan and Ivey v. Secretary of State for Employment* 1997 was whether a person who was the director and majority shareholder in a small private company could also be classified as an employee of the company for the purposes of statutory employment rights. Both companies became insolvent and went into receivership. Mr. Buchan as director and full-time employee of his company relied on ss166 and 186 of the Employment Rights Act 1996 and applied to recover arrears of wages, redundancy payments and payments in lieu of notice from the Secretary of State. Mr. Ivey the Managing Director and majority shareholder of his company applied to the Secretary of State for a redundancy payment. In both cases the tribunal held that the directors could not be classified as employees for the purposes of statutory employment rights. Even with a written contract of employment the tribunal held that as controllers of the company the directors were in *'every sense the company'*. *'He was a businessman carrying out the functions of a businessman rather than an employee behaving as such'*. *The EAT agreed and held that 'there is a distinction, properly recognised by the industrial tribunal between an individual running his own business through the medium of a limited company and an individual employee of a limited company who is subject to the control of the board of directors of that company.'*

The Court of Appeal subsequently disagreed with the decision of the EAT in *Buchan and Ivey v. Secretary of State for Employment* that an individual who holds the sole or controlling shareholding in a company cannot be regarded as an employee. In *Secretary of State for Trade and Industry v. Bottrill* 1999 the court held that all the facts must be considered to determine an individual's status one of which is the fact that he has a controlling interest in the company and that is likely to be decisive. But other factors include whether the contract of employment is genuine or a sham, whether the individual is in reality answerable only to himself and whether he is able to vote on matters in which he was personally interested such as his own employment. Here it was possible to conclude that there was a genuine contract of employment.

This approach is given further weight by the judgment in *Sellars Arenascene Ltd. v. Connolly* 2001 in which the Court of Appeal disagreed with the tribunal's decision that the service agreement between the applicant and the companies in which he held a controlling interest did not give rise to a contract of employment. While the fact that the applicant was a controlling shareholder is a significant factor the tribunal *'should not attach a significance to the factor which excludes a proper consideration of all other relevant factors'*. Here the service agreement was found not to be a sham and the applicant had behaved as an employee. Interestingly the court also disagreed with the tribunal's findings that the applicant's entrepreneurial skills and achievements were inconsistent with a position as an employee. *'If the skills and success attributed by the tribunal to the applicant were qualities which prevented a person in his position from enjoying the status of an employee, it would be a severe and unwarranted deterrent to business enterprise.'*

Workers and Employers

The most straightforward employment relationship, well recognised throughout the European Union, is that of the employer and the worker. Increasingly this status has been adopted by UK legislators to receive the protection of statutory rights. 'Workers' have been defined in a number of UK statutes, including the Working Time Regulations 1998.[6] Regulation 2(1) provides that:

'Worker' means an individual who has entered into or work under (or where employment ceased worked under);

(a) *a contract of employment; or*

(b) *any other contract whether express or implied and (if it is express) whether oral or in writing, whereby the individual undertakes to do or perform personally any work or services for another party to the contract whose status is not by virtue of the contract that of a client or customer of any profession or business undertaking carried on by the individual.*

It follows from the definition that as all employees will have a contract of employment under which they are required to provide personal services then they may also be classified as workers. Significantly however contractors would also be included provided they have or seek a contract to provide personal services. Individuals excluded are professional advisors and contractors who reserve the right to sub-contract or contract to provide an end product to which others will contribute. There are many self-employed individuals who will contract to provide their own personal services and who as a consequence are classified as 'workers'. The definition also encompasses the numerous casual contract workers who are often economically dependent on a sole employer.

> In *Byrne Brothers v. Baird* 2002 the EAT attempted to determine the status of self-employed building trade workers who had signed subcontractor agreements. The agreements set out the terms of engagement which made it clear that there was no obligation on the employer to offer or the contractor to accept work 'where the subcontractor is unable to provide the services the subcontractor may provide an alternative worker to undertake the services but only having first obtained the express approval of the contractor.' The agreement also provided that the subcontractor is not entitled to holiday pay, sick pay, or pension rights. The applicants were employed on this basis exclusively on a particular site working under the control of the company. As self-employed labour only subcontractors they paid their own tax having submitted accounts to the Inland Revenue. Their application to the tribunal claimed that as 'workers' they were covered by the Working Time Regulations and entitled to holiday pay. Applying the definition in Reg 2(1)[7] the tribunal discounted 2(1)(a) as there was no contract of employment but there was a contract for the purposes of 2(1)(b). The tribunal also found that the applicant did not offer their service as a business undertaking and they were obliged to perform work personally so they could be classified as 'workers' under the Regulations. The EAT agreed stressing that *'a limited power to appoint a substitute is not inconsistent with an obligation of personal service'.*

---

6. Also defined in s.54(3) National Minimum Wage Act 1998
7. Above

Here the understanding was that the services would be supplied personally other than in exceptional circumstances with the consent of the employer.

The classification is important because there is an increasing tendency to confer statutory rights on 'workers' rather than just 'employees' for example the right to a minimum wage, restrictions on working time and paid holidays.[8] Workers are covered by discrimination legislation[9] and under the Employment Rights Act 1996 are protected from unlawful deductions from their pay.[10] Legislation which applies to workers rather than just employees includes: The National Minimum Wage Act 1998; The Working Time Regulations 1998; The Public Interest Disclosure Act 1999; and the Part-Time Workers Regulations 2000. Significantly under s.23 Employment Relations Act 1999 authority is conferred on the Secretary of State for Employment to extend existing statutory rights to workers who are not employees. There is no doubt that this is a significant but as yet unused power to extend some or all of the long standing rights to 'workers' leaving only the 'genuinely self-employed' outside the statutory protection. There is a strong belief that the casual workers at the bottom of the employment ladder who are genuinely economically dependent should benefit from statutory employment rights. There is also a growing tendency in recent Acts and Regulations to confer rights exclusively on the narrower concept of the employee. The Maternity and Parental Leave Regulations 1999, the Fixed term Employee (Prevention of Less Favourable treatment) Regulations 2002 and the Flexibility Working (Eligibility Complaints and Remedies) Regulations 2002 all apply exclusively to employees.

The EAT in *Bryne* above provided an important insight into the policy behind the extension of employment rights beyond employees to 'workers'. The aim of extending protection in relation to working hours beyond employees is that 'workers' are often substantively and economically in the same position as employees with a similar degree of dependence. It is necessary to distinguish this type of worker from the genuinely independent contractor who would not require this type of legal protection. It may be that to distinguish between the genuine contractor and this *'intermediate category'* of worker it is necessary to consider the features of the engagement such as the degree of control, the exclusivity of the arrangement, the level of financial status the duration and payment and the equipment supplied.

Redrow Homes (Yorkshire) Ltd. v. Wright 2004 involved contract bricklayers, who claimed that they were 'workers' and thus entitled to paid annual holiday under the Working Time Regulations. The company claimed that there was no obligation to do work personally because their standard contract provided that 'the contractor must at all times provide sufficient labour' The Court of Appeal acknowledged that it does not necessarily follow from the fact that the work was done personally that there was a contractual obligation to do it personally. In this case, however, the correct construction of the contract was that it involved an obligation on the claimants to personally do the work. Relevant factors were that the company contracted with the applicants personally, they were paid individually and the items of work specified in the contract were not beyond the capacity of the applicants to do themselves. However the court also stated that *'employment tribunals should not be deflected from a consideration of the definition of 'worker' and from a consideration of terms of the contract in that context by general policy considerations as to the nature of employment and self-employment'.*

---

8. See Chapter 7
9. See Chapter 6
10. See Chapter 9

ntly a claim was made in *Bacica v. Muir* 2006 for annual holiday pay under the
ime Regulations. The claimant was a painter and decorator who worked under
̣ uction Industry Scheme Regulations (CIS) by which tax was deducted from his
earnings but he paid his own National Insurance. He had annual accounts prepared by his
accountant where expenditure was set against income and capital allowances provided for.
The EAT disagreed with the tribunal and decided not to classify the claimant as a worker
for the purpose of the Regulations. While the work was rendered on a personal basis the
claimant was a sole trader performing services as part of a business and so excluded from
the definition of a worker.

The legal status of individuals who operate sub-post offices was considered by the EAT in
Commissioners of Inland Revenue v. Post Office 2003. The EAT found overwhelming evidence
that they were not 'employees' of the Post Office including the lack of control and the
absence of personal service. The lack of personal service meant that they also failed to
satisfy the definition of 'worker'. The fact that a minimum of 18 hours personal service
each week was a requirement to qualify for a 'holiday substitution allowance' did not make
the contract one for personal service. In addition the definition of a worker excludes a
'business undertaking carried on by the individual' and plainly that is what a sub-postmaster
is doing with the Post Office as his client.

Distinguishing between the Employed and Self-employed

A large number of legal and economic consequences stem from the distinction between
employed and self-employed status and that is why it is crucial to be able to identify the
true nature of the employment relationship. Employment legislation and the common law
both recognise the distinction between employment under a *contract of service* and self-
employment under a *contract for services*. The distinction is a relatively straightforward one
to make in the majority of cases. It is only in a small proportion of cases that difficulties
arise, often where employers, or those they employ are seeking to achieve contractor
status for economic advantage or in order to evade legal responsibilities. The table on the
following page provides a summary of the major legal and economic consequences of the
employment classification.

The case-law on the following pages demonstrates that it is not only the parties to an
employment relationship who have an interest in an individual's employment status. The
State may also intervene for such purposes as National Insurance contributions, income
tax, and employee rights on an employer's insolvency. An individual may be required to
establish employee status to enjoy the benefits of statutory rights in relation to security of
employment or health and safety. By asserting a statutory right, such as the right to a
statement of employment terms to which an employee is entitled under the Employment
Rights Act 1996 s.1, an individual can bring the issue of status before a tribunal.[11]

While it should be stressed that in the vast majority of cases it is easy to recognise a
contract service and a contract for services the distinction between the contracts in borderline
cases is not so straightforward.

---

11. See later *Carmichael v. National Power* 2000

Contract of Service (Employed Persons)	Contract for Services (Self-employed)

Liability

An employer may be made vicariously liable for the wrongful acts of employees committed during the course of their employment.

As a general principle an employer may not be made liable for the wrongful acts of contractors he employs other than in exceptional cases.

Common Law Employment Terms

Numerous terms are implied into a contract of employment by the common law to regulate the relationship of employer and employee e.g. trust and confidence.

The common law is much less likely to intervene in the relationship of employer and contractor.

Health and Safety

A high standard of care is owed by an employer both under statute and the common law with regard to the health and safety of his employees.

While both the common law and statute recognise the existence of a duty of care by an employer in relation to the contractors he employs, at common law it is of a lesser standard than the duty owed to employees.

Statutory Employment Rights

A large number of individual employment rights are conferred on employees by statute which generally arise after a period of service e.g. the right to unfair dismissal protection; to redundancy payments; to belong to a trade union and take part in trade union activities; to protection in the event of the employer's insolvency; to guarantee payments, to security of employment after maternity, paternity, adoption leave; to statutory maternity pay; to a written statement of the main terms and conditions of employment and the right not to be discriminated against on the grounds of sex, race or marital status.

Contractors are traditionally excluded from the mass of individual employment rights conferred by statute. One notable exception however is the legislation in relation to discrimination, which protects the self-employed when they are providing personal services. Such workers are now more likely to benefit from statutory employment rights e.g.

* working time rights and paid holidays
* the national minimum wage
* public interest disclosure
* part-time workers regulations
* representation in disciplinary proceedings

Income Tax

The income tax payable by an employee is deducted at source by the employer under the PAYE (pay as you earn) scheme. An employee is referred to as a Schedule E tax payer.

The income tax of a self employed person is payable by the taxpayer and not his employer, on a lump sum basis (Schedule D) on a 'current year basis' of assessment. Schedule D taxpayers retain more favourable treatment in claiming reasonable expenses when assessed for tax. Furthermore an independent sub-contractor may have to charge VAT on services.

Welfare Benefits

Under the Social Security Act 1975 both employer and employee must contribute to the payment of Class 1 National Insurance contributions assessed on an earnings related basis, entitling the employee to claim all the available welfare benefits e.g. Job Seekers Allowance, statutory sick pay, industrial disablement benefit, state retirement pension.

Under the Social Security Act 1975 a self-employed person is individually responsible for the payment of lower Class 2 National Insurance contributions and has only limited rights to claim welfare benefits e.g. statutory sick pay.

One form of employment where there has been increasing doubt as to status is where individuals are placed to work for clients by registering with employment agencies. Agency workers constitute an increasing proportion of the atypical work-force and we will deal with their legal position under a separate heading.[12] Previously we mentioned s.23 of the Employment Relations Act 1999 which conferred power on the Secretary of State to extend the protection of employment legislation to a specified description of individual. As yet we await the use of this power but in *Montgomery v. Johnson Underwood Ltd.* 2001 Buckley J in the Court of Appeal drew attention to the considerable uncertainty concerning the status of individuals who find work through employment agencies and stated that the power under s.23 to extend statutory protection *'might be put to good use in this respect'*.

In the final analysis the determination of whether an individual is an employee or a contractor is a question of law for the courts rather than a question of fact involving placing sole reliance on the description of the contract given by the parties to it. In *Carmichael v. National Power Plc* 2000 the House of Lords confirmed that the decision whether an applicant is employed under a contract of employment is a question of law if the parties to the contract intended all the express terms to be contained in contractual documents. However *'when the intention of the parties, objectively ascertained has to be gathered partly from documents but also from oral exchanges and conduct, the terms of the contract are a question of fact'*. In the absence of perversity questions of fact are of course a matter for the tribunal with which the EAT and appellant courts should not interfere. In this case the House of Lords held that the tribunal was entitled to find that the parties conduct and surrounding circumstances indicated that when the applicants were not working there was no contract of employment and no mutual obligation to work or provide work. This case is considered later in the chapter.

The control test

The original test for employment status which still has significance today was at one time applied exclusively by the courts. In *Performing Rights Society Ltd. v. Mitchell and Booker* 1924, McCardie J. said that *'the final test, if there is to be a final test, and certainly the test to be generally applied, lies in the nature and degree of detailed control over the person alleged to be a servant'*. If an employer could tell his workers not only what to do, but also how when and where to do it, then the workers would be regarded as employees, employed under a contract of service. Today the courts adopt a much wider approach and take account of all the circumstances to determine a worker's status. This is not to say that control is no longer a significant factor, for it would be difficult to imagine a contract of service where the employer did not have the ultimate authority to control the work performed by the employee.

In *Montgomery v. Johnson Underwood* 2001[13] Buckley J said that *'a contractual relationship concerning work to be carried out in which one party has no control over the other could not sensibly be called a contract of employment'*. He further held that control is a fundamental part of the *'irreducible minimum of obligation for the existence of a contract of employment'*.

---

12. See later in the chapter
13. See later in the chapter

The multiple test

A more recent approach of the courts, which involves viewing all of the circumstances of the case to determine status, has been described in various ways as the mixed, or multiple test. It has its origins in the following case.

> In *Ready Mixed Concrete Ltd. v. Ministry of Pensions* 1968 MacKenna J, a single judge of the Queens Bench Division of the High Court,[14] had to decide the employment status of a driver for the plaintiff company. This was in order to determine the employer's responsibility in relation to the National Insurance contributions of its drivers. The Ministry of Pensions had rejected the employer's contention that its drivers were self-employed, despite the existence of written contracts of employment[15] which had attempted to create a contract for services rather than contracts of service. The declaration that the driver was self-employed was not decisive and all aspects of his job were considered, for instance the fact that the driver purchased the lorry from the company; had to maintain it; that pay was calculated on the basis of the driving work performed. All these factors pointed to the driver being a contractor. Others pointed to his status as an employee. He had to paint the lorry in the company colours, he had to use it exclusively for company business and he was required to obey reasonable orders. McKenna J stated that there is a contract of service if an individual agrees to provide his own work, submits to his employer's control and in addition the majority of the contractual provisions are consistent with a contract of service. This approach has since been referred to as the mixed or multiple test. On the facts the power to delegate work was regarded as a decisive indication that the drivers were self-employed under a contract for services.

The Court of Appeal recently reaffirmed the significance of McKenna J's test in *Montgomery v. Johnson Underwood Ltd.* 2001 *'In determining whether a contract of employment exists, the guidance of McKenna J in Ready Mixed Concrete (South East) Ltd. v. Minister of Pensions and National Insurance, approved by the Lord Chancellor in Carmichael v. National Power plc, is the best guide and should be followed by tribunals. This requires three conditions to be fulfilled:*

> (i) *agrees that, in consideration for a wage or other remuneration, he will provide his own work and skill in the performance of some service for his master, 'mutuality of obligation';*

> (ii) *he agrees, expressly or impliedly, that in the performance of that service he will be subject to the other's control in a sufficient degree to make that other master; and*

> (iii) *the other provisions of the contract are consistent with its being a contract of service.'*

The test set out in Ready Mixed Concrete permits tribunals appropriate latitude in considering the nature and extent of 'mutual obligations' in respect of the work in question and the 'control' an employer has over the individual. It does not permit those concepts to be dispensed with altogether. It directs tribunals to consider the whole picture to see whether a contract of employment emerges, although 'mutual obligation' and 'control' must be identified to a sufficient extent before looking at the whole.'

---

14. Sitting as an appellate court
15. 30 pages long

The status of self-employment cannot be achieved simply by including an express provision in a contract as in *Ready Mixed Concrete*. The courts will look to the substance of an employment relationship rather than the label applied by the parties in order to decide a worker's status.

> In *Ferguson v. John Dawson Ltd.* 1976 the plaintiff, a builder's labourer agreed to work as a 'self-employed labour only sub contractor' an arrangement commonly known as the 'lump'. When working on a flat roof he fell and suffered injuries. No guard rail had been provided, in breach of a statutory duty owed only to employees.[16] The High Court decided that the employer was in breach of this statutory duty towards the plaintiff and damages of over £30,000 were awarded. On appeal the employer argued that as the plaintiff was self-employed the statutory duty was not owed to him. It was the plaintiff's responsibility to ensure that the guard rail was in place. The Court of Appeal held, by a majority, that the plaintiff was in reality an employee and so entitled to the compensation awarded. The 'lump' was no more than a device to attempt to gain tax advantages and whilst a declaration as to employment status may be relevant, it is not the conclusive factor to determine the true nature of the employment relationship.

> A difficult case to reconcile with the decision in *Ferguson* 1976 is *Massey v. Crown Life Insurance Company* 1978. Here a branch manager of an insurance company, who also acted as a general agent, decided to become 'self-employed' on his accountant's advice, despite the fact that his duties remained unchanged. The Court of Appeal concluded that a change of employment status had in fact taken place so that he was unable to bring a claim for unfair dismissal. Lord Denning M R stated that if there is ambiguity in the relationship then this can be resolved with a declaration one way or the other.

Whilst there was a degree of ambiguity in the above case in the branch manager's original position as manager/agent, it was significant that here was a 'professional' man, having considered independent advice, making a declaration which he believed would be to his benefit. This is in contrast to the labourer in *Ferguson* 1976 who was unadvised and could not be said to have consciously chosen to be a contractor with the legal consequences that this involved.

> Consider also the decision of the Employment Appeal Tribunal in *Thames Television v. Wallis* 1979. Here a researcher, and later a reporter for a TV company, was taxed under Schedule D and treated as self-employed. This was despite the fact that there was detailed control over her work over which her employer had exclusive access. On her dismissal she claimed compensation for unfair dismissal alleging that in reality she had been employed under a contract of service. The EAT agreed stating that the original declaration as to status was *'only one consideration that had to be taken into consideration in determining her status'*. It was found possible to distinguish the above decision in *Massey* 1978 on the grounds that in *Massey* here had been a deliberate change in status whereas in Wallis the researcher's status was ambiguous from the outset.

Despite the existence of a clear agreement between the employer and the worker that he should be treated as self-employed this may nevertheless be regarded by the courts as a false designation and overturned.

---

16. Construction (Working Places) Regulations 1966

In *Young & Wood Ltd. v. West* 1980 the complainant, a sheet metal worker, asked his employer if he could be treated as self-employed. This was accepted and despite the fact that there was no difference between his working conditions and those of PAYE workers, he was paid without deductions of tax and was not given holiday entitlement or sick pay. Furthermore the Inland Revenue had accepted the change, resulting in an estimated tax advantage of about £500 over five years because of assessment under Schedule D rather than Schedule E. Stephenson L J seemed to cast doubt on Lord Denning M R's approach in *Massey* 1978 by stating that *'It must be the court's duty to see whether the label correctly represents the true legal relationship between the parties.'* The Court of Appeal found that as it was impossible to regard the complainant as in 'business on his own account' he was not self-employed but remained an employee. Consequently the tribunal had jurisdiction to hear his complaint of unfair dismissal.

The economic reality test

The approach was originally adopted by Coche J in *Market Investigations v. Ministry of Social Security* 1969 was a genuine attempt to distinguish between entrepreneurs and individuals who are economically dependent on a sole employer. *'Is the person who has engaged himself to perform there services performing them as a person in business on his own account. Matters of importance are whether the worker provides his own equipment, whether he hires his own helpers, what degree of financial risk he takes, what degree of responsibility he has for his investment and management and whether and how far he has an opportunity to profit from sound management in the performance of his task.'*

By asking the question whether the worker is *'in business on his own account'* or under the control of an employer under a continuing business relationship, the courts have found it possible to conclude that a relationship traditionally regarded as self-employment, namely that of a homeworker, was in reality a contract of service. Questions posed in applying this entrepreneurial test would include whether the individual was in business on his own, provides his own equipment, employs other workers and has a financial stake in the business.

> In *Airfix Footwear Ltd. v. Cope* 1978 the court held that homeworkers, employed to assemble shoe parts for a company using equipment supplied by them, were not contractors but employees. While the work was provided on a regular basis, the employer argued that there was no obligation to provide work and the worker could also refuse it. In the present case the employment relationship had continued over the seven year period. In reality the employer decided on the things to be done, the manner, means, and the time and place of performance. The homeworker should therefore be regarded as an employee.

> In *Nethermere (St. Neots) Ltd. v. Taverna and Another* 1984 the position of homeworkers was once again considered. Here a trouser manufacturer had paid a piece rate to homeworkers over a number of years. Machines for home use had been installed by the employer and work delivered daily. Following a dispute about holiday pay, the arrangement was terminated, and a claim for unfair dismissal brought by the workers. While the Court of Appeal confirmed that the law required mutual obligations for a contract of service in this situation, such mutuality was present in the continuing obligation of the employer to

provide and pay for work and the employees' obligation to accept and perform it. Despite the absence of strict legal obligations to carry out the work, by evaluating the practices which reflected the economic realities of the situation (economic and psychological pressures) the majority of the Court of Appeal concluded that the complainant homeworkers were employees.[17]

Mutuality of obligation

The so called *'mutuality of obligation'* in a contract of employment refers to the common understanding between an employer and an employee that they have an ongoing relationship under which work will be offered and personal service will be provided. There are mutual promises of further performance under the contract. If however there is a genuine understanding by the parties supported by an express provision in the contract which denies this mutuality there is unlikely to be a contract of employment. So held the Court of Appeal in *Stevedoring and Haulage Services v. Fuller* 2001.[18]

In *Wilson v. Circular Distributors Ltd.* 2006 the claimant, an area relief manager, was employed on terms and conditions which mirrored those in a standard contract of employment. His employer stressed however that there would be occasions when no work was available and no payment would be made. Having worked for 2 years for up to 4 days per week his position was terminated and he claimed unfair dismissal. The tribunal dismissed the complaint finding that the claimant was not an employee because the arrangement lacked mutuality of obligation mainly because there was no obligation on the employer to offer work. The EAT disagreed with the tribunal's reasoning confirming that under this arrangement there was mutuality of obligation. Under the terms, if the respondent had work available they were required to offer it to the claimant, and equally when it was offered, the claimant was required to do it. There was a contract of employment and the claimant was entitled to have his complaint of unfair dismissal heard.

Reliance on a pool of casual workers has long been a tradition in some sectors of business including the catering industry.

> The legal status of so called 'regular casuals' was put to the test in *O'Kelly and Others v. Trusthouse Forte plc* 1983. Here a banqueting department run by the employer was staffed in part by full time employees but mainly by so called 'casuals'. Among the casuals were 'regulars' who were given preference when work was available, were often expected to work very long hours and consequently had no other employment. The applicants in this case were 'regulars' but when they became trade union shop stewards they were told by the employer that their services would no longer be required. In a claim for unfair dismissal brought by the applicants, the first issue the industrial tribunal had to deal with was whether they were employed under a contract of service and so protected by the law relating to unfair dismissal. In determining their employment status the tribunal acknowledged that its role was to *'consider all aspects of the relationship, no feature being itself decisive, each of which may vary in weight and direction and, having given such a balance to the factors as seem appropriate determine*

---

17. See also *Duke v. Martin Retail Group plc* 1993
18. See later in the chapter

whether the person was carrying on business on his own account'. Applying this mixed or multiple test the tribunal isolated factors consistent with a contract of service including the lack of mutual obligations on the part of the employer to provide work and on the part of the worker to offer services (referred to as mutuality of obligation). In addition there was the custom and practice of the catering industry to employ large numbers on a casual basis. By placing most emphasis on the inconsistent factors the tribunal found that the applicants were not employees and therefore not entitled to statutory protection. The Court of Appeal later found it unable to interfere with the tribunal's decision given that the correct legal approach has been adopted.

While there is no doubt that the decision in *O'Kelly* supports the custom and practice of the hotel and catering industry and confirms the fact that a fundamental feature of the contract of employment is the requirement to provide work and offer services, it is nevertheless difficult to reconcile with previous decisions, in particular *Ferguson* 1976. The reality of *O'Kelly* is that the regular casuals were subject to the same control as full time employees. They often worked longer hours than full time staff and a failure to work when required had the dramatic consequences of removal from the regular casual lists. Having no alternative employment, capital equipment or profit sharing, it would be difficult to describe them as business people working on their *'own account'*. The decision has been criticised by eminent labour lawyers. Bob Hepple thought that the approach of the Court of Appeal failed to focus on the purpose of the statute, to confer protection on members of trade unions who are *'workers'*. The labour lawyer Gwyneth Pitt asked the question *'can it really be the case that casual workers at the bottom of the employment heap should not receive the protection of the law'.*

The House of Lord's decision in *Carmichael v. National Power* 2000 stresses the need for mutuality of obligation as the core of a contract of employment as a prerequisite for trust and confidence. Here power station guides who were recruited and trained by their employer were employed 'on a casual as required basis'. They often worked for 25 hours a week and were paid net after deductions of income tax and national insurance at the employed persons rate. They could refuse work under their contract and sometimes did. To establish their status a s.1 statement of terms of employment was requested of the employer. All employees are entitled to a s.1 statement. The tribunal thought that the guides were contractors due to the lack of mutuality of obligation and the EAT felt that as the final arbiter on a question of fact that decision should not be interfered with. The Court of Appeal however held that the ordinary meaning of the word 'on a casual as required basis' in these circumstances was that there was an implied term that the employee would provide a reasonable amount of guiding work and subject to the qualification of reasonableness the applicants would accept the work offered. This meant that the contract did impose mutual obligations to offer and to undertake work. Of course this interpretation of mutuality of obligation by the Court of Appeal majority differs significantly from the *O'Kelly v. Trust House Forte* approach which required a legal obligation to offer and accept work as the core of an employment contract. A further appeal to the House of Lords restored the Tribunal's decision.

Relying on evidence which established that there were numerous occasions when the guides were not available for work Lord Irvine drew the objective inference that when work was available the guides were free accept it or not as they chose and they would not be subject to any disciplinary action. This flexibility he felt suited both sides. The tribunal was entitled to decide from the documentation, the circumstances and the parties conduct that they intended their relationship to be governed by a contract when they were not working. The *case 'founders on the rock of absence of mutuality'*. The words employment on a casual as required basis do not in the opinion of Lord Irvine impose an obligation to undertake guiding work. Ld Hoffmann emphasised that the issue of status is a question of fact for the tribunal when the intention of the parties is to be gathered from documents, oral exchanges and conduct. *'I think that it was open to the industrial tribunal to find as a fact that the parties did not intend their letters to be the sole record of their agreement but intended that it should be contained partly in the letters, partly oral exchanges at the interviews or elsewhere and partly left to evolve by conduct as time went on.'* This would not be untypical of agreements by which people are engaged to do work, whether as employees or otherwise. On the basis the ascertainment of the agreement was a question of fact with which the EAT were right not interfere. Having accepted the tribunal's finding as to the lack of mutuality their decision that there was no contract of employment may not be disturbed. The guides could only succeed if their engagement created an employment relationship which subsisted when they were not working. While the House of Lords in *Carmichael* is saying that there could be no overall global contract of employment subsisting during the period of work inactivity because of the lack of mutuality there still remains the possibility of a services of short term contract of employment during work periods. A continuous period of such contracts could establish sufficient continuity for the purposes of statutory rights.

There are few examples of the courts deciding that mutuality and control is satisfied but that the contractual terms are inconsistent with a contract of employment.

The issue in *Curr v. Marks & Spencer* 2003 was whether a management trainer remained employed during a four year child break scheme that she had accepted following the termination of her maternity leave. Under the scheme she was required to work for a minimum period of two weeks full-time or the equivalent part-time for each year of the break for which she would be paid. She was required to resign her post but with the employer's commitment to offer her a similar management position at the end of the break. All her staff benefits were terminated and her pension was frozen. Subsequently after the applicant had returned to work it became necessary to determine her continuity of employment for the purposes of a redundancy payment. The Court of Appeal confirmed that during the break the applicant did not have a contract of employment despite having mutuality of obligation. *'There was mutuality of obligation by virtue of the requirement that the applicant work for a minimum of two weeks in each year of the child break, which implied an obligation on the employers to provide work for that period, and the employers' promise to pay her for that work. However, the terms on which it was agreed that the applicant would take a child break did not satisfy another of the essential conditions for the existence of a contract of employment, that the other provisions of the contract are consistent with its being a contract of service. The terms were quite unlike a normal contract of employment.'* It was the other essential condition of a contract of employment that the *'other provisions of the contract are consistent with it being a contract of service'* that had not been satisfied.[19]

In the final analysis the determination of a worker's status can only be made by asking a number of questions relating to the main features of the relationship such as the extent to which the individual is:

- providing personal services;
- under the employer's control;

---

19. One of the three conditions from Montgomery

- regarded as an integral part of the organisation;
- in business on his own account;
- providing tools and equipment;
- sharing in the profit and contributing towards the losses;
- able to delegate work;
- in agreement as to his status.

The Court of Appeal was faced with the issue of employment status in Hall *(HM Inspector of Taxes) v. Lorimer* 1994. Here the Inland Revenue claimed that a free-lance vision-mixer who worked for a number of production companies should be charged to income tax under Schedule E as an employee rather than Schedule D as a self-employed person. The reasoning behind the claim was that the vision-mixer provided no equipment for his work and had no financial status in the programmes upon which he worked. On his behalf it was argued that he took a financial risk in relation to payment for his work, he could also delegate work and had had a large number of different employers. The Court of Appeal agreed with the High Court that he was a self-employed person employed under a contract for services. The court stated that *'there is no single path in determining whether or not the contracts from which a person derives his earnings are contracts of service or contracts for services. An approach which suits the facts and arguments of one case may be unhelpful in another'.* The earlier decision of the High Court was approved of in particular the approach to this type of analysis that *'it is not a mechanical exercise of running through items on a check list to see whether they are present in, or absent from a given situation. The object of the exercise is to paint a picture from the accumulation of the detail. The overall effect can only be appreciated by standing back from the detailed picture which has been painted, by viewing it from a distance and by making an informed, considered, qualitative appreciation of the whole. It is a matter of evaluation of the overall effect of the detail which is not necessarily the same as the sum total of the individual details. Not all details are of equal weight or importance in any given situation. The details may also vary from one situation to another'.*

In *Lane v. Shire Roofing Company (Oxford) Ltd.* 1995, the Court of Appeal considered the issue of employment status in the context of a personal injury scenario. The complainant was Mr. Lane a general builder who traded under the name of PJ Building as a one man business. He was categorised as 'self-employed' for tax purposes working directly for clients and sometimes for other contractors. Shire Roofing was a roofing contractor whose owner Mr. Whittaker often hired men for individual jobs. In 1986 Mr. Lane was hired by Shire Roofing to work on a large roofing sub-contract. When that work was near completion Mr. Whittaker asked Mr. Lane to re-roof a porch in a private house. The job was agreed an they both visited the house to decide the fee and the equipment that was necessary to do the work. Because the cost of hiring scaffolding would have made the job unprofitable it was decided that Mr. Lane should use his own ladder to do the work. When carrying out the work Mr. Lane fell from the ladder and suffered severe head injuries. In an action claiming damages from Shire Roofing the High Court held that as Mr. Lane was a contractor he was owed no duty of care. Factors that the court thought were significant in reaching that conclusion included the fact that Mr. Lane had his own business, he was recognised as self-employed for tax purposes and he was working on a single job without supervision. In addition the court concluded that there was no evidence to support the finding of a breach of duty. The Court of Appeal disagreed with the High Court on both of the main issues and held that Mr. Lane as an employee was owed a duty of care by Shire Roofing which they had broken. As a consequence Mr. Lane was awarded £102,100 in damages. The court confirmed that in determining whether a worker is an employee or a contractor control is an important factor *'Whose business was it?'* – was the workman carrying on his own business, or was he carrying on that of his employers? The answer to this question may cover much of the same ground as the control test, such as whether he provides his own equipment and hires his own helpers, but may involve looking to see where the financial risk lies, and whether and how far the workman has an opportunity of profiting from sound management in the performance of his task. These questions must be asked in the context of who is responsible for the overall safety of those doing the work in question. The court felt that there are good policy reasons in the safety at work field to ensure that the law properly categorises between employees and independent contractors and recognises the employer/employee relationship when it exists because of the responsibilities that the common law and statutes place on the employer. Despite the fact that Mr. Lane was self-employed for tax purposes, his relationship with the employer was much closer to the 'lump', where workmen are engaged only for their labour and are clearly employees.[20]

The significance of this case is that it illustrates a pragmatic approach of the higher courts to the issue of employment status. By emphasising the importance of public policy in deciding a workers' status in the health and safety context, the court found it possible to categorise the worker as an employee and so owed a duty of care by his employer. This was despite the fact that a strict analysis of his contract might have produced a different conclusion. Certainly if the issue had been one of security in employment the result might well have been different.[21]

In Chapter 6 and Chapter 8 the potential vicarious liability of employers for the unlawful acts of their employees is explored. In this context, the designation of employee status is based largely around the element of control. In *Hawley v. Luminar Leisure plc* 2005 the High Court considered the potential liability of a nightclub owner for the unlawful conduct of a door steward under its control. The steward had violently punched the claimant causing severe injuries. He was in fact employed by a separate company, ASE Security Services Ltd., and his services supplied to the nightclub under a commercial contract. Applying the established tests of an employee relationship to the door steward proved to be fruitless given the lack of a contract, mutuality and personal service. Nevertheless the High Court held that for the purposes of vicarious liability the only significant test of employee status is one of control so as to make the door steward the deemed employee of the nightclub and the nightclub liable for his conduct.

Personal service

Personal service is the core of an employment contract. The Court of Appeal decision in *Express and Echo Newspapers v. Tanton* 1999 is in many ways a further confirmation of the judgment of McKenna J in *Ready Mixed Concrete v. Ministry of Pensions* 1968. Here a driver who had been an ex employee was re engaged as a driver on a self-employed basis. His contract contained a provision which stated 'in the event that the contractor is unable or unwilling to perform the services personally, he shall arrange at his own expense the services personally. While the driver did not sign the contract he worked in accordance

20. See earlier *Ferguson v. John Dawson* 1976
21. See earlier *O'Kelly v. Trust House Forte* 1983

with its terms and on occasion used substitute drivers. Other factors pointed to him being an employee including the requirement to wear a uniform and using the company's vehicles. By requesting a s.1 statement the driver was in essence asking the tribunal to confirm his status. The tribunal's decision that he was an employee giving emphasis to what occurred rather than the documentation was confirmed by the EAT as a permissible conclusion with no arguable point of law. On further appeal however the Court of Appeal held that the right to employ a substitute is inherently inconsistent with status as an employee. A contract of employment must necessarily contain an obligation on the part of the employee to provide services personally. Both the tribunal and the EAT had thought that the substitution clause was not fatal to their being a contract of employment. The Court of Appeal ruled that the right to provide a substitute is inherently inconsistent with employment status. Without such an irreducible minimum of obligation it cannot be said that there is a contract of employment.

> *Macfarlane v. Glasgow City Council* 2001 illustrates the fact that contemporary employment practices will continue to raise doubt in relation to employment status. Here qualified gymnastic instructors employed by the Council at sports centres were required under their contract to arrange for replacements if they were unable to work. The replacements were recruited from the Council's approved list and paid directly by the Local Authority. On the issue as to their legal status the tribunal held relying on Tanton above that *'although the picture was largely one of the applicants being employees, the fact that they could arrange for substitutes to attend on their behalf was inconsistent with the existence of a contract of employment and, on that basis alone, the applicants' claims were bound to fail'.* On appeal however the court held that a contract did not cease to be a contract for personal service simply because, in the absence of an express contractual term dealing with personal service or the use of substitutes, there was, as a matter of fact, a right to substitute in a limited sense. The instructors were required to provide personal service but in certain circumstances such as illness they were simply required to provide cover from the council's list of replacements.

To achieve a contract for services there must be a clear contractual term indicating that there is no requirement for the individual to do the work personally.

In *Staffordshire Sentinel Newspapers v. Potter* 2004 the claimant began working for the company as a home delivery agent in 1999 under a delivery agency agreement which stated that it was an agreement for services, not a contract of employment, and that the agent was an independent contractor. He also signed an agreement which contained a clause providing that he was not required to discharge his or her duties personally. Following the termination of his appointment in 2003, he presented a complaint of unfair dismissal. The employment tribunal concluded that he had been employed under a contract of service, rather than a contract for services, and could therefore proceed with his claim. The tribunal found that although he could substitute a third party in his place, that was not an unfettered right since the substitute had to meet with the company's approval, which had not always been given and, on one occasion, they had provided their own substitute. On appeal to the EAT, the company contended that, in view of his right to engage a substitute, Mr. Potter's contract lacked one of the irreducible minima of a contract of service, in that it was not a contract for personal service. The EAT held that in determining whether a contract includes the need for personal service, the critical question is what is the relevant contractual term. Where there is a clear express term in writing, it is not necessary to look at the overall factual matrix, unless the writing can be said to be a sham. However, where there is no clear express term in writing then it may be necessary to look at the overall factual matrix in order to find that term. In the present case, the employment tribunal was bound to find that the contractual term providing that the applicant was not required to do his work personally was inconsistent with a contract of service and that, it had no jurisdiction to entertain the applicant's complaint of unfair dismissal.

The decision of the Court of Appeal in *Stevedoring and Haulage Services v. Fuller* 2001 sheds further light on the dilemma for employers and represents a clear victory for form over substance. The case concerned the status of dock workers who after years of permanent employment accepted generous voluntary redundancy packages and then were taken on as casual workers. The letter offering casual employment made it clear to the workers that they would not be employees but would provide their services on *'an ad hoc and casual basis'* with *'no obligation on the part of the company to provide such work for you nor for you to accept any work so offered'*. A further document emphasised that *'you are not an employee and your services are being utilised only when mutually agreed'*. From 1996 the dock workers worked regularly and exclusively for the respondent and were given priority over other agency casual workers. After three years they applied for a s.1 statement in order to determine their status.[22] They succeeded in the tribunal and the EAT who found the applicants to be employees by finding an overarching contract of employment. Despite the documents, the tribunal held that by considering the evidence of how the parties had conducted themselves it was possible to imply terms indicating a mutual understanding that work would be offered and accepted, which provided for an irreducible minimum of obligation on both sides. The Court of Appeal however disagreed and found for the employer. The court stated that *'where the terms upon which casual work is offered and accepted expressly negative mutuality of obligation, there can be no global or overarching contract of employment. If there is no contract, one cannot be created by implying terms which water down the effect of the express terms so as to give it sufficient mutuality of obligation to pass the test necessary for establishing a contract of employment'*. Here the implied terms suggested by the tribunal *'flatly contradicted the express terms contained in the documents'*. As neither party was obliged to accept or offer work the tribunal's decision that the applicants were employees could not be sustained.

The message from *Stevedoring* is that an employer can avoid the risk of an overarching contract of employment where the terms upon which casual work is offered and accepted expressly negative mutuality of obligation. If the express terms of the agreement unequivocally contradicted implied terms based upon conduct, then the formal document takes priority.

Agency Workers

Agency workers comprise an increasingly significant proportion of the UK work force so it is necessary to determine their legal status in relation to the agency and its clients.

Some Employment Agencies are in the business of recruiting candidates for their clients, prospective employers. The employers are charged a fee for a successful placement from the agency and a contractual relationship as an employee or contractor is entered into between the candidate and the employer.

---

22. As in *Carmichael v. National Power* 2000

In recent years however there has been rapid growth in Employment Agencies which operate in a different way. Prospective staff are registered for work and placed with clients who pay the agency for their services. There are three parties to the arrangement:

- the agency;
- the worker; and
- the client end-user.

Under the agency contract it is the agency which then pays an hourly rate to the staff who have been placed. It is this group of individuals who may have an uncertain legal position particularly when then are placed almost exclusively with the same client for long periods. Having a contract with the agency and under the control of the client it is difficult for an agency worker to establish either party as his employer for the purposes of statutory rights. In addition to flexibility one of the main benefits of this arrangement for the clients is that the agency is perceived to be the employer for the purpose of statutory rights.

In *McMeechan v. Secretary of State for Employment* 1997 the complainant worked for an employment agency on a series of temporary contracts. There was a clear statement in his contract with the agency that he would provide his services *'as a self-employed worker and not under a contract of service'*. The agency contacted to offer him the opportunity to work on a self employed basis where there was a suitable assignment with a client but there was no obligation to offer work or indeed accept it. When the agency became insolvent the complainant sought to recover money owed to him under a statutory right as an employee of an insolvent business. The tribunal held that as a temporary, on the books of an employment agency, the complainant was not an employee. The EAT took a different view however deciding that *'Where there is a written contract between an employment agency and a worker whose services are provided by the agency to a third party client on a temporary basis, whether the contract is one of employment is a question of law to be determined upon the true construction of the document in its factual matrix. It is necessary to consider all the terms and conditions of the contract. The question is not determined by earlier judicial decisions on different contracts or the label which the parties themselves put on the relationship. The authorities do not lay down a general proposition of law that a worker who renders services under a series of temporary contracts with an employment agency does not have a contract of employment with the agency. The cases go no further than stating the general legal principles applicable to the question of whether a contract of employment exists and then proceeding to decide the individual case on the basis of the actual terms.'*

Here despite the label of self employed the totality of the written conditions of service between the complainant and the agency indicated that he was an employee of the agency. The Court of Appeal went on to hold that the EAT had adopted the correct approach and effectively overruled the previous decisions. A temporary worker can have the status of employee in respect of each assignment actually worked through an employment agency.

In *Costain Building & Civil Engineering Ltd. v. Smith* 2000 the EAT considered the status of an agency building worker who had been appointed a safety representative and then dismissed by the agency on the instructions of a builder client. The issue was whether he could claim automatic unfair dismissal as an employee dismissed as a safety representative. The EAT disagreed with tribunal and held that his apparent status as a contractor was genuine supported by factors such as no deduction of tax or national insurance, payment on invoice, no grievance procedure sickness or holiday pay. Certainly the appointment of the applicant as a safety representative could not make him an employee simply because they are required to be so.

Under s.134 of the Income and Corporation Taxes Act 1988 the agency is the employer for the tax purpose in respect of workers who are *subject to, or the right of, supervision, direction or control as to the manner in which they rendered services to the client.* Moreover agency workers were encouraged to form service companies to enable them to receive gross income for their services when payments were made from the company to the individual. Of course remuneration from the service company to the workers was subject to National Insurance and tax, broadly equivalent to self employed tax under Schedule D. Legislation known as IR3S from the Finance Act 2000 provides a mechanism to treat the worker as a Schedule E tax payer with Class I National Insurance Contributions.

> In *Montgomery v. Johnson Underwood Ltd.* 2001[23] the applicant was registered with an agency and worked for the same client company for over two years. She named both the agency and the client as respondent in her unfair dismissal claim. While the tribunal and the EAT both ruled that she was an employee of the agency the Court of Appeal took a different view. Endorsing the guidance provided in Ready Mixed Concrete Mr. Justice Buckley sets out the important principles of 'mutuality of obligation' and 'control' as the 'irreducible minimum of legal requests for a contract if employment to exist'. *'A contractual relationship concerning work to be carried out in which one party has no control over the other could not sensibly be called a contract of employment.'* Here the lack of control by the agency was fatal to the tribunal's decision that the applicant was the agency's employee.

In *Montgomery* above Buckley J referred to the statutory power of the Secretary of State under s.23 of the Employment Relations Act 1999 to extend the right not to be unfairly dismissed to a specified description of individuals and suggested that this power *'might be put to important use'* in respect of agency workers.

If the agency worker does not qualify as an employee of the agency, could he be employed by the client? In *Motorola v. Davidson* 2001 the EAT held that an agency worker was directly under the control of the client and therefore its employee. Mr. Davidson had been recruited by an agency and assigned to work at Motorola's site. Under his contract he was bound to comply with Motorola's instructions but had entered into no formal contract with them. Nevertheless the EAT agreed with the tribunal and found that the workers after two years service was under a sufficient degree of control of the client, Motorola, to be regarded as their employee, *'in circumstances in which, although the applicants had no direct legal right of control over the respondent under a contract they had made with him, he was bound by the terms of his contract with the employment agency who then assigned his services to the appellants to comply with all reasonable instructions and requests made by the appellants and control of what he did on a day-to-day basis lay with them'.*

So in *Motorola,* despite the written contract between the agency and the worker, the tribunal was prepared to find an unwritten contract of employment between the worker and the client based upon control. It can no longer be presumed that an agency worker has no

---

23. See earlier in the chapter

statutory rights against the client particularly if he is used over a long period and treated as an ordinary employee.

In *Hewlett Packard Ltd. v. O'Murphy* 2002 an employment tribunal was convinced that a long-standing arrangement[24] under which a computer specialist was supplied to a client and end user through an agency constituted a contract of employment for the purposes of unfair dismissal. This was despite the fact that the worker in question had contracted with the agency through his own service company and fees were payable for his services by the client to the agency and by the agency to the worker's company. The factors which supported the existence of a contract of employment included the degree of control exercised by the client and the long-standing nature of the relationship. On appeal the EAT rejected this analysis convinced that here the arrangement was deliberately structured to prevent there being a contract between the worker and the client *'In determining whether an individual who, either directly or through his own limited company, has hired himself out through the machinery of an agency to a third party is an employee of that third party, the task of an employment tribunal is first to ascertain whether there was a contract of any kind between the individual and the third party. If the individual fails to satisfy the tribunal that there was a contract of some kind, that is the end of a claim based on the assertion that he had entered into or worked under a contract of employment within the meaning of s.230 of the Employment Rights Act. Had the tribunal asked itself that question it would have been bound to have come to the conclusion that there was no contractual nexus between the applicant and the appellants and that, accordingly, he was not employed by them.'*

There may be compelling evidence that the end-user client integrates an agency worker into the workforce to such an extent that the overall picture is an employee relationship supported by an implied contract of employment. That was the conclusion of the Court of Appeal in *Franks v. Reuters Ltd.* 2003 where the agency worker was described as a temporary replacement. Lord Justice Mummery said *'whilst I would agree that a person cannot become an employee simply by reason of the length of time he does work for the same person … it is not irrelevant evidence in the context of an individual who sought a temporary placement through an employment agency, but was then allowed to stay working in the same place for the same client for over five years'.*

Dealings between parties over a period of years, as distinct from the weeks or months typical of temporary or casual work, are capable of generating an implied contractual relationship.

The Court of Appeal in *Dacas v. Brook Street Bureau* 2004 addressed the question of the legal position of temporary workers and those who recruit and make use of their services. The applicant, a cleaner, was registered with an employment agency under a temporary worker's agreement. She had worked exclusively and under the control of a council run hostel for a number of years while receiving payment from the agency. Her agreement with the agency expressly stated that its provisions shall not give rise to a contract of employment between the agency and the worker or the client and the worker. Following an incident at work the applicant's contract with the agency was terminated and she claimed unfair dismissal. The tribunal found no contract with the client and no intention to create a contract of employment with the agency. The EAT upheld the applicant's appeal that she was employed by the agency finding considerable control and mutuality of obligation. The provisions of the original agreement were no more than a label and not reflective of the true nature of the relationship.

---

24. Six years

Further appeal to the Court of Appeal provided a different analysis of the conflict. The tribunal was held to be correct in finding that the applicant was not an employee of the agency. The temporary workers agreement was not a contract of service as the irreducible minimum requirement of mutuality of obligation had not been satisfied. The agency had no obligation to provide work and the worker had no obligation to accept it and the agency had no control over the work carried out. There could however be an implied contract of employment with the client who did exercise control at the workplace through the management of the hostel. Mummery LJ explained the potential combination of transactions as a triangular arrangement involving an express contract for services between the applicant and the agency, an express contract between the agency and the client and an implied contract of employment between the client and the applicant. As an employee of the client the applicant would have the right not to be unfairly dismissed.

It is difficult to see how the requirement of mutuality of obligation was satisfied between the client and the applicant in the above case and the fact that payment was under the control of the agency is another concerning factor.

You should appreciate that Dacas above is a majority decision. Munby J in a dissenting judgment could not accept that the claimant could be an employee of the council. He felt that there could be no mutuality of obligation between an agency worker and an end-user for the purposes of satisfying the irreducible minimum requirement. The lack of mutuality was due to the fact that the claimant was paid by the agency and not the end -user. Any failure by the end-user to pay the agency would not have removed the obligation of the agency to pay the claimant. Without payment Munby J did not see how a contract of employment could be implied.' In deciding whether it has jurisdiction to hear and determine a claim for unfair dismissal, an employment tribunal must decide whether the applicant has a contract with the respondent and, if so, whether it satisfies the requirements of '*an irreducible minimum of mutual obligation necessary for a contract of service', i.e. an obligation to provide work and to perform it, coupled with the presence of control. In the absence of a contract, or of a contract having those features, the applicant cannot qualify as an employee, even though it may well be surprising not to regard the applicant as an employee. A tribunal must resist the temptation to conclude that an individual is an employee simply because he or she is not a self-employed person carrying on a business of their own'.*

Two further cases in 2005 illustrate the fact that the status of agency workers is still very much a controversial issue taxing the minds of our judiciary, each case turning on its own facts.

In *Bunce v. Postworth Ltd. t/a Skyblue* 2005 a welder entered into an agency contract with an employment agency.[25] The contract expressly provided that its terms 'shall not give rise to a contract of employment' and that suitable assignments would be arranged with client companies and there would be periods of no work. The claimant was not obliged to accept work, but when on assignment he was required to produce a weekly time sheet, signed by the client. The Agency was responsible for payment, subject to deductions for income tax and National Insurance. Under the agreement, he was entitled to paid annual leave but not to sick pay. The agreement also contained a clause requiring him, during an assignment, to 'Cooperate with the client's staff and accept the directions, supervision and instruction of any person in the client's organisation to whom he is responsible and conform to the client's rules and regulations and normal working hours and practice.'

---

25. Skyblue

The claimant was engaged by the Agency on that basis for a little over a year. During that time, he was sent to work on assignments for a number of companies engaged in railway maintenance, but he worked mostly for a client, Carillion Rail. Following complaints by Carillion Rail about alleged deficiencies in his work, the claimant was dismissed by the Agency. He subsequently presented a complaint of unfair dismissal contending that the agreement he had with the Agency constituted an umbrella contract and that a contract of employment with the agency was entered into each time he went on an assignment. Mutuality existed between the claimant and the agency because he was doing the work at their request, being paid by them, with the control element having been delegated to the client under the contract between the worker and the agency. Lord Justice Keene in the Court of Appeal was not convinced. He explained, *'the law has always been concerned with who in reality has the power to control what the worker does and how he does it'*. In this case, during the time when the claimant was working for the client, the agency could not exercise control. *'That is really fatal to his case'*, The fact that there was no obligation to provide work and the claimant could turn it down meant that there was no mutuality and he was not an employee of the agency.

Finally in *Royal National Lifeboat Institution v. Bushaway* 2005 the claimant registered with an employment agency after being made redundant. She was offered a temporary position as an administration assistant with the RNLI. She signed an agreement with the agency which described her as a 'temporary worker' and under which she agreed that she was not an employee of the agency or of the client. The agreement provided that there was no obligation on the agency to provide work, or on the temporary worker to accept any offer of work that was made. The letter of appointment with the RNLI confirmed that she would be providing her services as a self-employed person and that the agency would act as paying agency for the client, would be responsible for administering her income tax and NI contributions and would administer any accrual of statutory annual leave. She agreed to provide her services to the RNLI but it was also agreed that they were under no obligation to provide her with work and there was no obligation on her to perform any work for any particular number of hours or days in the week. The agreement provided that the engagement could be terminated immediately by written notice by either party. It further stated that: 'This agreement constitutes the whole agreement between the parties and any amendment to it shall be made in writing.' She worked as an agency worker up to 21 March and began as a permanent employee on 24 March, continuing in exactly the same role working under the same line manager. On becoming a permanent employee, she received a number of benefits including an annual salary, sick pay, additional holidays and access to the RNLI pension scheme. Her statement of particulars of her new employment described her period of employment as commencing on 24 March 2003.

She terminated her employment with effect from 27 February 2004 and subsequently claimed unfair constructive dismissal. The RNLI contested the claim on the grounds that she did not have sufficient service for making an unfair dismissal claim. The employment tribunal decided that the claimant did have the necessary qualifying service to bring a claim of unfair dismissal. According to the tribunal, although the documents purported to suggest that she was not employed either by the employment agency or by the RNLI, it was apparent from the authorities *'that a tribunal not only has to look at the written agreements which the parties concluded, but also at their conduct and how they operated the arrangement in practice. A label which the parties place on an arrangement is a helpful indication of the situation, but it is no more than that and the tribunal must look at the reality of the situation'*. The tribunal went on to examine the facts and concluded that there was a contract of employment in existence for the whole of the period when she was 'treated in the same way as any other employee'.

On appeal the EAT agreed with the employment tribunal that the claimant was an employee of the appellants throughout the period that she worked for them, including the initial period of five months when she was assigned to work for them in a temporary capacity by an employment agency, and that she therefore had the necessary qualifying period of service to bring a claim for unfair dismissal.

Conclusion

Despite the confused state of the case-law there do seem to be some guiding principles. When examining the end-user and the worker it is important to consider the overall picture rather than dissecting each element of the relationship. Also there should be a recognition that the intention of the parties may emerge over a period of time. The documentation may of course fail to represent the true substance of the relationship and a tribunal must examine the factual matrix to reach a decision. Matters such as control, the way the work is done, discipline and grievance powers, and the actual hours worked are all significant. Certainly an entire agreement clause will not prevent the tribunal examining the reality of the situation. Finally you should appreciate that an agency worker may be regarded as an employee from one stand point such as health and safety but not another.

The fact that there has been such litigation on the employed/self-employed distinction suggests that in the borderline cases and in particular, agency agreements, decisions are by no means clear cut. The courts are faced with the difficult task of maintaining a balance between the freedom of employers to offer employment on the terms that best suit their interest and the rights of workers, for the most part in an unequal bargaining position, to obtain the benefits of status as an employee. In the European Union employment law rights and duties tend to be conferred and imposed on 'workers' which would include employees or contractors providing personal service. As more rights in the UK are extended to workers the distinction between employees and contractors providing personal services will become less significant. Unfortunately the initial enthusiasm of the present Government to extend rights to workers has been replaced by a growing caution particularly when you consider recent legislative developments. In Chapter 7 we will consider the new right to request flexible working for parents of young children under the Employment Act 2002. This new right is restricted under the Act to employees as well as paternity and adoption leave. Similarly the Fixed Term Workers Regulations apply only to employees. It is to be hoped that recent concern about the increasing number of tribunal applications does not override the need to extend rights to economically active workers. Nevertheless we do await the responses to the consultative document on employment status for which there may be a legislative response on the issue of extending employment rights to atypical workers.

Further Reading

Clarke, Linda *Mutuality of Obligation and the Contract of Employment* (2000) 63 MLR 75.

Collins, H. *Employment Rights of Casual Workers – Carmichael v. National Power plc* (2000) 29 ILJ 73.

Davidov, G. *Who is a Worker?* (2005) 34 ILJ 57.

Fredman, S. *Labour Law in Flux: The Changing Composition of the Workforce* (1997) 26 ILJ 337-352.

Hepple, B. *Restructuring Employment Rights* (1986) 15 ILJ 69-89.

Jeffrey, M. *Not really Going to Work? Of the Directive on Part-time Work, 'Atypical Work' and Attempts to Regulate It* (1998) 27 ILJ 193.

McColgan, Aileen *The Fixed Term Employee (Prevention of Less favourable Treatment) Regulations* (2003) 32 ILJ 194.

Morris, Debra *Volunteering and Employment Status* (1999) 28 ILJ 249.

Murray, J. *Normalising Temporary Work: The Proposed Directive on Fixed Term Work* (1999) 28ILJ 269.

Chapter 4

Establishing the Contract of Employment

Having identified and distinguished between the main employment relationships in Chapter 3 it is now possible to focus attention on the legal process by which an employer recruits staff. In this chapter we will explore the *'cornerstone of a modern system of labour law, the contract of employment'*.[1] Despite the increased use of atypical employment relationships, the primary mechanism for recruiting both full-time and part-time staff remains the contract of employment. It is proposed to consider the legal position of part time staff, both employees and workers, in Chapter 7 as part of the work/life balance.

Both full-time and part-time employees are recruited by means of entering into a contract of employment. Despite the unique nature of such a contract the common law rules relating to formation, construction and discharge of contracts are largely applicable. It is a fundamental element of the law of contract that verbal promises that are intended to have legal consequences will have contractual effect. There is also a common law inference that promises made in a business context are presumed to have been intended to be legally binding.

The difficulty facing the Court of Appeal in *Judge v. Crown Leisure* 2005[2] was determining the legal impact of a promise made by a senior manager at a Christmas party to the claimant a junior operations manager. The promise related to salary increases within the organisation, in particular the intention to bring the salaries of all operational managers, including the claimant, in line. Subsequent letters by the senior manager referred to the verbal promise that he had made and when two years later full parity had not been achieved, the claimant resigned claiming unfair constructive dismissal. The Court of Appeal agreed with the EAT and the tribunal that the letters written by the senior manager were not an acknowledgement of an existing contractual commitment but rather confirming an intention to act. The words used at the Christmas party did not carry an intention to create legal relations but only a general intention to move towards parity of salary at some point. There was therefore no fundamental breach of contract for the purposes of constructive dismissal.[3]

---

1. Otto Kaun-Freund
2. See Chapter 1
3. See Chapter 10

The formation of an employment contract is the culmination of a recruitment process which will normally involve advertising for staff, submission of application forms, job interviews, negotiating terms of employment and selection of staff. Each stage of the recruitment process can be considered culminating in the contract of employment. Potential unlawful discrimination in the recruitment process is dealt with in Chapter 6.

Illegality

A contract of employment is unenforceable if it is illegal under statute or its objects are contrary to public policy at common law. Illegality can arise in the formation or during the continuance of the contract. The most common ground for illegality is when the parties agree to commit a fraud on the Revenue by means of tax evasion.[4]

> In *Napier v. National Business Agency* 1951 the plaintiff was employed on a salary of thirteen pounds per week with six pounds a week expenses when both parties were aware that genuine expenses would never exceed one pound. Following her summary dismissal the plaintiff claimed damages for wrongful dismissal. The Court of Appeal held that the contract was unenforceable as contrary to public policy. By contracting as they had *'the parties to it were doing that which they must be taken to know would be liable to defeat the proper claim of the Inland Revenue and to avoid altogether, or at least to postpone, the proper payment of income tax'.*

More recently in *Soteriou v. Ultrachem* 2004 a claim for unfair dismissal and subsequently wrongful dismissal was struck out by the High Court because the contract of employment was tainted with illegality. The claimant had been found to have made false statements to investigators from the Contributions Agency in an attempt to establish his employee status for the purposes of statutory rights. The High Court judge held that *'Where the contract at the basis of a claim for wrongful dismissal has already been adjudicated upon by the employment tribunal and found to be unenforceable because it was tainted with illegality, the tribunal's findings as to illegality operate as an issue estoppel. The issue of the legality of a contract of employment is the same before an employment tribunal in proceedings for unfair dismissal as it is before the High Court in a claim for wrongful dismissal. Accordingly, the High Court would be bound to find that the contract for breach of which the claimant sought to sue is unenforceable and the claim would be bound to fail.'*

An employer could seek to rely on the fact that a contract of employment is unenforceable on the grounds of illegality as a defence to a complaint of unfair dismissal. This was the case in *Lightfoot v. D & J Sporting Ltd.* 1996 where an employer had arranged to pay part of his gamekeepers wages to his wife so reducing the employee's tax liability and national insurance contributions. Despite the fact that the wife did genuinely assist her husband in his gamekeeping duties the tribunal concluded that the contract of employment was tainted by illegality, for the scheme to reduce tax liability had been adopted after seven years of employment. Accepting the reality of tax avoidance schemes the EAT disagreed with the finding of the tribunal that such schemes are necessarily unlawful. *'A scheme is not necessarily unlawful because its only purpose is to reduce the amount of lawful deductions that ought to be paid to the Inland Revenue or the Department of Social Security. That is the purpose of all legitimate tax avoidance schemes. If the scheme was entered into in good faith and was a proper*

---

4. Rather than tax avoidance which is lawful

method of reducing tax, open and above board, which either had been or would be disclosed to the Revenue, there is nothing unlawful about it.'

An illegal contract may not affect an employment claim that does not depend upon its existence, for instance the statutory tort of sex discrimination.[5]

> In *Hall v. Woolston Hall Leisure Ltd.* 2000 the Court of Appeal held that despite the fact that an employee knew from her payslips that her employer was defrauding the Inland Revenue and that her contract was therefore tainted with illegality, she was nevertheless entitled to compensation under the Sex Discrimination Act 1975 when she was unlawfully dismissed because of her pregnancy.

If an employer knowingly recruits an employee who is fraudulently claiming welfare benefits this will not only affect the validity of the contract but also constitute a criminal offence. Under s.8 of the Asylum and Immigration Act 1996 it is a criminal offence to employ someone aged 16 or over who does not have the right to work in the UK or do the type of work offered to them. Employers do have a statutory defence to the criminal offence of employing an illegal worker provided that they check and copy certain original documents before the employment commences. Such documents include a UK or European Economic Area passport, a national ID card or a UK residence permit. An employer who employs an illegal worker without carrying out the necessary checks is liable to be fined up to £5000 for each person they illegally employ.

The Recruitment Process

The recruitment process often begins when the employer places an advertisement indicating that staff are required. Statements of fact in the advertisement are classified as representations and if false and having induced a contract of employment, the innocent employee could seek a remedy for misrepresentation. In rare cases statements in the advertisement have been given the status of contractual terms or at least used as evidence to determine the express terms of employment.

> In *Holliday Concrete v. Woods* 1979 the job advertisement indicated that a fifteen-month contract was available. This was regarded as the period of employment rather than the employer's view that there was an understanding that the job would last as long on the project continued. Also in *Joseph Steinfeld v. Reypert* 1979 the EAT held that the fact that the job advertised 'sales manager' bore no relation to the actual job which was mainly clerical, amounted to a repudiatory[6] breach of the contract of employment.

A job advertisement may also place clear obligations on an employee so that if they are not fulfilled this will be a factor in determining the reasonableness of the employer's decision to dismiss as a result.

> In *Tayside Regional Council v. McIntosh* 1982 the job advertisement required a car mechanic to have a clean driving licence. Despite the fact that this was not inserted as an express term in an employment contract the subsequent dismissal of a mechanic who lost his licence was held to be fair.[7]

---

5. See Chapter 6
6. A significant breach justifying contractual termination
7. Under s.98(2)d Employment Rights Act 1996

Job advertisements must of course comply with equal opportunity law, the focus of Chapter 6.

The application form

Advertisements for job applications normally indicate that a prospective employee should complete an application form to assist in the selection process. While a significant feature of the employment contract is that it involves a relationship of trust and confidence it is not a contract uberrimae fidei (utmost good faith).[8] This means that there is no duty on an applicant to volunteer information which is not requested during the recruitment process, which includes the completion of the application form.

> In *Walton v. TAC Construction Materials Ltd*. 1981 the complainant was dismissed after working for thirteen months when the employer discovered that he was a heroin addict. During a medical inspection prior to employment the employee had answered 'none' when asked to give details of serious illnesses and failed to reveal that he was injecting himself with heroin. Both the tribunal and the EAT held that it was fair to dismiss the applicant firstly because of his deception and secondly in accordance with their policy not to employ anyone who was addicted to drugs. Although not relevant for the case the EAT considered whether the complainant should have disclosed his addiction for the purposes of employment and decided that *'it could not be said that there is any duty on the employee in the ordinary case, though there may be exceptions, to volunteer information about himself or otherwise than in response to a direct question'.*

The lesson from Walton (above) is that a prudent employer should comprehensively question a prospective employee, making full use of the application form and the interview, without relying on the applicant to provide unsolicited information of relevance to the application.

If a job applicant is deliberately dishonest on an application form this will normally make any subsequent decision to dismiss fair.

> In *Torr v. British Railways Board* 1977 the EAT held that the employers *'were justified in deciding to dismiss the employee as soon as they appreciated that he had obtained employment as a guard by dishonest concealment of a criminal conviction carrying a sentence of three years imprisonment, even though the conviction was as far back as 1958 and the employee had apparently been working satisfactorily as a guard for sixteen months'*. The sentence was of such a duration not to be covered by the Rehabilitation of Offenders Act 1974 and neither could the philosophy behind that Act be extended to render a dismissal in the circumstances unfair *'It is of utmost importance that an employer seeking an employee to hold a position of responsibility and trust should be able to select for employment a candidate in whom he can have confidence. It is fundamental to that confidence that the employee should truthfully disclose his history so far as it is sought by the intending employer.'*

In determining the fairness of an employer's decision to dismiss after discovering an employees mis-statement on an application form all the circumstances must be considered including the significance of the mis-statement, the length of employment and whether the work was satisfactory.

---

8. Such as partnership or insurance

In *Johnson v. Tesco Stores Ltd.* 1976 the application form stated that 'a misstatement as to date of birth, previous employment details etc., will render the application and any subsequent contract invalid.' When a mis-statement by the complainant as to his employment history was discovered, his job was terminated, despite having worked satisfactorily for eighteen months. The tribunal held that the effect of the clause could not be to make the employment contract void from the outset when the false statement was discovered. When the contract was terminated by the employer there was a dismissal which could be regarded as fair or unfair applying the law relating to unfair dismissal.[9]

Job interviews

The primary objective of the job interview from the employer's viewpoint is to assist in the selection process. It should be stressed however if a decision to employ an applicant is made it may be at this point that a formal offer is made and accepted and a contract concluded. Even in cases where an understanding is reached, subject to a formal written offer at a later stage, statements or promises made during the interview may be used to interpret the contractual terms or constitute express terms of the contract in themselves. Certainly it makes sense to ensure at the interview stage that a prospective employee is given a realistic picture of the terms and conditions of employment and what the job entails. Even statements such as promotion prospects could be regarded as contractual promises and terms of employment if they later prove to be unrealistic. Certainly a clearly worded job offer will override conflicting statements made in the job advertisement. In the event of conflict between oral statements and writing the writing will normally have primacy, but it is the intention of the parties which must be determined. The following case is instructive but nevertheless represents an exceptional decision.

In *Hawker Siddeley Power Engineering Ltd. v. Rump* 1979 the complainant was employed as a heavy goods vehicle driver in 1973 and signed a contract of employment which stated that he would be liable to travel all over the country. This obligation was confirmed in a later statement of terms of employment issued in 1976 and signed by the employee. In fact the complainant had made it clear when he took the job that because of his wife's illness he would not travel beyond the south of England and that had been orally agreed by a manager when he signed the contract. When finally in 1978 the complainant refused to obey an instruction to travel to Scotland and this led to his dismissal, one issue before the EAT was whether he was contractually obliged to do so. The EAT held that the promise to work only in the south was an oral contractual term. Here *'there was a direct promise by the employers which must have become part of the contract of employment because it was following upon the promise that the employee signed the contract'.* Even the subsequent written statement[10] which included a mobility clause signed by the employer was insufficient to exclude the oral term previously agreed. Here the employee *'had no notice that the oral term he had secured was going to form no part of his new contract. The mere putting in front of him a document and invitation for him to sign it could not be held to be a variation by agreement so as to exclude the important oral term which he had previously secured. Rather if there was a variation at all to the contract, it was a unilateral variation which was not binding upon the employee'.*

---

9. See Chapter 11
10. Under s.1 Employment Rights Act 1996

From an employer's perspective it is unsatisfactory to have a contract of employment composed of both written and oral terms. By inserting a clearly worded express term in the written contract it would be possible to confine the express mutual obligations of the parties to the content of the written document. In *White v. Bristol Rugby Ltd.* 2002 the contract of a professional rugby player expressly provided that *'Each party to this agreement now acknowledge that this agreement contains the whole agreement between the parties and that they have not relied upon oral or written representations made to them by other persons, its employees or agents.'* The Bristol Mercantile Court held that this clearly worded *'entire agreement'* clause effectively excluded any claim based upon oral terms outside the written agreement.

It could be argued that in the interests of certainty an *'entire agreement'* clause may also be beneficial from the employee's perspective. Such a clause would however have no impact in removing implied terms from the contract of employment, particularly those in relation to trust, confidence and safety.[11]

Conditional offers

Quite often an offer of employment is made conditional, for instance *'subject to the receipt of satisfactory written references'* or the *'passing of a medical examination'.* The contract can only normally be concluded in such circumstances by fulfilling the requirements of the condition.

> In *Wishart v. National Association of Citizens Advice Bureaux Ltd.* 1990 The Court of Appeal considered a case where the plaintiff had been offered the post of information officer *'subject to satisfactory references'* and then when the employer discovered his past attendance record withdrew the job offer. The issue before the Court of Appeal was whether the employer's decision to treat the references as unsatisfactory could be viewed objectively and tested by the standard of the reasonable person in the position of the employer. In fact the court decided that unlike medical opinion as to the employee's fitness which could be tested objectively, there was no obligation in law on the employer other than to decide in good faith whether the references were satisfactory. *'The natural reading of a communication, the purpose of which is to tell the prospective employee that part of the decision on whether he is firmly offered the post has yet to be made, is that the employer is reserving the right to make up his own mind when the references have been received and studied.'*

More recently in *Paul v. National Probation Service* 2004 an offer of employment was made subject to a satisfactory occupational health report. As a conditional offer the employer exercised his common law right to withdraw it pursuant to the report. While recognising the common law right to withdraw the offer the tribunal went on to decide that the claimant was entitled to challenge the withdrawal, as contrary to the Disability Discrimination Act[12]. The EAT disagreed with the tribunal however, deciding that that existence of a disability does not of itself substantially disadvantage a disabled person in comparison with persons who are not disabled merely because of the need for occupational health clearance.

---

11. See later in the chapter
12. See Chapter 6

If there is a dispute as to whether an appointment has been made or not it is only rarely that a court would grant a temporary injunction[13] to require the employer to allow the employee to remain in the post until the issue is settled at the full trial.

> This was the case in *Powell v. London Borough of Brent* 1987 where there was a dispute as to whether the appellant a council officer had been validly promoted. The employer alleged that the decision to promote her was not valid as it had not been confirmed. The Court of Appeal granted an interlocutory[14] injunction requiring the council employer to allow the officer to remain in the promoted post until it was determined at the trial of the action whether she had been validly and effectively appointed to the office in question. *'Although it is a general rule that there cannot be specific performance of a contract of service, part of the basis of which is that mutual confidence is a necessary condition for the contracts satisfactory working, the present case was exceptional. It is unlikely that a plaintiff will be able to satisfy the court that, despite strenuous opposition by her employers to her continuing in the job, nevertheless there subsists the necessary confidence to justify the making of an injunction. Sufficiency of confidence must be judged by reference to the circumstances of the case, including the nature of the work, the people with whom the work must be done and the likely effect upon the employee and the employer's operations if the employer is required by injunction to suffer the plaintiff to continue in the work.'* Here the fact that the claimant worked competently in the promoted post for over four months and there was no evidence of any defect in her work relationships enabled the court to grant the injunction pending the trial of the action.

If the acceptance of the job offer by the applicant is conditional, the normal contractual rules apply and it will be taken as a rejection and amount to a counter offer capable of acceptance or rejection. It is in the interests of both the employer and the employee that the express terms of employment are precise and clearly understood. It is then less likely that legal problems will arise in the future when contractual terms are possibly subject to change or it becomes necessary to bring the employment relationship to an end.[15]

Breach of contract

Once a contract of employment is concluded there is legal redress available if either party decides to back out of the contract and so commits a contractual breach. The unilateral withdrawal by an employer of an offer of employment, once accepted, will constitute a breach of contract, and the damages awarded could in exceptional cases exceed the wages due under the contractual notice period.

> In *Gill and Others v. Cape Contracts Ltd.* 1985 the plaintiffs gave up their present employment as insulation engineers in Northern Ireland to take up the offer by the defendants of six months work in the Shetlands on much higher wages. After confirming the arrangement the defendants then withdrew the offer of employment and the plaintiffs sued for damages. The Northern Ireland High Court awarded the men £2,500 damages each holding that *'the plaintiff insulation engineers were entitled to damages for breach of warranty by the defendants in*

---

13. Court order to retain the status quo
14. Temporary
15. See Chapter 5

> *circumstances in which the defendants failed to honour a representation to the plaintiffs forming a collateral contract that if they gave up their existing employment they would be employed by the defendant... for approximately six months at wages considerably in excess of their existing earnings... those representations formed a collateral contract to the contract of employment'.*[16]

It should be stressed however that the above scenario is rare and damages available against an employer in breach will normally be restricted to the wages due under the notice period. Also the courts will not, other than in exceptional cases, order specific performance[17] of a contract of employment, the remedy for breach by the employee is damages. In practice unless an employer has incurred substantial recruitment cost the cost of litigation would make an action against an employee in breach unwise. There is no right to bring a potential unfair dismissal claim without one years continuous employment unless the reason for dismissal is shown to be inadmissible such as related to pregnancy, trade union membership, statutory rights or health and safety.[18]

> In *Sarker v. South Tees Acute Hospitals NHS Trust* 1997 the employer withdrew a formal letter of appointment before the employee started work. The EAT held that the tribunal had jurisdiction to hear a claim for damages for breach of contract relating to the termination of the contract of employment under the Industrial Tribunals Extension of Jurisdiction Order 1994. An employee is defined as someone who has entered into a contract of employment despite not having started work so that a potential claim for unfair dismissal also arises if the reason for dismissal is shown to be inadmissible such as pregnancy or trade union membership. The EAT rejected the notion that here there was a contract for employment rather than a contract of employment. The employee had entered into a contract of employment to provide future service in consideration of remuneration and no further contract was required to confirm the relationship.

Legal Formalities and the Contract of Employment

Contrary to popular belief, apart from merchant seamen and apprentices, there is no legal requirement that a contract of employment be in writing. Under s.230 (2) of the ERA '*a contract of employment means a contract of service or apprenticeship whether express or implied and if express oral or in writing*'. While there are problems associated with identifying the terms of an oral agreement, or part oral and written nevertheless, given the fluid nature of a contract of employment there is no guarantee that a requirement to reduce the original contract to writing would solve all the problems of identifying and interpreting its content.

Under s.1 of the Employment Rights Act 1996[19] there is a statutory requirement on employers to provide their employees within two months of the commencement of employment with a written statement of the main terms of employment. The section originally applied to full-time employees[20] or part-time workers[21] after five years employment. Since 1996 the hours threshold has been removed and s.1 applies to both full-time and part-time employees.

---

16. See *Sarker v. South Tees* 1997 (below)
17. Court order requiring contractual performance
18. See Chapter 11
19. As amended by the Employment Act 2002
20. Employed for at least 16 hours per week
21. Employed for between 8 and 16 hours

Also certain classes of employees are excluded from s.1 including registered dock workers, Crown employees and employees who work wholly or mainly outside Great Britain. The object of s.1 is to ensure that employees have written confirmation and a source to scrutinise at least the main terms of their employment contracts. Employers can issue the statement in instalments but within the two months limit. The principal statement should contain certain information prescribed by section 1.[22]

Statutory Statement of Terms and Conditions of Employment

Particulars which must be included in the statutory statement include:

Reference to the parties and the dates on which the period of continuous employment began (stating whether a previous period of employment is included as part of continuous employment);

- the scale of remuneration and the method of calculation;
- the intervals at which remuneration is paid (whether weekly or monthly or some other period);
- the terms and conditions relating to hours of work;
- the terms and conditions relating to holidays and holiday pay (sufficient to enable the employee's entitlement to accrued holiday pay on the termination of employment to be precisely calculated);
- the terms and conditions relating to sickness or injury and sickness pay;
- the terms and conditions relating to pension and pension scheme;
- the length of notice which the employee is obliged to give and entitled to receive;
- the title of the job which the employee is employed to do or a brief description of the work;
- a note containing a specification of any disciplinary rules and the person to whom the employee can apply if dissatisfied with a disciplinary decision or for the purposes of redressing a grievance;[23]
- the name of the person to whom the employee can apply if he is dissatisfied with any disciplinary decision relating to him;
- the name of the person to whom the employer can apply to seek the redress of any grievance;
- any collective agreement which directly affects terms and conditions of employment.

Sections 35-38 of the Employment Act 2002 amends section 1 in relation to written particulars of employment. The requirement under s.1 to provide a note of disciplinary rules to a new employee requires that the note must now specify any procedure applicable to the taking of disciplinary decisions or refer to a document specifying such a procedure that is readily accessible. The statement must also specify a person to whom the employee may apply if dissatisfied with a disciplinary decision or a decision to dismiss. The statutory grievance procedure will also have to be included in the written statement. Significantly

---

22. See below
23. An important requirement under Employment Act 2002 (Dispute Resolution) Regulations 2004

the previous exception for employers with less than 20 employees not having to supply disciplinary rules and procedures was removed by s.36.

Also under the Employment Act 2002 there is now a power for an employment tribunal to award compensation in the case of a s.1 failure. There is also a tribunal discretion of making a two weeks pay award if it finds in favour of the employee but makes no award of compensation.

A section 1 statement may refer to other documents such as a staff handbook or written policy for the purposes of sickness provisions and pensions and a collective agreement for the purposes of notice provisions provided the employee has either a reasonable opportunity of reading such documents during the course of employment or they are readily accessible. It would also be permissible to include a disciplinary and grievance procedure in separate documents provided they are reasonably accessible.

Reference is made several times in s.1 to *'terms and conditions'* of employment and yet there has been no attempt in statute or common law to satisfactorily distinguish between these expressions. The prevalent view seems to be that *'terms'* are those parts of the contract that are mutually agreed, expressly or by implication and are found in the contract, collective agreements and occasionally in statutory provisions. *'Conditions'* on the other hand have a lower status and are unilateral instructions from the employer and will specify how and when employment duties are to be fulfilled. Conditions are usually found in work rules, disciplinary and grievance procedures and job descriptions.[24]

Section 1 requirements

To satisfy the requirements of s.1 it is not sufficient simply to be told or shown the above particulars of employment. The employer must present the employee with a document containing the information or at least make such a document available for inspection.[25] It should be stressed that a statutory statement is not the contract of employment but rather strong prima facie[26] evidence of its terms. Certainly the mere acknowledgement of its receipt does not turn the statement into a contract.

> In *System Floors (UK) Ltd. v. Daniel* 1982, Browne-Wilkinson J said in relation to the statement that *'It provides very strong prima facie evidence of what were the terms of the contract between the parties. Nor are the statements of the terms finally conclusive: at most, they place a heavy burden on the employer to show that the actual terms of the contract are different from those which he had set out in the statutory statement.'* This view of the status of the statutory statement was subsequently approved by the Court of Appeal in *Robertson v. British Gas Company* 1983 where it was held that if the written statement does not accurately reflect the agreed terms then the agreed terms prevail.
>
> In *Eagland v. British Telecommunications plc* 1992 the Court of Appeal held that when called upon to scrutinise the accuracy of a s.1 statutory statement the industrial tribunal cannot after all invent terms to cover matters not referred to, such as grievance procedures and holiday pay. LJ Leggatt suggested that he was

---

24. See later in the chapter
25. A collective agreement or a rule book
26. On the face of it

> '*unable to envisage circumstances in which it might become appropriate for an industrial tribunal to invent a term ... in the sense of determining either what term should have been agreed or what term would have been reasonable. If an essential term, such as a written statement must contain, has not been agreed, there will be no agreement. If it has it is the duty of the industrial tribunal where necessary to identify the term as having been agreed, whether expressly or by inference from all the circumstances including the conduct of the parties without recourse to invention*'.

Certainly while it is up to the contractual parties to agree the content of the contract of employment it is for the employer to provide the employee with a statutory statement of terms and conditions of employment. All the matters in s.1 should be included in the statement so for instance reference should be made to holidays, holiday pay, and accrued holiday pay rights. In *Morley v. Heritage* 1993 the employee argued that when his employment ceased he was entitled to 13 days accrued holiday pay relying on an implied term of his contract that if his employment terminated with accrued holiday entitlement he would be paid in lieu. The Court of Appeal made the important point that it was not necessary to imply a term into a contract of employment to satisfy the requirements of s.1. While the section does refer to a statement in relation to accrued holiday rights *it 'leaves it open to an employer to enter into a contract with an employee which contains no provision at all'*. Applying both the business efficacy test and the presumed intention of the parties the Court of Appeal held that there was no implied term entitling the employee to accrued holiday pay.[27]

While the statutory statement does not constitute the contract of employment the High Court held in *Lee and others v. GEC Plessey Telecommunications* 1993 that there is a heavy burden on a party who claims that the actual contract is different from the statutory statement.

Changing terms and conditions

Contractual terms we shall discover, are often the subject of change,[28] in which case an employer is obliged under s.4 to notify the employee of changes in the statement within one month of the change. An employer who fails to comply with obligations in relation to the statutory statement could be the subject of a complaint to an employment tribunal. Complaints are rare, and only arise usually in connection with other complaints, for instance in relation to unfair dismissal. Alternatively a complaint may have an ulterior motive for instance to establish an individual's status as an employee.[29] Finally it should be mentioned that those employers who provide their employees with a written contract of employment which covers all the matters which must be referred to in the statutory statement, do not have to supply their employees with a separate statutory statement. The writing should of course reflect what has been orally agreed by the parties.

> In *Discount Tobacco and Confectionery Ltd. v. Armitage* 1990 the complainant was a shop manageress with only a short period of continuous employment who enlisted the help of her trade union official to secure a written contract of

---

27. See later in the chapter
28. See Chapter 5
29. See *Carmichael v. National Power* 2000 Chapter 3

employment from her employer. When finally such a contract was issued, and she felt that it contained discrepancies, the complainant attempted to raise them with her employer. The response of the employer was to dismiss her, giving the reason for dismissal as lack of suitability or capability. This led to a complaint of unfair dismissal, the complainant alleging that the true reason for dismissal was her trade union membership which was automatically unfair under s.152 of the Trade Union Labour Relations (Consolidation) Act 1992. If trade union membership or activities is the reason for dismissal there is no need to qualify with continuous employment for protection against unfair dismissal. Both the industrial tribunal and the Employment Appeal Tribunal thought that there was no genuine distinction between trade union membership and making use of the essential services of a union officer and as a consequence the dismissal in this case was automatically unfair.

It is the statutory statement that is the source of many of the express terms in the contract of employment but some parts of the statement will not have contractual status. The House of Lords in *Johnson v. Unisys Ltd.* 2001 considered the status of the disciplinary procedure which would be part of a Statutory Statement. Failure to comply with the procedure would not give rise to a common law action for damage for breach of contract. Their lordships held that the disciplinary procedure *'was intended to operate within the scope of the law of unfair dismissal and was not intended to be actionable at common law'.*

The Contents of a Contract of Employment

A contract of employment is composed of its terms, the mutual promises and obligations of the parties to it. Contractual terms may be *express* and become part of the contract through the express agreement of the parties. Usually of course, there is simply agreement by the prospective employee to the standard terms dictated by the prospective employer or terms previously agreed between the employer and a trade union. Alternatively, contractual terms may be *implied* into the contract of employment by an external source such as a collective agreement. The major sources for implication we shall discover, are the courts and tribunals but occasionally terms are implied into contracts of employment by statutory provisions or through custom. Such mutual obligations have legal significance and a failure to comply with the requirement of a term of the contract could provide the innocent party with the option of securing legal redress.

An action for breach of contract may be brought to secure damages against the party in breach of a contractual term. If damages would not suffice to provide a remedy, an injunction could be sought to restrain the breach of contract. In such circumstances an *interlocutory*[30] *injunction* is often sought as a remedy. One rarely used option for an employee who feels that his employer is unreasonably requiring him to do work which is not part of his contractual obligations is to seek an injunction to maintain the status quo at work. A further option for an employee in these circumstances is to apply to the High Court for a declaration as to the legal position.

---

30. Temporary

Repudiatory breach

If a breach of contract is regarded as so serious as to be repudiatory, then the innocent party has the option of accepting the breach and terminating the contract. A repudiatory breach by an employer could, if accepted by the employee, entitle him to regard himself as constructively dismissed if he walks out as a result. Alternatively, a repudiatory breach by the employee could in some circumstances justify summary dismissal by the employer. Obviously there is no legal requirement for an employer or an employee to act upon a breach of contract.

A good example of an employer's repudiatory breach of contract could be a failure to pay the full salary of the employee. In *Cantor Fitzgerald International v. Callaghan* 1999 the Court of Appeal distinguishes between an employers failure to pay or delay in paying agreed remuneration and a deliberate refusal to do so. A wilful refusal to pay the agreed salary following perhaps a unilateral reduction in pay will undermine the entire foundation of the contract and constitute a repudiatory breach by the employer. Alternatively a delay or failure to pay due to a mistake or some temporary fault may not constitute a breach which goes to the root of the contract and redress would be limited to damages.

In the majority of cases of conflict or dispute between the employer and employee, the true legal position can only be assessed by identifying and analysing the express and implied terms of the contract. The contractual terms are usually the starting point for the analysis of a conflict scenario.

Express Terms

Express terms of a contract of employment are those that are expressly agreed by the employer and employee, and may be in writing or oral or a mixture of the two. Inevitably of course they tend to originate from the employer.[31]

The statutory statement of the main terms and conditions of employment will normally provide sound evidence of the express terms. As we have said even a job advertisement, an application form or a letter of appointment could contain contractual terms, as well as matters orally agreed in the interview. Express terms relate to matters such as *wages, hours, holidays, sick pay, job description, restraints, etc.* Of course, what has been expressly agreed by the parties may often require interpretation in the courts and employment tribunals. You should also appreciate that express terms rarely define fundamental matters such as the work quality or the pace of work effort.[32]

Well drafted express terms in a contract of employment will normally give the employer an absolute discretion over the performance of the contract. The contractual power of an employer to determine wage rises and bonuses is largely unfettered but the instructive case of *Clark v. Nomura International plc* 2000 indicates that there are some limits to contractual discretion. The claimant was a senior equities trader whose contract of employment provided for a discretionary bonus which was *'not guaranteed in any way, and is dependent upon individual performance'.* The claimant seemed to have performed very successfully from his

---

31. Because of the nature of the contract
32. Other than to require competence

appointment in July 1995 having received bonuses of over £2.5m in his first year. Following a relationship breakdown he was given three months notice in February 1997 and these proceedings arose out of the failure of the employer to award any bonus for the previous year despite the claimant's successful individual performance. Concerns about his behaviour was the reason put forward by the employer not to award a discretionary bonus, which the claimant alleged constitutes a breach of contract. On a proper construction of his contract he claimed that his financial performance was the precondition to the exercise of the discretion to award a bonus. Mr. Justice Burton in the High Court set out the general principle that *'an employer exercising a discretion which on the face of the contract of employment is unfettered or absolute will be in breach of contract if no reasonable employer would have exercised the discretion in that way'*. Previous case-law provided some assistance In *Clark v. BET* 1997 the court held that such a discretion should not be exercised capriciously. In *White v. Reflecting Roadstuds* 1991 it was held that the discretion should not be exercised without reasonable or sufficient grounds. Neither approach appealed to Mr. Justice Burton who concluded that the right test is one of *'irrationality or perversity'*. Here the terms of the contract required the employer to award a bonus to the claimant based upon individual performance. Having performed significantly well in financial transactions the court awarded the claimant £1.35m on the grounds that that would have been the bonus he would have received had the employers complied with their contractual obligations.

While a perversity rule, to control the employer's discretion in a contract of employment seems perfectly reasonable, in *Clark*[33] it also seems reasonable that the exercise of bonus discretion should also be subject to the overriding requirement of satisfactory contractual performance by the employee.

Contractual interpretation

It is the ordinary courts that generally but now not exclusively deal with disputes surrounding the interpretation of the terms of a contract of employment based upon an action for breach of contract. The majority of employment disputes however relate to statutory employment rights such as unfair dismissal, redundancy and discrimination and they are heard by employment tribunals and on appeal by the Employment Appeal Tribunal. Constructive dismissal is determined by applying a repudiatory breach test, so that it is inevitable that a tribunal is often faced with the vexed question as to the seriousness of a breach of contract by the employer.

A court or tribunal may be called on to determine the rights of the parties by interpreting the exact wording of the express terms of a contract of employment.

> In *Cole v. Midland Display Ltd.* 1973 the tribunal was faced with the problem of determining the meaning of the term, *'employed on a staff basis'* when it was applied to a manager. The tribunal held that the phrase meant that the employee was entitled to wages during periods of sickness or no work but in return the employee could be required to work overtime with out pay. In *McCaffrey v. A E Jeavons & Company Ltd.* 1967 an employee employed expressly as a *'travelling man'* in the building trade was held to be contractually obliged to move his place of employment anywhere in the country when required to by the employer. An

---

33. Above

employee whose job title was described as carrying out *'general duties'* in *Peter Carnie & Son Ltd. v. Paton* 1979 was held to be required to be very flexible in relation to the needs of his employer for the type of work to be carried out. In *Securicor Ltd. v. Reid and others* 1992 the EAT construed the express term that an employee was *'based at'* a certain location to mean that he could be required to work at any site within the area administered from that location. The employee could be required therefore, under the express terms of his contract to move from one site to another and if the employee refuses to move and is dismissed, he would not be entitled to a redundancy payment.

Later we will consider the role of custom and practice in relation to contractual terms. Certainly if there is ambiguity concerning the nature and extent of an express contractual term then evidence of custom and practice may indicate the parties true intentions and the proper interpretation of the term. In *Dunlop Tyres Ltd. v. Blows* 2001[34] the Court of Appeal regarded the practice adopted by the parties as to overtime payments for working statutory holidays as powerful evidence of the parties intentions.

The fact that an employee has a right to occupational sick pay contained in an express contractual term means that there would be a breach of contract if an employer purported to dismiss an employee who was in receipt of sick benefit unless the dismissal was on the grounds of gross misconduct. *Aspden v. Webb Poultry & Meat Group Ltd.* 1996 indicated that this may be the case even where the employee is served with the appropriate period of notice.

The Court of Session in *Hull v. General Accident, Fire & Life Assurance Co. plc* 1998 approved of the above decision but felt that in these circumstances redundancy could also be a lawful reason for dismissal. The High Court in *Villella v. MFI Furniture Centres Ltd.* 1999 held that there was an implied contractual term that where an employee was entitled to incapacity benefit, the employer would not terminate the contract except for a reason other than ill health, if the effect was to deprive the employee of incapacity benefit.

Overriding terms

Contract law dictates that an express term should prevail over an implied term dealing with the same matter however you should appreciate that certain implied terms such as health and safety and trust and confidence are fundamental in a contract of employment and will represent an irreducible minimum of obligation. There is an academic view that such terms represent the foundation of any contract of employment.[35]

There are also extreme circumstances where the courts have recognised that a fundamental implied term may take precedence over an express term.

The Court of Appeal decision in *Johnstone v. Bloomsbury Health Authority* 1991 held by a majority that an employer's implied obligation to ensure the health and welfare of his employees could be broken even where the employer was exercising an express option in the contract to require the employee to work a large number of hours overtime. The court felt that if the employer is aware that by requiring a junior doctor to work long hours his health is suffering, it

---

34. See later
35. See later in the chapter- trust and confidence

would be a breach of contract to impose such long hours on him despite the fact that it was authorised by an express term of the contract.

Work rules

It is common practice in many spheres of employment for the employer to issue work rules by printing notices or handing out rule books or staff manuals. Such rule books or manuals often contain instructions as to time-keeping, meal breaks, disciplinary offences and grievance procedure, sickness and pension rights, job descriptions, and the employer's safety policy. Although there is still some doubt as to the legal status of work rules, the present view is that such documents are unlikely to contain contractual terms. One school of thought is that work rules and manuals should be regarded as *conditions* rather than *terms* of employment, hence the expression, '*terms and conditions of employment*' and as such they should be subject to unilateral change by the employer. For example, while the number of hours worked would normally be the subject of express agreement and constitute a contractual term, instructions as to when these hours should be worked will normally be contained in a rule book and as a condition be liable to unilateral change.

> In *Cadoux v. Central Regional Council* 1986 the employee's contract of employment was to be subject to the Conditions of Service laid down by the National Joint Council for Local Authorities' Administrative, Technical and Clerical Services, as supplemented by the Authorities Rules, as amended from time to time. The issue in the case was whether, under the Authorities' rules, the employer was entitled to introduce a non-contributory life assurance scheme for staff and then subsequently unilaterally withdraw it. The Court of Session held that here the 'Authorities' Rules' were clearly incorporated into contracts of employment. They were however, made unilaterally by the employer, and although introduced after consultation, they were the 'Authorities' Rules' and not subject to mutual agreement. Consequently there was '*no limitation on the employer's right to vary, alter or cancel any of the provisions of the Rules. The reference to the Authorities Rules, "as amended from time to time", led to the clear inference that the employer could alter their rules at their own hand*'. In the present case therefore the employer was entitled unilaterally to withdraw the provision of the non-contributory life assurance scheme.

> In *Dryden v. Greater Glasgow Health Board* 1992 the EAT held that an employer was entitled to introduce a rule imposing a smoking ban at the workplace and the staff has no implied right to smoke.[36] '*An employer is entitled to make rules for the conduct of employees in their place of work within the scope of the contract and once it was held that there was no implied term in the contract which entitled the employee to facilities for smoking, the rule against smoking was a lawful rule.*'

> In *Secretary of State for Employment v. ASLEF (No 2)* 1972 Lord Denning expressed the view that rule books issued to railwaymen by their employers did not contain contractual terms but rather instructions to an employee as to how he was to do his work.

Where, however, a rule book or manual is given or referred to by the employer at the time the contract of employment is formed, the fact that the employee has agreed that it is to be

---

36. See Chapter 8

part of the contract and acknowledges that fact by his signature would more than likely give the rule book or manual contractual effect.

There is an inference that agreed employment policies such as no smoking in *Dryden*[37] and equal opportunities are non contractual.[38] However in *Taylor v. Secretary of State for Scotland* 2000 the House of Lords confirmed that an equal opportunities policy, negotiated with trade union representatives and then notified to employees by means of a circular, was incorporated into individual contracts of employment. Despite this ruling their Lordships held that there was no breach of contract when a prison officer was chosen for compulsory retirement because he was over the minimum retirement age.

Implied Terms

A contract of employment is composed of contractual terms that have been expressly agreed or incorporated into the contract by an extraneous source such as a collective agreement, the custom and practice of a particular trade or business, or the common law. To have a full appreciation of the content of a contract of employment you should be aware of the role of the common law in defining rights and duties of employers and employees. In addition to a large number of common law duties relating to such matters as good faith, confidentiality, health and safety, and obedience, which were originally tortious in origin, there is an increased willingness of the courts and tribunals to imply terms into employment contracts to deal with issues such as trust and confidence, mutual respect and sexual harassment.

The trust and confidence term is now regarded by the House of Lords as fundamental and the foundation of a contract of employment not capable of exclusion and capable of overriding conflicting express terms. In *Horkulak v. Cantor Fitzgerald* 2004 the Court of appeal emphasises the fact that principles of trust and confidence underpin the employment relationship. When paying a discretionary bonus therefore the employer in this case was bound to act rationally and in good faith as a matter of contract.[39]

Later when we consider the termination of employment, you will discover that the need to point to a clear repudiatory breach of the contract of employment to establish a constructive dismissal has encouraged judicial ingenuity in incorporating implied terms into the contract of employment which the tribunal or court may then declare that the employer has broken.[40]

Implied terms may originate from Statute, Custom and Practice and the Common Law.

Implied terms from statute

Apart from a few notable exceptions, statute is not a major source of implied terms of employment. On the creation of a contract of employment, however, a number of statutory rights arise almost immediately. Obvious examples include the right to a written statement of particulars of employment and ordinary maternity leave. Other rights, such as unfair dismissal and additional maternity leave attach to the contract of employment after a

---

37. Above
38. See below *Quinn & Others v. Colder Industrial Materials* 1996
39. See later in the chapter
40. See Chapter 10

period of continuous employment, usually one year. Most of these rights are under s.203 ERA non excludable and cannot be removed by an express term in the contract of employment.

An important example of a statutory term is provided by s.30 Employment Act 2002 which incorporates Statutory Dispute Resolution Procedures into all contracts of employment. Significantly it is not possible to contract out of this provision.[41]

Also under s.17 of the National Minimum Wage Act 1998[42] the minimum wage takes effect as a statutory implied term in a worker's contract and is enforceable by legal proceedings for breach of contract.

The High Court in *Barber v. RJB Mining (UK) Ltd. 1999* ruled that the maximum forty eight hour working week prescribed for workers in s.4(1) of the Working Time Regulations is a statutory implied term in all contracts of employment. This means that a breach of the regulations will constitute a breach of contract for which the employee could pursue a remedy such as a declaration and/or damages. Mr. Justice Gage said that *'It seems to be clear that parliament intended that all contracts of employment should be read so as to provide that the employee should work no more than an average of 48 hours in any week during the reference period.'*

Implied terms from custom and practice

If a particular work practice satisfies the criterion of being *'certain, notorious and reasonable'* then it may be regarded as a customary right and have the status of a contractual term. The EAT in *Henry v. London General Transport Services Ltd.* 2002 recently held that *'for a term to be incorporated into a contract of employment by way of custom and practice, the custom and practice so relied on must be reasonable, certain and notorious. Once the reasonableness, certainty and notoriety of the custom and practice is sufficiently proven it must be presumed that the term thus supported represents the wishes and intention of all relevant parties'.*

There are very few examples of terms established on the basis of a custom of the particular trade and workplace.

> In *Sagar v. Ridehalgh* 1931 for over 30 years an employer had made deductions from the wages of his weavers for bad workmanship and despite the fact that there was no reference to this practice in their contracts of employment or a relevant collective agreement it was upheld as a contractual term based upon custom.

While custom and practice is rarely used to justify the implication of terms it may nevertheless be significant in assisting in the interpretation of terms where there is ambiguity. In *Dunlop Tyres v. Blows* 2001 conflicting clauses in a collective agreement dealing with overtime payments and payments for statutory holidays were subject to scrutiny. For over 30 years the collective agreement had been applied so that salaried staff received the equivalent of 300% of the normal pay for working statutory holidays. From 1998 the employers took a different view of the agreement and paid double time rather than treble time. The conflicting interpretations were eventually considered by the Court of Appeal who found for the

---

41. See Chapter 11
42. See Chapter 9

employees by relying on custom and practice. *'Where the terms of a contract of employment are truly ambiguous it is open to the court to look at the practice adopted by the parties and to attach considerable importance to it as indicating the proper interpretation of the contractual terms. That practice is powerful evidence of the party's intentions to which the court can turn in order to resolve the ambiguity. Where there is a clearly established practice which continues before and after a contract is made the evidence of what happened before becomes relevant in determining whether any change in the position has been made.'* Here the incorporated terms were ambiguous so the established practice became part of the factual matrix against which the contract should be interpreted. By failing to pay treble time during the statutory holiday the employers were in breach of the Employment Rights Act 1996 s.13 and had made an unlawful deduction from wages.

Implied terms from the Common Law

The fact that common law implied terms confer rights impose duties on both parties to the employment relationship, suggests that they can be more meaningfully examined by considering each of them in turn in relation to both the employer and the employee. Most of the implied terms can be categorised under broad headings such as the wage/work bargain, health and safety, good faith, confidentiality, fidelity, the right to information, and trust and confidence.

The courts are careful to stress that terms are implied into contracts of employment by applying one of a number of common law tests. A term maybe implied if it is either:

- necessary to the functioning of the contract or;
- reflecting the obvious intention of the parties at the time the contract was concluded or;
- an inevitable incidence of the employment relationship.

The fact that a particular policy is regarded as custom and practice is used as a justification for an implied term. In *Duke v. Reliance Systems* 1982 it was held that a policy adopted unilaterally by management cannot become a term of employee's contracts on the ground that it is an established custom and practice, unless it is at least shown that the policy has been drawn to the attention of the employees or has been followed without exception for a substantial period. The issue in *Quinn and Others v. Calder Industrial Materials Ltd.* 1996 was whether the employers policy of paying enhanced redundancy payments supported the inference that it should be regarded as an implied term in employee's contracts. The fact that the policy had not been communicated to either the recognised[43] union or the employees helped convince the EAT that it had not been incorporated into individual contracts of employment as an implied term.

It does seem however that the courts and tribunals do find it possible to imply a term wherever it is thought necessary.

> In *Mears v. Safecar Security* 1983 the Court of Appeal held that if there is no express agreement on a matter, the courts are entitled to consider all the facts and circumstances of the relationship, including the parties' conduct, to determine whether a term should be implied into the contract of employment.

---

43. Recognised for the purposes of collective bargaining

In *Courtaulds Northern Spinning Ltd. v. Sibson* 1988 the Court of Appeal was called on to determine the nature and extent of an implied term in a contract of employment in relation to the place of work. Slade L J said that *'in cases … where it is essential to imply some term into the contract of employment as to place of work, the court does not have to be satisfied that the parties, if asked, would in fact have agreed the term before entering the contract. The court merely has to be satisfied that the implied term is one which the parties would probably have agreed if they were being reasonable'.* Implied terms may be subject to implied qualifications In *Prestwick Circuits Ltd. v. McAndrew* 1990 it was held that *'An implied right to order an employee to transfer from one place of employment to another must be subject to the implied qualification that reasonable notice must be given in all the circumstances of the case. Even where the proposed transfer involves a reasonable distance it is necessary to imply the qualification that the employee be given reasonable notice so as to preclude a contractual right of the employer to transfer the employee to some other place at a moment's notice. Whether the notice given in a particular case was reasonable is a question of fact and degree for the industrial tribunal to determine.'*

> In *Jones v. Associated Tunnelling Ltd.* 1981 the EAT held that a contract of employment cannot simply be silent on the place of work. If there is no express term, it is necessary to imply some terms into each contract of employment laying down the place of work in order to give the contract business efficacy. The term to be implied in that which in all the circumstances the parties, if reasonable, would probably have agreed if they had directed their minds to the problem.

The wage/work bargain

The role of the courts and tribunals in implying contractual obligations into contracts of employment is a fundamental feature of employment law. Employment conflicts sometime occur in determining whether a particular job function carries the status of a contractual duty even where job descriptions have been agreed by the parties. This conflict often arises during industrial action.

> In *Sim v. Rotherham Metropolitan Borough Council* 1986 the High Court had to decide whether the requirement of school teachers to provide cover for absent colleagues during normal school hours was an implied contractual obligation or merely a matter of goodwill. Refusing to provide such cover during a period of industrial action had led the employer to deduct an appropriate sum from the teacher's monthly salary. The High Court recognised that school teachers are a member of a profession and as such you would not expect their contracts to detail the professional obligations under their contracts. *'The contractual obligations of persons employed in a profession are defined largely by the nature of their profession and the obligations incumbent upon those who follow that profession. Teachers have a contractual obligation to discharge their professional obligations towards their pupils and their school. Cover arrangements, the court decided, are part of a teacher's professional obligations and the refusal of teachers to comply with them was a breach of contract.'*

In a contract of employment there is an implied duty on the employee to provide personal service for which the employer is obliged to provide a wage. At the appointed time therefore, an employee is required to present himself for work and be ready and willing to perform at the direction of the employer.

Beveridge v. KLM UK Ltd. 2000 confirms an important principle that there is a common law duty to pay wages which does not depend upon a contractual term. Here the applicant having completed a period of sick leave informed her employers that she wished to return to work with a supporting medical certificate. She was refused the right to return until passed fit by the employer's doctor six weeks later. Having exhausted her statutory sick pay the applicant claimed that this failure to pay her during the six week period was an unlawful wage deduction. The EAT disagreed with the tribunal and found there to be an unauthorised wage deduction.[44] *'An employee who offers her services to her employer is entitled at common law to be paid unless a specific condition of the contract regulates otherwise.'*

Absence from work without good reason would clearly constitute a breach of contract which would entitle the employer to adjust the wage accordingly. If the absence is due to industrial action there is a tendency for the courts and tribunals to deal with conflict over entitlement to a wage or a partial wage by applying strict contractual principles.

The principle of 'no work no pay' was reaffirmed by the House of Lords in *Miles v. Wakefield MBC* 1987. Here industrial action taken by Registrars involved them in refusing to carry out a proportion of their work, that of performing marriages, on Saturday mornings. While the Registrars attended for work on Saturdays and performed other duties the employer made it clear that wages would be deducted for Saturday morning hours if the employees were unwilling to perform the full range of their duties. The House of Lords upheld the employer's position that they were entitled to withhold the Saturday wage despite the fact that a substantial part of the work was performed. Lord Templeman said that *'in a contract of employment, wages and work go together, in an action by an employee to recover his pay he must allege and be ready to prove that he worked or was willing to work'.*

The Court of Appeal has also expressed the view that limited industrial action which involves non-performance of a part of an employee's contractual duties will prejudice an employee's claim for wages or even partial wages during the relevant period. This is certainly the case where the employer makes it clear that he does not condone part performance of the contract by the employee, so that he can regard any contractual duties performed as purely voluntary. By allowing the employee to come to work and carry out less than his full contractual duties the employer is not accepting a partial performance of the contract, and there is no requirement to prevent the employee working.

In *Wiluszynski v. London Borough of Tower Hamlets* 1989 an estates officer in the Council's Housing Department, as a result of an industrial dispute between NALGO and the Council, took part in limited industrial action which involved boycotting enquiries from council members. While the contractual duty was only a small but important part of the officer's workload, the response of the employer was to warn the officer by letter that if he carried on limited work it would be regarded as unauthorised and purely voluntary and wages would not be paid. The industrial action lasted five weeks, during which the officer was not paid and when it ended it took him two and a half to three hours to deal with the members' enquiries which had built up. The officer's claim for salary during the relevant period was upheld by the High Court on the basis that he

---

44. Under s.13 Employment Rights Act 1996

had substantially performed his contract and higher management were aware of that, acquiesced in it and took the benefit of the work. On appeal, however, a totally different view was expressed by the Court of Appeal. In these circumstances, the court held, an employee is entitled to dismiss an employer in repudiatory breach of his contract of employment or decline to accept the partial performance of the contract. Here the employer had made it clear that any work undertaken would be voluntary, so that the employee could not reasonably have been confused or misled by this statement. There was no question, therefore of the employer waiving the right not to pay by accepting the services rendered and no obligation to prevent the employee from working, particularly where there is a large workforce. In this case partial performance of the contract had not been condoned by the employer so that no wages were payable.

A unilateral decision by the employer to withhold wages without just cause constitutes a breach of the fundamental obligation under the contract and give the employee the right to accept the repudiatory breach and treat the contract at an end.[45] Such a breach does not however automatically terminate the contract.

In *Rigby v. Ferodo Ltd.* 1987 the employer attempted to impose a lower wage on the employees. On their behalf, the trade union made it clear to the employer that the lower wage was unacceptable and while the employees continued to work they nevertheless regarded the employer as in repudiatory breach of the contract of employment. When an action was brought to recover the unpaid wages, the House of Lords held that the employees were entitled to the full contractual wage from the time that the reduction was unilaterally imposed.

In *Cantor Fitzgerald International v. Callaghan* 1999 the Court of Appeal considered the consequences of an employer failing to pay the contractual wage. Such a failure is of course a breach of contract but the court felt that if it was due to an accounting error or a simple mistake then the breach would not be fundamental.[46] In a case where an employer unilaterally reduces the employee's pay or the value of a salary package however the *'entire foundation of the employment is undermined'* and may be regarded as a repudiatory breach.

Where work is subject to seasonal variations it has become a popular practice to employ staff on *annualised hours*. Usually a standard wage is payable for a notional number of hours per week, taking account of holiday entitlement, and when the annual hours have been worked in a given year, the employee becomes entitled to payment of overtime.

Such a system was adopted by collective agreement in *Ali v. Christian Salvesen Food Services Ltd.* 1997 providing that factory workers worked a notional 40 hour week with total annual hours of 1824. The issue before the Industrial Tribunal and then the EAT was whether in the event of contractual termination by reason of redundancy, an employee who had worked in excess of the notional 40 hour week for part of the given year was entitled to payment for the extra hours on a pro rata basis despite not having worked the 1824 annual hours.

---

45. See Chapter 9
46. Limited to damages as a remedy

The EAT disagreed with the tribunal's decision and found it possible to imply a term into individual contracts of employment providing that an employee whose employment was terminated by the employer before the end of the pay year to be paid for those hours worked in excess of the notional 40 per week. By not making these additional payments for pro rata hours the employers had made unauthorised deductions of wages contrary to the Wages Act 1986.[47] On further appeal to the Court of Appeal the court felt that the EAT was wrong in law to imply a term to that effect and in the absence of express provision for payment, in these circumstances the employees were not entitled to additional payment. The Court of Appeal held that if a collective agreement leaves a topic such as this uncovered, that is not a justification to imply a term into individual contracts to provide for this type of contingency. There may have been a conscious decision by those negotiating the agreement to leave complicated and controversial matters uncovered.

It is suggested that this somewhat surprising decision does seem to ignore the clear basis for implying a sensible term recognising the incomplete nature of the collective agreement and the obvious injustice of non payment for hours worked. Had the parties to the collective agreement, at the time it was negotiated applied their minds to the issue of payment in the event of premature termination for redundancy, their conclusion, it is suggested, would have been inescapable.

Provide work

While it seems that there is an obligation to pay the contractual wage, this does not carry with it a duty to provide the employees with work. The general proposition was illustrated by Asquith LJ in *Collier v. Sunday Referee Publishing Company Ltd.* 1940 when he said, *'Provided I pay my cook her wages regularly she cannot complain if I choose to take any or all of my meals out.'*

> If an employee's pay depends upon work being provided, for instance piece work, or commission, the court in *Devonald v. Rosser and Sons* 1906 held that the employer is under an implied obligation to provide sufficient work to enable a reasonable wage to be earned. The obligation to provide work would also apply where the employee's occupation is such that the opportunity to work is an essential feature of the contract because of the possibility of loss of reputation due to inactivity such as an entertainer in *Herbert Clayton v. Oliver* 1930.
>
> In *William Hill Organisation Ltd. v. Tucker* 1998 the Court of Appeal refused to grant an injunction to prevent an ex-employee taking up employment with a competitor and accept salary without work during a six month notice period. The court felt that *'whether there is a right to work is a question of construction of the particular contract in the light of its surrounding circumstances'*. Here the employer had a duty to provide the employee with work during the notice period so as to enable him to exercise his skills as a specialist in the field of spread betting.

---

47. Now Employment Rights Act

Health and safety

At common law an employer is obliged to provide his workers with a safe system of work. This common law duty encompasses an obligation to ensure that workers are provided with safe plant and appliances, appropriate safety equipment, safe work methods and safe fellow workers.

> In *British Aircraft Corporation v. Austin* 1978 the employer was held to be in breach of his implied duty of safety when he failed to investigate a complaint relating to the suitability of protective glasses for an employee. This conduct was held to be a repudiatory breach of the contract of employment sufficient to entitle the employee to terminate the contract and regard himself as constructively dismissed.

Employees themselves are under a duty to co-operate in relation to their own safety and that of their work colleagues. An employee who is unduly negligent in the performance of his work will be in breach of his employment contract and while he is unlikely to be sued by his employer, this could be used as a justifiable reason for dismissal. In *Lister v. Romford Ice and Cold Storage Co. Ltd.* 1957 the House of Lords held that an employee who caused injury by negligently reversing his lorry, was in breach of an implied term of his contract of employment.

> In *Walton & Morse v. Dorrington* 1997 the applicant, a non smoker, found that her smoking colleagues created a working environment which constituted a nuisance and a cause of discomfort. This was despite the fact that her employer had implemented a no smoking policy which restricted smoking activities in the building in which she worked. Following an ultimatum by her employer the applicant finally left indicating the smoking issue as the reason and claiming constructive unfair dismissal. The EAT confirmed the tribunal's decision that the employers were in breach of an implied term of the employee's contract of employment in requiring her to work in an environment which was affected by the smoking habits of fellow employees. *'It is an implied term of every contract of employment that the employer will provide and monitor for employees, so far as is reasonably practicable, a working environment which is reasonably suitable for the performance by them of their contractual duties.'* A further implied term recognised by the EAT was that an employer should *'deal timeously and properly with the employees grievance'* and in this case the attitude of the employer to the health concern demonstrated that they were in breach of that term.

The law relating to health and safety at work is examined in Chapter 8.

Good faith

Of all the implied duties, the duty of good faith and mutual respect is the most difficult to define precisely. This is because good faith is such a wide ranging concept and involves an obligation on the employee to respect confidences, obey reasonable instructions, take care of the employer's property, account for money received in the performance of duties and not disrupt the employer's business. An employer on the other hand must treat his workforce with respect, indemnify them for expenses incurred in the performance of their duties and when providing a reference, ensure that it is accurate and fair.

All employees have a duty of faithful service and any attempt by an employee to use his position for undisclosed personal gain, for instance by accepting bribes or making a secret commission, will constitute a breach of the employment contract.

In *Tesco Stores v. Pook* 2004 the defendant, a senior manager, was dismissed and then sued for substantial sums of money that had been paid by his employer under false invoices that he had concocted. He was subsequently convicted of theft and sentenced to a term of imprisonment. The High Court held that the payment received by the defendant employee from a company doing business with his employers was clearly a bribe. The payment inevitably gave rise to a conflict of interest and was also a secret commission.. The employers were also entitled to refuse to allow the defendant to exercise options which he held under an employee share option scheme after he had been suspended pending an investigation into his conduct but before his employment was terminated. It was an implied term of the scheme that the option would not be exercisable so long as the employee was in such breach of contract as would entitle the employer to terminate the contract of employment. The court stressed that senior employees and company directors have a positive obligation to disclose breaches of their fiduciary duties.

In *Item Software UK Ltd. v. Fassihi* 2003 the High Court found that a company director was in breach of the duty of good faith when he engaged in double-dealing by attempting to divert a commercial contract from his employer to a company which he controlled. In such circumstances the High Court held that the director was in breach of the 'super added' duty to disclose his own misdeeds as this was a clear case of fraudulent concealment and consequently a breach of contract. The director was in breach of his fiduciary duty not to make a secret profit and despite the fact that the employer was not aware of all of the directors misdeeds at the time of the dismissal, under the common law the employer could now rely on the earlier misconduct to justify the director's dismissal.

Reasonable orders

Part of the obligation of good faith requires an employee to submit to his employer's control and this involves obeying reasonable orders. What would constitute a reasonable instruction depends upon an objective interpretation of the employee's contractual duties both express and implied.

> In *Pepper v. Webb* 1969 the head gardener who responded to his employer's request to plant some flowers with the words, *'I couldn't care less about your bloody greenhouse or your sodding garden'* was held to be in breach of the implied duty to obey reasonable instructions.

The Court of Session established in *Macari v. Celtic Football Athletic Co. Ltd.* 1999 that an employee is in breach of contract if he fails to carry out a lawful and legitimate instruction. The fact that the employer may have some ulterior motive in giving the instruction is irrelevant. Even if an instruction is within the scope of an employee's duties, it may not be reasonable if it involves a risk of serious injury such as *Robson v. Sykes* 1938 or a breach of the criminal law. Certainly the duty of good faith would require an employee to be flexible and move with the times, so that an instruction to adopt work techniques involving new technology, after proper training has been given, would normally be regarded as reasonable.

In *Cresswell v. Board of Inland Revenue* 1984, Walton J said that *'there can really be no doubt as to the fact that an employee is expected to adapt himself to new methods and techniques introduced in the course of employment'*.[48]

It is important to distinguish however, between a change in work methods and change in the job itself which if not authorised or agreed to, could not be unilaterally imposed without a possible claim for a redundancy payment or compensation for unfair dismissal. A wilful refusal to obey a reasonable order could lead ultimately to a dismissal so we will return to the problem of reasonable instructions in Chapters 10 and 11.

Employees have an implied obligation to take care of their employer's property. An employee who negligently allows his employer's property to be stolen or causes it wilful damage will be in breach of his employment contract and liable to dismissal.

Industrial action

Given that the objective of industrial action is normally to cause disruption to the employer's business, an employee who takes part in a strike, go-slow, partial performance or even a 'work to rule' will be in breach of his contract of employment. Industrial action of itself involves a withdrawal of good faith so it is arguable that even an overtime ban, where there is no contractual obligation to work overtime, could be regarded as a breach of contract.

> In *Secretary of State for Employment v. ASLEF* 1972, the Court of Appeal held that wilful disruption of the employer's undertaking would amount to breach of this implied duty of good faith. Here the railwaymen were disrupting British Rail services by working to the letter of the British Rail rule book, but nevertheless were held to be in breach of contract. The employee's duty to cooperate was broken if their action had the effect of defeating the employer's commercial objectives.

> In *Ticehurst and Thompson v. British Telecommunications Plc.* 1992 the Court of Appeal considered the legality of the employer's act of withholding wages during a period of industrial action when staff refused to work normally. The Court held that wages could be withheld if employees are not ready and willing to perform in full their obligations under their contracts of employment and withdraw goodwill. *'There is an implied term to serve the employer faithfully within the requirements of the contract. This term must be implied into the contract if a manager is given charge of the work of other employees and who, therefore, must necessarily be entrusted to exercise her judgment and discretion in giving instructions to others and in supervising their work. Such a direction, if the contract is to work properly, must be exercised faithfully in the interests of the employer. There is a breach of the implied term of faithful service when the employee does an act or omit to do an act, which would be within her contract ... and the employee so acts or omits to do the act not in the honest exercise of choice or discretion for the faithful performance of her work but in order to disrupt the employer's business or to cause the most inconvenience that can be caused.'*

One tactic often employed by trade unions is an industrial dispute is to call for members to participate in half day or one day strikes over a period of time. Clearly by taking strike

---

48. See Chapter 5

action an employee is in breach of contract and the appropriate sum could be deducted from his wage. If however the employee in question is otherwise working normally during the dispute the employer would not be entitled to refuse to accept work or refuse to pay wages. Again in *Ticehurst and Thompson v. British Telecommunications plc* 1992 the Court of Appeal held that *'the plaintiffs evinced intention to take part in future in a rolling campaign of strike action would not be a sufficient ground, by itself, for the employers to refuse to let her continue to work during the dispute. If the only intention evinced by the plaintiff was to continue to respond to a strike call if and when called upon by the union to strike, then she would, in effect, have been saying to the employers that she was intending to perform the full range of her contractual duties until sometime in the future, which might not happen at all, when she would break her contract by going on strike. If, during the time that her services would be rendered, the employers would receive full value from those services, there was no reason why they should not perform their part of the contract'.*

Misconduct

While there is no implied obligation on an employee to reveal to an employer his own misconduct or deficiencies, the relationship of trust and confidence may demand that an employee in a managerial capacity should report the misconduct of others in the organisation. In *Sybron Corporation v. Rochem Ltd. and Others* 1983 the Court of Appeal held that an employee may be so placed in the hierarchy of an organisation so as to have a duty to report either his 'superior's' or 'inferior's' misconduct. Previously we said in *Tesco Stores v. Pook* 2004 that a senior employee has a duty to report his own breaches of contract.

Confidentiality

Good faith most certainly includes respecting confidences so there would be a clear breach of the contract of employment if the employee revealed confidential information relating to any aspect of his employer's business to a competitor, or made use of such information for his own purposes.

Business goodwill revealed in customer lists and accounts or trade secrets such as manufacturing processes or designs, are in the nature of rights in property which the employer is entitled to protect during the employment relationship and to some degree even after its termination. It is a question of fact in each case whether information could be classified or confidential but some guidance was provided in *Marshall Thomas (Exports) Ltd. v. Guinle* 1978 where relevant factors were identified:

- the owner of the information must reasonably believe that its release would benefit a competitor or cause detriment to himself;
- the owner must reasonably believe that the information is confidential and not already public knowledge;
- the information must be judged bearing in mind the practice of the particular trade or industry.

By relying on the duty of fidelity an employer could obtain an injunction to prevent an employee working for a competitor in his spare time or revealing confidential information to a competitor. Breach of confidence could also be a reason relied on by an employer to convince an employment tribunal that in the circumstances the decision to dismiss an employee was fair.

It has been argued that the implied term not to reveal or make use of confidential information acquired during the course of employment can extend beyond the termination of employment.

> Such a duty of confidentiality was alleged by the employer to bind his ex-employee in *Faccenda Chicken Ltd. v. Fowler* 1986. Here the defendant, having previously worked for the plaintiff as a salesman, set up business in competition. The defendant recruited a number of the plaintiff's staff and the majority of his customers were ex-customers of the plaintiff. The plaintiff then claimed damages from the defendant for using confidential sales information relating to prices and customer requirements in breach of his contract of employment. Both the High Court and the Court of Appeal dismissed the claim holding that the use of the information did not in this case involve a breach of contract. The Court of Appeal laid down a number of legal principles to be applied, where in the absence of an express term, an ex-employee makes use of information acquired during the course of employment. The duty of confidentiality in these circumstances is much more restricted than the general duty of good faith which covers a subsisting employment relationship. Also, such a duty will extend to information which is 'confidential' only in the sense that unauthorised use of it while the contract subsisted would be a breach of the duty of good faith. To determine whether information would fall within the implied term, it is necessary to consider the following:
>
> - the nature of the employment and the nature of the information;
> - whether the information can be easily isolated from other information which the employee is free to use; and
> - whether the employer stressed the need for confidentiality.

In Chapter 9 you will see that in certain circumstances a worker may disclose confidential information under the protection of the Public Interest Disclosure Act 1998.

A number of issues including confidentiality were considered by the High Court in *Nottingham University v. Fishel* 2000. The case concerned the head of a University's infertility clinic who had carried out private work at clinics abroad without his employers knowledge or consent. The High Court held that while he had broken his contract by not seeking permission there was no contractual loss from the breach. In addition here was no fiduciary duty on an employee to reveal such outside work in the absence of express provision in his contract. By using other university employees to pursue the work the doctor was in breach of contract.

It seems then that only genuine trade secrets are capable of protection by an implied term relating to confidentiality following the termination of employment. To achieve a greater degree of protection therefore, a prudent employer should ensure that an express restraint clause is inserted into the employment contract. Such a clause is of course an example of an express term in a contract of employment. Restraint clauses are given special treatment under the common law and are considered in Chapter 10.

Further guidance in relation to the implied duty on an employee to respect confidential information even on the termination of employment was provided in *Universal Thermosensors Ltd. v. Hibben* 1992. The court concluded that *'The contracts of employment between the plaintiff and the three defendants did not include any provision restraining their activities after their employment had ended. So when they left they were free to set up at once a directly competing business in the same locality. Further, they were entitled to approach the plaintiff's customers and seek and accept orders from them. Still further they were entitled to use for their own purposes any information they carried in their heads regarding the identity of the plaintiff's customers or pricing policies, provided they had acquired the information honestly in the course of their employment and had not for instance, deliberately sought to memorise lists of names for the purposes of their own business. What the defendants were not entitled to do was to steal documents belonging to the plaintiff, or to use for their own purposes confidential information contained in such documents regarding the plaintiff's customers or customer contacts or customer requirements or the prices charged. Nor were they entitled to copy such information onto scraps of paper and take these away and use the information in their own business.'*

It is only relatively recently that the courts and tribunals have recognised that an employee's duty to trust and respect his employer is in fact a mutual obligation in an employment relationship.

Trust and Confidence

Leading labour law commentators have welcomed the development of the implied term in relation to maintaining trust and confidence unreservedly. It exemplifies the core of the employment contract and was confirmed by the House of Lords as a term *'now established in employment law'*. Trust and confidence sets the contract of employment apart from commercial contracts for goods and services by recognising that an employment relationship involves more than simply a transfer of work for payment. In *Re Public Service Employment Relations Act* 1987 Dickson CJ stated that *'work is one of the most fundamental aspects of a persons life, providing the individual with a means of financial support and as importantly a contributing role in society. A persons employment is an essential component of his or her sense of identity, self worth and emotional well being'.*

The development of the implied term of trust and confidence can be traced back to case-law from the 1970s.

> In *Robinson v. Crompton Parkinson Ltd.* 1978 the EAT considered the contract of an employee who had been dismissed for theft from his employers for which he was prosecuted and then subsequently acquitted by the Magistrates Court. When no apology was forthcoming from his employer he resigned claiming constructive dismissal. The EAT held that a false accusation of theft without an apology constituted a breach of confidence and trust such as to amount to a repudiation of the contract of employment. *'In a contract of employment, there has to be mutual trust and confidence and if either party is in breach of that mutuality of confidence there may be a breach of contract.'*

Mutual respect has always been an important feature of an employer employee relationship and in some circumstances can be destroyed in an instant.

> In *Isle of Wight Tourist Board v. Coombes 1976* a personal secretary walked out of her job when she heard her manager declare in front of other staff that she is *'an intolerable bitch on a Monday morning'*. Such a statement destroyed the relationship of mutual trust and respect and constituted a repudiatory breach of her contract of employment.[49]

---

49. Constituting a constructive unfair dismissal

The definition of trust and confidence which is most usually quoted today has its origins in the following case. In *Woods v. W H Car Services (Peterborough) Ltd.* 1982 the EAT recognised that in every employment contract there is an implied term of great importance, that of trust and confidence between the parties. Such a term requires that employers *'will not, without reasonable and proper cause, conduct themselves in a manner calculated or likely to destroy or damage the relationship of trust and confidence between employer and employee'*. The words of Mr. Justice McCoombe in *Cantor Fitzgerald International v. Bird* 2002 are also helpful when he said that *'an employees loss of confidence in management is not the same as conduct by the employer calculated to seriously damage trust and confidence within the meaning of the implied term'*.

A breakdown in trust and confidence is usually evidenced by a course of conduct. In *Lewis v. Motorworld Garages Ltd.* 1985 over a long period the employer was guilty of consistently repudiating his employee's contract of employment by insisting on unilateral variations of it. These changes were in fact accepted by the employee so that they could not be raised to support an allegation of constructive dismissal. The Court of Appeal held that such imposed variations did, however, establish a course of conduct so that if an employee did not waive a subsequent breach he could also raise this previous conduct to show that the employer was in breach of the implied term of trust and confidence.[50]

The House of Lords in the landmark judgment in *Malik v. Bank of Credit and Commerce International SA* 1997 considered the significance of the implied term of trust and confidence in a contract of employment. The case arose from a claim by ex employees of the BCCI for stigma damages for pecuniary loss allegedly caused by the bank's breach of an implied contractual obligation of mutual trust and confidence. The employees claimed that the fraudulent practices of the bank ultimately leading to its dissolution, put them, as innocent employees, at a severe disadvantage in the job market. A unanimous decision of the House of Lords reversed the Court of Appeal and held that *'if conduct by the employer in breach of the implied term of trust and confidence prejudicially affects an employees future prospects so as to give rise to continuing financial losses, and it was reasonably foreseeable that such a loss was a serious possibility, in principle damages in respect of the loss should be recoverable'*. Also there is no requirement that the employee should while employed, be aware of the trust destroying conduct or that it should be directed at the employee in question.

The House of Lords confirmed that stigma damages may be recoverable by employees who had suffered a disadvantage in the labour market when the highly publicised dishonest conduct of their ex-employer placed them under a cloud. For a claim of damages to succeed it must be established:

(a) that the employer conducted a dishonest or corrupt business and this was capable of constituting a breach of the implied term of trust and confidence; and

(b) financial loss was suffered by employees as a consequence which was not too remote from the breach.

The test of breach of the trust and confidence term confirmed by Lord Steyn is whether the employers' conduct, so impacted on the employee that, viewed objectively, the employee could properly conclude that the employer was repudiating the contract.

---

50. The 'last straw argument' LB of *Waltham Forest v. Omilaju* 2005

The possibility of damages being awarded in such circumstances was then tested by a number of ex employees of the bank in *Bank of Credit and Commerce SA v. Ali* 1999. Here the High Court accepted that the employer had as a bank been guilty of systematic fraudulent activities over a long period and this amounted to a breach of the term of trust and confidence implied into the employee's contracts. However while there was a stigma attached to the employees as a result of the employer's conduct the employees had failed to establish that the publicity given to the bank's wrongdoing blighted their prospects of obtaining fresh employment and caused them financial loss. *'Where an employee claims that the employer's breach of trust and confidence term created a stigma which resulted in his being under a handicap in the labour market, damages are only recoverable if the "stigma in the market place" results in financial loss. Damages are not recoverable for the stigma itself. The onus is on the employee to establish on the balance of probabilities that the stigma was a cause of a job application not succeeding or the loss of an opportunity of obtaining a job or the loss of a job or a particular level of remuneration. It must not be merely the occasion for the loss.'*

A further decision of the Court of Appeal in the *Malik* saga provides further guidelines as to the circumstances in which stigma damages could be awarded because of a breach in trust and confidence by a pervious employer.

> In *Bank of Credit and Commerce International SA v. Ali and Others (No 3)* 2002 the Court of Appeal confirmed that where a claimant alleges stigma resulting from previous employment affecting employment prospects, it is for the claimant to prove that the stigma had a real or substantial effect on his chances of obtaining employment. But for the former employer's breach of trust and confidence would the claimants have secured employment is the relevant question. While there is no requirement to produce evidence from prospective employers as to the effect of stigma on particular job applications such evidence from an independent source would give powerful support to a claim. Certainly there is no presumption that stigma plays a part in adverse decisions made on job applications and each employee must prove that the stigma was a real or substantial cause of their failure to obtain new employment.

The House of Lords in *Malik* (above) provides a clear justification for the incorporation of a trust and confidence term. *'An employment contract creates a close personal relationship where there is often a disparity of power between the parties. Frequently the employee is vulnerable. Although the underlying purpose of the trust and confidence terms is to protect the employment relationship, there can be nothing unfairly onerous or unreasonable in requiring an employer who breaches the trust and confidence term to be liable if he thereby causes continuing financial loss of a nature that was reasonably foreseeable.'* The court emphasised that the trust and confidence term is a useful tool, *'well established now in employment law'*. In his judgment Lord Steyn gave full support to the term. He said that the evolution of the implied term of trust and confidence is a fact. *'It has not yet been endorsed by your Lordships House. It has proved a workable principle in practice. It has not been the subject of adverse criticism in any decided cases and it has been welcomed in academic writings. I regard the emergence of the implied obligation of mutual trust and confidence as a sound development.'*

Employers who have been guilty of conduct such as verbal or physical abuse of their employees or unilateral attempts to impose unreasonable changes in employment terms have found themselves in breach of this implied term.

> In *Hilton International Hotels (UK) Ltd. v. Protopapa* 1990 the complainant resigned from her job as a telephone supervisor in one of her employer's hotels

when she was severely reprimanded by her manager. The reason for the reprimand was her failure to obtain permission before making a dental appointment and the fact that it was *'officious and insensitive'* constituted a repudiatory breach of her contract of employment. The EAT confirmed that she was *'humiliated, intimidated and degraded to such an extent that there was a breach of trust and confidence which went to the root of the contract'.*[51]

It does seem that conduct that destroys the relationship of trust and confidence between the employer and employee is inevitably fundamental and constitutes a repudiatory breach of contract.

The Employment Tribunal in *Morrow v. Safeway Stores* 2002 held that conduct by the employer that amounted to a breakdown in trust and confidence could be found to be insufficiently serious to constitute a repudiatory breach of contract. The notion that there could be degrees of trust and confidence breakdown, some repudiatory and some not is a daunting prospect and the EAT thankfully disagreed with the tribunals reasoning *'In general terms a finding that there has been conduct which amounts to a breach of the implied term of trust and confidence will mean inevitably that there has been a fundamental or repudiatory breach going necessarily to the root of the contract.'*

There is a view that if the culture at a workplace encompasses a dictatorial and forceful management style then it may be appropriate to expect highly paid employees to accept foul and abusive language from their managers as part of the cut and thrust of working life.

In *Horkulak v. Cantor Fitzgerald International* 2004 the claimant, a highly paid City broker, on a fixed term contract, resigned his post after being subject to a hysterical verbal attack from his chief executive. The claimant claimed wrongful dismissal contending that the attack was the culmination of an inappropriate course of conduct constituting a breach of the implied term of trust and confidence. The employer argued that the claimant resigned because he could not cope with the pressures, tensions and demands which were properly incidental to his job. The Court of Appeal rejected the notion that the payment of high salaries excused the conduct complained of. Trust and confidence has emerged from the duty of cooperation and *'the particular role and status of an employee will define the character and degree of cooperation to which the contract of employment gives rise'.* Here the Chief executive's conduct demonstrated that he had lost faith in the claimant making his position intolerable. He left because his position had been undermined and was entitled to substantial damages for wrongful dismissal. The case provides us with one of the few examples of a constructive wrongful dismissal.

The Court of Appeal decision in *London Borough of Waltham Forest v. Omilaju* 2005 considers the novel point as to whether, for the purpose of establishing a breakdown in trust and confidence, the final straw act must of itself constitute a breach of the employment contract. The court held that 'in order to result in a breach of the implied term of trust and confidence, a *'final straw'*, not of itself a breach of contract, must be an act in a series of earlier acts which cumulatively amount to a breach of the implied term. Certainly the act does not have to be of the same character but it must contribute to a breach of trust and confidence.'

---

51. See *Brown v. Merchant Ferries Ltd.* 1998

Later in Chapter 10 when we consider the termination of employment, you will discover that the development of this particular implied term is tied to the doctrine of constructive dismissal because that is when it is usually alleged to have been broken. The employee must establish a repudiatory breach of the contract of employment by the employer to justify the contractual termination as a constructive dismissal.

It seems that the courts are now willing to rule that the implied terms of trust and confidence is capable of imposing a positive obligation on an employer and is not limited to a negative prohibition on conduct which could seriously damage the employment relationship.

> In *Transco v. O'Brien* 2002 the Court of Appeal confirmed that there would be a breakdown in trust and confidence resulting from a failure by an employer to offer an employee an enhanced contract of employment. Only the applicant had been excluded from the new contract solely because the employer had mistakenly believed him not to be a permanent employee. *'A reasonable belief is a state of affairs now held not to exist is not a ground for depriving an employee of improved terms of employment which would have been offered but for the error. It was plainly a breach of contract to treat the applicant as not being entitled to benefits resulting from him being a permanent employee when he was in fact a permanent employee.'*

If tribunal proceedings are brought for unfair dismissal caused by a breakdown in trust and confidence then it is unlikely that a separate claim for breach of contract or in tort would be sustainable. If injury to feelings compensation is not available in an unfair dismissal claim, could a claimant bring separate proceedings for damages on the basis of a breakdown in trust and confidence on the manner of dismissal.

In *Eastwood and Another v. Magnox Electric plc* 2002 both claimants had successfully established unfair dismissal on the grounds that they had been subjected to unreasonable treatment by their employer through harassment leading to unfair disciplinary proceedings. They then sought to bring a common law action for damages for breach of contract and in the tort of negligence alleging a breakdown in trust and confidence and psychiatric illness. The decision of the County Court to reject the complaints was upheld by the Court of Appeal. Relying on the House of Lords decision in *Johnson v. Unisys* 2001 it was held that the implied term of trust and confidence did not extend to matters within the purview of an employment tribunal considering unfair dismissal including those acts which occurred during the disciplinary proceedings *'Johnson plainly held that unfairness in the manner of dismissal of an employee does not give rise to a common law action whether it is founded in contract or tort, but must be the subject of employment tribunal proceedings. The implied terms of trust and confidence cannot be used in connection with the employer/employee relationships is terminated.'*

The ruling in *Johnson v. Unisys* 2001 was further elaborated by the Court of Appeal in *McCabe v. Cornwall CC* 2003. The facts revealed a similar scenario. Following a successful claim for unfair dismissal the claimant brought proceedings in the High Court seeking damages for psychiatric illness in respect of events leading up to the dismissal. The claim was based on the breach of the implied duty of mutual trust and confidence in respect of the initial suspension and the employer's failure to inform the claimant of the allegations against him or to carry out a proper investigation. Finding that the decision in *Gogay v. Hertfordshire CC* 2000[52] does not apply when dismissal follows the breach of duty the High

---

52. Below

Court held that the claim disclosed no cause of action. The activities complained of were all 'part and parcel' of the events leading up to the dismissal and therefore the principle established in *Johnson v. Unisys* 2001 precluded any common law claim.

The House of Lords has now ruled in *Eastwood v. Magnox Electric plc / McCabe v. Cornwall CC* 2004 that a common law claim for damages can only be brought where the cause of action has accrued before the dismissal as in cases such as *Gogay v. Hertfordshire Council* 2000. The only remedy in relation to the dismissal is the statutory unfair dismissal code. There could be a common law claim for the events leading up to the dismissal but not for the manner of the dismissal itself.

In almost all of the cases where a breakdown in trust and confidence is alleged by the employee there has been a termination of employment and the cause of action is a claim for constructive/unfair dismissal. There are now contemporary examples of legal proceedings brought by claimants attempting to secure damages under the common law against an employer for the breach of this implied term.

> An excellent example is provided by *Gogay v. Hertfordshire County Council* 2000. Here proceedings were brought in the High Court by a residential care worker who had been subjected to an allegation of abuse by a child in her care and so suspended during a period of investigation. This was despite the fact that the claimant had communicated concerns about the child to her superiors and received assurances about her own conduct. When the investigation concluded that there was no case to answer and the claimant was reinstated in her post she was unable to return to work due to clinical depression brought on by the suspension. The High Court held that the employers were in breach of the implied term of trust and confidence because they had no reasonable grounds for suspending the claimant and had failed to carry out a proper investigation of the circumstances before doing so. The Court of Appeal upheld the High Court's finding of a breach of the implied contractual duty. *'Whether the decision to suspend an employee amounts to breach of the implied term of trust and confidence depends upon whether there was reasonable and proper cause for the employer's action. It does not follow that an employee should be suspended because a local authority has reasonable grounds for making inquiries into allegations of child abuse. There is a distinction to be drawn between the process of investigating whether a child is at risk of significant harm and the process of dealing with an employee who may be implicated in that risk. It is a gross over-simplification to conclude that because some investigation is taking place in relation to the child the employee must inevitably be suspended.'*

Here there was almost a knee-jerk reaction to the allegation when there should have been more thought given as to what to do about the claimant, and particularly the possibility of a temporary transfer. Another important part of the ruling in this case related to the employee's appeal in relation to the £26,000 damages awarded by the High Court. The employer had contended relying on the House of Lords decision in *Johnson v. Unisys* that damages for breach of contract cannot be awarded for injury to feelings arising out of the manner of dismissal. This contention was rejected on two grounds. Firstly that here the claim was not for hurt feelings but for psychiatric illness and secondly that this was a suspension from employment rather than a dismissal.

The right to information

The right to information is another aspect of the requirement to maintain trust and confidence in an employment relationship. In *Scally v. Southern Health and Social Services Board* 1991 the House of Lords held that there is an implied term in a contract of employment imposing a duty on the employer to take reasonable steps to provide an employee with certain information. Here the information in question related to pension rights which had been negotiated on the employee's behalf but they had not been informed of the benefits they conferred. Four junior doctors sued their employer for loss sustained by them because of the failure of their employer to give them notice of the right to purchase added years of pension entitlement. *'It is necessary to imply an obligation on the employer to take reasonable steps to bring a term of the contract of employment to the employee's attention so that he may be in a position to enjoy its benefit where the terms of the contract have not been negotiated with the individual employee but result from negotiation with a representative body.'*

The obligation to inform does not extend to requiring an employer to guide an employee in the direction of the most beneficial pension.

> In *University of Nottingham v. (1) Eyett (2) The Pensions Ombudsman* 1999 the right for an employee to be given pension information by his employer so as to secure the most beneficial entitlement was tested in the High Court. Earlier the pension ombudsman had upheld a complaint that the employer was in breach of the implied term of trust and confidence by not alerting the employee as to the most beneficial course of action. On appeal the High Court held that the implied duty of mutual trust and confidence in a contract of employment does not include a positive obligation on the employer to warn an employee who is proposing to exercise important rights in connection with the contract of employment that the way in proposing to exercise them may not be the most financially advantageous.

The obligation to inform does not extend to requiring an employer to guide an employee in the direction of the most beneficial pension.

In *Crossley v. Faithful & Gould* 2004 the Court of Appeal confirmed that there was no implied term in the claimant's contract of employment imposing an obligation on the employers to take reasonable care for the claimant's economic well-being, and which required them to alert the claimant to the effect that resigning would have on his entitlement to benefits under a long-term disability insurance scheme. *'There are no obvious policy reasons to impose on an employer the general duty to protect his employee's economic well-being. The implied term proposed would impose an unfair and unreasonable burden on employers.'* Of course it would be different if an employer assumes the responsibility for giving financial advice to an employee. In those circumstances the employer is under a duty to take reasonable care in the giving of that advice. A general duty on an employer to protect an employee's economic well-being is also wholly inconsistent with the approach adopted by the House of Lords in *Scally v. Southern Health and Social Services Board*[53] and *Spring v. Guardian Assurance plc*. It was not for the Court of Appeal to take a big leap to introduce a major extension of the law in this area when, comparatively recently, the House of Lords had declined to do so.

---

53. Above

To suggest that to give an employment contract business effect it is necessary to imply an obligation on an employer to give his employees an annual pay rise would not be acceptable.

> In *Murco Petroleum v. Forge* 1987 the complainant, having had pay increases for the past ten years resigned when one year she did not receive a pay rise. She was the only employee not to receive a pay increase, her employer stating that her work was not satisfactory. The tribunal found there to be an implied term in her contract that she would receive an annual pay rise and failing to give her one without warning or criticism of her work, constituted a breach so as to justify constructive dismissal. This finding the EAT held was totally unreasonable. It was impossible to say that there is an implied term in a contract of employment that there will always be a pay rise. It *'is not part of the industrial structure and neither employer or unions would wish it to be so'.*

The right to a reference

While there is no duty to provide one, if an employee decides to supply his employee with a reference the employer should ensure that it is a fair and accurate assessment of the employee in question. There is no right to see a reference but an employee can access a reference which becomes part of a personnel file. Under the Data Protection Act 1998 an employee is entitled to see the entire contents of her personnel file held with her employer.[54] If it is alleged that the reference supplied contains a defamatory statement, the employee is entitled to raise the defence of qualified privilege which is effective, provided that the employer can show that the statements were made without malicious intent.

> In *Bartholemew v. London Borough of Hackney* 1999 the Court of Appeal ruled that an employer who provides a reference is under a duty to ensure that it is in substance *'true, accurate and fair'.* While it does not have to be full and comprehensive it must not give an unfair or misleading impression overall even if it is factually correct. A reference could be misleading although factually accurate, if it gives a false impression of the employee. Also *TSB Bank v. Harris* 2000 is the first reported case to hold that an employee was entitled to walk out of his job and claim constructive unfair dismissal because a reference provided by her employer was in breach of the implied term of trust and confidence. Here a reference was neither fair nor reasonable.

> In *Spring v. Guardian Assurance Plc* 1994 the Court of Appeal held that the giver of a reference owes no duty of care in negligence to the person who is the subject of the reference or in obtaining the information upon which it is based. On appeal to the House of Lords however in 1994 their Lordships took a different view. The case surrounded a reference which had been supplied for the plaintiff in which he was described as a man of 'little or no integrity and could not be regarded as honest' and that there was evidence of negligence in his work. Not surprisingly the plaintiff found it difficult to find employment and claimed damages against his ex-employer for the economic loss he had suffered as a result of the bad reference. His claim based on malicious falsehood failed because of the lack of malice and the failure to establish a contractual term which required references to be supplied with reasonable care. His claim in negligence succeeded in the High Court however and despite being reversed

---

54. Full disclosure within 40 days - potential fee £10

in the Court of Appeal has now been affirmed on final appeal to the House of Lords. By a majority of four to one their Lordships held that an employer giving a reference is under a duty to the subject of the reference to take reasonable care in compiling it or in obtaining the information on which it was based. If the subject of the reference suffers economic loss as a result of an employer's failure to meet this duty he can claim damages. Liability based on negligent misstatement could be established if:

1. *the damage was foreseeable and it occurred. An employer who gives a careless reference can foresee economic loss;*

2. *there was a certain proximity between the nature of the misstatement and the subject so as to create a duty situation. The relationship of employer and employee was sufficiently closer to give rise to a duty; and*

3. *the situation was one where it was fair just and reasonable to impose a duty of care. This was the case with the giver of a reference who should take reasonable care in compiling it.*

In *Kidd v. Axa Equity and Law Life Assurance Society plc* 2000 an employee made a claim against his ex-employer for damages on the ground that they had a duty of care to provide him with a reference making full and frank disclosure of all relevant matters and to ensure that the reference was fair and not misleading and that they were in breach of such a duty. The High Court rejected this claim and found that there was no duty to provide the claimant with a reference which was fair, full and comprehensive '*The duty owed by the giver of a reference to the subject of that reference, whether arising in tort or from contract, is a duty to take reasonable care not to give misleading information about him, whether as a result of the unfairly selective provision of information, or by the inclusion of facts or opinions in such a manner as to give rise to a false or misleading inference in the mind of a reasonable recipient. The giver of a reference owes no additional duty to the subject to take reasonable care to give a full and comprehensive reference, or to include in a reference all material facts.*' The court considered the proof necessary to establish a breach of the duty to take care not to provide misleading information in a reference. The claimant must establish: that the information was misleading; that this information was likely to have a material effect on the mind of the reasonable recipient to the claimant's detriment; and that the defendants were negligent in providing such a reference.

The nature and extent of the duty of care to provide an accurate and fair reference was considered by the Court of Appeal in *Cox v. Sun Alliance Life Ltd.* 2001. Here the claimant alleged that a reference supplied by his employer questioning his honesty was both negligent and in breach of a mutual agreement he had entered into to terminate his employment. The Court of Appeal found that the employers were negligent in providing a reference to subsequent employers of the claimant which relied upon allegations of dishonest conduct which they had not properly investigated. The court stated that '*discharge of the duty of care to provide an accurate and fair reference will usually involve making reasonable inquiry into the factual basis of the statements in the reference. A similar approach to that set out in British Home Stores Ltd. v. Burchell in relation to dismissal on grounds of misconduct is appropriate.*[55] *In order to take reasonable care to give a fair and accurate reference, an employer should confine unfavourable statements about the employee to those matters into which they had made*

---

55. See Chapter 11

reasonable investigation and had reasonable grounds for believing to be true. Although, in order to discharge the duty of care, an employer is not obliged to carry on with an inquiry into an employee's conduct after the employee has resigned, if an investigation is discontinued, unfavourable comments should be confined to matters which had been investigated before the resignation'.

It has been known for employers to retaliate against former employees who have made legal claims against them by refusing to provide a reference or labeling the employee as a troublemaker in the reference.

> In *Coote v. Granada Hospitality (No 2)* 2000 the EAT gave effect to a European Court of Justice ruling and held that under the Sex Discrimination Act it would be possible to make a complaint of victimisation in respect of events which occurred after the employment relationship has terminated. This would include failing to provide a reference because the complainant had brought earlier proceedings against the employer. Here the tribunal found that Ms Coote's former employers wrote a tardy and misleading reference because they bore a grudge in relation to her earlier sex discrimination claim.

Hopefully you will now have an appreciation of the legal principles relating to the formation and content of a contract of employment. In the next chapter we will turn to the vexed question as to how and in what circumstances the terms of a contract of employment may be changed.

Further Reading

Brodie, Douglas *Beyond Exchange: The New Contract of Employment* (1998) 27 ILJ 79.

Brodie, Douglas *Mutual Trust and the Values of the Employment Contract* (2001) 30 ILJ 84.

Brodie, Douglas *Protecting Dignity in the Workplace: The Vitality of Mutual Trust and Confidence* (2004) 33 ILJ 349.

Clarke, Linda *Mutual Trust and Confidence Fiduciary Relationships and the Duty of Disclosure* (1999) 28 ILJ 348.

Honeyball, S. *Employment Law and the Primacy of Contract* (1988) 17 ILJ 97.

Mr. Justice Lindsay *The Implied Term of Trust and Confidence* (2001) 31 ILJ 30.

Chapter 5

Changing Contractual Arrangements

Having formed the contract of employment in Chapter 4 it is logical in this Chapter to recognise its unique nature by demonstrating how it can adapt to the needs of the parties in a long-standing and fluid relationship. To what extent are employers constrained by the contract of employment when they require their staff to accept different job functions or new roles and responsibilities?

It is inevitable that the success and in some cases the survival of any business organisation in the public or private sector will depend on its ability to respond positively to legal, economic or social change. Here we will consider the legal position relating to changing contractual arrangements.[1] Human nature dictates that there will be a degree of opposition to change so it makes sense for an employer to attempt to manage the change process sensitively. This will involve supplying affected employees with information, engaging in consultation and seeking their acceptance of the proposed change. A contemporary feature of present day employment is the attempt by employers to introduce new contracts that in some spheres of employment represent a move away from collectively bargained terms and conditions of employment to individual or 'personal' contracts. Nevertheless, for millions of workers, represented by recognised trade unions, any changes to their working practices must still be negotiated with the appropriate collective bargaining agent, the trade union.

The legal position relating to changing contractual arrangements is the subject matter of this chapter.

One point should be stressed from the outset. Despite the contrary view of numerous employers, contracts of employment contain terms which cannot be unilaterally varied but depend upon mutual agreement to effect a change. It is highly unlikely that an employee would have the right to unilaterally change a contract of employment and so too an employer. In *WPM Retail Ltd. v. Lang* 1978 the complainant was promoted to area manager in 1974 with the right to earn an additional bonus based upon performance. After one bonus

---

1. See also Chapter 12

payment the employer sought to withdraw the right to a bonus unilaterally. The EAT held that the obligation to pay the bonus was a contractual term and remained in force until the employment was terminated. There was no question of the employee waiving his rights by remaining in employment. *'For as long as the employee goes on working in the same job, each time the employer does not pay the correct amount the employer incurs a liability which he will ultimately have to meet if the employee asserts his right to be paid the agreed amount.'*

In *Miller v. Hamworthy Engineering Ltd.* 1986 the plaintiff, a salaried fireman, made a claim for the net loss of wages which he suffered during periods of short-time working which was not agreed to by him or his union. While the County Court rejected his claim the Court of Appeal held that the employer was liable for the net loss of pay which he suffered as a result of being put on to short-time without the agreement of either himself or his union *'where there is an admitted contract of employment under which a salary is payable, if the provision as to payment of salary in that contract is to be displaced, the employers must show some agreed variation of the contractual term binding upon the employee'.*

There are employers who would unilaterally reduce wages to fund the cost of statutory rights such as paid holidays.

In *Davies v. M. J. Wyatt (Decorators) Ltd.* 2000 the EAT considered the employer's obligations imposed by the Working Time Regulations. When the Regulations came into force the employer here decided unilaterally to reduce the hourly rate of all employees to assist in meeting the cost of providing paid annual leave. The EAT held that the reduction in pay amounted to an unauthorised deduction from wages[2] *'An employer cannot unilaterally reduce an employee's contractual rate of pay in order to discharge the employer's liability under the Working Time Regulations to provide paid holidays. Unless there has been a consensual agreement, such a deduction cannot properly be made. The object of the Regulations is to confer a benefit upon employees.'*

Unilateral Change

In Chapter 4 we considered the expression *'terms and conditions of employment'* and said that conditions of employment cover numerous matters under the control of the employer such as disciplinary procedures, safety policy, meal breaks which are ultimately subject to unilateral change. The working environment and the rule book that applies to it are effectively under the control of the employer. The following case provides a classic example of the authority of an employer in relation to the rules of the workplace.

In *Dryden v. Greater Glasgow Health Board* 1992 the EAT held that an employer was entitled to introduce a rule imposing a smoking ban at the workplace and the staff had no implied right to smoke *'An employer is entitled to make rules for the conduct of employees in their place of work within the scope of the contract and once it was held that there was no implied term in the contract which entitled the employee to facilities for smoking, the rule against smoking was a lawful rule.'*

Also in *Hussmen Manufacturing v. Weir* 1998 an employee objected to the employer's unilateral change in the shift systems under which he was required to move from night

---

2. Employment Rights Act s.13

shift and suffer a consequential reduction in shift allowance payments. His claim of an unauthorised reduction in wages was rejected however on the grounds that the employers were unilaterally entitled to vary his conditions of employment and move him from one shift to another.

If the employer in the above case was attempting to introduce a shift system then that would normally involve contractual change which would require consent. To simply impose a shift system would be likely to constitute a breach in contracts of employment. While it would be prudent to consult before changing working rules, substantial alterations to the working environment can nevertheless be achieved unilaterally by an employer in this way.

Even where an employer's policy is non contractual a unilateral change by the employer must not have the effect of undermining trust and confidence. In *French v. Barclays Bank* 1998 the Court of Appeal considered the decision of an employer to change the terms of a bridging loan on staff relocation to the detriment of an employee. The relocation policy was incorporated in the staff manual. The court held that *'to seek to invoke a change of policy or a change in the terms on which loans are made to employees required to relocate, which has been applied to other employees over many years and appeared in the employer's staff manual at the time that the loan is made, is conduct on the part of the employer likely to destroy the confidence and trust between employers and their employees'.*

It seems therefore that even with unilateral rights to implement change an employer is still subject to the overriding duty not to undermine trust and confidence, otherwise there could be a repudiatory breach of contract.[3]

Usually an employer will expect that a Code of Practice will be unlikely to contain contractual terms and be subject to unilateral variation. A Code of Practice on staff sickness which contains procedures for monitoring and reviewing different categories of absence may be unilaterally amended by the employer.

So held the Court of Appeal in *Wandsworth London Borough Council v. D'Silva* 1998 disagreeing with the tribunal and the EAT's decision that the Code contained contractual terms subject to change through mutual agreement. The Court of Appeal held that *'whether a particular provision in an employer's Code of Practice is contractually binding depends upon whether it should properly be regarded as conferring a right on employees or as setting out no more than good practice which managers were intended to follow. In the present case the language of the provision in question did not provide an appropriate foundation on which to base contractual rights'.* The Code could be unilaterally changed by the employer.

Authorised Change

More significantly as a result of a change process in any organisation, an employer may wish that members of the workforce should accept an increase or decrease in hours or pay, different contractual duties or responsibilities, a change in job location or different job functions or work practices. A sensitive employer would usually seek their consent even where the workforce may be legally required to accept the change within their terms of employment. If express terms of employment authorise the employer to implement the change, then an employee is legally obliged to accept it provided the term is interpreted

---

3. See Chapter 4

reasonably. In *McCaffery v. A.E. Jeavons Ltd.* 1967 an employee employed expressly as a 'travelling man' in the building trade was held to be bound to move anywhere in the country.

It seems that it would be perfectly proper for an employer to expressly authorise the right to change a contractual term by reserving such a right in the contract. So for example an express mobility clause in a contract could authorise the employer to move the employee's place of employment from one part of the UK to another. If the clause is triggered and the employee is required to move, then as a consequence the contract of employment has changed because the employer has a new place of employment. In this way a unilateral change is authorised by the contract. Notice that the clause has authorised the change in the place of employment rather than the clause itself being changed to, for instance, 'the UK' to 'the world'.

> This process was alluded to by the Court of Appeal in *Wandsworth London Borough Council v. D'Silva* 1998.[4] The court stated that '*although contracts of employment generally can only be varied by agreement, either party can reserve the ability to change a particular aspect of the contract unilaterally by notifying the other party as part of the contract that this is the situation. However, clear language is required to reserve to one party an unusual power of this sort. In addition the court is unlikely to favour an interpretation which does more than enable a party to vary contractual provisions with which that party is required to comply. To apply a power of unilateral variation to the rights which an employer is given could produce an unreasonable result, which the courts in construing a contract of employment will seek to avoid*'.

The reference above to either party reserving the right to effect change has no real practicable impact when applied to employees. Given the nature of a contract of employment it is highly unlikely that an employee could negotiate a term that authorises unilateral change.

The guidance from the Court of Appeal is that while a well drafted mobility clause can authorise unilateral contractual change the courts will not enforce a clause purporting to confer on the employer an absolute power of unilateral variation of employee rights.

Even where there is a well drafted mobility clause in a contract of employment, for example, '*the bank may from time to time require an employee to be transferred temporarily or permanently to any place of business which the bank may have in the UK for which a relocation or other allowance may be payable at the discretion of the bank*', an employer must maintain trust and confidence when relying upon it. All contracts of employment contain the fundamental term relating to trust and confidence which effectively has the effect of controlling the exercise of a discretion conferred in the contract.

> In *United Bank Ltd. v. Akhtar* 1989 the employer was in repudiatory breach of an implied term of the contract of employment requiring reasonable notice when he sought to rely on the above mobility clause to require a junior bank employee to move from the Leeds branch to Birmingham after giving only six days notice. As a consequence the employee who refused to move without more notice could regard himself as being constructively dismissed. The EAT held that '*the tribunal was entitled therefore to imply a term that the employer's*

---

4. Above

discretion under the mobility clause was one which they were bound to exercise in such a way as not to render it impossible for an employee to comply with his contractual obligation to move. It was necessary to imply that requirement into the contract in order to avoid impossibility of performance'. The employer's conduct in relation to the transfer could be said to be in breach of the general implied contractual duty of trust and confidence.

The same principles apply when an employer attempts to rely on an express flexibility clause to transfer an employee from one job function to another.

In *White v. Reflecting Roadstuds Ltd.* 1991 the complainant worked for a number of years for the employer in the dispatch department of the company and then asked for a transfer to more highly paid but onerous work in the rubber mixing department. When he found the new work too demanding the employer eventually transferred the complainant to lighter work in the pressing department at a reduced wage. The complainant resigned claiming constructive dismissal, despite a clear flexibility clause in his contract of employment *'The company reserves the right when determined by requirements of operational efficiency, to transfer employees to alternative work and it is a condition of employment that they are willing to do so when requested'.* The tribunal held that the transfer amounted to a repudiatory breach of contract. The flexibility clause, the tribunal held, was subject to further implied terms, that firstly it would be exercised reasonably and secondly that there would be no reduction in pay if it was relied on. The EAT disagreed and held that there were no grounds to imply a term that requires that express terms in a contract are subject to a test of reasonableness when exercised or that a change in job functions that produces a wage reduction automatically constitutes a breach of contract. *'Where organisation and reorganisation are concerned, it is for management to reach decisions, provided they do so responsibly. This principle can be given effect within the legal framework of a clear contractual term on mobility or job transfer.'*

Explaining the ruling in *Akhtar* the EAT in *White*[5] also said that *'To imply a term that a transfer in accordance with an express flexibility or mobility clause should be handled reasonably would be to reintroduce the reasonableness test into constructive dismissal cases by the back door and would fly in the face of the authority of Western Excavating (ECC) Ltd. v. Sharp.*[6] *The decision of the EAT in United Bank Ltd. v. Akhtar could not be understood as implying a term that an employer should act reasonably in exercising his discretion under a contractual mobility clause. In Akhtar, the term found to be implied was that the employer should not exercise his discretion in such a way as to prevent the employee from being able to carry out his part of the contract.'*

Even with express authority to impose change there is an overriding requirement to maintain trust and confidence in the relationship.

In *St. Budeaux Royal British Legion Club Ltd. v. Cropper* 1995 there was an express clause in the contract of employment authorising the employer to change working hours on reasonable notice. On economic grounds the employer reduced working hours by five, giving employees six weeks notice of the change. The Tribunal and the EAT held that the reduction in hours was a fundamental breach

---

5. Above
6. See Chapter 10

of the implied terms in relation to trust and confidence and the resulting constructive dismissal was unfair.

A change in job duties may of course be authorised in a clearly drafted job description.

In *Land Securities Trillium Ltd. v. Thornley* 2005 Mrs. Justice Cox explained, *'Job descriptions are not prescriptive documents. They frequently fail to represent, … accurately or fully, the actual duties in fact undertaken by an employee in his or her post; and the duties are often described in vague terms so that, when interpreting them, a tribunal is required to put some flesh on the bones, as it were, in order to understand what exactly the employee's duties comprised.'* In the case before it the EAT considered the validity of a change to the duties of an architect from a hands on role to a managerial role which had the effect of de-skilling her. The change in job duties did not fall within the scope of a flexibility clause, which provided that the employee would 'perform to the best of your abilities any other duties which may reasonably be required of you and will at all times obey all reasonable instructions given to you'. The EAT held that such a clause did not give unfettered authority to require the applicant to undertake any duties they wished her to, but expressly imposed a requirement of reasonableness on the employers' request. *'Once it is found that the duties required by the appellants were unreasonably required of her … the fact that there may have been valid, commercial grounds, as opposed to a wholly arbitrary basis, for the appellants requiring her to undertake them, cannot in a contract of employment cure the unreasonableness of the requirement insofar as the employee is concerned … Once such a requirement is found to be unreasonable for that individual employee, a reasonable basis for making the request cannot mean that it is "reasonably required" of that employee.'* Here to impose the change was a repudiatory breach by the employer which constituted a constructive dismissal.[7]

Implied Terms

In Chapter 4 we saw that courts and tribunals have a wide discretion to imply terms into contracts of employment to give effect to the parties' intentions by more fully expressing the contractual bargain.

> In *Jones v. Associated Tunnelling Co. Ltd.* 1981, the EAT held that, in the absence of express terms to the contrary, there is an implied term in a contract of employment that the employer has the right to transfer the employee to a different place of work within reasonable daily commuting distance of his home.

By implying a term into employment contracts that employees should be flexible and adaptable and react positively to change, an employer is authorised to implement quite sweeping changes in job functions provided staff are given sufficient training to enable them to cope with the different demands placed upon them.

> In *Cresswell v. Board of Inland Revenue* 1984, employees sought a legal declaration that their employers had broken the terms of their contract of employment by introducing new technology and expecting them to adapt to it.[8] The High Court declared, however, that, provided they received adequate training, employees were expected to adapt to new methods and new techniques. There is a general

---

7. See Chapter 10
8. The Union was seeking a pay rise

contractual duty on employees to adapt to changing working methods. There was also a right for the employer to withhold pay for those employees who refused to conform to the new methods, for they are in breach of their contractual obligations.

The legal position is much more complex if the changing contractual arrangements are not expressly or impliedly authorised by the contract of employment. An obvious example would be the situation where an employer requires his staff to move from full-time to part-time work or accept a reduction in wages. Here the employer must seek the express or implied assent of his workforce or their trade union to the change and he cannot legally impose the change unilaterally.

Certainly by continuing to work under protest the employee is demonstrating his unwillingness to accept a proposed contractual change and is entitled to a period of grace during which he can assess his legal position.

In *Marriott v. Oxford District Co-operative Society Ltd.* 1969 a foreman supervisor was told by his employer that the position of foreman was no longer required and that his wages were to be reduced by £1 per week to reflect his loss of status. The employee continued to work under protest for three weeks before terminating his contract of employment by notice and claiming a redundancy payment. The Court of Appeal held, reversing the Divisional Court's judgment, that as there was no implied assent to the contractual change, it amounted to a repudiation of the contract of employment. The employee's reaction of continuing to work for a short period under protest was understandable and in no way constituted implied assent to the contractual change.

In *Henry v. London General Transport Services* 2002 the Court of Appeal considered the circumstances in which an employee could be taken to have affirmed a contract by his conduct. The court approved of the position set out by the EAT in *WE Cox Toner (International) Ltd. v. Crook* that *'provided the employee makes clear his objection to what is being done, he is not to be taken to have affirmed the contract by continuing to work and draw pay for a limited period of time'*. However if the employee does acts which are only consistent with the continued existence of the contract, these acts will normally show affirmation of the contract. Here despite initial objection to contractual change by continuing to work under new terms for two years it would be *'extremely difficult to conclude other than that the employees had accepted the revised terms of employment'*.

While it is possible for a contract of employment to expressly provide for its unilateral variation by the employer, very clear words would need to be used to achieve that objective.

In *Security and Facilities Division v. Hayes* 2001 the claimants were electricians who installed security systems and required to work away from home. The conflict with their employer arose when having failed to secure a reduction in allowance rates through collective bargaining the employer unilaterally reduced the subsistence allowance to a single flat rate. The employees sued in the County Court alleging breach of contract and their claim was upheld. On appeal the employer argued that such a unilateral variation was authorised by an implied contractual term provided it was triggered reasonably and not capriciously. The Court of Appeal upheld the decision and found the employer to be in breach of contract. *'Where parties to a contract of employment intend a provision allowing unilateral variation of the rate of allowance the contractual terms must provide unambiguously for that.'* Here there was nothing in the contract to authorise a unilateral change and it was highly improbable that the parties intentions were supportive of an implied term.

One option for an employee who feels that his employer is unreasonably requiring him to do work which is not part of his contractual obligations is to seek an interlocutory[9] injunction to maintain the status quo at work.

> In *Hughs v. London Borough of Southwark* 1988 a number of social workers applied to the High Court for an interlocutory injunction to stop their employers requiring them to staff community areas on a temporary basis and so terminate their normal hospital work. The High Court held that the employer's instruction was in breach of contract and the plaintiff social workers were entitled to an interlocutory injunction to restrain the breach. The Court of Appeal in *Powell v. The London Borough of Brent* 1987 had previously held that the court has power to grant an interlocutory injunction to restrain the breach of a contract of service provided that there was mutual confidence between the employer and employee. Here, despite the dispute, the employers retained confidence in the social workers. In this case the employers had *'failed to consult with the hospital or have taken sufficient steps in investigation properly to inform themselves as to the balance of work priorities. Although it is for managers to manage, that principle was flawed in the present case by their failure to inform themselves of the relevant considerations before deciding on priorities'.*

Collective Agreements and Change

In many spheres of employment, the process of negotiating and varying terms and conditions of employment is not carried on by employees individually bargaining with their employers but by employers and trade unions engaging in collective bargaining on their behalf. The product of collective bargaining is called a collective agreement which will normally contain, along with a number of other matters, specific reference to individual terms and conditions of employment. In *Adams v. British Airways* 1996 the Master of Rolls[10] was called upon to interpret a collective agreement and made the following comment. *'A collective agreement has special characteristics, being made between an employer or employer's organisation on one side and a trade union or trade unions representatives of employees on the other, usually following a negotiation. Thus it represents an industrial bargain, and probably represents a compromise between the conflicting aims of the parties, or "sides" as in this context they are revealingly called. But despite these special characteristics, a collective agreement must be construed giving a fair meaning to the words used in the factual context which gave rise to the agreement.'*

Over seventy five per cent of workers are still covered by collective agreements so that it is crucial to appreciate their legal standing and those parts of a collective agreement that are suitable for incorporation into individual contracts of employment. The legal status of collective agreements is referred to in the Trade Union and Labour Relations (Consolidation) Act 1992 which provides that such agreements are conclusively presumed not to be legally enforceable unless in writing and expressed to be so. As between the parties to a collective agreement therefore,[11] collective agreements while in writing are not usually expressed to

---

9. Temporary
10. Head of the Court of Appeal
11. The trade union or unions and employers or employer's association

be legally enforceable and are consequently not legally binding. Those parts of the collective agreement that are incorporated into individual contracts of employment will become legally enforceable however between the employer and employee.

The process of incorporation

The usual method of incorporation is by the individual contract of employment making express reference to the collective agreement or agreements. Statements such as *union conditions or subject to a national agreement* either in the contract of employment or even the statutory statements of the main terms and conditions of employment would normally suffice for the purpose of incorporation. It should be stressed however, that the agreed terms of employment prevail over the statutory statement.[12]

> In *Robertson and Jackson v. British Gas Corporation* 1983 the Court of Appeal held that an express reference in the contract of employment to the effect that 'incentive bonus conditions apply to the work carried on' made the payment of an incentive bonus a contractual obligation, the terms of which were to be found in the collective agreement which existed at the time of appointment. A conflicting reference in the statutory statement of particulars of employment to the effect that the bonus scheme could be unilaterally withdrawn by the employer had no significance.

The suggestion is, therefore, that collective agreements can only be varied by the parties to them rather than some unilateral act of the employer. Of course the employer is free to seek an individual's agreement that collectively agreed terms should no longer apply but to attempt to achieve that result unilaterally would result in a repudiatory breach of the contract of employment.

> In *Edinburgh Council v. Brown* 1999 the employer had agreed a policy on re-grading with the Unions and on express terms in individual contracts of employment incorporated that policy into the employee's contracts. As a consequence the unilateral withdrawal from that policy by the employer had no impact on individual employees who could still rely on contractual rights conferred under it. This meant that the employee was entitled to have his re-grading back dated to the date of his original application and the employers decision to unilaterally do away with retrospective on re-grading had no impact on individual contracts of employment.

In the absence of an express reference to collectively agreed terms in the contract of employment it may be that the courts will support their incorporation through the operation of custom and practice. If a custom and practice is established that changes may be effected through collective bargaining, then significant parts of the agreement will be incorporated as contractual terms.

> In *Henry v. London General Transport Service Ltd.* 2002 during a proposed management buy out the employer entered into an agreement with the recognised trade union which set out new and less advantageous terms and conditions of employment. The union held workplace meetings and informed the employer that the majority of staff accepted the changes but no formal ballot was held as

---

12. The s.1 Statement of terms and conditions

on previous occasions when changes were proposed. A number of staff at one particular workplace objected to the changed terms and called for a ballot, continuing to work under protest. Two years later some 60 staff claimed an unlawful deduction from wages at the Employment Tribunal. The claim was upheld the tribunal ruling that where fundamental changes were proposed in a collective agreement, then 'strict proof' was required to establish the custom and practice of consequential incorporation. Both the EAT and the Court of Appeal disagreed dismissing the notion that strict proof was required to justify the incorporation of a term. *'In order to establish a custom and practice, clear evidence of the practice is required ... the burden is upon the balance of probabilities and the word strict suggests a different and high standard. If a custom and practice is established that changes are incorporated into individual contracts of employment by collective bargaining it can be expected to cover all contractual terms.'* It was however a matter for the tribunal to decide whether a ballot was necessary to secure the staffs' consent to the changes rather than relying on the union's assurance that the majority of the staff had consented to the changes.

Appropriate terms

Part of the process of identifying the terms of a contract of employment must involve discovering those parts of a collective agreement which have been incorporated into individual contracts of employment. This is by no means an easy task, for it is a question of sorting out those parts of the agreement that deal with employer/trade union matters, for instance the machinery for collective bargaining, and those parts which have significance for individual employees, such as wage negotiations.

In *British Leyland (UK) Ltd. v. McQuilken* 1978 a collectively agreed redundancy scheme was negotiated between the employer and a trade union to deal with a massive reorganisation which involved employees in retraining and possible transfer to other work locations. When the employer failed to implement the agreed scheme in relation to the complainant, he resigned due to uncertainty about his future. To succeed in a claim for unfair dismissal it was necessary for the complainant to show that he had been constructively dismissed. Constructive dismissal is established by proving that the employer has been guilty of a significant breach of the employment contract. One issue in the case therefore, was whether by failing to implement the scheme the employer had been guilty of such a breach. The EAT thought not. The redundancy scheme was a long term plan dealing with policy rather than individual employment rights and was not therefore capable of incorporation into individual contracts of employment.

In *Lee and Others v. GEC Plessey Telecommunications* 1993 the High Court agreed that in appropriate circumstances the terms of a collective agreement relating to redundancy matters could be incorporated into individual contracts of employment. In order to decide whether this had occurred in a particular case, a court had to look for the 'necessary contractual intent on both sides of the bargain and also look at the content and character of the relevant parts of the collective agreements.' The court held that an employer has no right to withdraw unilaterally its employee's contractual entitlement to generous enhanced redundancy payments and that those entitlements were not extinguished by a later collective agreement because the terms of that agreement were not incorporated into individual contracts.

Further support for this approach was provided by *Anderson v. Pringle of Scotland Ltd.* 1998 where it was held that an employer was obliged to comply with the terms of a redundancy procedure which had been incorporated into the employee's contract of employment. Despite the fact that there was no express reference in the employee's contract to the redundancy procedure there was a reference to the fact that employment was in accordance with the collective agreement. This reference, the Court of Session held, was sufficient to incorporate the *'last in first out'* selection criterion into the employee's contract and ensure that the employee in question was secure in employment. In *Kaur v. MG Rover Group Ltd.* 2005 the Court of Appeal concluded that the job security provision in a collective agreement amounted to an expression of collective aspiration and not a provision intended by the parties to be incorporated as a binding term in individual contracts of employment.

It is a recognised principle under TUPE[13] that all the transferor's duties and liabilities in connection with a contract of employment go over to the transferee. The issue in *Whent v. Cartledge* 1997 was whether incorporated collective agreement terms are transferred along with subsequent amendments. The relevant bridging clause , including the words 'as amended from time to time' meant that the transferee employer was bound by changes in terms and conditions of employment negotiated after the transfer. The fact that the relevant bridging clause in *Ackinclose v. Gateshead MBC* 2005 simply provided that the relevant terms and conditions were 'in accordance with national agreements ' was insufficient to bind the transferee employer to new terms and conditions negotiated under a new collective agreement.

Subject to the approval of the Secretary of State for Employment, a collective agreement can replace certain of the statutory rights, for example, to a redundancy payment or guaranteed payment. In cases where approval is granted the statutory right is substituted by the right under the collective agreement which becomes legally enforceable as a term of the individual contract of employment to which it relates. Once identified as terms of individual contracts of employment it may still be necessary to interpret their nature and the scope of their application.

> In *Brigden v. Lancashire County Council* 1987 the Court of Appeal considered a term inserted into a lecturer's contract by a relevant collective agreement which provided that *'where a teacher is appointed under a Principal to take charge of adult education work in a particular centre or area where the unit total is 75, the teacher shall be graded not less than Lecturer Grade II'.* The complainant having been initially appointed at a lower grade argued that she should have been immediately upgraded when her work reached the appropriate level. She claimed that the employer was in breach of this provision and she was justified in claiming constructive dismissal which was unfair. The Court of Appeal however confirmed the decision of the EAT that the employer's were not in breach of contract. The relevant provision should be interpreted as *'applying only to an initial appointment'* and the *'fact that the work increases to the prescribed level does not create a new appointment'.*
>
> In *Davies v. Hotpoint Ltd.* 1994 the contracts of employment of factory workers employed by the respondents had the terms of a 1984 collective agreement incorporated within them. One term provided for guaranteed wages stating *'All*

---

13. The Transfer of Undertakings (protection of employment) Regs 1981 and 2006

hourly rated manual workers employed by the company for not less than four weeks shall be guaranteed employment for five days in each normal week. In the event of work not being available for the whole or part of the five days, employees covered by the guarantee will be assured earnings equivalent to their time rate for thirty nine hours' subject to the condition that "where approved short-time is worked as an alternative to redundancy ... the guarantee shall be reduced accordingly".' Despite union objections there were a number of occasions where the employer put workers on short-time, paying them less than the guaranteed minimum wage. The employees complained that the employers were in breach of the Wages Act in paying them less than the guaranteed wage without the approval of the union. The issue before the EAT therefore was whether the term *'approved short-time working'* meant that the employer could not unilaterally introduce it but needed the consent of the union. The EAT held that *'the use of the word "approved" indicated a requirement of the consent or agreement of someone other than the person making the decision to be approved. The word would be redundant if it meant "approved by the employer". Moreover since the context of the collective agreement was a guaranteed minimum wage negotiated between management and the union on behalf of the workforce, if the guarantee were to have any substance it could not have been the intention of the parties that it should depend solely on the unilateral decision of the employer to abandon the guarantee by deciding on short-time working'.*

The Court of Appeal considered the interpretation of a collective agreement in relation to the status of employees on the merger of two large organisations in the following case.

In *Adams and Others v. British Airways* 1996 a number of British Airways pilots as plaintiffs sought a ruling from the High Court that BA had wrongly interpreted a collective agreement that applied to them. Following BA's takeover of British Caledonian, 300 hundred of British Caledonian pilots joined BA and were given seniority above the plaintiffs. This was significant for the plaintiffs as seniority is important in determining promotion and choice of route. By giving the new pilots seniority based upon their experience the plaintiffs claimed that constituted a breach of their own contractual seniority rights. The clause of the collective agreement in dispute stated that in relation to *'new entrants', 'on initial appointment all pilots will enter service in the grade of first officer on point 000'.* For the plaintiffs it was argued that this clause was entirely unambiguous and meant that BA should install the new British Caledonian pilots as new entrants at the bottom of the ladder. The alternative argument was that the British Caledonian pilots were *not 'new entrants'* and the intention of the merger could not have been to rank senior British Caledonian pilots below junior pilots of BA. This argument was rejected by the High Court which held that the relevant clause was unambiguous and as new entrants by giving the British Caledonian pilots seniority BA were in breach of the plaintiff's contracts of employment. The Court of Appeal disagreed and held that the High Court had wrongly applied the literal working of the collective agreement to a merger situation. While the British Caledonian pilots were new entrants to BA as new employees, they were not *'new entrants'* to the Gatwick based airline undertaking of British Caledonian which BA had taken over. To regard the British Caledonian pilots as simply *'new entrants'* in the sense of new recruits of BA was absurd, they were in fact experienced employees of an airline which had been merged with another. There was nothing in the language of the collective agreement to indicate that it was intended to apply to the merger of two airlines. Accordingly the British Caledonian pilots should be entitled to seniority according to their years of service.

Imposed Change

If there is no agreement to a proposed change and the employer attempts to unilaterally impose a more onerous term on an employee, for example a wage cut, then the employee has a number of options. He could:

- accept the variation as a repudiatory breach of the contract, walk out and claim constructive dismissal;
- remain passive without protest and eventually be taken to have accepted the varied contract;
- continue to work under protest and sue for damages for breach of contract.

In *Rigby v. Ferodo Ltd.* 1988 the employee, in response to a unilateral wage cut, took the final option and sued for damages representing the unpaid wages. Both the High Court and the Court of Appeal agreed that there had been no mutual variation of the contract of employment so that the unreduced wage was payable and, further, that the damages should not be limited to the twelve week notice period under which the employee could have been dismissed. The House of Lords agreed and held that a repudiatory breach does not automatically terminate a contract of employment unless the breach is accepted by the employee as a repudiation. Damages were not limited therefore to the notice period of twelve weeks and the primary contractual obligation to pay the full wage survived.

The EAT has suggested that tribunals should be very cautious in reaching the conclusion that an employee had accepted a variation to his or her contract merely because he or she had continued working without any overt objection to the new terms.

In *Aparau v. Iceland Frozen Foods plc* 1996 new employers had issued new contracts to existing staff containing an express mobility clause. The complainant did not sign the new contract and continued working for twelve months so that when she objected to a mandatory transfer there was an issue as to whether the mobility clause was part of her contract. The decision of the EAT in *Jones v. Associated Tunnelling* was approved where it was stated that *'where there is a unilateral alteration by the employer of the terms of employment which has no immediate practical effect, there is a need for great caution before implying that the employee had consented to the variation by continuing to work without objecting to it'.* In the circumstances of this case there was no express mobility clause and no justification for implying a term. *'Although there must necessarily be some term as to place of employment in a contract of employment, there was no necessity to have any clause about mobility in the employee's contract. The nature of her work did not make such a clause necessary, nor was it needed in order to give the contract business efficacy.'*

The legal position relating to contractual variation was examined by the High Court in *Alexander v. Standard Telephones and Cables Ltd.* (no 2) 1991. Mr. Justice Hobhouse stated that *'Although an employer is not entitled unilaterally to vary a contract, it is always open to an employer, as a matter of contract, to say to his employee that after the expiry of the contractual notice period the employer will only continue the contract of employment on different terms.*

Such a notice is equivalent to giving notice to terminate the existing contract and offering a revised contract in continuation of and substitution for the existing contract. The period of notice has to be the notice that is required to terminate the existing contract. It is then up to the employee to decide whether he is willing to accept the revised terms.' It seems therefore that provided the correct notice is given, an employee could be contractually bound to accept a change in terms of employment. There must be an unequivocal termination of existing contracts however by the employer for the courts would be unlikely to imply a dismissal from a notice of variation.[14] An attempt by an employer to vary existing contracts unilaterally could be restrained by court action.

> In *Burdett-Coutts v. Hertfordshire County Council* 1984 the council employer attempted to vary the contracts of employment of a number of 'dinner ladies' by sending them a letter of 'amendment of contract of service', detailing the changes with a notice of when they were to take effect. The plaintiff employees made it clear that they were not prepared to accept the changes and sued for breach of contract. The High Court held that the employer's letter amounted to a repudiatory breach of contract. *'The plaintiffs were entitled to a declaration that the defendants were not entitled in law to vary unilaterally the terms of the plaintiffs' contracts of employment and to damages in the form of arrears of wages.'* The court was not prepared to construe the letter as a notice of termination. *'Nor could it be held that the plaintiffs, by staying at their posts and taking the lower sums paid to them, by implication had waived their right to treat their contract as having been brought to an end and by implication had entered into a fresh contract.'*

Termination of employment

In the absence of agreement therefore it seems that an employer who wishes to impose change must proceed by way of notice of termination with the offer of a new contract. An employee who is faced with a dismissal notice however, if qualified to do so, having one years continuous employment, would have the right to pursue a claim for unfair dismissal. This type of economic dismissal is potentially fair under the category *'some other substantial reason for dismissal'.*[15] Economic dismissals are covered in Chapter 11 but some of the issues can be dealt with here. By requiring such an employee to accept more onerous terms of employment an employer will be in repudiatory breach and if accepted by the employee this could constitute constructive dismissal and potentially an unfair dismissal.

> In *Hill Ltd. v. Mooney* 1981 the EAT held that an attempt by an employer to unilaterally alter his obligation to pay the agreed remuneration was a breach which went to the root of the contract and consequently constituted a repudiation of it. The complainant was entitled therefore to regard himself as constructively dismissed when he resigned following the employer's decision to unilaterally change the basis upon which sales commission was payable to him. *'Although a mere alteration in the contractual provisions does not necessarily amount to a fundamental breach constituting repudiation, if an employer seeks to alter that contractual obligation in a fundamental way such attempt is a breach going to the very root of the contract and is necessarily a repudiation. The obligation on the employer is to pay the contractual wages, and he is not entitled to alter the formula whereby those wages are calculated.'*

---

14. The validity of the change could be tested in an unfair dismissal complaint
15. S.98(1) Employment Rights Act 1996

In *Greenaway Harrison Ltd. v. Wiles* 1994 a telephonist who worked a split shift to fit in with her child care responsibilities was told to work a new shift pattern which was not compatible. Her employer warned her that unless she accepted the new shift pattern she would be dismissed with one month's notice. The complainant left claiming constructive dismissal which was unfair. The EAT upheld the finding that the case fell within a constructive dismissal because the decision to dismiss had already been taken before she left and this was a fundamental breach of contract.

The imposition of a radical change in job functions could indicate a breakdown in trust and confidence. The EAT held in *Brown v. Ministry of Defence* 1992 that to move the applicant after eighteen years service from his work as a boatman to work in a paint shop at a different work location would constitute a breach of the implied term of trust and confidence. The applicant was entitled to regard himself as constructively dismissed when he left as a result.

Unfair Dismissal

In the present employment climate the potential redress for a successful complaint of unfair dismissal will hardly compensate for the loss of secure employment. Rights in relation to unfair dismissal are considered later in Chapter 11 but the following cases provide an illustration of the approach to be adopted by tribunals. It seems that even public sector employers will still attempt to impose change with a threat of dismissal.

In *Wilson (HM Inspector of Taxes) v. Clayton* 2005 the claimant had his essential car user allowance withdrawn with a threat of dismissal if he did not agree to the change. The claimant was one of a large number of affected employees who did not agree to the removal of the allowance and he was subsequently dismissed. The unfair dismissal claim was upheld by the tribunal who made an order for their reinstatement.

> In *St. John of God (Care Services) Ltd. v. Brooks* 1992 following a reduction in State funding the response of the hospital employer was to attempt to reduce costs, and to assist in the process the staff were offered less favourable terms of employment. Such terms included a reduction in holidays, the abolition of overtime rates and the generous sick pay scheme and a freeze on pay levels. Employees were told they had a reasonable time to accept the new terms, but failure to do so would lead to dismissal. As a consequence three employees were dismissed, a further employee having walked out in response to the changes, claiming a repudiatory breach and constructive dismissal. In the event 140 out of 170 staff accepted the new terms of employment. The claim of unfair dismissal was upheld by an industrial tribunal who in determining the fairness of the employer's conduct asked the question whether the terms offered were those which a reasonable employer could offer and decided that they were not. On appeal however the EAT took a different view and held that the question as to fairness should also be considered in the light of the matters which occurred subsequent to the offer of new terms being made. In particular the fact that the vast majority of staff had accepted the change was significant as were the sound business reasons for the reorganisation.

Quite often the new terms of employment are offered following a reorganisation.

In *Catamaran Cruisers Ltd. v. Williams* 1994 the seven complainants were all employed by a cruise company which was taken over when in financial difficulties. The new employers offered new terms and conditions to the staff which were eventually approved by the Union and accepted by the majority of employees. The complainants rejected the new contracts, were dismissed and presented complaints of unfair dismissal. The employers relied on 'some other substantial reason' as the reason for dismissal and claimed that it was fair given that it was introduced for a sound business reason. Having compared the old contracts with the new contracts the tribunal held that as the new contracts were much less favourable and the company's financial position was not sufficiently serious to require the imposition of the new terms the dismissals were unfair. The EAT disagreed however and found that there was no principle of law that supported the approach adopted by the tribunal. It was necessary to examine the motives of the employer and *'satisfy itself that they are not sought to be imposed for arbitrary reasons. What has to be carried out is a balancing process'*. The tribunal should *'not look solely at the advantages or disadvantages but should also consider and take account of the benefit to the employers in imposing the changes'*. The question of reasonableness should be determined in the light of the fact that many employees accepted the new terms and the fact that the reorganisation was partly motivated by the need to give more emphasis to safety.

If the reorganisation involves implementing a policy of rationalisation then the fairness of any decision to dismiss must be considered in the light of the policy.

The issue in *Banerjee v. City and East London Area Health Authority* 1979 was whether having decided to replace two part-time consultants in a hospital with a full-time consultant, the decision to dismiss was reasonable as in accordance with the employer's policy of rationalisation. A decision to dismiss in these circumstances could be prima facie fair. The EAT said that *'A question such as that which arose in the present case is very largely a matter for the employer. If an employer can show to the satisfaction of the industrial tribunal that a certain policy has been evolved and that it was considered to be a matter of importance or to have discernible advantages to the organisation, then, subject to there being any effective cross examination, dismissal in accordance with that policy can be said to be for 'some other substantial reason.'* In 1979 the burden of proving fairness was on the employer,[16] however the EAT still provided instructive guidance on determining the issue of fairness in these circumstances. Certainly it is not enough to simply show that the decision to dismiss was reached in accordance with a particular policy. *'In a case involving dismissal following a policy of rationalisation, this involves other adducing evidence of the relevant minutes of how the decision to rationalise was made, of the pros and cons which were considered and if the importance which was attached to the different features which went into the decision; alternatively, a witness may be called who could show that the reason for the dismissal was that the company considered keeping on the dismissed employee and that the advantages of each course had been weighed.'*

In *Scottish Co-operative Wholesale Society v. Taylor* 1993 the EAT held that it was a question of fact based on all the circumstances to decide whether it is reasonable

---

16. A neutral burden of proof was introduced by the Employment Act 1980

for an employer when implementing a reorganisation to request an emp
move from full-time employment to part-time employment under a shif

Also the EAT in *Shevlin v. Coventry Free Church Homes for the A*
stressed that the circumstances of the reorganisation must be considered from
the viewpoint of both the employer and the employee. Insufficient thought had
been given to the impact of a change in a shift system on the employee's domestic
circumstances so that her complaint of unfair constructive dismissal was upheld
by the EAT when she left her job as a result.

One obvious question is whether an employee who has reluctantly accepted a new contract
can still maintain a claim of unfair dismissal.

In *Hogg v. Dover College* 1990 it was held that once action amounting to a
dismissal is established the fact that the employee has accepted a new contract
will not prevent a complaint of unfair dismissal. This complaint can be pursued
before an industrial tribunal while the applicant remains in the employment of
the same employer. Applying the rationale of *Hogg in Alcan Extrusions v. Yates*
1996 the EAT reached a similar conclusion when an employer unilaterally
changed contracts of employment. *'Where an employer unilaterally imposes radically
different terms of employment ... there is a dismissal ... if on an objective construction
of the relevant letters or other conduct on the part of the employer, there is a removal
or withdrawal of the old contract.'*

A significant recent trend in employment is the practice of employers offering employees
financial incentives to sign so called personal contracts and relinquish the right to trade
union representation for the purposes of collective bargaining. In *Wilson v. Associated
Newspapers Ltd.* 1993 the Court of Appeal held that this could constitute unlawful action
short of dismissal against those employees who refuse the offer. Now s.13 of the Trade
Union Reform and Employment Rights Act 1993 amends s.148 of TULRA(C)A 1992 so
that if an employer offers enhanced payments to employees who accept personal contracts,
provided that the aim of the employer was to change the relationship with a class of
employee this will not be unlawful in relation to those who do not accept the change.
Unlawful action short of dismissal is considered in Chapter 9. *Wilson v. The United Kingdom*
2002 is a claim arising out of this case which was taken to the European Court of Human
Rights. By using financial incentives to induce employees to surrender their trade union
rights it was alleged that this was a breach of Article 11. This Article provides that *'everyone
has the right to freedom of association with others, including the right to form and join trade
unions for the protection of their interests'*. The court held that by offering *'sweeteners'* in the
form of higher pay to prevent employees from making use of their trade union services,
employers are in breach of the Convention.

Further Reading

Brodie, Douglas *Beyond Exchange: The New Contract of Employment* (1998) 25 ILJ 79.

Clarke, Linda *Mutual Trust and Confidence Fiduciary Relationships and the Duty of Disclosure* (1999) 28 ILJ 348.

Collins, H. *Market Power, Bureaucratic Power and the Contract of Employment* (1986)15 ILJ 1.

Chapter 6

Equal Opportunity Law

This chapter and the next is devoted to a consideration of equal opportunity law in employment.[1] This involves an examination of discrimination law in particular in relation to sex, race, disability, sexual orientation, and religion. Inevitably as we have had sex and race discrimination law for almost a generation, this will be the main focus of attention. Nevertheless there have been significant developments in disability discrimination law and these will be reflected in the chapter. The first major discrimination claim based on sexual orientation began in March 2006. Discrimination law in relation to age will be introduced in 2006.[2] In addition there are equal opportunity objectives in legislative developments which support the work/life balance such as maternity leave, paternity leave, the rights of part-time workers and equal pay. They are the focus of Chapter 7. Unlawful discrimination may take place during the recruitment process, at the workplace, or when employment is terminated. In addition to UK legislation on discrimination we should also examine European Community law which is directly applicable in UK Courts and also incorporated into United Kingdom law by Statute and by Statutory Instruments. While this chapter is devoted to exploring unlawful discrimination law, you should appreciate from the outset that employers can still lawfully discriminate in recruitment in circumstances where the nature of the work justifies it.[3] In December 2005 the World Health Organisation announced a ban on the recruitment of smokers illustrating the fact that employers can lawfully adopt policies that have detrimental impact on specific sections of society.

Unfortunately as a consequence of discriminatory recruitment practices we have a workforce in the UK divided by sex and race. The tendency to stereotype sexes and races and also perceive jobs to have male or female characteristics means that discrimination in Britain is still widespread. Members of racial and ethnic minority groups generally occupy a low position in the occupational structure, concentrated in unskilled manual jobs and unrepresented in skilled manual jobs, managerial and professional occupations where there

---

1. A distinct legal subject
2. The Employment Equality (Age) Regulations 2006
3. See later in the chapter

are less likely to be flexible employment practices. Minority groups are found mainly in low paying industries such as clothing and textiles, in service sector jobs and in hospitals, shops and catering. Furthermore male black workers earn considerably less than male white workers and suffer a much higher rate of unemployment. Female workers are similarly concentrated in low paid unskilled jobs in a relatively small number of occupations including mainly clerical and related jobs and industries such as cleaning, catering and manufacturing. Because of child care responsibilities many women take part-time or casual work, often unskilled with poor pay and conditions. Part-time work is still rewarded pro-rata substantially less than full-time work (female part-time workers, 40% less than male full-time staff).

Nevertheless there are still relatively few complaints brought and success rates are consistently low. Studies have shown that there are numerous reasons for this, ranging from ignorance as to legal rights, insufficient support for claimants, difficulties of proof, and fear of victimisation. On the positive side however, there have been some notable successes recently which have caused change in employment practices. Unlawful discrimination has been found in a number of recent equal pay cases, in employment practices in relation to part-time workers, in unnecessary demands for British qualifications, in maximum age limits and in stringent language tests.

You will also see that changes in the law relating to the burden of proof in discrimination cases are of great assistance to prospective applicants. Also the lifting of the cap on compensation payable has focused the minds of employers in adopting employment practices than help to minimise the risk of legal action. Publicity given to recent substantial awards by Tribunals in discrimination cases inevitably focuses the minds of employers on their employment practices.[4] There is no doubt that there is a change in attitude, for there is increasing evidence that employers in the public and also in the private sector of the economy are adopting equal opportunity employment practices. Equal opportunity is an important issue in industrial relations, and the law can act as an important stimulus to both employers and trade unions to ensure that organisations adopt employment practices designed to combat discrimination.

Finally there is evidence of a new positive approach from the higher courts in dealing with applications claiming infringement of disability discrimination law. Indeed in certain jobs, disabled persons may be give priority in shortlisting and the anti discrimination law in relation to the disabled introduced in 1995 has been positively interpreted and substantially amended since October 2004.[5]

While the main focus of the chapter is discrimination law in relation to sex, race and disability, there are in addition laws which confer protection on those individuals who may suffer discrimination because of their past offences or trade union membership which deserve mention.

Offenders

Rather than stigmatising an individual for life because of his past conduct, the Rehabilitation of Offenders Act 1974 allows past offenders who have criminal convictions to regard them as 'spent' in certain circumstances. Imprisonment for 30 months or more can never be spent and in a number of professions even spent offences must be disclosed for instance

---

4. Compensation in excess of one million pounds
5. See later in the chapter

medicine, the law, teaching and local authority employment in connection with the provision of social services.[6] In *Wood v. Coverage Care Ltd.* 1996 the EAT held that the social service exception applied not only to social workers but to a range of employment opportunities relating to social service functions. Accordingly it was lawful to take account of spent convictions when deciding the suitability of an applicant for the posts of manager or bursar at a residential care home for persons over the age of 65. If the offence is spent then on a job application the past conviction need not be mentioned and the failure to disclose it is no ground for an employer to discriminate against individuals by refusing to employ them or by dismissing them for past offences. It is reasonable of course for an employer to expect full disclosure of information on a job application and this would most certainly include a prospective employee providing details of criminal convictions which were not spent. A failure to fully disclose details of previous employment or trade union activities however may not be regarded as fatal to the validity of the contract of employment.

> In *Fitzpatrick v. British Railways Board* 1991 the complainant obtained a job with British Railways Board and deliberately failed to provide full details of her previous employment and participation in trade union activities. When it became obvious to the employer that the complainant was, and had been a union activist, they dismissed her on the ground that she had obtained the job by deceit. The complainant then claimed that her dismissal was unfair as it was on the ground of trade union activities contrary to s.152 of the Trade Union and Labour Relations (Consolidation) Act 1992. If the reason for a dismissal is trade union membership or activities the then requirement of two years continuous employment to qualify for protection did not apply.[7] The Court of Appeal held that the true reason for the complainant's dismissal was her union activities in previous employment and the fear that these activities will be repeated in her present employment. *'An employer is in clear breach of the section if he dismisses an employee on the basis of previous trade union activities, when the only rational basis for doing so is the fear that those activities will be repeated in the present employment. Although the trade union activities referred to in the section are activities in the employment from which the employee alleges that he has been unfairly dismissed, what happened in the employee's previous employment may form the reason for dismissal in subsequent employment and therefore can be highly relevant to the question which an industrial tribunal has to answer under the section.'* Here the Court of Appeal felt that the reason for dismissal here was a fear of a repetition of the same conduct and in the circumstances it fell within the section and was therefore unfair.

Under the Trade Union and Labour Relations (Consolidation) Act 1992 s.137 it is unlawful to refuse employment because a person is or is not a trade union member. Also under the Act if a job advertisement indicates that trade union membership is a requirement and, then employment is refused it will be presumed to be for that reason if the applicant is not a trade union member.

---

6. The Sex Offenders Register

7. Now one years continuous employment

European Community Law

The right not to be discriminated against on the grounds of sex, race or marital status is one of the few individual employment rights that has not been weakened but rather strengthened over recent years. This has been mainly due to the impact of Community law and judgments of the European Court of Justice particularly in relation to gender. An examination of UK discrimination law must therefore take account of changes which required substantial amendments to UK legislation. In May 1999 the Amsterdam Treaty came into force and Article 141 strengthens the sex equality provisions to ensure equal opportunity and equal treatment. In addition a new Article 13[8] empowers the Council on the European Union to take appropriate action to combat discrimination based on sex, racial ethnic origin religion or belief, disability, age or sexual orientation in employment and vocational training. A number of Equal treatment Directives have been adopted by the UK Government and implemented by means of Regulations.[9]

While European Union Law did not provide protection from discrimination on the grounds of sexual orientation in *Smith and Grady v. United Kingdom* 1999 it was held that homosexuals may have rights under the European Convention on Human Rights. Here the European Court of Human Rights held that the Ministry of Defence had violated the private lives of members of the armed forces by carrying out investigations into their homosexuality and their subsequent discharge from the services.[10] The Equal Treatment Directive has had considerable impact on UK discrimination law and in *Johnston v. Chief Constable of the RUC* 1987 it was confirmed that the Directive was unconditional and sufficiently precise to be used by an individual against a member state or in a national court. An individual could not enforce the Directive against a private employer however.

In *P v. S* 1996 the European Court of Justice considered whether the Equal Treatment Directive applied to the case where a transsexual had been dismissed for a reason related to a sex change. Following the complainant's announcement that he intended to undertake gender reassignment, and the commencement of initial surgery, he had been dismissed. The European Court held that the Directive's principle of equal treatment required no discrimination on the grounds of sex and its scope should not be confined to a person's gender status but also to gender reassignment. A comparison should be drawn in such a case with the treatment the applicant received before undergoing the reassignment and after. Now the Sex Discrimination (Gender Reassignment) Regulations 1999 confer protection on individuals who suffer less favourable treatment because of their change in gender. The Regulations protect individuals against less favourable treatments at recruitment and in employment due to the fact that the person intends to change, is undergoing, or has undergone gender reassignment. The Regulations also prevent disparity of pay and benefits on these grounds.

In *Goodwin v. UK and I v. UK* 2002 the European Court of Human Rights found the UK to have broken the rights of two transsexual people under Article 8 and 12. As a result of these two cases the Gender Recognition Act 2004 was passed.[11] It establishes panels to deal with applications from transgender and transsexual people for legal recognition of

---

8. Inserted as Schedule 6 Treaty of Rome
9. E.g. The Sex Discrimination (Indirect Discrimination and Burden of Proof) Regulations 2001
10. See Chapter 1 Human Rights
11. In force April 2005

their acquired gender. This means that transsexuals can now invoke the full protection of the Sex Discrimination Act.

The Equal Treatment Directive 2002 has its origins in Article 141 and Article 2 of the Treaty of Rome which proclaims that *'equality between men and women'* is a *'task'* of the Community. Also Article 3(2) states that it is the aim of the Community to *'eliminate inequalities and to promote equality between men and women'*. The Directive places the objective of equality at the forefront by requiring all member states to proactively consider it in their decision making. New definitions of direct and indirect discrimination are introduced as well as definitions for sex related harassment and sexual harassment under Article 2. The impact of these new definitions will be considered later in the chapter. Importantly the new Directive covers pay claims so that a claimant will be able to bring an equal pay claim under the Sex Discrimination Act without the need for a comparator.[12] (see Chapter 7) Also you will see in Chapter 7 that unlawful treatment in relation to pregnancy leave and maternity is already covered by Statute. The fact that it will also constitute sex discrimination is important because there is no limit on the level of compensation that may be awarded. The Employment Equality (Sex Discrimination) Regulations 2005[13] made amendments to the Sex Discrimination Act 1975 to implement the Equal treatment Directive.

Age Discrimination

Age discrimination law was required to be introduced in 2003 under the Equal treatment Directive but the UK government was granted a three-year extension to allow full consultation. The Employment Equality (Age) Regulations will be in force on 1 October 2006. Individuals[14] of all ages will have the new right not to be discriminated against in employment or vocational training because of their age. The Regulations will create the standard unlawful acts of direct discrimination, indirect discrimination victimisation and harassment.[15]

Unlike other forms of discrimination however it will be possible for an employer to raise the defence of justification for direct as well as indirect discrimination. Employers can treat individuals differently because of their age if they can show that the treatment, provision, criterion or practice can be objectively justified as a proportionate means of achieving a legitimate aim. The defence will require strong supporting evidence. In this way a health and fitness test for employees could be objectively justified if the employer could show that a certain standard of health and fitness is a requirement of the job. It seems that length of service benefits such as incremental pay scales, enhanced sickness pay, additional annual leave and loyalty rewards will continue but for those dependent on more than five years service, they will have to be objectively justified.

The retirement age is to be set at 65 and compulsory retirement below that age will be unlawful unless the employer can establish that a lower retirement age is objectively justified. Employers will have an obligation to consider an employee's request to continue working beyond retirement and deal with it in a similar way to a request for flexible working.[16]

---

12. See Chapter 7
13. In force October 2005
14. Employees, contactors and job applicants
15. See later in the chapter
16. See Chapter 7

Entitlement to redundancy pay[17] and unfair dismissal rights[18] will no longer cease when the employee is aged 65.

Sex, Race, Sexual Orientation and Religious Belief

UK legislation on sex and race discrimination has been established for almost a generation. For sexual orientation and religious belief, the law is more recent, introduced as a result of the Equal Treatment Directive 2003. Its aim is to encourage employers to implement equality of opportunity in the recruitment process and at the workplace. The law on disability discrimination was introduced in 1995 and we will consider it separately later in the chapter.

While unlawful discriminatory acts are usually committed by employees, liability tends to fall on employers, who, because of vicarious liability, are ultimately responsible for their actions. Of course an employee who commits a discriminatory act will usually be in breach of contract and be subject to disciplinary action. In addition he could be joined as a defendant with the employer in any legal proceedings. Even if the employer establishes a defence to the legal action the employee at fault may still be made liable. In *Yeboah v. Crofton* 2002 the Court of Appeal confirmed that an employer can be made personally liable for acts of unlawful discrimination committed by him during the course of employment even though the employer establishes a defence to the complaint. The provision on aiding the employer's act if the employer is liable *'or would be so liable but for'* means that personal liability can arise despite the employer's defence.

The Race Relations Act 1976 and the Sex Discrimination Act 1975 as amended, identify similar categories of unlawful acts in relation to discrimination, namely direct discrimination, indirect discrimination, and victimisation. It is convenient to set out these unlawful acts of discrimination in tabular form as a means of comparison.[19] Recent amendments however have removed the mirror image. In particular the Sex Discrimination (Indirect Discrimination and Burden of Proof) Regulations 2001 has amended the definition of indirect sex discrimination giving it a wider application. Regulations 3 and 4 change the definition of sex discrimination by substituting a new s.1 and s.3 into the 1975 Act and in particular changing the scope of indirect discrimination. The need for a *'requirement or condition'* is replaced by the broader concept of a *'provision criterion or practice'*. Also it is no longer necessary to show an inability for a *'considerably smaller'* section to be able to actually comply but rather that the provision would be to the detriment of a considerably larger proportion of women than men and to the complainant. The amendments are intended to widen the scope of indirect discrimination, which you will see is presently very difficult to establish. The fact that both pieces of legislation were drafted in a largely similar fashion means that case-law involving the Sex Discrimination Act will also serve as an aid to the interpretation of the provision of The Race Relations Act. It is proposed therefore to consider the provisions of both Acts in unison despite the recent amendments.

17. See Chapter 12
18. See Chapter 11
19. See the next page

Definitions

The Sex Discrimination Act 1975 is concerned with discrimination on grounds of gender either by males against females, or vice versa, and on grounds of marital status by treating a married person less favourably than an unmarried person. In *Nemes v. Allen* 1977 an employer in an attempt to cope with a redundancy situation dismissed female workers when they married. This was held to be unlawful direct discrimination on the grounds of sex and marital status.

We now have discrimination law in relation sexual orientation in the form of the Employment Equality (Sexual Orientation) Regulations 2003, and religion in the form of the Employment Equality (Religion or Belief) Regulations 2003. As yet there have been few claims of indirect discrimination[20] on the grounds of religious belief. In *Williams-Drabble v. Pathway Care Solutions* 2005 a practising Christian who had to resign when her shifts at a residential care home were changed so that it was impossible for her to attend church on Sundays brought such a claim. While the rota change was held to be a provision, practice or criterion, which applied to all workers, it put people of the same religious belief as the claimant at a particular disadvantage. The employer had not justified the new arrangement as a proportionate means of achieving a legitimate aim. Indirect discrimination was established as well as a breakdown in trust and confidence for the purposes of constructive dismissal. In March 2006 a major tribunal claim was presented by an HSBC manager on the grounds of sexual orientation discrimination.

As we said earlier Employment Equality (Age) Regulations 2006 will be brought into force from 1 October 2006. The Regulations will follow the format of other employment equality regulations by creating the unlawful acts of direct and indirect discrimination on the grounds of age as well as victimisation and harassment. The usual exception will apply of genuine occupational requirement[21] where the individual's age is a genuine characteristic proportionate to the requirements of the particular case.[22]

The Race Relations Act 1976 is more complex in relation to those it protects and under s.3 is concerned with discrimination on racial grounds which, is based upon colour, race, nationality, or ethnic or national origin. In *Race Relations Board v. Mecca* 1976 an individual telephoned to apply for a job but when the employer discovered the applicant was black, he put the telephone down. This was held to be unlawful direct discrimination as the applicant had been denied the opportunity to apply for a job on racial grounds. In *Seide v. Gillette Industries* 1980 the EAT held that the term 'Jewish' can mean membership of a particular race or ethnic group as well as a religion. Also in *Mandla v. Dowell Lee* 1983 the House of Lords held that Sikhs were a racial group within the meaning of the Act.

---

20. See later in the chapter
21. In rare cases
22. See later in the chapter

Race Relations Act, 1976	**Sex Discrimination Act, 1975**
Direct Discrimination	
This occurs where one person: Treats another less favourably on racial grounds e.g. by segregating workers by race. s.1(1)(a)	This occurs when one person: Treats another less favourably on the grounds of sex or marital status e.g. by providing women with different working conditions or selecting married women first for redundancy. s.1(1)(a) s.3(1)(b)
Indirect Discrimination	
This occurs where one person: Requires another to meet a provision criterion or practice which as a member of a racial group is less easily satisfied because:	This occurs where one person: Requires another to meet a provision criterion or practice which as a member of a particular sex or as a married person is less easily satisfied because:
it is to the detriment of a considerably larger proportion of that racial group and not justified	it is to the detriment of a considerably larger proportion of women than men and not justified
There would therefore be indirect discrimination if an employer required job applicants to have been educated only in Britain. s.1(1)(b)	There would therefore be indirect discrimination if an employer advertised for a clerk who is at least six feet tall. s.1(1)(b) s.3(1)(b)
Victimisation	
This occurs where one person: Treats another less favourably because the other has given evidence or information in connection with, brought proceedings under, or made allegations under the Act against the discriminator. s.2	This occurs where one person: Treats another less favourably because the other has given evidence or information in connection with, brought proceedings under, or made allegations under the Act or the Equal Pay Act, 1970, against the discriminator. s.4

In *Northern Joint Police Board v. Power* 1997 the EAT held that discrimination against an English person or a Scottish person based on national origins is discrimination on racial grounds within the meaning of the Race Relations Act. National origins in the definition has a different meaning from nationality, which points to citizenship.

Wakeman v. Quick Corporation 1999 was an unusual case where British employees of a Japanese company in the UK claimed that they had been discriminated against on the grounds of race when the redundancy pay package they received was substantially less than that paid to Japanese secondees in comparable roles. The EAT dismissed the complaint on the grounds that local recruits were very different from secondees who were in the UK temporarily. Locally hired Japanese would be paid on the same scale as locally hired UK nationals. The Court of Appeal agreed and held that the higher level of pay was not attributable to nationality but rather the status of the staff as secondees.

Certainly to share a common language would not on its own be sufficient to establish a racial group.

In *Commission for Racial Equality v. Dutton* 1989 the Court of Appeal was required to determine whether the display of a sign at a public house saying 'sorry no travellers' unlawfully discriminated against gypsies on racial grounds contrary to the Race Relations Act 1976. The court held that gypsies could come within the definition of 'racial group' as an identifiable group defined by reference to ethnic origins, having a long shared history, customs, and unique dialect. There remains a discernible minority who have not merged wholly in the population and have not lost their separateness and self awareness as being gypsies.

In *Crown Supplies PGA v. Dawkins* 1993 the Court of Appeal held that Rastafarianism is no more than a religious sect and not an ethnic group for the purposes of the Race Relations Act. As a consequence when a Rastafarian is refused employment because of the way in which he wears his hair that does not amount to discrimination under the 1976 Act.

Unlawful acts

In relation to employment, any discriminatory practice which comes within any of the three categories (direct, indirect or victimisation) is unlawful. Section 6 of the Sex Discrimination Act and section 4 of the Race Relations Act are similar in format and relate to discrimination by employers in the recruitment process, at the workplace and in relation to the termination of employment.

Under s.6(1) It is unlawful for a person, in relation to employment by him at an establishment in Great Britain, to discriminate against a woman:

   (a)   *in the arrangements he makes for the purpose of determining who should be offered that employment, or*

   (b)   *in the terms on which he offers her that employment, or*

   (c)   *by refusing or deliberately omitting to offer her that employment.*

(2)   *It is unlawful for a person, to discriminate against her:*

   (a)   *in the way he affords her access to opportunities for promotion, transfer or training, or to any other benefits, facilities or services, or by refusing or deliberately omitting to afford her access to them, or*

   (b)   *by dismissing her, or subjecting her to any other detriment.*

Under s.4(1) of the Race Relations Act It is unlawful for a person, in relation to employment by him at an establishment in Great Britain, to discriminate against another:

   (a)   *in the arrangements he makes for the purpose of determining who should be offered that employment, or*

   (b)   *in the terms on which he offers him that employment, or*

   (c)   *by refusing or deliberately omitting to offer him that employment.*

(2)   *It is unlawful for a person, to discriminate against that employee:*

   (a)   *in the terms of employment which he affords him, or*

   (b)   *in the way he affords him access to opportunities for promotion, transfer or training, or to any other benefits, facilities or services, or by refusing or deliberately omitting to afford him access to them, or*

   (c)   *by dismissing him, or subjecting him to any other detriment.*

It is therefore unlawful for a person in relation to employment by him to discriminate in the arrangements he makes for the purposes of deciding whom should be offered employment, the terms on which it is offered or by refusing to offer employment. Also where there is an existing employment relationship it is unlawful for an employer to discriminate in the way he gives access to opportunities for promotion, transfer, training or any other benefits, or refuses to afford such access. Furthermore, it is unlawful to discriminate by dismissing the complainant or subject him to any other detriment.

Can a claim of discrimination be maintained against an ex-employer?

> In *Relaxation Group v. Rhys-Harper* 2003 the House of Lords dealing with three separate appeal cases considered whether a discriminatory act committed by an employer, following an employee's dismissal, can still fall within the Discrimination legislation. Their Lordships ruled that the employment relationship can endure beyond the employment contract and that it is unlawful to discriminate against a former employee so long as there is a 'substantial connection' between the discriminatory conduct and the employment relationship. This is conveniently the same test provided for in the new Discrimination Regulations on race, sex, disability, religion sexuality and sexual orientation. It is unlawful for an employer to discriminate against a former employee where 'the discrimination arises out of and is closely connected to a relationship between the complainant and the respondent which has come to an end. Three particular cases have led to the litigation. Discrimination was alleged in the post dismissal appeal procedure; the claimant was denied or aggrieved at the content of a reference; and the claimant alleged different treatment for similar ex employees.

While the majority of unlawful discrimination complaints are brought by individuals presently in employment, both s.6 and s.4 recognise that a job applicant may suffer discriminatory practices in the recruitment process, particularly in the arrangements made for the purposes of determining who should be offered employment. If the alleged discriminatory practice relates to employment policies then it is the role of the Commissions to bring a complaint against an employer rather than an individual.

> In *Tyagi v. BBC World Service* 2001 an ex-employee complained of a continuing act of unlawful discrimination on racial grounds by the respondents. The Court of Appeal confirmed however that a job applicant cannot complain of a policy of continuing discrimination. Interpreting s.4 the court said that the words '*in the arrangements which the employer makes for determining who should be offered employment*' make it clear that what is being complained about is not employment generally but the particular employment that is being offered.

The anti-discrimination legislation provides redress for those who 'contract personally to execute any work or labour'. In *Quinnen v. Hovells* 1984 the EAT confirmed that the legislation was not confined to employees therefore and would also protect the self employed provided they are supplying personal services.

The EAT in *Hill Samuel Investment Services Group Ltd. v. Nwauzu* 1994 held that an insurance agent employed on a commission only basis as a self employed person offering personal services was protected by the Race Relations legislation. The employer was found to be guilty of discrimination when the issue of the complainant's race influenced the decision to terminate his contract. The issue faced by the Court of Appeal in *Mingeley v. Pennock and Ivory* 2004 was whether a taxi driver who owned his own vehicle and paid a taxi firm a weekly sum of £75 to operate under its radio and computer system fell within the definition . While the driver decided his own hours of work, when he did so he was required to wear the taxi firm's uniform and adhere to its scale of charges. The court held that the driver was not employed under a contract *'personally to execute work or labour'* in circumstances in which there was no mutual obligation to offer or accept work. While this meant that the tribunal had no jurisdiction to hear a complaint of race discrimination the court did comment as to whether it was truly the intention of Parliament to exclude such working relationships from the legislation. The House of Lords held in *Percy v. Church of Scotland* 2006 that a minister's relationship with the church constituted employment for the purposes of the Sex Discrimination Act.[23]

Time limits

Complaints of unlawful discrimination are made to the employment tribunal. Now following the Employment Act 2002 (Dispute Resolution) Regulations 2004 the tribunal will only accept a claim of unlawful discrimination if the claimant has submitted a written grievance to her employer,[24] alleging discrimination, and then waited 28 days.[25]

The time limit for presenting a complaint is three months from the act or last act of discrimination. The time limit may need to be extended to enable the parties to comply with the requirements if the Employment Act 2002 (Dispute Resolution) Regulations 2004.[26] The tribunal has power to permit a claim presented out of time if it is just and equitable in the circumstances. While time begins to run from the date of the last act complained of, the statutes also provide that *'any act extending over a period shall be treated as done at the end of the period'*.

> In *Calder v. James Finlay Corporation* 1989 the employers operated a subsidised mortgage scheme which had an unwritten rule excluding women. An employee lodged a complaint of unlawful discrimination five months after she was refused a mortgage subsidy but within three months of leaving employment. The EAT held that as long as the complainant was an employee, and the scheme operated, it constituted discrimination against her in the way she was *afforded access to the scheme*. The last *act* of discrimination was when her employment terminated so that she was within the three month time limit for lodging a complaint.

> In *Barclays Bank v. Kapur* 1991 an employer's refusal to give its Asian employees the same favourable pension terms as its European employees was held to be a continuing discriminatory act extending over the period of employment until the employment terminated.

In considering the meaning of the phrase *'continuing act'* under the Race Relations Act the EAT held in *Sougrin v. Haringey Health Authority* 1991 the loss of wages resulting from an alleged discriminatory grading of a black nurse did not qualify *A "continuing act" is a rule or regulatory scheme which during its currency continues to have a discriminatory effect on the grounds of sex or race. In the present case, the industrial tribunal had not erred in distinguishing between the decision not to change the appellant's grade and the failure to pay the appellant the same as her comparator. The "rule" was that the appellant was paid according to her grade and*

---

23. S.82(1)
24. Step one procedure see Chapter 11
25. Rule 3(2)c Employment Tribunal Rules of Procedure 2004
26. By a further 3 months

her complaint was that he was not up graded when her appeal was heard. The fact that he continued to be paid less than her comparator was a consequence of the decision on appeal and was not of itself a continuing act of discrimination.'

Even in cases where there is no 'continuing act', the time should not begin to run until it is clear that an act of discrimination has occurred and the course of action has crystallised.

In *Clarke v. Hampshire Electro-Plating Co Ltd.* 1991 the complainant, a metal polisher who had seventeen years employment with the defendants enquired about a supervisors post within the company. On the 25 April he was told by a director that he was not the person he was seeking for that particular appointment. On the 4 September a white man was appointed to the post and after consulting with his union the complainant, a black man, brought proceedings for racial discrimination. The tribunal held that it did not have jurisdiction to hear the complaint as it was out of time. The act of discrimination occurred on the 25 April and when proceedings were commenced the three month time limit had expired. On appeal the EAT disagreed however stressing the obvious point that the cause of action depended upon the employer's decision to appoint someone of a different racial group to the post. *'In determining when the act complained of was done, the question is whether the cause of action had crystallised on the relevant date, not whether the complainant felt that he had suffered discrimination on that date. The phrase "the act complained of was done" indicates that there was at that time an act of discrimination and that the cause of action could properly be said to be complete at that time, because otherwise there would be no point in bringing proceedings. Every case must depend upon its own facts as to the clarity of the crystallisation of any cause of action! In the present case, if the appellant's cause of action had not crystallised on the date when his promotion application was rejected, then the date a white man was appointed would have crystallised the cause of action by providing the comparison.'*

In *Cast v. Croydon College* 1997 the complainant, an information centre manager, made a request to her employers for job sharing or part-time work when her maternity leave expired. The request was refused on the 26 March 1992 and following further requests was given written reasons for the employer's decision on the 14 May 1993. The complainant resigned in early June and complained of unlawful sex discrimination on the 13 of August. Both the tribunal and the EAT felt that the claim was out of time as the act of discrimination occurred on the first refusal of the complainant's request which was nearly a year and half before she made the claim. *'It could not be held that time began to run when the complainant resigned because she could not work part-time and claimed constructive dismissal on the basis that the act of discrimination complained of was the dismissal. The proper analysis was that there was a detriment at the date the request to work part-time was refused and the later resignation was a result of that detriment. The resignation did not create a fresh cause of action.'*

If the complainant is out of time the tribunal still has jurisdiction to hear the complaint if it is *'just and equitable in the circumstances'*.

In *Forster v. South Glamorgan Health Authority* 1988 the failure to present the complaint within the time limits was found to be understandable as it was due to a change in the law. In such circumstances the EAT held that whether or not it is *'suitable'* to hear a complaint out of time is a *'question of fact and degree for the tribunal to determine in each case'*. In *Hawkins v. Ball & Barclays Bank Plc* 1996 the EAT confirmed that the tribunal has a wider discretion to allow claims out of time under discrimination legislation than unfair dismissal law.[27] The EAT felt that the tribunal was entitled to find that it could be just and equitable to extend the three month limitation period on the grounds that the complainant received incorrect legal advice. In *Aniagwu v. London Borough of Hackney* 1999 the EAT was prepared to extend the three month time limit in a race discrimination case where the applicant had delayed presenting the claim because he hoped that an internal appeal procedure would resolve the matter

A copy of a complaint of unlawful discrimination must be sent to ACAS who will pass it on to a conciliation officer. It is the duty of the conciliation officer to attempt to resolve the conflict between the parties, if requested by them to do so, or if he feels that he has a reasonable prospect of success. If there is no settlement and the tribunal finds that there has been discrimination it can declare the rights of the parties, award compensation up to the unfair discrimination limits, and recommend action to be taken by the guilty party to reduce the adverse affects of the discrimination. A failure to respond to a recommendation without good reason could lead to an award of increased compensation. Enforcement and redress are considered later in the chapter along with the role of the Commissions. You should appreciate that the Commission for Racial Equality, the Equal Opportunities Commission and the Disability Rights Commission have a role to play in encouraging, advising and providing financial assistance to prospective litigants. Furthermore only the Commissions may bring proceedings in respect of certain unlawful acts including discriminatory advertising, unlawful instruction to discriminate and unlawful inducements to discriminate.[28]

Direct Discrimination

Direct discrimination occurs where one person treats another less favourably on the grounds of sex, race, sexual orientation or religious belief.[29] This is the unlawful act most usually relied upon by claimants. If the reason for the less favourable treatment is found to be personality rather than a discriminatory reason such as nationality, then the claim will be rejected.

In *Madden v. Preferred Technical Group* 2005 the Court of Appeal considered the finding of a tribunal that there had been no discrimination notwithstanding that there was evidence of less favourable treatment than a hypothetical comparator with no satisfactory explanation from the employer. The Court agreed that the tribunal was entitled to decline to draw an inference of discriminatory conduct on the grounds of race[30] when there were no facts upon which to base that conclusion. The Court stressed that *'Tribunals are not required to draw inferences. If they either think that there is no evidence from which inferences can properly be drawn, or if they think the evidence does not warrant the drawing of inferences, they should say so. Where a tribunal has found less favourable treatment and no adequate explanation for it, there is an obligation on the tribunal to say that it is not drawing an inference 'because', and then go on to explain, shortly and succinctly, why, on the particular facts, it is not drawing an inference of discrimination. At the same time, however, there will be*

---

27. See Chapter 11
28. See later in the chapter
29. S.1(1)(a) Sex Discrimination Act 1975, Race Relations Act 1976
30. That the claimant was Irish

cases where the 'because' will be that the tribunal have examined the facts, made findings about what has happened, identified its actual or hypothetical comparator and come properly to the conclusion either that the facts simply do not warrant the drawing of an inference or that there is no evidential basis upon which an inference can be drawn.'

Burden of proof

In an allegation of direct discrimination the formal burden of proof was on the claimant This is no longer the case. A European Directive on sex discrimination and the burden of proof has led to the Sex Discrimination (Indirect Discrimination and Burden of Proof) Regulations 2001. Regulation 5 provides.[31]

'Where on the hearing of the complaint, the complainant proves facts from which the Tribunal could ... conclude in the absence of an adequate explanation that the respondent ... had committed an act of discrimination against the complainant which is unlawful ... the Tribunal should uphold the complaint unless the respondent proves that he did not commit that act.'

This section constitutes a formal reversal of the burden of proof in sex discrimination cases. It is suggested however that while there is no formal reversal of the burden of proof in race cases the present approach to proof is very similar. The difficulty is of course that often direct evidence of discrimination is not available and consequently it is sufficient if the complainant can establish primary facts from which inferences of discrimination can be drawn. Evidence is necessary therefore to draw comparison with some person, actual or hypothetical who falls outside the relevant racial group or who was or would be treated differently by the employer.

Once the primary facts indicate a prima facie case of discrimination therefore *'the employer is called on to give an explanation and, failing a clear and specific explanation being given by the employer to the satisfaction of the industrial tribunal, an inference of unlawful discrimination from the primary facts will mean the complaint succeeds'.*

Certainly there is no burden on an employer to disprove race discrimination but once a prime facie case has been made out a tribunal is entitled to turn to an employer for an explanation of the facts.

> In *King v. The Great Britain–China Centre* 1991 the applicant who was Chinese and educated in Britain, failed to secure the post of deputy director of the China Centre despite her obvious qualifications for the job. She was not one of the eight candidates short-listed who were all white and no other ethnic Chinese person had ever been employed at the Centre. The Court of Appeal held that the tribunal was entitled to conclude that it was legitimate for them to draw an inference of discrimination on racial grounds in the absence of a satisfactory explanation by the employer.

The Court of Appeal in the above case produced some helpful guidelines in determining a claim of unlawful race discrimination.

- It is for the applicant to make out a case of race discrimination on the balance of probabilities.

---

31. Inserted as s.63A Sex Discrimination Act 1975

- Direct evidence of race discrimination is rare, it is rarely admitted and is often based on an assumption that the applicant may not fit in rather than be ill-intentioned.

- Outcomes will often depend upon inferences drawn from primary facts and these can include evasive or equivocal replies to a questionnaire.

- If there are primary facts which point to a finding of a difference in race and the possibility of discrimination, in the absence of a satisfactory and adequate explanation by the employer it is legitimate for a tribunal to infer that the discrimination was on racial grounds.

At the conclusion of all the evidence the tribunal should make findings as to the primary facts and draw such inferences as they consider proper. They should then reach a conclusion on the balance of probabilities bearing in mind both the difficulties which face a person who complains of unlawful discrimination and the fact that it is for the complainant to prove his or her case.

Inititially it was thought that the new Regulations simply reflected the decision in *King*[32] in relation to the burden of proof in sex discrimination cases. *Barton v. Investec Henderson Crosthwaite Securities* 2003 provides helpful guidance to the Regulations and the EAT's interpretation of their content indicates that they go further. Once that the tribunal is satisfied that a prima facie case has been established then it is compelled to find discrimination unless the employer proves that there has been no discrimination. *'The tribunal shall uphold the complaint unless the respondent proves that he did not commit that act.'* In order to discharge that burden of proof the EAT held that *'it is necessary for the respondent to prove, on the balance of probabilities, that the treatment was in no sense whatsoever on the grounds of sex'.* The requirement *'no discrimination whatsoever'* is compatible with Burden of Proof Directive.

Further, in *Igen v. Wong* 2005 The Court of Appeal made it clear that the formal reversal of the burden of proof in discrimination cases makes it harder for the employer to defend the claim. Once that the claimant has established facts from which there could be an inference of discrimination then he will succeed unless the employer can show that there is another ground for the treatment.

The EAT decision in *Riley v. Base (t/a GLI Heating)* 2005 shows how clearly the two stage burden of proof test should be applied to alleged cases of discrimination. Hear, the employer, a heating engineer, admitted that he would not physically abuse a female apprentice in the same way that he had a male apprentice.[33] This admission of abusive conduct established a clear fact at the first stage from which the tribunal could conclude discriminatory treatment. The tribunal must then find unlawful discrimination unless the employer can at the second stage provide an adequate explanation for his conduct. In this case he could not, so the tribunal was bound to find unlawful discrimination.

While there is no legal obligation as a employer to give reasons for not selecting a candidate for a job the discrimination legislation provides that following a complaint an employer could be required to complete a questionnaire in which reason for decision making are asked. The questionnaire is admissible in evidence and evasive responses by the employer in the questionnaire will influence the tribunal's findings.

---

32. Above
33. Beating him with the 'apprentice correction stick'

In *Brighton Borough Council and Bishop v. Richards* 1993 the fact that the employer had delayed for two and half months in completing the questionnaire without good reason was thought to be significant by the EAT. In looking to the council for an answer to a prima facie case of discrimination the tribunal was entitled to take account of the delay with the questionnaire, the failure to provide an explanation as to why the successful candidate had been selected, the fact that no notes had been made of the significant stages of the selection process and the failure to monitor the equal opportunities policy.

An employer must now respond within 8 weeks to a statutory complainant's questionnaire relating to any alleged act of discrimination or harassment in employment.[34]

One major difficulty facing a claimant is that proving discrimination may be impossible without access to documents which the employer holds. Since they may be confidential the applicant cannot have access to them unless the industrial tribunal chairman believes that they are relevant.

The Court of Appeal in *Nassè v. SRC* 1979 held that an industrial tribunal should not order or permit the disclosure of a report or reference, given and received in confidence, except in rare cases where, after inspection of the document, the chairman decides that it is essential in the interests of justice that the confidence should be overridden.

Less favourable treatment

Direct discrimination extends not only to acts based on sex but also decisions made on gender-based criteria. The intention of the alleged discriminator is immaterial and tribunals should focus simply on whether the act or decision satisfies the *'but for'* test. Would the complainant have received the same treatment but for his or her sex? In *Horsey v. Dyfed CC* 1982 the act complained of was a refusal by the employer to recommend a married female social worker for secondment in London. The reason for the refusal was the fact that the wife's husband was already working in London and the employer believed that on completion of her secondment she would not return. This assumption the EAT held was one based on sex and in the circumstances constituted direct discrimination.

The words *'on the grounds of'* sex, race or marital status in the statutes would cover the situation where the reason for discrimination was a generalised assumption that men, women, married persons, or persons of a particular race, possess or lack certain characteristics. In *Skyrail Oceanic Ltd. v. Coleman* 1981 two rival firms employed a man and woman who were subsequently married and for reasons of confidentiality, the woman was dismissed. The Court of Appeal held by a majority that, as the reason for dismissing the woman rather than the man was based on a general assumption that the man in a marriage is the breadwinner, and this is an assumption based on sex, this amounted to unlawful discrimination. In *Cockroft v. Restus Ltd.* 1989 the complainant was not selected for an interview as a warehouse assistant as the employer required someone that had physical strength and the work was therefore unsuitable for a *'young lady'*. The presumption that only a *'big strong lad'* would be qualified for the job was held to be unlawful discrimination on the grounds of sex. In fact the complainant whose hobbies included weight lifting clearly demonstrated that physical strength was not an exclusively male characteristic.

---

34. Employment Equality (Sex Discrimination) Regulations 2005

In *Brumfitt v. Ministry of Defence* 2005 the claimant, a corporal in the RAF military police, brought a complaint of sexual discrimination in respect of harassment and the process by which her complaint of harassment had been investigated. Both the tribunal and the EAT dismissed her complaint. Despite the fact that the language she had been exposed to on a training course was '*offensive and humiliating to her as a woman*' she had not been exposed to it because of her sex but rather the requirement to attend the course. Applying the '*but for*' test it could not be said that but for her sex she would have been treated any differently. The EAT confirmed that what the House of Lords said in *Pearce v. Governing Body of Mayfield School* 2003 is '*crystal clear*'. In all cases of sex discrimination, including sexual harassment, a male comparator whether actual or hypothetical is required. Here the House of Lords stressed the need for a comparator in a sex discrimination claim so that a female who was harasses because of her sexual orientation must be compared with a homosexual of the opposite gender for the purposes of establishing direct sex discrimination. Also as the harassment was at the hands of school pupils rather than the school staff, she could not rely on vicarious liability under s.41. The case of *Burton and Rhule* was wrongly decided, for it cannot be vicarious liability to fail to protect employees from the acts of third parties unless that failure is itself less favourable treatment on the grounds of the victim's sex.[35]

The relevant questions in any claim of direct discrimination are:

(i)   has the claimant been treated can favourably than the comparator with whom she falls to be compared and

(ii) has she been so treated on the grounds of her sex, race etc.

In *Moonsar v. Fiveway Express Transport Ltd.* 2005 the female claimant alleged sex discrimination on the grounds that she shared an office where on a number of occasions, male colleagues downloaded pornographic images and this constituted an affront to her dignity. The EAT found that as such conduct was potentially degrading to a woman it was prima facie evidence of less favourable treatment. The burden then shifts to the employer to explain otherwise and as the employer did not attend the proceedings and provide an explanation, then a finding of sex discrimination would be made. In *Madden v. Preferred Technical Group* 2005,[36] the Court of Appeal held that even if a tribunal finds that there is less favourable treatment of the claimant in a discrimination claim there is no requirement to draw an inference that the treatment is on the ground of race, for the purposes of the burden of proof. If the tribunal does not draw a inference, it is obliged to say so and then explain, shortly and succinctly why on the particular facts, it is not drawing an inference of discrimination. Here the less favourable treatment was found to be due to a personality clash between the claimant and his manager and had nothing to do with the fact that the claimant was Irish.

Where discrimination is alleged to have occurred as a result of the cumulative effect of a number of incidents, for instance in cases of sexual or racial harassment, it would be tempting to consider each incident in isolation to determine whether it was discriminatory. This approach to raising an inference of discrimination is the wrong one said the EAT in *Driskel v. Peninsula Business Services Ltd.* 2000 The EAT approved of an earlier decision where it was held that in '*deciding whether or not to infer race discrimination, tribunals should not look at each incident separately to assess whether it occurred on racial grounds as this*

---

35. See later in the chapter
36. See earlier in the chapter

would inevitably have the effect of diminishing any eloquence that the cumulative effect of the primary fact may have'. In cases of harassment the EAT said that the tribunal should find all the facts and then decide the totality of the successive incidents.

> In *Ace Mini Cars Ltd. and Loy v. Albertie* 1990 the EAT held that there was unlawful direct discrimination by an employer who refused to employ a black female minicab driver because he believed that she would be the subject of racial attacks.

If the employer puts forward a number of reasons for his conduct, some valid and some discriminatory, then provided the discriminatory reason was an important factor, there is unlawful discrimination.

In *Owen & Briggs v. James* 1982 a case involving race discrimination, the complainant was a young black girl who had applied for a job as a shorthand typist with a firm of solicitors. She was interviewed for the job but rejected. When the post was re-advertised some months later she re-applied, but when she arrived for her interview the employer refused to see her. The same day a young white girl was appointed to the post despite the fact that her shorthand speed (35 words per minute) was far inferior to the complainant's (80 words per minute). It was also established that one of the partners of the firm had said to the successful *candidate 'why take on a coloured girl when English girls were available'*. The applicant's unlawful direct discrimination on the grounds of race was upheld in the industrial tribunal and on appeal in the Employment Appeal Tribunal. On further appeal to the Court of Appeal by the employer, it was argued that there could be no unlawful discrimination unless the sole reason for the conduct was the racial factor. This argument was rejected, the court deciding that it is sufficient if race is an important factor in the employer's decision and accordingly the appeal was unsuccessful.

It is still necessary to establish for a successful claim of sex discrimination that the complainant was subjected to a detriment on the grounds of his or gender. It is entirely permissible for a tribunal to decided that while the act complained of may be offensive and a detriment it may be equally so for a man or woman.

> This was the decision of the EAT in *Stewart v. Cleveland Guest (Engineering) Ltd.* 1994 when the substance of a female worker's complaint was the practice of the male dominated workforce in a factory displaying pin ups and calendars featuring naked and semi naked women. The management of the factory thought the complaint trivial and it was only following union intervention that the pictures were removed. Nevertheless when the complainant suffered hostility from fellow workers for her action she resigned and complained of unlawful sex discrimination. The EAT agreed with the tribunal that even though it was possible to find that the complainant suffered a detriment there may be no sex discrimination. The display of the pictures could be equally offensive to men so that there was no less favourable treatment on the grounds of sex for the purpose of direct discrimination. The tribunal, as the industrial jury, was best placed to decide whether the employer had discriminated against the complainant.

> In *Smith v. Safeways plc* 1996 the Court of Appeal provided guidance as to the circumstances in which an employer's dress and appearance code would constitute sex discrimination. Here the employer had adopted an appearance code which applied to delicatessen staff but which operated differently for men and women particularly in relation to length of hair. The complainant was dismissed for refusing to have his ponytail shortened claiming that a woman in

a comparable position would surely be required to keep her hair clipped back. The majority of the EAT thought that the hair length rule was discriminatory and unlike a dress code it was a rule which extended beyond working hours. In an important judgment the Court of Appeal disagreed with EAT and emphasised that *'there is an important distinction between discrimination between the sexes and discrimination against one or the other of the sexes. Discrimination is not failing to treat men and women the same. If discrimination is to be established, it is necessary to show not merely that the sexes are treated differently, but that the treatment accorded to one is less favourable than the treatment accorded to another'.* Appearance codes should be even handed and will not be discriminatory if their content is different *'if they enforce a common principle of smartness or conventionality, and takes as a whole and not garment for garment or item by item, neither gender is treated less favourably in enforcing that principle'.* The guide provided by the court therefore is that there should be a package approach to the effect of an appearance code in deciding whether it is discriminatory.

In *Department for Work and Pensions v. Thompson* 2004 the EAT was called on to determine the legal validity of a dress code operated by Jobcentre Plus which required its entire staff 'to present a clean and tidy appearance and to dress in a business like way.' Men were required to wear a collar and tie and women were required merely to 'dress appropriately and to a similar standard.' The applicant, Mr. Thompson, refused to wear a collar and tie and having received a formal warning he brought a sex discrimination claim. The tribunal concluded that by requiring men to wear clothing of a particular kind the employer was treating them less favourably on the grounds of sex and compensation was awarded. On appeal however the EAT took a different view and held that the question for the tribunal was whether, in the context of an overarching requirement for staff to dress in a professional and businesslike way the level of smartness which the employer required, applying contemporary standards of conventional dress-wear could only be achieved by men wearing a collar and tie. If that could be achieved by men dressing otherwise than in a collar and tie then the lack of flexibility would suggest less favourable treatment because it would not be necessary to restrict the men's choice of clothing. You do wonder whether the tribunal should be the final arbiter of smart male dress-wear?

A useful tool to attack the credibility of the employer's denial of discrimination is statistical evidence. This is particularly so when the management decisions on matters such as promotion or access to benefits are based upon subjective criteria such as *excellence, potential* or *efficiency*. In *Owen & Briggs v. James* 1982[37] if the firm of solicitors could have shown that they had other black employees, this could have gone a long way towards enabling the tribunal to reach a contrary decision. In *West Midlands Passenger Transport Executive v. Singh* 1988 the Court of Appeal ruled that statistical evidence of the employer's record of appointing ethnic minority applicants in the past, is material as to whether he has discriminated on racial grounds against a particular complainant. This enables a tribunal to scrutinise the employer's stated reason for rejecting the complainant and test it against comparative evidence of the employer's overall record. Ethnic monitoring is recommended by the Race Relations Code of Practice and *'unless the monitoring was to be merely an academic exercise, there*

---

37. See earlier in the chapter

> *could be no purpose in the Code of Practice encouraging the production of statistics save to use them as some indication of whether racial discrimination was being practised or not'.*

The types of questions asked in interviews may be of relevance to determine whether there has been discrimination.

> In *Saunders v. Richmond on Thames LBC* 1978 the EAT confirmed that it is not in itself unlawful to ask a question of a woman which would not be asked of a man. Here in an interview for a job as a golf professional, the female applicant was asked whether there were other female golf professionals and whether she thought that men would respond as well to a woman golf professional as to a man. Her claim of unlawful discrimination when she was not appointed did not succeed. The existence of direct discrimination depended upon whether she was treated less favourably on the grounds of sex than a man. Here, while the questions demonstrated an out of date attitude, the industrial tribunal was entitled to find that they were not asked with the intention of discriminating.

Asking questions about domestic circumstances would not necessarily be discriminating particularly when they could be asked of both male and female candidates.

In *Adams v. Strathclyde Regional Council* 1989 an applicant for a post as senior lecturer was asked at her interview how many children she had and their ages. This question was held not to constitute unlawful discrimination given that it could have equally have been asked of a male candidate and had been asked simply to help put her at her ease in the interview despite having the very opposite affect.

An important issue is whether it is possible to be the victim of unlawful discrimination when any employee suffers less favourable treatment for failing to implement an employer's racist policy.

> In *Weathersfield Ltd. t/a Van and Truck Rental v. Sargent* 1999 the applicant had obtained a job as a receptionist for a van rental company and was told during her induction that she was to effectively discriminate against potential clients who were from ethnic minorities. Refusing to implement what she felt was a racist policy she left claiming constructive dismissal constituting unlawful discrimination. When she succeeded before the tribunal and the EAT the employer finally appealed to the Court of Appeal claiming firstly that there was no dismissal and secondly if there was less favourable treatment it was not on racial grounds. The court held that an employee is unfavourably treated on racial grounds if they are required to carry out a racially discriminatory policy even though the instruction concerned a different racial group to the complainants. The employee was entitled to leave because of the repudiatory conduct of the employer without notifying the employer of the reason. *'For many employees the more outrageous or embarrassing are the instructions given to them, or suggestions made to them, the less likely they may be to argue the point there and then. They may reasonably wish to remove themselves at the first opportunity and with a minimum of discussion. Leaving the employment without notifying the reason does not preclude a finding of constructive dismissal though it will usually make it more difficult to obtain such a finding.'*

It is also unlawful to show an intention to commit an act of discrimination in relation to employment. Therefore the publication of an advertisement which invites applicants for the post of salesman or barmaids would constitute unlawful discrimination.[38]

Under the EC 'Equal Treatment Directive' the UK is required to implement the principle of *'equal treatment for men and women as regards access to employment'. The directive also provides that 'there shall be no discrimination whatsoever on grounds of sex in the conditions, including selection criteria, for access to all jobs or posts'.*

> In *Dekker v. Stichting Vormingscentrum voor Jonge Volwassenen Plus* 1991 the European Court of Justice held that it is a breach of the directive to refuse to employ a woman because she is pregnant despite the fact that this could mean grave financial consequences for the employer. If a woman receives less favourable treatment because she is pregnant this is direct discrimination and there is no need to establish that a man in comparable circumstances would not have been treated better. Pregnancy dismissals are considered in Chapter 7.

> In *Webb v. EMO Air Cargo (UK) Ltd. (No 2)* (1996) the European Court of Justice held that it amounts to sex discrimination to refuse to employ a woman who due to her pregnancy cannot immediately perform the job. This was the case in *Malburg v. Land Macklenburg Vorpommen* 2000 where a nurse was refused a permanent post in a heart clinic because being eight weeks pregnant she could not work in an operating theatre for health and safety reasons. The European Court of Justice held that this was unlawful sex discrimination.[39]

Sexual and Racial Harassment

Following the Equal Treatment Directive there is now a statutory definition of harassment which applies to all forms of discrimination. Harassment is defined in s.3A Race Relations Act 1976, the Equal Opportunities (Sex Discrimination) Regulations 2005, s.3B Disability Discrimination Act 1995, s.5 Employment Equality (Religion or Belief) Regulations 2003 and s.5 Employment Equality (Sexual Orientation) Regulations 2003.

Harassment occurs when, on the grounds of another person's race, ethnic or national origins, gender, disability, sexual orientation or religion of belief, a person

…engages in unwanted conduct which has the purpose or effect of:

(a) violating that other person's dignity; or

(b) creating an intimidating, hostile, degrading, humiliating or offensive environment for him.

Such conduct shall be regarded as having the effect specified in (a) or (b) only if, having regard to all the circumstances, including in particular the perception of that other person, it shall reasonably be considered as having that effect.

Racial harassment could amount to discrimination on racial grounds and constitute unlawful direct discrimination under the Race Relations Act. The European Race Directive 2000

---

38. See later in the chapter
39. See Chapter 1

usefully defines racial harassment as occurring when '*unwanted conduct relating to racial or ethnic origin takes place with the purpose of or effect of violating the dignity of a person and of creating an intimidating, hostile, degrading, humiliating or offensive environment*'.

Sexual harassment while originally not referred to specifically in the Sex Discrimination Act has been held to constitute unlawful direct discrimination for which an employer could be made vicariously responsible. The EC Resolution on the Protection of the Dignity of Men and Women at Work defines sexual harassment as conduct of a sexual nature, or other conduct based on sex affecting the dignity of men and women at work which is:

- unwanted, unreasonable and offensive to the recipient;
- used as a basis for employment decisions; or
- such as to create an intimidating, hostile or humiliating work environment for the recipient.

The Code recommends that employers should facilitate a climate of opinion at work which inhibits sexual harassment. This could involve the issuing of a policy statement which is communicated and promoted through training. Also employers should adopt clear and precise procedures for dealing with complaints including sympathetic counsellors and incorporating independent and objective investigations. A range of conduct which could constitute sexual harassment emerges from the case-law including:

- physical attacks;
- brushing against the victim;
- making suggestive statements or telephone calls;
- pressurising the victim to enter into a sexual relationship;
- sending the victim suggestive material.

In *Scott v. Commissioners of Inland Revenue* 2004 the Court of Appeal stressed that a balanced, common sense approach must be taken to sexual harassment and sometimes a careful explanation of the effect of the behaviour complained of to the alleged harasser, together with a warning, will be enough to end the matter. The tribunal had been wrong to trivialise the complaint of sexual harassment made against the claimant, for sexual harassment is always a serious matter in the workplace that must always be addressed. Incidents that are trivial in themselves can become serious if they are recurrent, and the employer ignores them at his peril. '*This was exactly the kind of situation which, if management ignores or trivialises it, can make the workplace a source of tension and unhappiness and escalate into formal disputes. The problem was that, the disciplinary wheels having been set prematurely and unnecessarily in motion against the applicant, nobody seemed willing or able to halt them.*'

Reed and Bull Information Systems Ltd. v. Stedman 1999 was considered in Chapter 4 as an illustration of how the failure of an employer to investigate alleged incidents of sexual harassment constituted a breach of the implied term of trust and confidence. The bullying behaviour of the manager with sexual overtones amounted to harassment as a course of unacceptable and unwelcome conduct which pervaded sexual innuendo and a sexist stance. This was despite the fact that there was no single incident capable of constituting sexual harassment. The view of Mr. Justice Morison the retiring President of the EAT provides helpful guidance to tribunals to identify unlawful sexual harassment. '*The essential characteristic of sexual harassment is that it is words or conduct which are unwelcome to the recipient and it is for the recipient to decide for themselves what is acceptable to them and what they regard as offensive. Because it is for each individual to determine what they find unwelcome or offensive, there may be a gap between what a tribunal would regard as acceptable and what the individual in question was prepared to tolerate. It does not follow that the complaint must be dismissed because the tribunal would not have regarded the acts complained of as unacceptable. It is particularly important that the tribunal should not carve up the case into a series of specific incidents and try and measure the harm or detriment in relation to each. Once unwelcome sexual interest has been shown by a man to a woman, she may feel bothered about his attentions which, in a different context would appear quite unobjectionable. There may be difficult factual issues to resolve as to whether conduct is unwelcome. Some conduct, if not expressly invited, could be described as unwelcome. A woman does not have to make it clear in advance that she does not want to be touched in a sexual manner. At the lower end of the scale, a woman may appear, objectively, to be unduly sensitive to what might otherwise be regarded as unexceptional behaviour. But because it is for each person to define their own levels of acceptance, the question would then be whether by words or conduct she made it clear that she found such conduct unwelcome. Provided that any reasonable person would understand her to be rejecting the conduct of which she was complaining, continuation of the conduct would, generally, be regarded as harassment.'*

Vicarious liability

An employer may be made vicariously liable for the action of his employees committed during the course of employment and this would include sexual, racial, sexual orientation or religious harassment constituting unlawful discrimination.[40] In fact if sexual harassment constitutes less favourable treatment, it could also amount to unlawful direct discrimination on the grounds of race, sex, sexuality or religion. Liability for sexual harassment is imposed vicariously on the employer.

Under s.41(1) Anything done by a person in the course of his employment shall be treated for the purposes of this Act as done by his employer as well as by him, whether or not it was done with the employer's knowledge or approval.

> *(2)   Anything done by a person as agent for another person with the authority (whether express or implied, and whether precedent or subsequent) of that other person shall be treated for the purposes of this Act as done by that other person as well as by him.*
>
> *(3)   In proceedings brought under this Act against any person in respect of an act alleged to have been done by an employee of his it shall be a defence for that person to prove that he took such steps as were reasonably practicable to prevent the employee from doing that act, or from doing in the course of his employment acts of that description.*

In *Canniffe v. East Riding of Yorkshire Council* 2000 the complainant brought a sex discrimination case against her employer based upon a set of serious acts of sexual harassment by a work colleague. The employer accepted that they were vicariously liable under s.41(1) but sought to establish a s.41(3) defence. They argued that better implementation of policies about sex discrimination and harassment would have had no effect on the criminal assault carried out by the perpetrator and the tribunal agreed. On appeal however the EAT did not believe that the employer had established a s.41(3) defence. *'The proper approach is first to identify whether the respondents took any steps at all to prevent the employee from doing the act*

---

40. See Chapter 8 Vicarious Liability

or acts complained of in the course of employment and secondly, having identified the steps, to consider whether there were any further acts that they could have taken which were reasonably practicable.'

An action against the harasser could of course be brought in tort and if his conduct constitutes a criminal offence there could be a prosecution. Under the Sex Discrimination Act however he may only be made liable as a secondary party.

This means that if the harasser is acting outside the course of employment the victim could not claim against him under the Sex Discrimination Act. Alternative actions in tort for the victim include assault and battery and more significantly the increasing recognition of a separate tort of harassment. In *Burnett v. George* 1992 the Court of Appeal recognised a separate tort of impairment of health caused by the intentional molestation of another. Here, and in *Khorasandjian v. Bush* 1993 an injunction was granted to restrain threats made by telephone. In the later case the Court of Appeal went some way to recognising a tort of personal injury by molestation.

Under s.42(1) A person who knowingly aids another person to do an act made unlawful by this Act shall be treated for the purposes of this Act as himself doing an unlawful act of the like description.

Usually the harasser will escape liability under the Act if the employer rebuts the allegation of vicarious liability. However if the employer establishes a s.41(3) defence by showing he has taken reasonably practicable steps to prevent harassment it seems that the harasser could still be liable under s.42(2). So despite the employer's defence, if vicarious liability is established the employee who committed the unlawful act of sex discrimination is liable for it. So held the EAT in *AM v. LWC 2. SPV* 1999 where a police officer was held to be liable for his own discriminatory act.

> In *Yeboah v. Crofton* 2002 the Court of Appeal confirmed that an employer can be made personally liable for acts of unlawful discrimination committed by him during the course of employment even though the employer establishes a defence to the complaint. 'The provision on aiding the employer's act if the employer is liable *'or would be so liable but for'* means that personal liability can arise despite the employer's defence.

For the purposes of vicarious liability employment has an extended meaning[41] so that an employer would be responsible for the actions of self employed workers who were personally executing work or labour such as sales representatives or building workers. The need to establish *'course of employment'* seems to be less onerous in sexual harassment cases and it seems to be sufficient to show that the misconduct occurs during the normal interaction of employees at the workplace. This approach is necessary if women are to be protected at the workplace. It is difficult however to reconcile with the decision in *Irving & Irving v. The Post Office* 1987 where a distinction was drawn between the employee who acts in the course of his employment and the employee who takes advantage of the opportunity provided by his employment in order to commit the wrongful act. Now however, as a result of the important decision of the Court of Appeal in *Jones v. Tower Boot* 1997 it seems that in race discrimination cases also the expression *'course of employment'* should be given its *'everyday meaning'* and extend to acts committed during working hours.

---

41. S.82(1)

In *Chief Constable of the Lincolnshire Police v. Stubbs* 1999 the EAT upheld the tribunal's decision that a police officer was acting in the course of his employment when he subjected a fellow officer to sexual harassment contrary to the Sex Discrimination Act 1975. The EAT found the employer vicariously liable despite the fact that the conduct complained of occurred at social events outside the police station. The tribunal had decided that such gatherings were extensions of the working day and so within the course of employment for purposes of liability.

The victim of sexual harassment at the workplace has a potential claim for unlawful direct sex discrimination, victimisation or even unfair dismissal where appropriate. Under the Trade Union Reform and Employment Rights Act 1993 tribunals can now make restricted reporting orders in cases involving sexual misconduct, to protect the identity of those making or affected by the allegations. Breaking such an order is a criminal offence punishable by a fine of up to £5,000.

In *Bracebridge Engineering Ltd. v. Derby* 1990 the EAT held that a single act of sexual harassment was a 'detriment' to the complainant within the meaning of s.6 of the Sex Discrimination Act. *'A single incident of sexual harassment, provided it is sufficiently serious, clearly falls within the proper intention and meaning of the statute as it is an act of discrimination against a woman because she is a woman.'* When the act of sexual harassment took place the perpetrators were supposedly engaged in exercising their disciplinary and supervisory function and were consequently within the course of their employment for the purpose of vicarious liability. Here when the employee had left her job because of the treatment she received and her employer's failure to treat her allegations seriously, this also amounted to a constructive dismissal which was unfair.

In *Insitu Cleaning Co Ltd. v. Heads* 1995 the EAT considered whether a single act of verbal sexual harassment is sufficient to found a complaint of direct sex discrimination. Here the complaint related to a derogatory remark made by a young male manager in a meeting and directed at the complainant, a female area supervisor. Despite the fact that the remark referred to complainant's breasts the employer argued that it was not sex related and therefore could not amount to direct discrimination. The EAT agreed with the tribunal that the employer was vicariously liable for the sexual harassment which constituted direct sex discrimination. *'The appellant's argument that the remark was not sex-related in that a similar remark could have been made to a man, for example, in relation to a balding head or beard, was absurd. A remark by a man about a woman's breasts cannot sensibly be equated with a remark by a woman about a bald head or a beard. One is sexual, the other is not. The industrial tribunal was entitled to find that the respondent suffered a detriment as a result of the remark. Detriment means no more than disadvantage. For the boss's son to make a sexual remark causing distress to a female employee nearly twice his age was a form of bullying and not acceptable in the workplace in any circumstances. As the European Commission Code of Practice on measures to combat sexual harassment makes clear, such conduct is likely to create an intimidating, hostile and humiliating work environment for the victim.'* The EAT confirmed that one incident of verbal sexual harassment can constitute direct discrimination depending on its seriousness.

Unfortunately this eminently sensible view of gender specific words being inherently discriminatory against a female, and different from the abuse of a male, was not followed in *Pearce v. Governing Body of Mayfield School* 2003.[42] Here a teacher had been driven out of her job by a campaign of homophobic abuse from her pupils. Applying the male comparator test the House of Lords held that there was no evidence that a male homosexual would have been treated less favourably so that there was no discrimination. The EAT had also given a narrow view of the responsibility of the school for the conduct of its pupils. *'Before finding a school or any similar body to have subjected an employee to discrimination, not only must the steps be identified which the school failed to take and could have taken, but also there must be a conclusion that taking those steps would have prevented or reduced discrimination, so as to hold that the school was guilty of subjecting its employee to discrimination by the absence of those steps being taken.'*

This is a view which is disappointing, given that many labour theorists would suggest that sexist language or gender specific abuse is inherently or automatically discriminatory.

Normally sex and race discrimination cases require a comparative approach but in harassment scenarios the courts have established an exceptional category where conduct is regarded as *sex or race specific*. Both the EAT and the Court of Appeal held in *Sidur v. Aeorospace Composite Technology Ltd.* 2000 that when the applicant was racially abused and assaulted on a works outing the conduct of the harasser was race specific. The Court of Appeal felt however that when the employer dismissed the applicant as well as the harasser for being violent and so contravened company policy, this was not race specific conduct. This harsh interpretation of the policy however did lead to a finding of unfair dismissal.

It is inevitable that in a claim for sexual harassment the employment tribunal will award compensation for hurt feelings and decide the level that is appropriate whether or not compensation is payable under any other head. In *Sharifi v. Strathclyde DC* 1992 the EAT held that £500 was at or near the minimum for hurt feelings. Certainly conduct which causes distress should be reflected in the level of compensation and substantial awards should be made if the harassment leads to depression, resignation or transfer. In *Cobbold v. Sawyer t/a Immigrants Advisory Bureau* 1993 the complainant was a seventeen year old who walked out of her first job as a result of sexual harassment by her manager. Her claim off sex discrimination was upheld and the meagre award of £150 for hurt feelings was increased by the EAT on appeal to £750.

Increasingly the tribunals are recognising that injury to feelings should be more substantially compensated and that awards should also be made against individually named harassers.

> In *Whitehead v. Isle of Wight NHS Trust and Others* 1999 a female paramedic was awarded £67,337 including £37,500 for injury to feelings when she was subjected to sexual harassment and her employers had failed to deal with the problem. She suffered stress and ill health as a result and was awarded £2,500 personally against the harasser.

> In *Burton and Rhule v. De Vere Hotels* 1996 the EAT held that two black waitresses who were employees at a hotel had suffered sexual and racial harassment when they were required to work in a banqueting hall during Bernard Manning's performance as guest speaker. Their employer, the hotel, could be held vicariously liable for subjecting the staff to racial abuse and sexual harassment by a third party if the employer had sufficient control to minimise the harm by adopting good employment practice. *'An employer subjects an employee to the detriment of*

---

racial harassment if he causes or permits harassment serious enough to amount to a detriment to occur in circumstances in which he can control whether it happens or not. A persons subjects another to something if he causes or allows that thing to happen in circumstances where he can control whether it happens or not. Foresight of the events, or the lack of it, is not determinative of whether the events were under the employer's control.'

The decision in Burton is included despite the fact that in *Brumfitt*[43] the EAT felt that it was wrongly decided in the context of vicarious liability.

Indirect Discrimination

Indirect discrimination, a more subtle form of discrimination than direct discrimination, is designed to cover overt yet not blatant acts of discrimination. A complaint of indirect discrimination could be brought under the UK legislation or the Equal Treatment Directive if applicable. Indirect discrimination occurs where a person requires another to meet '*a provision, criterion or practice*' which as a member of a particular sex, race, sexuality or religious belief is less easily satisfied.[44] This is because the proportion of those of that type who can comply with it is smaller, and it is to the complainant's detriment. This new definition was introduced under the European Race Directive and the Sex Discrimination (Indirect Discrimination and Burden of Proof) Regulations 2001.

The words '*requirement or condition*' from the original definition have been replaced with the words '*a provision, criterion or practice*' which have a much wider connotation. The new words indicate that almost any aspect of a person's job which has a disparate impact and is not justifiable could come within the definition. This could include matters such as recruitment criterion where employers identify essential or desirable qualities for the successful applicant. While the phrase 'requirement or condition' suggested a mandatory requirement , the new definition indicates that a discretionary criterion could be indirectly discriminatory. It was held in *Perera v. Civil Service Commission* 1981 that in an allegation of indirect discrimination it is necessary to show that the requirement or condition is mandatory rather than one of a number of criteria which the employer would take into account. Also in *Meer v. London Borough of Tower Hamlets* 1988 the requirement was alleged to be job selection criteria, one of which was to have experience working in Tower Hamlets. The fact that this particular criteria was not mandatory meant that it could not constitute a requirement for the purposes of indirect discrimination. Under the new definition the criterion for selection could fall within the definition of indirect discrimination.

As yet there have been few claims of indirect discrimination on the grounds of religious belief. In *Williams-Drabble v. Pathway Care Solutions* 2005 a practising Christian who had to resign when her shifts at a residential care home were changed so that it was impossible for her to attend church on Sundays brought such a claim. While the rota change was held to be a provision, practice or criterion, which applied to all workers, it put people of the same religious belief as the claimant at a particular disadvantage. The employer had not justified the new arrangement as a proportionate means of achieving a legitimate aim. Indirect discrimination was established, as well as a breakdown in trust and confidence for the purposes of constructive dismissal.

---

43. See earlier in the chapter
44. S.1(1)(b) Sex Discrimination Act and Race Relations Act

For the purposes of showing that the proportion of the complainant type who can comply with the condition is smaller there is no need to produce elaborate statistical evidence, but rather a common sense approach is to be encouraged. Nevertheless to succeed it is necessary to show that the proportion who can comply is considerably smaller.

> In *Price v. Civil Service Commission* 1978 the complainant alleged indirect discrimination on the grounds of sex because far fewer women than men could comply with the age limits of seventeen and a half to twenty eight to qualify as an eligible candidate for the executive officer grade. By comparing the proportion of qualified women with the proportion of qualified men, it is obvious that as a larger number of women of that age group will be likely to be having or bringing up children, then the proportion who can comply with the age requirement is less. The EAT held that as the proportion who can comply in practice is less and the requirement was not justifiable, there was unlawful indirect discrimination.

Even where indirect discrimination is established there are no damages payable if it is shown to be unintentional. So, unlike direct discrimination, the intention of the alleged discriminator is relevant. Where the fundamental purpose of the claim is to secure compensation for the victim there is little point in presenting a complaint where there was no intention to discriminate.

> In *Tickle v. Governors of Riverview CE School and Surrey County Council* 1994 the tribunal held that damages are available for unintentional indirect discrimination if the claim is brought under the Equal Treatment Directive. Here, as the teacher involved was employed by a local authority, an emanation of the state, the Directive was applicable.

Although no damages are payable for unintentional indirect discrimination in practice under the statute it is the employer who must satisfy the burden of establishing that the requirement or condition was not applied with the intention of treating the claimant less favourably. In *Walker Ltd. v. Hussain* 1996 the EAT held that an employer had indirectly discriminated against Muslim employees by refusing to allow staff to take holidays during the busy season and so preventing the claimants from taking a day off work to celebrate a religious holiday. The EAT supported the tribunal's award of £1000 for injury to feelings having taken account of the nature of the detriment, the claimants length of service, work record, upset and distress caused and the imposition of final written warning when they took the day off. Stressing the burden of proof on the employer under the statute the EAT held that an act of indirect discrimination is applied intentionally at the time of the act if the person (a) wants to bring about the state of affairs which constitute the unfavourable treatment and (b) knows the prohibited result will follow from his acts. It is permissible for a tribunal to infer that an employer wants to produce certain consequences from his acts if he knows what those consequences will be.

It is a question of fact in each case to determine the proportion of the complainant's group who can comply with the requirement or condition in practice. By deciding what proportion of the complainant's group can comply and comparing that figure with the proportion of qualified persons who can comply but fall outside the group, it is possible to decide whether it is considerably smaller.

> In *Fulton v. Strathclyde Regional Council* 1986 the employer decided that certain social work posts should be exclusively for full-time staff. Of the basic grade social workers the statistics showed that 90% of the women could comply with

the full-time requirement and all of the men. It was held on a complaint of indirect discrimination that 90% is not *'considerably smaller'* than 100% and so the claim must fail.

Now following the Sex Discrimination (Indirect Discrimination and Burden of Proof Regulations) 2001 there is a changed wording to the phrase *'considerably smaller proportion of women who can comply'*. The new wording *'to the detriment of a considerably larger proportion of women than men'* is much more straightforward and simply showing that the provision, criterion or practice is to the womans detriment will suffice.

The success of an indirect discrimination claim will turn on the choice of the pool for comparison.

> In *Pearse v. Bradford MC* 1988 one 'requirement' of eligibility to apply for a post as a senior lecturer in a college was that the applicant was presently a full-time employee of the local authority in the college. This 'requirement' was claimed to be indirectly discriminatory, the complainant alleging that the proportion of women who could comply with it, 21.8% of the academic staff, was considerably smaller than the proportion of men, 46.7% of the academic staff. The EAT held that the correct pool for comparison was not all of the full-time academic staff but rather those academic staff who had appropriate qualifications for the post. Consequently the statistical evidence put forward by the complainant was inappropriate and she had failed to show that the requirement of being employed full-time had a disproportionate impact on the qualified women. The argument that the pool for comparison must be extended to those eligible to apply, could not be accepted, for it would be irrational to ignore the fact that appropriate qualifications were a pre-requisite to apply for the post.

The definition of indirect race discrimination also requires the complainant to have suffered a detriment and the requirement or condition must not be justifiable. The fact that the complainant has been adversely affected by the condition is sufficient to establish a detriment.

> In *Clymo v. Wandsworth LBC* 1989 the issue before the EAT was whether the failure to extend job sharing to managerial positions within the respondent council constituted indirect sex discrimination. Both the complainant and her husband were employed as librarians by the defendant council. The complainant had a more senior position with managerial responsibilities and following maternity leave she applied to share her job with her husband so that they could share child care between them. The council's job sharing policy covered non-managerial positions. Her request was consequently refused, and she resigned and presented a claim for unlawful indirect discrimination. Both the industrial tribunal and the EAT rejected the claim. The EAT held that the unavailability of job sharing was not a denial of access to a *'facility'* since no such facility was currently available. Neither was the complainant subjected to a detriment by being refused access to a facility which was not available and the provision of an advantage which is not available to others is not a detriment.

It is open however for the defendant to show as a question of fact that in all the circumstances the requirement is justifiable.

In *Hardys & Hansons plc v. Lax* 2005 the Court of Appeal considered the test of justification in an indirect discrimination claim and found that a tribunal should make its own judgment as to whether the employer has shown that an indirectly discriminatory provision, criterion, or practice is objectively justified. Here a recruitment manager returning from maternity leave wished to return on a job share or part-time basis and was refused as no such role was available. When she was dismissed for redundancy she brought a claim for indirect sex discrimination and succeeded in the tribunal. On appeal the employer raised the reasonable response test to justify the decision to refuse the work proposal. The Court of appeal rejected this approach and held that the tribunal must make its own judgment as to whether a proposal is reasonable having undertaken a fair and detailed analysis of the working practices and business considerations involved. A decision by an employer in good faith that a flexible work proposal is not practicable could still constitute sex discrimination. Also in *British Airways plc v. Stamer* 2005 BA was held to have indirectly discriminated against a female pilot by refusing to reduce her hours by 50%.

In *Singh v. Rowntree Mackintosh* 1979 the complainant objected to a 'no beard rule' operated by confectioners, which was alleged to be indirectly discriminatory against Sikhs. Here the EAT held that while the rule was discriminatory, it was a justifiable requirement on the grounds of hygiene, supported by medical advice, and therefore not unlawful. The burden of proof was on the employer to justify the requirement or condition and here the tribunal recognised that in adopting standards *the employer must be allowed that independence of judgment as to what he believes is a common expedient in the conduct of his business. Certainly the requirement must be more than convenient but need not be necessarily essential.*

If a person produces reasons for doing something which would be acceptable to right thinking people as sound and tolerable reasons for so doing, then he has justified his conduct.

In *Hampson v. Department of Education and Science* 1989 Balcombe L J held that to determine whether a condition is justifiable or not, an objective standard is required in each case. *'Justifiable' 'requires an objective balance to be struck between the discriminatory effect of the condition and the reasonable needs of the party who applies that condition'.*

In *Cobb v. Secretary of State for Employment and Manpower Services Commission* 1989 on a complaint of unlawful indirect discrimination, the tribunal held that the eligibility criteria for admission to the Community Programme, which included receipt of the appropriate social security benefit, had a disproportionate impact on women in general and married women in particular. Nevertheless the EAT confirmed that the tribunal is entitled to find that such a criterion is justifiable in the circumstances without reliance on a mass of statistical or sociological evidence but rather by taking a broad and rational view of the circumstances. *'In a case of indirect discrimination it is for the respondent to satisfy the tribunal that the decisions which he took were objectively justified for economic, administrative or other reasons. It is for the tribunal to decide what facts it found proved and to carry out the balancing exercise involved, taking into account all the surrounding circumstances and giving due emphasis to the degree of discrimination caused against the object or aim to be achieved, the principle of proportionality.'*

The fact that a claim of indirect sex discrimination may also be founded upon Article 141 of the *Treaty of Rome* and the Equal Treatment Directive is no better illustrated than by a direct challenge to national legislation brought by the Equal Opportunities Commission in 1994. In a momentous judgment in 1994 the House of Lords ruled by a majority of four to one that UK legislation that gives part-time workers, predominantly women, less protection than full-time workers, predominantly men, is incompatible with European Union law as to equality between employees.

> In *R v. Secretary of State for Employment, ex parte the Equal Opportunities Commission* 1994 the House of Lords considered the Employment Protection (Consolidation) Act 1978 which confers statutory rights relating to unfair dismissal and redundancy on full-time employees who have been continuously employed for two years. When compared with the position of part-time employees (employed between eight and sixteen hours) who qualify for such statutory rights after five years employment, the Lords held that such provisions indirectly discriminate against women.

The Equal Opportunities Commission the Commission for Racial Equality and Disability Rights Commission have issued Codes of Practice to provide guidance to employers as to how to avoid discrimination particularly in recruitment. While the Codes are not law they are admissible in evidence in any proceedings under the legislation. An employer who complies with the Codes is more likely to avoid liability. One recommendation that employers should adopt is to monitor their recruitment processes, for resultant statistics could be used to overturn an inference of discrimination. Certainly this would be useful information to enable an employer to comply with the questionnaire procedures available to an individual considering or having brought proceedings under the discrimination legislation. It is of course much more difficult to challenge recruitment decisions as discriminatory when informal recruitment methods are used because of the secrecy attached to them. Quite often jobs are filled without advertising or interviewing with staff appointed on the basis of personal recommendations. In these circumstances if ethnic minorities or a particular gender do not have access to these informal networks then they will continue to be under represented.

Victimisation

Protection from victimisation at the workplace is a fundamental right for potential equal opportunity claimants and has been greatly enhanced by a recent House of Lords decision. Victimisation you will remember is less favourable treatment because the claimant has given evidence or brought proceedings under the legislation.[45] The Court of Appeal has long held that for a victimisation claim to succeed the claimant must establish a conscious motive on the part of the discriminator. In *Nagarajan v. London Regional Transport* 1999 the House of Lords found no justification from the language of the legislation to interpret victimisation in this way. To establish discrimination by way of victimisation it is necessary to establish that the less favourable treatment suffered was *'significantly influenced'* or an *'important cause'* of the fact that the claimant had brought proceedings against the employer. Here the applicant had been victimised in respect of an unsuccessful application for a vacancy because the interviewers were consciously or subconsciously influenced by the fact that he had brought proceedings. The House of Lords recognised that unconscious

---

45. S.2 Race Relations Act, s.4 Sex Discrimination Act

prejudice may be just as prevalent as deliberate discrimination *'All human beings have preconceptions, beliefs, attitudes and prejudices on many subjects. It is part of our make-up. Moreover, we do not often recognise our own prejudices. Many people are unable or unwilling, to admit even to themselves that actions of theirs may be racially motivated. An employer may genuinely believe that the reason why he rejected an applicant had nothing to do with the applicant's race. After careful and thorough investigation of the claim, members of an ET may decide that the proper inference to be drawn from this evidence is that whether the employer realised it at the time or not, race was the reason why he acted as he did.'*

A further development in the law of victimisation is provided by the case of *Coote v. Granada Hospitality Ltd.* (No 2) 2000. Here the complaint was brought by an ex employee who claimed that her employers reluctance to provide her with a reference was a reaction to her previous claim for unlawful discrimination. The EAT ruled that as the Sex Discrimination Act only applies to discrimination during the course of the employment relationship it did not have jurisdiction to hear the complaint. Following a reference to the European Court of Justice however the EAT decided that the Sex Discrimination Act 1975 could be interpreted as protecting ex employees against victimisation. In *Chief Constable of West Yorkshire v. Khan* 2001 the House of Lords declared the correct approach to determining victimisation. It is necessary to compare the treatment that the complainant received with the treatment afforded to other employees who had not done a protected act. Crucially however it is also necessary to decide the reason for the treatment, in this case the failure to give a police officer a reference, when they were normally provided on request for those seeking alternative employment. The question was whether the failure to supply a reference was linked to the officer's outstanding race discrimination case. Was the action of the complainant the real reason that the alleged discriminator gave him the less favourable treatment.

Unlawful discrimination in this form is intended to protect employees at the work place who are given less favourable treatment by the employer for bringing a complaint or giving evidence on behalf of a complainant. It is the fear of victimisation that often prevents employees from taking or supporting legal action against an employer. Possible victimisation and sensational reporting are reasons why many employees who suffer sexual harassment from a superior decide not to seek legal redress. In *Northampton County Council v. Dattani* 1994 the complainant's employers promised to investigate a complaint that she has not been selected for a period of paid study leave. When the employer received notification of her claim under the Race Relations Act the investigation was dropped. The EAT upheld the tribunal's ruling of unlawful victimisation.

Lawful Discrimination

Both the Sex Discrimination Act 1975 and the Race Relations Act 1976 identify circumstances where it is lawful to discriminate in the recruitment of staff.[46] They are referred to as instances of genuine occupational qualification (goq). It should be stressed from the outset that goq defence only applies to the making of a job offer or access to promotional, training or other benefits. It does not apply to subjecting to a detriment or dismissal.

---

46. See also the Employment Equality (Sexual Orientation) Regulations 2003, and the
    Employment Equality (Religion or Belief) Regulations 2003

In *Timex v. Hodgson* 1981 however, the EAT took a broad view of goq and applied it to a situation where a man had been selected for redundancy rather than a woman of shorter service. The employer's reason for selection was that the remaining job had been revised to come within the goq relating to considerations of decency. The EAT held that the goq applied because the discrimination was not attached to the dismissal but failure to offer the man the revised job.

If a job applicant shows on the balance of probabilities that an act of direct or indirect discrimination has occurred it is open to an employer to establish as a defence that being of a particular sex or racial group is a genuine occupational requirement. To do this the employer must establish that the job falls within a number of identified categories. It would not be sufficient to argue that the employer was simply motivated to recruit from a particular sex or race to achieve a more balanced workforce.

In *Etam plc v. Rowan* 1989 the complainant was refused a job as a sales assistant because the employer argued he could not carry out all the duties of the post because as a man he could not enter the fitting rooms in a shop which sold female clothing. The EAT agreed with the tribunal's finding that the complainant could have performed the majority of the job functions and there were plenty of female sales assistants who could enter the fitting rooms should that prove necessary. The complainant had suffered sex discrimination and the goq provided no defence.

The categories of genuine occupation requirements under the Sex Discrimination Act s.7(2) are as follows:

(a) *the essential nature of the job calls for a man for reasons of physiology (excluding physical strength or stamina) or, in dramatic performances or other entertainment, for reasons of authenticity, so that the essential nature of the job would be materially different if carried out by a woman; or*

(b) *the job needs to be held by a man to preserve decency or privacy because: it is likely to involve physical contact with men in circumstances where they might reasonably object to its being carried out by a woman, or the holder of the job is likely to do his work in circumstances where men might reasonably object to the presence of a woman because they are in a state of undress or are using sanitary facilities; or*

(ba) *the job is likely to involve the holder of the job doing his work, or living, in a private home and needs to be held by a man because objection might reasonably be taken to allowing to a woman:*

(c) *the nature or location of the establishment makes it impracticable for the holder of the job to live elsewhere than in premises provided by the employer, and: the only such premises which are available for persons holding that kind of job are lived in, or normally lived in, by men and are not equipped with separate sleeping accommodation for women and sanitary facilities which could be used by women in privacy from men, and it is not reasonable to expect the employer either to equip those premises with such accommodation and facilities or to provide other premises for women; or*

(d) the nature of the establishment, or of the part of it within which the work is done, requires the job to be held by a man because it is, or is part of, a hospital, prison or other establishment for persons requiring special care, supervision or attention;

(e) the holder of the job provides individuals with personal services promoting their welfare or education, or similar personal services, and those services can most effectively be provided by a man; or

(f) the job needs to be held by a man because it is likely to involve the performance of duties outside the United Kingdom in a country whose laws or customs are such that the duties could not, or could not effectively, be performed by a woman.

The goq under s.7(2)(a) would not apply if it is shown that the employer has a stereotyped assumption about the physical abilities of men and women. It would be permissible under this subsection to recruit a female actor or male model or a female for a chat line.

The decency or privacy goq under s.7(2)(b) can only be raised if in the circumstances it is not practical to employ a man or a woman.

In *Wylie v. Dee & Co. (Menswear) Ltd.* 1978 the tribunal rejected the goq defence under s.7(2)(b) on the basis of physical contact between the sexes raised by a menswear shop manageress who argued that a female applicant would be prevented from taking customer's inside leg measurements. The tribunal thought that such measurements were often known, could be estimated or easily taken by a male colleague.

One feature of this goq is that *'reasonable objection might be taken if the job holder were of a different sex.'*

In *Secretary of State for Scotland v. Henley* 1983 the decency or privacy goq was raised as a defence to recruit a male as a hall governor in a men's prison on the grounds that the job holder might have to be present in the toilet areas or where the men might be in a state of undress. The fact that no objection had been raised by the men helped the tribunal decide that the goq did not apply.

In *Neal v. Watts* 1989 the tribunal held that there was no unlawful discrimination when the complainant was refused a job as a nanny. Here the goq under s.7(2)(ba) applied because of the likely contact between the male applicant and the child's mother when the baby was bathed in the bathroom. Being a woman was a goq for the job.

In *Sisley v. Britannia Security Systems Ltd.* 1983 the EAT provided guidelines as to what is meant by 'living in' premises for the purposes of s.7(2)(c) and disagreeing with the tribunal felt that twelve hour shift workers who were provided with beds for rest periods did not qualify. *'The words 'to live in' involve the concept of residence either permanent or temporary and do not cover the cases where an employee is obliged to remain on the premises for a limited period of time. We think that whether there is the necessary feature of residence is a question of fact and degree in every case.'*

The categories of genuine occupational requirement in race discrimination are set out in s.5(2) of the Race Relations Act 1976:

(a)   the job involves participation in a dramatic performance or other
      entertainment in a capacity for which a person of that racial group is required
      for reasons of authenticity; or

(b)   the job involves participation as an artist's or photographic model in the
      production of a work of art, visual image or sequence of visual images for
      which a person of that racial group is required for reasons of authenticity; or

(c)   the job involves working in a place where food or drink is (for payment or not)
      provided to and consumed by members of the public or a section of the public
      in a particular setting for which, in that job, a person of that racial group is
      required for reasons of authenticity; or

(d)   the holder of the job provides persons of that racial group with personal services
      promoting their welfare, and those services can most effectively be provided by a
      person of that racial group.

In *London Borough of Lambeth v. Commission for Racial Equality* 1990 the EAT
held that the goq defence under s.5(2)(d) exception provides a defence only if
the post advertised is for the provision of personal services, and the particular
racial groups of the holder of the post and persons to whom the services are
provided are sufficiently identified so as to establish that they are both of the
same racial group. Here the fact that the local authority's advertisement related
to posts which were of a managerial and administrative nature which involved
very little contact with the public meant that they should not be confined to
applicants of Afro-Caribbean or Asian origin. The intention of this exception
under the 1976 Act *'envisaged circumstances where there was direct contact, mainly
face to face or where there could be physical contact, and where language, cultural
understanding and religious backgrounds were of material importance'.* Subsequently
the Court of Appeal agreed with the EAT that the holders of the jobs advertised,
being managerial positions, did not provide personal services promoting the
welfare of persons of a particular racial group.

In *Tottenham Green Under Fives Centre v. Marshall (No2)* 1991 the scope of the
goq defence under s.5(2)(d) relating to personal services was further examined.
The case arose out of the complainant's application for the post of nursery
worker which was rejected on the grounds that the employer wished to recruit
an Afro-Caribbean worker and a white person he was not suitable. The employer
raised the goq defence to the complaint of unlawful discrimination claiming
that *'personal services'* applied. The personal services involved in the job were
maintaining a cultural background link for the children of Afro-Caribbean
background who attended the centre; dealing with these children's parents; reading
and talking to the children in a West Indian dialect and having an awareness of
their skin and healthcare needs. The industrial tribunal rejected the defence
deciding that there was no evidence that a nursery worker of any ethnic origin
could not render the required services. An appeal was upheld by the EAT however
which laid down number of guidelines:

▪   the question for the tribunal in deciding whether the goq applied was not
    whether the personal services promoting the child's welfare could not be
    provided by a person of another racial group but by which group could the
    service be most effectively provided;

- in answering that question the tribunal had to carry out a delicate balancing exercise bearing in mind the need to guard against discrimination and promoting racial integration;
- if the tribunal accepted a conscious decision of a responsible employer to commit an act of discrimination and rely on a goq and that decision was based on a genuinely held and reasonably based opinion that applying a goq would best promote the welfare of the recipient of the personal services, then the tribunal should give considerable weight to the employer's decision.

Positive action

In addition to these specific instances where the sex or race of an employee is regarded as a genuine occupational requirement there are provisions in the Sex Discrimination Act and the Race Relations Act which enable employers and others (trade unions, employer's organisations and professional bodies) to achieve a more balanced work force. Employers are authorised to take positive action to encourage females or members of a particular racial group to apply for positions in their organisations where they are under-represented in those jobs. The requirement for positive encouragement to do certain work under the Sex Discrimination Act is that during the previous twelve months there were no or comparatively few women doing that type of work. Under the Race Relations Act it must be shown that either no members of the racial group are doing the work in question at the organisation or that the proportion of that group who do that work is small among those employed, or among the population of the area from which recruitment normally takes place. Of course it is one thing positively to encourage applicants from under-represented groups by stating in a job advertisement that applications from ethnic minorities or women will be particularly welcomed. If it is shown however than an employer is attempting to limit recruitment exclusively to the members of a racial group, where there is no genuine occupational requirement, then this will be unlawful.

> In *Hughes and Others v. L B Hackney* 1986 the defendant council advertised for gardeners stating that applicants from ethnic minority people would be warmly welcomed. Subsequently three white applicants for the jobs were told that the posts were only open to applicants who were ethnic minority members. The tribunal found that to limit job recruitment in this way was not authorised by the legislation, and in fact in this particular case neither was the criterion for encouraging applicants from a particular racial group satisfied. The defendant council had argued that the proportion of ethnic minorities doing work of this kind was small in comparison with the population of the recruitment area. This argument was rejected by the tribunal who found that the population area should not be restricted to Hackney for a substantial number of workers were recruited from outside the borough.

> In *Kalanke v. Freie Hansestadt* 1995 the European Court of Justice confirmed that the Equal Treatment Directive does not permit affirmative action. However in *Lommers v. Minister von Landbouw Natuurbeheer en Vissey* 2002 the European Court of Justice ruled that a policy under which an employer provided female employees only with access to nursery places for their children at work, while denying male employees with children the same facility except in cases of emergency did not breach the Equal Treatment Directive. This was because the policy was adopted as a positive action measure.

Disability Discrimination

Disability discrimination legislation was first introduced in 1995 in the form of the Disability Discrimination Act, supported by the Meaning of Disability Regulations 1996. In the field of employment small employers were originally not covered but importantly since 1 October 2004 all employers are subject to the Act. Extensive amendments were made to the Act by the Disability Discrimination Act 1995 (Amendment) Regulations 2003.[47] In addition there have been further amendments under the Disability Discrimination Act 2005.[48] In addition to the legislation there is a statutory Code of Practice, recently redrafted by the Disability Rights Commission. The provisions of the Code may be used in evidence and must be taken into account by a tribunal if relevant to the questions in the proceedings before it.

Unfortunately the law is complex but this is inevitably so when you consider what the Act is attempting to achieve. Mummery LJ in *Clark v. TDG Ltd. t/a Novacold* 1999 said that '*anyone who thinks that there is an easy way of achieving a sensible, workable and fair balance between the different interests of disabled persons, of employers and of able-bodied workers, in harmony with wider public interests in an economically efficient workforce, in access to employment, in equal treatment of workers and in standards of fairness at work, has probably not given much serious thought to the problem.*'

The purpose of the disability legislation is to achieve equality of outcome between disabled and non-disabled people. Both the legislature and significantly the courts recognise that to achieve that goal, employers are sometimes required to introduce differential treatment for disabled people. In the significant House of Lords decision of *Archibald v. Fife Council* 2004, Baroness Hale said that '*the Disability Discrimination Act is different from the Sex Discrimination and Race relations acts in that employers are required to take steps to help disabled people which they are not required to take for others. The Act does not regard the differences between disabled people and others as irrelevant. It does not expect each to be treated in the same way. The duty to make adjustments may require the employer to treat a disabled person more favourably to remove the disadvantage which is attributable to the disability. This necessarily entails a measure of positive discrimination*'. In this significant judgment the House of Lords has recognised the challenges faced by disabled people in employment and instructed employers to take a proactive approach in dealing with those with disabilities.

Employers have clear statutory duties under the legislation and may be made potentially liable for any one of the unlawful Acts. In *Abbey Life Assurance Ltd. v. Tansell* it was held that contract workers could claim against their 'principals'. '*It is more probable that parliament intended to confer than to deny protection from discrimination in cases where the supply of the employee was made by his company to the principal through an employment agency.*' From October 2004 most employment spheres are protected by the legislation including the police, prison officers and fire fighters. Time limits for presenting a complaint are consistent with other discrimination legislation. Claims must be brought within three months of the act complained of but this period can be extended to accommodate the requirements of the Employment Act 2002 (Dispute Resolution) Regulations 2004.[49]

---

47. In force October 2004
48. In force October 2005
49. By a further 3 months

The circumstances in employment where the unlawful discriminatory acts may occur are largely similar to other forms of discrimination and include arrangements for offering employment, terms and conditions and benefits at work and dismissal or any other detriment. The test for a detriment was propounded by the House of Lords in *Shamoon v. Chief Constable of the RUC* 2003. As long as a reasonable employee in the claimant's position would or might take the view that the treatment was in all the circumstances to his or her detriment the test for detriment will be satisfied. The perception of the reasonable employee test was applied in *Jenkins v. Windsor Park Legoland* 2003 where the employee was presented with a long service award, consisting of a model that depicted his disability.

The new Regulations expressly provide that constructive dismissal and the non-renewal of a fixed term contract fall within the definition of dismissal. Also the DDA can now extend to post employment events arising out of and closely connected with employment. If a dismissal turns out to be discriminatory that does not always mean that it will be unfair under the Employment Rights Act 1996. The issue of unfair dismissal must be assessed separately according to the 1996 Act.[50]

As with other discrimination legislation the vicarious liability of employers for the actions of individuals under their control is expressly provided for. Under s.58(1) anything done by a person in the course of his employment shall be treated as if done by the employer, whether or not it is done with the employer's knowledge or approval. It is a defence[51] for an employer to show that it took such steps as were reasonably practicable to prevent the employer from doing the act complained of. Case-law in relation to course of employment etc from sex and race discrimination law is relevant to the interpretation of the Act.

Proof of disability discrimination

Originally under s.5 there were three types of discrimination. Now, following the 2003 Amendment Regulations a fourth category of direct discrimination has been created. It is also now unlawful under the Act to harass a disabled person. The types are: Breach of duty by failure to make a Reasonable Adjustment; Disability Related Discrimination; Direct Discrimination; and Victimisation.

To establish a complaint of unlawful discrimination it is necessary to:

- Provide clear evidence that the claimant is protected by the legislation as a disabled person
- Provide clear evidence that the employer has committed one of the four unlawful acts
- Ensure that the employer fails to raise a successful defence.

As with other discrimination legislation[52] there is a reversal of the burden of proof in disability discrimination cases. Tribunals must adopt a two stage approach to establish disability discrimination. They will normally wish to hear all the evidence together, including the respondent's explanation, before deciding whether the requirements of each stage have been satisfied. The claimant is not required to prove discrimination but rather establish a prima facie case which, if proved, shifts the burden of proof to the respondent. If the

---

50. See Chapter 11
51. Under s.58(5)
52. Under s.17A(1C)

respondent fails to establish a satisfactory explanation that there was no discrimination, then the tribunal is bound to draw an inference of discrimination. To assist in providing evidence in support of a claim applicants can serve a questionnaire on their employer within three months of the act complained of and if the employer fails to reply to the questionnaire within eight weeks, without a reasonable excuse, the tribunal is entitled to draw an adverse inference.

Protected persons

Other than for victimisation discrimination, the protection of the Act only extends to those individuals categorised as disabled persons and have or at the relevant have had a disability under the legislation. A non-disabled person could however suffer victimisation because they have given evidence on behalf of a disabled person. Disability is defined in s.1 and schedule 1 as *'a physical or mental impairment which has a substantial and long term adverse affect on the persons ability to carry out normal day to day activities'*.

Inevitably this definition has been the subject of extensive judicial scrutiny. It has three core elements.

- The person must have a physical or mental impairment.
- The impairment must have an adverse effect one or more of the eight capacities in Schedule 1.
- The adverse effect must be substantial and long term.

The Disability Discrimination Act 2005 has amended the 1995 Act to redefine *'disability'* to cover workers suffering from multiple sclerosis, HIV infection and cancer from the point of diagnosis. In addition the requirement that a mental illness must be *'clinically well recognised'* in order to constitute a mental impairment has also been removed.

> In *McNicol v. Balfour Beatty Rail Maintenance Ltd.* 2002 the Court of Appeal helpfully said that in the context of the Act, impairment bears its ordinary and natural meaning. In schedule 1 of the Act an impairment is taken to affect the ability of a person to carry out normal day to day activities only if it affects: mobility, manual dexterity, physical coordination, continence, ability to lift and carry heavy objects, speech hearing or eyesight, memory or the ability to concentrate, learn or understand or perception of the risk of physical danger.

Obviously a claimant would be expected to provide clear medical evidence to establish a disability In *Ekpe v. Commissioner of Police of the Metropolis* 2001 the EAT provided some guidance on the meaning of disability. Here the applicant claimed that she could not do her keyboard job because she had a physical impairment consisting of a wasting of the intrinsic muscles of her right hand. Despite hearing evidence of a long list of tasks she could not do including housework, cooking cleaning and applying make-up the Tribunal had decided the applicant's impairment did not have a substantial adverse affect on her ability to carry out normal day to day activities. Most of the tasks could be carried out to some degree particularly with increased use of the left hand. The EAT disagreed and found that the applicant was a disabled person. Rather than solely considering each example of impairment the Tribunal should have asked whether, taking the evidence as a whole , the impairment had an adverse effect on either or both manual dexterity and the ability to lift objects. Also *'normal activities'* for the purposes of the Act should be regarded as anything which is not abnormal and for a woman this could include putting rollers in her hair and applying make-up. In *Kirton v. Tetrosyl* 2003 the Court of Appeal considered the meaning of the requirement that the impairment must result from the progressive condition. The employee suffered from prostate cancer and surgery resulted in urinary incontinence. Both the tribunal and the EAT felt that the surgery was an intervening event and had caused the progressive condition. The Court of Appeal disagreed however and ruled that the incontinence was the result of the cancer. Here there was a sufficient link between the cancer and the surgery required. There could however be a different result in other medical scenarios.[53]

The Statutory definition is also supplemented by the Meaning of Disability Regulations 1996. Regulation 3(1) provides that addiction to *'alcohol, nicotine, or any other substance is to be treated as not amounting to an impairment for the purposes of the DDA'*. Regulation 4 also excludes some mental illnesses which are clinically well recognised including *a tendency to set fires or steal, commit sexual or physical abuse of other persons, exhibitionism and voyeurism.* Guidance issued by the Secretary of State and the Disability Rights Commission states that under the Act it is not necessary to determine how an impairment was caused, even if the cause is a consequence of a condition excluded by the Regulations e.g. liver disease caused by alcohol dependency. In *Power v. Panasonic UK Ltd.* 2003 the tribunal felt that the core issue was whether the applicant's clinical depression was brought on by alcohol abuse or vice-versa. The EAT disagreed deciding that *'it is not material to a decision as to whether a person has a disability … to consider how the impairment was caused, what is material is to ascertain whether the disability which they have at the material time is a disability within the meaning of the Act or whether it is an impairment excluded by the Regulations'.*

A further complication is that the excluded matters under the Regulations are to be interpreted as *'freestanding conditions'* and not the direct result of an impairment under the Statutory definition. In *Murray v. Newham CAB* 2003 the applicant had been turned down for volunteer work on the grounds that it was thought he could not cope with the stress attached to the job. He claimed disability discrimination alleging that the rejection was related to the fact that he had served a prison sentence for stabbing a neighbour when diagnosed as a paranoid schizophrenic. His condition was now controlled by treatment and appropriate medication. The EAT held that the applicant's tendency to violence was not an excluded condition because it was a consequence of paranoid schizophrenia and thus a manifestation of his disability. The difficulty with the above decision is that most of the excluded conditions reveal conduct associated with another mental disorder, which may then fall within the definition. This wide interpretation means that a claimant will simply have to show that a prima facie excluded condition such as a tendency to physical or sexual abuse of other persons, is a physical manifestation of a mental or physical impairment.

The EAT in *Dunham v. Ashford Windows* 2005 considered the term *'Mental Impairment'* and found that there is a clear distinction between a mental impairment consisting of learning difficulties, a mental handicap and mental illness. The case involved a claimant who had learning difficulties and was found by the tribunal to be outside the legislation. The EAT felt that a tribunal hearing a mental impairment case based on learning difficulties should look for expert evidence of an identified condition. They observed that *'it is unlikely to be sufficient for a claimant to put his case only on the basis that he had difficulties at school or is "not very bright".* Tribunals are likely to look for expert evidence as to the nature and degree*

---

53. Now see the 2005 amendments to the definition in relation to cancer

of the impairment claimed and for evidence of a particular condition (which may have a specific or a generalised effect on function).'

It should be stressed that while claimants under the new 2005 amendments will no longer have to show a clinically well-recognised illness, they will still have to establish, by evidence, that they have a mental impairment.

In *Goodwin v. The Patents Office* 1999 the EAT reversed the tribunals decision and found that a paranoid schizophrenic who was dismissed because of his behaviour was a disabled person under the Act. The EAT laid down helpful guidelines, stressing the need to interpret the legislation with its object in mind and relying on non statutory sources such as Codes of Practice issued by the Secretary of State. The evidence should be examined in the light of four different conditions.

1.   Does the applicant have an impairment which is either mental or physical.

2.   Does the impairment affect the applicant's ability to carry out normal day-to-day activities focusing on the things that the applicant cannot do or only do with difficulty?

3.   Is the adverse effect substantial taking account of how the applicants 'manage' and considering the impact of taking medication.

4.   Is the adverse affect long term?

Certainly the determination of whether a condition has a substantial effect on a person's ability to carry out normal day-to-day activities can only be achieved by evidence. This is particularly so if the applicant has a progressive condition such as cancer, multiple sclerosis, muscular dystrophy or infection by the human immunodeficiency virus. It may be sufficient to show that contracting the condition has an immediate effect on the person's ability to carry on normal day-to-day activities and the prognosis is that it will have a substantial effect at some time in the future. In *Mowat Brown v. University of Surrey* 2002 the EAT considered the impact of a progressive condition and held that to establish a substantial adverse effect medical evidence would have to be used and in some cases *'it may be possible to discharge the onus of proof by statistical evidence.'*

In *Vicary v. British Telecommunications plc* 1999 the EAT held that tribunals should use their own judgment when making an assessment of the effect of an impairment, and should not rely on the opinion of medical experts. *'In deciding whether someone has a disability a tribunal should focus on what the worker cannot do, not on what he can do. The fact that someone can mitigate a disability does not mean that he is not disabled.'* A controversial provision of the Act relates to 'deduced effects'[54] provides that *'an impairment which would be likely to have a substantial adverse effect on the ability of the person concerned to carry out normal day to day activities, but for the fact that measures are being taken to improve or correct it, is to be treated as having that effect'.* The provision acknowledges the fact that an individual may have an impairment which is classified as a disability despite the fact that it is controlled or corrected by treatment. This would include a disability such as paranoid schizophrenia controlled by drugs. In *Woodrup v. London Borough of Southwark* 2003 the Court of Appeal was reluctant to invoke this provision without clear expert evidence of the disability. The court stated that *'those seeking to invoke this particularly benign doctrine should not readily expect to be indulged by the tribunal of fact'.*

---

54. Under Schedule 1 para 6

Under the Act[55] the expression *'long term effect'* means a period of at least 12 months but even where the impairment has ceased it should be treated as having a long-term effect if it is likely to recur.

The Unlawful Acts

Following the Disability Discrimination Act (Amendment) Regulations 2003 there are now four potential unlawful acts under the legislation.

1.   Failure to make Reasonable Adjustments
2.   Disability Related Discrimination
3.   Direct Discrimination
4.   Victimisation Discrimination

1. Failure to make reasonable adjustments

Failure to make reasonable adjustments is unique to this form of discrimination and the central core of disability legislation. It was originally contained in s.6 but is now amended and found in ss.4A and 18B following the 2003 Regulations. As Baroness Hale said when it is triggered it is a duty on employers to take steps to help a disabled person which they are not required to take for others.

The original duty applied only in relation to arrangements made by or on behalf of the employer. Since October 2006 the new wider duty under s.4B applies to any provision, criterion or practice applied by or on behalf of the employer and puts the disabled person at a substantial disadvantage in comparison with a non disabled person or a person with a different disability. There is no doubt that the wider definition shifts the focus of reasonable adjustments from physical features at the workplace to the employer's policies and practices.

Where any physical features of the premises occupied by the employer, place the disabled person concerned at a substantial disadvantage in comparison with persons who are not disabled, it is the duty of the employer to take such steps as is reasonable, in all the circumstances of the case, for him to have to take in order to prevent the feature, provision, criterion or practice having that effect. The Disability Rights Commission in its Code of Practice suggests that the wider duty applies to arrangements for determining to whom employment should be offered, terms and conditions of employment and arrangements on which employment, promotion, transfer or training or any other benefit is offered or afforded. Inevitably there will be both formal and informal workplace practices and policies that may have a discriminatory effect.

In such circumstances the employer is under a duty to take such steps as are reasonable to change the provision, criterion or practice to prevent its discriminatory impact. Proactive strategies could include altering the hours of work, transferring the individual to another place of work, arranging training or mentoring and providing support. Examples include conducting meetings in such a way that a deaf person could participate and ensuring support for a returning worker to help with loss of confidence following the onset of a disability. In *Kenny v. Hampshire Constabulary* 1999 the EAT said that the duty to make reasonable adjustments applied only to job related matters, so that assistance to get to and

---

55. Schedule 1

from work fell outside the duty. More recently in *Rothwell v. Pelikan Hardcopy Scotland Ltd.* 2006 the EAT held that an employer's failure to consult with the employee prior to dismissing him on health grounds amounted to a failure to make a reasonable adjustment. Lady Smith said that *'it is plain from a reading of Archibald v. Fife Council alone that a tribunal cannot make a finding that less favourable treatment of a disabled person is justified under the Act unless it is satisfied that any reasonable adjustment that an employer has a duty to make have been carried out'.*

The Act now[56] sets out a list of relevant factors to which the tribunal should have regard in determining reasonableness. Such factors include, practicability, cost, resources, financial support, and the nature of activities carried on by the employer. The Act[57] also provides examples of reasonable steps which include: making adjustments to premises or equipment; reallocating duties, providing a supervisor, mentor, reader, or interpreter; transferring to other work or workplace; altering hours, training manuals ; and allowing absence during working hours for rehabilitation or treatment.

Reasonable adjustments can inevitably mean more favourable treatment to enable disabled persons to function as well as others. An employer may have to make inquiries to find out what he needs to do to ameliorate the disadvantage. The EAT in *Mid Staffordshire General Hospital Trust v. Cambridge* 2003 held that this duty incorporated a requirement to carry out a risk assessment to decide the steps that need to be taken in relation to a disabled person. *'A proper assessment of what is required to eliminate a disabled person's disadvantage is a necessary ... fulfillment of the duty and part of it.'*[58]

A good example of a failure to make reasonable adjustments is provided by *London Borough of Hillingdon v. Morgan* 1998 where the employer failed to allow an employee to work from home until she readjusted to work following a period of sick leave. The size and resources of the employer were such that a staged return to work should not be out of the question. Also in a significant case, *Nottingham CC v. Meikle* 2004, the Court of Appeal ruled that the employer had failed to make reasonable adjustments to a pay policy which, after six months absence, reduced wages to one half in circumstances where the absence was due to disability.

Importantly the House of Lords in *Archibald v. Fife Council* 2004 explained the duty to make reasonable adjustments. This is now the leading case on reasonable adjustments and disability discrimination. The relevant arrangement was the express or implied contractual term that anyone who is incapable of fulfilling their job description is liable to be dismissed. Here the applicant was substantially disadvantaged when compared with her non disabled colleagues because she became liable to be dismissed. She had been employed as a road sweeper but could no longer walk following the onset of a spinal disability. The Court of Session held that the duty to make reasonable adjustments did not include a requirement to provide her with the opportunity to be interviewed for a different job without competitive interview under the employer's rules. The House of Lords disagreed and in a judgment, previously referred to, Baroness Hale provided a positive interpretation of the requirements of the disability legislation. She said that *'The duty to make adjustments may require the employer to treat a disabled person more favourably to remove the disadvantage which is*

---

56. S.18B(1)
57. S.18B(2)
58. See also *Southampton City College v. Rendall* 2006

attributable to the disability. This necessarily entails a measure of positive discrimination.'
Here the duty to make adjustments encompasses a requirement to override the employer's
rules and give the claimant the chance to fill an existing vacancy for which she was qualified,
at a slightly higher grade, without competitive interview. To the extent that the duty to
make reasonable adjustments requires it the employer is not only permitted but obliged to
treat a disabled person more favourably than others.

The Court of Appeal applied *Archibald* in *Smith v. Churchills Stailifts plc* 2006 and provided
helpful guidance as to the appropriate comparator for reasonable adjustment purposes.
The court confirmed that the reasonable adjustment test is objective. Lord Justice Kay
emphasised that in determining reasonableness regard is to be had, amongst other things
to *'the financial or other costs which could be incurred by the employer in taking the step and
the extent to which it would disrupt any of the employer's activities'* .

2. Disability related discrimination

Under s 3(1)A[59], this form of unlawful act remains unaltered by the 2003 Regulations. An
employer discriminates against a disabled person if he, treats the individual less favourably
and does so for a reason which relates to the person's disability and cannot show that the
treatment is justified. The test for disability related discrimination is from Mummery LJ
in the Court of Appeal decision, *Clark v. TDG Ltd. (t/a Novacold)* 1999. In dismissal cases
the two stages are firstly whether the claimant was dismissed for a reason related to his
disability. If so the second stage is did the employer treat him less favourably than it would
treat others to whom that reason did not apply. Significantly if a person is unfairly dismissed
for a disability related reason, then the compensation awarded should be assessed under
the Disability Discrimination Act rather than the Employment Rights Act 1996.

Establishing a disability related reason is a question of fact in each case. It need not be the
only reason for the treatment so long as it is an effective reason. For the purposes of this
unlawful act and establishing less favourable treatment no like for like comparisons are
needed as in direct sex and race discrimination. This means that if the employer has a
policy that applies equally to the disabled and others it may still have a discriminatory
impact. If the policy provides for a reduction in pay after six months sick leave and a
disabled person is off work for that period as a result of his disability, there is no need to
compare his circumstances with a non disabled person who would suffer similar treatment.
Here the reason that the disabled person suffered the pay reduction is the disability which
caused the sick leave absence.[60]

In *O'Neill v. Symm & Co. Ltd.* 1998 the EAT held that disability related discrimination
only applied when the employer knew that the worker had a disability but this ruling has
now been disapproved. In *Heinz Co Ltd. v. Kenrick* 2000 the employee was dismissed after
a long period of illness later diagnosed as chronic fatigue syndrome of which the employer
was unaware. The EAT felt that nevertheless the dismissal was related to his disability and
as the employer had not adequately considered possible alternative employment the
discrimination was unjustified. The Act *'requires the employer to pause to consider whether
the reason for some dismissal they have in mind might relate to the disability and, if it might,
to reflect upon the Act and the Code before dismissing'*.

---

59. Originally s.5(1)
60. See *Nottingham City Council v. Meikle* 2004

The test for detriment is whether a reasonable employee in the claimant's position would or might take the view that the treatment was in all the circumstances to his or her detriment. This was certainly the position in the bizarre case of *Jenkins v. Windsor Park Legoland* 2003.[61] Here the EAT agreed that the claimant had been discriminated against on the grounds of his disability when as part of a long service award ceremony he was presented with a model depicting his disability, a withered arm. The aim was to present models which were designed to show the award winner in a work related environment. The employer's argument that it was difficult to represent the claimant's job as a team leader because of the lack of work related items was in fact accepted by the tribunal but then rejected by the EAT.

A significant feature of disability related discrimination is that it can be justified as a defence. Justification now only applies to disability related discrimination and must be by reference to a reason which is both substantial and material to the circumstances of the particular case. In *Baynton v. Saurus General Engineering Ltd.* 1999 the EAT held that *'the circumstances of the case related to both the employer and the disabled employee and the tribunal must carry out a balancing exercise between the two'*. In *Smith v. Churchills Stairlifts* 2006 the Court of Appeal said that the test for justification, unlike reasonable adjustments is partly subjective. In relation to justification the task of the tribunal is *'to consider the materiality and substantiality of the employer's reason'*.

Jones v. Post Office 2001 is an important judgment of the Court of Appeal which addresses the approach to establishing the defence of justification. Given the wide definition of disability s.3(1)A[62] it is often the issue of justification that is the key question in a disability dispute. Here the employer admitted discrimination in taking an insulin dependent post office worker off driving duties but sought to justify the decision. Referring to the words *'substantial and material'* the court held that all facts should be considered including the results of a risk assessment based upon medical advice. Adopting the *'band of reasonable response test'* from the test of fairness in unfair dismissal, if an employer acts upon the results of a proper risk assessment, provided that the decision is not perverse then it will be enough to establish the defence of reasonable justification. In *Collins v. Royal National Theatre Board* 2004 the Court of Appeal has doubted the low threshold of justification set out in the *Jones* Case.[63] The court held that the Act does not permit a breach of the duty to make reasonable adjustments to be justified by factors which were already taken into account in deciding whether an adjustment was reasonable.

In *Murray v. Newham CAB* 2003 the EAT considered the defence of justification. Importantly the EAT draws a distinction between the standard of investigation for existing employees, which should be rigorous, and what is appropriate for job applicants. Adopting a well known test from unfair dismissal law the EAT found that the tribunal should only interfere with the decision of a prospective employer where the employers investigations are outside the reasonable responses by a reasonable prospective employer in the circumstances. Failure to carry out reasonable investigations would make the less favourable treatment unjustified. To justify the decision an employer must show that it was based upon material it had before it at the time the decision was made.

---

61. See earlier in the chapter
62. Originally s.5(1)
63. Above

3. Direct discrimination

This form of discrimination is analogous to direct discrimination in relation to sex and race discrimination where there is less favourable treatment than that of a real or hypothetical comparator. Under s. 3A (5) a person directly discriminates against a disabled person if, on the ground of the disabled person's disability, he treats the disabled person less favourably than he treats or would treat a person not having that particular disability whose relevant circumstances, including his abilities, are the same as, or not materially different from those of the disabled person.

The comparison will be between the disabled person and the non disabled person in similar circumstances. In the previous example of the sick leave policy the comparison would be with a non disabled person who was absent for six months and if there was no less favourable treatment, then there is no direct discrimination.

Direct discrimination will cover rare cases where disability is a significant factor in the treatment or generalised assumptions about the disabled person for example, a blanket refusal to employ anyone with a mental impairment in a particular post. This form of discrimination cannot be justified. Case-law on race or sex direct discrimination is relevant to assist in the interpretation.

4. Victimisation

This unlawful act is designed to protect those who assist a prospective claimant under the Act and suffer less favourable treatment as a result. Under s.55 victimisation occurs when a person treats another less favourably than he would treat others of similar circumstances for a prohibited reason. The prohibited reasons are that:

- The person has brought proceedings under the Act.
- The person has given evidence or information in connection with such proceedings.
- The person has made an allegation under the Act.

It is also a prohibited reason if the reason for the treatment is a suspicion that the individual has done or intends to do any of the above acts. Victimisation cannot be justified and the claimant does not have to be disabled to present a complaint.

In line with other discrimination legislation from October 2004 it is unlawful for employers to subject disabled workers or job applicants to harassment. Harassment is defined in s.3B. A person subjects a disabled person to harassment where, for a reason which relates to the disabled person's disability, he engages in unwanted conduct which has the purpose or effect of violating the disabled person's dignity, or creating an intimidating, hostile, degrading, humiliating or offensive environment for him.[64]

Enforcement and Remedies

Discrimination law in employment may be enforced by individual, having raised a grievance, making a complaint to an employment tribunal. Also both the Commission for Racial

---

64. See earlier in the chapter

Equality, the Equal Opportunities Commission and the Disability Rights Commission have a role to play in the enforcement of the law, and where certain unlawful acts are alleged, their role is an exclusive one. The process and time limits relating to the presentation of a complaint were considered earlier in the chapter.

If despite the attempts at conciliation the claimant decides to go ahead, there is a special pre-tribunal procedure to assist in the effective presentation of the complaint and access to information.

The remedies available to a tribunal who felt that a complaint has been made out are:

- an order declaring the rights of the parties;
- an order requiring the respondent to pay the complainant damages subject to the upper limit for unlawful dismissal claims;
- a recommendation of action to be taken by the respondent to reduce the adverse effect of discrimination.

A failure by the respondent without reasonable justification to comply with a recommendation may lead to an award of increased compensation. In the case of indirect discrimination if the respondent proves that the provision, criterion or practice was applied without any intention to discriminate, then no compensation will be awarded.

> In *Noone v. North West Thames Regional Health Authority* 1988 the Court of Appeal confirmed that awards for incidents of racial discrimination were subject to the same rules as awards for damages for personal injury in respect of any other breach of statutory duty. Here the complainant was 'devastated' by the discriminatory act and suffered a severe injury to feelings which should be acknowledged by the award of damages. Nevertheless bearing in mind that she suffered no actual loss, the award of £5,000 was too high and should be reduced to £3,000.

The Sex Discrimination and Equal Pay (Remedies) Regulations 1993, formally removed the ceiling on compensation for unlawful sex discrimination and set out the method of calculating the interest. In 1993 it was also recognised that thousands of women who had been dismissed from the armed forces because they were pregnant can claim sex discrimination. The fact that the ceiling on compensation was lifted dramatically increased the significance of the potential claims and tens of thousands of pounds have been awarded. Tribunals have recognised that injury to feelings in such cases can include the emotional effect of discharge from the services evidenced by feelings of humiliation, isolation, loss of status and career aspirations and personal hurt. The notion that a higher level post should carry with it a higher award of compensation was recognised in *Sharifi v. Strathclyde Regional Council* 1992.

The statutory ceiling on a compensatory award for race discrimination was lifted under the Race Relations (Remedies) Act 1994. If a complaint is well founded then the tribunal must decide whether it is 'just and equitable' to award damages. The damages should reflect a sum of injury to feelings and the pecuniary loss subject to the ceiling. Damages for injury to feelings should compensate the complainant for the insult and humiliation suffered. In *Browne v. Cassell* 1972 Ld Diplock said that *'where salt is rubbed into the wound by high handed malicious insulting or offensive conduct additional compensation may be awarded by way of aggravated damages'.*

In *Alexander v. Home Office* 1988 the Court of Appeal considered an appeal against an award of compensation for injury to feelings where a complaint of race discrimination had been established. Increasing the award from £50 to £500 the Court of Appeal gave some indication as to the principles to be applied in assessing damages in race discrimination cases. LJ May said that *'The objective of an award for unlawful racial discrimination, as with any other awards of damages, is restitution. Where the discrimination has caused actual pecuniary loss, such as the refusal of a job, then the damages referable to this can be readily calculated. Damages for unlawful discrimination, however, are not limited to the pecuniary loss that can be specifically proved and it is impossible to say what is restitution for the injury to feelings, humiliation, and insult. The answer must depend on the experience and good sense of the judge and assessors. Awards should not be minimal, because this would tend to trivialise or diminish respect for the public policy to which the Act gives effect. on the other hand, just because it is impossible to assess the monetary value of injured feelings awards should be restrained. To award sums which are generally felt to be excessive does almost as much harm to the policy and the results which it seeks to achieve as do nominal awards. Moreover injury to feelings, which is likely to be of a relatively short duration, is less serious than physical injury to the body or the mind which may persist for months or for life. The injury to feelings for which compensation is sought must have resulted from knowledge of the discrimination. Although damages for discrimination will in many cases be analogous to those for defamation, they are not necessarily the same. In the latter, the principal injury to be compensated is that to the plaintiff's reputation and it is doubtful whether this will play a large part in discrimination cases. On the other hand, if the plaintiff knows of the racial discrimination and that he has thereby been held up to "hatred, ridicule or contempt", then the injury to his feelings will be an important element in the damages. In the substantial majority of discrimination cases the unlawful conduct will cause personal hurt, in the sense of injury to feelings, or of preventing the plaintiff from working in more congenial conditions, or of preventing the plaintiff from obtaining a better, more remunerative job. However, unless the court can and feels it right to draw an inference that the discrimination will cause a plaintiff 'hurt' of a particular kind, the mere fact that a defendant is guilty of racial discrimination is not in itself a factor affecting damages.'*

In *Orlando v. Didcot Power Station Sports and Social Club* 1996 the EAT held that in a sex discrimination case in assessing injury to feelings, the willingness of the employer to admit that it has acted in breach of the discrimination legislation may help to reduce the hurt which is felt, in that it can spare the complainant the indignity and further hurt of having to rehearse the nature of her treatment. Such a reduction in *'hurt'* can of course be reflected in the level of damages awarded.

The decision in *Armitage Marsden and the Prison Service v. Johnson* 1997 provides an indication of the level of compensation payable in cases or race discrimination. The complainant was a prison officer who had been subjected *to 'appalling treatment'* by two work colleagues including racist remarks, false accusations and biased treatment. The EAT upheld the tribunal's award of £20,000 for injury to feelings with an additional £7,500 aggravated damages for the malicious nature of his employers attitude. A further award of £500 was made against each of the officers in question on the grounds that they had victimised the complainant and aided the employer to discriminate. The EAT summarised the relevant principles for assessing awards for injury to feelings.

(1) Awards for injury to feelings are compensatory. They should be just to both parties. They should compensate fully without punishing the respondent. Feelings of indignation at the respondent's conduct should not be allowed to inflate the award.

(2) Awards should not be too low, as that would diminish respect for the policy of the anti-discrimination legislation. Society has condemned discrimination and awards must ensure that it is seen to be wrong. On the other hand, awards should be restrained, as excessive awards could be seen as the way to untaxed riches.

(3) Awards should bear some broad general similarity to the range of awards in personal injury cases. This should be done by reference to the whole range of such awards, rather than to any particular type of award.

(4) In exercising their discretion in assessing a sum, tribunals should remind themselves of the value in everyday life of the sum they have in mind. This may be done by reference to purchasing power or by reference to earnings.

(5) Tribunals should bear in mind the need for public respect for the level of awards made.

The above decision in Armitage was applied by the EAT in *Chief Constable of West Yorkshire Police v. Vento (No2)* 2002 where in upholding a complaint of sex discrimination when a probationary policewoman was not confirmed in her post, the Employment Tribunal had awarded her £65,000 including £50,000 for injury to feelings and £15,000 for aggravated damages. This was held by the EAT to be too high and the award was reduced to £30,000 composed of £25,000 for injury to feelings and £5,000 for aggravated damages.

In *Sheriff v. Klyne Tugs (Lowestoft) Ltd.* 1999 the Court of Appeal held that a claimant may recover compensation for any injury caused by discrimination both mental and physical from the Employment Tribunal. The Court also noted that in negligence proceedings for personal injury a claimant would have to show that the injury was reasonably foreseeable. In discrimination statutes there is no such requirement and it is sufficient if it is shown that the act of discrimination caused the injury.

Pecuniary loss which is quantifiable includes the loss of wages, the loss of opportunity to work and the loss of advantage on the labour market. While such cases may be *'few and far between'* the EAT ruled in *Zaiwalla v. Walia* 2002 that aggravated damages can be awarded against an employer because of his conduct in defending a discrimination complaint. Here aggravated damages of £7,500 were awarded against a firm of solicitors for defending sex discrimination proceedings in a manner which was designed to be *'intimidatory and cause the maximum unease and distress to the applicant'.*

In *British Telecom plc v. Reid* 2004 the Court of Appeal upheld an award of £2000 aggravated damages in addition to compensation for hurt feelings, when a complaint of racial harassment was established. The aggravated damaged had been awarded to reflect the fact that the employer had promoted the harasser during the long period of internal investigation of the applicant's grievance. The Tribunal was entitled to find that such a promotion indicated high handed action and one that was insulting to the applicant.

Exemplary damages[65] were thought to be available where a public employer was guilty of offensive conduct or a private employer discriminates for profit.

In *Gibbon v. South West Water Services Ltd.* 1992 the Court of Appeal indicated that exemplary damages are not available for all civil wrongs. The court held

---

65. To punish the respondent

> that an award of exemplary damages could only be made for torts which existed prior to 1964 when *Rookes v. Barnard* established the right to exemplary damages in defined circumstances.

As the statutory torts of discrimination were not created until the mid 1970s it seems that exemplary damages are not therefore available.

> In *Deane v. London Borough of Ealing* 1993 the EAT held that it was bound by the above decision and found that the statutory tort of race discrimination under the Race Relations Act 1976 does not carry with it the possibility of an award of exemplary damages.

> In *Ministry of Defence v. Meredith* 1995 the EAT held that exemplary damages are not available for breach of the Equal Treatment Directive. Punitive damages are not usually available for tortious liability and the Directive is a tort *'comparable ... with statutory tort of discrimination under the Sex Discrimination Act'* for which exemplary damages are not available.

> Finally in *British Gas Plc v. Shama* 1991 the EAT confirmed that there are limits to the extent that tribunals have power to make recommendations to reduce the adverse affects of unlawful discrimination. While the tribunal had found that the complainant had been the victim of direct racial discrimination when she was not promoted, the tribunal had no power to recommend that she should be promoted to the next suitable vacancy.

Enforcement of the legislation is also the role of the Commissions who having instituted a formal investigation and, being satisfied that unlawful discriminatory acts or practices have taken place, may issue a non-discrimination notice on any person. Such a notice will require the person on whom it is served not to commit the acts complained of and also comply with any required changes in conduct. The Commissions may seek an injunction to prevent repeated discrimination within five years of the non-discrimination notice becoming final.

Only the CRC, the EOC or the DRC can initiate proceedings under the legislation alleging discriminatory advertising which indicates an intention to discriminate. A job advertisement which indicates a racial or sexual preference such as 'steward' or 'waitress' would contravene the legislation without further explanation. Both the publisher and the advertiser could be made liable for a discriminatory advertisement but the publisher would have a defence if he can establish that he reasonably relied on a statement by the advertiser that the advertisement was not unlawful.

> In *Cardiff Women's Aid v. Hartup* 1994 it was confirmed that only the Commission for Racial Equality can bring proceedings for racially discriminating advertising. The important point was made however that it is still possible for an individual complainant to use a discriminatory advertisement as evidence of direct discrimination in the recruitment process.

The present power to conduct formal investigations is that they may be instigated for any purpose in connection with the Commission's duties. The terms of reference for an investigation must be drawn up by the Commission and general notice of the holding of an investigation served. To assist the investigatory process, power to require a person to furnish written information or to give oral evidence and produce documents is also conferred. On completion of an investigation the Commission must prepare a report within which it can make recommendations for changes in policies or procedures to individuals or organisations, and recommendations for changes in the law to the Secretary of State. Such investigations may also lead to the issue by the Commission of a non-discrimination notice on any person. This would be the case where the individual is committing or has committed an unlawful discriminatory act or has applied or operated an unlawful discriminatory practice. Only the Commission may bring proceedings before the county court in respect of certain unlawful acts, namely discriminatory advertising, unlawful instructions to discriminate and unlawful inducements to discriminate under ss.30 and 31 of the Race Relations Act 1976.

> The meaning of ss.30 and 31 were considered by the EAT in *C.R.E. v. Imperial Society of Teachers of Dancing* 1983. Here there had been a request by an employer to a school's head of careers that no coloured students should be sent to fill a job. The EAT held that there had been no instruction to discriminate under s.30 because the instructor had no authority over the instructed. Nevertheless there had been a contravention of s.31, for the request was an attempt to induce an infringement of the Race Relations Act.

Where an unlawful act is committed by an employee in the course of his employment, we said earlier that the principles of vicarious liability apply and the employer is also made liable for the act whether or not it is done with his approval. It is a defence for an employer to prove that he took such steps as were reasonably practicable to prevent the employees from doing that act or from doing, in the course of his employment, acts of that description. Such steps would certainly include full implementation of the Commission for Racial Equality Code of Practice on discrimination.[66] Furthermore an employer is not liable unless the discriminatory act is done in the course of employment. Vicarious liability for discrimination in the workplace is considered in more detail in Chapter 8.

Further Reading

Bowers & Moran *Justification in Direct Sex Discrimination Law* (2002) 30 ILJ 307.

Connolly, Michael *The Sex Discrimination (Indirect Discrimination and Burden of Proof) Regulations 2001* (2001) 30 ILJ 375.

Davies, Jackie *A Cuckoo in the Nest? A Range of Reasonable Responses. Justification and the Disability Discrimination Act 1995* (2003) 32 ILJ 164.

Hughs, Pauline *Disability Discrimination and the Duty to make Reasonable Adjustments* (2004) 33 ILJ 358.

Manknell, David *Discrimination on Grounds of Sexual Orientation Harassment and Liability for Third Parties* (2003) 32 ILJ 297.

Oliver, Hazel *Sexual Orientation Discrimination* (2004) 33 ILJ 1.

Rowland, Dianne *Discrimination and Constructive Dismissal* (2001) 30 ILJ 381.

Vickers, Lucy *The Employment Equality (Religion or Belief) Regulations 2003* (2003) 32 ILJ 188.

Disability Discrimination Who is Protected? (2004) 745 IRLB 3.

---

66. New Code in force from April 2006

Chapter 7

Work/Life Balance

A continuing feature of the present Government's employment policies is the long-term plan of promoting law, which directly or indirectly assists workers to balance their work with their home life responsibilities. While the public debate surrounding family friendly policies is well documented, and will no doubt continue to be so, I do not propose to add to it. The aim of this chapter is to explain the present law. It should be appreciated that there will be further developments in the next few years. The present Government has a goal that paid maternity leave will be increased from six months to one year before the end of the present Parliament. Fathers will also get the right to share paid leave with mothers and this move should reduce the level of maternity discrimination, but it seems that the present view is that transferring maternity leave between parents would prove to be unworkable. A widening of the right to request flexible working to carers of sick and disabled adults and possibly the parents of older children is also a possibility.

A start is to be made under the Work and Families Bill 2006. UK fathers are to be given some of most generous paternity rights in the world. While the proposed changes are fiercely opposed by opposition groups it is estimated that up to 400,000 men a year will qualify for the leave to be introduced in April 2007. Currently the majority of men take up the present two weeks paternity leave but over half are paid their full salary by their employers rather than paternity pay. There will be a power to introduce new paternity leave for fathers enabling them to benefit from leave and statutory pay if the mother returns to work after 6 months but before the end of her maternity leave period. Significantly new mothers will be entitled to 9 months maternity leave and pay from April 2007 and a then possibly a years leave from 2009.

This chapter is a recognition that there is a body of law, in addition to employment status[1] and discrimination law,[2] which impacts most significantly on the work/life balance. This body of law includes rights and responsibilities in relation to:

---

1. See Chapter 3
2. See Chapter 6

- Working time and paid holidays.
- Part-time working and fixed term contracts.
- Maternity, paternity, parental and adoption leave, time off.
- Flexible working.

Significant changes in employment rights in relation to maternity and paternity leave as well as the right to request flexible working were introduced by the Employment Act 2002. The *'work and family'* provisions contained in the Employment Act 2002 are the result of one of the most extensive public consultations to ever precede new legislation. This chapter will begin by examining the law relating to working time, a significant development for those workers on the lower rungs of the employment ladder attempting to balance home and working life. The right to be paid the national minimum wage is also fundamental for the low paid and is dealt with in Chapter 9.

Working Time

The saga of the Working Time Directive was mentioned in Chapter 1. The present government sought to implement the Directive in the Working Time Regulations 1998. As with the minimum wage the Regulations apply not just to employees but to workers, but as we discovered earlier[3] identifying workers is not always straightforward. In *Willoughby v. County Home Care Ltd.* 1999 a freelance care assistant was able to establish that she was a worker for the purposes of the Regulations and able to claim accrued holiday entitlement.

Workers in transport, sea fishing, off-shore oil and gas work and junior doctors in training were originally excluded but this has changed. Under the Regulations there is a maximum working week of 48 hours and a standard reference period for average hours of work of 17 weeks. It is possible for a worker to agree to work in excess of this limit in a written agreement subject to a right to terminate the agreement on notice. Strict records must be kept of all such agreements and how they operate.

> In *Barber v. RJB Mining (UK) Ltd.* 1999 the High Court provided an important ruling on the interpretation of specific Working Time Regulations and their enforcement. Here a number of mine workers claimed that they had been required to work in excess of the 48 hour working week over a 17 week reference period and had refused the employer's request to sign an 'opt out' agreement until wage negotiations had been completed. When required to continue working in breach of the Regulations the workers began proceedings in the High Court seeking a declaration of their rights and an injunction. The employers argued that redress under the Regulations the exclusive jurisdiction of employment tribunals and a worker who was required to work in breach of the Regulations could only claim he was suffering a detriment or dismissal in accordance with ss.45A and 101A of the Employment Rights Act. The High Court disagreed and found that Regulation 4(1) imposes contractual obligations on an employer and could be enforced in the civil courts *'The plaintiff was entitled to a declaration that having worked in excess of the permitted hours during the relevant reference period they need not work until such time as their average working time fell within the limits specified in Reg. 4(1).'* An injunction however was not appropriate

---

3. See Chapter 3

given that any detriment caused could be remedied by a complaint to a tribunal under s.45A of the Employment Rights Act 1996.

There is an entitlement to a minimum rest break of 20 minutes after 6 hours work which may be taken by workers.

One of the issues in *Gallagher v. Alpha Catering Services Ltd.* 2005 was whether 'downtime', when employees were not actually doing any work, would qualify as a rest break for purposes of the Working Time Regulations. The workers in question were employed to load and unload food and drink to aircraft and between loading assignments, they were required to remain in radio contact with their employers and were at their disposal during a period referred to as 'downtime'. The Court of Appeal held that *'A "rest break" is an uninterrupted period of at least 20 minutes which the worker can use as he or she pleases. A period of downtime where, as in the present case, the worker remains at the employer's disposal cannot be a rest break. The worker must also know at the start of a rest break that it is such. A period of downtime cannot retrospectively become a rest break only because it can be seen after it is over that it was an uninterrupted period of 20 minutes.'*

'Time work' for the purposes of the National Minimum Wage Regulations can also include time that a worker is available for work although not actually working.

> In *British Nursing Association v. Inland Revenue* 2002 the Inland Revenue National Minimum Wage Compliance Team had took the view that emergency 'bank' nurses employed to be available on night shift were entitled to be paid the national minimum wage for all the hours that they were on duty. Working from home they were required to deal with telephone calls but when not doing so could carry out other activities such as reading or watching television. The Court of Appeal upheld the EAT ruling stating that it was self evident that the employees were working. *'No one would say that an employee sitting at the employer's premises during the day waiting for more calls was only working in the sense of only being entitled to be remunerated during the periods when he or she was actually on the phone.'*

Annual leave

For the first time the right to annual leave is included in legislation so that all workers are entitled to four weeks paid leave. Unfortunately there is evidence that this minimal right to take an annual holiday is being flouted by unscrupulous employers who are counting the 8 bank holidays as part of the statutory leave.[4] Effectively this reduces the annual leave to 12 days and is an issue that the government has committed itself to address. There was a qualifying period of 13 weeks before a worker could accrue annual leave entitlements. However there was a successful challenge to the validity of the qualifying period made to the European Court in *R v. Secretary of State for Trade & Industry ex parte BECTU* 2001.

As a result the Regulations were amended by the Working Time (Amendment) Regulations 2002 so that a worker is allowed to take one twelfth of their annual holiday entitlement for each month worked rounded to the nearest day. This amendment effectively means that holiday entitlement accrues from the commencement of employment so that if a worker

---

4. There is no statutory right to take bank holidays

leaves during the first few months of employment he will be entitled to pro rata holiday pay. Annual leave will also accrue during ordinary and additional maternity leave.[5]

In *Commission of Inland Revenue v. Ainsworth* 2005 the Court of Appeal ruled that workers on long term sick leave, who are no longer entitled to sick pay,[6] do not qualify for annual holiday pay under the Working Time Regulations.

To qualify the individual must satisfy the definition of 'worker' and in *Bacica v. Muir* 2006 the claimant was excluded from holiday pay as a self employed sole trader, despite the fact that he was offering personal service.

To enforce the right to paid leave a complaint may be made to an employment tribunal within three months of an unreasonable refusal and compensation which is just and equitable may be awarded for an infringement of the right.

> In *Davies v. M. J. Wyatt (Decorators) Ltd.* 2000 the EAT provided a supportive ruling on the employers obligations imposed by the Working Time Regulations. When the Regulations came into force the employer decided unilaterally to reduce the hourly rate of all employees to assist them in meeting the cost of providing paid annual leave. The EAT held that the reduction in pay amounted to an unauthorised deduction from wages[7] *'An employer cannot unilaterally reduce an employee's contractual rate of pay in order to discharge the employer's liability under the Working Time Regulations to provide paid holidays. Unless there has been a consensual agreement, such a deduction cannot properly be made. The object of the Regulations is to confer a benefit upon employees.'*

On the termination of employment an employee is entitled to be paid arrears of holiday pay. To calculate a day's holiday pay it is necessary to divide a worker's annual salary by the number of working days rather than by reference to calendar days. So held the EAT in *Leisure League UK Ltd. v. Maconnachie* 2002 supporting the universal practice that a weeks holiday pay should reflect a weekly wage. A dispute relating to pay due on the termination of employment could be raised in a tribunal on a complaint of wrongful dismissal[8] or unlawful deduction from wages.

Any attempt to exclude or limit the effect of the Regulations is rendered void by virtue of Regulation 35.

In *MPB Structures Ltd. v. Munro* 2003 the Court of Session was faced with the dilemma of determining whether an employer could fulfil his statutory obligation to provide paid annual leave by including an allowance of 8% of the hourly rate for holiday pay as part of the wage. It was then the employee's responsibility to retain the appropriate amount of the advance payment for the holiday period. The court found that the rolled up holiday pay was contrary to the Working Time Regulations. Referring to the Working time Directive the court held that the right to holiday pay is part of a single health and safety entitlement and that it is essential that payment should be made in association with the taking of leave. Inevitably, paying a rolled up rate discouraged workers from taking their holidays, was

---

5. See later in the chapter
6. But remain employed
7. Contrary to s.13 Employment Rights Act 1996
8. See Chapter 10

contrary to the Regulations[9] and therefore void under Regulation 35(1). The EAT set guidelines in *Marshalls Clay Products v. Caulfield* 2003 but the whole issue of the legality of rolled-up pay was referred to the European Court of Justice to determine whether it is compatible with the Working Time Directive.

Subsequently the EAT, in a group of cases under the name *Wiggens v. North Yorkshire CC* 2005 has issued further guidance to ensure that rolled-up holiday pay meets the requirements of the Working Time Regulations. Crucially the provision for rolled up holiday pay must be clearly incorporated into the contract of employment and represent a genuine addition to the rate of pay for the purpose of holidays. The actual percentage of pay allocated should be identified in the contract and preferably also on the pay slip. Also records of holidays should be kept and reasonably practical steps taken to ensure that holidays are taken within the relevant holiday year.

Part-time Working

A significant trend of employment over the last decade has been the growth of reliance on part-time working and the self employed. There are approximately six million individuals working part-time in the UK and significantly the vast majority of them are women. While as a general rule self employed workers tend to work longer hours than employees, there are nevertheless over a half a million[10] self employed part-timers in Britain. As we have already seen in Chapter 3 many self employed individuals offer personal service and may be classified as *'workers'* with increasing statutory protection.

It is still the case that the vast majority of part-time workers in the UK are women, many of whom find part-time work practicable because of family commitments. It does seem reasonable therefore to consider the law relating to part-time and fixed term work in this chapter as a major issue in the maintenance of work/life balance. Since the mid 1990s the courts have recognised that to distinguish between full-time and part-time staff in relation to employment rights is prima facie discriminating and this has led to statutory intervention. Prior to 1995 the qualifying period to acquire certain statutory rights was much longer for employees considered to be part-time working for less than 16 hours per week. Also those employed under fixed term contracts rather than indefinite contracts could have statutory rights excluded by their contracts of employment.[11] Employers across the full range of occupational categories offer part-time employment but there are particular concentrations of the six million part-time workers in;

- sales and services (check out operators, cleaners, catering assistants, porters);
- teaching and health professionals (school teachers, lecturers, nurses, physiotherapists);
- personal services (cooks, bar staff, hairdressers, domestic staff);
- clerical and secretarial (clerks, typists, computer operators).

Clearly while a number of part-time workers would prefer the opportunity to enter full-time employment a significant proportion of part-time workers choose to work part-time

---

9. Reg 16(1)
10. 10% of the workforce
11. No longer so see Chapter 10

because of the impracticability of full-time hours, given their other work or family responsibilities.

Previously a full-time employee was anyone who worked under a contract of employment for sixteen hours a week or more and as an employee such a person enjoyed the full range of statutory employment rights, generally after a period of continuous employment. In relation to part-time workers the position was that statutory rights could be acquired after five years continuous service for those employed under a contract for between 8 and 16 hours per week. Following the momentous decision of the House of Lords *in R v. Secretary of State for Employment ex parte EOC and Another* 1994 the legal position of part-time workers changed dramatically. Their lordships ruled that UK legislation conferring statutory rights on full-time workers and not part-timers in relation to redundancy and unfair dismissal was indirectly discriminatory against women and incompatible with European Community Law.

Where full-time employment is offered, but only on a temporary basis, perhaps to cover for an employee on maternity leave or secondment, the fact that there is an understanding as to the temporary nature of the work is important in determining the rights of the parties when the contract is terminated. Certainly the dismissal of a temporary worker eligible to present a claim for unfair dismissal is not automatically 'fair', but it could be regarded as such if the employer has acted reasonably in the circumstances in reaching his decision to dismiss. This would be the same for an employee who is required to serve out a probationary period and is dismissed having worked for the necessary period of continuous employment to qualify to present a claim for unfair dismissal. The use of fixed term contracts is considered later in the chapter. They are an increasingly popular device giving employers flexibility when they are faced with volatile markets. Factors such as economic pressure are used to attempt to justify the use of zero hours contracts where staff are provided with work, often on a daily basis when there is a demand for their services. The premature termination of a fixed term contract can also prove to be a costly exercise for employers.[12]

Part-time employees

The rights of part-time employees have now largely been brought into line with full-time staff by legislation. This was achieved by the Employment Protection (Part-time Employees) Regulations 1995. Under these Regulations the hours thresholds are abolished so that all distinctions in statutory employment rights based on the number of hours worked no longer apply. This means that part-time employees can rely on the same amount of continuous service as a full-time employee to qualify for rights relating to redundancy pay, unfair dismissal, written reason for dismissal, notice and maternity leave. Necessarily any statutory payments due to a part-time employee is calculated on a pro-rata basis.

All part-time employees are protected by discrimination law, and to comply with European Community law all part-time women are entitled to ordinary weeks maternity leave. Now all part-time employees with one years continuous service will also qualify for additional maternity leave.

---

12. See Chapter 10

Part-time workers

While the position of full-time women at the workplace has improved in recent years those who work part-time have fared considerably worse. Their rate of pay is disproportionally lower than full-time men and they do not enjoy the fringe benefits of full-time work including pension, sick pay, company cars, meal subsidies, child care and recreation facilities. Inevitably the rates for part-time workers are often poor because they are usually concentrated in workplaces where poor pay is standard. Some improvement in the position of part-time workers may result from the Part-Time Workers Directive which was implemented into UK law by the Part-Time Workers (Prevention of less Favourable Treatment) Regulations 2000. Whether the Regulations achieve their aim *'to ensure that part-timers are no longer discriminated against'* is debatable.

Under Regulation 5 a part-time worker has the right not to be treated less favourably by his employer than the employer treats a comparable full-time worker where the less favourable treatment is on the grounds that the worker is a part-time worker and is not justified on objective grounds.

An obvious but significant point is that the Regulations apply not only to employees but to the broader category of 'worker'. However for the Regulations to apply there must be a comparable full-time worker. A comparable worker is one who is engaged in the same or broadly similar work having regard to whether they have a similar level of qualification, skills and experience. Also the comparator must be employed by the same employer and on the same type of contract for instance indefinite or fixed term.

The only exception is where a full-timer goes part-time and makes a comparison with his own previous terms, or has returned to work after an absence of less than one year to the same or similar job. In either case the claimant can compare with a notional comparator. The comparator principle therefore is a major weakness in the Regulations for the vast majority of part-time workers who do not have full-time equivalent. To determine less favourable treatment the pro rata principle applies to the following benefits:

- Must not have a lower basic rate of pay than comparable full-timers unless it can be justified on objective grounds.
- Will be entitled to receive pay at overtime rates once they have worked the same number of hours as full-timers.
- Will be entitled to the same sick pay and maternity rights (pro rata).
- Will be entitled to equal access to occupational pension schemes.
- Will be entitled to the same training opportunities as full-timers.
- Will be entitled to the same annual holidays and potential leave (pro rata).
- Will be treated no less favourably when being selected for redundancy.

Matthews & Others v. Kent & Medway Towns Fire Authority 2004 (Court of Appeal) 2006 (House of Lords) In a majority decision the House of Lords in March 2006 has ruled that retained fire-fighters, as part-time workers, are employed under the same type of contract as their full-time colleagues and engaged in the same or broadly similar work. The majority felt that they operated under the same type of contract and disagreed with the tribunal that had found there were *'measurable additional job functions, which included educational preventative and administrative tasks carried out by the full-time staff but not by the retained fire-fighters'*. Here the House of Lords has provided a positive interpretation of the Regulations which will encourage other part-time workers to compare their position with full-time colleagues. When deciding whether work is of the same or broadly similar the tribunal should focus on the similarities in the work rather than the differences.

The Regulations also provide that part-timers can apply to their employers for a written statement of reasons if they believe that they are being treated less favourably than comparable full-timers.

Unfortunately it does seem that the comparator principle will make the Regulations redundant in relation to most part-time workers. Those who may benefit are full-time workers opting to go part-time who retain their terms and conditions after maternity leave or where there is a change in child-care arrangements.

Fixed Term Employees

An increasingly popular method of recruiting employees is to offer employment on a fixed term contract. In cases where staff are required to cover for long term illness or maternity leave or they are required for a particular project, a limited term arrangement for six months or a year has obvious benefits for the employer. Many employers believe that by offering fixed term employment they have an opportunity of measuring the employees' capability and it is then possible to exercise options on the expiration of the contract. In these cases the fixed term is almost a probationary period. In longer fixed term contracts it was also possible to exclude redundancy rights.[13] From the worker's perspective the fixed term contract would usually mean less security at work and more often than not less favourable terms and conditions of employment. Well over a million people in the UK work on limited term contracts and the majority of them are women. Following a European Directive, Regulations have been made to improve the legal position of fixed term contract holders to bring them in line with those on indefinite contracts.

The Fixed Term Employees (Prevention of less Favourable Treatment) Regulations 2002 These Regulations made under s.45 Employment Act 2002 are designed to implement the EC Fixed Term Work Directive. Following a public consultation on fixed term work practices it became obvious that there are considerable pay disparities between fixed term employees and permanent employees and many examples of less favourable terms and conditions generally.

Unfortunately the Regulations apply almost exclusively to employees despite pressure to extend them to 'workers. Among the reasons for not including the broader category of 'worker' include:

- The Directive applies to workers who have an employment contract.
- The framework agreement expressly excludes temporary agency workers.
- Many casual workers are already covered by the Part-Time Workers Regulations (see above).

The Regulations apply to:

- Seasonal or casual workers such as employees at children's summer camps and agricultural workers and shop assistants at Christmas.

---

13. No longer so

- Employees on fixed term contracts covering for maternity, paternity and sick leave.
- Employees hired for a specific task whose contract expires on completion of the task.

A permanent employee is an individual who is not employed under a fixed term contract.

A fixed term contract is defined as a contract of employment that under its provision determining how it will terminate in the normal course will terminate:

- On the expiration of a specified term.
- On the completion of a specific task.
- On the occurrence or none occurrence of a specified event.

Other than the attainment of normal retirement age the definition has been broadened to cover individuals who are employed to complete a project or who work until a specified event occurs such as its withdrawal of finding for a post. Under Reg. 2(1) the right to equal treatment depends upon a comparison with a *comparable permanent employee*.

Such a person must at the relevant time:

- Be employed by the same employer as the complainant.
- Be employed on the same or broadly similar work.
- Work or be based at the same establishment.

So in line with the Part-Time Workers Regulations equal treatment depends upon finding a comparable full-time employee. Where there is no comparable permanent employee in the same establishment one who satisfies the first two requirements and who works or is based at a different establishment will suffice.

An employee whose employment has ceased is not a comparable permanent employee. If there are permanent employees who do comparable work on different contracts then the complainant must select a comparator bearing in mind that there could be objective reasons for different treatment. Permanent employees however are not entitled to equal treatment with similar fixed term employees.

Less favourable treatment

The right to equal treatment is expressed under Regulation 3 as not to be treated less favourably than a comparable permanent employee;

- as regards the terms of employment; or
- by being subjected to any other detriment by an act or omission of the employer.

The less favourable treatment must relate to the fixed term status of the employee and cannot be justified on objective grounds. The Regulations provide specific examples of matters covered including the need for a service qualification to qualify for a condition, the opportunity to receive training or to secure permanent employment in the establishment. The 'pro rata principle' should be applied to determine less favourable treatment so that in relation to pay the fixed term employee should be entitled to such proportion as received by a comparable permanent employee as is reasonable having regard to the complainants lengths of service and to the terms upon which pay or other benefits is offered.

Guidance from the DTI suggests that benefits such as season ticket, season ticket loans, health insurance or staff discount cards, gym membership, holidays, bonuses and training should be available on a pro rata basis. Particular forms of less favourable treatment would include: selecting fixed term employees for dismissal or redundancy solely because of their status; Providing permanent employees with better promotion opportunities. There is a right to be informed by the employer of available vacancies in the establishment.

In *Department for Work and Pensions v. Webley* 2005 Regulation 3 was used to challenge a policy operated in job centres that temporary employees had their employment terminated after 51 weeks, regardless of whether there was a demand for their services. The Court of Appeal held that non renewal of a contract cannot by itself constitute less favourable treatment. Lord Justice Ward said that *'once it is accepted, as it must be, that fixed term contracts are lawful it seems to me inexorably to follow that the termination of such a contract by simple effluxion of time cannot constitute less favourable treatment by comparison with a full-time employee'.*

There is no less favourable treatment under Regulation 4 *'if the terms of a fixed term employee's contract of employment, taken as a whole, are at least as favourable as the terms of the comparable permanent employee's contract of employment'.* There would be a good reason for treating the employee less favourably if it was necessary and appropriate to achieve a legitimate business objective. The approach adopted should be to consider the employee's overall package giving individual benefits an objective monetary worth and considering their overall value. Then if the employer can show that the total package of terms and conditions is at least equal to the value of the comparable permanent employee then the differences may be justified. Even in cases where there are missing benefits it could still be possible to objectively justify their exclusion.

While the Regulations do not refer to pensions once again the DTI guidance suggests that they are covered and while it would not always be necessary to provide fixed term employees with access to occupational pension schemes this should be decided on a case by case basis.

The Regulations provide that a fixed term employee who feels he may have suffered less favourable treatment may, under Regulation 5, request a written statement from the employer giving particulars of reasons for the treatment within 21 days. Such statement is admissible in evidence in the tribunal and failure to provide it or providing a statement that is evasive will lead the tribunal to draw inferences that it considers just and equitable. There is no requirement to provide a statement in a dismissal scenario where s.92[14] provides a right to a statement of the reasons for dismissal.[15] To dismiss an employee for a ground connected with the Regulations is[16] automatically unfair regardless of the length of service. Also the right not to be subjected to a detriment under Reg. 6 is based on one the specified grounds in Reg. 6(3). They are that the fixed term employee:

- Brought proceedings under the Regulations or requests a written statement.
- Gave evidence or information in connection with proceedings.
- Alleged an infringement of the Regulations.
- Refused to forge a right conferred by the Regulations.

---

14. Employment Rights Act 1996
15. See Chapter 11
16. Under Regulation 6

- Refused to sign a workforce agreement for the purposes of the Regulations.

It is also automatically unfair[17] to select an employee for redundancy if the reason is one specified above however selection for redundancy solely on the basis that employees are on fixed term contracts may be justified. It should be stressed that in addition to the right not to suffer a detriment a fixed term employee may simply bring a complaint to an employment tribunal that the employer has infringed his right not to suffer less favourable treatment under Regulation 3. The complaint must be brought within three months of the less favourable treatment or detriment and in the case of a series of acts, within three months of the last of them. If the complaint is upheld the tribunal can declare the rights of the parties, recommend action and award compensation. Compensation should be considered on a *just and equitable* basis but unlike discrimination there is no award for injury to feelings.

Successive fixed term contracts

Under Regulation 8 some fixed term contracts may in the future be regarded as permanent in the following convoluted circumstances:

- where the employee is employed under a fixed term contract (contract A) and that contract has previously been renewed or extended; or
- where the employee has previously been employed by the same employer on a fixed term contract before the start of contract A.

In the above circumstances any provision in contract A restricting its duration *'shall be of no effect'* and the employee shall be a *'permanent employee'* only if the employee has been continuously employed under the contract or under that contract and a series of fixed term contracts for a period of four years or more excluding any period of employment before 10 July 2002. In 2006, therefore, there will be numerous fixed-term contracts being regarded as permanent.

If the above applies then the employment will be permanent unless the fixed term contract was objectively justified. Justification is to be determined when contract A was renewed or if not renewed when it was first entered into. A fixed term employee will become permanent on the date on which he acquires four years continuous employment or the date on which contract A was entered into or last renewed if later. If an employee considers that by virtue of a succession of fixed term contracts under Reg. 8 he should no longer be treated as fixed term but permanent he can[18] request a written statement from his employer confirming his status. The employer has 21 days to respond with reasons and any conflict may be resolved by an application to the employment tribunal for a declaration. Section 203 of Employment Rights Act applies to the Regulations restricting the right to contract out, by rendering such an agreement void.

---

17. Under Regulation 6(4)
18. Under Regulation 9

Maternity Rights

An employee has a number of statutory rights in relation to having a family:

- The right not to be dismissed for pregnancy or a reason connected with it or to suffer a detriment.
- The right to maternity leave and pay.
- The right to paternity leave and pay.
- The right to adoption leave and pay.
- The right to return to work after pregnancy or childbirth.
- The right to request flexible working.
- The right to time off for antenatal care.

Since the mid 1970s pregnant employees have had security of employment rights. In the UK while we have some of the longest maternity leave periods in the European Union our Statutory Maternity Pay Scheme is one of the least generous. There is now some provision for paternity and adoption rights introduced by the Employment Relations Act 1999 and the Employment Act 2002. Also under the 1999 Act there is a right not to suffer a detriment on the grounds of pregnancy, childbirth or maternity inserted as s.47C of the Employment Rights Act 1996. The rights provide an alternative to claim for sex discrimination and should provide wider protection covering detrimental treatment. There are a number new family friendly proposals in the Work and Families Bill with extended maternity and paternity leave to be introduced in 2007 and 2009. Novel mechanisms such as '*keeping in touch days*' will enable those taking leave to go into work without losing rights. Employers will also have the right to contact employees on leave to ease their return to work and notice to return will be extended to two months.

Despite the very basic nature of the right to maternity pay and leave, legislative provisions governing the right were difficult to interpret and were described by Browne-Wilkinson J as of '*inordinate complexity, exceeding the worst excesses of a taxing statute*'. He further observed that this was especially regrettable bearing in mind that they are regulating the rights of ordinary employers and employees. Hopefully the new legislation will make the rules more straightforward for those who have to interpret them. There are inevitable problems of interpretation, particularly when you consider how successive governments have changed and added to the maternity legislation. A further added complication is the fact that there may be contractual entitlements which would supersede the statutory rights. We will deal with the law relating to pregnancy dismissals before we consider maternity rights.

Pregnancy Dismissal

If an employee is dismissed because of her pregnancy then this will constitute unlawful sex discrimination under s.6(2) of the Sex Discrimination Act 1975. As such a claim could attract unlimited compensation it should always be considered.[19]

A dismissal because of the employee's pregnancy or because of a reason connected with the employee's pregnancy would also constitute automatically unfair dismissal[20] under s.99 of the Employment Rights Act 1996 and this applies regardless of the length of service of the employee.

---

19. See Chapter 6
20. See Chapter 11

A dismissal of a woman is automatically unfair if the reason for it is either:

- That she is pregnant or a reason connected with pregnancy such as a miscarriage.

- That she has given birth or a reason connected with the birth and she was dismissed during maternity leave.

- That she took maternity leave.

- That she gave the employer a medical certificate stating she was incapable of work after the end of the maternity period and her contract was terminated within four weeks of the end of maternity leave.

- That she is suspended from work on maternity grounds.

- That she was made redundant during maternity leave and without an offer of suitable alternative employment.

The expression *'any reason connected with pregnancy'* was given a wide interpretation by the House of Lords in a judgment on earlier legislation, which further emphasises the importance of this statutory right.

> In *Brown v. Stockton on Tees* BC 1988, the complainant was a care supervisor who, along with three others, was told that her employment would terminate on a given date. All four staff were given the opportunity of applying for three posts, each of one years duration, and they all applied. The complainant who was pregnant at the time of her interview was the unsuccessful candidate and so the only one made redundant. This was despite the fact that there was no criticism of her work and one of the successful candidates had less service with the council. While she successfully claimed unfair dismissal before the industrial tribunal the decision was reversed by the EAT and the Court of Appeal. Both appellate bodies upheld the decision to dismiss on the grounds that the employer had acted reasonably and fairly for the purpose of s.57(3)[21] and this was the appropriate section where the principal reason for dismissal was redundancy. The House of Lords disagreed, however. Their Lordships held that the dismissal contravened the Act as automatically unfair where the reason for dismissal is that the complainant is pregnant or in any other reason connected with her pregnancy. Ld Griffiths in reviewing the history of equal opportunities legislation said that *'it must be seen as a part of social legislation passed for the specific protection of women and to put them on an equal footing with men'*. While recognising the inconvenience caused to employers in coping with maternity leave and security of employment, he said that *'it is part of the price that has to be paid as a part of the social and legal recognition of the equal status of women in the work place. If an employer dismisses a woman because she is pregnant and he is not prepared to make arrangements to cover her temporary absence form work he is deemed to have dismissed her unfairly. There is no reason why the same principle should not apply if in a redundancy situation an employer selects the pregnant woman as the victim of redundancy in order to avoid the inconvenience of covering her absence from work in the new employment he is able to offer others who are threatened with redundancy'.*

In *Intelligent Applications v. Wilson* 1992 the applicant's absence during maternity leave revealed a genuine redundancy situation when it became obvious that her work could be carried out by existing staff. She claimed unfair dismissal when she was notified that she

---

21. The test of fairness – now s.98(4) Employment Rights Act 1996

was being dismissed for redundancy because of over capacity. The EAT agreed with the tribunal that this dismissal was automatically unfair because the reason for dismissal was connected with her pregnancy. The connection arose because the redundancy originally occurred as a result of the reallocation of duties and this came about because of the maternity leave which of course was granted due to her pregnancy.

Failure to consult in a redundancy situation where the redundant employee was on maternity leave was a feature in *McGuigan v. T. Baynes & Sons* 1997. Following a selection exercise a female solicitor was chosen for redundancy while on maternity leave and the EAT held that the dismissal was both unfair and constituted direct sex discrimination. But for her pregnancy the employer would have consulted her and less favourable treatment on the grounds of pregnancy did not require a male comparator.

In *Caledonia Bureau Investment and Property v. Caffrey* 1998 the complainant failed to return to work at the end of her 14 week maternity leave because of post-natal depression and submitted a medical certificate. When her illness ran to six weeks her employer dismissed her on the grounds of ill health with pay in lieu of notice. She complained of unfair dismissal and sex discrimination and succeeded on both counts in the employment tribunal. On appeal the EAT held that her dismissal for failing to return to work on the expiration of her maternity leave due to post-natal depression was for a reason connected with her pregnancy within the meaning of s.99[22] and automatically unfair. The EAT confirmed that the section is not limited to dismissals during the pregnancy and maternity leave but also where the contract of employment has been expressly extended. Such a dismissal was also held to be unlawful sex discrimination. '*Where a woman is dismissed by reason of an illness which is related to being pregnant, or having given birth, which illness arises or emerges during the course of the maternity leave period, the dismissal is still discriminatory even though it takes place after the expiry of that period, on the basis that at the time of dismissal she suffered from an illness from which a man could not suffer and thus was treated differently from her male counterparts.*'

A dismissal by reason of pregnancy is unlawful under the Sex Discrimination Act 1975[23] and would also infringe the Equal Treatment directive.

> In *Shomer v. B & R Residential Lettings Ltd.* 1992 the Court of Appeal considered a complaint of sex discrimination by a complainant who claimed that she had been dismissed on account of her pregnancy. Employed as a negotiator the complainant had been provided with a company car but she disobeyed a clear instruction by the managing director to deliver up the car for her employer's use while she was aboard on holiday. When she returned from holiday she found she had received a notice of dismissal. Her complaint of sex discrimination was based on the fact that prior to the holiday the complainant had informed the managing director that she was pregnant and this she alleged was the true reason for the dismissal. The Court of Appeal disagreed with the majority finding of the industrial tribunal that there was unlawful discrimination The Court confirmed that the for determining sex discrimination was to ask '*whether the woman would have received the same treatment as a man but for her sex. A tribunal is entitled to find discrimination even if there is not direct evidence, if there is some evidence from which they can properly draw an inference that a woman has been dismissed because of her pregnancy, whereas she would not be dismissed were she not pregnant and a man in comparable circumstances would not*

22. Employment Rights Act 1996
23. See Chapter 6

have been dismissed'. All the circumstances should be taken into account in drawing the hypothetical comparison including in a case such as this the fact that there was serious misconduct. If a hypothetical man would have been dismissed for such misconduct there was no discrimination and the tribunal's decision could be regarded as perverse.

The European Court of Justice has now cast doubt on this approach and it now seems that despite the fact that pregnancy is unique to one sex, unfavourable treatment on the grounds of pregnancy is automatically discrimination on the grounds of sex. There is no longer any need to compare the treatment of a pregnant woman with that of a hypothetical male. Such a ruling greatly strengthens the position of women so that a refusal to employ a woman because of the financial costs of the pregnancy can no longer be justified. This decision was reached in a Dutch case called *Dekker v. Stichting Vormingscentrum Voor Jonge Volwassenen (VJV Centrum)* 1991 and this interpretation of the Equal Treatment Directive should be followed by national courts in the UK.

> In *Webb v. EMO Air Cargo* 1994 the European Court of Justice was called upon to give a ruling on the issue. The complainant had been employed by a small firm to replace an employee who was due to take maternity leave in six months time. It was envisaged that the complainant could become a permanent employee but when three months after starting work she also became pregnant the employer decided to dismiss her. The English domestic courts including the House of Lords had held that if a comparable man had been recruited in similar circumstances and became unavailable for work for a similar period due to some medical reason he would also have been dismissed. On that basis there was no unlawful discrimination. The European Court however held that there could be no question of comparing the situation with that of a man. Pregnancy was not in any way comparable with a pathological condition there being a clear distinction between pregnancy and illness. The termination of the complainant's employment contract on the grounds of her pregnancy could not be justified by the fact that she was prevented on a purely temporary basis from performing the work for which she had been engaged. It is unlawful therefore for an employer to recruit an employee for an indefinite period and then dismiss her when she becomes pregnant, even if she was initially employed to replace another pregnant employee.

In the light of this ruling by the European Court the House of Lords finally decided in her favour in *Webb v. EMO Air Cargo (UK) Ltd. (No 2)* 1995. A decision to dismiss by reason of pregnancy therefore will constitute direct discrimination and given that the maximum level of compensation has been removed in sex discrimination cases it could provide a more significant remedy than unfair dismissal.

> The EAT in *O'Neill v. Governors of St. Thomas More RCVA Upper School* 1996 upheld a complaint of unfair discrimination against a school which had dismissed a religious instruction teacher during her maternity leave when it became known that the father of her child was the local Roman Catholic priest. The EAT rejected the contention that the motive for the dismissal was the paternity of the child and the applicants position at the school. These reasons it was held were all related to the pregnancy which was the dominant reason for the dismissal.

> The EAT also held in *Caruana v. Manchester Airport* 1996 that the failure to renew a fixed term contract on the grounds that the applicant would not be

available for work due to her pregnancy constituted sex discrimination. Here the new contract was an extension of a continuing employment relationship and to disqualify it from the protection of discrimination law *'would be a positive encouragement to employers to impose a series of short term contracts to avoid the impact of discrimination law, rather than offer a continuous and stable employment relationship'*. The applicant in this case was self employed and did not therefore qualify for protection under unfair dismissal law.

If the underlying cause of the dismissal is the fact that the employee is absent on maternity leave that will constitute unlawful sex discrimination. In *Rees v. Apollo Watch Repairs Plc* 1996 the complainant secretary was dismissed while on maternity leave because her employer found that her temporary replacement was more efficient. The EAT applied the decision of the House of Lords in *Webb (No 2)* and rejecting the test of the comparable male found the dismissal constituted discrimination on the grounds of sex. *'The protection afforded to women on maternity leave would be drastically curtailed if an employer was able to defeat a complaint of direct discrimination by a woman who, during such absence, discovers that her employer prefers her replacement, a state of affairs which has arisen solely as a result of her pregnancy and therefore of her sex.'*

If the tribunal finds reasons for dismissal other than pregnancy then it could decide there has been no discrimination. In *Berrisford v. Woodward Schools Ltd.* 1991 the complainant, a matron at a girls boarding school run by a Church, was dismissed when she informed the headmaster that she was pregnant but had no plans to marry. The decision to dismiss was taken, not because the matron was pregnant, but because her pregnancy demonstrated extra-marital sex. As male employees at the school were subject to the same code of conduct a majority of the EAT held that the tribunal was entitled to find that the dismissal was not discriminatory. There was no less favourable treatment as *'evidence of extra-marital sexual activity would have been treated as a ground for dismissal just as much in a man as in a woman'*. Furthermore as the dismissal was not for pregnancy, it was not in breach of the EC Equal Treatment Directive.

In *Hardman v. Mallon t/a Orchard Lodge Nursing Home* 2002 the tribunal had held that there could be no discrimination for failure to carry out a risk assessment in relation to a pregnant woman whose job involved lifting because no such assessment was carried out in respect of men. The EAT reversed this decision by holding that failure to conduct a risk assessment in respect of a pregnant woman falls within the umbrella of pregnancy discrimination which is automatic sex discrimination.

Maternity Leave

The right to secure employment for a pregnant employee has been embodied within legislation for a quarter of a century. Numerous amendments to the maternity rules have added to their complexity but under the Employment Relations Act 1999 an attempt was made to simplify the rules and the procedure. More significant changes are included in the Employment Act 2002[24] and the numerous Regulations made under it. There will be further changes introduced as a result of the Work and Families Bill 2005 coming into force in 2007 and 2009.

---

24. The 2002 Act

For the present maternity rights are conferred on employees and not on the self employed or workers, and under the Employment Protection (Part-Time Employees) Regulations 1995 the right to maternity leave now extends to part-time employees also. If an employee has a contractual right to maternity leave which is more beneficial than the statutory rights, then the employee can take advantage of the most beneficial right.

The core of maternity law remains within the Employment Rights Act 1996 to which substantial amendments and additions have been made by the 2002 Act. New Regulations under the 2002 Act have been made as well as amendments to the Maternity and Parental Leave Regulations 1999. In addition to changes to maternity leave and pay the 2002 Act and Regulations made under it introduce the rights to:

- Maternity leave and pay on the birth of a child.
- Paternity leave on the birth or adoption of a child.
- Adoption leave and pay on the placement of a child for adoption.
- Parental leave for qualifying employees.

The Civil Partnership Act 2004 came into force in December 2005. The Act provides for the registration of civil partnerships between same sex couples, giving them the right to be treated in the same way as spouses in relation to certain legal rights. Civil partners are now entitled to take paternity and adoption leave and pay and request flexible working to care for their partner's child.[25]

Maternity leave periods

Originally the right to maternity leave depended on an employee qualifying through continuity of employment. Now all pregnant employees are entitled to maternity leave irrespective of their length of employment or hours of work, with additional periods available for those with continuity of employment. There is a compulsory two-week period[26] of maternity leave starting with the birth, and it is a criminal offence for an employer to fail to ensure that this leave is taken

A distinction is made between ordinary maternity leave (OML) and additional maternity leave (AML). From 2003 OML was increased from 18 weeks to 26 weeks to begin at any time commencing with the start of the 11th week before the expected week of childbirth. During OML the employee is entitled to the same terms and conditions[27] had she not been away from work.[28] She may also be entitled to statutory maternity pay (SMP), which we will examine later. If an employee is absent with a pregnancy related illness at any time after the beginning of the 4th week before the Expected Week of Confinement then maternity leave starts automatically.

Additional maternity leave (AML) is a further fixed period of leave of 26 weeks commencing the day after the last day of OML. While all pregnant employees are entitled to OML, to

---

25. See later in the chapter
26. Four weeks for factory workers
27. Apart from the right to pay
28. Annual leave will accrue

qualify for AML it is necessary to have 26 weeks of continuous service on or before the 15th week before the expected date of childbirth. Under the present system it is possible to have an overlap between the ordinary and additional leave periods so one of the governments objectives is to introduce fixed periods of leave so the employers and employees can have greater certainty as to the periods and consequence of employee absence.

Under the present rules then the maternity leave periods for employees with 26 weeks continuous service are 26 weeks OML plus statutory maternity pay (SMP) followed by 26 weeks AML unpaid. The assumption is that if a woman is entitled to AML she will take it and so be absent for one year. There remains a requirement to serve notice of pregnancy, the expected week of childbirth (EWC) and the date she intends to start her leave in or before the 15th week before the EWC or as soon as is reasonably practicable. If requested the employee must produce a medical certificate and while the failure to give proper notice is no longer fatal without it absence could be regarded as unauthorised and this could constitute a disciplinary matter. There is a duty on the employer to respond within 28 days setting out the expected date of return.

Although a woman's contract of employment continues during AML, she is only entitled to a limited number of terms and conditions. The fundamental implied term in relation to trust and confidence remains in operation along with the right to notice and the benefit of procedures in relation to discipline and grievance. Statutory holiday rights still accrue during AML. In *Visa International v. Paul* 2003 the EAT held that an employer had fundamentally broken the implied term of trust and confidence for the purposes of a constructive dismissal when he failed to notify her when on maternity leave, of a vacancy, for which she would have applied had she been made aware of it.

Hoyland v. Asda Stores Ltd. 2005 demonstrates the distinction between a pregnant employee off work with a pregnancy related illness and an employee on maternity leave. The former must be treated as if she is at work while the latter is off work with protected status. The case surrounded the entitlement to a bonus payment which was paid pro rata for part-time staff and to full-time staff where there were absences of eight weeks or more. The claimant's absences during maternity leave exceeded eight weeks, and her bonus was reduced accordingly. The EAT agreed with the tribunal that the employers had not subjected the claimant to a detriment within the meaning of s.47C[29] or been guilty of sex discrimination. Other than a bonus entitlement for the two week compulsory maternity period there could be a reduction for the ordinary maternity period.

The right to return to work

The position is straightforward in relation to ordinary maternity leave for there is an assumption that the employee will return to her original job and no notice is required. If a woman wishes to return to work either before the end of the ordinary or additional maternity leave periods she must give the employer 21 days notice. Once the date of birth is known then the additional leave weeks can be calculated if it is relevant. There are notification provisions in relation to additional leave bearing in mind that the mother may have a change of heart and employers need to plan ahead. Not earlier than 21 days before the end of the ordinary leave period the employer may request written notification of:

---

29. See later in the chapter

1.   the date of birth; and

2.   whether she intends to return to work after the additional maternity leave.

There is a request to reply with 21 days but failure to do so will not result in a loss of rights but could constitute a disciplinary matter.

Previously a woman who suffered a detriment because she took maternity leave would have had to present a complaint of sex discrimination. Now the Regulations extend the right to complain to a tribunal because of detrimental treatment by an employer because a woman:

-   Is pregnant or has given birth.

-   Has taken the benefit of ordinary or extended maternity leave.

-   Has taken time off for antenatal care.

-   Is subject to a relevant statutory recommendation (e.g. a risk assessment).

The right to return from ordinary leave is to the original job on terms and conditions which are no less favourable. The right to return after additional leave is to the same job that she was employed to do, or if that is not reasonably practicable, to another job which is both suitable and appropriate in the circumstances.

Statutory Maternity Pay (SMP)

The period of entitlement to statutory maternity pay is to 26 weeks. Also the rate of pay remains 90% of the average weekly wage for the first six weeks but no longer underpinned by a statutory minimum for the remaining 20 weeks. The rate payable is the lower of 90% of the average weekly wage and weekly rate prescribed in Regulations (£106). For the vast majority then the rate will be 90% of average weekly wage for 6 weeks and £106 per week for the remaining 20 weeks. Under s.20 notice should be given to the employer of the potential liability to pay SMP of 28 days or as soon as is reasonably practicable. Employers can offset SMP against any allowable payments due to be made to the Inland Revenue depending on their National Insurance liability.

In *Alabaster v. Barclays Bank plc* 2005 the European Court of Justice held that the statutory maternity pay average weekly earnings calculation should take account of wage rises that were, or would have been, awarded to the claimant between the start of the 8 week period for calculating maternity pay and the end of her maternity leave.[30]

Paternity Leave

The right to paternity leave is a recognition that employees with paternity responsibilities should be entitled to take paid time off around the birth of a child for whom they have responsibility. Entitlement is determined upon the basis of the employee's relationship with the child whether as biological father, married or partner of the same sex or not, but some who lives with the mother in an enduring family relationship and has responsibility for the upbringing of the child.

The right is contained in s.1 of the Employment Act 2002 and is inserted in the Employment Rights Act 1996 as 80A-80C. There are also detailed provisions in the Paternity and

---

30. 1986 Regulations amended by the Statutory Maternity Pay (General) Regulations 2005

Adoption Leave Regulations regulating the statutory right for employees to take paternity leave on the birth of a child or placement of a child for adoption for the purposes of caring for the child or supporting the mother. In addition to the relationship requirement the employee must also have a minimum of 26 weeks continuous service with the same employer by the end of the 15th week before the expected week of childbirth.

The right is to two weeks leave taken within 56 days of the birth date and triggered by a notice of intention served on the employer. The notice must contain details of the EWC, the period of leave and its commencement date and include a signed declaration that the employee fulfills the conditions of entitlement. During the period of the leave the employee is entitled to all the contractual benefits except wages and salary and can return to the same job. If there is a contractual scheme for paternity leave the employee may take advantage of the most beneficial scheme. There are new rights not to suffer a detriment or dismissal because the employee took paternity leave creating a new category of automatic unfair dismissal.

Employees with one years service are also entitled to take parental leave as well as paternity leave. It is envisaged that the parental leave period will be taken after paternity leave as one consecutive period. For the moment parental leave remains unpaid.[31]

Paternity pay

Provisions for statutory paternity pay SPP is inserted into the Social Securities Contributions and Benefits Act 1992 by s.2 of the Employment Act 2002 and also supported by Regulations. Entitlement to SPP generally mirrors the entitlement to statutory paternity leave but there is a lower earnings limit and those employees who do not qualify will be able to claim income support. Written notice of at least 28 days is required to claim SPP with a self declaration as to entitlement. The weekly rate will be the same statutory maternity pay the lower of £106 or 90% of the employees normal weekly earnings. In most cases therefore it will be £106 per week. In fact the majority of fathers that take paternity leave are paid their full wage by their employer for the two week period. Employees with one years service will also be able to take parental leave which remains unpaid as well as paternity leave.

Adoption Leave

The right to take adoption leave is inserted into ss. 75A-75D of the Employment Rights Act by Employment Act 2002.[32] For the first time there will be a statutory right for employees to take adoption leave around the time of the placement of a child for adoption. The new rules are aimed to mirror as close as possible the existing provisions for maternity leave on childbirth. Consequently there is an ordinary adoption leave period (OAL) and an additional adoption leave period (AAL). To qualify for OAL an employee must first be matched with a child for the purposes of adoption and secondly have 26 weeks of continuous employment ending with the matching week.

Adoption leave is not available for the adoption of a child already known to the family such as a stepson or even a foster child who is adopted by his carer. The person legally adopting the child is entitled to the leave but in the case of a married couple, jointly adopting, either

---

31. See later
32. s.3

qualified person is entitled to take the time off work. Originally only married couples could jointly adopt but this has changed in the Adoption Children Act 2002. OAL will last for 26 weeks commencing with the date of placement or within 14 days of the expected date. AAL is an additional period of 26 weeks which commences from the last date of OAL so the total period of leave could be a year. An employee qualifying for OAL is entitled to take AAL but significantly it is unpaid.

Subject to further amendments if the placement is terminated then the qualifying employee is entitled to a further 8 weeks leave within the remaining leave period. This provision differs from maternity leave where the employee is entitled to the full period of leave and pay if the child dies or is stillborn. To support the provisions in the Employment Rights Act 1996 there are Regulations providing for the notice requirement, evidence and notice of adoption, and the Matching Certificate which mirrors the Medical Certificate of Pregnancy. The proposed period of 7 days notice of placement does however seem a short period to trigger what could be a years absence from work.

Regulations provide that during the adoption leave period the employee is entitled to the benefit of the terms and conditions of employment which would have applied had she not been absent other than those in relation to remuneration. The employee must also carry the burden of obligations that arise during that period. Practically then the employee will continue to accrue holiday entitlement and other benefits that depend on the length of service. Returning from OAL the employee is entitled to return to the same job with seniority, pension etc intact. The position on retaining from AAL is similar to returning from Additional Maternity Leave. The right to return is to the same job that she was employed to do or if that is not reasonably practicable to another job which is both suitable and appropriate in the circumstances. If an employee is entitled to AAL it is assumed that she will take it and 28 days notice is required if she intends to return to work earlier.

It will be unlawful to subject an employee to a detriment because she has taken adoption leave and if dismissed for that reason the dismissal will be automatically unfair. There are two circumstances where dismissal will not be automatically unfair:

(a) if the employer has fewer than five employees and it is not reasonably practicable to allow an employee on adoption leave to return to a job that is both suitable and appropriate; or

(b) it is not reasonably practicable to allow the employee to return to a job that is both suitable and appropriate and an associated employer offers such a job and that offer is unreasonably rejected.

As with maternity and paternity leave if there is a contractual right to adoption leave then the employee should take advantage of the most favourable right.

There are Regulations in relation to Statutory Adoption Pay (SAP) and once again the aim is to mirror the rules for Statutory Maternity Pay. SAP is payable for the OAL period for which the employee will have qualified. The weekly rate of payment will be the smaller of £106 or 90% of the employees normal weekly wage. This is the same rate as Statutory Paternity Pay and the lower rate of Statutory Maternity Pay.

Parental Leave

The right to parental leave was inserted into the Employment Rights Act 1996 by the Employment Relations Act 1999 and the detail is contained in the Maternity and Parental Leave Regulations. The Regulations contain the key elements of parental leave which will apply to all qualifying employees with the aim of encouraging employers to draw up their own schemes to suit the needs of their organisations. A contractual scheme that is in force prior to the Regulations will continue to be binding in so far as it is equivalent to or more favourable than the statutory scheme. The model scheme in the Regulations will apply as a default scheme is the employer fails to produce their own.

The right extends to employees with one years continuous employment who have responsibility for a child and the leave is for the purpose of 'caring for that child'. The birth certificate will normally provide evidence of the employee's responsibility for children born or adopted after 15 December 1999. The key age is up to five years from birth or adoption and the amount of leave is 13 weeks for each child. Under the Regulations employees may take a minimum of one week at a time up to four weeks in one year. A minimum of four weeks notice of intention to take two weeks parental leave must be given and longer notice for longer periods of leave. Because the leave is an entitlement granted in respect of the child an employee who changes employer without having taken the full leave entitlement may transfer any remaining leave to the new employer. Before taking that leave however the employee would have to re-qualify by working for a full year for the new employer.

Employers cannot refuse to grant leave but may postpone it for up to six months if the operation of the business would be substantially prejudiced if the employee took leave during the period identified in the notice. The contract of employment continues during the period of the leave in particular implied terms relating to trust and confidence and confidential information continue to apply but there is no right to be paid. The employee is entitled to the benefit of terms and conditions which would have applied had not he not been absent. There is a right not to suffer a detriment or be dismissed for taking parental leave.

The Regulations on parental leave envisage the period of leave to be in multiples of one week. This was intended to prevent parental leave from being taken on a day-by-day basis. In *Rodway v. South Central Trains Ltd.* 2005 an employee who asked to take one day's parental leave to look after his child, was disciplined when he took the day off anyway when permission was refused. An employment tribunal upheld his complaint under s.47A but the EAT overruled the decision. The Court of Appeal held that parental leave under the statutory scheme can only be taken for a minimum of one week or in blocks of weeks. The court commented that '*one can readily see that employers might well prefer to be able to make arrangements for temporary employees to cover for a week during an employee's absence, rather than to face the problems arising from an employee being absent for a single day or two odd days*'. Unfortunately the decision seems to ignore the practicalities of child care responsibilities.

Time off for antenatal care

Under s.55(1) Employment Rights Act 1996 an employee who is pregnant and on medical advice who makes an appointment to attend at a place for antenatal care has the right not to be unreasonably refused paid time off to enable her to keep the appointment. If challenged, the employee should be prepared to verify that she is pregnant by producing a medical certificate to that effect and producing an appointment card. This does not apply when the employee's appointment is the first during her pregnancy.

Once again, an employee who feels that the employer is infringing her right, may complain to an employment tribunal within three months and the tribunal has power to make a declaration and award compensation.

Time Off for Dependents

The right to time off for dependents was introduced as a result of the Parental Leave Directive in force from 1999. The aim of the Directive was to give workers time off for urgent family reasons in cases of sickness or accident making the presence of the worker indispensable. This right along with maternity paternity and adoption leave is a further example of the government's commitment to family friendly policies in the working environment. Schedule 4 of the Employment Relations Act 1999 adds a new s.57A to the Employment Rights Act 1996 containing the provision. The right is to a reasonable amount of time off during working hours to take action in the following circumstances:

- To provide assistance when a dependent falls ill, gives birth, is injured or assaulted.
- To make arrangements for the provision of care for a dependent who is ill or injured.
- Upon the death of a dependent.
- Due to the unexpected disruption or termination of the arrangements for the care of a dependent.
- To deal with an incident involving a child during the time when an educational establishment has the care of that child.

Significantly the rights to time off in the above circumstances does not carry with it any right to be paid during the period of time off. Also the period is that which is reasonable and so left to the interpretation of a tribunal in a case where enforcement is necessary. A complaint may be made[33] within three months of an unreasonable refusal and compensation which is just and equitable may be awarded for an infringement of the right. A requirement of s.57A in relation to dependent care leave is to inform the employer of the reasons for the absence as soon as reasonably practicable.

In *QUA v. John Ford Morrison Solicitors* 2003 the EAT gave helpful guidance in determining what would constitute reasonable time off for the purposes of s.57A. *'In determining what is a reasonable amount of time off work the disruption or inconvenience caused to an employer's business by the employee's absence are irrelevant factors which should not be taken into account. The operational needs of the employer cannot be relevant to a consideration of the time an employee reasonably needs to deal with an emergency circumstance of the kind specified.'*

In *Truelove v. Safeway Stores plc* 2004 an employee who requested a day off work at short notice failed to fully explain the reason for her proposed absence. Nevertheless the EAT found that sufficient information had been given to the employer to support the request. The EAT stated that the provision was intended to allow parents faced with sudden and difficult circumstances to take time off to care for dependents. They were not required to articulate their reasons to their employer with any formality provided the employer could understand that something had happened, affecting the relevant dependent, which made it necessary to leave work urgently.

---

33. Under s.57B

Suspension from work on medical grounds

This right arises also after one month's continuous employment and provides that an employee is entitled to be paid for up to twenty six weeks during which the employee is suspended from work on medical grounds. The suspension must be in consequence of a requirement imposed under statute or a Code of Practice issued under the Health and Safety at Work Act 1974. Basically then, if an employee is suspended due to a relevant health hazard, he is entitled to be paid provided he is available for work, has complied with any reasonable requirements imposed by the employer and has not unreasonably refused an offer of suitable alternative employment. Once again the right is enforced by means of a complaint to an industrial tribunal within three months of any day to which it is claimed. The tribunal can order the employer to make a payment of any remuneration due if it finds the complaint made out.

Flexible Working

The right to request flexible working was introduced by s.47 of the Employment Act 2002 inserted as ss.80F and 80G of the Employment Rights Act 1996. The dual aim is to make the lives of parents with young children easier and enable them to retain their skills in the workplace, *'For the first time the law will facilitate a dialogue between parents and their employers about working patterns that better meet parents childcare responsibilities and employer's need.'* Under the Work and Families Bill the right to request flexible working will be extended to carers and possibly those with older children from 2007.

Employers are under a legal duty to consider application for flexible working from employees who are parents of children under six years of age or of disabled children under 18. To qualify an employee must have 26 weeks of continuous service on the date of application. The right does not extend to workers.[34] Also the employee must have a sufficiently close relationship with the child in question as biological parent, guardian, adopter or foster carer, married/partner or civil partner of such a person and live with the child. He must also have responsibility for the upbringing of the child.

Inevitably there are many requests for flexible working when maternity leave comes to an end, either to job share or to work part-time. In Chapter 6 we saw that a refusal of such a request could constitute unlawful indirect sex discrimination.

To request flexible working the employee must submit a formal application detailing the working patterns applied for and its impact on the employer with a qualification statement. The application must be dealt with by the employer in accordance with the Regulations and can only be refused on one or more of a number of grounds.

- The burden of additional costs.
- The detrimental effect on ability to meet customer demands.
- The inability to reorganise work among existing staff.
- The inability to recruit additional staff.
- The detrimental impact on quality or performance.
- Insufficiency of work during the periods the employee proposes to work.

---

34. See Chapter 3

- Planned structural changes.

- Such other grounds as may be specified in Regulations. There are important procedural requirements in relation to dealing with an application involving the holding of a meeting within 28 days with the employee and a representative. Notice of its decision should be made within 14 days with a right to appeal within a further 14 days.

One of the main purposes of the initial meeting is to discuss possible alternative compromise arrangements and to enable agreement to be reached the parties could agree an extension of time limit to consider feasibility.

The right to a flexible working consideration is enforced by means of a complaint to an employment tribunal[35] within three months of an alleged breach of statutory duty or the date when the employee was notified of his unsuccessful appeal. A complaint based on a decision to reject the application should rest upon an allegation that the decision was made on incorrect facts. Inevitably the employee must have exhausted the employer's appeal route and initiated the grievance procedure before a complaint will be tolerated by a tribunal. If the tribunal decides that the complaint is well founded it will make a declaration to that effect and may order a reconsideration of the application and make an award of compensation to the employee. It seems therefore that the tribunal's jurisdiction to scrutinise the employer's decision making is limited to assessing whether the correct procedure was followed and whether the grounds for the decision making were based upon correct findings of fact. The aim is that employers will consider requests seriously and fairly so that issues of commercial viability should not be subject to challenge.

We now have a positive interpretation of the flexible working rules. *Commotion Ltd. v. Butty* 2006 considers the role of the tribunal in scrutinising the employer's decision making when a request for flexible working has been made. The employees initial request had been turned down and so she made a formal request under s.80F. She wished to reduce her full-time hours to a three-day week when, as a grandmother, she became legally responsible for her grandchild. The employer refused the request and an appeal on the grounds that to allow it would have a detrimental impact on performance at the warehouse at which she worked. The claim was brought to the tribunal under s.80H(1)(6) that the decision by her employer to reject the application was based on incorrect facts. The EAT held that in investigating a refusal of flexible working the tribunal is entitled to investigate the evidence to see whether it is based on incorrect facts. This involves an examination of the circumstance surrounding the situation and an enquiry as to the effect the granting of the request would have had. Here the tribunal was entitled to find that the evidence did not support the employer's assertion that allowing the claimant to work on a three-day week would have a detrimental effect on performance. Accordingly the tribunal was entitled to find that the employer was in breach of the flexible working provisions.

It is inevitable in a chapter called work/life balance decisions have to be made as to the material appropriate for inclusion. You should appreciate that throughout the text there are issues dealt with, particularly in relation to statutory rights that could be interpreted as in some way supporting the needs of individuals who are attempting to balance home and working life.

---

35. Under s.80H

Further Reading

Fredman, Sandra *Women at Work: The Broken Promise of Flexicurity* (2004) ILJ 299.

Honeyball, Simon *Pregnancy and Sex discrimination* (2000) 29 ILJ 43.

McColgan, Aileen *Family Friendly Frolics ? The Maternity and Parental Leave etc. Regulations 1999* (2000) 29 ILJ 125.

McColgan, Aileen *Missing the Point: The Part-Time Workers Regulations 2000* (2000) 29 ILJ 260.

The Employment Act 2002: the family friendly provisions (2002) 695 IRLB 2.

Chapter 8

Health and Safety at Work

Any treatment of the law relating to employment should involve an examination of health and safety law. Here the topic is given detailed consideration in an attempt to address its complexity and reflect the high priority that should be given to the aim of securing a safe working environment. In addition while health and safety law is embodied within the UK legislation and common law it is an area of law that has been subjected to dramatic change due to our membership of the European Community. Legal duties in relation to health and safety are imposed with the aim of encouraging a safe working environment and when you consider the high number of deaths and injuries as well as diseases contracted at the workplace in the UK, enforcement of health and safety law should be a priority. Potential primary and secondary liability under the Common law and Statute for psychiatric injury caused by stress at work is dealt with in this chapter.

In the United Kingdom legal intervention in the field of health and safety has a long history and the earliest examples of employment legislation, the nineteenth century Factories Acts, were designed to ensure that a slender cushion of legislative protection was provided for those categories of workers at particular risk. The criminal codes in relation to health and safety law were contained in numerous statutes and statutory instruments e.g. the Factories Act 1961, the Office Shops and Railway Premises Act 1963. Eventually in 1972 the Robens Committee on Safety and Health at work criticised this fragmented state of the law. As a result of the Robens Committee recommendations the Health and Safety at Work Act 1974 was passed.

The Act is still the core legislation and the original aims were to:

- Lay down general duties applicable across the industrial spectrum.
- Provide a unified system of enforcement under the control of the Health and Safety Executive and local authorities.
- Create the Health and Safety Commission to assist in the process of changing attitudes and producing detailed regulations applicable to each industrial sector backed up by Codes of Practice designed to give guidance as to how general duties and specific regulations could be satisfied.

By imposing legal duties on employers, employees, contractors, manufacturers and others backed up by criminal sanctions, the 1974 Act is designed to achieve minimum standards of conduct and so addressing the risk of injury and enhancing the welfare of those at the workplace. In addition to criminal sanctions however the possibility of civil redress must also be considered so that those injured at the workplace have a further avenue of redress to secure compensation by relying on common law principles.

European Community Law

As previously stated UK businesses also operate in a European legal framework and health and safety issues are an established part of European Community social policy. Since the adoption of the Single European Act 1986 the regulation of Health and Safety at work in the UK as been refined by European Community law initiatives. In 1990 the Chairman of the Health and Safety Commission said that *'the European Community has now to be regarded as the principal engine of health and safety law affecting the UK not just in worker safety but also major hazards and most environmental hazards'*. Article 22 of the Single European Act 1986 added a new Article 118A to the Treaty of Rome and so introduced a new concept *'the working environment'*. Following the Amsterdam Treaty this Article is now contained within Article 137.

> Article 137 provides that *'Member States shall pay particular attention to encouraging improvements especially in the working environment, as regards the health and safety of workers and shall set as their objective the harmonisation of conditions in this area, while maintaining the improvements made.'*

The significance of Article 137 is that it incorporates the qualified majority procedure rather than unanimity for the adoption of health and safety provisions by the Council of Ministers. *'In order to help achieve the objective laid down in the first paragraph, the Council acting by a qualified majority on a proposal from the Commission, in co-operation with the European Parliament and after consulting the Economic and Social Committee, shall adopt, by means of directives, minimum requirements for gradual implementation, having regard to the condition and technical rule obtaining in each of the Member States.'*[1]

This means that despite the objection of individual member states the majority view as to setting health and safety standards throughout the European Community will prevail. Furthermore the European Parliament has suggested that the expression *'working environment'* in Article 137 should be given a wide definition so that it could embrace matters such as the arrangement of a workplace as well as physical and psychological conditions at work. The working environment provisions were also acknowledged by the acceptance of the Charter of Fundamental Rights of Workers as an integral part of the development of the internal market.

Health and Safety Regulations

In order to implement numerous directives a number of Regulations have been produced. In addition, practical guidance in the form of Codes of Practice have also been produced to ensure compliance with the Regulations which have been in force from the beginning of 1993.

---

1. Paragraph 2

The Regulations apply to virtually all work activities and place duties on employers in relation to their employees and in some circumstances to the public and self employed contractors in relation to themselves and others who may be affected by their acts or omissions. The Regulations are very comprehensive however it should be stressed that the main focus is initially to promote awareness and enforcement is not likely unless:

- *the risks to health and safety are immediate and evident, or*
- *employers appear deliberately unwilling to recognise their responsibilities to ensure the long term health, safety and welfare of employees and others affected by their activities.*

The Health and Safety (Consultation with Employees) Regulations 1996 require employers to consult with employees who are not covered by safety representatives appointed by recognised unions[2] under them. They are a top up to the 1977 Regulations aimed to secure compliance with the Health and Safety Framework Directive which states that *'Employers shall consult workers and/or their representatives and allow them to take part in discussions on all matters relating to health and safety at work.'* There is no doubt that the Health and Safety Commission concluded that those new Regulations were necessary following two decisions of the European Court of Justice on the acquired rights directive and collective redundancies directive where the obligation to consult other than where there are recognised trade unions was confirmed.

The Management of Health and Safety at Work Regulations 1992 are aimed at improving health and safety management and apply to almost all work activities in Great Britain and offshore. Under them employers are required to adopt a well organised and systematic approach to comply with their statutory duties in relation to health and safety. In pursuing this objective employers are required to:

- Carry out a risk assessment of health and safety so that preventive and protective measures can be identified. While there is an existing obligation in the Health and Safety at Work Act for employers of five or more employees to prepare a written health and safety policy there is now an additional obligation on them to record the findings of the risk assessment.
- Make arrangements for putting into practice the health and safety measures that follow from the risk assessment. These arrangements will include planning, organisation, control, monitoring and review and must be recorded by employers with five or more employees.
- Appoint competent people to help devise and implement the appropriate measures and ensure that employees including temporary workers are given appropriate health and safety training and understandable information.
- Provide appropriate health surveillance for employees and set up emergency procedures where the risk assessment shows it to be necessary.
- Consult employees safety representatives, provide facilities for them and co-operate with other employers sharing the same working environment.

Risk assessments[3] should identify hazards and then evaluate risks which should be remedied as soon as possible. The assessment should be carried out by health and safety personnel or suitably qualified line managers. It should be comprehensive covering organisational, job,

---

2. For collective bargaining
3. See Chapter 7

workplace and individual factors and where possible include the participation of individual employees and safety representatives.

Following amendments to the 1992 Regulations resulting from the Pregnant Workers Directive[4] employers are required to address the health risks of pregnant mothers. This involves carrying out a risk assessment, considering preventative measures, attempting to avoid the risk of altering working conditions and suspending the woman on full pay if no suitable alternative work is available.

> In *Day v. T Pickles Farms Ltd.* 1999 the EAT held that the obligations in the Regulations are triggered by employing a woman of childbearing age rather than waiting for an employee to become pregnant. Interestingly the EAT also held that failure to carry out a risk assessment could constitute a 'detriment' for the purposes of the Sex Discrimination Act and provide a right to damages for the injury caused by the employer's failure.

> The EAT in *Hardman v. Mallon t/a Orchard Lodge Nursing Home* 2002 confirmed that failure to conduct a risk assessment in respect of a pregnant woman who lifted as part of her job was automatic sex discrimination *'construing the Sex Discrimination Act by reference to the Equal Treatment Directive and the Pregnant Workers Directive, it is not necessary for the treatment of a pregnant woman to be compared with the employer's treatment of a comparable male employee, or non pregnant female employee. If the basis of the treatment is pregnancy it is unlawful irrespective of the comparable treatment of men'.*

In relation to employees, the Regulations require them to follow health and safety instructions and report dangers. Finally as far as the management of health and safety is concerned it should be recognised that there is an overlap between the Regulations and some existing requirements contained in duties and Regulations. A specific Regulation will replace a general duty but there is no requirement to for instance carry out two risk assessments for the purposes of different Regulations. A civil claim for damages for breach of statutory duty based on the Management of Heath and Safety at Work Regulation 1992 was rejected by the Court of Session in *Cross v. Highlands and Islands Enterprise* 2001 which held that the statutory duties created by the Regulations did not give rise to a civil right of action.

The Provision and Use of Work Equipment Regulations 1992, were replaced by the Provision and Use of Work Equipment Regulations 1998. Under the 1998 Regulations general duties are placed upon employers in relation to equipment used at work and minimum requirements are identified to apply to all industries.

The expression *'work equipment'* is given a very wide definition and covers machinery of all kinds ranging from a hand tool to a complete plant. The *'use'* of such equipment includes all activities ranging from installing and repairing to transporting and dismantling.

It should be stressed that employers who already use 'good practice' in the use of work equipment will find themselves in compliance with the new Regulations.

The general duties will require an employer to:

- Assess working conditions in particular risks and hazards when selecting work equipment.

---

4. See Chapter 7

- Ensure that equipment is suitable for its use and that it conforms with EC product safety directives.

- Give staff adequate information, instruction and training and maintaining equipment in efficient working order and a good state of repair.

- Ensure that work equipment is maintained in an efficient state, in efficient working order and in good repair.

The above duty was interpreted by the Court of Appeal in *Stark v. the Post Office* 2000. The equipment in question was a postman's bicycle which had suffered a wheel lock when part of the brake had broken and became lodged in the front wheel. The court rejected the postman's claim for damages both under the common law and the Regulations on the grounds that the brake defect would not have been disclosed on a routine inspection or even a rigorous examination of the bike. The Court of Appeal took a different view construing the regulation as imposing an absolute duty on the employer. Establishing that the mechanism failed to work efficiently and that failure caused the accident is sufficient to impose liability. The court emphasised that absolute liability in these circumstances was the position under previous legislation and the relevant Directive makes it clear that *'the Directive does not justify any reduction in levels of protection already achieved in member states'.*

In addition to the general duties the Regulations also contain specific requirements in relation to equipment which will replace existing Regulations. They include:

- Guarding of the dangerous parts of machines.

- Protection against specific hazards such as articles or substances, fire risks and explosion.

- Ensuring adequate lighting, maintenance, warnings, stability, control systems and control devices.

The Manual Handling Operations Regulations 1992 are aimed at preventing injuries which occur at the workplace due to the mishandling of loads by incorrect lifting, lowering, pushing, pulling, carrying or simply moving them about. Such operations should have been identified in the risk assessment. The Regulations require an employer to ensure that:

- There is a genuine need to move a load and that manual handling is necessary rather than mechanical means.

- The weight size and shape of the load is assessed along with the working environment and the handler's capabilities.

- In so far as is reasonably practicable the risk of injury is reduced by for example reducing the load, employing mechanical means or training the handler.

The aim of the Workplace (Health Safety and Welfare) Regulations 1992 is to replace numerous parts of existing legislation including the Factories Act 1961 and the Office Shops and Railway Premises Act 1963. They cover many aspects of health safety and welfare at the workplace in particular the working environment which includes temperature, ventilation, lighting, room size, work stations and seating. Facilities at the workplace are covered which includes toilets, washing, eating and changing facilities, drinking water, clothing storage, rest areas and facilities along with the need for cleanliness and effective removal of waste. Specific aspects of safety are included in particular relating to safe passage of pedestrians and vehicles, windows and skylights, doors, gates and escalators and floors.

The Workplace Regulations[5] requires that where a person has to wear specialist clothing for the purposes of work then suitable and sufficient changing facilities should be provided. The High Court recently decided that specialist clothing should not be limited to distinct uniforms but should be interpreted to include *'any clothing which would not ordinarily be worn other than for work even if it is worn coming to and from work. As a consequence it did include a postal workers uniform and allowing women to change in the toilets did not satisfy the requirements of the Regulations'.*

Under the Personal Protective Equipment at Work Regulations 1992 protective equipment includes protective clothing, eye foot and head protection, harnesses, life jackets and high visibility clothing. Where risks are not adequately controlled by other means there is a duty to provide PPE free of charge for employees exposed to risks. The PPE provided must provide effective protection as appropriate to the risks and working conditions, take account of the worker's needs and fit properly. Further Regulations are necessary to comply with a separate EC directive on the design certification and testing of PPE. The present Regulations require an assessment of risks to determine the suitability of PPE; the provision of storage facilities; adequate training information and instruction; appropriate methods of cleansing maintenance and replacement and effective supervision to ensure its proper use. In a general statement the Regulations provide[6] that *'every employer shall ensure that any personal protective equipment provided to his employees is maintained (including replaced or cleaned as appropriate) in an efficient state, in efficient working order and in good repair'.*

In *Fytche v. Wincanton Logistics plc* 2004, a tanker driver delivering and collecting milk was issued with safety boots with steel toecaps to protect his feet in case something heavy fell on them. When his tanker got stuck in the snow and he dug it free, one of his boots leaked through a tiny hole and as a result, he suffered frostbite and part of his toe had to be amputated. He brought proceedings, claiming a breach of the Regulations to keep his equipment in good repair. He failed in the county court, High Court and the Court of Appeal, on grounds that the Regulation only requires the employer to maintain or repair the equipment so as to guard against the risk for which they were supplied. By a majority the House of Lords also rejects the claim. Lady Hale and Lord Walker, both dissenting, thought that a boot with a hole in it is not in good repair. The majority decision however was that the duty to keep the equipment efficient and in good repair is not an absolute one. It relates to the purpose of protecting against the relevant risk, and not to any other risks which might arise. In this case, the employee was not expected to expose himself to severe weather conditions and was not issued with boots for that purpose. An employer has a continuing duty to maintain the equipment so that it continues to be suitable. Lord Hoffmann, in the leading decision, reasons, however, that *'Reg. 7 cannot, by means of the repairing obligation, require the employer to provide equipment which he need not have provided in the first place.' 'In the present case, the claimant had been provided with boots with steel toecaps because his employers considered that there was sufficient risk of heavy things falling on his feet and, notwithstanding the hole, they remained adequate for that purpose. Accordingly, the damage sustained by the claimant when freezing water seeped through the hole was not the consequence of any breach of statutory duty on the part of the employers.'*

The Health and Safety (Display Screen Equipment) Regulations 1992 apply where an individual habitually uses display screen equipment as a significant part of normal work. Duties are imposed on employers if equipment is used for the display of text, numbers and

---

5. Regulation 24
6. Regulation 7(1)

graphics but some systems are excluded including transport systems for public use, cash registers, window typewriters and portable systems not in prolonged use. The duties require employers to:

- assess display screen work stations and reduce risks revealed;

- ensure that minimum requirements are satisfied in relation to the display screen, keyboard, desk and chair, working environments and task design and software;

- plan the work so that there are changes of activity and appropriate breaks; and

- provide information and training for display screen users, eye testing and special spectacles if needed.

There is no doubt that under these Regulations in particular, employers will have to incur considerable expense to ensure that equipment meets the basic minimum requirements. Existing work stations must be brought up to standard and the costs of eye testing spectacles and insurance must all be borne by the employer.

Enforcement of Health and Safety Law

Enforcement of the safety legislation is in the hands of the Health and Safety Executive and local authorities which have a number of powers at their disposal. The main power is to appoint inspectors who have authority to enter premises, take samples and require information to be given. The breach of a general duty or a specific regulation under the Health and Safety legislation is a criminal offence. This can lead to a prosecution in the criminal courts. Less serious offences are dealt with summarily in the Magistrates Court and those of a more serious nature are tried on indictment[7] in the Crown Court. Conviction in summary proceedings carries a fine of up to £20,000, or for an indictable offence, an unlimited fine and/or up to two years imprisonment. The fundamental aim of those enforcing the law is to encourage a positive attitude to health and safety at the workplace rather than to take numerous employers through the criminal courts. There is no doubt however that some employers resent the economic cost of health and safety and it may only be the threat of criminal prosecution, that will cause the more recalcitrant employers to respond. Unfortunately enforcement remains inadequate due to under resourcing of the Inspectorate.

In May 2005 an NHS Trust was successfully prosecuted by the Health and Safety Executive for a breach of s.2 of the Health and Safety at Work Act in failing to provide sufficient care for one of it's staff. The case was referred to the Crown Court from the Magistrates who felt that their powers of punishment, a fine of up to £20,000, were too limited. The South West London and St. Georges' Mental Health NHS Trust was found guilty of a series of systematic failures which led to a psychiatric nurse being battered to death by a schizophrenic patient. The failures which were seriously unacceptable and incompetent, included leaving a nurse to supervise an aggressive patient with no walkie-talkie or personal alarm and with insufficient training in restraint techniques. Justifying the £28,000 fine the judge reflected that a large fine might be appropriate for a profitable organisation. Here the NHS needed funds and a substantial fine would result in a reduction of healthcare or further injection of taxpayers money.

---

7. Triable with a jury

Notices

One of the major innovations of the Health and Safety at Work Act was the introduction of constructive sanctions. A Health and Safety Inspector who believes that an employer is contravening one of the statutory provisions may serve on that person an improvement notice requiring that the contravention be remedied within a specific period of not less than twenty one days. The notice will specify the provision which is contravened and state how it is being broken. In cases where the contravention involves an immediate risk of serious injury, the inspector may serve a prohibition notice which will direct that the particular activity is terminated until the contravention is rectified. Such a notice may take immediate effect or be deferred for a specified time. Failure to comply with a prohibition notice, for example by using a machine which has been identified as a serious source of danger, is an offence triable on indictment in the Crown Court.

While liability is generally associated with fault the courts have recently confirmed that even where there was little evidence of personal blame, an occupier of factory premises may still be held liable under the Factories Act 1961 if he fails to make his premises as safe as is reasonably practicable for all persons who may work there, even if they are not employees.

> In *Dexter v. Tenby Electrical Accessories Ltd.* 1991 contractors were employed by the defendants to install fresh air fans at their factory premises and for this purpose an employee of the contractor was required to work for a period on the factory roof. Despite the fact that the defendants were unaware that the employee was working on the roof they were nevertheless liable as occupiers of the factory when he suffered injuries after falling through it. The Health and Safety Executive charged the defendant with a contravention of s.29(1) of the Factories Act 1961 which provides *'there shall, so far as is reasonably practicable, be provided and maintained safe means of access to every place which any person has at anytime to work, and every such place shall, so far as is reasonably practicable, be made and kept safe for any person working there'*. While the Magistrates accepted the argument that the defendants had no control over the employee's place of work and there was no case to answer, this was rejected on appeal by the prosecution to the Divisional Court. The Appeal court held that lack of knowledge was no defence and if a person is ordered by his employer, a contractor, to work on a factory roof, the occupier of the factory is liable under the Act if the roof is in an unsafe condition.

General duties

Most of the general duties contained in the 1974 Act impose on a number of different categories of person, a standard of care based on the idea of reasonable practicability. The most important general duty is that contained in s.2(1). Section 2(2) identifies matters to which the duty extends:

Under s.2(1) It shall be the duty of every employer to ensure, so far as is reasonably practicable, the health, safety and welfare at work of all his employees.

> (2) *Without prejudice to the generality of an employee's duty under the preceding subsection, the matters to which that duty extends includes in particular-*

(a) *the provision and maintenance of plant and systems of work that are, so far as is reasonably practicable, safe and without risks to health;*

(b) *arrangements for ensuring, so far as is reasonably practicable, safety and absence of risks to health in connection with the use, handling, storage and transport of articles and substances;*

(c) *the provision of such information, instruction, training and supervision as is necessary to ensure, so far as is reasonably practicable, the health and safety at work of his employees;*

(d) *so far as is reasonably practicable as regards any place of work under the employer's control, the maintenance of it in a condition that is safe and without risks to health and the provision and maintenance of means of access to and egress from it that are safe and without such risks;*

(e) *the provision and maintenance of a working environment for his employees that is, so far as is reasonably practicable, safe, without risks to health, and adequate as regards facilities and arrangements for their welfare at work.*

The scope of the general duty, contained in s.2, qualified by the words *'reasonably practicable'* is difficult to determine. However the meaning of this phrase is obviously crucial in determining the scope of an employer's duty. It would be wrong to assume that it imposes a standard of care comparable with the duty to take reasonable care at common law. The statutory duty requires the employer to take action to ensure health and safety unless, on the facts, it is impracticable in the circumstances. This has been taken to mean that in determining the scope of general duties cost-benefit considerations must be taken account of.

In *Associated Dairies v. Hartley* 1979 the employer supplied his workers with safety shoes which they could pay for at £1 per week. An employee who had not purchased the shoes suffered a fractured toe when the wheel of a roller truck ran over it. There was an obvious risk to workers from roller trucks in the employer's warehouse. Accordingly an improvement notice was served on the employer requiring him to provide his employers with safety shoes free of charge (estimated cost £20,000 in the first year and £10,000 per annum thereafter). The Court of Appeal held that while such a requirement was practicable in all the circumstances of the case, it was not reasonably so, bearing in mind the cost in relation to the risk of injury. The improvement notice was therefore cancelled, the court confirming that in relation to the general duty, practicability alone is not the test, for it is qualified by the term 'reasonable'.

Since then there is evidence that the courts have adopted a more positive approach to the interpretation of the general duties under s.2(1) and s.2(2).

In *Bolton Metropolitan Borough Council v. Malrod Insulation Ltd.* 1993 a prosecution was brought against the defendant contractors under the general duty in s.2(1) and for failing to provide and maintain safe plant under s.2(2)(a). Following an inspection, an electrically driven decontamination unit, used by the contractors, was found to have defects which could cause electric shocks to those who used it. Following a conviction the defendants appealed on the grounds that the duties owed under s.2 only applied when the employee is at work and at the time of the alleged offences work had yet to begin. The Crown Court, upheld the appeal agreeing with the defendant's interpretation of the section. On further appeal the Divisional Court rejected this interpretation and held that the use of the *'at work'* in s.2(1) could not on any common sense basis mean that the duty to provide safe plant only arises when men are actually at work. This would mean that the health and safety inspectorate would be powerless to act if they discovered unsafe machines on an inspection at the end of the working day. The duty is to *'provide plant'* which is safe, subject to the question of reasonable practicability.

The fact that a working practice adopted by employers is universal within the industry is not conclusive evidence that the general duty under s.2(1) has been discharged. The High Court in *Martin v. Boulton and Paul (Steel Construction) Ltd.* 1982 held that a universal practice whilst of great weight, is not conclusive evidence that it was not reasonably practicable to use some other and safer method. *In R. v. Associated Octel Co. Ltd.* 1997[8] the Court of Appeal gave further guidances as to reasonable practicability stressing the subjective nature of the concept *'what is reasonably practicable for a large organisation employing safety officers or engineers contracting for the services of a small contractor on routine operations may differ markedly from what is reasonably practicable for a small shopkeeper employing a local builder on activities on which he has no expertise'.*

Safety representatives

A further requirement of s.2 for employers other than those with less than five employees is the obligation to prepare and revise a written statement of their general policy on health and safety and bring this statement to the notice of their employees. The statement should be more than a bland statement of responsibilities but rather a genuine attempt to identify specific health and safety problems of the employer in question and the arrangements that have been made to deal with them. Matters to be included would cover inspection procedures, emergency arrangements, safety precautions, consultative arrangements and training. Under the Safety Representatives and Safety Committee Regulations 1977 it is only recognised trade unions who have the exclusive right to appoint safety representatives and request the creation of safety committees. The functions of safety representatives are laid down in the 1977 Regulations and include the investigation: of hazards and employee complaints, making representations to the employer, to carry out inspections and attend safety committees.

If safety representatives are appointed under s.2 then it is the duty of an employer to consult with such representatives in order to promote health and safety at the workplace. In many cases this will involve consultations with safety committees which have the function of reviewing measures taken to ensure health and safety at work. Safety representatives have a number of powers, including the right to inspect the workplace and require the establishment of a safety committee. The Trade Union Reform and Employment Rights Act 1993 inserted a right on safety representatives which is included in the Employment Rights Act 1996. Under s.44 safety representatives have the right not so suffer a detriment for carrying out their health and safety functions. By Regulation, a safety representative is entitled to paid time off work to undergo such training as is reasonable in the circumstances.

8. See later in the chapter

Duty to non-employees

Both employers and those who are self employed are required, in the words of s.3(1), to *'conduct their undertakings in such a way, in so far as is reasonably practicable, to protect persons other than their own employees from risks to their health and safety'*. This would require an employer to give anyone who may be affected, information relating to health and safety risks arising from the way in which the business is run.

> In *Carmichael v. Rosehall Engineering Works Ltd.* 1983 an employer was found to be in breach of his duty under s.3(1) when he failed to provide two youths on a work experience programme with suitable clothing for carrying out a cleaning operation using flammable liquid. The failure to give proper instruction and information, as to the possible risks to their health and safety, was a factor which led to the death of one of the boys when his paraffin soaked overalls burst into flames.

Those to whom an employer owes a duty under s.3(1) include contractors and employees of independent contractors.

> In *R v. Associated Octel Co. Ltd.* 1997 the defendant employer was convicted of an offence under s.3(1) when an employee of a contractor engaged to carry out maintenance and repair work suffered severe injury when working at the defendant's chemical plant. On appeal the employer argued that under s.3(1) an employer is not liable for the acts of independent contractors over whom he has no control. The Court of Appeal held that the employer had been correctly convicted. *'The cleaning, repair and maintenance necessary for carrying on the employer's business or enterprise is part of the employee's conduct of its undertaking within the meaning of s.3(1) so as to impose a duty of care with regard to persons not in its employment, whether it is done by the employer's own employees or by independent contractors. The ingredients of an offence under s.3(1) are that the accused is (i) an employer (ii) who so conducts his undertaking (iii) as to expose to risk of health and safety (iv) a person not employed by him (v) who may be affected by such conduct of the accused's undertaking. If there is actual injury as a result of the conduct of that operation, there is prima facie liability subject to the defence of reasonable practicability.'* A further appeal to the House of Lords was also dismissed. In relation to determining whether the work involved came within the definition under s.3(1) Lord Hoffman said *'The employer is under a duty s.3(1) to exercise control over an activity if it forms part of the conduct of his undertaking. The existence of such a duty cannot therefore be the test for deciding whether the activity is part of the undertaking or not. Likewise, the question of whether an employer may leave an independent contractor to do the work as he thinks fit depends upon whether having the work done forms part of the employer's conduct of his undertaking. If it does, he owes a duty under s.3(1) to ensure that it is done without risk - subject, of course to reasonable practicability, which may limit the extent to which the employer can supervise the activities of a specialist independent contractor. Although the case was very much on the borderline, here there was evidence upon which the justices could find that having the asbestos sheets removed was part of the employer's undertaking. The facts were a matter for them and their decision should not have been disturbed.'*

In determining reasonable practicability under s.3(1) it is necessary to consider the extent of control over the contractor, the requirement of instruction as to work methods and safety measures, the degree of risk and the competence and experience of the workmen.

> Guidance as to the interpretation of s.3 was provided by the Court of Appeal in *R. v. Mara* 1987. Here the defendant, Mr. Mara, a director of a cleaning company called CMS Ltd., was convicted of an offence in that he had permitted a breach of his company duty under s.3. The company had failed to conduct its undertaking in such a way as to ensure that persons not in its employment were exposed to health and safety risks. The facts were that the cleaning company had contracted to clean premises owned by International Stores plc on weekdays. This involved using electrical cleaning machines. As the loading bay could not be cleaned because it was in constant use, it was agreed that employees of International Stores should do the work using CMS equipment. One Saturday morning whilst using a CMS cleaning machine, a Store's employee was electrocuted due to the defective condition of the machine's cable. Mr. Mara was convicted and fined for an offence under s.3. On appeal however it was submitted that as the incident occurred on a Saturday morning, when the cleaning company did not work, it was not *'conducting its undertaking'* at all, and so could not be in breach of its duty. The Court of Appeal rejected the submission however, holding that s.3 could not be limited to situations where a company's undertaking is in the process of actively being carried on. The way in which CMS Ltd. conducted its undertaking was to clean during weekdays and leave their equipment for use by their client's employees, at weekends. By failing to ensure that its equipment was safely wired the company was in breach of its s.3 duty to its client's employees. Consequently the director had rightly been convicted of an offence.

This case provides an example of a rare prosecution brought against an individual director of a company rather than the company itself. Under the Act proceedings may be taken against a director of a company which, with his consent or due to his negligence committed an offence. In a prosecution brought against Mr. Chapman in 1992 whose company had contravened a prohibition notice, the Crown Court used its powers under the Company Directors Disqualification Act 1986 to ban him from being a company director for two years in addition to a £5,000 fine and a £5,000 fine on the company.

Duty for premises and machinery

By virtue of s.4 a general duty is imposed on those who control work premises to ensure *so far as is reasonably practicable the safety of the premises, any means of access and exit from the place of work, and of any plant or substance provided for use on the premises.*

The duty extends to persons in control of non-domestic premises which are made available as a place of work and is owed to those who are not their employees.

> Under s.4(2) *'It shall be the duty of each person who has control of non-domestic premises or of the means of access thereto or therefrom or any plant or equipment in such premises, to take such measures as is reasonable for a person in his position to take to ensure, so far as is reasonably practicable, that the premises, all means of access available for use by persons using the premises and any plant or equipment in such premises is safe and without risk to health.'*

In *H M Inspector of Factories v. Austin Rover Group Ltd.* 1989 the defendants were prosecuted for a breach of s.4(2) when the employee of a contractor working on the defendants' premises was killed following a sudden flash fire where he was working. A combination of breaches of safety instructions had contributed to the cause of the fire and at the original trial the defendants were convicted of a s.4(2) offence for failing to take precautions which would have constituted 'reasonable measures' and been 'reasonably practicable' for a person in the position of Austin Rover. On appeal and then further appeal to the House of Lords however, it was held that in determining the reasonableness of the measures to be taken under s.4(2) account must be taken of the extent of control and knowledge of the occupier in relation to the actual use to which the premises are put. *'If the premises are not a reasonably foreseeable cause of danger, to anyone acting in a way which a person reasonably may be expected to act, in circumstances which reasonably may be expected to occur during the carrying out of the work, or the use of the plant or substance for the purpose of which the premises were made available, it would not be reasonable to require an individual to take further measures against unknown and unexpected risks.'*

A successful prosecution under s.4(2) requires the proof of:

- unsafe premises and a risk to health;
- the identity of the individual having control of the premises; and
- the fact that the person in control ought reasonably to have taken measures to ensure safety.

On proof of these three matters the onus then shifts to the accused to show that it was not reasonably practicable to take such measures. As in the present case, the defendant could not have reasonably foreseen the unknown and unexpected events which made the premises unsafe, they would not be held to be in breach of s.4(2). Lord Jauncey made the important point that the *'safety of premises was not an abstract concept. It must be related to the purpose for which the premises were being used at any one time. Some premises might be unsafe for any normal use, for instance because of large unguarded holes in the floor or unstable walls. Other premises might be completely safe for the purposes for which they were designed but completely unsafe for other purposes, for example, an upper floor warehouse designed to a loading capacity of x lbs might become unsafe if loaded to a capacity of 2xlbs. If A made the warehouse available to B who used it within the designed loading capacity, it could not be said that the warehouse was unsafe and a risk to health under s.4(2) because B at some future date exceeds that capacity contrary to A's instructions'.*

A further general duty imposed on those who control work premises is to *use the best practicable means to prevent the emission of offensive substances and to render harmless and inoffensive those substances emitted.*

Those who design, manufacture, import or supply any article for use at work are required under s.6 in so far as is reasonably practicable to ensure the article's safety, to carry out necessary testing and examining and provide sufficient information about the use of the article at work to render it safe and without risks to health.

Finally there is a general duty on every employee while at work under s.7 to take reasonable care for the health and safety of himself and of other persons who may be affected by his acts or omissions at work and to cooperate with employers in the discharge of their health and safety duties. Those employees who act in disregard of health and safety should be counselled but in the end dismissed if they are a danger to themselves or others.

Certainly there is no room to be complacent about compliance with health and safety law for of the 5000 or so deaths at the workplace over the last ten years in the UK, the Health and Safety Executive estimated that over 70% are due to the failure of companies to provide workers with adequate safety equipment, training, supervision and instruction as they are bound to do under the legislation. Lack of enforcement, particularly against individual directors or managers is a particular cause for concern and the small number of prosecutions that are brought against companies only result in a limited fine in the Magistrates Court.

Civil Redress

A further major objective of the law relating to health and safety at the workplace is to provide a means by which those who have suffered injury may recover compensation. Since the mid 1960s, state benefit has been available for employees who suffer injury from accidents arising out of and in the course of employment or contract prescribed industrial diseases. If injury is caused through fault however, whether of the employer or a fellow worker, an injured person can bring a claim for damages through the courts. If it can be shown that injury has occurred as a result of a failure to comply with a regulation under the Health and Safety at Work Act 1974 or some other statutory obligation, for instance under the Factories Act 1961, then a claim could be brought for damages under a civil action for breach of statutory duty. This action has the status of a separate tort and can provide a means of redress for persons who suffer harm as a result of a breach of a duty imposed by statute. In addition claims may be brought by employees alleging the breach of statutory duties under discrimination legislation where they have suffered physical or psychiatric injury. Later in the chapter you will see that recently the Protection from Harassment Act 1997 has been held to provide a potential cause of action for breach of statutory duty in circumstances when an employee suffers from the bullying of a fellow worker.

Common Law Negligence

An alternative course of action for an employee who has suffered harm due to the fault of his employer or a fellow employee is to base a claim on common law negligence. Under the common law, an employer owes a legal duty of care to ensure the health and safety of his employees and this duty takes effect as an implied term of the contract of employment. The potential of an employer to incur liability may arise in two ways. Primary liability arises when the employee is injured as a result of the employer's own act or default by failing to take reasonable care. Vicarious liability arises when the injury occurs as a result of the negligent conduct of a fellow employee for whom the employer is responsible. We will examine both forms of liability.

Primary Liability

An employer is required to take reasonable care with regard to the safety of his employees by providing a safe system of work. The provision of a safe system of work involves an obligation to provide safe fellow employees, safe plant and equipment, safe working premises and safe working methods. If an employer is in breach of his common law duty to take reasonable care, and damage in the form of injury is caused as a result, he will be liable. According to Lord Brandon in *McDermid v. Nash Dredging and Reclamation Co. Ltd.* 1987 the provision of a safe system of work has two aspects. *'(a) the devising of such a system and (b) the operation of it.'* Additionally the *'essential characteristic of the duty is that if it is not performed it is no defence for the employer to show that he delegated its performance to a person, whether his servant or not his servant, whom he reasonably believed to be competent to perform it. Despite such delegation the employer is liable for the non performance of the duty'.*

It should be stressed that in civil proceedings it is often the case that a claim is based upon both the breach of a common law duty and for breach of statutory duty if relevant.

> In *Smith v. Vange Scaffolding & Engineering Company Ltd. and Another* 1970 the plaintiff scaffolder suffered injury when he fell over a welding cable when walking back from his place of work. The High Court held that the employee's immediate employers were liable for breach of their common law duty of care because they were aware of the dangerous state of the site where their employees worked. In addition the employers were in breach of their statutory duty imposed, by Regulation 6 of the Construction (Working Places) Regulations 1966, to provide a suitable and sufficient access to and exit from the claimant's place of work.

Certainly there is no intention that statutory regulation is designed to supersede the common law so that even if an employer has complied with a regulation, for instance to supply his workers with safety equipment, an employee is still entitled to pursue a claim under the common law if he is injured due to a failure to wear it.

> In *Bux v. Slough Metals* 1973 the plaintiff lost the sight of one eye as a result of a splash from molten metal when he was pouring it into a die. While safety goggles had been supplied, the plaintiff refused to wear them because they misted up, and no attempt was made to persuade him otherwise. The Court of Appeal held that while the employer had provided suitable goggles for the purpose of safety regulations, they were nevertheless negligent under the common law. The evidence suggested that the plaintiff would have followed clear instructions to wear the goggles, and that the question whether or not an employer's common law duty of care extended to instructing, persuading or insisting on the use of protective equipment depended on the facts. By failing to make use of the goggles the plaintiff was guilty of contributory fault and damages were reduced by forty percent.

As far as safety equipment is concerned, the contemporary view seems to be that the common law duty to make it available and ensure that employees are aware of it does not necessarily carry with it any further obligation to inspect it or insist that it is worn. Obviously there is some obligation on the employee to take some responsibility for his own safety by ensuring that safety equipment is renewed when necessary.

> In *Smith v. Scott Bowyers Ltd.* 1986 the plaintiff, who was just twenty years of age, and employed by the company for nineteen months, suffered injury when he slipped on the greasy factory floor. To help minimise the risk the employer provided the workers with wellington boots with diamond ridge soles and they were renewed on request. Having already replaced one pair of boots the accident was due to the plaintiff's failure to renew the replacement pair which had also worn out and were a danger. In an action for damages for breach of the employer's duty of care, the High Court found that the failure of the employers to emphasise the danger and carry out checks of the safety equipment made them in breach

of the legal duty of care they owed to the plaintiff. Damages were to be reduced by one third however, due to the plaintiff's contributory fault. On appeal however, the Court of Appeal reversed the decision and held that there was no breach of the employer's duty to take reasonable care. The failure of the employee to renew the boots was due to his own lack of care and could not be taken as the fault of the employer. *'The employer's duty to provide employees with properly designed Wellington boots would not be filled out with any further obligation to instruct them to wear them or to inspect the condition of the soles from time to time.'*

In *Pape v. Cumbria County Council* 1991 the plaintiff had been employed as a cleaner by the council for many years and her job involved the use of chemical cleaning materials and detergents. While rubber gloves were supplied, they were rarely used, the employer failing to point out the dangers of frequent contact of the skin with cleaners or encouraging the use of gloves. In 1982 the plaintiff was diagnosed as suffering from dermatitis and told by a consultant to protect her skin at work. This she did but her medical condition deteriorated so that all her skin became infected and in 1989 she gave up her job as a result. Mrs Pape claimed damages against her employer for negligence in that her dermatitis resulted from exposure to chemicals in the course of her employment and the employer was in breach of a clear duty to warn of the dangers and persuade staff to take preventative measures. The High Court awarded her £58,000 in damages stating that *'there is a duty on an employer to warn cleaners of the dangers of handling chemical cleaning materials with unprotected hands and to instruct them as to the need to wear gloves all the time. The argument on behalf of the defendant that an employer's duty to his office cleaners is fully discharged when he provides them with gloves could not be accepted'.* The risk of dermatitis was not an obvious risk to the cleaners but should be appreciated by a reasonable employer.

The common law duty encompasses an obligation to provide safe plant and appliances. If an employer was aware that machinery or tools are not reasonably safe, and an employee is injured as a result, the employer will be in breach of his duty under the common law.

In *Bradford v. Robinson Rentals* 1967 the employer provided an unheated van for the employee, a 57 year old, to make a 400 mile journey during the winter, which would involve him in at least 20 hours driving. The court held that the employer was liable for the employee's frost bite, which was the type of injury that was reasonably foreseeable from prolonged exposure to severe cold and fatigue. The court also confirmed that even if the plaintiff had been abnormally susceptible to frost bite he would still be entitled to succeed under the rule that the defendant must take his victim as he finds him.

In the past an employer could satisfy his duty to provide safe equipment by showing that he purchased the equipment from a reputable supplier and that he had no knowledge of any defect. Now however, following the Employers Liability (Defective Equipment) Act 1969, injury occurring to an employee under those circumstances may be attributed to the deemed negligence of the employer. If damages are awarded against the employer then it is up to him to seek a remedy from the supplier of the defective equipment.[9]

---

9. *Knowles v. Liverpool City Council* 1993

The obligation to provide a safe system of work also encompasses a requirement to provide safe fellow employees. If there are untrained or unskilled people employed at the workplace then a higher standard of care is owed by the employer to ensure their safety and the safety of those who work with them. The conduct of fellow employees of contributing to an unhealthy working environment by smoking could be the responsibility of the employer in relation to an employee who suffers damage to health through passive smoking. The judgment in *Dryden v. Greater Glasgow Health Board* 1992[10] makes it clear that an employee who smokes cannot insist on an implied term entitling him to smoke or have access to smoking facilities. If a no smoking policy is introduced for a legitimate purpose, the health and welfare of the staff, the fact that it makes life difficult for smokers is of no consequence. The later case of *Walton and Morse v. Dorrington* 1997[11] establishes a clear duty on employers in relation to the health of non smokers to ensure that they do not suffer the effects of passive smoking.

The duty to provide safe fellow employees exists irrespective of any issue of the employer's vicarious liability[12] for the actions of his employees. If an employee is injured through the negligence of some third party then the court must decide in the circumstances whether this constitutes a breach of the employer's duty of care and so imposing liability.

> In *Reid v. Rush & Tompkins Group* 1989 the plaintiff driver claimed that his employer was in breach of their duty of care in failing to insure him or advising him to obtain insurance cover when driving abroad. The plaintiff had suffered severe injuries as a result of an accident which occurred in Ethiopia resulting from the negligence of another driver. Both the High Court and the Court of Appeal were reluctant to impose liability on the employer for the loss sustained by the employee. '*It was impossible to imply into the plaintiff's contract of service any term a breach of which would entitle him to recover damages from the defendants for the loss he sustained. There was no basis on the facts as pleaded for holding that the defendants gave an implied undertaking to insure his plaintiff against the risk of uncompensated injury caused to him, while acting in the course of his employment in Ethiopia, by third party drivers.*'

The employer's common law duty also imposes an obligation to provide safe working methods and safe working premises. To determine whether an employer is providing safe working methods, it is necessary to consider a number of factors including: the layout of the work place; training and supervision; warnings; and whether protective equipment is provided.

It should be stressed that the common law duty on an employer is to take reasonable care, and if he gives proper instructions which the employee fails to observe then the employer will not be liable if the employee is then injured.

> In *Charlton v. Forrest Printing Ink Company Ltd.* 1980 the employer gave proper instructions to an employee who was given the job of collecting the firm's wages. The instructions required the employee to vary his collecting arrangements to prevent robbery. The employee failed to do this and suffered severe injury when he was robbed. The Court of Appeal held that the employer was not liable

---

10. See Chapter 4
11. See Chapter 4
12. See later in the chapter

as he had taken reasonable steps to cut down the risk. The normal industrial practice of firms of that size in that area was to make their own payroll collection rather than employ a security firm. The employers *'did what was reasonable in the circumstances to eliminate the risk and no more could have been expected of them. They could not be held liable for the injuries incurred by the employee'.*

It should be stressed that the common law duty is not one of strict liability but rather a duty to take reasonable care in the circumstances.

In *Latimer v. AEC* 1953 after a factory was flooded, the employer asked his workforce to return, warning them of the dangerous state of the factory floor. Sawdust had been used to cover most of the damp areas but not enough was available, and the plaintiff slipped, and was injured. To determine whether the employer had broken the common law duty of care he owed his employees the court weighed the cost of avoiding the injury against the risk of injury and held that the employer had acted reasonably in the circumstances.

In *Dixon v. London Fire and Civil Defence* 1993 the fire authority was held not to be in breach of its common law duty of care to an officer who slipped and fell as a result of a wet floor. The fact that water had leaked on to the floor of the fire station from an appliance did not constitute negligence for such an occurrence was endemic in the fire service and appeared to be insoluble.

If the plaintiff is a trained professional it may be reasonable to allow the employer to rely on the plaintiff's expertise without the need for warnings or instruction.

In *Pickford v. Imperial Chemical Industries* 1998 a secretary who suffered *repetitive strain injury* due to her secretarial duties claimed that her employer had been negligent in failing to instruct her about the need for rest breaks and work organisation to alleviate the need for long periods of typing. By a majority decision the Court of Appeal reversed the decision of the High Court and found that the employer was in breach of the duty of care he owed to his employee. A majority of the House of Lords however reversed the Court of Appeal and confirmed the decision of the High Court and dismissed the claim. They felt that the claimant, as a general secretary had a number of duties other than typing and would have organised her own rest periods from the word processor. In addition they thought that the medical evidence was insufficient to prove that her condition was caused by repetitive movements while typing.

The courts have recognised that to require an employee to work long hours, which is related to health problems, could put an employer in breach of his common law duty.

In *Johnstone v. Bloomsbury Health Authority* 1991 the claimant, a senior house officer, was required to work forty hours by his contract with an additional average of forty eight hours per week on call. He alleged that some weeks he had been required to work for one hundred hours with inadequate sleep and as a consequence he suffered from stress, depression, diminished appetite, exhaustion and suicidal feelings. It was claimed that the employers were in breach of the legal duty to take reasonable care for the safety and well being of their employee by requiring him to work intolerable hours with deprivation of sleep. The majority of the Court of Appeal held that an employer's express contractual rights had to be exercised in the light of their duty to take care of the employee's safety and if the employer knew that they were exposing an employee to the risk of injury to health by requiring him to work such long hours, then they should not require him to work more hours than he safely could have done.

Although only a majority decision, the Court of Appeal by this judgment is recognising that the implied objective of health and safety in an employment contract may override a clear express contractual right in relation to the hours of work.[13]

The standard of care owed by an employer will vary with regard to each individual employee. A young apprentice should be provided with effective supervision while this may not be required for an experienced employee.

> In *Paris v. Stepney BC* 1951 the plaintiff, a one-eyed motor mechanic, lost the sight of his good eye while working at chipping rust from under a bus. Despite there being no usual practice to provide mechanics with safety goggles, the court decided that they should have been provided to the plaintiff. The defendants were liable as they could foresee serious consequences for the plaintiff if he suffered eye injury. *'The special risk of injury is a relevant consideration in determining the precautions which the employer should take in the fulfilment of the duty of care which he owes to the workman.'*

What is the legal position of an employee, aware of a risk to his health from carrying on a work activity, nevertheless wishes to carry on working. The principle of law established by the Court of Appeal in *Withers v. Perry Chain Co. Ltd.* 2005 is that there is no legal duty to dismiss an employee in these circumstances simply because there is some risk to the employee in doing the work and that an employee is free to decide what risks he or she will run.

In *Coxall v. Goodyear Great Britain Ltd.* 2002 the Court of Appeal considered the case of an employee who suffered occupational asthma caused by constant fumes at work. He had complained and been examined by the works doctor who recommended that he should be moved to a different work activity. Unfortunately an administration failure meant that the employee's care manager was unaware of the recommendation and the employee continued the work exacerbating the illness. The Court of Appeal upheld the Withers principle recognising that *'although employers responsibilities towards their workforce have grown over the years, societies increasing respect for the freedom of the individual is a countervailing consideration'*. It was however, said the court the actual nature and extent of the known risk that is the principal consideration in determining whether or not any particular case falls within the Withers principle. *'An employer is not immune from liability if an employee known to suffer intermittently from vertigo or epileptic fits was allowed to continue working as a spiderman.'* Here the relevant management staff thought that the claimant should cease work so the employer was under a duty to take him off the job, or, as a last resort to dismiss him.

The third element in establishing liability under the common law is to show that there is a causative link between the breach of duty and the damage suffered. We will examine this link in the next section on psychiatric illness caused by stress at work.

> In a landmark decision, *Fairchild v. Glenhaven Funeral Services Ltd.* 2002 the House of Lords has reached a positive decision in relation to those who contracted

---

13. See overriding terms Chapter 4

mesothelioma as a result of their negligent exposure to asbestos dust. The Court of Appeal had held that the disease is not cumulative and could be caused by a single exposure to asbestos fibres. As a consequence if there were a number of employers potentially at fault, liability could not be pinpointed on the causation principle. This ruling has been reversed by the House of Lords which held that the claimant must be entitled to recover damages against any or all of their former employers. *'Any other outcome'* said Lord Nicholls *'would be deeply offensive to instinctive notions of what justice requires and fairness demands'*. Their Lordships held that the conventional test of causation can be departed from in special circumstances where justice so requires by importing an element of joint liability. Here it was sufficient that the employer's breach of duty materially increased the risk that the claimant would contract the disease.

Psychiatric illness caused by stress

There is an increased recognition that individual employees may suffer stress as a direct result of their work. If an employer has reason to believe that this is the case and takes no steps to alleviate the problem there is now authority to suggest he could be in breach of the common law duty of care.

> In *Walker v. Northumberland CC* 1995 the High Court held that a local authority was in breach of duty if care to a senior social worker who was required to cope with an increased workload despite the fact the employer was aware of his susceptibility to mental breakdown. Mr. Justice Coleman said that *'An employer owes a duty to his employees not to cause them psychiatric damage by the volume or character of the work which they are required to perform. Although the law on the extent of the duty on an employer to provide an employee with a safe system of work and to take reasonable steps to protect him from risks which are reasonably foreseeable has developed almost exclusively in cases involving physical injury to the employee, there is no logical reason why risk of injury to an employee's mental health should be excluded from the scope of the employer's duty. The standard of care required for performance of that duty must be measured against the yardstick of reasonable conduct on the part of a person in the employer's position. What is reasonable depends on the nature of the relationship, the magnitude of the risk of injury which was reasonably foreseeable, the seriousness of the consequences for the person to whom the duty is owed of the risk eventuating, and the cost and practicability of preventing the risk. The practicability of remedial measures must take into account the resources and facilities at the disposal of the person or body who owes the duty of care, and purpose of the activity which has given rise to the risk of injury.'*

It should be noted that a material fact in deciding liability in the Walker case was that the claimant complained of his employer's breach of duty in relation to a second nervous breakdown which was reasonably foreseeable. Previously Mr. Walker had suffered a breakdown due to the stress caused by his heavy workload which was not reasonably foreseeable and for which there would have been no breach of duty. By allowing Mr. Walker to be exposed to the same workload as before however the employer should have appreciated that he was as a result of the first breakdown more vulnerable to psychiatric damage.

Employers should be aware of the causes of stress and can achieve that by carrying out a full assessment of:

- factors that could lead to stress including the stress levels of particular job functions;
- training requirements for staff, particularly those changing job functions;
- individual needs and the requirement to record individual progress; and
- potential signs of deterioration due to work loads.

In *White v. Chief Constable of South Yorkshire Police* 1999 a claim for damages in the tort of negligence was brought by police officers who suffered post traumatic stress disorder as a result of attending the dead and injured following the Hillsborough disaster in 1987. They claimed that their employer owed them a duty of care as employees/rescuers to avoid exposing them to increasing risk of physical or psychiatric injury. Claims by police officers who had actually dragged dead and injured spectators from the scene and risked injury themselves had earlier been conceded and settled by their employers. By a majority the Court of Appeal held that a duty of care was owed to those officers at the ground who suffered psychiatric harm as rescuers and the primary victims of their employer's negligence. On further appeal to the House of Lords the decision was reversed by a majority and the door seems to be closed on further expansion of potential liability for psychiatric loss. The police officers could not be classified as primary victims of the defendants negligence for it does not follow that a duty to avoid causing physical harm extends to psychiatric injury except in stress related cases such as *Walker v. Northumberland County Council* 1995. Here the harm resulted from a traumatic experience as a secondary victim and as the police officers lacked the close ties of love and affection with the victims a duty of care could not extend to them. Also to qualify as rescuers their psychiatric harm must result from a fear of foreseeable physical injury and this was held not to be the case here.

In *Young v. Post Office* 2002 the Court of Appeal considered a further claim of psychiatric illness resulting from occupational stress. Mr. Young was a long-standing workshop manager employed by the Post Office who in 1994 was beginning to show signs of stress and prescribed anti-depressants. By 1997 he indicated that he needed help which he did not receive and subsequently that year he suffered a nervous breakdown and was off work for four months. During his absence Mr. Young was counselled by management and told he could return to work on a flexible basis with plenty of support. When he did return promises that had been made to him were not kept and eventually in 1997 he suffered a further psychiatric illness leading to early retirement. His claim for damages was upheld in the County Court and he was awarded £94,000. The employer appealed contending that there was no breach of duty as they had taken reasonable steps to enable Mr. Young to return to work and that they were unaware he was suffering further stress. They also raised the defence of contributory fault. The Court of Appeal upheld the decision. They held that *'where an employee has already suffered from psychiatric illness resulting from occupational stress it is plainly foreseeable that there might be a recurrence if appropriate steps are not taken when the employee returns to work. The employer owes the employee a duty to take such steps and to see that the arrangements made are carried through'*. Here the broken promises indicated a breach of duty. Also while a claim of contributory fault is theoretically possible the claimant could not be blamed for doing his best to do his work.

Stress injury guidelines

The Court of Appeal, in particular Lady Justice Hale, has laid down a significant judgment on the circumstances when liability may be imposed on an employer for psychiatric injury caused by stress. Her 16 propositions to assist in deciding stress liability have been approved by the House of Lords on appeal under the case name *Barber v. Somerset Council* 2004 and are now applied by the lower courts.

In *Sutherland v. Hatton* 2002, (*Barber v. Somerset* 2004) the Court of Appeal provides important new guidelines for determining employer liability for psychiatric illness caused by workplace stress. In her extensive and thought provoking judgment Lady Justice Hale[14] indicated that the employer's duty to take steps to safeguard an employee is only triggered when the indications are plain enough for any reasonable employer to recognise that something must be done. The test then should be familiar, it is one of reasonable foreseeability in relation to the particular employee and the nature of the occupation should be of no relevance. An employer is entitled to assume that his employees can withstand the normal pressures of the job unless the employer knows of some particular problem or vulnerability. *'An employee who returns to work after a period of sickness without making further disclosure or explanation to his employer is usually implying that he believes himself fit to return to work which he was doing before.'* Emphasising that the test of foreseeability is a duty owed to individual employees and not some notional outsider, Lady Justice Hale indicated that it is not the occupation but rather the interaction between the individual and the job that causes the harm. Factors likely to be relevant include *'the nature and extent of the work done by the employee. Is the workload more than normal for the particular job? Is the work particularly intellectually or emotionally demanding for the particular employee? Are the demands being made of this employee unreasonable when compared with the demands made of others in the same or comparable job? Are there signs that others doing comparable jobs are suffering harmful levels of stress? Is there an abnormal level of sickness or absenteeism in the same job or department? Secondly there are signs of impending harm to health from the employee himself. Has he a particular problem or vulnerability? Has he already suffered from illness attributable to stress at work? Have there recently been frequent or prolonged absences which are uncharacteristic of him? Is there reason to think that these are attributable to stress at work, for example because of complaints or warnings from him or others? If the employee or his doctor makes it plain that unless something is done to help there is a clear risk of a breakdown in mental or physical health, then the employer will have to think what can be done about it'.* Having decided that the risk of harm to health from stress is foreseeable it is then necessary to consider whether the employer has broken the duty of care by taking into account what he did and what he failed to do. The employer is only in breach of duty if he fails to take reasonable steps applying the usual criterion of:

- the magnitude of the risk and the justification for running it;
- the gravity of the harm that might occur;
- the cost and practicability of preventing it.

Lord Justice Hale suggested steps that might be taken by the employer including *'giving the employee a sabbatical; transferring him to other work; redistributing the work; giving him some extra help for a while; arranging treatment or counselling; or providing "buddying" or mentoring schemes to encourage confidence. Whether it is reasonable to expect the employer to take such steps depends upon factors such as the size and scope of the employer's operation, its resources, whether it is in the public or the private sector, and other demands placed upon it, such as the interests of other employees at the workplace. It may not be reasonable to expect the employer to rearrange the work for the sake of one employee in a way which prejudices the others. An employer who tries to balance all these interests by offering a confidential advice service, with*

---

14. Now Baroness Hale

referral to appropriate counselling or treatment of services, to employees who fear that they may be suffering harmful levels of stress is unlikely to be found in breach of duty, except where he has been placing totally unreasonable demands upon an individual in circumstances where the risk of harm was clear'.

Finally if a breach of duty is shown then it is necessary to show that the particular breach caused the harm. It is not enough to simply show that occupational stress caused the harm but that the breach of duty caused the ill health or made a material contribution to it when the circumstances show that the harm level had more than one cause she said that *'the employer should only pay for that proportion of the harm suffered which is attributable to his wrongdoing, unless the harm is truly indivisible. It is for the defendant to raise the question of apportionment. Where the breach of duty has exacerbated a pre-existing disorder or accelerated the effect of a pre-existing vulnerability, that will be reflected in the assessment of damages, as will the chance that the employee would have succumbed to a stress-related disorder in any event'.* In the four cases that were the subject of the appeal, none of the judges at County Court level had applied these principles properly. As a consequence the judgments for the employee in three of the cases were reversed and the employer's appeal against the award of damages would be allowed. In one of the cases the Court of Appeal upheld the decision of the County Court by applying the principles of law laid down in the Court of Appeal judgment.

The practical implications of the *Sutherland* decision are that it will now be much more difficult for employees to succeed in a stress at work claim. The crucial question is whether the employer is aware of the problem or vulnerability otherwise the employer can assume that the employee can withstand the normal pressures of work. Certainly by offering a confidential advice service the employer will be offered a fair degree of protection against potential claims.

In *Bonser v. RJB Mining* 2004 The Court of Appeal stressed that *'in order to succeed in a claim for damages for psychiatric illness caused by stress, a claimant must establish not simply that it was reasonably foreseeable that overwork would lead to stress but that it would lead to a breakdown in the stressed employee's health'.* To establish liability therefore there must be clear evidence to put the employer on notice that the employee's workload would lead to stress and crucially that it was reasonably foreseeable that it would lead to a breakdown in health. *Hartman v. South Essex Mental Health and Community Care NHS Trust* 2005 was a decision of the Court of appeal in six cases dealing with work-related stress. The Court reaffirmed the Hale guidelines on determining reasonable foreseeability for psychiatric injury caused by stress at work. The court stressed however that it is not right to attribute to an employer knowledge of confidential information disclosed by an employee to the employer's occupational health department.

Applying the guidance in *Sutherland* the Court of Appeal in *Harding v. The Pub Estate Co* 2005 felt that despite the fact that a pub manager had obviously suffered personal injury caused by his stressful work the county court was wrong to impose liability on the employer. The test is whether the injury to the particular employee was reasonably foreseeable in the light of what the employer knew or ought to have known. Here the evidence did not show that the employee had put the employer on notice of the health risks and as a result there was no breach of duty. Here the evidence *'failed to get within striking distance of activating the trigger'.*

The fact that the employer is aware of the long hours worked by the claimant could be relevant evidence that the risk of psychiatric injury is foreseeable. In *Hone v. Six Continents*

Retail Ltd. 2006 the Court of Appeal upheld a finding that it was reasonably foreseeable that a pub manager would suffer psychiatric injury if he continued to work long hours without adequate support. The court applied the clear and workable test propounded by Baroness Hale in *Sutherland*, in particular her seventh proposition to trigger a duty to take steps. '*The indications of impending harm to health arising from stress at work must be plain enough for any reasonable employer to realise that he should do something about it.*' Here the fact that the landlord had refused to sign an opt-out from the 48 hour limit and had persistently complained about his working hours and lack of support was sufficient to justify the conclusion that harm to his health was reasonably foreseeable.

In the section on vicarious liability[15] you will see that there have been dramatic developments in the potential statutory liability of an employer where the psychiatric illness is caused by the conduct of a fellow employee. In particular by relying on the Protection from Harassment Act 1997 and breach of statutory duty an employee does not have the burden of establishing that the injury was reasonably foreseeable.

Defences available to the employer

In very exceptional cases the claimant may be taken to have consented to the risk of injury and the defence of 'volenti non fit injuria'[16] established.

> In *Imperial Chemical Industries v. Shatwell* 1965 two employees, both experienced shot firers, in contravention of specific safety instructions, fired a shot causing injury to both of them. The House of Lords held that the employer could rely on volenti as an absolute defence to the action, due to the act of gross disobedience.

It is more likely that the employer will be able to rely on the Law Reform (Contributory Negligence) Act 1945 which provides a partial defence. If the employer can show that the injured employee contributed to his injury by his own fault then damages may be reduced to '*such extent as the court thinks just and equitable having regard to the claimants share in the responsibility for the damage*'.

If the employer can show that the injured employee contributed to his injury by his own fault then damages may be reduced to '*such extent as the court thinks just and equitable having regard to the claimants share in the responsibility for the damage*'.

You will remember that in the case of *Bux v. Slough Metals* 1973[17] the damages awarded were reduced by 40% to reflect the employees contributory fault. Alternatively the claim of contributory fault was rejected by the Court of Appeal in *Young v. The Post Office* 2002[18].

The legal responsibility of an employer extends to where an employee under his control causes harm to a fellow employee or a third party by some wrongful act. This is by virtue of vicarious (substituted) liability, an important feature of an employer's responsibility to which we should devote some attention.

---

15. See later in the chapter
16. No wrong is done to one who consents to injury
17. Earlier in the chapter
18. See earlier in the chapter

Vicarious Liability

As stated previously there are some situations where the law is prepared to impose vicarious[19] liability on an individual who is not at fault for the commission of the wrongful[20] act of another. The best known example of this situation is the common law rule which imposes vicarious liability on employers in respect of torts committed by their employees during the course of their employment. Accordingly, if one employee by his negligent act causes harm to a fellow employee, then in addition to the possibility of pursuing a legal action against the employee at fault, he may have the further option of suing his employer, who will have become vicariously liable if the negligent act occurred during the course of employment. The same principle applies equally where the injuries are caused by an employee to some third party. However, while employers have a choice as to whether they insure against the risk of injury to third parties, under the Employer's Liability (Compulsory Insurance) Act 1969, an employer is statutorily required to insure himself in respect of injuries caused by his employees to their colleagues.

The imposition of vicarious liability does not require proof of any fault on the employer's part, or any express or implied authorisation to commit the wrongful act. All that must be proved for the purpose of vicarious liability is:

(1)   an actionable wrong committed by the worker;

(2)   that the worker is an employee;

(3)   that the wrongful act occurred during the course of his employment.

What then is the *theoretical* basis for imposing liability in these circumstances? A number of reasons have emerged, such as he who creates and benefits from a situation should assume the risk of liability arising from it. There is also the idea that if an organisation embarks on an enterprise and as a result harm is caused by one member of the organisation or a third party, it should be the responsibility of the organisation to compensate for the harm. It is after all the employer who selects and controls the employees who work for him. The employer has the responsibility of training staff and can of course dismiss those whose work is performed incompetently. The practical reason for vicarious liability is of course that if the employee were solely liable he would have to insure himself, and the cost of this would be indirectly borne by the employer in the form of higher wages. Under the present system insurance costs are borne directly by the employer who, as a principle of sound business practice, will normally carry adequate insurance.

To determine an employer's liability it is first necessary to establish the employment status of the worker who is alleged to have committed the wrongful act. This is because the legal position differs dramatically depending on whether the worker is employed as an employee under a contract of service rather than as a self employed contractor under a contract for services. Usually this issue may be settled without argument but in the small proportion of cases where there is doubt the courts are left with the task of identifying the true contractual status of the worker.

---

19. Substituted
20. Tortious

While it is settled law that an employer can only be made vicariously liable for the acts of its employees, recent case law suggests that the test of an employee for the purposes of personal injury liability is much wider than for statutory rights.[21]

In *Hawley v. Luminar Leisure plc* 2005 the High Court considered the potential liability of a nightclub owner for the unlawful conduct of a door steward under its control. The steward had violently punched the claimant causing severe injuries. He was in fact employed by a separate company, ASE Security Services Ltd., and his services supplied to the nightclub under a commercial contract. The claimant was wise to sue both the nightclub and ASE because at the time of the legal proceedings ASE had been voluntarily wound up. In addition ASE's insurers successfully denied liability as they had only provided cover for accidental injury. The claimant was therefore left with the nightclub owner as defendant. Applying the well-known tests of an employee relationship to the door steward proved to be fruitless given the lack of a contract, mutuality and personal service. Nevertheless the High Court held that for the purposes of vicarious liability the only significant test of employee status is one of control so as to make the door steward the deemed employee of the nightclub. In vicarious liability cases the usual tests for employment status are ignored so that despite the lack of a contract and payment, the nightclub could be made vicariously liable for the conduct of the doorman.

A recent decision of the Court of Appeal stressed the control test as a justification for imposing liability on more than one employer. The case arose in the context of damage caused as a result of the negligence of an employee of a sub contractor who worked under the control of a head contractor. In *Viasystems (Tyneside) Ltd. v. Thermal Transfers (Northern) Ltd.* 2005 the Court of Appeal raised the prospect of dual vicarious liability where an employee was under the control of more than one employer. The Court said that the proper approach was to decide in respect of each employer separately, whether it had the general power to control the actions of the employee. If there was a positive answer to that question then the rationale for vicarious liability applied and that employer would be responsible. There was no reason why that rationale should not be applied to two employers at the same time. If they both had power to direct the employer they should be jointly liable. *'For dual vicarious liability, equal contribution may be close to a logical necessity. Vicarious liability derives from the relationship between the employee and the employers, the critical relationship being the employers' right, and theoretical obligation, to control the relevant activity of the employee. If the relationships yield dual control, it is highly likely that the measure of control will be equal, for otherwise the court would be unlikely to find dual control.'*

Course of employment

As a general principle an employer is vicariously liable for the tortious acts of his employees committed during the course of their employment. The phrase *course of employment* has produced numerous interpretations in the courts, but essentially it concerns the question of whether the employee was doing his job at the time of the *act*. It should be emphasised that an employee will have both express and implied authority to perform work for his employer and while he will normally have no authority to commit torts, he may nevertheless be guilty of a tortious act in the performance of his authorised duties. The traditional test applied by the courts[22] was to ask whether at the time of the unlawful act the employee was doing something authorised or something reasonably incidental to an authorised act.

---

21. See Chapter 3
22. Before Lister 2001 see later

In *Century Insurance Ltd. v. Northern Ireland Road Transport Board* 1942 a tanker driver while delivering petrol at a garage, lit a cigarette and carelessly threw away the lighted match which caused an explosion and considerable damage. His employer was held to be vicariously liable for his negligence as the employee had acted within the course of his employment. By supervising the unloading, the employee was doing his job, but by smoking he was doing it in a grossly negligent manner.

Even if an employee is carrying out an act outside the basic obligation of his contract of employment, his employer may nevertheless be made vicariously liable if the act is carried out for the benefit of the employer. In *Kay v. ITW* 1968 the employee injured a colleague when he negligently drove a five ton diesel lorry which was blocking his way. Despite the fact that he was contractually authorised to drive only small vans and trucks, his employer was held to be vicariously liable for his action. Also in *Iqbal v. London Transport Executive* 1974 a bus conductor had clearly stepped outside the course of his employment when he drove the bus and injured the plaintiff so that his employer could not be held responsible. In *Ilkiw v. Samuels* 1963 however the employer could be held liable for the driver's negligence when he allowed an unauthorised person to drive.

If an employee is doing something of purely personal benefit at the time of the negligent act then he may be regarded, to quote from the colourful language of the Victorian era as *'off on a frolic of his own'*, and his employer will not be responsible.

> The facts of *Fennelly v. Connex South Eastern Ltd.* 2001 illustrate conflict that may arise as a result of the frustration caused by the UK railway system. It involved a passenger who failed to show his ticket to an inspector and when asked to do so was quite offensive. When he attempted to walk away the inspector barred his way and eventually when the ticket was produced it was snatched from him. Further words of abuse were exchanged and eventually the inspector physically assaulted the passenger by dragging him to the ground. Subsequent proceedings were brought in the High Court alleging that the defendants were vicariously liable for the assault which had been carried out during the course of the inspector's employment. The High Court disagreed finding that while the inspector had acted within his authority when checking the ticket and blocking the passenger, at the time of the assault he was going about his own business rather then is employers. He was as we have said *'off on a frolic of his own'* at the time of the tortious act. The Court of Appeal disagreed and held that the High Court Judge had adopted the wrong approach. *'Whether an action was taken in the course of employment requires looking at the job being done by the employee in general terms, not by narrowly dividing each step and task that he performs and then asking whether each step was authorised by the employer.'* Here the inspector's job was to deal with the public. The assault sprang directly from the altercation, which was being conducted by the inspector for his employer and was all part of the same incident.

The work connection test

The difficulty with associating course of employment with job function is that the more heinous the act of the employee the less likely the employer will be made liable for it. That is why the recent liberal approach of the House of Lords to the issue of vicarious liability is to be welcomed The common law test for vicarious liability has now moved much closer to the test when applied in relation to statutory torts, such as sex discrimination. The House of Lords have propounded the new *'work connection test'*. Was the worker's tort so closely connected with his employment, that it would be fair and just to hold the employer vicariously liable? In the following case the employee's conduct was unfortunately, the exact opposite of his authorised work, so could hardly be said to be connected to it.

In *Lister v. Hesley Hall Ltd.* 2001 The House of Lords declared the correct approach to be taken in determining the vicarious liability of an employer for the wrongful acts of his employees. The case involved abuse by a housemaster of vulnerable boys in his care in a residential home. The claims were based on the allegation that the employer had actual or constructive knowledge of the abuse and/or was negligent in failing to take measures to prevent it. In the High Court the claim was upheld on the basis that failure by the abuser to report harm to the boys was a failure to carrying out a duty to them and the defendants were vicariously liable for that failure. The court did not impose vicarious liability for the sexual abuse because that was held to be an independent act outside the course of employment for which the employer was not responsible. The Court of Appeal allowed the employers appeal holding that if the assault was outside the course of employment then a failure to report the wrongful conduct could not be within the scope of the employment. In a significant judgment the House of Lords allowed the appeal against the employer and found the employer vicariously liable for the torts of their employee. *'In determining whether an employee's wrongful act has been committed in the course of his employment so as to make the employers vicariously liable, the correct approach is to concentrate on the relative closeness of the connection between the nature of the employment and the employee's wrongdoing. The question is whether the employee's tort was so closely connected with his employment that it would be fair and just to hold the employers vicariously liable. The conventional test formulated by Salmond, which deems as within the course of employment a wrongful and unauthorised mode of doing some act authorised by the employer, does not cope ideally with vicarious liability for intentional wrongdoing. Salmond also observed, however, that an employer is liable even for acts which he has not authorised provided they are so connected with acts which he has authorised and they may rightly be regarded as modes, albeit improper modes, of doing them.'* Here the employee's position as warden involved work that created a sufficiently close connection between the acts of abuse and the tasks he was employed to do and the duties he was required to perform.

In *Mattis v. Pollock* 2003 the employer, a nightclub, had employed an unlicensed doorman to keep order and discipline at the club. He was encouraged to act in an intimidating manner and the employer had colluded with the employee's aggressive behaviour at the club on previous occasions. The claim related to a serious stabbing incident at the club involving the doorman and resulting in life threatening injuries to a customer. The stabbing was the culmination of an unpleasant revenge incident and the issue was whether it could be treated in isolation from previous events. Was the employee's tort so closely connected with the employment that it would be fair and just to hold the employer liable? Under the previous test the more serious the employee's tortious act, then the less likely it was that the employer would be found vicariously liable for the act. Here the Court of Appeal disagreed with the High Court and ruled that vicarious liability was established. The court also felt that on the facts it would also have been possible to find the employer personally liable for the injuries.

The extent to which an express prohibition by the employer will prevent vicarious liability will depend upon the nature of the prohibition. If it merely attempts to instruct the employee how he is to do his job, the employee may still be within the course of his employment for the purposes of vicarious liability.

> In *Rose v. Plenty* 1976 a milkman, contrary to an express prohibition, engaged a thirteen year old boy to help him deliver the milk. The boy was subsequently injured by the milkman's negligent driving and sued both the milkman and his employer. The Court of Appeal held that despite the prohibition of the employer, he remained vicariously liable as the milkman had acted within the course of his employment. Scarman LJ having considered the prohibition stated that *'There was nothing in the prohibition which defined or limited the sphere of his employment, the sphere of his employment remained precisely the same as before the prohibition was brought to his notice. The sphere was as a roundsman to go the rounds delivering milk, collecting empties and obtaining payment. Contrary to instructions the roundsman chose to do what he was employed to do in an improper way. But the sphere of his employment was in no way affected by his express instructions.'*

It seems therefore that only an express prohibition which effectively cuts down the *sphere of employment* will prevent the establishment of vicarious liability. The fact that contemporary courts seem to favour the idea of a very wide sphere of employment in individual cases, severely limits the opportunity of employers to restrict liability by express instruction. It is only by deciding the authorised parameters of an individual's job, and deciding that the act complained of fell outside these parameters that vicarious liability can be successfully denied.

While it may be reasonable for an employee to use a degree of force in protection of his employer's property, or to keep order, an employee who commits an assault which has no connection with his work will be solely liable for his conduct.

> So in *Warren v. Henleys Ltd.* 1948 the employer was held not to be vicariously liable for a physical attack by a petrol pump attendant on one of his customers. The claim that the attendant was acting within the scope of his employment was rejected, for while the attack developed out of an argument over payment for petrol, it was in reality motivated by an act of private vengeance.

Certainly to impose liability on an employer for the tortious or criminal acts of an employee under his control, there must be a connection between the act complained of and the circumstances of employment. The fact that employment gives the employee an opportunity to commit the wrongful act is insufficient to impose vicarious liability on the employer.

> In *Heasmans v. Clarity Cleaning Company* 1987 the Court of Appeal found it possible to absolve the defendant cleaning company from liability for the acts of one of their cleaners who, while employed on the plaintiff's premises, used the plaintiff's telephone to make international telephone calls to the value of £1411. The mere fact that the cleaner's employment provided the opportunity to fraudulently use the plaintiff's telephone was not itself sufficient to impose liability on the defendant.

Statutory Torts

An employer can be vicariously liable for statutory torts such as sex, race disability, sexuality or religious belief discrimination, committed by employees during the course of employment, unless he can show that he took such steps as were reasonably practicable to prevent the employee from committing the act of discrimination. A contentious issue is the extent to which an employee can be regarded as acting within the course of employment when committing an act of racial or sexual harassment.

In *Irving & Irving v. Post Office* 1987 the complaint of race discrimination was based on the conduct of an employee of the post office who when sorting the mail had written a racially insulting comment on a letter addressed to his neighbours who were of Jamaican origin. The issue before the Court of Appeal was whether the employee was acting in the course of his employment so that the Post Office could be made vicariously liable for the discriminatory act. The employee's act of writing on the mail was clearly unauthorised so the question was whether the act was an unauthorised mode of doing an authorised act. Here the misconduct formed no part of the postman's duties and could not be regarded as an unauthorised way of performing his work. *'An employer is not to be held liable merely because the opportunity to commit the wrongful act had been created by the employee's employment, or because the act in question had been committed during the period of that particular employment'.*

In *Bracebridge Engineering v. Derby* 1990 the complainant was the victim of serious sexual harassment by her supervisor which constituted unlawful discrimination. The employer was vicariously liable for the misconduct as at the time the act of sexual harassment took place the perpetrators were supposedly engaged in exercising their disciplinary and supervisory functions and were in the course of their employment. Here the court applied a liberal interpretation of course of employment.

In *Jones v. Tower Boot Co Ltd.* 1997 the EAT held that racial taunts of fellow workers were not an unauthorised wrongful act connected with employment so as to make the employer vicariously liable. *'The phrase in the course of employment has a well established meaning in law. The nub of the test is whether the unauthorised wrongful act of the servant is so connected with that which he was employed to do as to be a mode of doing it. That has to be judged by reference to all the circumstances of the case. Applying that test to the facts of the present case, the acts complained of, including the deliberate branding with a hot screwdriver and whipping, could not be described by any stretch of the imagination, as an improper mode of performing authorised tasks.'* Adopting a sensible pragmatic approach to this type of case, the Court of Appeal, in giving emphasis to the object of the legislation gave the phrase *'course of employment'* different interpretation from that applied when potential vicarious liability is determined in relation to common law tort. For the purposes of statutory torts, such as race discrimination the court held that course of employment should be given an everyday meaning so that if an employee commits an act of race discrimination at the workplace his employer would be held liable. Now as a result of *Lister v. Hesley Hall* 2001[23] the common law approach to course of employment is much closer to that applied in cases of statutory torts. The question is simply whether the employee's tort was so closely connected with his employment that it would be fair and just to hold the employers vicariously liable.

---

23. See earlier in the chapter

This novel approach to the liability of employers for the statutory torts of their employees was further tested in *Chief Constable of the Lincolnshire Police v. Stubbs* 1999. Here the EAT upheld the tribunal's decision that a police officer was acting the course of his employment when he subjected a fellow officer to sexual harassment contrary to the Sex Discrimination Act 1975. The EAT found the employer vicariously liable despite the fact that the conduct complained of occurred at social events outside the police station. The tribunal had decided that such gatherings were extensions of the working day and so within the course of employment for the purposes of liability.

In *Pearce v. Governing Body of Mayfield School* 2003 the House of Lords stressed the need for a comparator in a sex discrimination claim so that a female who was harasses because of her sexual orientation must be compared with a homosexual of the opposite gender for the purposes of establishing direct sex discrimination. Also as the harassment was at the hands of school pupils rather than the school staff, she could not rely on vicarious liability under s.41.[24]

The issue in *Sidhu v. Aerospace Composite Technology Ltd.* 2000 was whether the events on a family day out organised by the employer would be regarded as within the course of employment. The Court of Appeal thought not as the employees were not at their place of work during working hours and the majority of participants were family and friends. The Employment Tribunal had correctly applied the statutory test for vicarious liability and their conclusion that the incident was not in the course of employment was a finding of fact that should not be interfered with.

While there is no doubt that this interpretation of *'course of employment'* represents a dramatic but sensible change of the law of vicarious liability in relation to statutory torts it should be stressed that there is a possible defence to a statutory claim. The employer can avoid responsibility if he can prove that he had taken such steps as were reasonably practicable to prevent the employee from committing the unlawful act.[25]

Harassment

A highly controversial development which is potentially of concern to employers is the extent to which they are potentially liable under statute for the bullying and harassment[26] of employees under their control. If the claim is for psychiatric injury caused by a fellow employee, can a claimant maintain an action for damages against an employer relying on vicarious liability for breach of the Protection from Harassment Act 1997. The requirement to prove foreseeability under the common law is circumvented if the courts are willing to accept a cause of action based upon the statutory liability of the employer.

The thorny issue faced by the Court of Appeal in *Majrowski v. Guy's and St. Thomas's NHS Trust* 2005 was the extent to which a victim of bullying at work could rely on the Protection of Harassment Act Here the claimant was employed by the Trust as a clinical audit co-ordinator. He alleged that, whilst working in that post, he was bullied, intimidated and

---

24. The statutory defence
25. s.41 see Chapter 6
26. See Chapter 6

harassed by his departmental manager, acting in the course of her employment by the Trust. The bullying took the form of excessive criticism, ostracism, abusive conduct and the setting of unreasonable targets. Because of difficulties in establishing foreseeability under the common law and complying with the relatively short limitation periods, the claim was brought against the Trust under s.3 of the Protection from Harassment Act. This section could provides a civil remedy where the manager's conduct amounted to harassment in breach of s.1 of the Act for which the Trust, as her employers, were vicariously liable.

The claim was rejected by the county court on the grounds that the Act does not permit the imposition of vicarious liability for breach of its provisions. On appeal It was submitted that, having regard to the recent decision of the House of Lords in *Lister v. Hesley Hall Ltd.* (i) an employer is vicariously liable where an employee's unlawful act in the course of employment is sufficiently closely connected with the employer's business; (ii) there is no good reason of principle or policy to distinguish between statutory and common law civil wrongs when applying that form of vicarious liability; (iii) it is immaterial that the act in question may also constitute a statutory criminal offence; and (iv) unless the context and wording of the legislation creating the statutory tort in question compels otherwise, an employer should normally be vicariously liable for an employee's statutory tort committed in the course of his employment. In the case of the Protection from Harassment Act, it was submitted that there was no good policy reason why vicarious liability should not apply to breaches of the Act.

The Court of Appeal held that employer may be vicariously liable for a breach of a statutory duty imposed on an employee. '*Vicarious liability is not confined to common law claims. Once it is accepted that the nature of vicarious liability is absolute in the sense that the employer is put into the employee's shoes and, though blameless, may be held liable for a common law tort or other wrong satisfying the new broader test, there is, as the House of Lords have now expressly held, no logical basis for differentiating between the legal categories of an employee's wrong. What matters is the closeness of the connection between the offending conduct of the employee with the nature and circumstances of the employment. Thus, it is immaterial whether the conduct in respect of which a claimant seeks to hold an employer to account is a breach of a common law or a statutory duty, and whether or not it is a criminal offence as well as a civil breach.*'

Employers may be vicariously liable under s.3 of the Protection from Harassment Act for their employees' acts of harassment of third parties, including fellow employees, committed in the course of employment. Lord Justice Auld adds that the reasoning in this case would apply '*not only where one employee, in the course of his employment, harasses another employee, but also where an employee, in the course of his employment, harasses an outsider, say a customer of his employer or some other third party with whom his work brings him or her into regular contact*'.

There was a significant dissenting judgment by Scott-Baker LJ who said that the Protection from Harassment Act was not intended to impose civil liability on an employer for acts of harassment perpetrated by an employee.' *The Act is aimed at unconscionable behaviour essentially by one individual to another. The statutory duty is personal in nature and not one which, in the event that the prohibited conduct happens to occur in the workplace, the employer is to be treated as standing in the shoes of an employee perpetrator. The fact that the perpetrator of harassment may be doing so within or from the workplace is entirely incidental to the primary purpose of the legislation which is to stop the harassment and provide the machinery for doing so, rather than to award compensation in those cases which would not otherwise be covered by the common law. There is nothing to suggest that Parliament was looking to the employer to provide a monetary remedy for a lower threshold of damage to the victim than would be the case apart from the statute.'* He said that the common law of negligence provides claimants with an adequate framework for claiming damages against employers for injury caused by stress at work in the nature of harassment. *'Vicarious liability for breach of the Protection from Harassment Act by an employee would be a considerable extension on the employer's liability at common law. In particular, there is a lower threshold for damages under s.3 of the Act. The Act is concerned with the effect of harassment on the mind of the victim and any anxiety caused by the harassment qualifies for an award of damages. This is in sharp distinction to stress at work claims where the threshold for an award is identifiable psychiatric injury, which has to be foreseeable injury following from a breach of duty on the part of the employer.'*

This decision thus provides an alternative potential remedy against the employer for employees who claim to have been bullied at the workplace. Significantly there is no equivalent defence of reasonable steps as in discrimination legislation. A further appeal in the case, will be heard by the House of Lords in 2006.

Further guidance on the statutory tort of harassment created under the Protection from Harassment Act was provided by the Court of Appeal in *Banks v. Ablex Ltd.* 2005. Here the claimant ceased work because she was suffering from a depressive disorder of moderate severity which rendered her unfit for work. She claimed damages in the county court against her employers on the grounds that the disorder and her loss of employment were caused by the conduct towards her of a fellow employee and the employers' failure to prevent that conduct. The Court of Appeal held that the claimant had not been harassed by a fellow employee in breach of s.1 of the Protection from Harassment Act In the present case, the judge was entitled to find that the alleged harassment of the claimant by another employee on one particular occasion when he shouted, swore and gesticulated at her could not of itself satisfy the requirements of the statutory tort, and that prior to that occasion, nothing had occurred which could properly be described as harassment of the claimant by the other employee.

In order to establish harassment in breach of s.1, a claimant has to show that the alleged offender pursued a course of conduct amounting to harassment and which he knew or ought to have known amounted to harassment, having regard to whether a reasonable person in possession of the same information would think the course of conduct amounted to harassment. Thus the conduct, which includes speech, must be intentional and such as to harass the other individual, but in deciding what the alleged offender knew or ought to have known at the relevant time, on the basis of the information available to him, the court applies an objective standard. Misconduct on one occasion will not suffice and since the misconduct did not occur on two occasions, the judge was entitled to conclude that the allegation of harassment was not made.

The increasing practice of employees contracting out areas of work to contractors and sub contractors has important implications when determining liability for injuries caused due to negligence at the workplace.

> In *Sime v. Sutcliffe Catering Scotland Ltd.* 1990 an employee brought a claim alleging negligence by the above catering company when, carrying out her work as a canteen assistant she slipped on some food dropped by a fellow worker and suffered injury. The case was complicated by the fact that the employee was not directly employed by the catering company but by a paper manufacturer.[27]

---

27. *Tullis Russell and Co.*

Previously the paper manufacturer had contracted out the management of the canteen to the above company, but following pressure from the trade union, had agreed to retain existing canteen staff, including the employee. It was never established whether the worker who had dropped the food was an employee of the catering company or not. The issue therefore was whether the catering company could be held liable vicariously to a worker for the possible negligent act of a worker who they did not employ. The Scottish Court of Session held that responsibility should be with the employer in control. Although not directly employed by the catering company, whether the employer relationship is '*such as to render the company liable for the negligence depends upon whether the substitute employer has sufficient power of control and supervision purely to be regarded as the effective employer at the critical time*'. As the '*whole day to day management of the catering operation and staff was undertaken by the catering company and the canteen manager had complete control over the way in which all the canteen workers did their job*'... and '*since one of the employed persons caused the accident by being negligent in dropping food stuff onto the floor and failing to clean it up the company had to accept responsibility for that negligence*'. The fault of the injured employee was also recognised and damages were reduced by 20 % to reflect her contributory negligence. '*Where a person is working in or near a kitchen where a number of people are working with food or dirty dishes and where it is quite predictable that food might be spilt it is reasonably necessary that a look out be kept for any wet or slippery patches on the floor.*'

Independent contractors

Generally vicarious liability has been confined to the employer/employee relationship and where contractors are employed, responsibility for their wrongful acts is solely their own. The justification for not extending vicarious liability to employers of contractors, other than in exceptional cases, stems from the fact that the contractor is not subjected to his employer's control in the same way as an employee. One important exception, which in recent times has assumed significance, is the situation where the contractor has been employed to carry out a statutory duty imposed on the employer. This is because of the recent move towards requiring public bodies to put out many of their statutory functions for competitive tender among contractors and so the possibility of imposing liability on employers for the tortious acts of a contractor have increased significantly. The law in this area is not new.

The case of *Hardaker v. Idle District Council* 1896 remains the leading authority in relation to the delegation of statutory duties. The council acting under a statutory power to construct a sewer, employed a contractor to carry out the work. The contractor negligently pierced a gas main and the plaintiff's property was damaged by the resultant explosion. In an action by the plaintiffs against the contractor and the council employer, the court held that in exercising their statutory power the council owed an overriding duty to the public. This duty was to construct a sewer so as not to damage the gas main and put the public at risk. The council could not discharge this duty by simply employing a contractor to carry out the work, and accordingly they remained responsible to the plaintiff for its breach.

There are then certain legal duties that cannot be delegated, and if the wrongful act of a contractor constitutes a breach of such a duty, owed by an employer to a third party, then the contractor's employer may be made vicariously liable for the default.

> In *Rogers v. Nightriders* 1983 a mini cab firm undertook to provide a hire car to the plaintiff for a journey and did so by engaging a contractor driver. The plaintiff was injured in an accident which was caused as a result of the negligent maintenance of the mini cab by the contractor. In an action against the mini cab firm the court held that it was not liable, as an employer could not be made vicariously liable for their contractor's default. On appeal however, it was held that as the employer had undertaken to provide a vehicle to carry the plaintiff, and since they ought to have foreseen harm to the plaintiff if the vehicle was defective, they owed a duty of care to the plaintiff to ensure that the vehicle was reasonably fit. Such a duty could not be delegated to a contractor and accordingly the employers were liable for breach of the primary duty that they owed to her.

This case is a further example of the distinction that must be drawn between vicarious and direct or primary liability previously considered. By providing a negligent contractor, the employer in *Rogers v. Nightriders* had failed to fulfill a direct duty of care he owed to those he could reasonably foresee being affected.

The responsibility for the conduct of a loaned employee is an important issue. The loaned employee could include the seconded employee from a multi-national company to a subsidiary or a skilled employee of a subcontractor leant to a head contractor because of his expertise. The prospect of dual vicarious liability raised in Viasystems is an interesting development.[28] The court said that dual responsibility provides a coherent solution to the problem of the borrowed employee. Both employers are using the employee for the purposes of their business. Both have a responsibility to select their personnel with care and to encourage and control the careful execution of their employees' duties. Thus dual vicarious liability is likely to be imposed in a situation where the employee in question is so much a part of the work, business or organisation of both employers that it is just to make both employers answer for his negligence.

Further Reading

Barrett, Brenda *Employers Liability for Stress at the Workplace* (2003) 33 ILJ 343.

Brodie, Douglas *Health and Safety, Trust and Confidence Some Further Questions* (2003) 33 ILJ 261.

Lewis, David *How should Safety Concerns be handled* (2003) 33 ILJ 42.

Lewis, Richard *The Overlap between Damages for Personal Injury and Work Related Benefits* (1998) 27 ILJ 1.

Parsons, Chris *Employers Liability Insurance How Secure is the System* (1999) 28 ILJ 109.

Ridley and Dunford *Corporate Killing Legislating for Unlawful Death* (1997) 26 ILJ 99.

Employers Liability after Hatton v. Sutherland (2004) 34 ILJ 182.

---

28. See earlier in the chapter

Chapter 9

Statutory Employment Rights and Continuity of Employment

In this chapter it is proposed to examine a number of the many statutory employment rights and obligations which apply to employees[1] in the workplace and the rules relating to establishing a continuous period of employment, particularly on a business transfer. The specific statutory rights we will concentrate cover the payment of wages, including equal pay, the national minimum wage, sickness, disclosure of matters of public concern, and trade union membership and activities. The majority of all employment rights depend upon the existence of a valid contract of employment involving an employer/employee relationship but we have already seen that more contemporary rights such as the minimum wage, maximum working hours paid annual holidays and public interest disclosure are conferred on the wider category of 'workers'.

To qualify for a number of the statutory rights, an employee must establish a minimum period of continuous employment. It is considered appropriate therefore to consider the law relating to continuity of employment including business transfer at this point and then deal with some of the major statutory rights and obligations that apply in a subsisting employment relationship.

Continuity of Employment

To qualify for the majority of statutory employment rights, an employee, full or part-time, must establish a period of continuous employment. In addition to calculate statutory redundancy pay or the basic award for unfair dismissal it is necessary to refer to the period of continuous employment. To calculate this period it will be necessary to establish the date of the commencement of employment and if relevant the effective date of termination. Issues such as breaks in continuity and the change of an employer may have to be addressed

---

1. And sometimes workers

and the increasing practice of employing individuals on a succession of fixed term contracts over a period of time. The relevant rules on continuity are contained in primary and secondary legislation and are often the subject of judicial interpretation.

Periods of continuous employment to qualify for the above statutory rights vary from one month to three months and as long as two years to qualify for a redundancy payment or one year to present a complaint of unfair dismissal.

The basic rules to establish the period of continuous employment are contained in ss.210-219 of the Employment Rights Act 1996. Under s.211 an employee's period of continuous employment begins with the day on which the employee starts work. Under s.212(1) any week during the whole or part of which an employee's relations with his employers are governed by a contract of employment counts in computing the employee's period of employment. Continuity is preserved while the contract of employment is in existence so that absence from work due to sickness, injury, pregnancy, or temporary cessation of work will count as periods of continuous employment.

> In *Sweeney v. J & S Henderson Ltd.* 1999 it was alleged that the complainant's continuity of employment was broken when he resigned and tried employment with a different employer but then obtained re-employment all in the same week. The EAT confirmed that s.212 (1) plainly contemplates that continuous employment can include gaps and the reason for the gap is immaterial. Here continuity was preserved because during the relevant week there was at least one day governed by a contract with the relevant employer.

Earlier in Chapter 4 we said that if the contract of employment is illegal then any statutory rights which would otherwise have accrued due to continuous employment are unenforceable. Certainly if an employee is aware of the illegality surrounding his employment contract, by participating further in the contract he may prejudice his rights to pursue statutory rights.

> In *Ali Begacem v. Turkish Delight Kebab House* 1987 the applicant was paid between £90 and £120 in cash and received no pay slip. While he was informed by the DSS that no National Insurance contributions had been paid and by the Inland Revenue that no tax had been deducted the applicant merely mentioned the matter to his employer and was satisfied with a cursory response. The EAT upheld the tribunal's decision to dismiss the applicant's unfair dismissal complaint on the grounds that the contract was illegal and the applicant was at fault in not making further enquiries as to his legal position.

Any period that the contract operates illegally will not count towards the period of continuous employment for the purposes of statutory rights.

> In *Hyland v. J H Barber (North West) Ltd.* 1985 it was held that a contract of employment became illegal during a four week period when a tax-free lodging allowance was paid. This period could not therefore count toward continuity for the purposes of statutory rights.

Following the important decision of the House of Lords in *R v. Secretary of State for Employment ex parte EOC* 1994 the legal position of a part-time employee in relation to continuity for the purposes of unfair dismissal and redundancy is now the same as a full-time employee. The previous longer qualification period was held to be indirectly discriminatory under EC law and the UK government, committed to amending the legislation, achieved this in the Employment Protection (Part-Time Employees) Regulations 1995.

Even if the employee is away from work without a contract, continuity is not broken if he returns and the absence was under s.212(3) because the employee was:

(a) incapable of work through sickness or injury up to 26 weeks;

(b) absent from work through a temporary cessation of work;

(c) absent from work in circumstances such that, by arrangement or custom, he is regarded as continuing the employment for any purpose.

The issue in *Curr v. Marks & Spencer* 2003[2] was whether a management trainer remained employed during a four year child break scheme that she had accepted following the termination of her maternity leave. Under the scheme she was required to work for a minimum period of two weeks full-time or the equivalent part-time for each year of the break for which she would be paid. She was required to resign her post but with the employer's commitment to offer her a similar management position at the end of the break. All her staff benefits were terminated and her pension was frozen. Subsequently, after the applicant had returned to work, it became necessary to determine her continuity of employment for the purposes of a redundancy payment. The Court of Appeal confirmed that during the break the applicant did not have a contract of employment despite having mutuality of obligation. The second issue was whether the employee preserved her continuity during the child break under s.212(3)c. The court held that for the section to operate there must be a mutual recognition by the arrangement that the employee, though absent from work, nevertheless continues in the employment of her employer. An intention that there should be some continuing relationship is not sufficient to meet the requirements of the section. Here none of the features of the relationship showed that the employee was mutually regarded as continuing in the employment.

> In *Booth v. United States of America* 1999 the applicants were employed by the United States Army under a series of fixed term contracts with a break of at least two weeks between each contract. The breaks were designed to prevent the applicants securing sufficient continuity of employment for the purposes of redundancy and unfair dismissal. The applicants argued that the breaks fell within s.212(3)(c) of the 1996 Act which provides that absence from work by arrangement or action is regarded as continuing of employment. This argument was rejected by the EAT who felt the employee's clearly did not want the employment relationship to continue and there was no evidence to suggest that there was a custom or arrangement that it should continue, merely an expectation that the applicants would be re-employed. '*If by so arranging their affairs, employers lawfully are able to employ people in such a manner that the employees cannot complain of unfair dismissal or seek a redundancy payment, that is a matter for them. It is for the legislators, not the courts, to close any loopholes that might be perceived to exist.*'

Unfortunately here the EAT failed to consider the substance of these employment practices and declare them to be devices or shams. The new Regulations relating to the rights of fixed term employees were examined in Chapter 7 and would apply in the above case.

---

2. See Chapter 3

Temporary cessation of work

It has been argued that the expression *'temporary cessation of work'*[3] should apply to preserve continuity of employment where there has been a succession of fixed term contracts.

> In *Ford v. Warwickshire County Council* 1983 a *'part-time temporary'* teacher in a further education college claimed that as she had been employed from September 1971 to July 1979 on a succession of fixed term temporary contracts which terminated each July and then recommenced in the September, the periods of summer vacation when she was not employed should count as temporary cessation of work. It was necessary to establish the period of continuous employment to maintain a claim for unfair dismissal and a redundancy payment. While the industrial tribunal, the EAT and the Court of Appeal all found that the continuity was broken each summer and the teacher was not absent from work but simply unemployed, the House of Lords on final appeal took a different view. The Lords held that the applicant's absence from work during the summer vacation could properly be described as *'on account of a temporary cessation of work'*, particularly when there was a regular pattern of employment and continuity was not broken.

In deciding whether a cessation of work is temporary or not, it is necessary to take account of all the relevant circumstances, in particular the length of period of absence in the context of the period of employment as a whole. In *Flack v. Kodak Ltd.* 1986 the Court of Appeal held that a long gap in the course of employment over a number of years may be considered temporary in the circumstances of the case.

Certainly to determine whether there has been a temporary cessation of work, the whole history of the employee's intermittent employment must be considered bearing in mind the nature of the industry in which he was employed. A failure by the tribunal in *Olla v. Sutcliffe Catering (UK) Ltd.* 1995 to take account of an employee's history of employment was held by the EAT to be fatal in deciding whether a three month break constituted a temporary cessation of work.

> In *Tipper v. Roofdec Ltd.* 1989 the EAT held that continuity of employment is not broken even if there is a change of work, and that the precise reason for the change of work is irrelevant. Here a lorry driver who could no longer drive because of a twelve month driving ban was offered and accepted labouring work by his employer. Terminating the job as a driver on the Friday and then being re-employed as a full-time labourer on the Monday meant that there was continuity of employment. Accordingly the driver had sufficient service to be able to claim a redundancy payment when he was dismissed when the labouring job came to an end.

Continuity may also be preserved if the absence is due to an established arrangement or custom.[4] The arrangement could cover leave of absence, secondment or even being placed on a reserve list of employees. In some industries employers rely heavily on a pool of casual or temporary employees who may be called upon subject to production or seasonal demands. Many temporary workers have a long period of service with their employers but

---

3. s.212(3)b
4. s.212(3)b

with numerous breaks in employment. Such breaks in employment could constitute temporary cessation of work or absences due to custom and practice which under s.212(3) would not break continuity of employment for the purposes of statutory rights. In *Hygena Ltd. v. Cook and Others* 1996 a furniture manufacturer maintained a pool of temporary employees to fill full-time absences. When choosing workers from the pool a custom developed that priority should be given to the longest serving pool members. The EAT held that the purpose of the pool was to provide the employer with access to skilled and experienced workers when required and the fact that priority was given to long serving members was consistent with regarding them as continuously employed for the purpose of statutory rights, despite breaks in employment.

In *London Probation Board v. Kirkpatrick* 2004 an employee who was dismissed and then reinstated on internal appeal was held to retain continuity under an 'arrangement' for the purposes of s.212(3).

Under s.216 periods of industrial action which involve no work due to strikes or lock outs will not count towards the period of continuity but will not break it.

Under the Employment Protection (Continuity of Employment) Regulations 1993 a dismissed employee's continuity of employment is preserved under the relevant legislation if she is reinstated or re-engaged by the employer or an associate following ACAS conciliation, a compromise agreement, or the order of a tribunal.

Change in the Employer

It is generally only continuous employment with the same employer that is calculated to determine an employee's length of continuity of employment for the purpose of statutory rights. If an employee changes his job then previous periods of employment with the old employer are ignored for the purposes of calculating continuity with the new employer. Under the common law this is also the position when the employer changes because the business is sold. The effect of the change is to discharge the contracts of employment with the old employer and start afresh with new contracts of employment with the new employer. There are however a number of exceptions to this rule, in particular contained in:

(a) section 218 of the Employment Rights Act 1996; and

(b) the Transfer of Undertakings (Protection of Employment) Regulations 1981. (new TUPE Regulations 2006[5]).

It should be stressed from the outset that these are complex provisions with a considerable degree of overlap, so that a business transfer could be covered by both s.218 of the 1996 Act and the TUPE Regulations. Also both s.218 and the 1981 Regulations[6] only apply to the take-over of a business as a going concern rather than a sale of the business assets which could include the employees. Continuity will be broken in such circumstances and the employees affected will negotiate new contracts with the transferee employer. They will also have the right to proceed against their old employer in relation to the termination of their original contracts for wrongful dismissal, unfair dismissal or redundancy payments where appropriate. It should also be stressed that the majority of business take-overs in

5. In force April 2006
6. And 2006 TUPE

England and Wales are effected by acquiring the shares of a limited company in which case the contracts of employment of the company employees will remain unaffected by the business transfer.

Under s.218(2), if a trade or business or an undertaking is transferred from one person to another, the period of employment in the trade or business or undertaking shall count as a period of employment with the transferee and the transfer shall not break continuity. Furthermore under s.218(4) continuity will not be broken if the employer dies and the employee is kept on by the Personal Representatives or trustees of the estate.

> The EAT in *Williams v. Evans* 1992 decided that the sale of a member's club to an individual proprietor was a business transfer for the purposes of the Act. It was not simply a sale of business assets but the transfer of a going concern and *'the reality of the situation is that the club is carrying on'*. As a consequence the continuity of employment of the club's sole employee was not broken by the transfer and she was qualified to present a complaint of unfair dismissal.

For a s.218(2) transfer, continuity is preserved only if the new business carried on is the same as the old business.

> In *Macer v. Abafast Ltd.* 1990 the EAT in considering the section decided that *'provided that there has been a valid transfer of a business from A to B then the continuous period of service with A may be added to the continuous period of service of an employee with B so as to establish a qualifying period of employment'*. The EAT stated there are four essentials to the section:
>
> - the transfer of the business;
> - employment by the owner before the transfer and after the transfer;
> - a period of service with the old owner and new owner which is continuous;
> - the combined periods of service satisfying the statutory qualification period.

This interpretation of s.218(2) suggests that the fact that the employee is not employed in the business *'at the time of the transfer'* does not necessarily break continuity. A gap in employment by the old employer and the new employer which is related to 'the transfer' is permissible, but if it is too long it may not be viewed as related to the 'machinery of the transfer' and so break continuity. In interpreting these provisions, the court *'should lean in favour of that interpretation which best gives effect to the preservation of continuity of service and hence the preservation of the rights of the employee and so obviate and discourage a tactical manoeuvre which seeks to avoid the clear intention of Parliament'*.

> In *A & G Tuck Ltd. v. Bartlott and A & G Tuck (Slough) Ltd.* 1994 the issue was whether the complainant's employment and consequently continuity had been preserved and transferred when he remained in the employment of the transferor at the time of the transfer and joined the transferee two weeks later. The EAT held that the tribunal was correct to conclude that nevertheless the section *'applied to circumstances in which the complainant entered the transferee's employment in connection with the transfer and after a gap which was related to the machinery of the transfer'*.
>
> In *Justfern Ltd. v. Dingerthorpe and Others* 1994 the complainant a college lecturer made a claim for unemployment benefit when his college employer closed down. One week later the college was purchased and reopened with the complainant

accepting re-employment. Despite the gap in employment of more than a week and the claim for benefit, the EAT held that the employee was still employed in the business at the time of the transfer. *'A liberal construction of the words at the time of the transfer accords with the evident policy of the legislature to preserve continuity of employment'.* The section operated, moreover to preserve continuity of employment even though the termination of employment by the original employer was for commercial reasons of insolvency rather than as a step in the transfer of the business. The motivation for the termination of the employment by the transferor employer is not in direct significance. The question is whether there was a transfer of a business in relation to which an employee's employment can also be regarded as transferred. It is a necessary implication of that the business and the employment of the relevant employee should survive sufficiently as to be susceptible to transfer. If the old employer closes down the business so completely that the new employer was effectively starting a new business, that necessary implication would not be satisfied.

Section 218(5) deals with a change in business partners, personal representatives or trustees who employ any person and provides that the employee's period of employment at the time of the change shall count as a period of employment after the change and continuity is not broken.

Employers are treated as associated if one is a company of which the other (directly or indirectly) has control or if both companies are under the control (directly or indirectly) of a third person. Under section 218(6), if an employee is transferred from one employer to an *'associated employer'* then continuity of employment is preserved. Under section 231 Employment Rights Act 1996 any two employers are to be treated as associated if one is a company of which the other (directly or indirectly) has control, or if both are companies of which a third person (directly or indirectly) has control. Continuous employment for associated employers may be aggregated in computing an employee's total period of service for the purpose of statutory rights.

> In *Hancill v. Marcon Engineering Ltd.* 1990. The employee in question had worked abroad for an American firm and then returned to the United Kingdom to work for a British Company which eventually dismissed him. Both undertakings were wholly-owned subsidiaries of a Dutch Company. In order to show the requisite period of continuous employment to qualify to bring a complaint of unfair dismissal the employee sought to include his period of employment with the American firm in the computation. The industrial tribunal however rejected the claim that the American firm was an *'associated company'*, as it was not a *'Limited Company'* as required by the section. This strict interpretation of the term *'company'* was not followed in the EAT which concluded that *'it is difficult to see quite how 'Inc' differs in its constituent parts from a company incorporated under the Companies Act. It seems to us that it would be entirely appropriate in the application of this branch of the law to contracts of employment that if the overseas subsidiary is a company which in its essentials is to be likened to a company limited under the Companies Act, then it would be right, fair and indeed in accordance with the principles of presumption of continuity under the Act that the company should be recognised as a company for the purpose of the definition section of associated employer'.* Concerned that without such an interpretation there would be obvious possibilities of transferring employees to overseas subsidiaries and so preventing them from acquiring statutory

employment rights dependent on continuous employment, the President of the EAT said that *'our task is to look to the true intent of the legislation and so to interpret the provisions of the Act and so far as we can properly do so as to give effect to that intention. It seems to us here that a coach and four could easily be driven round a few corners and then straight through the provision of this legislation if the word 'company' were only to include a UK Ltd. Company when the overseas vehicle is to all intent and purposes identical'.*

The TUPE Regulations 1981 and 2006

Further rights relating to the preservation of continuity were contained in the Transfer of Undertakings (Protection of Employment) Regulations 1981. These Regulations were passed to give further protection to workers in a business transfer and as so, give effect to the Acquired Rights Directive. The principal aim of the Regulations was to ensure that on the transfer of an undertaking, the contractual rights of the employees, including continuity, are preserved. The present Regulations are replaced by the Transfer of Undertaking (Protection of Employment) Regulations 2006 which apply to any transfer that takes place after 19 April 2006.

The broad aim of the Acquired Rights Directive was to preserve workers continuity of employment on a business transfer. While the TUPE Regulations were passed to implement the Directive there is no doubt that the prevailing Government view in the 1980s was to substantially nullify the effect of the Directive. There is not doubt however that over the years a series of domestic and European judgments have attempted to strengthen the Directive but we are left with a highly complex and contradictory legal position. We now have a new Acquired Rights Directive 2001 which has led to a revised TUPE 2006 following a period of consultation. The new TUPE 2006 aims to implement the Acquired Rights Directive of 2001 and codify existing case-law to address the uncertainties in the interpretation of TUPE 1981. The concerns of the judiciary were expressed by May LJ in *Adi (UK) Ltd. v. Willer* 2001. He said that *'It is clear that the state of European and domestic authorities is unsatisfactory. The concept of transfer is now a judicially constructed fiction derived from the purpose of the Directive and the Regulations to safeguard the rights of employees. The requirement in Article I of the Directive for the transfer to result from a legal transfer or merger has been emasculated out of existence by purposive judicial interpretation.'*

The TUPE 2006 amendments aim to:

- Increase certainty by helping the parties to a relevant transfer know whether they are covered so that they can apportion risk.
- Reduce the scope for litigation and reduce the legal costs of the transfer.
- Reduce the risk of being undercut on employment costs in competitive tendering situations.

The Regulations apply to employees. An employee is defined as *'any individual who works for another person whether under a contract of service or apprenticeship or otherwise but does not include anyone who provides services under a contract for services'.*

In *Cowell v. Quilter Goodison Company Ltd.* and *QG Management Services Ltd.* 1989 the Court of Appeal held that an equity partner for a firm which had transferred its business could not count his prior service as a partner for the purposes of showing two years' service as an employee to qualify for a claim of unfair dismissal. An equity partner does not work for another person under a contract of service and nor does he have an employment relationship with any or all of the partners. His relationship is governed by the definition of a partnership under the Partnership Act under which partners are required to provide services under a contract for services for the benefit of the partnership.

What is a TUPE transfer

One of the most litigated issues under TUPE was the application of the Regulations and what constituted a relevant transfer. The new TUPE 2006 attempts to expand the definition of relevant transfer to include service provision changes, where there was a major area of uncertainty as to when the Regulations applied. Much depended upon the nature of the arrangements before and after the change and whether or not the change was asset dependent[7] or labour intensive.[8] Under TUPE 2006 there will be a deemed transfer if before the change there was a dedicated group of people providing the service other than on a one off basis. This means that the transfer of labour intensive services without assets will be included. Changes to service provision would include outsourcing,[9] changes to the contractor or bringing a service back in-house.[10] The party responsible for carrying out the service before the change will be treated as the transferor and after the change, treated as the transferee.[11]

Under TUPE 2006 therefore the definition of relevant transfer has been expanded to include service provision changes.

1. There must be a dedicated team of people whose principal purpose is to carry out the services of the client

2. The activities must be carried out other than in connection with a specific single contract e.g. organising a conference.[12]

3. The activities are not for the procurement or supply of goods e.g. supplying food for the works canteen.

In future there will be two ways that TUPE can apply where there is a change in service provider.

1. Under the *Main Definition* the change may amount to a relevant transfer if the entity has retained its identity. Or

2. Under the *Service Provision Change* definition if the activity remains the same and the relevant conditions are met. Under this definition the entity is not required to retain its identity and the fact that a major part of the workforce is not taken on or the service is to be carried out differently is irrelevant.

Hopefully the wider definition will increase certainty and reduce the scope for litigation.

---

7. Such as catering
8. Such as cleaning
9. Where an employer contracts out the service
10. Insourcing
11. See later in the chapter
12. It is less clear whether a long term project is included as a single event

Originally the 1981 TUPE Regulations only applied to business transfers which were of a 'commercial venture'. Following the decision of the European Court of Justice in *Dr Sophie Redmond-Stitching v. Bartol* 1992 it became necessary to bring the TUPE Regulations in line with the Acquired Rights Directive and the Regulations were amended by the Trade Union Reform and Employment Rights Act 1993. Following the TURERA amendments the Regulations apply to all relevant transfers rather than just where the undertaking is a commercial venture. The defective implementation of the Acquired Rights Directive in TUPE so that 'non-profit making undertakings' were excluded was confirmed by a ruling of the European Court of Justice in *Commission of the European Communities v. UK* in 1994. As a result, all those employees whose jobs were lost or accepted inferior terms and conditions of employment resulting from the contracting out of public services prior to the TURERA amendments had potential claims. The argument is that had the law been properly implemented their position would have been safeguarded. Such claims however should have been lodged within three months of the TUPE amendments coming into force, subject to the tribunal's discretion. Alternatively there is a potential action against the Government under the Francovitch principle for failing to properly translate the Directive into national law.

> In *Kenny and others v. South Manchester College* 1993 the High Court ruled that the contracting out by the Home Office of the education service at a young offenders institution is a transfer covered by the TUPE Regulations. The further education college that won the contract was therefore bound by the terms and conditions in the contracts of the existing staff who were previously employed by the local authority.

Both the European Court of Justice in *Rask and another v. ISS Kantineservice A/S* 1993 and the Court of Appeal in *Dines and others v. Initial Health Care Services and Pall Mall Services Group Ltd.* 1993 make it clear that a business which comprises of only the provision of labour is capable of being an economic entity within the meaning of the TUPE Regulations and the Business Transfer Directive.

> In *Rask and Christensen v. ISS Kantineservice A/S* 1993 the European Court of Justice ruled that the Business Transfer Directive may cover the contracting out of a canteen service even though the service is incidental to the transferors main business and the transferee receives only a fixed fee for running the service. If a transfer which falls within scope of the Directive has occurred, the transferors rights and obligations in relation to the affected employees are transferred to the transferee. The transferee cannot therefore alter the date on which the employee's wages are paid or the constituent parts of their wages unless the transferor would have had the same rights in a non transfer situation.

> In *Workman and Birckley v. Servisystem Ltd.* 1994 the EAT held that when cleaning services at a local authority college are transferred from the council to a private contractor and then to another contractor, this was the transfer of an 'economic entity' to which the TUPE Regulations applied. As a consequence two cleaners who moved on two occasions to the contractors retained their continuity of employment for the purposes of their complaints of unfair dismissal.

Following amendments to TUPE Regulations in 1993 all new transfers are covered by the Regulations even if they do not involve a transfer of property or relate to a non-commercial venture. This means that almost all public sector contracting out scenarios are now covered by the Regulations.

Equally there is not a transfer of an undertaking merely because assets are disposed of. The relevant question is whether the business was transferred as a going concern indicated by the fact the new employer continues the same activities. An important question is whether on the transfer the business retains its identity. All the circumstances surrounding the transfer must be considered including the type of business, the proportion of employees transferred, the impact on customers/clients, and the extent to which tangible and intangible business assets are transferred. In a significant case the judgment the European Court of Justice *in Suzen v. Zehnacher Aebaudereinigung GmbH Krankenhausservice and Another* 1997 held that the Business Transfer Directive *'does not apply to a situation in which a person who had entrusted the cleaning of premises to a first undertaking, terminates the contract and for the performance of similar work enters into a contract with the second undertaking, if there is no concomitant transfer from one undertaking to the other of significant tangible or intangible business assets or taking over by the new employer of a major part of the workforce, in terms of their numbers and skills, assignment by the predecessor to the performance of the contract'.*

Suzen was applied by the Court of Appeal in *Adi (UK) Ltd. v. Willer* 2001 where the issue before the court was whether a change of service contractor amounted to a TUPE transfer. Adi had provided a security service at a shopping centre but gave up the contract and some of the existing staff were employed by the incoming contractor. Deciding that neither the workforce nor any significant assets were part of the transfer both the tribunal and the EAT held that TUPE did not apply. The Court of Appeal agreed that the mere loss of a service contract to a competitor does not necessarily indicate a TUPE transfer. One of the main factors in deciding whether there has been a transfer of an economic entity is whether the majority of the employees were taken over by the new employer. Of relevance is the Court of Appeal's decision in *ECM (Vehicle Delivery) Service Ltd. v. Cox* 1999 that an employer who does not take on existing employees to avoid the application of TUPE cannot rely on that fact to show there is no TUPE transfer. Applying *ECM* the Court of Appeal held that *'if the economic entity is labour intensive such that, applying Suzen there is no transfer if the workforce is not taken on, but there would be if they were, the tribunal is obliged to treat the case as if the labour had transferred if it is established that the reason or principal reason for this was to avoid the application of TUPE. However there is no positive burden on the person arguing against the transfer to establish the reason for not taking on the workforce'.* Here there would have been a TUPE transfer if the workforce had been taken on or the reason for not taking them on was the employer adopting a TUPE avoidance strategy.

RCO Support Service v. Unison 2002 is a Court of Appeal decisions on when TUPE applies where there is a change of service contractors. The EAT's decision was upheld that TUPE applies where there is a change in hospitals providing inpatient care within the same NHS Trust area and new contractors took over the provision of cleaning and catering, despite the fact that almost none of the workforce was taken on by the transferee. Explaining the decision in the light of *Suzen* Ld Justice Mummery said that *Suzen* does not mean *'that as a matter of community law there can never be a transfer of an undertaking in a contracting out case if neither assets not workforce are transferred'.* All the relevant factors have to be taken account of and the workforce is only one factor and not conclusive. The decisive issue is whether the transferred entity retains its identity. Confirming the *ECM* principle the Court of Appeal also said that the reason why the employees were not taken on is a relevant circumstance in determining whether the identity was retained. Here the fact that the transferors cleaners would be employed by the transferee if they resigned from their old jobs and accepted new terms and conditions with the transferee, was regarded as relevant evidence pointing to a retention of identity.

Duty on transferor to inform transferee of employee liability information

Under TUPE 1981 there was no duty on the transferor employer to provide workplace information to the transferee employer. Under TUPE 2006 Reg 11, in an attempt to encourage transparency and combat sharp practice, the transferor has a duty to provide information in writing to the transferee in good time (at least two weeks) before the transfer and update it before completion. This information will include the identities of all transferring employees and details of all rights, liabilities, powers and duties that arise under or in connection with the transferring contracts of employment.. The transferor can no longer rely on the Data Protection Act 1998 to resist providing the names of employees. While transferees should ensure they have disclosure provisions in the purchase agreement, this is nevertheless a significant new protection. It will be of most relevance on a re-tendering transfer where the second generation contractor is unlikely to have any contractual connection with the outgoing contractor. Also the transferee may find it difficult to negotiate protection in the purchase contract because the transferor is a public authority or an administrator in an insolvency situation. Under the new Regulations the transferee may claim against the transferor in the ordinary courts for a failure to comply with this obligation and the transferor could be ordered to pay up to a maximum of £75,000 as a penalty. (A minimum award of £500 per employee.)

Duty to inform and consult employees

There was conflicting case-law as to whether potential liability for failure to consult with employee representatives[13] prior to a TUPE transfer passed by virtue of Reg 5 from the transferor to the transferee. The EAT in *Kerry Foods Ltd. v. Kreber* 2000 ruled that the duty to consult is a right which arises from individual worker's contracts and is therefore covered by Reg 5 and passed to the transferee. The maximum compensation for failing to consult was increased from 4 weeks pay to 13 weeks pay, so that there could be a substantial liability on the transferee.

Under TUPE 2006 Reg. 15, for non transferring employees of either the transferor or the transferee, the liability to inform and consult rests with the relevant employer. For transferring employees, the transferor and the transferee will be jointly and severally liable for any failure to inform and consult, unless the failure is due to the fact that the transferee did not provide the required information, in which case he is solely responsible. A transferor will be able to join a transferee in any legal proceedings for failure to consult a relevant trade union. It does make sense that the parties should address the issue in the transfer transaction and ensure that they are indemnified for liability that may arise because of the other parties failures.

Collective Agreements

The EAT in two cases in 1997, *BET Catering Services Ltd. v. Ball and Others and Wheat and Others v. Cartledge Ltd.* held that under Regulation 5, on a TUPE transfer from the public sector to the private sector, a collective agreement under which pay rates were varied transferred to a private contractor without modification or amendment. This meant that a

---

13. Trade unions

private employer who was not a party to the collective agreement was bound to pay collectively bargained rates of pay to the transferred employees as their terms and conditions remained the same after the transfer.

> In *Bernadone v. Pall Mall Services* 2000 the Court of Appeal held that tortious liability transfers under TUPE. Therefore a transferee is liable for any negligence or breach of statutory duty by the transferors in connection with a claimant's accident at work prior to the transfer of the undertaking. The obligations of a transferor to compensate an employee as a consequence of negligence by the employer arises *'in connection with'* the employee's contract of employment within the meaning of the TUPE since the duty of care arose by virtue of the contract of employment. Of great practical significance was the further ruling that the right to be indemnified under the employers liability insurance policy was also transferred along with the undertaking. Reg 5(2). TUPE confers on the transferee the right of an indemnity under the insurance policy between the transferor and their insurers in respect of the employee's claim. The position is therefore satisfactory for the transferee as the transferor is obliged by statute to have the relevant employer's liability insurance cover.

A question of considerable practical importance on a business transfer is whether TUPE would preserve the employee's right to share in profits earned by the former employer. Also is there any obligation on the transferee to create a comparable profit sharing scheme.

> In *Unicorn Consultancy Services Ltd. v. Westbrook* 2000 the EAT upheld a finding that the employees were entitled to profit related pay earned by the date of the transfer and the transferee was liable for this under TUPE. While the employee's acquired right should be an obligation on the transferee there was no obligation under TUPE for the transferee to replicate the former employers scheme.

More recently a purposive approach to the interpretation of the TUPE Regulations has been recommended bearing in mind their purpose *'to protect workers and safeguard their rights upon a change of employer.'* The right to participate in profit sharing or share option schemes may be a significant part of an employee's remuneration, and the question as to whether such a right is automatically transferred in a TUPE scenario is an important one.

> In *MITIE Managed Services Ltd. v. French and Others* 2002 the claimants contended that they remained contractually entitled to participate in a Sainsburys profit sharing scheme when the undertaking in which they worked was subject to a relevant transfer from Sainsburys Supermarkets Ltd. to Pitney Bowes Management Services Ltd. The Employment Tribunal held that as the profit sharing clause was incorporated into the claimant's contracts the transferee was bound by it and the claim was upheld. On appeal however the EAT took a more pragmatic view stressing that in attempting to safeguard workers' rights on a transfer it was required to adopt a broad approach that achieved results rather than taking a position which was absurd or impossible to administer. As the transferee could not issue shares in Sainsburys or have access to commercially sensitive information the entitlement to the profit sharing scheme was impossible to perform and would produce a result which was absurd and unjust. Here there was an entitlement on transfer, but to an equivalent or comparable scheme, rather than literally the Sainsburys scheme. In reaching its conclusion the EAT held that previous authorities to the effect that the exact clause must be transferred are confined to the particular factual circumstances of each case.

Employee rights on a TUPE transfer

Under Regulation 5(1) the transfer of an undertaking *'shall not operate so as to terminate the contract of employment of any person employed by the transferor ... but any such contract ... shall have effect after the transfer as if original made between the person so employed and the transferee'*. This means that the contract of employment still subsists after the transfer and consequently continuity of employment is preserved. This process under the Regulations of preserving rights by deeming that a contract *is 'as if originally made between the person so employed and the transferee'* is an attractive one.

Under Regulation 5(2) *'all the transferor's rights, powers, duties and liabilities under or in connection with ... the contract shall be transferred to the transferee; and anything done before the transfer is completed by or in relation to the transferor in respect of that contract ... shall be deemed to have been done by or in relation to the transferee'*. This means that an employee can pursue his rights against the transferee business even where breaches of contract occur prior to the transfer. If an employee objects to the transfer he will not be transferred and his contract will terminate. By showing that the transfer would have a detrimental affect on his contract however such an employee could claim constructive dismissal by reason of the transfer under Regulation 5(5).

Under TUPE 2006 if there is a service provision change then the transferee will inherit the employees assigned to the undertaking together with all the rights, obligations and liabilities arising in relation to their contracts of employment.[14] This is the case regardless of how the transferee organises his existing workforce, so if they are earmarked for the new tasks then the transferee will have to embark on a redundancy exercise in relation to the transferred staff. The intention under TUPE 2006 is to protect jobs so it may be necessary for the transferee to redeploy the incoming employees in other roles at the workplace.

Under TUPE 1981 only changes to terms and conditions of employment unconnected to the transfer were permitted. This is still the case under TUPE 2006 so if the reason for the change is the transfer it will be void. Under TUPE 2006 however the transferee employer and the employee can agree changes connected to the transfer if such changes are for an economic, technical or organisational reason entailing changes in the workforce.[15] The harmonisation of terms and conditions will not qualify as an ETO reason.

Importantly an employee may treat his contract as terminated by dismissal with notice if the transfer involves a substantial change in working conditions which are to his detriment. Alternatively the employee may terminate in a constructive dismissal scenario by accepting the employer's repudiatory breach for unilateral changes resulting from the transfer. There was some doubt as to whether a transferor could be liable for constructive dismissal if an employee opted out of a transfer because the transferee did not provide equivalent pension provision. Under TUPE 2006 Reg 10 the transferor is not at risk in this situation. Employees are provided with some protection under the Pensions Act 2004[16] which requires the transferee to make matching contributions of 6% of pay into a stakeholder scheme or provide benefits worth at least 6% of pensionable pay.

---

14. Excluding occupational pensions
15. The ETO reason
16. s.258

Dismissal in connection with a TUPE transfer

The 1981 Regulations provides some degree of protection to employees who are dismissed on the transfer of a business undertaking. Under the Regulations it is provided that the dismissal of an employee before or after a relevant transfer is to be regarded as automatically unfair if by reason of the transfer or for a reason connected with the transfer. This remains the position under TUPE 2006 Reg 7.

The dismissal is prima facie fair however, under Reg 8(2), if it is for an *economic, technical or organisational reason* entailing change in the workforce and so regarded as *some other substantial reason* for the purpose of s.98(1) or for redundancy under s.98(2) Employment Rights Act 1996.[17] If the decision to dismiss is regarded as reasonable under s.98(4) it is fair.[18] This will remain the position under TUPE 2006 Reg 7.

> Guidance in relation to the interpretation of economic, technical or organisational reason was provided by the EAT in *Wheeler v. Patel & J. Golding Group of Companies* 1987. Here the unfair dismissal claim by a sales assistant against the purchaser of the shop where she worked was rejected because she had been dismissed before the contractual date set for completion of the sale. In relation to the phrase an *economic reason* for dismissal the EAT felt that like technical or organisational reasons *it must be a reason which relates to the conduct of the business*. A desire to obtain an enhanced price for the business or to achieve a sale is not a reason relating to the conduct of the business. This limited meaning given to the *phrase 'economic reason'* reflects the fact that if a broad literal interpretation were given to it, the majority of dismissals by transfers in such circumstances would be regarded as for an *economic reason*. Here the dismissal, in order to comply with the requirement of an intending purchaser, was not for an *economic reason*, for it did not relate to the conduct of the business, rather the vendor's desire to sell. As the vendor had not shown that the dismissal was for an economic technical or organisational reason, the unfair dismissal claim against the vendor was upheld.

The Court of Appeal in *Whitehouse v. Chas A Blatchford & Sons* 1999 agreed with the EAT in *Wheeler* above and found that the words *economic, technical or organisational reason entailing changes in the workforce* clearly means that the reason must be connected with the future conduct of the business as a going concern. Here the transferee business needed to reduce the number of technicians to secure the award of a contract as so the complaints dismissal could be categorised as for an economic or organisational reason within the meaning of Reg 8(2) end the employee had a defence to the complaint.

A dismissal caused by or connected with the transfer of a business for the purpose of the Regulations will be fair if the reason for dismissal is an *organisational one* entailing changes in the workforce.

> The changes imposed upon the complainant in *Crawford v. Swinton Insurance Brokers* 1990 on the transfer of business were held to be so radical that when she resigned as a result of them she could regard herself as constructively dismissed. From a clerk/typist who worked mainly at home, she was offered

---

17. See Chapter 11
18. See Chapter 11

other work, with the changed function of selling insurance. The tribunal further held however that the changes imposed were dictated by the new employer's organisational requirements, and to offer new standard conditions to existing staff was a *'change of the workforce'* for the purpose of the Regulations . Such a finding was approved by the EAT which held that there can be a *'change in the workforce'* if the same people are kept on but given different jobs. In the case of a constructive dismissal following an organisational change however, it is the tribunal's function to *'identify the principal reason for the conduct of the employer which entitled the employee to terminate the contract and then determine whether the reason is an economic, technical or organisational one entailing changes in the workforce'.*

An important transformation of the law relating to liability for dismissals on a business transfer was brought about by the House of Lords' decision in *Lister v. Forth Dry Dock and Engineering Company Ltd.* 1989. Here the Lords held that liability for a dismissal by the vendor prior to the transfer, will pass to the purchaser, if the employee has been unfairly dismissed for a reason connected with the transfer. In order to give effect to the EC Employee Rights on Transfer of Business Directive, Regulation 5(3) which provides that liability is to be transferred only where the employee *is 'employed immediately before the transfer'* is to have the words added *'or would have been so employed if he had not been dismissed'* in the circumstances described in the Regulation. The effect of this change is that an employee who is dismissed solely because of a transfer is automatically passed to the transferee but if the employee is dismissed for an economic, technical or organisational reason then liability will not pass unless the employee was still employed at the time of transfer. Without such an interpretation, employees in cases like this would be left with *'worthless claims for unfair dismissal'* against an insolvent employer. This potential liability is incorporated in TUPE 2006 Reg 4.

In cases where there is a relevant transfer for the purposes of the Regulations and a dismissal before the transfer by the transferor, it was thought that under Regulation 5(2) the act of dismissal was deemed to have been done by the transferee who would be responsible for the dismissal.

In *Allen v. Stirling DC* 1994 the EAT indicated that Regulation 5(2) while imposing liability on the transferee does not necessarily remove it from the transferor. The EAT held that *'there are no words which can be said to exclude the transferor's liability apart from the word 'transferred' itself and some addition or qualification such as the word 'instead' or an equivalent had to be added to that word for liability to go to the transferee instead of the transferor'.*

Further guidance as to the operation of Regulations 8 and 5 was provided by the EAT in *Kerry Food Ltd. v. Creber* 2000. The applicant's employer went into receivership and eventually the business was purchased by Kerry Food Ltd. who acquired the company's brand name and goodwill. None of the remaining staff were employed by Kerry but applying the Court of Appeal's decision in *Elm (Vehicle Delivery Service) v. Cox* 2000 the EAT nevertheless held that a transfer had occurred, the employment of staff being only one of the relevant factors to take account of. Further guidance provided by the EAT included:

- any dismissal by a transferor due to an impending transfer is automatically unfair and the employee should proceed against the transferee. Issues about economic, technical or organisational reasons (ETO) do not arise if the transfer was the principal reason for the dismissal;

- if the main reason for the dismissal by the transferor is an ETO reason the employee can claim unfair dismissal against the transferor;

- if the transferee dismisses the employee he can claim automatic unfair dismissal against the transferee if the dismissal was connected with the transfer or unfair dismissal against the transferee for an (ETO) reason.

The Payment of Wages

We considered the payment of wages and salaries in Chapters 4 as the employer's fundamental obligation under a contract of employment. Here it is proposed to examine statutory rights in relation to the payment of wages, in particular protection in relation to unlawful deductions and the National Minimum Wage. Over 20% of claims before employment tribunals are concerned with unlawful deductions from wages.

Earlier when we explored the formation of a contract of employment in Chapter 4, it was stated that while there is no legal requirement that an employment contract be in writing, under s.1 of the Employment Rights Act 1996, an employee is entitled to be supplied with a written statement of the main terms and conditions of employment. Section 8 of the 1996 Act further provides that every employee has the right to be given a written itemised pay statement at the time or before wages or salary are paid. Following the Employment Protection (Part-time Employees) Regulation 1995, part-time employees are also entitled to a written itemised pay statement. Certain particulars must be included on the statement:

- the gross amount of the wages or salary;

- the amount of any variable and fixed deduction and the purpose for which they are made;

- the net amount of the wages or salary; and

- where different parts of the net amount are paid in different ways, the amount and method of each part-payment.

In relation to fixed deductions a further option is for the employer to provide his employees with a standing statement of fixed deductions. If this statement is kept up to date on an annual basis then the employee need only include the aggregate amount of fixed deductions in the pay statement. If an employer fails to comply with a s.8 obligation to provide a complete and accurate itemised pay statement, the remedy for an employee is to make an application[19] to the employment tribunal within three months for a declaration to that effect.

> In *Coates v. John Wood & Company* 1986 the tribunal took the view that as the employee in question had never been denied the right to an itemised statement, and details of deductions had been shown to her whenever requested, then s.8 had not been infringed. On appeal however, the EAT disagreed and made a declaration to the effect that there had been non compliance with the statutory

---

19. Under s.11

right. The EAT stated that '*s.8 establishes an inherent right which creates an inherent obligation on an employer to provide the employee with an itemised pay statement at or before the time at which any payment of wages or salary is made and that right exists whether or not the employee exercises any claim under it*'.

Unlawful deductions

The provisions of the Act are designed to extend beyond those working under a contract of service and would cover apprentices and even contractors provided they were performing personal services. This is a good example of a major part of the Employment Rights Act that applies to workers as well as employees.

Under section 13(1)[20] *An employer shall not make any deduction from any wages of any worker employed by him unless:*

(a) *the deduction is required or authorised to be made by virtue of any statutory provision or a relevant provision of the worker's contract; or*

(b) *the worker has previously signified in writing his agreement or consent to the making of the deduction.*

An employer should not receive any payment from any worker employed by him unless the payment satisfies one of the conditions set out in paragraphs (a) and (b) of section 13(1).

In *Fairfield Ltd. v. Skinner* 1993 the EAT considered an employer's argument that the Act only permits a tribunal to interpret contractual terms to determine whether a deduction is authorised and not investigate the facts of the case to see whether the deduction is justified. The EAT ruled that is perfectly proper for a tribunal to decide that while a deduction is contractually authorised on the evidence before it the deductions were not justified.

The expression wages is given a wide definition under the Act and includes under s.27(1) any fee, bonus, commission, holiday pay or other emolument referable to his or her employment whether payable under his or her contract or otherwise. Wages would also include non contractual bonuses, payment in pursuance of reinstatement or re-engagement orders.[21] and numerous statutory payments in lieu of wages such as guarantee payments, time off payments, sick pay and maternity pay. The Act[22] excludes a number of payments including those made by way of an advance for a loan or wages, expenses, pension allowance and redundancy.

In *Kent Management Services Ltd. v. Butterfield* 1992 the EAT agreed with the tribunal's view that a commission and bonus scheme, which was expressly described as '*discretionary*', '*ex gratia*' and '*non contractual*' constituted wages under the Act. Despite the fact that the Act stated that non contractual bonuses were considered to be wages once they had been paid the EAT nevertheless held that a non contractual commission, once calculated but not paid was still wages under the Act. The commission was a sum payable '*in connection*' with the worker's employment since it was within the reasonable contemplation of both parties that in ordinary circumstances it would be paid.

---

20. Originally contained in the Wages Act 1986
21. See Chapter 11
22. s.27(2)

In *Robertson v. Blackstone Franks Investment Management Ltd.* 1998 the Court of Appeal held that commissions that became payable after termination of a contract were wages under the Act.

In *Edinburgh Council v. Brown* 1999 the EAT held that a re-grading policy between the employer and a Trade Union in a collective agreement had become incorporated into individual contracts of employment. Accordingly the failure to implement the policy in relation to the claimant so that his new wage following a re-grading was backdated to the date of approval constituted an unauthorised deduction from his wages in contravention of s.13.

More recently in *Four Seasons Healthcare v. Maughan* 2005 the claimant, a nurse, was suspended without pay during an investigation of his alleged misconduct of abusing a patient. Subsequently he was charged with a criminal offence and given bail. There followed a successful prosecution leading to a two-year sentence of imprisonment. On a claim for unlawful deductions from his wages during the period of suspension the EAT rejected the employer's argument that the contract of employment had been frustrated by reason of him being charged with a criminal offence or alternatively being given bail pending the trial. The employer's disciplinary process did envisage dismissal in these circumstances and the EAT felt that it was open to the employer to terminate the contract. The contract survived the criminal charge and the granting of bail so that the failure to pay wages during the period of suspension amounted to an unlawful deduction from wages.[23]

Following a number of conflicting decisions it now seems that payments made in lieu of notice following a summary dismissal are not 'wages' under the Act.

In *Delany v. R J Staples* 1990 the Court of Appeal upheld both the EAT and the tribunal in deciding that a claim for payment in lieu of notice was in effect a claim for damages for wrongful dismissal and so did not come under the Wages Act. The House of Lords attempted to clarify the position by identifying the various payments that could be made on contractual termination most of which fell outside the Act. There is no payment of wages if:

- The contract of employment expressly provide for summary termination with payment in lieu of notice.
- There is a mutual agreement on summary termination for a payment in lieu.
- There is a summary dismissal and payment in lieu is tendered in respect of proper notice.

Their lordships did decide however that the Act does apply if the employer gives proper notice but tells the employee that he need not work and gives wages attributable to the notice period in a lump sum.[24] Here there is no breach of contract by the employer and the employment continues until the notice expires, the lump sum being an advance of wages.

It is now possible of course to use the contractual jurisdiction of the employment tribunal to pursue a claim for wrongful dismissal and claims for payment in lieu as well as retaining the right to sue in the ordinary courts.

---

23. See Chapter 10
24. Garden leave

Lawful deductions

A deduction for the purposes of the Act covers any shortfall in payment of the amount properly payable leaving aside errors of computation. This includes any deductions which an employer alleges that he is entitled to make, but also disputes about whether wages are due or the amount payable.

The Act excludes a number of deductions or payments from its provision and under section 14(1) the unlawful act under section 13 does not apply to a deduction from a worker's wages made by his employer, where the purpose of the deduction or payment is the reimbursement of the employer in respect of any overpayment of wages or expenses or deductions for specified purposes such as disciplinary proceedings, industrial action or court orders.

> In *Home Office v. Ayres* 1992 The EAT suggested that the s.14(1) exception had to be read as if the word lawful was inserted in the provision so that if it is claimed by an employer an employee is entitled to raise a number of defences. The employee could argue that there was *'no overpayment, incorrect amount of deduction; the purpose of the deduction was not to reimburse; or some defence under the general law to the claim to deduct'.*

It now seems however that this is not the approach to be adopted when s.14 is raised. The determination of the question in any given case as to whether a deduction falls within s.14 and is lawful does not fall within a tribunal's statutory jurisdiction. Rather it is a common law contractual matter subject to proceedings in the ordinary courts.

> In *Sip (Industrial Products) Ltd. v. Swinn* 1994 the complainant was dismissed for dishonesty relating to a fraudulent claim for expenses. The employer then deducted a sum of money due to him in respect of wages and holiday pay against the money he had dishonestly obtained. A complaint was presented that this deduction was in breach of the Wages Act[25] to which the employer argued that the deduction constituted a reimbursement. The tribunal held that the deduction was not a reimbursement therefore was not a lawful deduction. On appeal the EAT said that it was not part of the tribunal's jurisdiction to decide the lawfulness of the deduction. *'An industrial tribunal has no jurisdiction to enquire into or determine the issue of the lawfulness of a deduction of a kind falling within one of the categories of the section'. The section disapplies the provision off the Act where there is any deduction lawful or unlawful falling within one of the specified categories. Where a deduction is made in these circumstances the appropriate procedure is to institute proceedings in the civil courts for alleged breach of contract and recovery of the sum deducted.'*

If a deduction is made the tribunal must ask whether the sum was properly payable or not.

> In *Grey May (CF&C) v. Dring* 1990 the employer refused to pay accrued holiday pay on dismissal relying on an express term in the employee's contract that it was not payable if the dismissal was for gross misconduct. The pay was held to be properly payable as the EAT did not believe that the facts constituted gross misconduct.

---

25. Now s.13

The Court of Appeal's decision in *Delany v. Staples* 1990[26] confirms that if wages are properly payable and not paid, then non payment is to be regarded as a deduction and the industrial tribunal has jurisdiction to determine the issue *'a dispute on whatever ground, as to the amount of wages properly payable cannot have the effect of taking the case outside the Act. It is for the industrial tribunal to determine that dispute, as a necessary preliminary to discovery whether there has been an unauthorised deduction. Having determined any dispute about the amount of wages properly payable, the industrial tribunal will then move on to consider and determine whether, and to what extent, the shortfall in payment of that amount was authorised by the Statute or was otherwise outside the statutory provision'.*

There is a deduction of wages under the Act if an employer unilaterally revises or reduces any element of a worker's wage whether temporarily or permanently.

In *Bruce and Others v. Wiggins Teape (Stationery) Ltd.* 1994 the employer unilaterally withdrew enhanced contractually agreed overtime rates and the employees continued to work overtime in protest. The EAT said that the issues in this type of case were identifying the wages, deciding whether a deduction had been made and determining whether the deduction was unlawful. The EAT confirmed that *'no valid distinction is to be drawn for the purposes of the Wages Act between a deduction from wages on the one hand, and a reduction of wages on the other. Overtime payments are wages so the question is whether for whatever reason, apart from an error of computation, the worker is paid less than the amount of wages properly payable to him. In the present case, the amount of wages properly payable to the employees included the enhanced overtime rate'.* There had been no express or implied acceptance of the reduced overtime rates and as the employer had no contractual right to reduce wages the Act was applicable. In *Rigby v. Ferodo* 1987 the court confirmed that a worker could continue to work under protest without impliedly accepting a reduction in wages. Here the deductions were unauthorised and unlawful.

In *Beveridge v. KLM UK Ltd.* 2000 the applicant having completed a period of sick leave informed her employers that she wished to return to work with a supporting medical certificate. She was refused the right to return until passed fit by the employer's doctor six weeks later. Having exhausted her statutory sick pay the applicant claimed that this failure to pay her during the six week period was an unlawful wage deduction. The EAT disagreed with the tribunal and found there to be an unauthorised wage deduction. *'An employee who offers her services to her employer is entitled at common law to be paid unless a specific condition of the contract regulates otherwise.'*

Error of computation

In *Yemm v. British Steel* 1994 four shift workers made a complaint under the Wages Act[27] claiming they had not been paid the correct shift allowance for a three month period and this constituted an unlawful deduction. The employers maintained that the correct shift allowance had been paid reflecting a change in shift patterns. The tribunal held that the under payment was due to an error of computation and not

---

26. Previously mentioned
27. Now s.13

therefore deemed to be a deduction from wages. Under the Act it is defined as an *'error of any description on the part of the employer affecting the computation by him of the gross amount of the wages that are properly payable by him to the worker on that occasion'*. The EAT disagreed with the tribunal and found that here there was no error of computation *'An employer who makes a conscious decision not to make a payment because he believes that the contract entitles him to take that course is not making an error of computation ... he may be mistaken about the terms and the effect of the contract but such an error cannot be characterised as an error of computation. If it could then in every case involving a contractual dispute about entitlement to pay it would be open to the employer to take the point and say that the Wages Act had no application to the facts of such a dispute.'*

The decision of the EAT in *Morgan v. West Glamorgan County Council* 1995 provides further guidance in relation to the meaning of the expression 'error of computation' under the Act. The EAT stated that: *'A deduction from wages made in consequence of a deliberate decision, even if that decision is legally erroneous, is not a deduction which is attributable to an "error of computation" within the meaning of the Act. Although the Act refers to an "an error of any description", it does not include an error of law. It must be (a) an "error" on the part of the employer and (b) an error which affects the computation of gross wages. An "error" is a mistake, something incorrectly done through ignorance or inadvertence. "Computation" of wages is a matter of reckoning the amount, of ascertaining the total amount due by a process of counting and calculation. In the present case the reduction in the employee's wages was attributable to a deliberate decision to demote him and reduce his salary. Although that decision was itself the result of an erroneous or mistaken view of the legal and factual position, the reduction in salary and the consequent deduction from the wages paid to the employee were attributable to that decision and not to any error of computation. The short fall was a "deduction" from wages within the meaning of the Act. If there was no right to demote him the employee remained in his original position and the amount of wages which were properly payable by the employers remained the same. Since the employers paid him less than he had previously been paid the amount of the deficiency fell to be treated as a deduction.'*

Lawful deductions are those which are:

- authorised by statute; or
- covered by a contractual term; or
- previously consented to in writing.

Statutory authorisation would cover deductions for income tax, national insurance and attachment of earnings orders. Contractual authorisation means a written contractual term transferred to the worker prior to the deduction. The term must authorise the deduction so that a tribunal could be called on to determine whether it is justified. Certainly an employer cannot rely on a term of the contract which is a contractual variation which took effect before the conduct which led to the deduction.

If management and union negotiations produce oral agreements as to proposed variations of individual contracts of employment, the variations will be effective from the date of the oral agreement rather than the date that a collective agreement is reduced to writing and signed by the parties.

A third way a legitimate deduction can be made is to rely on the previous consent in writing of the worker that the deduction could be made. Once again the consent must be given before the conduct which gives rise to the deduction occurs.

In *Discount Tobacco and Confectionery v. Williamson* 1993 on the consent authorising the deduction was given after the considerable stock shortages had been discovered so the EAT held that the authorisation did not make the deductions lawful.

In *Pename Ltd. v. Paterson* 1989 a deduction of one week's pay from a worker who had left without giving notice was held to contravene the Act. This was despite the fact that the employee had orally agreed to such a deduction in these circumstances and had that confirmed in a letter. Such deductions are unlawful unless the employer positively signifies his consent in writing.

National Minimum Wage

One of the commitments of the labour government was to extend the floor of workers rights and introduce minimum wage legislation in line with other member states. This was done by virtue of the National Minimum Wage Act 1998. As with wage deduction rights, the minimum wage legislation applies not just to employees but to workers generally, so that an employer will not avoid its impact by simply designating staff as contractors or casuals.

The Act adopts a wide definition of worker as *an individual who has entered into, works under or who has worked under a contract of employment or any other contract where the individual undertakes to do or perform work or services for another party whose status is not by virtue of the contract that of a client or customer of any profession or business undertaking carried on by the individual.*

The Act also extends to a homeworker who is defined as 'an individual who contracts with a person, for the purposes of that person's business, for the execution of work to be done in a place not under the control or management of that person'.

We said in Chapter 3 that the aim of the definition is to exclude all but the genuinely self employed operating as businesses from its ambit. A worker is an individual who offers personal service other than through a business and so would include a casual, agency worker, or those employed under zero hours contracts. In *Edmunds v. Lawson* 2000 a pupil barrister claimed that she should be classified as a worker and so entitled to the national minimum wage. While the High Court accepted that her apprenticeship contract brought her within the statute the Court of Appeal disagreed and held that the pupillage contract that she had entered into did not make her a worker for the purposes of securing a minimum wage.

The 1998 Act contains the basic framework of the statutory scheme supported by the National Minimum Wage Regulations 1999 which detail the applicable rate and the method of calculation. The present rate is £5.05p per hour from October 2005[28]. One of the most controversial aspects of the Minimum Wage Regulations is to reduce the standard minimum rate of pay for those aged between 18-21. The present rate is £4.25 per hour.[29] Also there is no requirement stipulating an annual uprating or even a review. Inevitably there is a requirement on the employer to maintain appropriate records which are subject to inspection and it is a criminal offence to fail to do this or indeed fail to pay the minimum wage.

---

28. Increasing to £5.35 from Oct 2006
29. Increasing to £4.45 from Oct 2006

Following the ruling of the European Court of Human Rights in *Nerva v. United Kingdom* 2002 it seems that tips left by customers in the form of additions to cheques or credit cards, and then distributed, are payments made by the employer to the employee and are therefore accountable for the purposes of a statutory minimum wage. This is not the case if tips are left in cash because they are not payable to the employer.

Under s.17 of the Act the right to a minimum wage takes effect as a contractual term so that an individual worker could potentially commence proceedings for its breach. In *Barber v. R.J.B. Mining (UK) Ltd.* 1999[30] the High Court held that the maximum 48 hour working week contained in the Working Time Regulations take effect as a statutory implied term in all contracts of employment.

The National Minimum Wage Regulations provide that where a worker by arrangement sleeps at or near a place of work, '*time during the hours he is permitted to sleep shall only be treated as time work when the worker is awake for the purposes of working*'.

> *Scottbridge Construction* v. *Wright* 2003 deals with the issue as to whether a night watchman, whose main function was to respond to an alarm, was entitled to be paid the national minimum wage for the long hours he worked which included sleeping time. The Court of Session held that the above Regulation applies where an employer specifically arranges a number of hours sleeping time with his employee. The claimant fulfilled the basic requirement of his job if he was present, even when asleep, and as a consequence he was entitled to the minimum wage for all of those hours. The Court of Session agreed with the EAT which had held that it is ' *Wholly inappropriate for the employer when requiring the employee to be present for a specific number of hours, to pay him only for a small proportion of those hours in respect of the amount of time that reflects what he is physically doing on the premises.*'

In *Inland Revenue v. Bebb Travel plc* 2002 the EAT ruled that an enforcement notice under s.19 of the National Minimum Wage Act cannot require an employer to pay minimum wage arrears to former employees who have left the employment in question before the notice was issued. Of course as the failure to pay the minimum is a breach of contract there would be nothing to prevent ex employees bringing their own proceedings for unpaid arrears.

Equal Pay

Equal opportunity legislation relating to the sexes was originally contained in the Sex Discrimination Act 1975 and the Equal Pay Act 1970 and while both Acts have been considerably amended, not least because of the UK's membership of the European Union, they still remain the cornerstones of equal pay law. While the Equal Pay Act is concerned with pay and related matters arising from the contract of employment, as we have seen[31] the sex discrimination legislation covers non financial matters from the contract or any other matter not dealt with in the contract of employment. In cases of doubt a decision as to the relevant legislation must be left to the Employment Tribunal.

---

30. See Chapter 7
31. See Chapter 6

At present there is still widespread inequality in the way men and women are financially rewarded for the work that they do and general agreement that the status of women must be improved. A conservative interpretation of the equal pay legislation in the courts and a tendency to employ women exclusively in low paid jobs so that comparisons are difficult to make, has meant that the law has provided little assistance in redressing the balance. By restricting the Equal Pay Act to cases where *'like work'* or *'work rated as equivalent'* can be shown, many women in low paid jobs were effectively excluded from a remedy. Despite the introduction of the Equal Pay Amendment Regulations 1983 applicants have still found it necessary to turn to European Community law to maintain a successful claim. Certainly the Treaty of Rome and various European Community Directives have had considerable impact in the field of equal pay.

European Community Law

Article 141 of the Treaty of Rome imposes a requirement of equal pay for equal work and by virtue of the European Communities Act 1972. This Article is directly applicable to the UK. As early as 1976 the European Court of Justice in *Defrenne v. Sabena* ruled that Article 141, which lays down the principle of equal pay for equal work, is directly enforceable by every employee and against every employer throughout the Member States. *Macarthys v. Smith* 1981 also confirmed that Article 141 is directly enforceable in domestic courts who in theory should apply the law of the national state first. In *Pickstone v. Freemans plc* 1988 the House of Lords held that a complainant could rely on domestic or European law in attempting to secure a remedy. There is no doubt that a wide interpretation of equal pay rights is achievable by applying Article 141 rather than the Equal Pay Act[32] (see later in the chapter).

Under the Treaty of Rome each member state is required to bring its domestic law into line with Community law. As we saw in Chapter 1 this is achieved mainly by Directives from the European Community outlining the law which member states should then adopt. An example is the Equal Pay Directive which expands the principle of equal pay in Article 141. A failure to incorporate a Directive into domestic law could be pointed out by the European Court of Justice.

> In *Commission for the European Communities v. The United Kingdom* 1982 the Commission successfully argued that UK law had not *adopted 'the necessary measures'* to adopt the Equal Pay Directive. Under existing British law a worker's claim that work is of equal value would have to be dropped if the employer refused to cooperate by not introducing a job classification system. This decision led to an amendment in UK Equal Pay law by the 1983 Equal Pay Amendment Regulations.

This whole process of effecting change on a reluctant member state by means of EC Directives laying down the law and the state being left with the form and method of implementation can be very drawn out. Attempts have been made therefore to enforce European Directives directly in national courts. The European Court of Justice has ruled that a Directive may be relied on by an individual before a national court where the Directive is *'sufficiently precise and unconditional'*. Such actions however are limited to where the respondent is a government authority acting *'as an employer'*. The rationale for

---

32. See later in the chapter

restricting the direct enforcement of European law to government authorities is that it is the member states' responsibility to bring its own domestic law into line and private employers should not be made responsible for that failure. A member state of the European Union may not take advantage of its own failure to comply with Community law.

The principle of equal pay in Article 141 has been invoked by male workers who as fathers have claimed that payments made exclusively to new mothers were consequently discriminatory.

> In *Abdoulaye v. Regie National Des Ursines Renault SA* 1999 the collective agreement for Renault workers provide for full pay for women on maternity leave and a bonus of Ff. 7,500. Male workers complained that it was discriminatory under Article 141 not to offer the same bonus to new fathers. The European Court of Justice emphasised that the principle of equal pay presuppose that male and female workers whom it covers are in comparable situations and that is obviously not the case. It is not contrary to Article 141 to make a lump sum payment to female workers on maternity leave, notwithstanding that they receive full pay during that period, where that payment is designed to offset the occupational disadvantages which arise for those workers as a result of being away from work.

This directive has been held to be unconditional and sufficiently precise to be relied upon by an individual and applied by the national courts against such a body.

> In *Worringham v. Lloyds Bank* 1982 the European Court of Justice ruled that a contribution to a retirement benefits scheme paid by the employer in the name of the employee by addition to his gross salary is pay under Article 141 of the Treaty. This meant that women were to be treated the same as men in relation to the repayment of pension contributions on the termination of employment.

The Equal Pay legislation is not just concerned with pay discrimination but covers discrimination in all aspects of an employees' contract of employment including holiday entitlement and sick leave provision. The definition of '*pay*' under Article 141 is even wider and covers '*the ordinary basic or minimum wage or salary and any other consideration whether in cash or kind, which the worker receives*'.

> In an extremely important decision the European Court of Justice in *Barber v. Guardian Royal Exchange Assurance Group* 1990 held that pensions are pay within the meaning of the directly enforceable provisions of Article 141 of the Treaty of Rome. This means that an occupational pensions scheme that discriminates on the grounds of sex and offends Article 141 may be declared unlawful.

The dramatic impact of the above ruling therefore is that pension benefits cannot discriminate on the grounds of sex, and any condition differing according to sex contravenes Article 141. Pensions must now be equated with pay and if rates are determined by gender criteria they are now unlawful. People must be treated as individuals rather than members of gender groupings so that in determining pay and pensions the fact that statistically women live longer, or take more sick leave than men, should be disregarded in determining levels of sick pay or pension benefits. Also despite the present difference in the State pension age, as a result of this case, pension ages under occupational schemes must be equalised. The court further confirmed that the Treaty takes precedence over Directives so that Social Security Directives which permitted the implementation of equal treatment in occupational pension schemes to be deferred, are consequently overridden by the decision.

Finally the court has decided that the principle of equal pay applies to each element of remuneration and is not satisfied by a comprehensive assessment of overall pay. This means that differences in contractual terms between men and women employed on equal work cannot be offset against each other. Applying the equality clause therefore, each aspect of the contract of employment must be equalised.

In *Lawrence v. Regent Office Care* Ltd. 2002 the European Court of Justice held that Articles 141 is not limited to situations where men and women worked for the same employer. Article 141 applies where the difference in pay can be attributed to a style source. Applying this ruling the tribunal in *Robertson v. Department for Environment, Food & Rural Affairs* 2005 decided that civil servants in one Government Department could compare their pay with those of another. The EAT and the Court of Appeal disagreed however finding that common employment was insufficient without that single source element. Pay policy and bargaining rights varied from department to department and this negated the single source requirement.

Under the new Equal Treatment Directive a claimant will be able to bring an equal pay claim under the Sex Discrimination Act without the need for a comparator. This will be a dramatic development in equal pay law.

Equal Pay Act claims

The main objective of the Equal Pay Act 1970 is to secure equal treatment for men and women in the same employment in relation to terms and conditions of employment. Originally certain terms were excluded from the operation of the Act including those affected by laws relating to the employment of women. In fact such laws are gradually being removed.[33] Terms *'affording special treatment to women in connection with pregnancy or childbirth'* are still outside the province of the Act and so a man has no right to paternity leave (other than unpaid parental leave) in circumstances where a woman is entitled to maternity leave.[34] Also, terms *'related to death or retirement, or to any provision made in connection with death or retirement'* are also excluded. This would not cover terms related to the *'membership of an occupational pension scheme'*.

The mechanism by which the Equal Pay Act attempts to achieve its objectives is the *'equality clause'*. The Equal Pay Act is one of the few employment law statutes that actually implies a term into a contract of employment. Under the Act *if the terms of a contract under which a woman is employed at an establishment in Great Britain do not include (directly or by reference to a collective agreement or otherwise) an equality clause they shall be deemed to include one.*

Under the equality clause a woman has the right to equal pay with a man if either:

- she is employed on *'like work'* with a man in the same employment;
- she is employed doing *'work rated as equivalent'* with a man following a job evaluation study; or
- she is employed to do work of *'equal value'* with a man in the same employment in terms of the demand placed upon her.

---

33. The Sex Discrimination Act 1986
34. See Chapter 7

There are therefore three avenues upon which a claim could be based, 'like work', 'work related or equivalent' or 'equal value'. Equal value was introduced by the Equal Pay Amendment Regulations 1983. A claim based on equal value can only be considered where there is no basis for a claim on 'like work' or 'work rated as equivalent'. The starting point for a claimant under the Equal Pay Act is to identify an individual male 'comparator' with whom she wishes to claim equal pay. This man must be employed on work which is the same or broadly similar to her own.[35]

A finding of inequality in pay structures can have dramatic consequences for an employer. By a majority the Court of Appeal in *Derbyshire v. St. Helens MBC* 2005 held that a letter sent to employees claiming equal pay and pointing out that if they succeeded there would be redundancies, did not constitute unlawful victimisation under the Sex Discrimination Act.[36] Here there was felt to be an honest and reasonable attempt by the employer to compromise proceedings under the Equal Pay Act.

Like work

The problem of using the concept 'like work' as a criterion for achieving fair treatment for women at the workplace, is that in fact large numbers of women workers are often at establishments where there are no male employees upon which to draw comparisons. Accordingly, the definition of 'like work' has been given a 'broad brush approach' interpretation by courts and tribunals.

> Section 1(4) provides that a *'woman is to be regarded as employed in like work with men if, but only if, her work and theirs is of the same or a broadly similar nature and the differences (if any) between the things she does and the things they do are not of practical importance in relation to terms and conditions of employment: and accordingly in comparing her work and theirs regard shall be had to the frequency or otherwise with which any such differences occur in practice as well as to the nature and extent of the differences'.*

Insignificant differences in work and vague or unrealistic responsibilities are to be ignored therefore, in deciding whether individuals are engaged in like work.

> In *Electrolux v. Hutchinson* 1977 female workers engaged in broadly similar work to their male counterparts were held to be entitled to equal pay, despite that the men alone would be required to work overtime, at weekends or at night. The fact that the men were rarely called on to do extra work was a major consideration.

The decision as to whether similar work is being carried on demands not a comparison between the contractual obligations of the parties, but rather a consideration of the things actually done and the frequency with which they are done.

> In *Coomes (Holdings) Ltd. v. Shields* 1978 the female counter clerks in bookmakers shops were paid a lesser rate of pay than their male counterparts. The employers sought to justify the differences on the grounds that the male employees had extra duties, including acting as a deterrent to unruly customers and transporting cash between branches. The Court of Appeal held that, in deciding the question

35. Like work or work rated as equivalent
36. s.4 see Chapter 6

as to *'like work'*, it was necessary to consider the differences between the things the men and women were required to do. Furthermore, it was necessary to consider the frequency with which such differences occur in practice. Finally, the court must consider whether the differences are of any practical importance. This approach should enable the court to place a value on each job in terms of demands placed upon the worker, and if the value of the man's job is higher he should be paid an increased rate for the job. In the present case the differences were not of sufficient importance to justify a different rate of pay.

In *Thomas v. National Coal Board* 1987 the EAT held that for the purposes of determining 'like work' there was no implicit requirement that a selected male comparator should be representative of a group. It was possible therefore to compare the terms and conditions of female canteen assistants with the only male canteen attendant. The EAT also held however that the tribunal was entitled to find that the additional responsibility of the male attendant in working permanently at night alone, and without supervision, was a *'difference of practical importance in relation to terms and conditions of employment'* and so not *'like work'* for the purposes of the Act.

Work rated as equivalent

The second means by which an equality clause will operate is if the employer has carried out a job evaluation study or work rating exercise and the women's work is rated as equivalent to that of a man employed at the same establishment. The study must be carried out in accordance with the Act which provides in s.1(5) that *'a woman is to be regarded as employed on work rated as equivalent with that of any men, if but only if, her job and their job have been given an equal value in terms of the demands made on a worker under various headings (effort, skill, decision making etc.) on a study undertaken with a view to evaluating in those terms the jobs to be done by all or any of the employees in an undertaking or group of undertakings'.*

To maintain an equal pay claim based upon job evaluation therefore it is necessary that a valid study has been carried out adopting one of the principal job evaluation methods laid down by ACAS. The fact that both trade unions generally and a number of employers are wary of job evaluation studies and there is still doubt as to whether an employer is bound to implement a scheme which has been carried out, means that equal pay claims based on work rated as equivalent are relatively rare.

The comparison

For both *'like work'* and *'work rated as equivalent'* it is left to the woman rather than her employer, to choose the male comparator but such a person must be typical and cannot be a hypothetical person. The comparison could even be with the man whom the woman replaced provided there was only a short break between this occurring. Both the applicant and the comparator must be employed which includes employees and contractors providing personal services.

A further requirement is that the comparison must be between the applicant and another in the *'same employment'* which would include the same establishment. Comparison with an individual employed by the same or associated employer at a different establishment is also permissible provided common terms and conditions of employment are observed at both establishments.

> In *Leverton v. Clwyd County Council* 1988 the complainant, a nursery nurse, sought to compare herself with higher paid clerical staff employed at different establishments by the council. To prevent a comparison the employers argued that common terms and conditions of employment were not observed for the relevant employees despite the fact that they were covered by the same collective agreement. In particular the nurses worked a 32.5 hour week and had 70 days annual holiday compared with the comparator's 37 hour week and 20 days basic holiday. Both the tribunal and the EAT felt that these differences were sufficient to defeat the contention that there were common terms of employment observed at the different establishments and so the claim failed. By a majority the Court of Appeal agreed. '*Although common terms and conditions of employment does not mean "identical" terms and conditions, as that would defeat the whole purpose of the legislation, there must be a sufficient element of common identity to enable a proper comparison to be made.*'

The above case gives considerable support to the notion of cross establishment comparison where the applicant and the comparator are covered by the same collective agreement. This is particularly significant in the public sector where national agreements prevail and even in the private sector where employers have multi-site operations and employees with standard terms and conditions of employment.

> In *British Coal Corporation v. Smith* 1996 the House of Lords considered s.1(6) in relation to a claim by female canteen workers and cleaners for equal pay for work of equal value where the comparators were surface mineworkers or clerical workers employed at different establishments. The court found that the cleaners were in the 'same employment' as their male comparators because they were 'common terms and conditions of employment' despite minor differences. It is sufficient, the court stated '*for the applicant to show that her comparators at another establishment and at her establishment were or would be employed on broadly similar terms. Whether any differences between the woman and the man selected as the comparators are justified depends on s.1(3), where the onus is on the employer. It would be far too restrictive a test to exclude the inquiry under s.1(3) unless the terms and conditions of the men at the relevant establishments were common in the sense of identical*'.

Earlier we said that an equal pay claim based on Article 141 may be easier to establish then relying on the Equal Pay Act. Certainly a claim based on the Act relies heavily on the complainant identifying an appropriate male comparator. A claim under Article 141 can have a broader basis however and the European Court in *Handels-og Kontorfunktion-aerenes Forbund i Danmark v. Dansk Arbejdsgiverforening (acting for Danfoss)* 1989 said that the complainant must establish a prima facie case of discrimination and usually reliable statistical evidence of average pay differences will suffice. It is then left to the employer to explain the differences on non discriminatory grounds. It is the industrial tribunal which must determine the validity and reliability of the statistical evidence and whether a good explanation is put forward by the employer. The onus under Article 141 falls on the employer to provide employees with as much information as possible about their pay systems showing how pay increments are obtained and how job evaluation and performance related pay schemes operate. In *Diocese of Hallam Trustee v. Connaughton* 1996 the EAT held that under Article 141 it was possible for a woman to compare her pay with her male successor.

Equal value

In cases where the provisions of *'like work'* and *'work rated as equivalent'* do not apply, a further option is to rely on an equality clause based on work of equal value added by the Equal Pay (Amendment) Regulations 1983. The equal value route is crucial in achieving the goal of equal pay for there are numerous areas of work even of a professional nature, which tend to be female dominated with relatively low rates of pay. Under the Regulations a woman is employed on work, which is, in terms of the demands made on her (for instance under such headings as effort, skill and decision making), of equal value to that of a man in the same employment. In such circumstances the equality clause has the effect of modifying less favourable terms in the woman's contract to bring them in line with the man's contract and inserting any beneficial terms in a man's contract into the woman's contract of employment. If a complaint is presented, the tribunal has no jurisdiction to hear the case unless it is satisfied either that there are no reasonable grounds for determining that the work is of equal value or it has required a member of the panel of independent experts to prepare a report with respect to that question and has received that report. The panel is designated by the Advisory, Conciliation and Arbitration Service (ACAS) but must not comprise officers or members of that body.

In an unexpected decision the Court of Session in *South Ayrshire Council v. Morton* 2002 ruled that not only does an equal pay claim not have to be confined to the claimants own employer it does not even have to be limited to a comparison with someone in the same service as set out in *Defrenne No 2*. In the case before it the court held that a female head teacher employed by a local Education Authority in Scotland could compare herself with a male head teacher employed by a different Scottish Education Authority. The reasoning behind the decision was that Article 141 applies where the parties pay is covered by a national collective agreement. In a disappointing decision however the European Court of Justice ruled in *Lawrence v. Regent Office Care Ltd.* 2002 that it was possible for female catering staff who were contracted out to private contractors to compare themselves with male employees who remained with the local authority as they were still in the *'same service.'* Disappointingly however, the court ruled that Article 141 does not apply *'where the differences identified in the pay conditions of workers performing equal work of equal value cannot be attributed to a single source'.* In such circumstances the court held that work and pay of the workers cannot be compared. Surely however it is the contractor who is responsible for the inequality, as he reduced the wage, and so the contractor is the proper person to restore the equal treatment.

There would be no reasonable grounds for determining that the work is of equal value if different values have been given to the work and that of the male comparator following a study and there is no evidence that the evaluation was made on a system which discriminated on the grounds of sex.

> In *Bromley v. H J Quick Ltd.* 1987 the employer had commissioned an independent job evaluation study under which grading boundaries were decided. Despite a different ranking under the study, a number of female clerical workers brought an equal value complaint comparing their work to male managers. The tribunal decided that because of the job evaluation study there were no reasonable grounds for determining that the work was of equal value. On appeal on behalf of the women it was argued that the job evaluation did not fall within the requirement of the Regulations because the study in question was non analytical and the Regulation demanded an analysis of the characteristics of each job. It

was also argued that if there was any ground for alleging discrimination which cannot be dismissed, the tribunal must refer the case to an independent expert. Both arguments were rejected by the EAT. Stressing that it was necessary for a tribunal to examine carefully the job evaluation scheme upon which the employer relies, the EAT felt that the study in question, although having blemishes, was valid. *'Although systems which are not analytical and which are based on a "felt fair" hierarchy or a paired comparison on a 'whole job' basis are much more vulnerable to sex discrimination, the proposition that any job evaluation study which is not analytical is thereby invalid , could not be accepted.'*

In *Springboard Sunderland Trust v. Robson* 1992 the EAT held that where a job evaluation scheme has been used as a basis for a grading structure then jobs which fall within the same grade should attract the same pay. This is despite the fact there may be wide variations within the grade and yet minimal differences at the boundaries of the grades.

An important equal value claim considered by the House of Lords was the decision in *Hayward v. Cammell Laird Shipbuilders Ltd.* 1988. Here a female canteen assistant, employed at a shipyard, claimed that she was doing work of equal value to male comparators, who were shipyard workers paid at the higher rate for skilled tradesmen in the yard. An independent evaluation convinced the tribunal that the women's work was of equal value. However when comparing all her terms and conditions of employment with the male comparator which revealed a free canteen lunches and two additional days holiday, the tribunal found that she was not entitled to a higher rate of pay. The approach was upheld by the EAT and the Court of Appeal but on final appeal to the House of Lords, the decision was reversed. The Lords suggested that individual contractual terms should be compared with similar provisions in the comparator's contract and a decision reached as to their respective merits. One such term related to pay, and a comparison could be drawn between the complainant's basic pay and the male comparator's. Despite the fact that when looked at as a whole, the complainant's contract was no less favourable.

The above ruling suggests therefore that if a woman can point to a term of her contract which is less favourable than a term of a similar one in the man's contract she is entitled to have that term made not less favourable irrespective of whether she is less favourably treated as a whole.

The Court of Appeal in *Degnan v. Redcar & Cleveland BC* 2005 considered *Hayward v. Cammell Laird* [37] in particular the rule that an applicant cannot only choose her comparator but claim equality on a term by term basis. In the case before the court, certain female employees sought equal pay with agreed comparators who were male gardeners, refuse workers and road workers. Obviously the female workers claimed the highest bonuses and attendance allowances appropriate to the different work groups. The effect would have been to make them higher paid than all the comparators. The court limited the females to a comparison with one comparator on their remuneration package. They could choose the most advantageous, but would not be allowed to cherry pick the most favourable aspects of pay among the various groups.

---

37. Above

The important decision of the European Court of Justice in *Enderby v. Frenchay Health Authority* 1993 has gone some way to remove some of the obstacles facing women seeking equal pay for equal value. The claim was brought by the complainant, a NHS speech therapist, a profession dominated by women, who sought pay comparable with NHS clinical psychologists and principal pharmacists, professions which were male dominated. The EAT struck out the claim finding no direct discrimination and holding that the level of pay was dictated by collective bargaining arrangements. The European Court rejected this view however and proposed a more realistic burden of proof for those attempting to establish equal value claims. The complainant is required to establish a prima facie case and can do this by showing that the work is of equal value, that there is a significant pay differential, and that the lower paid workers are almost exclusively women and the higher paid are men. The burden then shifts to the employer to show that the pay differential is based on objectively justified factors unrelated to sex discrimination.

In *Enderby v. Frenchay Health Authority and Secretary of State for Health* 2000 the Court of Appeal made an important decision on the consequences of making an equal value finding. The issue in dispute was whether an equality clause under s.1(2) should operate so that the relevant term of the woman's contract of employment *'should be treated as so modified as to be no less favourable'* than her male comparator so that her salary should mirror the comparator on the incremental pay scale. The alternative argument was that having decided that the speech therapist should be put on the higher incremental scale, then they should be placed at the incremental point commensurate with their years of service. The Court of Appeal agreed that the claimant should mirror her comparator on the incremental pay scale and therefore enter the scale at the lower point rather than at a more favourable point. The fact that the speech therapist had greater length of service and experience played a significant part in her establishing that she was doing work of equal value to her comparator and was entitled to equal pay.

Defence

At this point it is convenient to consider the main defence to an equal pay claim. An equality clause shall not operate in relation to a variation between the woman's contract if the employer proves that the variation is genuinely due to a material factor which is not the difference of sex. If the claim is based on an equality clause relying on *'like work'* or *'work rated as equivalent'* then there must be a material difference between the woman's case and the man's for the defence to operate. For claims based on equal value however, it is slightly different and the factor may be a material difference.

In *Snoxell and Davies v. Vauxhall Motors* 1977 the EAT held that an employer cannot establish a defence, that the variation between the woman's contract and the man's contract was genuinely due to a material difference between her case and his, when it can be seen that past discrimination has contributed to the variation. Even if the original discrimination occurred before the effective date of the Act *'it cannot have been the intention of the legislation to permit the perpetuation of the effect of the earlier discrimination'*.

Genuine material differences would include a consideration of factors such as the place of employment or academic qualifications of the individual involved.

> In *Rainey v. Greater Glasgow Health Board* 1987 the House of Lords held that the word 'material' means 'significant and relevant' and the difference had to be between the woman's case and the man's. The decision involves a consideration of all the relevant circumstances and they might go beyond personal qualifications, skill, experience or training. It could be that the difference was reasonably necessary to achieve some result such as economic necessity or administrative efficiency and was not directly related to the personal characteristics of the individual involved.

> In *R v. Secretary of State for Social Services and Others ex parte Clarke and Others* 1988 speech therapists sought to compare their work to that of clinical psychologists and pharmacists. The response of their employer, the Health Authority was to point to the National Health Service (Remuneration and Conditions of Service) Regulations 1974 which provide that officers' remuneration which has been negotiated and approved by the appropriate body is the sum payable and the employer was bound to pay the salary in accordance with the Regulations. Even if their work was of equal value, the pay variation was *'genuinely due to a material factor which is not the difference of sex',* the material factor being the requirement that the employers comply with the Regulations. On a judicial review of the tribunal's decision, the Divisional Court of the Queen's Bench Division held that the mere fact that the applicants' pay had been approved under Regulation did not provide a defence to an equal pay claim. Whether an employer had satisfied the defence required evidence and the simple assertion that the employers were bound by law to pay the salaries was not enough.

A complaint in relation to equal pay may be presented to a tribunal by an individual, an employer and in certain circumstances, by the Secretary of State for Employment. If the tribunal finds that a claim has been established, it can make a declaration to that effect and award up to two years' back pay to the successful applicant. The burden of proof rests with the complainant and it is for the employer to establish a defence.

The two year limit on arrears of remuneration under the Equal Pay Act was held by the EAT in *Levez v. T H Jennings (Harlow Pools) Ltd.* (No 2) 1999 to be in breach of Article 141 and therefore unenforceable. Individuals who are successful in equal pay claims may therefore be able to claim up to six years back pay in accordance with the general limitation period.

Sickness

While there is no legal requirement to continue to pay wages to an employee who is absent from work due to illness, it is often the case that an express term of the contract of employment will make provision. The contract could provide that full wages are payable to the employee during a specified period of sickness and then a proportion of the pay in cases of long absence, depending on length of service. In the absence of an express term, the courts are reluctant to imply a right to sick pay.

In *Mears v. Safecar Security* 1983 the plaintiff who had been employed as a security guard for fourteen months, had been absent from work for half that period and received no sickness benefit. On a complaint brought to require the provision of a statutory statement of the main terms and conditions of employment including reference to the right to sick pay, the Court of Appeal held that a term requiring the payment of sick pay should only be implied into a contract of employment after considering all the facts and circumstances. Here no such term would be implied into the contract.

Under the Social Security Contributions and Benefits Act 1992 an employee is entitled to be paid statutory sick pay (SSP) by the employer during periods of absence from work due to illness. Employers are obliged to administer the scheme in relation to qualified employees and there is no provision for contracting out. Also, significantly, the Statutory Sick Pay Act 1994 abolished the employers' right to reimbursement of 80% of sums paid out by way of SSP. There is relief however for small employers to which the reimbursement rules still apply. Small employers get 100% reimbursement of SSP payments made from their NIC payments but only in respect of sick absences of four weeks or more.

The maximum entitlement under the scheme is to twenty eight weeks SSP in any three year period. To qualify for a payment the claimant must be an employee, which would include an office holder or even someone in part-time employment, and both man and women are eligible up to the age of 65. The claimant must satisfy three conditions:

(1) *There must be a period of incapacity for work (PIW) and that is a period of four or more consecutive days of incapacity which may include Sundays and holidays.*

(2) *The period of incapacity must fall within a period of entitlement (PE). A PE commences with the PIW and ends on the occurrence of the first of the following:*
   ▪ *the day the employee returns to work;*
   ▪ *after twenty eight weeks during a three year period;*
   ▪ *the termination of the contract of employment;*
   ▪ *when a pregnant employee reaches the beginning of the eleventh week before the expected week of confinement; or*
   ▪ *the day the employee leaves the European Community or is detained in custody.*

(3) *Statutory Sick Pay is only payable in respect of qualifying days in any PIW. They are normally agreed with the employer and include all days which are normal working days.*

The first three qualifying days are waiting days for which no SSP is payable. From the fourth qualifying day SSP becomes payable the weekly rate for which is calculated according to the claimant earnings.

If there is any conflict as to entitlement, the matter can be referred to an insurance officer (civil servant) who will give a written decision, with possible appeal to a local Appeal Tribunal, and from there to a Social Security Commissioner. When we consider the termination of employment and unfair dismissal, we shall see that long term sickness could amount to a fair reason for dismissal[38] or result in a contract of employment being brought to an end by the operation of the doctrine of frustration.[39]

---

38. See Chapter 11
39. See Chapter 10

Rights in Relation to Trade Union Membership and Activities

A number of rights are conferred on employees by the Trade Union and Labour Relations (Consolidation) Act 1992 in relation to the membership of independent trade unions and taking part in their activities.

- The right not to refused employment on grounds relating to trade union membership under s.137 TULR(C)A 1992 is illustrated in Chapter 6.

- The right not to be dismissed on grounds relating to trade union membership or activities under s.152 TULR(C)A 1992 is considered in Chapter 11.

Here it is proposed to examine the right not to have action short of dismissal taken against an employee on grounds related to union membership or activities.

Action short of dismissal

Under TULR(C)A 1992 s.146(1) An employee has the right not to have action (short of dismissal) taken against an individual by his employer for the purpose of:

(a) preventing or deterring him from being or seeking to become a member of an independent trade union or penalising him for doing so; or

(b) preventing or deterring him from taking part in the activities of an independent trade union at any appropriate time, or penalising him from doing so; or

(c) compelling him to be or become a member of a trade union.

The section requires the proof of an intention by the defendant to deter the complainant from trade union membership or activities. The words *'for the purpose of'* suggest that the employer has an object which he desires to be achieved.

> In *Gallacher v. Department of Transport* 1994 the Court of Appeal held that there had been no breach of the section when the employer indicated that to gain promotion to a senior post it was necessary for the applicant to demonstrate management skills and this would involve a return to a line job. The fact that the effect of such a requirement would prevent the applicant continuing his full-time union duties did not put the employer in breach of the section. *'The word "for the purpose of" in the section connote an object which the employer desires or seeks to achieve. The purpose of an action must not be confused with its effect.'*

There is no requirement for an employee to qualify by means of a period of continuous employment to take action under s.146. An individual who believes that the section has been contravened may present a complaint to a tribunal within three months of the act complained of and if the complaint is well-founded the tribunal will make a declaration to that effect and may award compensation. The type of action envisaged by s.146 would include demotion, suspension or withholding financial benefits from an employee because of his trade union activities. In the few reported cases, the courts have accepted less serious conduct by the employer as infringing s.146.

> In *Brassington v. Cauldon Wholesale* 1977 three members of the TGWU presented a complaint that the conduct of their company chairman constituted action short of dismissal because of trade union membership. During a recognition enquiry, the chairman, had threatened the trade union representatives to the

effect that he would rather close the factory than recognise the union. The EAT upheld the complaint that such a threat was action short of dismissal for the purpose of deterring employees from becoming or remaining members of an independent trade union.

In *Carlson v. The Post Office* 1981 the EAT held that 'penalising' for the purposes of the section cannot be limited to the imposition of a positive punishment or to a financial penalty. Here the refusal of a parking permit because of trade union membership subjected the individual to a disadvantage and that was sufficient to amount to penalising' him for the purposes of the section.

In *British Airways v. Clark* 1982 trade union representatives were disciplined for attending a trade union meeting without permission. The EAT held that this amounted to action short of dismissal. Furthermore, the three month's time limit in presenting the complaint was held to run from the date of the final appeal against the decision to discipline the men rather than the date of the original hearing.

A major source of conflict in relation to the section was whether the right is restricted to preventing action targeted against an employee or an individual or whether it extends to protect an employee who is discriminated against on the basis of his membership of a trade union or of a particular trade union.

The matter was considered by the Court of Appeal in *Ridgeway and Fairbrother v. National Coal Board* 1987. Here employees complained that as members of the National Union of Mineworkers they had directly suffered when they did not receive a pay increase that had been restricted to members of the Union of Democratic Mineworkers. The Court reversing the decision of the EAT held that the NUM employees had been discriminated against directly because of their membership of a particular trade union for they did not receive the pay increase which was a direct loss to them as individuals. Accordingly their right not to have action taken against them as individuals for the purpose of preventing or deterring them from being a member of an independent trade union (the NUM) had been infringed.

In *Farnsworth Ltd. v. McCoid* 1999 the employer exercised the right in a collective agreement to derecognise the claimant as a shop steward because of his conduct. The claimant's allegation of a breach of s.146 was upheld by the Court of Appeal which found that the derecognition was action taken against him as an individual with the meaning of s.146(1).

Under s.148 when an employee complains to an industrial tribunal about an alleged breach of s.146 it is for the employer to show the purpose for which the action was taken against the employee.

In *Palmer v. Associated British Ports* 1993 and *Wilson v. Associated Newspapers Ltd.* 1993 the Court of Appeal held that the employers had infringed s.146 in relation to certain trade union members who had refused to accept personal contracts and give up their rights to union representation in collective bargaining. By withholding pay rises from such members the employer was penalising them for trade union membership and this constituted unlawful action short of dismissal.

In an immediate response to the judgment s.148(3) was inserted into TULR(C)A 1992 by s.13 of the Trade Union Reform and Employment Rights Act 1993.

> *Under s.148(3) In determining what was the purpose for which action was taken by the employer against the complainant in a case where–*
>
> *(a)   there is evidence that the employer's purpose was to further a change in his relationship with all or any class of his employees, and*
>
> *(b)   there is also evidence that his purpose was one falling within s.146.*
>
> *the tribunal shall regard the purpose mentioned in paragraph (a) (and not the purpose mentioned in paragraph (b)) as the purpose for which the employer took the action, unless it considers that the action was such as no reasonable employer would take having regard to the purpose mentioned in paragraph (a).*

The effect of the new s.148(3) is that even if an act may at first seem to amount to a breach of s.146 it is nevertheless open to the employer to show that it had another purpose, for instance to effect a change under s.148(3)(a) and that is the purpose which must prevail.

The amendment therefore severely limits the scope of s.146 as protection for trade union members if an employer is determined to derecognise a union, establish single union bargaining or introduce personal contracts (see Chapter 5).

Time off for trade union officials to carry out trade union duties

The right to paid time off for trade union officials was considerably narrowed by the Employment Act 1989 and is now contained in s.168 of TULR(C)A 1992.

> *Under s.168(1) An employer shall permit an employee of his who is an official of an independent trade union recognised by the employer to take time off during his working hours for the purpose of carrying out any duties of his, as such an official, concerned with*
>
> > *(a)   negotiations with the employer related to or connected with matters falling within section 178(2) (collective bargaining) in relation to which the trade union is recognised by the employer, or*
> >
> > *(b)   the performance on behalf of employees of the employer of functions related to or connected with matters falling within that provision which the employer has agreed may be so performed by the trade union.*
>
> *(2)   He shall also permit such an employee to take time off during his working hours for the purpose of undergoing training in aspects of industrial relations*
>
> *(3)   The amount of time off which an employee is to be permitted to take under this section and the purposes for which, the occasions on which and any conditions subject to which time off may be so taken are those that are reasonable in all the circumstances having regard to any relevant provisions of a Code of Practice issued by ACAS.*

The Code of Practice referred to by the section is ACAS Code of Practice 3: Time Off for Trade Union Duties and Activities.

A trade union official would include anyone appointed to be a representative of members of an independent trade union, for instance, a steward, safety representative or branch secretary. It seemed that the *words 'concerned with industrial relations between employer and employees'* were not to be interpreted too strictly.

> In *Beal v. Beecham Group Ltd.* 1982 the issue was whether attendance by seven union officials of the ASTMS at a National Advisory Committee for the Beecham group, with the object of planning a co-ordinated strategy to ensure minimum allowances and health and safety standards for all employees of the various groups was a duty *'concerned with industrial relations'.* It was held that to restrict the duty to when officials are actually engaged in transacting industrial relations business is too narrow an interpretation. Here the meeting in question was designed to make concrete policy decisions as to how industrial relations should be negotiated in the future and attendance was a duty for which time off should be allowed.

> In *Young v. Carr Fasteners* 1979 when the employer set up a pension scheme for the staff, a steward of the recognised trade union went on a course to the trade union college entitled *'Pensions and Participation'.* In deciding whether she was entitled to paid time off, the EAT held that the question to be asked was whether what the trade union official was seeking to do was to undergo training in some aspect of industrial relations relevant to the carrying out of her duties. Advising and negotiating on pension rights was as much industrial relations as advising on wages and she was entitled to paid time off.

This broad view of industrial relations training and duties taken by industrial tribunals led the government to intervene and considerably narrow the scope of the right in the Employment Act 1989, now included as s.168 TULR(C)A 1992. In s.168(1) above reference is made to s.178(2) which relates to collective bargaining matters for which the trade union is recognised.

As a result of the amendments it seems that there is no right to paid time off for matters in respect of which the union is not recognised by the employer unless the employer has specifically agreed that the union may act on behalf of the employees. The right to time off depends on whether the trade union is recognised and the extent of recognition is crucial in determining the purposes for which time off can be claimed. Nevertheless there is still a view that s.168 should be broadly interpreted.

> In *STC Submarine Systems v. Piper* 1993 the complainant branch secretary of the TGWU asked for paid time off to attend a training course on sex discrimination in pension plans. This request was refused and he claimed that this was in breach of statutory rights to paid time off. The TGWU is independent and recognised for collective bargaining purposes by the employer. Also one of the complainant's roles was to advise company employees on pensions and he was also on the consultative committee of the company's group pension scheme. The issue was whether the training course was relevant to his function as branch secretary concerned with negotiations about terms and conditions of employment. To assist in its deliberation the industrial tribunal referred to the 1991 Code of Practice relating to time off which states that time off could be considered for training particularly where an official has special responsibilities. The EAT agreed with the tribunal that time off should have been given emphasising that the phrase special responsibilities was useful and tended to show that they may well be functions which were part and parcel of the efficient carrying out of an official's position and were incidental to the office, even

though they did not fall within a strict interpretation of the word *'duties'*. The argument that the pension scheme was not negotiable was also rejected by the EAT who decided that information the branch secretary gave to shop stewards about pensions was nevertheless relevant to their negotiations.

In *Ryford Ltd. v. Drinkwater* 1996 the EAT considered the operation of s.168 in relation to the right of a trade union official to take time off for the purpose of trade union duties. To establish a breach of s.168 the EAT prescribed that the official had to establish on the balance of probabilities, that a request for time off was made, that it came to the notice of the employer's appropriate representative, and that they either refused it, ignored it or failed to respond to it. Obviously the employer must be aware of the request before he can 'fail' to 'permit' time off.

Trade union officials are entitled to be paid for time off approved under s.168

> Under s.169(1) *An employer who permits an employee to take time off under section 168 shall pay him for the time taken off pursuant to the permission.*
>
> (2) *Here the employee's remuneration for the work he would ordinarily have been doing during that time does not vary with the amount of work done, he shall be paid as if he had worked at that work for the whole of that time.*
>
> (3) *Here the employee's remuneration for the work he would ordinarily have been doing during that time varies with the amount of work done, he shall be paid an amount calculated by reference to the average hourly earnings for that work.*

If the section is infringed then the claimant is entitled to compensation.

In *Skiggs v. South West Trains* 2005 the tribunal found that the employers were in breach of their duty to allow the claimant time off during working hours to carry out his union duties. The tribunal made a declaration to that effect but refused to make an award of compensation to the claimant under s.172(2) of the Trade Union and Labour Relations (Consolidation) Act 1992 which provides that: 'The amount of the compensation shall be such as the tribunal considers just and equitable in all the circumstances having regard to the employer's default in failing to permit time off to be taken by the employee and to any loss sustained by the employee which is attributable to the matters complained of.' Here the tribunal found that the claimant had suffered no loss of wages and there was no evidence to suggest that he had suffered any injury to his feelings. The EAT disagreed. Where the statute provides that compensation is to be awarded having regard not only to 'any loss sustained by the employee' but also to the employer's default, 'compensation' is wide enough to include the concept of a cash reparation to the individual for the fact that a wrong has been done to him, independently of any special consequential loss he can prove he has also suffered. The wording of s.172(2) contemplates that there may be compensation having regard to the employer's default even in the absence of proof of consequent financial or other loss.

Time off for trade union members to take part in trade union activities

A member of a recognised independent trade union has under s.170(1) the right to be given reasonable time off during working hours to take part in a trade union activity.

Again the relevant Code of Practice is ACAS Code of Practice 3: Time off for Trade Union Duties and Activities (1991).

Following the Employment Protection (Part-Time Employees) Regulations 1995 this right applies to all employees whether or full-time or part-time.

Specifically excluded from the expression *'trade union activity'* is industrial action whether or not in contemplation or furtherance of a trade dispute.

> In *Luce v. Bexley LBC* 1990 the EAT held that for the purposes of this section the lobbying of Parliament in connection with proposed legislation which affected the teaching profession was not a 'trade union activity' which enables a member of the National Union of Teachers to take time off work. While the lobbying of Parliament could amount to a *'trade union activity'* in appropriate circumstances, if it merely has the object of conveying political and ideological objections to proposed legislation, that could not be regarded so. For the purpose of the section the role of the industrial tribunal was: *'first to decide whether on the facts the request fell within the section, and then it had to apply the provisions of reasonableness'.*

Public duties

An employee, whether full-time or part-time, is entitled by virtue of s.50 of the Employment Rights Act 1996 to take time off during working hours to undertake certain public duties such as in the capacity of a Justice of the Peace or a local councillor. Once again the amount of time off must be reasonable bearing in mind the amount of time off needed to perform the public duty and the effect of the absence on the employer's business.

> In *Borders Regional Council v. Maule* 1993 the EAT provided some guidance as to how the section should be interpreted so that *'time off'* is reasonable in the circumstances. The EAT thought that the onus lay with the employee to plan absences and through discussion with the employer scale down the level of commitment to produce a pattern which is reasonable in the circumstances. *'In determining whether an employer was in breach of the section in refusing to permit an employee to take time off for public duties the statute requires the tribunal to consider the whole circumstances including the number and frequency of similar absences which have been permitted by the employer.'*

Time off to look for work or arrange for training

If an employee with two years service is dismissed by reason of redundancy, he is entitled, before his notice period expires, to be allowed to have a reasonable amount of paid time off during working hours to search for new employment or make arrangements for training for future employment. If such time off is unreasonably refused, the employee may within three months present a complaint to an employment tribunal who may declare that fact if they feel the claim is well founded, and award compensation.

Disclosure of Public Interest Matters

The Public Interest Disclosure Act 1998 was brought into force on July 2 1999 its provisions being incorporated into the Employment Rights Act 1996. Its aim is to provide protection for workers who wish to speak out about matters of public concern. Notice that the Act confers protection on a 'worker' which would include a full-time or part-time employee and a contractor providing personal services as well as agency workers. Fear of unjustifiable disciplinary action or victimisation has in the past deterred workers from making known matters of public concern and the aim of this legislation is to provide them with some degree of protection. Health and safety issues should always be raised and addressed without fear of intimidation, particularly where staff are temporary or on short term contracts. There is evidence that disasters such as Piper Alpha, The Herald of Free Enterprise and Clapham Junction would have been prevented if a different culture of raising genuine concerns about health and safety had been in place. More recent concerns about the standard of some of the work carried out in the health service also points to the need to encourage whistle-blowing for the protection of the public.

Under the Act protection is offered to a whistle-blower provided that the disclosure is proportionate and made in good faith on a matter of public concern. Two key considerations are:

- the subject matter of the disclosure;
- to whom the disclosure is made.

Only a disclosure which is the reasonable belief of the worker and relates to one of six specified categories may qualify for protection, called 'qualifying disclosures'. The categories are contained in s.43B:

- actual or apparent breaches of the criminal law;
- a failure to comply with a legal obligation;
- a miscarriage of justice;
- endangering of an individuals health and safety;
- damage to the environment;
- concealment of any of the above.

  Parkins v. Sadexho Ltd. 2002 concerned the interpretation of *'qualifying disclosure'* when it is applied to a failure to comply with a legal obligation. The EAT held that an alleged breach of health and safety obligations could give rise to a breach of contract which would count as a failure to comply with a legal obligation.

The Act differentiates between disclosure to an employer or other responsible person and disclosure to outsiders. In relation to employers a worker who makes a qualifying disclosure is protected under s.43C provided he acted in good faith and reasonably believes that the information tends to show the malpractice or misconduct.

There are numerous regulatory bodies who may have an interest in hearing certain disclosures such as the Health and Safety Executive and the Financial Services Authority. A worker who makes a qualifying disclosure to such a body will be protected if he acts in good faith and reasonably believes that the malpractice falls within the matters for which the body is responsible and reasonably believes that the information disclosed and allegations in it is substantially true. It should be stressed that it is the employer who needs to be in the position to establish that the employee has a clear ulterior motive.

In *Street v. Derbyshire Unemployed Workers Centre* 2004 following her dismissal for gross misconduct the claimant alleged unfair dismissal for making a protected disclosure. The Court of Appeal held that while the disclosures were qualifying, they had not been made in good faith and were motivated by personal antagonism to a superior member of staff. It is the employer who needs to be in the position to establish a clear ulterior motive[40] to successfully raise a defence. The Court of Appeal endorses the EAT ruling that it is not the purpose of the statutory provisions '*to allow grudges to be promoted and disclosures to be made in order to advance personal antagonism*'. It rejects the contention that 'in good faith' merely means 'with honest intention'.

If disclosure is made externally on a wider scale then under s.43G there are significant additional requirements before protection is offered in such cases. The subject of the disclosure must be exceptionally serious or the workers must show that they reasonably believe that they will be victimised for making the disclosure internally or that there will be a cover up. In addition the disclosure must be reasonable in the circumstances. Certainly there will be no protection if disclosure is made for personal gain or for example to the press rather than to the police who could address the issue. A worker has the right under s.47B not to be victimised for making a protected disclosure. In cases involving dismissal an employee has the right to claim unfair dismissal with no qualifying period and no upper limit on potential compensation. If it is established that the applicant has been dismissed as a result of making a protected disclosure then under s.103A the dismissal will be automatically unfair.[41] Termination of employment and the common law and statutory rights that arise are the subject of the remaining chapters of the text.

Further Reading

Lewis, David *Whistle blowing at Work. On what Principles Should Legislation be Based* (2000) 30 ILJ 169.

Simpson, Bob *A milestone in the Legal Regulation of Pay. The National Minimum Wage Act 1998* (1999) 28 ILJ 57.

Simpson, Bob *Implementing the National Minimum Wage* (1999) 29 ILJ 171.

---

40. There could be multiple motives
41. See Chapter 11

Chapter 10

The Termination of Employment

Legal conflict between employer and employee arises most usually when the employment relationship comes to an end. Important statutory rights in relation to security of employment such as the right not to be unfairly dismissed and the right to redundancy payments, all depend upon showing that the employment relationship was terminated by means of a dismissal. For this purpose therefore, it is necessary to explore the various modes of termination of the employment relationship and identify when a dismissal, whether express or implied has occurred. In this chapter we will also consider the common law claim of wrongful dismissal and the issue of post contract terms.

Dismissal and Notice

If either an employer or an employee wishes to terminate a contract of employment they are required to comply with the contractual requirements in relation to notice. Generally the length of the contractual notice period will depend upon the nature of the employment and may increase in relation to the number of years' service. In addition one of the first significant statutory employment rights introduced under the Contracts of Employment Act 1963, provided for statutory minimum periods of notice that apply where the contract is silent, or provides for less favourable periods.[1] Also you will remember from Chapter 4 that the statutory statement of the main terms and conditions of employment supplied under s.1 of the Employment Rights Act 1996 will stipulate the minimum notice period to which the employee is entitled.

> Under s.86 [2] *The notice required to be given by an employer to terminate the contract of employment of a person who has been continuously employed for [one month] or more:*
>
> > (a) *shall be not less than one week's notice if his period of continuous employment is less than two years;*

---

1. S.86 Employment Rights Act 1996
2. Employment Rights Act 1996

    (b)   *shall be not less than one week's notice for each year of continuous employment if his period of continuous employment is two years or more but less than twelve years; and*

  (c)   *shall be not less than twelve weeks' notice if his period of continuous employment is twelve years or more.*

(2)   *The notice required to be given by an employee who has been continuously employed for [one month] or more to terminate his contract of employment shall be not less than one week.*

It is only if the contractual notice period is less than the statutory minimum period that the statutory minimum period will apply. This minimum period is often triggered in the case of employees who have been employed for twelve years or more and are entitled to 12 weeks notice under s.86. Sometimes employers still limit the contractual period to one month no matter what the length of service. Following the Employment Protection (Part-Time Employees) Regulations 1995, the right to a statutory minimum period of notice extends to part-time employees regardless of their hours of work.

One further complication is that if the contract is silent as to the notice period, there is an implied term under the common law that the notice given will be reasonable and such a notice period may, in exceptional cases, exceed the statutory minimum. Certainly the seniority of the employee, the nature of his job, and the length of service could dictate that a relatively long period of notice is required. In *Hill v. Parsons & Company Ltd.* 1972 a senior engineer was held to be entitled to notice of six months under the common law, well in excess of the statutory rights.

> *Masiak v. City Restaurants (UK) Ltd.* 1999 is a case we will consider later in Chapter 11 in relation to automatic unfair dismissal. The applicant chef walked out of his job for safety reasons and claimed both unfair dismissal and damages for wrongful dismissal in breach of contract. The tribunal concluded that his claim for damages for wrongful dismissal must fail because he did not have the requisite period of employment to entitle him to any statutory period of notice. The EAT disagreed and upheld the claim for damages for breach of contract confirming that no period of continuous employment is required for the common law claim of damages for wrongful dismissal. *'At common law every employee is entitled to reasonable notice of termination, that is a term to be implied into each contract of employment in the absence of any express term as to notice.'*

There is nothing to prevent an employee from waiving his right to notice or, in fact, accepting a lump sum payment in lieu of the notice period to which he is entitled. It is usual now for employers to include an express term in the contract of employment authorising the payment of wages in lieu of notice. If the dismissal is by reason of misconduct or capability it does make sense for an employer to terminate the relationship as soon as possible. Failure by the employer to comply with notice requirements would entitle the employee to bring an action for damages in the ordinary courts or now in the employment tribunal based on breach of contract. Such a claim is known as 'wrongful dismissal' referring to the wrongful manner in which the contract of employment has been terminated.

Wrongful Dismissal

The common law claim for wrongful dismissal is based entirely on a breach of contract and is a cause of action which may be brought before an employment tribunal.[3] McLachlin J. in the Supreme Court of Canada in *Wallace v. United Grain Growers Ltd.* 1997 said that: '*The action for wrongful dismissal is based on an implied obligation in the employment contract to give reasonable notice of an intention to terminate the relationship (or pay in lieu thereof) in the absence of just cause for dismissal ... A "wrongful dismissal" action is not concerned with the wrongness or rightness of the dismissal itself. Far from making dismissal a wrong, the law entitles both employer and employee to terminate the employment relationship without cause. A wrong arises only if the employer breaches the contract by failing to give the dismissed employee reasonable notice of termination. The remedy for this breach is an award of damages based on the period of notice which should have been given.*'

Wrongful dismissal therefore is concerned with the process of dismissal and whether an employee is given the contractual or statutory notice, or other rights to which he is entitled.[4]

Summary dismissal occurs when the contract of employment is terminated instantly without notice and it is prima facie wrongful. Such a dismissal is justifiable under the common law, however, if it can be shown that the employee is in repudiatory breach of the contract of employment because of his *gross misconduct*. By summarily dismissing, the employer is accepting the repudiatory breach of the employee and treating the contract as discharged.

Whether the alleged misconduct may be classified as gross is a question of fact and degree, but it would normally include serious misconduct such as disobedience, neglect, dishonesty, or misbehaviour. Certainly early cases must now be viewed with caution. The summary dismissal of a housemaid in *Turner v. Mason* 1854 because she went to visit her sick mother in contravention of her employer's instructions was held not to be wrongful, but would be unlikely to constitute gross misconduct in the present day. There is of course nothing to prevent an employer categorising misconduct in a disciplinary policy and providing realistic examples of gross misconduct.

In *Neary and Neary v. Dean of Westminster* 1999 the issue before Ld Jauncey of Tullichettle[5] was whether an alleged breakdown in trust and confidence[6] amounted to gross misconduct for the purposes of summary dismissal. He stated that '*conduct amounting to gross misconduct justifying summary dismissal must so undermine the trust and confidence which is inherent in the particular contract of employment that the employer should no longer be required to retain the employee in his employment. Whether particular misconduct justifies summary dismissal is a question of fact. The character of the institutional employer, the role played by the employee in that institution and the degree of trust required of the employee vis-à-vis the employer must all be considered in determining the extent of the duty of trust and the seriousness of any breach thereof. It could not be accepted that when financial wrongdoing is alleged, nothing short of deliberate dishonesty or deceit will constitute gross misconduct*'.

A fundamental question that is often asked is whether the employment relationship can survive the nature of the misconduct.

---

3. Since 1998
4. Such as holiday pay
5. Acting as a special commissioner
6. See Chapter 4

In *Pepper v. Webb* 1969 the action of the head gardener in wilfully disobeying a reasonable order was sufficient to amount to gross misconduct and provide grounds for summary dismissal, despite the contract of employment providing for three months' notice. It should be stressed, however, that the reaction of the gardener in this case represented the culmination of a long period of insolence, and the isolated use of choice obscenities by an employee to an employer may not amount to gross misconduct if there is provocation. Also, in *Laws v. London Chronicle* 1959 an employee who disobeyed an express order of her managing director was nevertheless held to be wrongfully dismissed in the circumstances. The employee had acted out of loyalty to her immediate superior when she walked out of an editorial conference despite the express instruction of her managing director to remain. The action of a betting shop manager in *Sinclair v. Neighbour* 1967 in borrowing £15 from the till and leaving a IOU, contrary to express instructions, was regarded as sufficient grounds to justify summary dismissal.

In *Denco Ltd. v. Joinson* 1991 the EAT felt that if an employee uses an unauthorised password in order to enter a computer known to contain information to which he is not entitled that of itself is gross misconduct which could attract summary dismissal. In such cases the EAT thought it desirable that the management should stress that such dishonesty will carry with it severe penalties. The EAT stated that *'Unathorised use of, or tampering with, computers is an extremely serious industrial offence. If an employee uses an Unauthorised password in order to enter or attempt to enter a computer known to contain information to which he is not entitled, that of itself is gross misconduct which prima facie will attract summary dismissal. The employee's motive is immaterial. It is a question of "absolutes" and should be compared with dishonesty. An analogy may be drawn with a situation where an employee enters the management offices of a company where he has no right to be, goes into an office, sees a key on the desk which he knows is the key to a filing cabinet containing information to which he is not entitled and thereafter opens the cabinet and takes out a file. It is desirable, however, that management should make it abundantly clear to the workforce that interfering with computers should be reduced to writing and left near the computers for reference.'*

In *Briscoe v. Lubrizol Ltd.* 2002 the alleged repudiatory conduct was the failure of an employee on long term disability leave to attend meetings and discuss his position following the insurers refusal of his claim for benefit. The majority of the Court of Appeal held that the conduct justified summary dismissal *'In the present case, the claimant's repeated lack of response to and cooperation with the employers' reasonable requests and instructions was well capable of being characterised as gross misconduct and of being properly treated by the employers as a repudiation by the claimant of his contract of employment. The judge was fully entitled to come to the conclusion that the claimant no longer intended to fulfill his part of the contract. The employers were not under a duty to warn the claimant that if he did not make contact with them he might be dismissed. The test for gross misconduct or repudiation is that set out in Neary v. Dean of Westminster the conduct must so undermine the trust and confidence which is inherent in the particular contract of employment that the employer should no longer be required to retain the employee in his employment.'*

In determining whether an employer is entitled to dismiss summarily for gross misconduct it is usually necessary to interpret the employee's contract of employment. In *Dietman v. London Borough of Brent* 1988 following a critical report on the performance of a senior social worker in relation to the death of child her employer instantly dismissed her without notice, payment in lieu of notice, or an opportunity to defend herself in a disciplinary hearing. This was despite the fact that the council's contractual disciplinary procedure was that in the case of more serious offences the employee should be invited to a formal disciplinary meeting and be represented. Her contract also provided that 'any breach of disciplinary rules will render you liable to disciplinary action which will normally include immediate suspension followed by dismissal, or instant dismissal for offences of gross misconduct'. Gross misconduct was defined as misconduct of such a nature that the authority is justified in no longer tolerating the continued presence at the place of work of the employee who commits an offence of gross misconduct. On a claim for wrongful dismissal the High Court held that on a proper construction of these terms the employer was not entitled to dismiss the employee without giving her the right to a disciplinary hearing. On appeal the council argued that the employee's gross negligence constituted gross misconduct under the contract and instant dismissal without suspension or a disciplinary hearing was permissible. This argument was rejected by the Court of Appeal who felt that in relation to gross misconduct the agreed procedure was suspension pending the outcome of a disciplinary hearing and this construction was in accordance with the ACAS Code of Practice. Furthermore the Court of Appeal agreed that gross negligence did not constitute gross misconduct as defined in the contract. Gross negligence lacks the element of intention and is conduct which is neither dishonest or disruptive but rather a serious failure to perform professional duties to the required standard. This case also made a helpful statement as to the legal impact of a wrongful dismissal in relation to the contract of employment. '*A wrongful dismissal does not unilaterally determine the contract of employment. The contract remains in force until the repudiatory breach is accepted by the employee. In the two most comprehensive considerations of authority, the judgments of the Vice-Chancellor in Thomas Marshall (Exports) Ltd. v. Guinle and Buckley LJ in Gunton v. London Borough of Richmond-upon-Thames, the "unilateral view" was rejected and the "acceptance view" preferred. In addition, the long line of cases in which injunctions were granted to prevent an employer terminating a contract of service were incompatible with the "unilateral view". The "acceptance view" was therefore to be regarded as correct, so that in a proper case where there has been a wrongful dismissal, the court can prevent, by injunction, the implementation of that dismissal until, for instance, the proper procedures laid down in the contract have been followed.*'

Horkulak v. Cantor Fitzgerald 2004 provides one of the few examples of a constructive wrongful dismissal.[7] The claimant brought his fixed term contract of employment to an end prematurely when he accepted the employer's repudiatory breach of the implied term of trust and confidence. A significant issue in the case was whether the claimant could recover damages to reflect the substantial bonus he would have earned under the contract. The employers thought not, given that the bonus was discretionary. The Court of appeal disagreed finding that such discretion was subject to the implied term that it would be exercised genuinely and rationally As the claimant had earned his bonus a nil award therefore seemed inappropriate. In assessing the damages to reflect the bonus that should have been paid the court had the unenviable task of putting itself in the shoes of the employer. '*The bonus clause was contained in a contract of employment in a high-earning and competitive*

---

7. See constructive dismissal later in the chapter

activity in which the payment of discretionary bonuses is part of the remuneration structure. The objective purpose of the bonus was plainly to motivate and reward the employee in respect of his endeavours to maximise commission revenue, and the condition precedent that the employee should still be working for the employers demonstrated that the bonus was to be paid in anticipation of some future loyalty. The provision was necessarily to be read, therefore, as having some contractual content, i.e. as a contractual benefit to the employee, as opposed to being a mere declaration of the employers' right to pay a bonus if they so wished, a right which they enjoyed regardless of contract. Although the clause left the amount of the bonus at large, it provided for a process of attempted mutual agreement prior to the making of any final decision. This emphasised the employers' obligation to consider the question of payment of a bonus, and the amount, as a rational and bona fide, as opposed to an irrational and arbitrary, exercise when taking into account such criteria as the employers adopted for the purpose of arriving at their decision. Failure so to construe it would strip the bonus provision of any contractual value or content in respect of the employee whom it was designed to benefit and motivate and would fly in the face of the principles of trust and confidence which have been held to underpin the employment relationship.'

The courts have recognised that a summary dismissal could occur despite the fact that an employee is already under notice of dismissal. In *Stapp v. Shaftesbury Society* 1982 there was held to be a summary dismissal when an employee, already serving a notice of dismissal, was sent a letter by the employer asking him to *'relinquish your duties with effect from today'.*

The remedy for a successful claim of wrongful dismissal is an action for damages amounting to the loss of wages payable during the notice period.

> In *Addis v. Gramophone Company Ltd.* 1909 the House of Lords ruled that when a servant is wrongfully dismissed from his employment, the damages for the dismissal cannot include compensation for the manner of the dismissal, for his injured feelings, or for the loss he may sustain from the fact that the dismissal in itself makes it more difficult for him to obtain fresh employment.

It seems therefore that if an employer pays the employee an appropriate lump sum on summary dismissal, which represents a full payment of pay in lieu of notice, there would be little point in bringing a claim for breach of contract as no further damages would be payable. In *Cox v. Philips Industries* 1975 there was some retreat from this somewhat harsh position. Here the plaintiff was dismissed and given five months' salary in lieu of notice. He nevertheless sued for further damages for breach of contract. Prior to his dismissal the plaintiff had been demoted to a position of less responsibility and relegated to duties which were vague and inadequately expressed and this constituted a breach of his contract of employment. The High Court held that *'it was in the contemplation of the parties that such a breach of contract would expose the plaintiff to the degree of vexation which he did in fact suffer frustration and sickness). Although it was argued by the defendants that damages for such a breach should only be awarded in funeral, wedding and holiday cases, there was no reason in principle why they should not apply to a case like the present one. Thus the plaintiff would be awarded £500'.*

> In *Bliss v. South East Thames Regional Health Authority* 1985 the Court of Appeal re-emphasised the ruling of the House of Lords in *Addis v. Gramophone Company Ltd.* 1909 and reversed the decision of the High Court in the case before it to award damages to a consultant orthopaedic surgeon who had suffered frustration, vexation, and distress from the repudiatory breach of contract by his employer.

> *'The general rule laid down by the House of Lords in Addis v. Gramophone Company Ltd. is that where damages fall to be assessed for breach of contract rather than tort, it is not permissible to award general damages for frustration, mental distress, injured feelings or annoyance caused by the breach. Unless and until the House of Lords has reconsidered its decision in Addis, the view taken in Cox that damages for distress, vexation and frustration could be recovered for breach of a contract of employment if it could be said to have been in the contemplation of the parties that the breach would cause distress was wrong.'*

You will remember that in the important House of Lords decision in *Malik v. BCCI* 1997[8] the court confirmed that damages could be awarded for breach of trust and confidence caused by the stigma attached to working for an employer who had been guilty of serious misconduct.

> In *Johnson v. Unisys Ltd.* 2001 the applicant having succeeded in an unfair dismissal claim made a further claim for substantial damages for wrongful dismissal alleging that because of the manner of dismissal he had suffered a mental breakdown and was unable to work. The Court of Appeal felt that the claimant was not entitled to damages in these circumstances. The court reaffirmed that where there is an express dismissal Addis remains authority for the principle that damages for wrongful dismissal cannot include compensation for the manner of the dismissal, for the employee's injured feelings or for the loss he may sustain from the fact that the dismissal itself makes it too difficult to obtain new employment. The court stressed that the House of Lords decision in *Malik v. BCCI* 1997 did not overrule Addis and dealt with the breach of the implied term of trust and confidence rather than the manner of dismissal. A further appeal to the House of Lords was also dismissed. Their lordships felt that it would be improper for the courts to develop a common law remedy relating to the manner of dismissal when the legislature has already created a statutory remedy in relation to unfair dismissal. Under the statutory scheme the compensatory award gives the employment tribunal a broad jurisdiction to award what they consider is just and equitable but subject to a statutory limit. *'In an appropriate case it is open to an employment tribunal to award compensation for distress, humiliation, damage to reputation in the community or to family life ... and also open to a tribunal to compensate an employee for financial loss following from psychiatric injury which is said to be a consequence of the manner of dismissal.'* Given the statutory remedy the House of Lords felt that it was *'inappropriate to imply the implied terms of trust and confidence to a dismissal. The implied term of trust and confidence is concerned with preserving the continuing relationship between employer and employee ... and does not apply to the way the relationship is terminated'.*

The judgment of the House of Lords significantly closes the door on the possibility of an employee receiving damages at common law for the manner of dismissal when this has caused harm to health or employment prospects. The House of Lords felt that the statutory regime of unfair dismissal with maximum compensation levels expressed Parliament's intention and should be given priority.[9]

A contract of employment could make provision for a minimum period of notice on termination, and also provide that the employer *'may make a payment in lieu of notice'.*

---

8. See Chapter 4
9. See Chapter 11

In *Cerberus Software Ltd. v. Rowley* 2001 the applicant was employed by a company which had inserted such a provision in his contract of employment that the contract was determinable by six months notice and that *'the employer may make a payment in lieu of notice to the employee.'* When he was dismissed summarily without any notice payment on an allegation of serious misconduct, the applicant brought a claim for damages for wrongful dismissal. The claim succeeded but a major issue of contention was the employer's assertion that the applicant was under a duty to mitigate his loss and to reduce the damages. As the applicant had found alternative employment during the notice period then under the normal rules for the calculation of damages credit should be given for his actual earnings. Both the tribunal and the EAT disagreed however deciding that the duty to mitigate does not apply as the claim here was for a sum due under the contract not subject to deduction. By a majority the Court of Appeal disagreed and found for the employer The court held that the contractual provision merely gave the employer a discretion as to whether to make a payment in lieu and that is inconsistent with the employee having a contractual right to be paid. In breaking the notice requirement by dismissing summarily the employers were in breach of contract and the employee was entitled to damages for wrongful dismissal *'the measure of damages earned had the employment continued according to contract subject to the ordinary rule that the employee must minimise his loss by using due diligence to find other employment'*. In a dissenting judgment Sedley LJ adopted the finding that by not allowing the employee to work his notice and summarily dismissing him without cause the employer elected to pay the salary in lieu under the termination clause and so has created a debt which was not covered by the mitigation rule.

In *Cerberus* as the summary dismissal was with insufficient cause the dismissal was unlawful. Nevertheless employers should always consider including an express provision in the contract of employment permitting the payment of wages in the event of summary dismissal. Such a provision ensures a lawful dismissal with an early effective date of termination and retaining the validity of any restraint clause.[10]

If the contract included a provision which imposed a clear duty on the employer to make a payment in lieu of notice then the duty to mitigate would not arise.

The contract could also make provision for its summary termination on the occurrence of a particular event. In *T. & K. Home Improvements Ltd. v. Skilton* 2000 a double glazing sales director had a term in his contract which provided that if he failed to make sales targets *'you may be dismissed with immediate effect'*. The employer sought to trigger the clause with no notice or wages in lieu and the employee claimed breach of contract. The Court of Appeal held that the claimant was entitled to three months pay in lieu of notice when he was dismissed in such circumstances. The power to dismiss with immediate effect did not override the employee's contractual right to notice. It did have the effect of terminating the employee's right to work but did not destroy all other contractual rights.

There is an increasing practice for senior post holders in organisations to negotiate long periods of notice to terminate their contracts of employment. Inevitably a substantial sum

---

10. See later in the chapter

would become payable if an employer wishes to terminate such a contract without giving the notice to which the employee is entitled under the contract.

> In *Clark v. BET Plc* 1997 following a takeover the chief executive of BET was dismissed without the three years notice to which he was entitled under his contract. Liability for wrongful dismissal was not denied by the employer but the parties litigated in the High Court over the level of damages. The plaintiff's contract of employment provided that his considerable salary should be reviewed annually and increased at the boards discretion. In addition the contract stated that 'The executive will participate in a bonus arrangement providing a maximum of 60% basic salary in any year'. For the previous five years the plaintiff was given a 10% salary increase and the maximum bonus. The High Court held that the damages for wrongful dismissal should reflect a 10% salary increase over the three year notice period, for the plaintiff had a contractual right to an annual upward adjustment in salary. A 50% bonus of salary for each of the three years was also payable as a realistic assumption of the plaintiff's position had he stayed with the company, The figure of £2.85 million paid in damages demonstrates the need for careful drafting in the contracts of high earners.

It is obvious in some cases that the employer has dismissed without notice to prevent the employee acquiring sufficient continuous employment for the purposes of qualifying for an unfair dismissal complaint. In *Stapp v. Shaftesbury Society* 1982 the court held that if there is no adequate reason which would justify summary dismissal, and if by the summary dismissal the employee as a consequence is deprived of his right to bring a claim for unfair dismissal by shortening the relevant period of continuous employment, the employee could have a remedy at common law for unfair dismissal. The measure of damages payable *'might include the loss of the right to complain of unfair dismissal which the employee would have had, had he not been summarily dismissed'.*

> *Raspin v. United News Shops* 1999 is the first case where the EAT has confirmed that an award of damages can be made against an employer to reflect the fact that a wrongful dismissal prevented an employee from acquiring the necessary service to qualify to make a complaint of unfair dismissal. The damages should equate with the loss which could be the opportunity to succeed in an unfair dismissal claim against the employer.

The reasoning in *Raspin*[11] was followed by the Court of Appeal in *Silvey v. Pendragon* 2001 involving a similar breach of contract claim. Here a longstanding employee had been summarily dismissed with 12 weeks wages paid in lieu of notice. The complaint related to the fact that had the employee been required to work his notice that would have taken him past his 55th birthday and substantially increased his pension rights. The court held that while employment ceases on the payment of wages in lieu, that does not have any bearing on the basis for awarding damages, which included what the employee would have qualified for had he served his notice period.

In *Harper v. Virgin Net* 2004 an employee who was wrongfully dismissed, one month before reaching the one year qualifying period for an unfair dismissal complaint was held to have no claim in damages for the loss of the statutory right to claim unfair dismissal. Here there was a breach of a contractual notice period but it does seem that under *Raspin*

---

11. Above

v. United News Shops Ltd. 1999 a claim based upon a breach of contractual disciplinary procedures could support a claim for such damages.

> In *The Wise Group v. Mitchell* 2005 a programme manager for a registered charity was dismissed with one month's wages in lieu of notice. Her contract started on the 10 June 2002 and was terminated on the 1 May 2003. The contractual notice period had been adhered to but under the contract there was no provision to pay wages in lieu of notice. The dismissal was therefore in breach of contract but the employer argued that the employee had suffered no loss as a consequence of the wrongful dismissal. As the reason for dismissal, essentially obstructive behaviour and inability to adjust to changes, would be categorised as misconduct, the employee was contractually entitled to participate in the employer disciplinary procedure which involved a full investigation and a hearing. The EAT held that the claimant was entitled to damages for the period that her employment would have lasted had the employer implemented the disciplinary process as he should have. In addition she was entitled to damages for breach of contract based on the positive outcome of statutory unfair dismissal proceedings had the decision of the disciplinary process led to her dismissal. The EAT stressed that these loss of opportunity damages were not based upon common law unfair dismissal but rather the common law claim of wrongful dismissal.

The implication is that there is a distinction between the breach of a contractual notice period and the failure to comply with contractual disciplinary procedures. In a premature breach of notice dismissal the employment relationship is terminated but where there is failure to comply with a disciplinary process the relationship continues for the purpose of qualifying for statutory rights.

It has been argued that in the case of a dismissal in breach of contract, where the employer ignores disciplinary and appeals procedures the employee in question should be able to rely on the implied contractual rights not to be unfairly dismissed. Damages equivalent to the compensatory award for unfair dismissal were awarded in such circumstances by the tribunal in *Fosca Services (UK) Ltd. v. Birkett* 1996. The tribunal held that while the employee could not claim unfair dismissal because he did not have sufficient service *'the effect of the terms of the contract of employment in this case is to give Mr. Birkett the right not to be unfairly dismissed as a right under his contract'*. On appeal the EAT strongly reversed the decision and made it clear *'It was not open to the chairman to imply a term of the contract that the respondent would enjoy the equivalent of the statutory right not to be unfairly dismissed. None of the recognised tests for implying such a term are made out. The fallacy, in our judgment, in the chairman's reasoning is to disregard the normal common law rules as to loss in cases of wrongful dismissal. That loss is limited to the sums payable to the employee had the employment been lawfully terminated under the contract. Once a dismissal has taken place, as was accepted and found in this case, it is irrelevant to consider what might have happened had a contractual disciplinary procedure been followed. An employer is entitled to dismiss on contractual notice at common law for whatever reason.'*

It may be that there are grounds for alleging that the summary dismissal of the employee is both wrongful and unfair. In such a case it would technically be possible to pursue a common law claim for wrongful dismissal based upon breach of contract and claim under statute for unfair dismissal in the employment tribunal. The Court of Appeal in *O'Laoire v. Jackel International Ltd.* 1991 confirmed that the High Court was wrong to deduct an award of the maximum compensation for unfair dismissal (then £8,000) from the damages recoverable by the plaintiff in an action for wrongful dismissal for loss of earnings during the notice period. *'Unless the defendants can prove a double recovery for the same loss, there is no basis for setting off an unfair dismissal compensatory award against common law damages for wrongful dismissal. For the rule against double recovery to be involved, it must be shown that the plaintiff would be obtaining compensation under two heads for the same loss.'*

A number of cases in the 1980s culminating in *Robb v. London Borough of Hammersmith and Fulham* 1991 suggest that in cases involving a dismissal in breach of contract an interlocutory[12] injunction to restrain the dismissal and preserve the contract of employment so compelling the employer to go through the contractual disciplinary procedure may be the most effective remedy. Here an injunction was granted by the High Court against the employer to restrain the dismissal and treat the plaintiff as suspended on full pay until the contractual disciplinary procedure had been complied with. The employer was clearly in breach of contract and while there was no longer trust and confidence between employer and employee the injunction was workable.

There are other examples of the High Court exercising its equitable jurisdiction to grant an injunction to restrain the implementation of a dismissal notice where contractual procedures have not been exhausted. In *Irani v. Southampton and South West Hampshire Health Authority* 1985 a part-time ophthalmologist was given six weeks notice of termination when there proved to be irreconcilable differences between himself and his consultant. He applied for an interlocutory injunction to restrain his employer from implementing the notice claiming that his employer had failed to follow the collectively agreed disputes procedure incorporated into his contract. Impressed by the reasoning in *Hill v. Parsons* the High Court granted the injunction stressing the fact that there was still complete confidence in the plaintiff as an employee and that damages would not be an acceptable remedy *'Were the court to decline to grant the injunction sought, in effect it would be holding that an authority in the position of the defendant was entitled to snap its fingers at the rights of its employees under the conditions of service.'*

Normal contractual principles would suggest that *an 'unaccepted breach of contract is a thing writ in water'* and if the letter of dismissal is a repudiatory breach of contract it is not effective until the breach is accepted by the employee. As far as the Employment Rights Act 1996 is concerned however, such a letter can unilaterally terminate a contract of employment.

In *Marsh v. National Autistic Society* 1993 the High Court confirmed that a contract of employment repudiated by the employer can no longer subsist in practice as the employee has been excluded from the employment. The contract does not continue on until either the repudiatory breach has been accepted by the employee or the contract has been terminated lawfully by proper notice. The employee in this case had no right to payment of salary up until the time the contract was lawfully terminated.

In cases where a fixed term contract is prematurely brought to an end by the employer's repudiatory breach, a claim for damages for breach of contract may be the more appropriate avenue for redress, for the sum due under the unexpired term of the contract may be well in excess of the possible compensation available for unfair dismissal.[13] Such claims are more prevalent with the increased use of limited term contracts which are usually terminated by mutual consent.

---

12. Temporary
13. Subject to the requirement to mitigate the loss

Statutory Dismissal

For the purposes of unfair dismissal the meaning of 'dismissal' is defined in s.95 of the Employment Rights Act 1996.

Section 95(1) provides that: *an employee shall be treated as dismissed by his employer if, but only if;*

(a) *the contract under which he is employed is terminated by the employer, whether it is so terminated by notice or without notice, or*

(b) *where under the contract he is employed for a fixed term, that term expires without being renewed under the same contract, or*

(c) *the employee terminates the contract, with or without notice, in circumstances such that he is entitled to terminate it without notice by reason of the employer's contract.*

The section envisages a dismissal arising expressly, under s.95(1)(a), impliedly under s.95(1)(b) and constructively when the employee terminates the contract in response to the employer's conduct under s.95(1)(c).

Express Dismissal

Under s.95(1)(a) an express dismissal occurs where the employer terminates the contract of employment with or without notice. This is the most usual form of dismissal.

We have already said that an employer is normally required to give the employee notice in accordance with the terms of the contract or least the statutory or common law minimum period. For a dismissal with notice, therefore, there should be no room for any misunderstanding in relation to the employer's intentions. In cases of alleged summary dismissal, however, where there is no notice, there have been claims by the employer that it was not his intention to dismiss but rather merely to discipline. While the words, 'you're dismissed, fired, sacked', etc. leave little doubt as to the employer's intentions, if he uses more colourful language, perhaps to register his discontent with the employee, the argument that there has been no express dismissal could have some merit.

In *Tanner v. D. T. Kean* 1978 the complainant had been told that he could not use the company van outside working hours. When the employer discovered that he was doing so, after abusing the employee, he said to him, 'that's it, you're finished with me'. The EAT held that in deciding whether the words or actions of the employer amounted to a dismissal, all the circumstances should be considered. *'A relevant and perhaps the most important question is how would a reasonable employee in all the circumstances have understood what the employer intended by what he said and did?'* Here the words spoken in the heat of the moment indicated a reprimand rather than a dismissal.

In *Rees v. Apollo Watch Repairs Plc* 1996 the employer wrote to an employee who was taking maternity leave stating that *'I am no longer able to guarantee that you are able to return ... I am unable to keep the job for you.'* This letter was held to be an express dismissal.

The custom and practice of the trade are also considerations to bear in mind to determine the interpretation to be placed on the language used.

In *Futty v. Brekkes Ltd.* 1974 the tribunal was called on to place an interpretation on the quaint language used on the Hull dock. During an altercation with his foreman the complainant fish filleter was told, 'If you do not like the job, fuck off'. The complainant took this as a dismissal, left, and found a job elsewhere. For the purposes of an unfair dismissal claim the employer argued in his defence that there had been no dismissal. Here the words were to be considered in the context of the fish trade, and in these circumstances were taken to mean that if you do not like the work you are doing, clock off and come back tomorrow. The custom of the fish trade was that, for a dismissal, the language used was clear and formal. The tribunal agreed with the employer's view and held that the complainant had terminated his own employment by deciding on this occasion that he would leave and subsequently find himself alternative employment.

What is the legal position if an employee is expressly dismissed. He then invokes the contractual disciplinary process and the decision to dismiss is revoked and replaced with a lesser sanction such as a demotion. In *Roberts v. West Coast Trains* 2004 this was the scenario, with the added complication that the claimant had presented an unfair dismissal complaint before the decision to demote and he wanted to pursue it. The Court of Appeal agreed with the tribunal and the EAT that the claim could not be heard. Here there was no dismissal. The effect of the decision on appeal was to revive retrospectively the contract of employment terminated by the earlier decision to dismiss, so as to treat the employee as if he had never been dismissed. Because the contractual procedure allowed the employers to demote, there was no termination of the previous contract.

If the conduct of the employer demonstrates a firm and settled intention to treat the contract of employment as at an end, then this would constitute an express dismissal for the purpose of the Act.[14]

In *Boyo v. London Borough of Lambeth* 1995 following an allegation of fraud made against an accountant, his employer the local authority, wrote to him stating that his action had effectively frustrated[15] his contract of employment and as a consequence his salary was to cease at the end of the month. The Court of Appeal held that despite the assertion of frustration, a firm and settled intention to stop paying salary and treat the contract as at an end constituted a dismissal. The meaning and effect of the letter did not depend upon the accuracy of the legal reasoning upon which it was based.

It should be noted, of course, that a failure to treat employees with respect could indicate a breakdown in trust and confidence[16] so as to entitle an employee to walk out and regard himself as constructively dismissed.[17]

An important development in the law relating to express dismissal is the notion that if an employer unilaterally imposes a fundamental change in employment terms that could constitute an express dismissal from a previous contract of employment. This possibility was first recognised in *Hogg v. Dover College* 1990 where a Head of Department was informed that he would in future be employed as a part-time teacher on half his previous salary. The EAT concluded that *'both as a matter of law and common sense, he was being told that his former contract was from that moment gone. There was no question of any continued*

---

14. S.95(1)a
15. See later in the chapter
16. See Chapter 4
17. See later in the chapter

performance of it. It is suggested, on behalf of the employers, that there was a variation, but again, it seems to us quite elementary that you cannot hold a pistol to somebody's head and say henceforth you are to be employed on wholly different terms which are in fact less than 50% of your previous contract'.

Applying the rationale of Hogg in *Alcan Extrusions v. Yates* 1996 the EAT reached a similar conclusion. Here staff had objected to a fundamental change in shift patterns which affected overtime and holidays. When the change was imposed unilaterally a number of staff responded by claiming that it constituted a fundamental breach of contract tantamount to dismissal. Continuing to work under protest they lodged unfair dismissal clauses and the EAT supported the tribunal's decision that the staff had indeed been expressly dismissed from their previous contracts. The EAT concluded *'that the applicants former contract of employment providing for employment in jobs with a steady and predictable pattern of shift employment were removed from them and replaced by an altogether more demanding and previously uncontemplated regime of rolling shift pattern work which the applicants were certainly not obliged to undertake by their contracts of employment.... Where an employer unilaterally imposes radically different terms of employment, applying the principle in Hogg v. Dover College, there is a dismissal under s.95(1)(a)) if, on an objective construction of the relevant letters or other conduct on the part of the employer, there is a removal or withdrawal of the old contract'.*

Rai v. Somerfield Stores 2004 addressed the issue as to what constitutes a notice of dismissal for the purposes of s.111(3) of the Employment Rights Act.[18] Here a letter from the employer informed the employee that if he did not return to work by a given date his employment would be treated as having been terminated. Such an ultimatum was held not to be a notice of dismissal and does not terminate the employment. It is giving information to the employee that if he does not turn up for work on the due date his employment will be terminated on that date.

The significance of classifying a change of contract as an express dismissal rather than a fundamental breach for the purposes of constructive dismissal[19] is that an employee may lodge a claim for unfair dismissal and yet retain his status in an employment relationship, albeit under the new contract.

The date of dismissal may be significant, particularly in relation to time limits.[20] A dismissal does not take effect until the employee is told or has been given a reasonable opportunity of reading the notice of dismissal.

Implied Dismissal

Previously we said that if a limited term contract is terminated by either party prematurely without good reason, or authorisation under the contract, then an action may lie for damages for breach of contract. If the contract runs its course however, under s.95(1)(b) there is an implied dismissal of the employee when the term expires. Potentially therefore if the limited term contract is not renewed the employee is entitled to present a complaint of unfair dismissal.

---

18. See time limits Chapter 11
19. See later in the chapter
20. Three months from the effective date of termination to lodge a complaint

Previously, if the limited term contract was for the performance of a task or a contract to last until an event occurs and so designed to terminate when the task is completed, or the event occurs, it could not be classified as a fixed term contract for the purposes of s.95 (1)(b). The contract would be discharged by performance when the task was fulfilled or the purpose came to an end. The fact that there was no dismissal in such circumstances effectively excluded all statutory rights such as unfair dismissal and redundancy.

Now under the Fixed Term Employees (Prevention of less Favourable Treatment) Regulations 2002[21] the termination of such contracts will constitute a dismissal under s.95(1)(b).

The Employment Rights Act 1996 previously provided that an employer under a fixed term contract could expressly exclude unfair dismissal and redundancy rights. Under s.197(1) the right to claim unfair dismissal did not apply to a fixed term of one year or more which has expired, if the parties had previously agreed in writing to exclude unfair dismissal rights. This section was amended by the Employment Relations Act 1999 which removed the right to contract out of unfair dismissal in fixed term contracts. Of course in the majority of fixed term arrangements the reason for non renewal of the contract may be redundancy which is potentially a fair reason for dismissal. Also as the right to exclude redundancy payments from fixed term contracts was unaffected by the Employment Relations Act 1999 Act most employers would ensure that a fixed term contract of employment contained such an exclusion.

Section 197 of the ERA has now been repealed by the Fixed Term Employees (Prevention of Less Favourable Treatment) Regulations 2002. It is no longer possible to waive the right to a redundancy payment in fixed term contracts of two years or more. Existing contracts and renewals of contracts which contain waivers will remain valid, however, the position is unclear if the renewed contract is less than two years or if there is a succession of fixed term contracts each of which is less than two years. It is suggested that during the transitional period, to maintain a waiver the renewed contract must be for a period of two years.

Constructive Dismissal

In many cases it may seem superficially that the contract of employment has been terminated by the employee's conduct in 'walking out' and treating the contract as at an end. Where however, the reason for leaving was due to the conduct of the employer or those under his control, it may be that the employee could show that the employer is responsible for the contractual termination. In such circumstances an employee could argue that he has been dismissed under s.95(1)(c). Such a dismissal is commonly referred to as a constructive dismissal and if established will usually provide the applicant with sufficient evidence to secure a remedy for unfair dismissal.

> In *Edwards v. Surrey Police* 1999 Mr. Justice Morison, President of the EAT, examined the circumstances of a constructive dismissal scenario and concluded that there must be a clear indication by the employee's words or conduct that the employment relationship has terminated. He felt that *'an employee alleging constructive dismissal, must communicate to the employer the fact that they are terminating their employment. It is not an infrequent occurrence that employees find their working life intolerable, walk out in a huff, but do not intend to bring*

---

21. See Chapter 7

their employment relationship to an end. Unless there has been a proper communication by the employee of the fact that they are regarding themselves as no longer employed, whether by words or conduct their employment relationship has not terminated'.

Originally the test for determining whether a constructive dismissal had taken place was to judge the reasonableness of the employer's conduct according to the language of s.95(1)(c). Since *Western Excavating (ECC) Ltd. v. Sharp* 1978 however, the Courts have rejected that approach as being too vague and now the so called 'conduct test' is to be applied based upon strict contractual principles. The aim of the conduct test is to bring some degree of certainty to the law by requiring the employee to justify his leaving as a response to the employer's repudiatory conduct. Ld Denning MR stated that *'If the employer is guilty of conduct which is a significant breach going to the root of the contract of employment, or which shows that the employer no longer intends to be bound by one or more of the essential terms of the contract then the employee is entitled to treat himself as discharged from any further performance.'*[22]

A breach by the employer of the express terms of the contract of employment covering such matters as wages, job location, contractual duties and job description, normally comes about when the employer unilaterally attempts to impose a change on the employee without his consent. In *Hill Ltd. v. Mooney* 1981 the EAT held that an attempt by an employer to unilaterally alter his obligation to pay the agreed remuneration was a breach which went to the root of the contract and consequently constituted a repudiation of it. The complainant was entitled therefore to regard himself as constructively dismissed when he resigned following the employer's decision to unilaterally change the basis upon which sales commission was payable to him. *'Although a mere alteration in the contractual provisions does not necessarily amount to a fundamental breach constituting repudiation, if an employer seeks to alter that contractual obligation in a fundamental way such attempt is a breach going to the very root of the contract and is necessarily a repudiation. The obligation on the employer is to pay the contractual wages, and he is not entitled to alter the formula whereby those wages are calculated.'*

In *Reid v. Camphill Engravers* 1990 the breach complained of was the failure of the employer to pay the statutory minimum rate of remuneration set out in the Wages Council Order. Such a breach was of a sufficiently serious nature to be repudiatory and justify a constructive dismissal when the employee resigned as a result. The issue in the case however was whether the breach, having continued for three years, had been affirmed by the employee. The EAT held that in the case of a continuing breach the employee is still entitled to refer to the initial breach to show constructive dismissal. *'In any event where an employer has a statutory obligation to make the appropriate weekly payments, it is not open to an employee to agree and affirm the contract for a lower sum in wages than decreed by Parliament. In the present case therefore affirmation by the complainant could not apply.'*

In a constructive dismissal scenario it has been suggested that the employee must leave in circumstances that make it clear that he is leaving because of the employer's breach of contract and not for some other reason. In *Holland v. Glendale Industries* 1997 the EAT said that the statutory definition of constructive dismissal should be considered in the light of ordinary contractual principles. Where one party by his conduct repudiates the contract

---

22. Now recognised as the appropriate test

and the other party wishes to rely on the repudiation the latter must make it clear that he is accepting the repudiation and that is the reason for the termination of employment. This requirement as a matter of law has been overruled by the Court of Appeal in *Weathersfield Ltd. t/a Van and Truck Rental v. Sargent* 1999. This case involved an employee who left her employment because of a racially discriminatory instruction from her employer.[23] The court clearly stated that in a claim of constructive dismissal there is no requirement as a matter of law that an employee must state his reason for leaving. *The holding of the EAT in Holland v. Glendale Industries that constructive dismissal cannot be established unless it is made clear to the employer that the employee is leaving because of the employer's repudiatory conduct was incorrect as a principle of law.*

Even in a case where the employee resigns with notice there may be evidence that the resignation is a response to the employer's repudiatory breaches of contract and so constitute a constructive dismissal.

> In *Jones v. F. Sirl & Son (Furnishers) Ltd.* 1997 the manageress of the furnishing store with almost 30 years service resigned when she was offered and accepted a post with a rival company. In fact she claimed that her resignation was triggered by her employer who over a period of months had unilaterally changed her terms and conditions of employment by removing job functions, withdrawing allowances and reducing pension rights. The tribunal rejected her claim of constructive unfair dismissal on the grounds that while the employer had broken her contract, she had not resigned as a result. The EAT disagreed and held that the question for the tribunal in this type of case was whether the fundamental breaches of contract were the effective cause of the resignation but not necessarily the sole cause *'In a situation of potentially constructive dismissal, particularly in today's labour market, there may well be concurrent causes operating on the mind of an employee whose employer has committed fundamental breaches of contract.'* Here the tribunal would have been bound to conclude that on the evidence before it the main operative cause of the employee's resignation was the serious breaches of her contract by the employers.

By demoting an employee and failing to provide him with suitable office accommodation an employer could be held to be in fundamental breach of the contract of employment. Such an employee could accept the repudiatory breach and regard himself as constructively dismissed.

> This was the case in *Wadham Stringer Commercials (London) Ltd. & Wadham Stringer Vehicles Ltd. v. Brown* 1983 where a fleet sales director was effectively demoted to no more than a retail salesman. At the same time he was moved from reasonable accommodation to an office 8ft x 6ft with no ventilation, next to the gentleman's lavatory. As a consequence the employee eventually resigned and claimed a constructive dismissal which was unfair. The EAT agreed that there had been a fundamental breach of contract, accepted by the employee, and following *Western Excavating (ECC) Ltd. v. Sharp,*[24] a constructive dismissal. The employer's argument that their actions were the result of economic necessity were relevant, but only in deciding the reasonableness of their conduct for the purposes of the test of fairness or for the purpose of assessing the level of compensation in an unfair dismissal claim.

---

23. See also Chapter 6
24. See earlier

In *Brown v. Merchant Ferries Ltd.* 1998 the Northern Ireland Court of Appeal considered the circumstances of an employee who had resigned from his position as manager because of his employer's conduct. He claimed that his position had been 'completely undermined' because of the abusive conduct of his general manager and the lack of consultation about his future role following a reorganisation of the business. The Appeal Court disagreed with the tribunal and found there to be insufficient repudiatory conduct to warrant a finding of constructive dismissal. Applying Ld Steyn's test from *Malik v. BCCI SA* 1997 '*whether the employer's conduct so impacted on the employee that viewed objectively the employee could properly conclude that the employer was repudiating the contract*'. The court felt that the employer's conduct here while unsettling was not repudiatory.

If it is custom and practice in an organisation to demote an employee where his competence is in issue, this may not constitute a fundamental breach of contract for the purposes of constructive dismissal.

In *Vaid v. Brintel Helicopters Ltd.* 1994 the applicant, a helicopter pilot, who held the rank of senior captain, was demoted to co-pilot for a period of two years following a potentially dangerous incident which reflected on his competence. As a consequence the applicant resigned and complained of constructive unfair dismissal. The EAT agreed with the tribunal that there was an implied term in the applicant's contract which allowed for demotion and in these circumstances no fundamental breach of contract for the purposes of constructive dismissal.

The need to look for a clear breach of contractual term in applying the conduct test has encouraged both tribunals and courts in the absence of relevant express terms to imply terms into a contract of employment. It is the need therefore to accommodate the doctrine of constructive dismissal that has encouraged judicial ingenuity in applying the business efficacy test to find implied obligations in employment contracts. An excellent example is provided by the need to maintain trust and confidence in the employment relationship. In *Courtaulds Northern Textiles Ltd. v. Andrew* 1979 the EAT stated that '*there is an implied term in a contract of employment that the employers will not, without reasonable and proper cause, conduct themselves in a manner calculated or likely to destroy or seriously damage the relationship of confidence and trust between the parties*'. Here a comment made to the complainant by his assistant manager that 'you can't do the bloody job anyway' which was not a true expression of his opinion was held to justify the complainant in resigning and treating himself as constructively dismissed. While criticism of a worker's performance would not necessarily amount to repudiatory conduct so as to lead to constructive dismissal, here telling the employee that he could not do his job, when that was not a true expression of opinion, was conduct which was '*likely to destroy the trust relationship which was a necessary element in the relationship between the supervisory employee and his employers*'.

In many cases the employee resigns in response to an act which is the 'last straw' and the culmination of a long period of events which have caused the employee distress. In such circumstances it would be perfectly valid for a tribunal to consider whether the events, taken together, constitute a breach of the implied term of trust and confidence, and so justify a finding of constructive dismissal. Certainly it is a breach of the implied obligation of mutual trust and confidence for an employer to fail to treat an allegation of sexual harassment with due seriousness and gravity, and in such a case an employee is entitled to resign and treat herself as constructively dismissed. A good example is provided by *Reed and Bull Information Systems Ltd. v. Stedman* 1999. Here the complainant was a secretary who alleged that she had suffered sexual harassment by her manager and when she was forced to leave her employment as a result, that constituted constructive dismissal and an act of discrimination under s.6(2) of the Sex Discrimination Act 1975. The EAT held that while she had made no formal complaint about the conduct she had complained to her work colleagues and the personnel department were aware of her deteriorating health. By failing to investigate the incident the employer was in breach of the implied term of trust and confidence and when she was forced to leave as a result, this amounted to a constructive dismissal and an act of discrimination within the meaning of s.6(2) of the Sex Discrimination Act.

In *London Borough of Waltham Forest v. Omilaju* 2005 the Court of Appeal emphasised the fact that 'a last straw' act must contribute to the cumulative breach of the trust and confidence term. While the act may be relatively insignificant and not unreasonable, it must not be entirely trivial. The significant point is that the act need not of itself constitute a breach of contract The question is whether the cumulative effect of a series of acts amount to a breach of the implied term of trust and confidence.

It is a common law principle that an innocent party should respond to a repudiatory breach of contract otherwise he could be taken to have affirmed the contract by implication. For serious breaches of employment contracts by employers however involving health and safety or trust and confidence, it may not be practicable for the innocent party to accept the breach and terminate the contract. In *Walton and Morse v. Dorrington* 1997 the fact that the employee did not resign when she suffered the breach was not fatal to her claim. She left when she obtained alternative employment but this still constituted a constructive dismissal. *'Having regard to the employee's length of service and to the fact that she needed the money from her employment because of family commitments the tribunal was entitled to conclude that she had not affirmed the contract by delaying a few weeks in order to find alternative employment before acting on the breach.'*

Similarly, failing to treat an employee fairly in relation to a disciplinary matter could constitute repudiatory conduct for the purposes of constructive dismissal.

> In *British Broadcasting Corporation v. Beckett* 1983 the complainant was a scenic carpenter who having been found guilty of an act of negligence which jeopardised the safety of others was dismissed, and then following an internal appeal, demoted. Refusing to accept the offer of a post as maintenance carpenter the complainant resigned, claiming constructive dismissal. The EAT confirmed that the imposition of a *punishment 'grossly out of proportion to the offence'* can amount to a repudiation of a contract of service. Here the conduct of the employer amounted to a fundamental breach of his contractual obligations to justify a finding of constructive dismissal that was also unfair.

> In *Greenaway Harrison Ltd. v. Wiles* 1994 the EAT held that a telephonist who refused to accept a radical change in her shift pattern and was threatened with dismissal was entitled to leave and regard herself as constructively dismissed. The threat of dismissal constituted an anticipatory breach of contract by the employer.

> There was also a radical change in *Kerry Foods Ltd. v. Lynch* 2005. The claimant refused to move from a 5 day week to a 6 day week with a reduction in holiday entitlement. He was told that if he did not agree to the change his current employment would be terminated and he would be offered re-engagement on

the new terms. The claimant left before the notice expired claiming unfair constructive dismissal. The tribunal held that the proposed changes constituted a breakdown in trust and confidence and a constructive dismissal. The EAT took a different view of the facts deciding that an employer's service of a lawful notice of termination coupled with an offer of continuous employment on different terms cannot of itself amount to a repudiatory breach of contract. Here the claimant's resignation before the expiry of the notice period could not give rise to a constructive dismissal.

Employers have a clear duty in relation to the health of non-smokers so that if smoking is allowed at the workplace this could constitute a breach of the employer's duty towards passive smokers.

> In *Walton & Morse v. Dorrington* 1997[25] The EAT held that a secretary who had left her employment because of the affects of smoking at the workplace had been constructively dismissed. There was no requirement to point to a deterioration in her health but rather establish the repudiatory breach of an implied term in relation to maintaining a suitable working environment. Mr. Justice Morison referred to the Health and Safety at Work Act to assist in formulating the implied term. '...*It seems to us that a good starting point for the implication of a term of the sort that the tribunal had in mind is s.2 of the Health and Safety at Work Act 1974. It is to be stressed that his case was not concerned with health and safety, in the sense that there was no evidence before the tribunal that being exposed to tobacco smoke is in fact injurious to the health of those who have to endure it. On the other hand, s.2(2)(e) of the 1974 Act is concerned with the employer's duty to provide and maintain a working environment for his employees that is reasonable safe, without risk to health, and is adequate as regards facilities and arrangements for their welfare at work .... We ourselves would be inclined to the view that the correct implied term to deal with the complaint in this case is that the employer will provide and monitor for his employees, so as is reasonably practicable, a working environment which is reasonably suitable for the performance by them of their contractual duties.*'

The failure by an employer to deal promptly and fairly with an employee's grievance as in *Walton* above, by providing and implementing a grievance procedure, could amount to a repudiatory breach of contract.

An employer is of course vicariously responsible for the actions of his employees within the scope of their employment so that if a supervisor in reprimanding an employee does so in a reprehensible manner this can be taken to be *the 'employers' conduct'* for the purpose of constructive dismissal.

> In *Hilton International Hotels (UK) Ltd. v. Protopapa* 1990 an employee resigned when she was subjected to an officious and insensitive reprimand not justified by her conduct. The industrial tribunal held that she was *'humiliated intimidated and degraded to such an extent that there was breach of trust and confidence which went to the root of the contract'.* The employer nevertheless appealed against the finding of constructive dismissal arguing that the person who had carried out the reprimand, while a supervisor, had no authority to effect a dismissal. This

---

25. Above

the EAT found was an irrelevant consideration and restated the general principle that an employer is bound by acts done in the course of a supervisory employee's employment. *'Therefore, if the supervisor is doing what he or she is employed to do and in the course of doing it behaves in a way which if done by the employer would constitute a fundamental breach of the contract between the employer and employee, the employer is bound by the supervisor's misdeeds.'*

Morrow v. Safeway Stores 2002 is another example of a public reprimand leading to a resignation. Here the applicant, a production controller in a supermarket, was publicly criticised by her store manager and as a consequence walked out. The tribunal accepted that this conduct constituted a breakdown in trust and confidence but then found that the breach of contract was not sufficiently serious to be repudiatory for the purposes of constructive dismissal. The EAT disagreed and held that conduct which undermined trust and confidence constituted a repudiatory breach of the implied term *'In general terms a finding that there has been conduct which amounts to a breach of the implied terms of trust and confidence will mean inevitably that there has been a fundamental or repudiatory breach going necessarily to the root of the contract.'*

The above decision of the EAT is to be welcomed. It would be a daunting prospect to have to measure the degree to which trust and confidence has broken down and distinguish between repudiatory and non repudiatory breaches of contract. The approach to be followed is that adopted in *Brown v. Merchant Ferries.*[26] If the conduct is not sufficiently serious there is no breach of the implied term.

The issue in *Stanley Cole v. Sheridan* 2003 was whether the imposition of a final written warning that was *'grossly out of proportion to the misconduct'* could amount to repudiatory conduct for the purposes of constructive dismissal. The EAT that here such a step was a disproportionate response to the employee's conduct in absenting herself from work for a short period without permission following an altercation with another employee. The imposition of a final written warning is capable of amounting to repudiatory conduct on the part of the employer. A final written warning is a severe penalty which is given for conduct which just stops short of that justifying dismissal. It is often imposed when a dismissal is an obvious and permissible sanction but, for reasons personal to the employee, is not imposed. It involves a real penalty in that there is a risk that should the employee commit any other offence during the currency of the final written warning, however minor it may seem to be on its own, it may justifiably be taken to give grounds for dismissal. A final written warning may be regarded by an employee as a statement that an employer has in mind dismissal, and just pulls back from the brink.

It would be acceptable for an employee to serve notice in a constructive/unfair dismissal scenario, in which case the contract of employment will expire when the notice period runs out.[27] This expressly provided for in s.95(1)(c).

Having established that an employer has been guilty of repudiatory conduct for the purpose of constructive dismissal, this will normally lead to finding that the dismissal was also unfair. Fairness however, is to be judged by applying different criteria to the circumstances of the case rather than contractual breach and it is still open for an employer to justify the

---

26. Above
27. See *Jones v. Sirl* 1997 above

reasons for his conduct and convince a tribunal that he had acted fairly.[28] In *Savoia v. Chiltern Herb Farm* 1982 there was a constructive dismissal when the employee resigned after being moved from one job and offered another but there were background facts which the Court of Appeal held were wholly favourable to the employer and could justify the tribunal finding that the dismissal was in fact a fair one.

> In *Durrant and Cheshire v. Clariston Clothing Co. Ltd.* 1974 there was a complaint of unfair constructive dismissal when textile machinists who had been provided with free transport to work by their employer had the service withdrawn on the grounds that it was uneconomical. The withdrawal was held to be the breach of an important term of the contract sufficient to justify constructive dismissal. However the tribunal further held that the dismissals were for some other substantial reason and because of economic considerations, fair.

> A fair constructive dismissal is also liable to arise in the case of a reorganisation. In *Genower v. Ealing, Hammersmith & Hounslow Area Health Authority* 1980 the applicant was an administrative assistant who objected to a departmental transfer under a reorganisation. He claimed that the new post was a complete waste of his specialised knowledge and experience and subsequently resigned. The Court of Appeal; upheld the tribunal's finding that the circumstances of the proposed transfer constituted a constructive dismissal when the applicant resigned as a consequence. Also as the restructuring of the business involving the movement of staff had been carried out sensitively, the tribunal was entitled to find in relation to the applicant that there had been a full consideration of his position and that the dismissal was for some other substantial reason and fair.[29]

The EAT acknowledged in *Greenhof v. Barnsley Metropolitan Council* 2006 that there may be circumstances where the breach of a statutory obligation to make reasonable adjustments might not be regarded as repudiatory for the purposes of constructive dismissal. In the case before it however there was a serious breach because the employer should have given the employee duties that he could cope with without stress. Accordingly when he resigned as a result, there was a breakdown in trust and confidence for the purposes of constructive dismissal.

If there is no statutory dismissal under s.95(1), a contract of employment could nevertheless terminate by operation of the doctrine of frustration, by a clear resignation, or by the mutual agreement of the parties to it. We should examine each in turn.

Frustration

There is no dismissal for the purposes of s.95 if it can be shown that the contract of employment has been brought to an end through the operation of the common law doctrine of frustration. Frustration occurs where, due to a change in circumstances, performance of the contract becomes impossible or radically different than the performance envisaged by the parties when they made the contract. The specified events upon which a claim of frustration could be based are limited generally to long illness, and imprisonment. Certainly the distinction between the termination of a contract of employment by dismissal and termination by frustration is of critical importance. The view of the Court of Appeal in

28. See Chapter 11
29. See Chapter 5 and Chapter 11

London Transport Executive v. Clarke 1981 and subsequently the EAT in *Norris v. Southampton City Council* 1984 was that frustration could arise only where there is no fault by either party. In the latter case, therefore, where the employee's misconduct made him liable to be sentenced to a term of imprisonment, the contract of employment was not frustrated but rather the employee was guilty of a repudiatory breach which, if accepted by the employer, could lead to a dismissal. Such a blatant repudiation of the contract would, of course, normally result in a finding that the dismissal was fair. These cases suggest therefore that frustration should be limited to situations where the employee is prevented through illness or accident from performing the work required of him.

> In *Shepherd & Company Ltd. v. Jerrom* 1986 however, the Court of Appeal considered the position of an apprentice plumber who was sentenced to Borstal training for a minimum period of six months.[30] Failure to dismiss him in accordance with standard procedures for apprentices led the tribunal and the EAT to find that he had been constructively dismissed unfairly and so entitled to compensation. The Court of Appeal disagreed however and held that the four year apprenticeship contract had been frustrated by the six month sentence.

While a successful claim for unfair dismissal may have been difficult to swallow in the above case it does seem that the doctrine of frustration was stretched to cover a change in circumstances brought about by the conduct of the employee rather than circumstances over which the parties had no control. The imposition of a prison sentence would normally provide sufficient evidence of misconduct upon which the employer could rely to justify a fair dismissal.

More recently in *Four Seasons Healthcare v. Maughan* 2005 the claimant, a nurse, was suspended without pay during an investigation of his alleged misconduct of abusing a patient. Subsequently he was charged with a criminal offence and given bail. There followed a successful prosecution leading to a two-year sentence of imprisonment. On a claim for unlawful deductions from his wages during the period of suspension, the EAT rejected the employer's argument that the contract of employment had been frustrated by reason of him being charged with a criminal offence, or alternatively being given bail pending the trial. The employer's disciplinary process did envisage dismissal in these circumstances and the EAT felt that it was open to the employer to terminate the contract. The contract survived the criminal charge and the granting of bail so that the failure to pay wages during the period of suspension amounted to an unlawful deduction from wages.[31]

It is difficult in any given case to say whether the circumstances of an illness are such that it is no longer practical to regard the contract of employment as surviving. Obviously the seriousness and length of the illness are crucial factors but generally all the circumstances are relevant, including the nature of the job, the length of employment, the needs of the employer and obligations in relation to replacement, and the conduct of the employer.

> In *Notcutt v. Universal Equipment Company* 1986 the Court of Appeal considered the position of a worker who, two years from retirement and with 27 years' service, suffered an incapacitating heart attack with a medical prognosis that he would never work again. A finding that the contract was terminated by frustration meant that the employee was not entitled to sick pay during his statutory period

---

30. 6 months to 2 years
31. See Chapter 9

of notice. The court held that *'there is no reason in principle why a periodic contract of employment determinable by short or relatively short notice should not in appropriate circumstances be held to have been terminated without notice by frustration, according to the accepted and long established doctrine of frustration in the law of contract. The coronary which left the complainant unable to work again was an unexpected occurrence which made his performance of his contractual obligation to work impossible and brought about such a change in the significance of the mutual obligations that the contract if performed would be a different thing from that contracted for'.*

We saw in Chapter 6 that if an illness falls within the definition of a disability then under the Disability Discrimination Act 1995 the dismissal of a disabled person may be required to be justified by the employer bearing in mind the need to make reasonable adjustments.

If a contract of employment is frustrated by the operation of the common law then no further rights can survive under it.

> *Sharp v. McMillan* 1998 provide further guidance as to the consequences of a frustrated employment contract and whether an employment relationship can exist outside of a contract. The claimant was a joiner who because of a hand injury was unfit for work and was given formal notice that his contract was frustrated because of ill health. Because of potential pension benefits however the company agreed to keep him 'on the books'. Subsequently the employee claimed a redundancy payment and notice payments from the employer. The EAT held that the applicant's contract of employment had indeed been frustrated by his inability to work and was a consequence at an end by operation of the law. It is possible however to then enter into an arrangement falling short of a contract under the umbrella of employment. The practice of keeping such employees on the books, has been recognised in case-law and in s.212(3)(c) in relation to continuity of employment.[32] As the contract of employment had been terminated by operation of the law then there was no dismissal and consequently no right to notice payments or a redundancy payment.

Resignation

There is no dismissal if the employee expressly terminates the contract of employment by resigning. A resignation will usually be express but could be implied from conduct provided that it is clear and unambiguous. Once given, a notice of resignation like a dismissal cannot be withdrawn unilaterally. A change of heart must be mutually agreed to override the resignation.

If clear words of resignation are used even if designed as a threat it may be that an employer is entitled to take them literally.

> In *Sothern v. Franks Charlesly* 1981 the Court of Appeal had no difficulty in disagreeing with the EAT's finding that an employee's words 'I am resigning' are ambiguous and when relied on by an employer should not be regarded as a dismissal. The EAT held that the words 'I am resigning' are not ambiguous. *'They are in the present tense and indicate a present intention of resigning. They*

---

32. See Chapter 9

*have the same meaning as 'I am resigning now' or 'I resign'. The words do not mean
I am going to resign in the future. She was not pushed into the decision, not an
immature employee and no evidence that the words were spoken in the heat of the
moment.'* Resignation by an employee should have normal legal consequences
and terminate the employment relationship.

In *Kwik-Fit v. Lineham* 1992 as a direct consequence of issuing a written warning
to a depot manager in accordance with the company's disciplinary procedure,
he walked out in protest. While the employer took the view that the manager
had resigned he nevertheless presents a complaint of unfair dismissal. The EAT
held that where words or action of resignation are unambiguous an employer
can accept them as such unless there are 'special circumstances'. *'Words spoken
or action expressed in temper or in the heat of the moment or under extreme pressure,
or the intellectual make-up of an employee may be such special circumstances.'* In a
case such as this, where there are special circumstances, an employer is required
to allow a reasonable period to elapse, perhaps a matter of days, before accepting
a resignation to determine an employee's true intention.

The correct question to ask in deciding whether a resignation constitutes a dismissal is
'Who really terminated the contract of employment'.

In *Ely v. YKK Fasteners (UK) Ltd.* 1993 the employee had given notice of his
intention to resign at some time in the future and such a notice, the Court of
Appeal held, was insufficient to bring the contract of employment to an end.
When the employer in this case acted upon the notice however, and gave the
employee a termination date, despite the fact that the employer was relying on
a termination by resignation it was possible for the tribunal to interpret the
circumstances as constituting a termination by express dismissal for the purposes
of unfair dismissal.

In *BAA plc v. Quinton* 1992 the EAT confirmed that a clear resignation can only
be withdrawn with the approval of the employer.

In *Sovereign House Security Services Ltd. v. Savage* 1989 a security officer was
told that he was to be suspended pending police investigations into theft of
money from his employer's office. The fact that the applicant told his superior
that he was 'jacking it in' was held by the Court of Appeal to amount to a clear
resignation.

There will normally be a contractual provision as to the length of notice to be given and, in
addition, there is a statutory minimum period of one week[33] where the employee has at
least one month of continuous employment. Failure to comply with notice requirements is
a breach of contract for which the employee could be made liable in damages. Employers
rarely sue in these cases due mainly to the problem of quantifying their loss which would
include the additional cost of advertising for and hiring a replacement during the notice
period.

The unilateral act of resigning must be distinguished from the consensual termination of
employment which normally involves an exchange of consideration, e.g. a lump sum in
return for the loss of the job.

---

33. Under s.86(2)

Mutual Termination

It is a fundamental principle of contract law that a contract can be terminated by the mutual agreement of the parties, and such an agreement constitutes a second contract. Fixed term contracts in particular are most usually terminated by the agreement of the parties. In the world of football management the premature termination of a manager's fixed term contract is often agreed to the mutual satisfaction of the parties, involving a sum of compensation to the outgoing manager or to his employer by a third party employer. The impact of a genuine voluntary mutual termination of the contract is that there is no dismissal for the purposes of unfair dismissal and redundancy payments.[34]

Considerable support was given by the courts to the view that if the employer and employee mutually agree that the contract of employment should terminate on the happening or non-happening of a specified event, then the contract would terminate automatically on its occurrence, and there would be no dismissal for the purposes of statutory rights. Such agreements were regarded as variations of existing contracts of employment.

> In *British Leyland v. Ashraf* 1978 the employee was given five weeks' unpaid leave to return to Pakistan on condition that he expressly agreed that if he failed by a given date to return to work, 'your contract of employment will terminate on that date'. The EAT held that a failure by the employee to return to work on the due date amounted to a consensual termination of the contract of employment and consequently not a dismissal for the purposes of unfair dismissal.

> The validity of automatic termination clauses must now be seriously in doubt following the judgment of the Court of Appeal in *Igbo v. Johnson Matthey Chemicals Ltd.* 1986. The case concerned a similar extended leave clause to that in Ashraf with a provision for mutual termination of the contract of employment in the event of non-compliance. Both the tribunal and the EAT, applying *Ashraf* held that there was no dismissal and, therefore, no unfair dismissal rights despite the fact that the employee had a medical certificate to explain her failure to return to work on the due date. Reaching a different conclusion the Court of Appeal held that the tribunal and the EAT were wrong in law and that the Ashraf decision should be overruled. The conclusion was reached by applying s.140(1) of the Employment Protection (Consolidation) Act 1978[35] to automatic termination clauses. The section stipulates that any provision in an agreement shall be void '*in so far as it purports … to limit the operation on of any provision of this Act*'. By limiting the right not to be unfairly dismissed, automatic termination agreements offended the section and were therefore void. To allow reliance on such clauses would mean that, '*the whole object of the Act could be easily defeated by the inclusion of a term in a contract of employment that if the employee was late for work on any day, no matter for what reason, the contract should automatically terminate. Such a provision would virtually limit the operation of the section, for the right not to be unfairly dismissed would become subject to the condition that the employee was on time for work*'.

It should be stressed that the operation of this section will not prevent the parties to an employment contract reaching agreement as to the termination of the contract by mutual

---

34. See Chapter 12
35. Now s.203 Employment Rights Act 1996

consent not contingent upon the happening or non-happening of an event. Accordingly if the parties to a contract of employment, without duress and after taking proper advice, enter into a separate contract, supported by good consideration, with the objective of terminating the employment relationship by mutual consent, the contract will be valid and enforceable.

> Such was the case in *Logan Salton v. Durham County Council* 1989. Here the complainant was a social worker who, as a result of disciplinary hearings, had been redeployed by his employer. In a statement to be considered at a further disciplinary hearing the complainant was given notice of a number of complaints against him and a recommendation that he be summarily dismissed. Prior to that meeting his union representative negotiated on his behalf a mutual agreement to terminate his employment with the Council. By that agreement the employment contract was to terminate in seven weeks' time and an outstanding car loan of £2,750 wiped out as a debt. Despite the fact that the agreement was signed by both parties, the complainant subsequently complained to an industrial tribunal that he had been unfairly dismissed. It was argued that a dismissal had occurred in law, for the mutual agreement to terminate was either void as an agreement entered into under duress, or void because its effect was to remove statutory protection, similar to *Igbo v. Johnson Matthey Chemicals Ltd.* Both these arguments were rejected by the industrial tribunal and on appeal by the EAT. The EAT found that this case could be distinguished from Igbo as here there was a separate contract rather than a variation of an existing contract of employment, and the termination of employment did not depend upon the happening of some future event. Furthermore, the fact that the appellant was aware of the employer's recommendation of dismissal did not constitute duress, bearing in mind the financial inducement. *'In the resolution of industrial disputes, it is in the best interests of all concerned that a contract made without duress, for good consideration, preferably after proper and sufficient advice and which has the effect of terminating a contract of employment by mutual agreement (whether at once or at some future date) should be effective between the contracting parties, in which case there probably will not have been a dismissal.'*

A common scenario in employment is the situation where an employee is offered a substantial change in employment or alternatively a severance deal involving a lump sum payment and pension rights.

> In *Kirkland v. Mercedes-Benz UK Ltd.* 1993 this was the choice facing the complainant a field service engineer who had 24 years service with his employer. After taking legal advice the complainant wrote to his employer rejecting the change in employment and confirming that he wished to remain employed. He also stated in his letter that the consequence of his decision was that his contract would be terminated and he would be entitled to a severance payment. The company responded by confirming that he had chosen the severance option and set a date for his contractual termination. Subsequently the complainant claimed unfair dismissal and the issue before the tribunal was whether there had been a dismissal. Both the tribunal and the EAT found that there was no dismissal deciding that the complainants letter, while ambiguous, seemed to acknowledge the termination of employment by means of an acceptance of the severance payment. His letter should be treated as a voluntary acceptance of a mutual termination rather than an acknowledgment of dismissal.

A final scenario worthy of mention is the situation where an employee, already serving notice of dismissal, agrees with his employer to terminate the notice period prematurely, perhaps to take up alternative employment. For the purposes of unfair dismissal[36] and redundancy[37] despite the agreement to release the employee from the contract there is still a dismissal.

Post Contract Terms

There is an issue as to whether certain contractual terms may remain enforceable following the termination of the contract of employment. The best example is the contract in restraint of trade which contains an express term which purports to survive the contract.

Such express terms found in many contracts of employment is a clause which purports to restrict the freedom of the employees, on the termination of employment, from engaging in a competing business or working for a competitor for a specified period. Provided such a clause is inserted to protect a genuine proprietary[38] interest of the employer and is reasonable in extent, the express restraint will be valid and enforceable. A restraint clause which purports to restrict the free choice of an ex-employee as to the employment options open is prima facie void as a contract in restraint of trade. Such a contract is nevertheless valid and enforceable if reasonable in the circumstances because:

(a) *the employer has a genuine proprietary interest worthy of protection such as clientele, confidential information, or trade connection; and*

(b) *the restraint clause is drafted in such a way that it is no wider than is reasonably necessary to achieve the desired objective.*

If the court is satisfied that the purpose of the restraint clause is no more than to prevent healthy competition then it will be declared void and of no legal effect.

> In *Strange v. Mann* 1965 the manager of a bookmakers agreed not to engage in a similar business to that of his employer with in a twelve mile radius on the termination of his employment. In an action to enforce the clause, the court held that, as the bookmaker had little or no influence over the firm's clientele and in fact communicated with them mainly by telephone, the employer had no valid interest to protect. As the primary aim of the clause was simply to prevent competition it was declared void.

The validity of a restraint clause will depend initially upon whether the employer has legitimate trade secrets worthy of protection. In *FSS Travel and Leisure Systems Ltd. v. Johnson* 1998 the Court of Appeal agreed that there was an unreasonable restraint of trade when an employer sought to enforce a restrictive covenant against a computer programmer. The court felt that the covenant was simply an attempt to control a former employee's skill, expertise and knowledge gained during employment.

A distinction must be drawn between an attempt by an employer to prevent his ex-employee revealing trade secrets or lists of clients to competitors and simply preventing an ex-employee putting into practice the knowledge, skills and abilities that he acquired during his period of employment.

---

36. S.95(2)
37. S.136(3)
38. Property

Having identified a proprietary interest worthy of protection, the next step is to analyse the restraint clause to discover whether it is reasonable in the circumstances. A number of factors are deserving of attention to assist in the analysis, such as the area of the restraint, the length of time it is to run and the nature of the work that the employer is attempting to restrain. The wording of the restraint clause is therefore crucial, for if it is too extensive in the geographical area of protection, or too long in time, it will be unenforceable. Each case turns on its own facts and all the circumstances are considered.

> In *Fitch v. Dewes* 1921 a lifetime restraint on a solicitor's clerk from working for another solicitor within a radius of seven miles of Tamworth Town Hall was nevertheless held to be valid. The House of Lords felt that the modest area of the restraint which the employer relied on for his clientele justified even a lifetime restraint.

If a restraint clause is drafted in such a way that it purports to prevent the ex-employer from obtaining non-competitive employment then it will be declared void.

> In *Fellows & Sons v. Fisher* 1976 a conveyancing clerk employed by a firm in Walthamstow agreed that for five years after the termination of employment he would not be employed or concerned in the legal profession anywhere within the postal district of Walthamstow and Chingford or solicit any person who had been a client of the firm when he had worked there. Not only was the five year restraint thought to be too long, bearing in mind the large population in the areas identified, but the attempt to exclude any work in the legal profession, which would include legal work in local government and the administration of justice, was also thought to be unreasonable and the restraint was declared void.

> A different attitude to restraint clauses is illustrated by the decision of the Court of Appeal in *Littlewoods Organisation v. Harris* 1978. Here the defendant was employed as a director by Littlewoods, a large company which competes with Great Universal Stores Ltd. for the major share of the mail order business in the United Kingdom. As a consequence, the defendant agreed in his contract of employment that he would not, for a period of twelve months after its termination, enter into a contract of employment with Great Universal Stores Ltd. or any subsidiary company. Littlewoods, by such a restraint clause was seeking to protect confidential information of which the defendant was aware, relating to the preparation of their mail order catalogue. As Great Universal Stores operated all over the world it was argued that the restraint clause was wider than reasonably necessary to protect Littlewoods' interest in the UK. A majority of the court held however that restraint clauses should be interpreted bearing in mind their object and intention. As a proper construction, the clause was intended to relate to the UK mail order business only and was therefore valid and enforceable.

It is crucial to the validity of a restraint clause that the employer limits its extent to protect the clientele and business locations which apply to the employee's term of employment. It would be unreasonable for an employer to attempt to prevent competition in geographical locations into which it has not yet operated.

> In *Greer v. Sketchley Ltd.* 1979 the restraint clause purported to prevent the employer competing nation-wide when in fact the employer's business was limited to the Midlands and London. The argument that an employer is entitled to seek protection in geographical areas in which he intends to expand, was rejected.

In *WAC Ltd. v. Whillock* 1990 the Scottish Court of Session emphasised that restrictive covenants must be construed fairly and it is *'the duty of the Court to give effect to them as they are expressed and not to correct their errors or to supply their omissions'*. Here the clause in question specifically prevented any ex-company-shareholders for two years carrying on business in competition with the company. The clause did not impose any restriction on the right of an employee to be a director or employee of another company which carried on business in competition and so could not prevent the employee/shareholder from becoming a director of a competing company.

In *J. A. Mont (UK) Ltd. v. Mills* 1993 the Court of Appeal restated the general principle that restrictive covenants which are two wide should be declared void and of no legal effect and the courts should not strive too urgently to find implied limitations on the terms of such covenants to enable them to be enforced.

In *Dentmaster (UK) Ltd. v. Kent* 1997 the High Court felt that a restraint clause was too wide when it purported to restrain the ex-employee from soliciting the trade of any customers of his employer whom he had dealt with during the course of his employment, from its very commencement. On appeal however the Court of Appeal disagreed and said that such a clause is not bound to be found invalid particularly in view of the short restraint period of six months.

If a restraint clause is drafted in such a way that it is reasonable in extent, then provided it does not offend the public interest it will be binding and can be enforced by means of an injunction. In practice such injunctions are rarely granted for the very presence of the clause acts as a sufficient deterrent.

There have also been a few exceptional cases where the courts have determined that part of a restraint clause is unreasonable but other separate parts of the clause are reasonable and would be valid and enforceable. In such circumstances, rather than declare the whole clause to be void and unenforceable, the courts have severed the unreasonable part of the contract and, provided that what remains can stand alone, declared it to be valid and enforceable.

In *TFS Derivatives Ltd. v. Morgan* 2005 a City equity broker was subject to term which did not allow the broker for a period of six months following termination to *'undertake, carry on or be employed, engaged or interested in any capacity in either any business which is competitive with or similar to a relevant business within the territory, or any business an objective or anticipated result of which is to compete with a relevant business within the territory'*. The High Court rather than holding that the restraint an unreasonable restraint of trade, severed the words 'or similar' and upheld the restraint clause.

In *Living Design (Home Improvements) Ltd. v. Davidson* 1994 the employer attempted to restrain a promotions manager's employment activities for period of six months on the termination of her employment *'however that comes about whether lawful or not'*. The contract also attempted to deal with the possibility of the restraint being found unreasonable and void by providing for the unlawful content to be severed from the agreement. Such clauses the Court of Session held were in themselves unreasonable and would not be enforced. A wrongful dismissal in breach of contract will always have impact on the validity of a restraint clause. Also it is for the courts to determine the extent to which severance is applicable. *'The court should not strike out words where to do so would alter the scope and intention of the agreement. Moreover, in the case of a* covenant by an employee, there should be severance only if the enforceable part is clearly severable and, even then, only where what it struck out is of trivial importance or technical and not part of the main import and substance of the clause.'

The argument in *P. R. Consultants Scotland Ltd. v. Mann* 1996 was that to restrain an ex employee for 12 months after termination of employment from soliciting customers was unenforceable because the restrictive covenant was to apply upon termination of employment *howsoever caused*. This meant that the covenant was to apply even if the employee was dismissed unlawfully as in *Living Design v. Davidson* above. The Court of Session rejected this interpretation and held that the expression *howsoever caused* could be taken to apply only to the many lawful ways a contract of employment could be terminated. On the balance of convenience the court was prepared to grant an order enforcing the covenant and preventing the employee operating the account of an important ex client of his previous employer.

The Court of Appeal in *Credit Suisse Asset Management Ltd. v. Armstrong* 1996 considered the impact of a garden leave clause and indicated that *'by means of such a clause employers are able to obtain protection from competition by people who wish to leave their employment but who may have confidential information or important contacts with customers or clients which the employer wishes to terminate before the end of the period of notice'*. Here the court held that a period of six months garden leave could be followed by a legally enforceable six month restraint clause. While the existence of garden leave may be a factor in determining the validity of a restraint clause in this case a period of twelve months protection was not unreasonable.

In *Symbian Ltd. v. Christensen* 2001 the Court of Appeal ruled that a clearly worded restraint clause providing for garden leave was legally effective. The clause in question prohibited the employee from working in any business which competed with that of the employer for a period of six months following the termination of employment. The employer could also require the employee to take garden leave during the period of notice whether given by the employer or the employee. Such a clause could be enforced by means of an injunction to the extent necessary to protect the legitimate interest of the employer and in a manner which would not constitute an unreasonable restraint of trade. Here the injunction could properly be granted to prevent the employee from working for a particular competitor during the period of the garden leave.

It now seems that if an employer wishes to have the option of requiring an expressly dismissed employee to take garden leave during the notice period then he should provide for this possibility in the contract of employment. In *William Hill Organisation Ltd. v. Tucker* 1998 the Court of Appeal refused to grant an injunction to prevent an ex-employee taking up employment with a competitor and accept salary without work during a six month notice period. The court felt that *'whether there is a right to work is a question of construction of the particular contract in the light of its surrounding circumstances'*. Here the employer had a duty to provide the employee with work during the notice period so as to enable him to exercise his skills as a specialist in the field of spread betting.[39]

---

39. See Chapter 4

An employee may be discharged from obligations arising from a restriction covenant it is established that there was a wrongful dismissal or a resignation arising from the acceptance of a repudiatory breach of contract by the employer.

> The High Court held in *Dairy Crest Ltd. v. Wise* 1994 that the conduct of the employer which led to the employee's resignation, was a breach of the implied duty of trust and confidence and consequently a repudiatory breach of covenant. Accordingly the court refused to grant an injunction to prevent the ex-employee from operating a milk round which would otherwise have been in breach of a restrictive covenant not to solicit ex-customers.

One final issue that may be addressed in relation to restraint clauses and contractual terms generally is the extent to which they remain enforceable when clearly expressed in an original contract of employment but not re-stated on various promotions within the organisation.

In *Marley Tile Co. Ltd. v. Johnson* 1982 the defendant's original letter of appointment contained a number of clearly expressed restraint clauses designed to prevent him seeking employment from rival organisations or competing for a period of twelve months after the termination of his employment. On a promotion to area manager some years later, the defendant agreed similar restraint clauses but then, when made a unit defendant resigned and took up employment with a rival firm within one month, his employer sought an interlocutory injunction to enforce the restraint clause. The Court of Appeal held that covenants which form part of the employee's original contract applied to his subsequent appointment as a unit manager, despite the failure to refer to them expressly. Lord Denning MR expressed the position when he said that, *'All that had happened in the present case was that the defendant had been promoted in the same company. Both parties would assume that the original terms of employment, including the restrictive covenants, would continue unless something was said to the contrary.'* Stressing this important point in relation to the variation of a contract of employment, Eveleigh L J said that, *'The defendant's appointment as a unit manager was varied. No reference was made in the memorandum and letter of appointment to the motor car which the defendant continued to have, or to telephone expenses, or to lunch and subsistence allowances, all of which were matters dealt with in the previous formal agreement.'* In fact the covenants, although part of the contract, were held to be void and unenforceable because they were thought to be too wide in area and extent.

Further Reading

Brodie, Douglas *Wrongful Dismissal and Mutual Trust* (1999) 28 ILJ 249.

Fodder and Freer *The Effect of Contractual Provision for Payment in Lieu of Notice* (2001) 30 ILJ 215.

Leach, D. *Development in Recoverable Damages for Wrongful and Unfair Dismissal* (2003) IRLB 3.

Reynold, Frederic and Palmer, Anya *Proving Constructive Dismissal : Should one be concerned with what was in the employer's mind?* (2005) 34 ILJ 96.

Chapter 11

Unfair Dismissal

The introduction of the right not to be dismissed without good reason in the Industrial Relations Act 1971 was a recognition that an employee has a stake in his job which cannot be extinguished simply by serving contractual notice. Security of employment is the core statutory right of employees. In the same way that a tenant may in certain circumstances acquire security of tenure in his home and resist the enforcement of a notice to quit unless it is reasonable in the circumstances, an employee, through continuous employment, can acquire security in his job. The right not to be unfairly dismissed is intended to act as a constraint on employers who feel they have the authority to hire and fire as they please. The extent to which the law of unfair dismissal achieves the objective of constraining management prerogative is arguable.

Certainly over the last thirty five years unfair dismissal has developed into a highly complex area of law, recognised as such as early as 1977 by Philips J. in *Devis & Sons Ltd. v. Atkins 1977*, when he said, *the expression 'unfair dismissal' is in no sense a common-sense expression capable of being understood by the man in the street*. The contemporary approach to termination of employment is to encourage employers to implement their own dispute resolution procedures to encourage parties to avoid litigation or make use of the alternative ACAS Arbitration Procedure. Following the Employment Act 2002 all employers are required to implement the Employment Act 2002 (Dispute Resolution) Regulations which came into force in October 2004. We will consider the new statutory procedures about disciplinary matters and employee grievances, and the consequences for failing to adhere to them, later in the chapter.

The Statutory Right

The present unfair dismissal law is contained in the Employment Rights Act 1996 as amended. The right not to be unfairly dismissed is perhaps the most fundamental of all statutory employment rights and inevitably that it is necessary to devote a reasonably lengthy chapter to a consideration of the law. Having considered the role of the Employment Tribunal in Chapter 2 you should appreciate that the emphasis in unfair dismissal complaints is very much on the primary facts of the particular claimant's case. As the final arbiter on questions of fact it is of the highest importance that flexibility in the tribunal should be retained and that the evaluation of an employer's conduct should be left exclusively to the tribunal in its capacity as an industrial jury.[1]

Under s.94(1) *in every employment to which the section applies, every employee shall have the right not to be unfairly dismissed by his employer.*

An employee is entitled to have a complaint of unfair dismissal heard before an employment tribunal even if the employer offers to pay the maximum compensation recoverable with no admission of unfair dismissal.

> In *Telephone Information Services Ltd. v. Wilkinson* 1991 the EAT held that *'An employee has a right to a claim of unfair dismissal decided by an industrial tribunal. Such a claim is not simply for a monetary award; it is a claim that the dismissal was unfair. The employee is entitled to a finding on that matter and to maintain his claim to the tribunal for that purpose. He cannot be prevented from exercising that right by an offer to meet only the monetary part of the claim. If that were so, any employer would be able to evade the provisions of the Act by offering to pay the maximum compensation. If employers wish to compromise a claim, they can do so by admitting it in full but they cannot do so by conceding only part of it.'*

Having established that a prospective applicant is classified as an employee for the purpose of s.94(1),[2] it is then necessary to determine whether the employee is otherwise qualified to present a claim for unfair dismissal to enable the tribunal to have jurisdiction over the complaint.

Qualifications

Prior to 1995 a distinction was drawn between full-time and part-time employees. Full-time employment meant working under a contract of employment which involves work for sixteen hours or more per week and a full-time employee qualified with two years continuous service.[3] An employee who had a contract which provides for employment for between eight and sixteen hours had to work continuously for five years or more to qualify. Significantly this provision was held to be indirectly discriminatory and contrary to European Community Law by the House of Lords in *R v. Secretary of State for Employment ex-parte the EOC* 1994.

In 1995 the Employment Protection (Part-Time Employees) Regulations came into force and abolished the thresholds distinguishing between full-time and part-time employment. All part-time employees, regardless of the number of hours that they work, enjoy the same statutory rights as full-time employees.

The period of continuous employment for an employee to qualify for unfair dismissal protection is contained in s.108(1).

> Under *s.108(1) ..., section 94 does not apply to the dismissal of an employee unless he has been continuously employed for a period of not less than one year ending with the effective date of termination.*

---

1. See *East Berkshire Health Authority v. Matadeen* Chapter 2
2. See Chapter 3
3. Now one years continuous service

To fall within the provisions of s.94 then an employee had to show continuous employment in a job, and not an excluded category of work. The minimum period of continuous employment is not less than one year ending with the effective date of termination. This is the date that the contract of employment actually comes to an end. If a summary dismissal[4] is unjustified it may be necessary to add the statutory period of notice onto the date of dismissal. If the employee can establish that the reason for dismissal is inadmissible and automatically unfair,[5] for instance pregnancy or trade union activities, then the period of continuous employment does not apply.[6] Unfortunately there are now numerous exceptions to the one year rule and we will deal with them later in the chapter.

The issue in *Pacitti Jones v. O'Brien 2005* was whether a 'year' under s.108 means 12 calendar months. Even though a calendar month generally runs from a date in one month to the corresponding date in the succeeding month, the court ruled that the day on which the employee started work is to be included in the period. This means that if employment starts on 3 March 2005 then if notice of dismissal terminates on 2 March 2006 then the service requirement is satisfied.[7]

A further requirement[8] is that if on, or before, the effective date of termination, the employee has reached the 'normal retiring age' or, if more than the age of 65,[9] then there is no right to present a claim.

The normal retiring age can be higher than the contractual retirement age. In *Royal and Sun Alliance Insurance Group plc v. Payne* 2005 the EAT held that the normal retiring age cannot be lower than the contractual retirement age. Any attempt by an employer to unilaterally impose a normal retiring age lower than the contractual retirement age will be in breach of contract and invalid. Establishing the normal retiring age is determined by ascertaining the reasonable expectation of employees in the relevant group as to the age at which they can be compelled to retire. An employee's reasonable expectation would be that they would not be compulsorily retired before reaching their contractual retirement age.

Under the Employment Equality (Age) Regulations 2006 such a restriction will be removed as discriminatory. From October 2006, the legal position as to retirement and unfair dismissal rights will change. The Regulations envisage a national default retirement age of 65 and are proposing that anyone who is dismissed by reason of retirement from age 65 onwards will not be entitled to claim unfair dismissal. This change will bring many more employees under the protection of unfair dismissal law. Those individuals who have a contractual retirement age agreed at over 65 may however be affected by such a change. The present age restriction for unfair dismissal is subject to a legal challenge and we await a ruling of the House of Lords in March 2006.

In addition to qualifying through service, an employee must not fall within one of the excluded categories of employment.

- Persons employed in the police force.
- Share fishermen e.g. members and crew paid by a share of the profits.

---

4. See Chapter 10
5. See later in the chapter
6. s.108(3)
7. Otherwise an employee would need to serve 366 days to qualify
8. Under s.109(1)
9. Whether male or female

- Employees who work ordinarily outside Great Britain.

In *Crofts v. Cathay Pacific Airways* 2005 the Court of Appeal had to decide whether airline pilots, based in England but employed by a Hong Kong registered company were employed in Great Britain. The court held that despite the fact that they flew Cathay Pacific their contract base in England meant that the tribunal had jurisdiction.

In relation to seamen, '*a person employed to work on board a ship registered in the United Kingdom*', they are also excluded if '*the employment is wholly outside Great Britain*'.

In *Wood v. Cunard Line Ltd.* 1990 a seaman was employed under an agreement extended into England, for employment on a British registered ship, but the ship never visited the United Kingdom. The issue was whether he was employed 'wholly outside' Great Britain bearing in mind he was employed in England and spent his leave there. The Court of Appeal held that as he only worked on board the ship outside British waters he was employed wholly outside Great Britain and not qualified to bring a complaint of unfair dismissal.

- Employees covered by a designated dismissal procedure agreement.
- Certain registered dock-workers.

Time Limits

Another issue in relation to jurisdiction is whether the complaint was made to the tribunal within the time limits. The procedure involved in presenting a complaint of unfair dismissal is considered in detail Chapter 2. An employee must initiate proceedings by submitting an ET1 form to the Central Office of Employment Tribunals or Regional Office of Employment Tribunals within three months of the effective date of termination. The completed form can be presented by hand, by post or submitted on-line. A crucial issue is whether the complaint has been presented within the statutory time limit under s.111.

> Under s.111(2), an employment tribunal shall not consider a complaint under this section unless it is presented to the tribunal before the end of the period of three months beginning with the effective date of termination or within such further period as the tribunal considers reasonable in a case where it is satisfied that it was not reasonably practicable for the complaint to be presented before the end of the period of three months.

Section 111(2) provides therefore that a tribunal will not have jurisdiction to hear a complaint unless it is presented within three months '*beginning with*' the '*effective date of termination*'.

The initial attitude of the courts and tribunals was that time limits in relation to tribunal complaints should be interpreted strictly. Popplewell J. in *Foster v. South Glamorgan Health Authority* 1988 expressed the attitude of the EAT when he said '*It has been the practice of industrial tribunals and this appeal tribunal, to apply the limitation periods with very great strictness. They go to jurisdiction. The rather leisurely pace at which proceedings in the High Court and elsewhere are conducted have no place in industrial tribunals or this appeal tribunal.*'

Recently you will see that there has been a softening of the approach of tribunals to time limits, the aim being to rarely deny a complaint where the employee has made a reasonable attempt at raising his grievance with the employer. Under the Employment Act 2002 (Dispute Resolution) Regulations 2004 the time limit in relation unfair dismissal claims can now be extended by a further three months where the parties continue to implement disciplinary or grievance procedures. Also a complaint will not be entertained by the tribunal unless the claimant has given the employer a reasonable period[10] to respond to the grievance in a constructive dismissal scenario.

A significant feature of unfair dismissal procedure is that it is possible for an employee who is dismissed with notice to lodge a complaint of unfair dismissal when still employed and serving out the notice period.[11] If following a dismissal with notice and a subsequent complaint, there is a summary dismissal, the Court of Appeal held in *Patel v. Nagesan* 1995 that the original complaint is unaffected. *'Once s.111(4) bites, there is a valid complaint which the tribunal has to consider. There is nothing in the section to suggest that the employer, whether deliberately or not, can invalidate the complaint by proceeding at a later date to dismiss summarily.'*

Obviously deciding the effective date of termination is a pre-requisite to establishing the time limits for initiating proceedings. The mandatory requirement to comply with the Employment Act 2002 (Dispute Resolution) Regulations 2004 inevitably extends the termination date to accommodate their operation.

Effective Date of Termination

The expression *'effective date of termination'* means for most purposes the date that the employment actually terminates.

> *Under s.92(6) the 'effective date of termination'*
>
> *(a)   in relation to an employee whose contract of employment is terminated by notice, means the date on which the notice expires;*
>
> *(b)   in relation to an employee whose contract of employment is terminated without notice, means the date on which the termination takes effect; and*
>
> *(c)   in relation to an employee under a contract for a fixed term, which expires without being renewed under the same contract, means the date on which that term expires.*

> In *McMaster v. Manchester Airport plc* 1998 it was held that the effective date of termination cannot be earlier than the date on which the employee receives the knowledge that he is being dismissed.

In a resignation/constructive dismissal scenario the effective date of termination is the date that the decision to leave the employment is communicated.

> In *Edwards v. Surrey Police* 1999 the Employment Tribunal held that in a constructive dismissal scenario the effective date of termination was the date that the applicant had drafted her letter of resignation, the 17 July 1997. Accordingly when she presented her application alleging unfair dismissal on the 17 October she was time barred. On appeal the EAT held that the tribunal was wrong to decide that the effective date of termination was the date that the applicant had decided she no longer wished to work for the employer and drafted her letter of resignation. For a constructive dismissal the EAT thought that there must be a proper communication, by words or conduct, to the effect

10. 28 days
11. s.111 (4)

that the employment has terminated. Mr. Justice Morison said that *'before a contract can be terminated there must have been communication by words, or by conduct, such as to inform the other party to the contract that it is at an end. An employee alleging constructive dismissal therefore must communicate to the employer the fact that they are terminating their employment. It is not an infrequent occurrence that employees find their working life intolerable, walk out in a huff, but do not intend to bring their employment relationship to an end'.*

It seems that for a summary dismissal, whether or not in breach of contract, the effective date of termination is the date of dismissal.[12]

In *Stapp v. The Shaftesbury Society* 1982 the Court of Appeal held that the 'effective date of termination' means the actual date of termination of the employment whether or not the employee was wrongfully dismissed. Here the effect of a summary dismissal with wages paid in lieu of one month's notice was to make the effective date of dismissal the date of termination of employment and so the employee had insufficient continuous employment to bring a claim for unfair dismissal.

There is one exception to the rule that the effective date of termination is when the employee actually leaves work.

Under s.92(7) where the contact of employment is terminated by the employer and the notice required by section 86 to be given by the employer would, if duly given on the material date, expire on a date later than the effective date of termination the later date is the effective date of termination.

Section s.92(7) provides therefore that the effective date of termination can be extended beyond the date of dismissal if the employer has been dismissed wrongfully and denied his right to the minimum period of statutory notice under s.86.[13] In that case the effective date of termination is postponed to the date on which the statutory notice would have expired.

What then is the position when an employee is summarily dismissed for gross misconduct, with wages in lieu of notice? Is that sufficient to preclude the operation of s. 92(7) and so extend the effective date of termination by the statutory minimum notice to which the claimant is entitled under s.86.

In *Lanton Leisure Ltd. v. White and Gibson* 1987 the EAT thought not and held that simply to designate a dismissal as one for gross misconduct was not sufficient to prevent a claimant from extending the effective date of termination by the minimum notice period. It is for the tribunal to decide whether the alleged misconduct was sufficient to warrant summary dismissal.

In *Batchelor v. British Railways Board* 1987 the Court of Appeal held that a dismissal expressed to be 'with immediate effect' takes effect on that date even if it is in breach of a contractual disciplinary procedure. The effective date of termination is the date that the actual termination of the contract took place whether unlawful or not.

---

12. s.92 (1) b
13. See Chapter 10

In *Valeo Distribution (UK) Ltd. v. Barber* 1992 the applicant was a warehouseman who was summarily dismissed by his employer for poor time-keeping by a letter he received on the 20 July 1991. Having started work on the 7 August 1989 the first issue before the tribunal, and subsequently the EAT, was whether the applicant met the two year qualification period. The tribunal held that as the letter of dismissal did not allege gross misconduct to trigger summary dismissal the applicant was entitled to notice under s.86. This notice brought the effective date of termination forward so that he had qualified with two years service. On appeal the EAT referred to *Stapp v. Shaftesbury Society* which held that the effective date meant the actual date of termination and similarly held that *'it does not matter whether or not the notice of dismissal or dismissal without notice constituted a breach of contract the section operates irrespective of whether, as a matter of contract, the employer ought to have given some notice or a longer time'.* The letter brought the employment to an end on the 20 July which was the effective date of termination. While s.92(7) allows the effective date of termination to be extended in some cases by the statutory notice period, this would have only added one week to the applicants period of employment so that he would still be unable to qualify to claim unfair dismissal.

Finally it should be mentioned that the effective date of termination can be a date agreed expressly by the parties and the tribunal will accept that this is the relevant date. In *Lambert v. Croydon College* 1999 the effective date of termination was held to be the agreed date of termination rather than the date of the agreement and as a consequence a subsequent claim for unfair dismissal was time barred.

Reasonable Practicability

Section 111(2)(b) further provides that a tribunal may hear a complaint presented outside the time limits if it is satisfied that it was not reasonably practicable to present the claim in time. The exercise of this discretion by tribunals has been the issue in a number of cases. In *Palmer and Saunders v. Southend on Sea Borough Council* 1984 the Court of Appeal held that in construing the expression *'reasonably practicable'*, the best approach is to read 'practicable' as the equivalent of 'feasible' and to ask *'was it reasonably feasible to present the complaint to the industrial tribunal within the relevant three months'.* Also the court stressed that the issue is one of fact for the employment tribunal and it is seldom that an appeal from its decision will lie.

> In *St. Basil's Centre v. McCrossan* 1991 the application to complain of unfair dismissal was posted in Birmingham on Friday 19 May but did not arrive at the Central Office of Industrial Tribunals in London until Tuesday 23 May which was one day late. The EAT held that the tribunal could decide that it was not reasonably practicable for the complainant to be presented in time as the evidence suggested that the applicant could have expected the complaint to arrive within the time limit. *'Where an unfair dismissal application is posted within the three months time period but arrives after that period has expired, the question to be determined is whether the claimant would reasonably have expected the application to be delivered in time in the ordinary course of the post. This is a question of fact for the industrial tribunal to determine on the evidence.'*

Application to the tribunal can now be submitted on line.

In *Initial Electronic Security v. Advic* 2005 the application was transmitted 8 hours before the expiration of the time limit but despite appearing in the sent message folder it was not received. When this was discovered a week later the application was made in writing and hand delivered. The employment tribunal found that it was reasonable for the claimant to assume that her email would be received on the day it was sent and she had no reason to suspect or believe that the message and claim form had not been sent. As a result the tribunal held that it was not reasonably practicable to present her complaint before the three-month time limit expired. The EAT agreed applying the principle that the reasonable expectation of the sender of a claim form by post is that it will be received by the tribunal in the ordinary course of post. Also the reasonable expectation of the sender of an electronic mail communication is that, in the absence of any indication to the contrary, it will be delivered and will arrive within a very short time after transmission, normally 30 or 60 minutes.

The requirement that time limits must be complied with is a stringent one and solicitors representing complainants should take all reasonable steps that applications are presented in time and should *'employ some system of checking that replies which might reasonably be expected within certain periods have in fact been received and that the conduct of business is taking a normal course'.* In *Camden & Islington Community Services NHS Trust v. Kennedy* 1996 the cut off date was 27 December. The application was posted by a solicitor on the 19 December and on the 30 January the solicitors enquired by phone and were told the application had not been received. In reversing the tribunal's decision the EAT held that here the conduct of the solicitor was not sufficient to show that he took all steps that were reasonably practicable to comply with the time limits. *'A competent solicitor practising in this field must be taken to appreciate the vital importance of complying with time limits strictly and having in place a system designed to ensure that such limits are complied with at the time they are supposed to be complied with.'*

Where illness is used as a ground for not presenting a complaint within the limitation period the courts have suggested that a disabling illness which falls near the end of the period should carry more weight. So held the Court of Appeal in *Schultz v. Esso Petroleum* 1999 which overlooked the fact that the claimant was in a fit state to start proceedings during the earlier part of the limitation period. Usually it is not 'reasonably practicable' to present the complaint prematurely but rather attempt to avoid litigation by pursuing alternative remedies.

In some cases it could be argued that the reason for the delay in presenting the claim was due to the time involved in investigating facts which give rise to the belief that the dismissal is unfair.

> In *Churchill v. Yeates & Son Ltd.* 1983 the reason relied on by the employer for dismissal was redundancy, but subsequently the applicant discovered that someone else was doing his old job. In addition to alleging that the process of dismissal was unfair because of lack of consultation or warning, etc., the applicant presented his claim for unfair dismissal out of time when he discovered that someone else had been engaged to do his job. The tribunal ruled that as the claim of unfairness based on the true reason for dismissal was not related to unfairness due to the process of dismissal, it was reasonably practicable for the applicant to present his claim within the time limits. This somewhat harsh decision was reversed by the EAT who held that *'ignorance of a fact, the existence of which is fundamental to the right to claim unfair dismissal, can amount to circumstances which render it not reasonably practicable for a complaint of unfair*

dismissal to be presented within the three month limit'. This is the case even if there are other grounds which could have formed the basis of a timely complaint. Here the new factual allegation challenged the honesty and genuineness of the reason for dismissal given by the employer and was fundamental to the success or failure of the claim.

It does seem therefore that if a ground for presenting a complaint for unfair dismissal came to light outside the three month time limit, then provided the complaint is presented within a reasonable period thereafter it will not be time barred. The Court of appeal in *Marley (UK) Ltd. v. Anderson* 1996 confirmed that this is the case even where more than one ground for presenting a complaint is alleged. *'The questions posed by s.111(2)(6), reasonable practicability of presentation within time and the reasonableness of any subsequent period elapsing before presentation, are both matters to be weighed separately, ground by ground and fact by fact, under each head of unfair dismissal upon which a complaint or complaints is or are founded.'* New facts emerge which indicate a different reason for dismissal a complaint could still be made but only within a reasonable period and in *James W. Wood Ltd. v. Tipper* 1990 the Court of Appeal said that a delay of four weeks or more once the true facts had emerged should be regarded as longer than a reasonable period.

The fact that an applicant relied on bad advice from a skilled advisor was not an excuse to present a claim out of time.

> In *Riley v. Tesco Stores Ltd.* 1980 the reason that the dismissed employee put forward for not presenting an unfair dismissal claim within the three month period was that she had relied on the advice of a skilled advisor. Following a dismissal for alleged theft from her employer, she was advised by the Citizens Advice Bureau that she could not proceed with her complaint of unfair dismissal until after the criminal proceedings had run their course. Almost ten months after the effective date of termination, when she was acquitted of the charge against her, she presented a claim for unfair dismissal which both the tribunal and EAT held could not be heard as it was out of time. Having engaged a *'skilled advisor'* it was reasonably practicable for her to present the claim within the three month time limit. This decision was upheld by the Court of Appeal. The court found that if a claim is presented out of time due to ignorance of rights it is the role of the tribunal to consider the circumstances of the mistaken belief and any explanation for it, including advice taken, and then ask whether the ignorance or mistake is reasonable. If either the applicant or his skilled advisor was at fault, or unreasonable, then it was reasonably practicable to present the claim in time.

More recently there is evidence that tribunals should adopt a more user-friendly approach to late applications.

In *Marks & Spencer v. Williams-Ryan* 2005 The Court of Appeal felt that s.111(2) of the Employment Rights Act, should be given a liberal interpretation in favour of the employee. The court agreed with the tribunal that had held that the claimant's lack of knowledge of the three month rule in an unfair dismissal complaint meant that it was not reasonably practicable for her to present the claim within the time limits. By the time that she had exhausted the internal appeal process she was out of time and presented her application with a covering letter one month late. Other factors included the misleading advice that she had received from the Citizens Advice Bureau and her employer which, together with her lack of knowledge, convinced the tribunal to exercise it's discretion in her favour.

It should be stressed however that this case preceded the changes made to the rules on time limits by the Employment Act 2002 (Dispute Resolution) Procedures introduced in October 2004.[14]

Where redundancy is the reason relied on for dismissal and an employer subsequently appoints a replacement for the job in question, this may provide the complainant with evidence that this was not the true reason for dismissal.

> In *Machine Tool Research Association v. Simpson* 1988 the complainant, aware that staff reductions were planned, accepted the decision that she was dismissed by reason of redundancy. Subsequently, however, when she discovered that in fact she had been replaced, she had good reason to doubt that redundancy was the true reason for dismissal and presented a claim for unfair dismissal but, unfortunately, some three days outside the statutory three month time limit. Both the industrial tribunal and the EAT felt that the tribunal had jurisdiction to hear the complaint, as it had not been reasonably practicable for the applicant to present the claim in time. The Court of Appeal agreed and held that it was not reasonably practicable to present a complaint where during the three month limitation period there were crucial or important facts unknown to the applicant which subsequently become known and gives rise to a genuine belief that he may have a claim. To establish that it was not reasonably practicable to present the claim in time, the applicant must satisfy three stages of proof.

- It was reasonable for him not to be aware of the relevant fact which would help establish the claim.
- Knowledge of the fact has been reasonably gained in the circumstances and that knowledge is crucial in promoting the belief that the applicant may have a substantive claim.
- Acquisition of that knowledge must be crucial to the decision to bring a claim.

Statutory Dispute Resolution

Obviously it makes sense for employers and employees to resolve any conflict they may have informally without resorting to statutory procedures. If there is an issue relating to employee's poor performance[15] or bad behaviour then an informal discussion pointing out the required standards of behaviour[16] may be sufficient to resolve the issue. If however there is no resolution or the matter is a serious one, then it may be appropriate to call a formal meeting where both sides are heard and represented. The decision at such a meeting could be a formal or written warning for the employee. If the situation does not improve then the statutory procedures should be adopted with a view of dismissal.

The Employment Act 2000 and the Employment Act 2002 (Dispute Resolution) Regulations 2004 introduced new dispute resolution procedures that apply to all employers. The procedures are designed to encourage parties to avoid litigation by resolving differences through proper internal procedures and imposing sanctions if they do not. The aim is to encourage employers and employees to discuss problems openly before resorting to a

---

14. See next section
15. Capability
16. Misconduct

claim before a tribunal. They came into effect in October 2004 requiring employers to have procedures for dealing with disciplinary matters and employee grievances. There is a statutory obligation on employers to notify their staff as to the new rights and procedures. This could be done verbally, by email,[17] and on posters and notices. Notice should also be included in the s.1 statutory statement of particulars of employment.[18] Interestingly, s.30 of the Employment Act 2002 incorporates the statutory procedure into all contracts of employment as an implied term and it is not possible to contract out of this provision. Failure by an employer to comply with the requirement to devise a statutory procedure will therefore constitute a breach of contract for which an individual employee could seek redress.

The main aim is to discourage tribunal claims where the parties have not implemented the dispute resolution regulations. Under s.32 of the Act a complaint may not be made to a tribunal in relation to a matter to which the statutory grievance procedure applies, unless the employee has complied with step one of the grievance procedure or 28 days have not expired since the employee did so. This means that the tribunal will not accept an ET1 claim unless the employer has had a reasonable opportunity to respond to the perceived grievance. Failure to complete the grievance procedure due to the employee's fault will entitle the tribunal to reduce any compensatory award by between 10% and 50%. Section 32 will not apply to unfair dismissal claims where there is a threat of violence or serious personal harassment so as to make it dangerous to comply with step 1.[19] The requirements of the section will apply to cases of constructive dismissal where the employee walks out in response to the employer's repudiatory breach of contract. In those circumstances a step one grievance should be submitted.

Sections 29 to 34[20] and the 2004 Regulations set out the new statutory dispute resolution procedures and the consequences of failure to comply with them. One controversial point was to whom the new procedures would apply. Under Employment Act 2002[21] the statutory procedure applies to employees rather than the wider category of 'workers'.[22] There are two statutory dispute resolution procedures, a disciplinary procedure and a grievance procedure.[23] For both discipline and grievance there is a standard procedure and a modified procedure. The modified procedure is only intended to be used in cases of gross misconduct where there has already been a dismissal. The standard procedure has three steps and the modified procedure has two.

The standard dismissal and disciplinary procedure

Three steps are undertaken under the standard procedure.

1. The employer must provide a written statement identifying the perceived misconduct, the characteristics or circumstances that led it to contemplate disciplinary action or dismissal and then send it to the employee inviting him to respond at a meeting.

---

17. The intranet
18. See Chapter 4
19. Only in rare cases
20. Employment Act 2002
21. s.40
22. See Chapter 3
23. Schedule 2 Employment Act 2002

2. Except where there is disciplinary action in the form of a suspension, a meeting must take place before action is taken. Before the meeting the employee must have been informed of the allegations against him and given a chance to reflect and prepare a response. After the meeting the employer must inform the employee of the decision and rights of appeal if appropriate.

3. Despite any appeal the dismissal or disciplinary action can still be implemented before the appeal meeting. After the appeal the employer must inform the employee of its final decision.

While the standard procedure will apply in all circumstances including individual redundancies it will not apply to collective redundancies which are covered by s.188 of the Trade Union and Labour Relations Act 1992.[24] Also it is not appropriate for some collective or constructive dismissals and summary dismissals for gross misconduct where the modified procedure would be more appropriate.

The modified procedure

This procedure is intended to apply only to cases where the employee has already been dismissed for gross misconduct. There are two steps.

1. The employer is required to set out in writing the alleged misconduct, the evidence for suggesting that the employee is culpable and his right to appeal. This statement containing the reasons for dismissal must be sent to the employee also informing him of his rights to appeal.

2. If the employee wishes to appeal against the decision he must inform the employer and an appeal meeting must be held which be should attend. After the appeal meeting the employer must inform the employee of its decision.

The procedure that applies therefore either standard or modified will depend upon the employer's decision to dismiss rather than the nature of the employees misconduct.

The standard grievance procedure

An employee who believes that he has a grievance that has not been resolved should follow the standard grievance procedure. It applies if an employee is aggrieved about action that the employer has taken against him that does not involve his capability or conduct. A grievance is defined in the regulations as a complaint by an employee about action which his employer has taken or is contemplating taking in relation to him. Relevant matters for grievance procedures include: complaints about the conduct of work colleagues; warnings and investigatory processes; potential detrimental or repudiatory conduct by the employer which could lead to constructive dismissal. Even where there is a dismissal, if the employee has a grievance about notice or accrued holiday payments they should follow the modified grievance procedure.

Schedule 2 of the Employment Act 2002 sets out the statutory grievance procedures and again there are two forms the standard procedure and the modified procedure when a dismissal has already occurred.

---

24. See Chapter 12

Once again the standard procedure has three steps.

1. The employee must set out the grievance and the basis for the grievance in writing and send it to the employer.

2. Having had a reasonable period to consider its response the employer must invite the employee to a meeting to discuss the grievance and the employee should attend. The decision of the meeting must be communicated to the employee and the rights of appeal.

3. If an appeal is requested it must go ahead with a further meeting the decision of which must be communicated to the employee.

A number of recent cases have been reported which assist in the interpretation of the Regulations

In *Shergold v. Fieldway Medical Centre* 2006 the EAT has provided some helpful guidance as to what would constitute a valid step one grievance letter. Here the claimant wrote a three page letter setting out her reasons for resigning. She did not ask for it to be treated as a grievance but nevertheless the employer invited her to a meeting to discuss the issues. The tribunal held that this did not amount to a step one grievance letter but was simply a resignation letter. The EAT disagreed and held that there is no formality in a statutory standard grievance letter. The requirements are minimal and all that an employee needs to do is to set out her complaint in writing for step 1. It is at step 2 that the basis for the grievance should be clarified and so the original setting out of the grievance is not required to be so particularised. It is not necessary to make it plain in the written document that it is a grievance, or is an invocation of a grievance procedure. The statutory procedures should rarely debar a complaint or even result in an employer being liable for automatic unfair dismissal. Burton P said '*the danger is obvious that the kind of pernickety criticism of the form or content of the writing exemplified here can result in an employee being barred from the judgment seat entirely*'.

In *Galaxy Showers v. Wilson* 2006 the claimant had sent a letter to his manager complaining that he had been given a verbal warning about his conduct without any proper investigation or formal disciplinary proceedings. The EAT agreed with the tribunal that the letter of resignation contained a statement of his grievance against the employer for the purposes of step 1. Here the substance of the claimant's grievance was his objection to being put through a disciplinary process which was not appropriate. The EAT felt that in any case in which '*the substance of the complaint has been raised and in which there has been subsequent discussion about the complaint, it is likely that the statutory requirements will have been fulfilled*'.

Finally in *Mark Warner Ltd. v. Aspland* 2006 the EAT confirmed that it is irrelevant that the grievance letter deals with other matters, it may still satisfy the requirements of step 1. Also the action taken could be by the employee's agent[25] and the employee does not have to send the letter personally. Here a letter from the employee's solicitor complaining that the employers had failed to accept the findings of an earlier tribunal and that the claimant had been bullied and discriminated against fulfilled the statutory requirement.

---

25. A solicitor

Modified grievance procedure

The modified procedure applies when the dismissal has already occurred and has two stages.

1. The employer must set out the grievance in writing and send it to the employer.
2. The employer must set out its response in writing and send it to the employee. Grievances which could arise in relation to the termination of employment could relate to payments due in relation to notice, holiday pay or even redundancy.

A draconian sanction is to be imposed on employers who dismiss and fail to comply with the statutory procedures. Under the Employment Act 2002[26] a new section 98A(1) is inserted into the Employment Rights Act, under which an employee is to be regarded as automatically unfairly dismissed if the statutory disciplinary procedures apply to the dismissal and the procedure has not been completed due to the failure of the employer. Unlike other cases of automatic unfair dismissal the employee will have to fulfill the usual qualifying period of one years continuous service.

While under the Act the failure to comply with the statutory disciplinary procedure can make the dismissal automatically unfair, it also inserts s.98A(2) into the Employment Rights Act 1996 which provides that failure by an employer to follow a procedure in the dismissal of an employee shall not be regarded by itself as making the employer's action unreasonable if the employer shows that it would have dismissed the employee even if the procedure had been followed. This means that the failure to follow a procedure other than the statutory procedure will not in itself make the dismissal unfair.

In *Perkin v. St. George's Healthcare NHS Trust* 2005 the EAT confirmed that even where there is a finding of unfair dismissal because of procedural impropriety, the tribunal can apply the principle in *Polkey v. Dayton Services* and reduce the compensation payable because of the claimant's contributory fault. Here the tribunal felt that there was a 100% chance that the claimant's employment would have terminated if a fair procedure had been adopted and his compensatory award would be reduced accordingly. Now following s.98A, the impact or the *Polkey* principle is diminished. If under s.98A the employee is dismissed and the employer fails to follow the statutory procedure in full, and it is not the employee's fault, the dismissal is automatically unfair and the employee is entitled to a minimum of four weeks pay as compensation. Section 98A also provides that if an employer fails to comply with any additional part of its own procedure in relation to the dismissal, this will no longer be regarded, by itself, as making the employer's action unreasonable if it can be shown that he would have been dismissed in any event.

The *Perkin* interpretation means that the *Polkey* reduction can only apply if the employer fails to follow the minimum statutory procedure, but not it's own, and fails to show on the balance of probabilities that the dismissal was inevitable because there is a chance that the employee would have been dismissed in any event.

The Act also contains general requirements in relation to all statutory procedures, emphasising that there should be no unreasonable delays with open and accessible meetings.[27] A meeting also constitutes a hearing for the purposes of s.10 of the Employment Relations

---

26. s.34(2)
27. Schedule 2

Act 1999 so that a worker may be accompanied in a disciplinary or grievance meeting if the worker reasonably requests to be represented.

In *Skiggs v. South West Trains* 2005 The claimant was asked to attend an interview with his manager investigating a grievance but he refused to do so without appropriate representation. He was told that he was not entitled to representation because it was only an investigatory interview, not a disciplinary hearing. The tribunal found that the meeting inquiring into the grievance against the claimant was not a 'disciplinary hearing' within the meaning of s.13(4) of the Employment Rights Act, which provides that: 'For the purposes of s.10 of the Employment Relations Act a disciplinary hearing is a hearing which could result in – (a) the administration of a formal warning to a worker by his employer; (b) the taking of some other action in respect of a worker by his employer; or (c) the confirmation of a warning issued or some other action taken.' The tribunal rejected the argument that the interview fell within that definition because it might lead to some further disciplinary process which, in light of his record, could lead to some action of a disciplinary nature against him. The EAT agreed with the tribunal that the interview remained at all times an investigative interview and that there was therefore no right to representation. *'Whether a discussion or meeting between management and a worker takes on the character of a "disciplinary hearing" within the meaning of s.13(4) of the Employment Rights Act, so as to give rise to the right to be accompanied, depends on the nature of the meeting itself and not on the description either or both parties attach to it, or its possible consequences.'* The EAT accepted that an interview which starts out as a preliminary factual inquiry may be transformed at some point into a disciplinary hearing. Whether that point of transformation has been reached must be a question of fact and degree in each individual case for the tribunal of fact hearing it to make. In the present case, the tribunal was entitled to conclude on the evidence before it that the interview remained at all times an investigative hearing.

If an employer fails to comply with a relevant statutory procedure then the tribunal has jurisdiction[28] to adjust a compensation award as a sanction. An adjustment would be relevant when the claim concerns a matter to which a statutory procedure applies and it was not completed before the proceedings were commenced. This non completion could be due to a failure by the employer or the employee so that an award could be adjusted up or down by between 10% and 50%. In exceptional cases an adjustment of less than 10% could be made. The right to adjust the award should be applied before any other adjustment is made to an award.

The legal process of pursuing a complaint of unfair dismissal before a tribunal was considered in Chapter 2. A copy of the ET1 and ET3 having been sent to ACAS, a conciliation officer is appointed to get in touch with both parties in an attempt to resolve the conflict over a fixed period and reach an amicable settlement. It should be stressed that in many cases an agreement is reached because of the intervention of the conciliation officer. While he is under a statutory duty to endeavour to promote a voluntary settlement of the complaint by encouraging an agreement to reinstate the employee, or make a payment of compensation, there is no requirement for the parties to co-operate or even communicate with him.[29]

If following case management the claim proceeds to a full hearing, the burden of proof is on the claimant to show that he has been dismissed unless that is conceded. The various

---

28. Under s.31
29. 42% of cases settled in 2003

forms of dismissal under s.95 and the alternative means by which a contract of employment may be brought to an end were examined earlier in Chapter 10.

Having established that a dismissal has occurred, it then falls to the tribunal to determine the reason for dismissal, whether it is a reason categorised in the Employment Rights Act 1996 and, if so, whether the dismissal is fair or unfair and redress where appropriate. In this chapter therefore in order to appreciate the process by which a claim of unfair dismissal is determined it is necessary to consider:

- the reason for dismissal;
- whether the reason constitutes a statutory reason;
- the various tests of substantive and procedural fairness; and
- the potential redresss.

Reason for Dismissal

To assist in a claim for unfair dismissal, the claimant is entitled, following a written request, to be provided by the employer with the reason or reasons for dismissal.

> *Under s.92(1) An employee is entitled to be provided by his employer with a written statement giving particulars of the reasons for the employee's dismissal:*
>
> (a) *if the employee is given by the employer notice of termination of his contract of employment;*
>
> (b) *if the employee's contract of employment is terminated by the employer without notice; or*
>
> (c) *if the employee is employed under a contract for a fixed term and, that term expires without being renewed under the same contract.*

This right applies therefore when there is an express dismissal or dismissal by reason of the expiration of a limited term contract which is not renewed. An employee who alleges constructive dismissal has no right to a written statement. To trigger the right the employee must request the statement in writing and it should be provided within fourteen days. Under s.92 (4) there is no need to make such a request if the dismissal occurs while the employee is pregnant or after childbirth.[30]

The written statement provided under this section is important evidence of the employer's reason or reasons for dismissal. The period of continuous employment to qualify for this statutory right is one year.[31] Following the Employment Protection (Part-Time Employees) Regulations 1995 the right applies to part-time employees regardless of their hours of work. If an employer unreasonably fails to comply with a request the employee may present a complaint to the tribunal.[32] The tribunal may declare the reasons for dismissal and also compensate the employee with an award of two weeks' wages if it finds that the claim is well founded. Originally the section provided that the claimant had to show that the employer also unreasonably refused to provide a statement. This is no longer a requirement.[33]

---

30. Including maternity or adoption leave
31. Under s.92(3)
32. Under s.93(1)
33. Since 1993

In *Kent County Council v. Gilham and Others* 1985 the Court of Appeal held that following a request for a statement of the reason for dismissal, it is acceptable for an employer to make a response which refers to earlier communications. That is, providing the covering letter specifically refers to the earlier communication, and it does contain the reason or reasons for dismissal.

The purpose of the statutory right to compel the employer to supply the employee with the reason or reasons relied on for dismissal is to enable the employee to scrutinise them in advance of the proceedings and also to tie the employer down to that reason in any subsequent proceedings. The Act requires an employer to state truthfully the reason that he was relying on in dismissing the employee so that the employee does not start with the disadvantage of not knowing the reason for dismissal if he wishes to pursue a claim for unfair dismissal.

In *Harvard Securities plc v. Younghusband* 1990 the EAT held that whether or not the employer is telling the truth in identifying the ground relied upon does not involve an examination of the justification for the dismissal. Here the tribunal had held that as the written reason referred to divulging confidential information, it was untrue under because the information in question could not in any sense be regarded as confidential. This, the EAT decided, was the wrong approach. *'There is no need under the section to embark upon a consideration of whether the reason was intrinsically a good, bad or indifferent one ... whether the employees were correct in describing the information in question as 'confidential' was irrelevant to the identification of the reason upon which they relied for dismissing the employee.'*

In *Catherine Haigh Harlequin Hair Design v. Seed* 1990 it was held that an employment tribunal has no jurisdiction to hear a complaint that the employer has not provided a dismissed employee with a statement of the particulars of the reason for dismissal unless there has been a request by the employee for the particulars.

Statutory Reasons for Dismissal

The formal burden of proof on the claimant in an unfair dismissal complaint is to establish the fact of dismissal under s.95 whether express, implied or constructive. It is then the turn of the respondent employer to show that the reason for dismissal falls within the Statute. If the claimant is relying upon an inadmissible reason for dismissal such as pregnancy then it is the claimant who must establish the reason for dismissal. The heart of unfair dismissal law is contained in s.98, and it is to this section we must devote some attention.

Under s.98 (1) In determining for the purposes of this Part whether the dismissal of an employee was fair or unfair, it shall be for the employer to show:

    (a) what was the reason or, if there was more than one, the principal reason for the dismissal; and

    (b) that it was a reason falling within subsection (2) or some other substantial reason of a kind such as to justify the dismissal of an employee holding the position which that employee held.

(2) In subsection (1)(b) the reference to a reason falling within this subsection is a reference to a reason which:

    (a) related to the capability or qualifications of the employee for performing work of the kind which he was employed by the employer to do, or

(b) *related to the conduct of the employee, or*

(c) *was that the employee was redundant, or*

(d) *was that the employee could not continue to work in the position which he held without contravention (either on his part or on that of his employer) of a duty or restriction imposed by or under an enactment.*

Under the section therefore it clearly states that it is the employer who must show the reason or principal reason for the dismissal[34], and that the reason falls within one of the four categories of admissible reasons identified in s. 98(2) or is a substantial reason under s. 98(1) of a kind such as to justify the dismissal of an employee holding the position which that employee held. If the employee establishes the true reason for dismissal, and that it falls within one of the five admissible statutory reasons,[35] then the dismissal will be declared to be prima facie[36] fair. The final determination of fairness is achieved by applying the test of reasonableness contained in s. 98(4).

If the claimant alleges an inadmissible automatically unfair reason for dismissal then if he has less than one years continuous employment he will need to establish the jurisdiction if the tribunal is to hear the complaint. The burden of proof would in those circumstances be on the claimant to establish that the reason for dismissal falls within an inadmissible category such as pregnancy, trade union membership or linked to health and safety etc. Inadmissible reasons for dismissal have grown dramatically in recent years as they are attached to new employment rights such as the minimum wage. We will consider them later in the chapter.

Guidance in relation to the application of s.98 was provided by Lord Bridge in *West Midlands Cooperatives Society v. Tipton* 1986, who said that there are three questions which must be asked in determining whether a dismissal is fair or unfair.

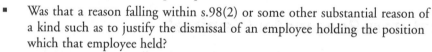

- What was the reason (or principal reason) for the dismissal?
- Was that a reason falling within s.98(2) or some other substantial reason of a kind such as to justify the dismissal of an employee holding the position which that employee held?
- Did the employer act reasonably or unreasonably in treating that reason as a sufficient reason for dismissing the employees for the purpose of s.98(4)?

The burden of proving, on the balance of probabilities, the real reason for dismissal, and that it is a statutory reason falling within s.98, is upon the employer. Failure to establish this true reason may make the decision to dismiss unfair.

In *Timex Corporation v. Thomson* 1981, the complainant, a long serving manager, was selected for redundancy following a re-organisation of managerial posts. The reasons for his selection were lack of engineering qualifications and unsatisfactory job performance. The tribunal concluded that the true reason for his dismissal was not redundancy but incompetence, and held the dismissal to be unfair. The EAT confirmed that the tribunal was entitled to find that they were not satisfied that the employer had put forward the true reason for dismissal. *'Even where there is a redundancy situation it is possible for an employer to use such*

34. Under s.98(1)a
35. Identified in s.98
36. On the face of it

a situation as a pretext for getting rid of an employee he wishes to dismiss. In such circumstances the reason for dismissal will not be redundancy.' Here the employer had not satisfied the burden cast by the section and so the dismissal was consequently unfair.

Clearly then if the tribunal is convinced that the reason put forward by the employer is not the true reason that was in his mind at the time of the dismissal, then it is entitled at this stage to decide that the dismissal is unfair.

> In *Price v. Gourley* 1973 the complainant worked in a cake shop and, after seven years' service, received top wages for her grade. She was dismissed and when she asked for a reason was told by the manager that it was *'just one of those things'.* At the tribunal the employer alleged that the reason was incompetence, but as he failed to show any deterioration in her work it did seem unreasonable that it was seven years before he took any action. The true reason for dismissal the tribunal held was simply that the employer was attempting to reduce overheads by replacing a well-paid employee with a junior on lower pay. As the alleged reason was not the true reason, and cost cutting was not a reason falling within the statute, the dismissal was consequently unfair.

If an employer decides not to rely on a justifiable reason for dismissal and rather chooses to put forward another reason that proves to be unjustifiable, then the result may be a finding of unfair dismissal. Ironically the fact that the employer could have relied on a valid reason to dismiss will not prevent a tribunal from making an award of compensation if the dismissal is found to be unfair.

> In *Trico-Folberth Ltd. v.Devonshire* 1989 the employer decided on compassionate grounds to withdraw a dismissal by reason of poor attendance and substitute instead a dismissal on the grounds of medical unfitness. While the original reason was perfectly justifiable the dismissal on the ground of a medical condition was unfair because of the failure of the employer to investigate and consult. The Court of Appeal confirmed that the dismissal was unfair, and whether or not the employer could have dismissed for another justifiable reason would not affect the amount of compensation awarded.

If a number of allegations are put forward in support of the reason for dismissal it is important that they are all established by the evidence.

> In *Smith v. City of Glasgow DC* 1987 the tribunal considered a number of complaints against the applicant challenging his competence and capability and despite its ruling that one significant complaint had not been established the tribunal held that the decision to dismiss was fair. Following subsequent appeals to the EAT and the Court of Session, the House of Lords eventually found for the applicant and ruled that the tribunal's decision disclosed an error of law. The court held that *'as a matter of law a reason cannot be treated as sufficient reason for dismissal where it has not been established as true or that there were reasonable grounds upon which the employer could have concluded that it was true'.* Here as the unsubstantiated reason had formed part of the reason for dismissal the decision to dismiss was as a consequence unfair.

Having decided the true reason for dismissal it is then necessary for the employer to establish that it falls within one of the four statutory reasons contained in s.98(2) or is some other substantial reason of a kind to justify dismissal under s.98(1). In practice it is rare for an employer to fail to show that the reason is categorised in the Act, so that the reason will in most cases be prima facie fair. The crucial issue is whether the reason relied on satisfies the test of substantive and procedural fairness in s. 98(4).

Potentially Fair Reasons for Dismissal

It is a question of legal analysis to determine which part of s.98 the reason given by the employer falls into. An error of characterisation of the reason by the Employment Tribunal can be rectified by the EAT on appeal, but only in exceptional cases.

In *Wilson v. Post Office* 2000 the employer had stated the reason for dismissal as *'incapability'* by reason of unsatisfactory attendance record. The Employment Tribunal wrongly found that to be a reason falling within s.98(2)(a) relying on the word capability. Both the EAT and the Court of Appeal held that as the reason for dismissal related to the applicant's attendance record it fell within s.98(1)(b) as *'some other substantial reason'*. The Court of Appeal stressed however that even if the tribunal proceeded upon an incorrect basis the appellate body should only rarely interfere with its decision making. *'Only in an extreme case, one that is very clear, will it be possible for an appellate body properly to say that an employment tribunal would inevitably have reached a particular conclusion when in the original case, albeit proceeding upon an incorrect basis, the employment tribunal had come to the contrary conclusion. An employment tribunal is not merely a fact finding body, it is an industrial jury. This is not merely a phrase but a concept that has to be taken seriously.'*

The fact that an employer relies upon the wrong statutory reason is not fatal to the employer's defence as the tribunal may substitute the more appropriate statutory reason. In *Pay v. Lancashire Probation Service* 2004 the applicant probation officer was dismissed for his inappropriate sexual activities of a public nature. While the employer advanced misconduct[37] as the reason for dismissal the tribunal held that it was for some other substantial reason.[38]

In *Perkin v. St. George's Healthcare NHS Trust* 2005[39] the claimant was dismissed for a reason related to his personality and brought an unfair dismissal claim against the Trust. The Court of Appeal considered the decision of the tribunal to catergorise the dismissal of the claimant NHS Trust finance director because of his manner and management style as being for a reason relating to his 'conduct' within the meaning of s.98(2)(b) rather than for 'some other substantial reason' within s.98(1)(b). The court concluded that that the *'tribunal's failure to categorise the reason properly was not fatal to its reasoning or to the safety of its decision'.* In the present case, there was material on which the tribunal could find that the claimant could not work harmoniously with his colleagues and, therefore, whilst it would have been preferable if the tribunal had analysed the case as falling within some other substantial reason rather than conduct, the tribunal was entitled to conclude that the employers had a potentially fair reason to dismiss him.

---

37. Under s.98(2)b
38. Under s.98(1)
39. See later in the chapter

Capability or qualification[40]

For the purposes of this reason *'capability'* is assessed by reference to *skill, aptitude, health or any other physical or mental quality*.[41] The majority of cases where capability is the reason relied upon relate to incompetence or ill health. Where an allegation of incompetence is established through evidence, in determining the reasonableness of the employer's decision to dismiss for the purposes of substantive fairness it is also necessary to examine the reasons for the alleged incompetence.[42] This could involve a consideration of the employer's appraisal processes, the amount of training and supervision required, and the extent to which employees are given the opportunity to improve their performance. Obviously there are degrees of incompetence, but even one serious lapse could be sufficient to justify a dismissal.

> In *Taylor v. Alidair Ltd.* 1978 the applicant pilot was dismissed when as a result of an error of judgment, the passenger plane he was flying landed so hard that serious damage was caused to the plane. The Court of Appeal held that *'the company has reasonable grounds for honestly believing that the applicant was not competent'*. As a result of this serious act of incompetence the belief was reasonably held, and the dismissal was consequently a fair one.

If incapability is alleged, due to the ill health of the employee, once again reasonableness of the employer's decision to dismiss must be viewed by the extent to which it is an informed judgment bearing in mind the various options available. Earlier in Chapter 10 we considered the extent to which a long illness can amount to a frustration of the contract of employment.

> In *Links and Co. Ltd. v. Rose* 1991 the reason for dismissal was capability related to ill health. The Court of Session re-emphasised that an employer reaching a decision to dismiss in those circumstances must act reasonably for the dismissal to be fair. *'Therefore, in deciding whether an employer acted fairly or unfairly in dismissing an employee on grounds of ill health, an industrial tribunal must determine as a matter of fact and judgment what consultation, if any, was necessary or desirable in the known circumstances of the particular case; and whether or not that consultation process was adequate in all the circumstances. If it was not adequate, the dismissal will be unfair.'*

If an employee is permanently unfit for work due to a medical condition, provided the employer has carried out a thorough investigation the illness could constitute a fair reason for dismissal. Of course there could now be a requirement to consider a reasonable adjustment under the Disability Discrimination Act 1995.[43]

> In *London Fire & Civil Defence Authority v. Betty* 1994 the claimant was retired from the fire service on medical grounds when he suffered a nervous breakdown. The tribunal found that the dismissal was unfair because the reason for the complainant's condition was the treatment he received from his employer. The EAT took a different view however and found the dismissal to be fair. *'An employer does not disable himself from fairly dismissing an employee whom he has*

---

40. Under s.98(2)a
41. Under s.98(3)
42. See later s.98(4)
43. See Chapter 6

> *injured. The employer's duty to act fairly in dismissing an employee on the grounds of ill health is unaffected by consideration as to who was responsible for the employee's unfitness for work. The question is whether the dismissal was fair having regard to the employee's medical condition and the enquiries and procedures which the employer made and used before deciding to dismiss.'*

If the reason for dismissal is related to 'qualifications' of the employee this is taken to mean *'any degree, diploma or other academic, technical or professional qualification relevant to the position which the employee held'.*

> In *Blackman v. The Post Office* 1974 the employee was recruited for a particular job on an unestablished basis. A collective agreement provided that such employees' employment should only be continued if the employee passed a written aptitude test. Despite showing aptitude for the job, the employee failed the test three times. The tribunal held that either capability or qualification could be a ground relied on for a fair dismissal.

There is no doubt however that *'qualification'* has in mind matters relating to aptitude or ability so that a mere licence permit or authorisation is not such a qualification, unless it is substantially concerned with the aptitude or ability of the person to do the job.

> In *Tayside Regional Council v. McIntosh* 1982 the loss of a valid driving licence when the employee is contractually obliged to have one was held to be substantially connected with his ability to do the job and fair reason for dismissal.

Misconduct[44]

Misconduct as a reason for dismissal covers a wide range of circumstances including such matters as lateness, absenteeism, insubordination, breach of safety rules and immorality. Of course the gravity of the misconduct, and the steps taken by the employer to address it, are crucial factors in determining whether the decision to dismiss for misconduct is a reasonable one or not.[45] Misconduct at work is not a new concept has been held to include:

- breach of exclusivity and trust and confidence - *Scottish Daily Record and Sunday Mail v. Laird* 1996;
- stealing from the employer – *Trust House Forte Hotels v. Murphy* 1977;
- a breach of safety instructions – *Wilcox v. Humphries & Glasgow* 1976;
- refusal to obey reasonable instructions – *Atkin v. Enfield HMC* 1975;
- refusal to stop wearing a provocative badge – *Boychuk v. Symons Holdings* 1977;
- immorality – *Wiseman v. Salford City Council* 1981;
- drunkenness – *Connely v. Liverpool City Council* 1974; and
- absenteeism – *Hutchinson v. Enfield Rolling Mills Ltd.* 1981.

Even misconduct outside of work could be classified under this head as the reason for dismissal, and provided the misconduct has some impact on the employee's job, the dismissal could be justified.

---

44. Under s.98(2)b
45. See later s.98(4)

In *P v. Nottinghamshire County Council* 1992 the claimant was dismissed from his job as assistant groundsman when he was convicted of an offence of indecent assault against his own daughter who was a pupil at the school where he worked. The Court of Appeal confirmed that the employer was entitled to take the view that the employee could not continue in employment which brought him into even casual contact with young girls.

Certainly, for private conduct to be used as the reason for dismissal it has to be of exceptional gravity and capable of damaging the employee's business.

In *Pay v. Lancashire Probation Service* 2004 a probation officer working with sex offenders was dismissed after his employers, a public body, discovered that he was involved in activities including the merchandising of products connected with bondage, domination and sado-masochism and that he performed shows in hedonist and fetish clubs. Photographs of him involved in acts of bondage, domination and sado-masochism were available on the internet. The employers took the view that these activities were incompatible with his role and responsibilities as a probation officer. Mr. Pay complained that his dismissal was unfair in that it entailed an infringement of the Human Rights Act. The EAT held that the employment tribunal had not erred in holding that dismissal of the applicant did not constitute an infringement of his rights under the Human Rights Act to respect for his private life and to freedom of expression.[46]

Misconduct is of course the most prevalent reason put forward by employers in complaints of unfair dismissal and it will be considered in some depth in relation to the issue of fairness.

Redundancy[47]

The employer may show that the reason for dismissal was that the employee was redundant. Essentially a redundancy situation arises when an employer closes part or all of his business operation, the purposes for which the employee was employed, or alternatively the requirements of the business for workers of a particular kind have ceased or diminished. The interpretation of the complex definition of redundancy is explored in some depth in Chapter 12 on redundancy payments. You will see that as a result of the House of Lords decision in *Murray v. Foyle Meat* 1999 it is much easier for an employee to establish that redundancy was the reason for dismissal. For the purposes of unfair dismissal however, not only must the dismissal be by reason of redundancy but the selection of the employee in question must also be fair.[48] Consequently if in a redundancy selection the employer failed to observe agreed industrial practice, this could render a decision to dismiss on grounds of redundancy unfair. The fairness of a decision to dismiss by reason of redundancy is examined in Chapter 12. The redundancy reason envisages a potentially fair dismissal despite the fact that the employee is not at fault.

---

46. See Chapter 1
47. s.98(2)c
48. Under s.98(4)

Employment in contravention of the law[49]

For the purposes of this limited category it must be shown that it would be illegal to continue to employ the employee in question. A good example is where driving is an integral part of the employee's work and he is disqualified from driving, for example *Fearn v. Tayford Motor Company Ltd.* 1975. As usual the reasonableness of the employer's decision to dismiss must be viewed in the light of the particular circumstance, not least the availability of alternative work.

> In *Gill v. Walls Meat Company Ltd.* 1971 to have continued to employ the complainant, who worked on an open meat counter would have infringed Food Regulations, for he had grown a beard. After refusing to shave it off and also an offer of alternative work, the tribunal held that the decision to dismiss was a fair one.

Some other substantial reason[50]

This final category of reason is used to include reasons for dismissal which do not fall neatly into the previous categories. Of course it is not every *other reason* which will be included within s.98(1)b so that the dismissal in *Price v. Gourley* 1973[51] for a cost cutting exercise was held not to be a reason of a substantial kind to justify the dismissal for the purposes of s.98(1)b. Nevertheless the approach seems to be that if the employer puts forward a genuine reason, which he honestly believes to be substantial, it will fall in this category. It would be permissible for an employer to require his staff to accept change for economic considerations and this could lead to a dismissal for some other substantial reason.

In *Perkin v. St. George's Healthcare NHS Trust* 2005 the Court of Appeal felt that a dismissal on the grounds of the claimant's personality should be catergorised as for some other substantial reason rather than on the grounds of misconduct. '*Although "personality" of itself cannot be a ground for dismissal, an employee's personality may manifest itself in such a way as to bring the actions of the employee within s.98. Whether, on the facts of a particular case, the manifestations of an individual's personality result in conduct which can fairly give rise to the employee's dismissal, or whether they give rise to some other substantial reason of a kind such as to justify the dismissal of an employee holding the position which the employee held, the employer has to establish the facts which justify the reason or principal reason for the dismissal.*' Here while there was no evidence of any failure in the claimant's competence, many colleagues and external agents had difficulty with his manner and management style.[52]

> A clash of personalities in the office was held to be a substantial reason of a kind to justify dismissal in *Treganowan v. Robert Knee & Company Ltd.* 1975. Here the complainant was dismissed because the atmosphere in the office where she worked had become so hostile that it was seriously affecting the employer's business. The prime cause of the trouble was the complainant, whose constant reference to her private life seriously upset her colleagues who felt that they could not work with her.

---

49. s.98(2)d
50. s.98(1)b
51. See earlier
52. See later in the chapter

If the reason for dismissal is related to unacceptable periods of absence because of illness then s.98(1) may be relied on as the reason for dismissal.

> In *Wharfedale Loudspeakers Ltd. v. Poynton* 1993 the complainant was eventually dismissed after having been given three written warnings in relation to her long periods of absence due to genuine illness. The EAT held that in these circumstances some other substantial reason could be relied on as the reason for dismissal which was potentially fair.

Certainly the refusal of an employee to accept an alteration in terms of employment has been held to fall within this category. In *St. John of God (Care Services) Ltd. v. Brooks* 1992 the EAT held that a reorganisation in a hospital which involved offering staff less favourable terms of employment fell within the category of some other substantial reason for dismissal when some staff were dismissed for failing to accept changes in their contracts of employment.[53] In *Ellis v. Brighton Cooperative Society* 1976 the applicant was dismissed for refusing to accept a new working system following a reorganisation. The EAT held that *'where there has been a properly consulted-upon reorganisation which, if it is not done, is going to bring the whole business to a standstill, a failure to go along with the new arrangements may constitute "some other substantial reason"'*. Here the employer had acted reasonably in requiring that all the staff should co-operate with the change in working methods.[54] In *Copsey v. WWB Devon Clays Ltd.* 2005 the Court of Appeal agreed that the employer had compelling economic reasons for requiring that the employees accept a change in hours and they had done everything that they reasonably could to accommodate the claimant who objected to Sunday working.

If an employee is employed under a fixed term contract which expires then this will constitute a dismissal for the purposes of the Act.[55] A complaint of unfair dismissal could be made if such an employee is unfairly rejected when applying for a new post involving broadly similar duties. In such circumstances it would be wrong to limit the application of the test of fairness[56] s.98(4) to the act of dismissal but rather the fairness of the decision not to select for the new job should also be judged. In *Oakley v. The Labour Party* 1988 the claimant was told that when her fixed term contract expired it would not be renewed and that following a re-organisation she could apply for a new post, which involved a broadly similar job. She complained of unfair dismissal when she was not selected for the new post. The Court of Appeal held that her interview for the new job was no more than a charade, for the employer had clearly decided beforehand that she should not be appointed. Restructuring was merely a pretext to get rid of the complainant and so, inevitably, the employer's conduct was unreasonable and unfair.

In rare cases the pressure on an employer to dismiss an employee comes from some third party source such as a trade union, customers or clients and even fellow employees. They may claim that the employee has been guilty of some objectionable conduct, that there is an insoluble personality conflict, or that the reason for the pressure is based upon some rational or irrational fear of HIV contagion. In this type of case the employer could rely on some other substantial reason as the reason for dismissal. The issue of fairness of a dismissal in these circumstances will depend largely on the conduct of the employer who should have made practical and genuine efforts to resolve the conflict. The circumstances should be

---

53. See Chapter 5
54. See Chapter 5
55. Under s.95(1)b
56. Under s.98(4)

investigated and there should be consultation with the parties concerned with a view to reaching a solution. The employers should consider solutions other than dismissal, for instance, a relocation of work. Dismissal under third party pressure is only fair if after investigation there is a valid and serious complaint or the goodwill of a third party is so important that dismissal is the only sensible commercial decision.

> In *Courtaulds Northern Spinning Ltd. v. Sibson* 1988 the third party pressure came from the TGWU who wanted the complainant an HGV driver dismissed, or moved to another depot, when he left the union. The complainant refused the employer's instruction to move to another depot a mile away and resigned, claiming a constructive dismissal which was unfair. Both the tribunal and the EAT found that there was unfair dismissal but the Court of Appeal disagreed deciding that the employer had an implied right to move the complainant from one depot to another, within reasonable commuting distance, and the reason for the move was irrelevant. Accordingly there was no breach of contract by the employer and therefore no constructive dismissal.

A decision to dismiss based purely on economic considerations could constitute *some other substantial reason* and fall within the band of reasonable responses of a reasonable employer.

> In *Saunders v. Scottish National Camps* 1980 the complainant, a handyman employed at a children's holiday camp, was dismissed when the employer discovered that he was a homosexual. The reason for dismissal was that the employee indulged in homosexuality and it was unsuitable to employ someone of that tendency in children's camps. Both the tribunal and the EAT found the dismissal to be fair. They decided that a large proportion of employers in this situation would perceive that the employment of a homosexual should be restricted where there is close contact with children. This is despite the fact that such a view may not be rational, or supported by evidence which is scientifically sound. There is no doubt however that the continued employment could have proved to be an economic liability for the employer, bearing in mind the views of certain parents.[57]

The Test of Fairness

Once the employer has shown that the principal reason for dismissal is prima facie fair it is then necessary for the tribunal to determine the heart of the issue, whether the employer acted reasonably in the circumstances. For this purpose it is necessary to apply the test of fairness not only to the substantive reason for dismissal but to the dismissal process.

> The test of fairness is contained in s.98(4) which provides that the determination of the question of whether the dismissal was fair or unfair, having regard to the reason shown by the employer, shall depend on whether in the circumstances (including the size and administrative resources of the employer's undertaking) the employer acted reasonably or unreasonably in treating it as a sufficient reason for dismissing the employee, and that question shall be determined in accordance with equity and the substantial merits of the case.

---

57. See Chapter 1 Human Rights Act 1998

Substantive Fairness

This important test involves an assessment of the employer's conduct from the viewpoint of substantive fairness and procedural fairness. Here we will consider substantive fairness and deal with procedural fairness later in the chapter. Inevitably the test of fairness has been the subject of judicial interpretation since its introduction in 1971[58] and you should appreciate that there have been a number of approaches as to how it should be applied.

An important issue in deciding the reasonableness of the employer's conduct is determining the date upon which fairness of the decision to dismiss is to be tested. There is case-law, notably the decision of the House of Lords in *Devis & Sons Ltd. v. Atkins* 1977 which seem to suggest that the reasonableness of the decision to dismiss should be assessed at the date when notice to terminate the employment was given and nothing that happened afterwards could have any effect upon the fairness of the decision to dismiss. While this is acceptable in relation to matters discovered after dismissal by the employer, which could support his decision to dismiss, the fact that in *West Midland Cooperative Society v. Tipton* 1986 the employer refused the employee his contractual right of appeal could be taken into account to decide the fairness of his conduct. Certainly matters which come to light during the appeal process may be taken into account in considering the overall *'equity and substantial merits of the case'*. The House of Lords ruled in the Tipton case that a dismissal is unfair if the employer unreasonably treats the reason as a sufficient reason to dismiss or when he maintains that decision at the conclusion of an appeal process. By totally denying an employee a contractual right to appeal against a decision to dismiss, the dismissal could also be held to be unfair.

> In *Stacy v. Babcock Power Ltd. (Construction Division)* 1986 after an initial warning in November 1983, the applicant was given a notice of redundancy in February 1984 that his contract would terminate on the fourth of May 1984. The decision to dismiss by reason of redundancy was incontestably fair when given, but in April 1984 the employer secured a contract which provided new opportunities for employees to do work of the kind that the applicant had been doing, and at a nearby location. Despite these fresh employment opportunities the applicant's contract was terminated without any offer of re-engagement. On a claim for unfair dismissal the tribunal held that the circumstances which arose after the decision to dismiss in February were irrelevant and the decision to dismiss was consequently fair. On appeal however the EAT reversed the decision and took the view that the process of dismissal was not complete until the notice had expired and a dismissal which was fair when the notice was given could become unfair by the date of its expiry. Here *'fair industrial practice would have required the respondents to offer the complainant, as a long standing employee, the opportunity of new employment before filling all the vacancies with newly recruited employees'*. Failure to offer fresh employment made the decision to dismiss unfair.

We said that the reason or reasons relied on by the employer to justify a dismissal must be the reason which the employer had in mind at the time of the dismissal. In *Patinson v. March Consulting Ltd.* 1997 the Court of Appeal suggested that the reason given at the time of giving notice to the employee cannot be divorced from the reason relied on when the dismissal actually occurs. This means that it is necessary to take account of circumstances

---

58. Industrial Relations Act 1971

which occur during the notice period including relevant facts or correspondence. In this case the applicant had been told at the time of notice that his position would become redundant because of a possible new post which had yet to be determined. The fact that the new post had been settled during his notice period was a 'fact' which could be used to support the reason for dismissal. Sir Iain Glidewell said that *'There is nothing in the statute or the authorities which prevent an employer who is required to give an employee a long period of notice, and who reasonably anticipates that at the end of that period a decision will have been made or facts will exist which will render the employee's services unnecessary, from giving a notice in anticipation of that decision or those facts and giving what he expects to happen on the reason for dismissal.'*

Further support for considering the reason for dismissal in the light of the dismissal process is provided by *Alboni v. Ind Coope Retail Ltd.* 1998 where the Court of Appeal held that a tribunal is not only entitled but is bound to have regard to events between notice of dismissal and the date that dismissal took effect both in determining the reason for dismissal and whether the employers acted reasonably in the circumstances in treating it as a reason for dismissal.

Where there are multiple reasons for dismissal it must be determined which is the principal one for the purposes of applying s.98(4).

> As recently as 1989 the Employment Appeal Tribunal in *Post Office Counters Ltd. v. Heavey* 1989 found it necessary to confirm that in an unfair dismissal complaint, while the burden of showing the reason for the dismissal is on the employer, the requirement of acting reasonably is not subject to any burden of proof. It is not for the employer to *show* or for the tribunal to be *satisfied* the employer acted reasonably in dismissing the employee. Rather the burden of proof was made neutral by the Employment Act 1980.

> In *Boys and Girls Welfare Society v. McDonald* 1996 the EAT stressed the neutral burden of proof in a complaint of unfair dismissal and confirmed that there is no onus of proof on the employer to satisfy a tribunal as to reasonableness. The tribunal must ask itself whether the dismissal falls within the range of reasonable responses.

'Fairness' then has to be judged by the employment tribunal acting as an industrial jury applying the words of s.98(4). The tribunal is not an arbitrator and has no jurisdiction to substitute its own views of reasonableness for the employer's but must adjudicate upon what a reasonable employer would have done in the circumstances. Useful guidelines in relation to the approach to be adopted in applying s.98(4) were provided by the EAT in *Iceland Frozen Foods v. Jones* 1982. Here Brown Wilkinson J. suggested that the approach which should be adopted by tribunals.

- The starting point should always be the words of the section themselves.
- In applying the section a tribunal must consider the reasonableness of the employer's conduct, not simply whether they consider the dismissal to be fair.
- In judging the reasonableness of the employer's conduct an industrial tribunal must not substitute its decision as to what was the right course to adopt for that of the employer.

- In many, though not all, cases there is a band of reasonable responses to the employee's conduct within which one employer might reasonably take one view, another quite reasonably take another;
- The function of the tribunal, as an industrial jury, is to determine whether in the particular circumstances of each case the decision to dismiss the employee fell within the band of reasonable responses which a reasonable employer might have adopted. If the dismissal falls within the band the dismissal is fair, if the dismissal falls outside the band it is unfair.

This approach to the application of s.98(4) has been widely adopted.

In *Rentokil v. Mackin and Another* 1989 the EAT emphasised that the function of an employment tribunal in an unfair dismissal case is to act as an industrial jury and determine whether in the circumstances the decision to dismiss falls within the band of reasonable responses which a reasonable employer might have adopted. Such a test does not mean however that such *'a high degree of unreasonableness be shown so that nothing short of a perverse decision to dismiss can be held to be unfair within the section'*. Here the EAT refused to interfere with the decision of an industrial tribunal that an employer had acted unfairly when he dismissed two employees who had admitted helping themselves to a milkshake while working in the kitchen of one of the employer's clients.

In deciding whether it is within the band of reasonable responses to dismiss for misconduct outside the workplace the gravity of the misconduct must be considered and the impact it may have on the employer's business.

In *Singh v. London County Bus Service Ltd.* 1976 the applicant who drove a one-man operated bus, was convicted of dishonesty committed outside the course of his employment for which he was dismissed. The EAT held that misconduct does not have to occur in the course of work to justify a dismissal, so long as it would affect the employer when he is doing his work. For the purposes of the job, honesty was a fundamental requirement, so that an employer could fairly dismiss an employee who was found guilty of an offence of dishonesty.

In *Mathewson v. R. B. Wilson Dental Laboratory Ltd.* 1988 the EAT considered the case of a dental technician who was arrested and charged with being in possession of a small amount of cannabis while on his lunch break. When he returned to his place of work he informed his employers who subsequently dismissed him. The employers sought to justify their decision to dismiss on the grounds that it was not appropriate to employ someone engaged in the skilled work that he did who was using drugs. Additionally his conduct was a bad example to junior staff. The EAT held that the tribunal had not acted unreasonably in dismissing the applicant on the grounds that he had been arrested and charged with a drugs offence. On the information the employer had, particularly the admission of guilt, the decision to dismiss fell within the band of reasonable responses which a reasonable employer might have adopted.

In *Hamilton v. Argyll & Clyde Health Board* 1993 the claimant was a chief hospital technician who was dismissed following an allegation that she had torn up a request card for a respiratory test on a patient so that the test was not carried out. Following an investigation the employer concluded that she had committed the guilty act and dismissed her for gross misconduct. The misconduct complained of, the employer believed, fell within the definition of misconduct set out in the employer's disciplinary procedure as 'conduct on the part of the employee which affects the relationship between the employee and the employer to such an extent that the employee can longer reasonably be retained in employment'. The finding of a fair dismissal in the tribunal was challenged on appeal on the grounds that the employer had, in response to a union request, considered the employee for employment within some other sphere within the organisation. As the employment relationship had not been destroyed by the misconduct, the misconduct could not be classified as 'gross' within the definition. This argument was rejected by the EAT which upheld the tribunal's decision. *'Willingness by an employer to offer re-employment is not inconsistent with a conclusion that an employee has been guilty of gross misconduct. What is gross misconduct must be considered in relation to the particular employment and the particular employee. There is no necessary inference that because an employee has been guilty of something which falls to be regarded as gross misconduct in relation to their actual employment, they must necessarily be considered unsuitable for any employment with the employer whatsoever.'*

Reasonable belief

If the reason for dismissal is connected with the employer's belief in the culpability of an employee, then to act reasonably the employer must have made due investigation and enquiry in order to equip himself with sufficient information to arrive at an *'honest belief'* in the employee's guilt.

In *British Home Stores Ltd. v. Burchell* 1978, Arnold J. set out a threshold test which requires that in a case of dismissal on grounds of misconduct the employers must establish three stages:

(1)   that they believed that the employee was guilty of the misconduct;

(2)   that they had reasonable grounds to sustain that belief; and

(3)   that they had carried out as much investigation into the matter as was reasonable in the circumstances.

This test has been subsequently approved by numerous courts and tribunals and still goes to the root of the question as to whether an employer has a sound basis for the allegations of misconduct which have been made. In *Beedell v. West Ferry Printing Ltd.* 2000 the EAT approved the *Burchell* test confirming that stage one related to the reason for dismissal and the employer's belief in it and will satisfy s.98(1) or s.98(2) stages 2 and 3 relate to reasonable grounds for that belief based upon a reasonable investigation and relates to s.98(4), the test of fairness.

For the purposes of s, 98(4) the Burchell test requires reasonable decision making and fair process. There is no requirement of proof on the balance of probabilities that the allegations made against the employee have been established. Rather, the employer must have a genuine belief that the employee committed the misconduct and had reasonable grounds to sustain that belief and to have conducted an investigation that is fair and proportionate to the employer's capacity and resources. In *Perkin v. St. George's Healthcare NHS Trust* 2005 the Court of Appeal held that the Burchell test was appropriate where the dismissal was by reason of a perceived personality conflict between the claimant and his work colleagues. This was despite the fact that here the dismissal was for some other substantial reason rather than for misconduct.

In *Santamera v. Express Cargo Forwarding* 2004 the applicant was suspended on full pay following allegations of bullying and harassment. At her disciplinary hearing the applicant asked that she be given the opportunity to cross-examine those who had made statements against her, but the employer refused her request. The finding of the hearing was that the applicant was guilty of gross misconduct and should be summarily dismissed. Her appeal against that decision was dismissed. On her complaint of unfair dismissal the EAT upheld the finding of fair dismissal by the tribunal. *'In a dismissal case based upon conduct it is sufficient for the employer to have a genuine belief that the employee behaved in the manner alleged, that he had reasonable grounds to sustain that belief and to have conducted an investigation which is fair and proportionate to the employer's capacity and resources.'*

In *British Railways Board v. Jackson* 1994 the claimant, a buffet car steward, who had fourteen years service with British Rail, was summarily dismissed when he was discovered to have bread and bacon in his possession at the beginning of his early morning shift without a satisfactory explanation. The reason for dismissal was contravening the BR rule relating to the possession of goods for the purposes of engaging in trade or business for his own benefit. Following a disciplinary hearing the complainant was summarily dismissed for gross misconduct. Both the tribunal and the EAT felt that the employer had *'jumped the gun'* in that the complainant was challenged in the locker room and had not taken the food onto the train. This conclusion was held to be flawed by the Court of Appeal who stated that the *'question which the tribunal had to determine was whether it was reasonable for the employers to find that the employee intended, in breach of the rules, to trade for his own advantage in the goods found in his possession. It was the wrong approach to adopt a legalistic stance and ask whether technically the BR rule had been infringed and conclude: that the employer had "jumped the gun"'.* To determine whether dismissal was a reasonable response the employer was entitled to take into account:

- the prevalence of this type of conduct among stewards;
- the need to deal with it severely as a deterrent;
- the conduct of the employee in not owning up and put forward unconvincing explanations.

Despite the facts that there was no completed act of dishonesty and the complainant had a long period of service with a good record, the dismissal could be held to be a reasonable response to the misconduct.

The reasoning of the EAT in *Farrant v. The Woodville School* 1998 in a misconduct case is somewhat surprising given the requirements of equity and *'substantial merits'* in decision making. Here the decision of school management had been to implement a reorganisation by requiring the applicant technician to move from one department to another when he refused to move he was dismissed for gross misconduct. Subsequently it was discovered that the employer was not entitled to move the applicant under the terms of his employment contract. Nevertheless the EAT upheld the tribunal's finding of a fair dismissal and felt that the lawfulness of the instruction to move was not decisive in determining the fairness of the dismissal. A genuine of mistaken belief that the applicant was guilty of from misconduct in refusing the new work was a sufficient ground to act reasonably in dismissing him. *'Although the employers were not entitled under the terms of his contract to require the employee to work to the new job description, it was not unreasonable of them to act on the advice they received as to the lawfulness of that instruction, and that having regard to the compelling need for the reorganisation and the fact that the employee had been given ample warning of the employer's intention and ample time to discuss his concerns with them, on balance the dismissal was fair.'*

In a case of admitted dishonesty it is tempting to assume that an employer is entitled to rely on this type of misconduct as a sufficient ground from dismissal without further investigation.

In *John Lewis v. Coyne* 2001 however despite the fact that the employer's disciplinary code provided that dishonesty is *'normally regarded as serious misconduct and normally leads to dismissal'* the tribunal was sympathetic to the applicant who was dismissed for making personal telephone calls without permission. *'Using an employer's telephone for personal calls is not necessarily dishonest. The test of dishonesty is not simply an objective one, What one person believes to be dishonest may in some circumstances not be dishonest to others. Where there may be a difference of view of what is dishonest, the best working test is that propounded by Lord Chief Justice Lane in R v. Ghosh. In summary, there are two aspects to dishonesty, the objective and the subjective, and judging whether there has been dishonesty involves going through a two-stage process. First it must be decided whether according to the ordinary standards of reasonable and honest people, what was done was dishonest. If so, then secondly, consideration must be given to whether the person concerned must have realised that what he or she was doing was by those standards dishonest.'* Here it was not necessarily obvious that using the employers' telephone for personal calls was *'dishonest'* and much depended upon the circumstances of the particular case. However, the employers did not investigate the question of the applicant's dishonesty. They assumed it from the making of any personal calls, putting it into the same category, in effect as stealing money. *'An employee who uses the employers' telephone lines for personal calls is not immune from properly conducted disciplinary action which may result in dismissal. However, the duty on the employers to act fairly and reasonably requires that they should investigate the seriousness of the offence in the particular case.'* Since in the present case they had failed to do so, the tribunal was entitled to find the employers' procedures leading to dismissal were not fair.

If an employee is dismissed for alleged misconduct the employer is normally obliged to investigate the circumstances and this is the case even where an employee is already under a final written warning.

In *FMU v. Sutheran* 1993 the complainant, who has already had a final written warning, was dismissed when she became involved in a heated argument on the shop floor. The EAT held that it was wrong to dismiss her without investigating the circumstances but compensation would be reduced by 50% to reflect her contributory conduct.

It would be tempting to presume that evidence of disparate treatment of different employees would constitute unfairness but this is not always the case. The tribunal is required to focus on the individual circumstances of the case before it and evidence that the treatment he received was not on a par with that meted out in other cases is only relevant in three sets of circumstances. *'Firstly, it may be relevant if there is evidence that employees have been led by an employer to believe that certain categories of conduct will be either overlooked, or at least will not be dealt with by the sanction of dismissal. Secondly, there may be cases where evidence made in relation to other cases supports an inference that the purported reason stated by the employers is not the real or genuine reason for dismissal. Thirdly, evidence as to decisions made by any employer in truly parallel circumstances may be sufficient to support an argument, in a particular case, that it was not reasonable on the part of the employer to visit the particular employee's conduct with the penalty of dismissal and that some lesser penalty would have been appropriate in the circumstances.'* So held the EAT in *Hadjioannou v. Coral Casinos Ltd.* 1981 where a blackjack inspector had been dismissed for breaching a company rule not to socialise with club members. The EAT upheld the tribunal's decision that the dismissal was fair despite the fact that other employees had broken the rule and not been dismissed. It was plainly open to the tribunal to take the view that none of the particular cases could really be regarded as similar to the applicant.

In *Strouthos v. London Underground* 2004 the Court of Appeal held that length of service is a factor which can properly be considered in deciding whether the reaction of an employer to an employee's conduct is an appropriate one.

Blanket dismissals

There have been cases where the employer is aware that at least one of a number of employees is guilty of some act of default but even after a thorough investigation he cannot trace the culprit.

In *Monie v. Coral Racing Ltd.* 1980 in a case involving alleged dishonesty, the employer was held to have acted fairly when he decided to dismiss both employees when only one of them may have been responsible for the guilty act.

In *Whitbread & Company plc v. Thomas* 1988 the justifiability of so called 'blanket dismissals' was called in question. Here the employer's off licence, which was staffed by three part-time assistants had been plagued with stock losses for many years. Despite a number of formal warnings and a temporary transfer of all three staff to other shops, when they returned to work at the off-licence in question the losses continued. Without any suggestion of dishonesty the three staff were dismissed for failing to prevent the stock losses. The complaint of unfair dismissal was upheld by the industrial tribunal which felt that dismissal was not a reasonable option open to the employer. The principle relating to blanket dismissals applied in *Monie v. Coral Racing* 1980 did not apply here as the present case did not involve dishonesty. The EAT disagreed however and held that the Monie principle could apply where the reason for dismissal was capability or conduct, although such a case would be exceptional. An employer could dismiss all the members of a group where he cannot identify the individual responsible for the act when three conditions are satisfied.

- the act must be such that if committed by an identified individual it would justify dismissal, and

- the tribunal must be satisfied that the act was committed by one or more of the group, and

- the tribunal must be satisfied that there has been a proper investigation by the employer to identify the person or persons responsible for the act.

Here then the decision to dismiss after a thorough investigation was within the band of reasonable responses open to a reasonable employer and accordingly fair.

The approach to be adopted by tribunals in relation to *'blanket dismissals'* was further considered and refined by the EAT in *Parr v. Whitbread plc t/a Thresher Wine Merchants* 1990. The case concerned the theft of £4,600 from an off-licence where the evidence suggested that one of four employees could have been responsible, but the employer had found it impossible to discover the guilty party. All four employees were dismissed and one of them, the branch manager, presented a claim for unfair dismissal. Both the tribunal and the EAT found the dismissal to be fair. The dismissal of a group of employees in such circumstances is justified provided that the employer's beliefs at the date of dismissal are based on solid and sensible grounds and the tribunal is able to find in the evidence that:

- An act had been committed which if committed by an individual would justify dismissal.

- The employer had made a reasonable, sufficiently thorough investigation into the matter and with appropriate procedures.

- As a result of that investigation the employer reasonably believed that more than one person could have committed the act.

- The employer had acted reasonably in identifying the group of employees who could have committed the act and each member of the group was individually capable of doing so.

- As between the members of the group the employer could not reasonably identify the individual perpetrator.

If a tribunal finds the facts and applies the relevant law in reaching a decision as to the fairness or otherwise of a decision to dismiss, then as we said in Chapter 2 it is only in exceptional cases that an appellate body can overturn its decision on the grounds of perversity[59] or where the primary facts are not supported by the evidence.[60]

In 1999 Mr Justice Morison, the retiring President of the EAT cast serious doubts about the approach of the courts to assess the validity of a decision to dismiss, particularly in cases of misconduct.

In *Haddon v. Van Den Bergh Foods* 1999 Mr. Justice Morison in the EAT provide a different analysis of the approach to s.98(4). The facts of the case reveal a bizarre management style. The applicant was to receive a good service award after 15 years service where food and drinks would be served. The presentation was to take place over a two hour period during the applicant's shift. He received mixed messages about returning to work after the presentation and on the day having consumed alcohol he decided not to return to work for the one and a half hours necessary to complete his shift. Subsequently the applicant was dismissed for failing to carry out a proper and reasonable instruction, an offence categorised in the company's disciplinary procedure as

---

59. See *East Berkshire HA v. Matadeen* 1992 Chapter 2
60. See *City of Edinburgh DC v. Stephen* 1977 Chapter 2

gross misconduct for which no warning was necessary. Despite believing that many employers would not have dismissed in these circumstances the tribunal held that it could not be said that a reasonable employer would not have done so and held that the dismissal fell within the band of reasonable responses and was consequently fair.

The President of the EAT held that the band of reasonable response test developed as a test to determining fairness under s. 98(4) should no longer be applied. He referred to the test as *'an unhelpful gloss on the statute'* stating that the test of fairness should be applied *'without embellishment and without using mantras so favoured by lawyers in the this field'*. The approach signals a return to using employment tribunals as true industrial juries applying their own industrial experience and judgment in deciding the fairness of an employer's decision making. The significant question is still whether a reasonable employer with those resources would have decided to dismiss but in answering it a tribunal is entitled to take account of what it would have done in the circumstances. Mr. Justice Morison emphasises that the test of fairness is still an objective one he merely recognises that *'it is neither reasonable not realistic to expect the objective question to be answered without the tribunal members having first asked what they would have done and since the tribunal is composed of people who are chosen to sit as an industrial jury applying their own good sense of judgment, what the tribunal themselves would have done will often coincide with their judgment as to what a reasonable employer would have done'*.

Unqualified approval of Mr. Justice Morison's approach to s.98(4) was provided by the EAT in *Wilson v. Ethicon Ltd.* 2000. The Employment Tribunal had decided that the decision to dismiss an employee for failing to carry out a testing procedure fell within the band of reasonable responses open to an employer after conducting a reasonable inquiry into the misconduct. This test, first enunciated in *British Home Stores v. Burchell*,[61] was not applied by the EAT which adopted the *Haddon* approach and endorsed the statements of Mr. Justice Morison. In cases of misconduct dismissal it is essential to address the whole question of reasonableness in terms of s.98(4) and *'stand back from the decision of the employer and assess in the knowledge of what was known to him at the time whether or not the dismissal was reasonable in the circumstances'*. Here the nature of the misconduct viewed against the employee's impeccable record should have led the employer to consider alternative remedies such as a written warning.

Certainly a return to emphasising the role of the tribunal as an *'industrial jury'* and so using its own knowledge and expertise to judge the actions of the reasonable employer is to be welcomed. Also by failing to apply the words of s.98(4) relating to *'equity and substantial merits'* tribunals did not always do justice to the applicant employee. Cases such as *Saunders v. Scottish National Camps* 1980[62] which support management prerogative to take economic decisions at the expense of innocent employees can hardly be regarded as just and equitable.

One of the reasons that Mr. Justice Morison accepted the need for a new approach was the belief that the band of reasonable response test had led tribunals to applying almost a perversity test. This was never the original intention and there is case-law authority which rejects that interpretation. In *Rentokil Ltd. v. Machin* 1989[63] the tribunal held that two

---

61. See earlier
62. See later
63. Above

employees who had taken milkshakes from the kitchen of the employer's client were unfairly dismissed. The employer appealed arguing that such an act of dishonesty and consequential loss of trust would surely amount to conduct which would lead to a dismissal within the band of reasonable responses. The EAT disagreed and unequivocally rejected the notion of fairness equating with perversity. *'The test of whether an employer's decision to dismiss falls within the band of reasonable responses of a reasonable employer does not mean that such a high degree of unreasonableness be shown so that nothing short of a perverse decision to dismiss can be held to be unfair.'*

The President of the EAT, Lindsay J. was given the opportunity to pronounce on the *Haddon* approach to fairness in *Midland Bank v. Madden* 2000 He was unequivocal in declaring that it is only the Court of Appeal or higher tribunal that can dispense with the *'reasonable response test'*. However a tribunal is free to substitute its own views for those of the employer as to the reasonableness of dismissal as a response to the reason shown for it. In misconduct cases the *Burchell* test should be applied and a tribunal is free to substitute its own views for those of the employer in coming to a view on each of the three parts of the test. It seems therefore that his view was not very different from Morison in *Haddon*.

The controversy over the correct approach to be taken to assess the fairness of misconduct dismissals now seems to be resolved, firstly by the EAT and secondly by the Court of Appeal itself.

> The EAT in *Beedell v. West Ferry Printers Ltd.* 2000 reasserted the significance of the band of reasonable response test and stressed that an employment tribunal should not put itself in the position of management to decide whether they would have dismissed an employee or not. Here the complainant, who had an impeccable employment record had been dismissed for fighting at work. The tribunal concluded that the employer's response to dismiss in this marginal case was not unreasonable despite the fact that the tribunal would not have dismissed in the circumstances. Reviewing the previous trilogy of cases the EAT held that where they follow earlier binding precedents of the Court of Appeal they add nothing and where they differ they cannot be sustained. Relying on the authorities the EAT is bound to apply the reasonable response test until modified or abandoned by the Court of Appeal.

Having reaffirmed the reasonable response test from *Iceland Frozen Foods* the EAT also supported the proposition from that case that the tribunal must not substitute its decision as to the right course of action to adopt for that of the employer. Holding that the tribunal's decision disclosed no error of law the claimant's appeal was dismissed.

> In *Post Office v. Foley and HSBC Bank plc* (formerly *Midland Bank plc) v. Maddon* 2000. the Court of Appeal overruled the decisions of the EAT in both *Madden* and *Haddon* and re-emphasised the primacy of *the 'range of reasonable response test'*. Lord Justice Mumery held that the approach in *Iceland Frozen Foods* and *Burchell* was to be applied and that *Haddon* was an unwarranted departure from previous case-law.

The Court of Appeal has reaffirmed the position pre Haddon but there is no doubt that the approach adopted by Morison J had its supporters and has provoked a constructive debate as to the correct approach to applying s.98(4).

It was made clear in *Iceland Frozen Foods* and cases such as *Rentokil Ltd. v. Machin* 1989[64] that the statutory provision did not require '*such a high degree of reasonableness to be shown that nothing short of a perverse decision to dismiss can be held to be unfair within the section*'. While there will be cases where there is only one reasonable response '*where there is room for reasonable disagreement among reasonable employers as to whether dismissal for the particular misconduct is a reasonable or unreasonable response it is helpful to consider the range of reasonable responses*'.

Human rights

In Chapter 1 we considered the extent to which unfair dismissal law[65] is subject to the European Convention on Human Rights. In relation to Public Authorities the Convention is directly applicable and can override the operation of the Employment Rights Act 1996.

In *Pay v. Lancashire Probation Service* 2004 the applicant probation officer was dismissed for his inappropriate extreme sexual activities of a public nature. The EAT held that the tribunal was right to begin with an examination of s. 98(4) but in a case where an employee is trying to enforce Convention Rights directly against a public authority then the tribunal should deal with those rights first. Here the inappropriate public acts were insufficient to prevent the engagement of a right to a private life.

In *X v. Y* 2003 the applicant was a development officer who worked with young offenders. When off duty he received a police caution for an act of gross indecency with another man in a public place. He did not disclose the caution and later when his employer became aware of the event he was subject to disciplinary proceedings that led to his summary dismissal for gross misconduct. The tribunal dismissed the applicant's claim for unfair dismissal finding that the employer's response fell within the band of reasonable responses for the purposes of s.98 (4). The tribunal also rejected the applicant's claim that s.98 (4) should now be regarded as subordinate to the European Human Rights Convention,[66] particularly Articles 8 and 14 in relation to the right of privacy and family life and not to suffer discrimination on any ground. The perceived incompatibility between s. 98(4) and the Human Rights Convention was the subject of an appeal to the EAT. While agreeing that s. 98(4) should be interpreted as far as possible in line with the convention, the EAT found that sexual activity in a public place does not come within the ambit of the right to respect for private life in Article 8. Also there was no discriminatory treatment for the purposes of Article 14, the applicant's sexuality not being an issue in this case. There was no evidence of perversity in the tribunal's reasoning that the tribunal's decision to dismiss fell within the band of reasonable responses.

McGowan v. Scottish Water 2005[67] raises the issue as to the means by which an employer can acquire evidence of fraudulent conduct by an employer. Here the claimant was employed at a water treatment plant and lived in a tied house nearby. Suspecting that he was falsifying his time sheet, the employer decided to employ private investigators to carry out a surveillance of his working week. For this purpose the investigation filmed the claimant's house and their evidence eventually led to the applicants dismissal. The claimant argued that his

---

64. See earlier
65. Particularly s.98(4)
66. See Chapter 1
67. See Chapter 1

dismissal was unfair as an infringement of his Article 8 rights of respect for his private and family life. Both the Tribunal and the EAT disagreed concluding that there had been no breach of Article 8. The conduct of the employer, bearing in mind the gravity of the offence investigated, was entirely reasonable and proportionate.

Having considered the general approach to be adopted by tribunals in determining its issue of substantive fairness it is now necessary to consider procedural fairness in the light of any disciplinary procedure adopted and applied by the employer

Procedural Fairness

In addition to determining fairness in relation to the reasons relied upon, the process of determining the reasonableness of the employer's decision to dismiss necessarily involves a consideration of the procedure implemented by the employer in relation to the dismissal. The requirement of a fair procedure is part of the test of fairness in s.98(4) so that a significant default in procedure could persuade a tribunal to uphold a complaint of unfair dismissal despite the fact that there was a substantively fair reason for dismissal. Also early in this chapter we examined the Employment Act 2002 and the Employment Act (Dispute Resolution) Regulations 2004 which introduces new statutory dispute resolution procedures in order to encourage parties to avoid litigation by resolving differences through proper internal procedure. These procedures are now in force and failure to comply with statutory processes will have serious consequences for the employer and the employee.[68]

There is also a Code of Practice drawn up by ACAS on *'Disciplinary Practice and Procedures in Employment' 2000*. The Code provides that employees should be fully informed of disciplinary rules and procedures and the likely consequences if the rules are broken. Also the Code identifies the essential features of a disciplinary procedure so that in cases of misconduct, at some point, the employee should be given the opportunity of putting his side of the case accompanied by a representative from a trade union or otherwise. The procedure should have built in a process involving formal and informal, oral and written, first and final warnings. In *Lock v. Cardiff Rail* 1998 the EAT held that the employer's decision to dismiss for a one off act of misconduct was perverse bearing in mind the employer's failure to implement the ACAS Code. The Code forms the basis on which the employee's conduct should be judged. The graver the misconduct the less requirement there would be to implement a system of warnings. Also, where warnings are given for less serious matters they should be recorded but then after a period of satisfactory conduct eventually disregarded. If a dismissal occurs because of the breach of a final written warning the warning must be in force for the employer to place reliance on it.

> In *Bevan Ashford v. Malin* 1995 the complainant had been issued with a final written warning about his work on the 29 January 1992. The warning was to remain in force for 12 months *'from the date of this letter'* and stated that any reoccurrence of the behaviour in question would be grounds for dismissal. On the 29 January 1993 a further behavioural problem arose and at a disciplinary hearing on the 3rd of February a decision was taken to dismiss the complainant on the basis that the final written warning was still in force. This interpretation of the warning the tribunal and EAT believed to be incorrect. The warning had

---

68. See earlier in the chapter

'come into effect on 29 January 1992, had expired at midnight on 28 January ?
and, accordingly, was not in force on 29 January 1993 when the incident which
to the dismissal occurred'.

The need to comply strictly with disciplinary procedures to justify a dismissal as fair was
a feature of the approach of tribunals to reasonableness in the 1970s but by the end of the
decade there was a change in approach. In *British Labour Pump v. Byrne* 1979 the EAT
formulated *the 'no difference principle'* under which procedural defects could be overlooked.
If, despite the non-compliance with a disciplinary procedure, the employer could show
that, on the balance of probabilities, the same course would have been adopted, the tribunal
was entitled to find the decision to dismiss a fair one.

A change in attitude was expressed by the House of Lords in the important case
of *Polkey v. A. E. Dayton Services Ltd.* 1987. Here, the 'no difference principle'
was overruled. The basic facts of the case were that the claimant, a van driver,
employed by the defendants for over four years, was without warning or
consultation, handed a letter of redundancy. His claim of unfair dismissal was
based on the employer's failure to observe the statutory code of practice which
provides for warning and consultation in a redundancy situation. Despite there
being *a 'heartless disregard'* of the code, the tribunal, EAT and the Court of
Appeal all found that the dismissal was fair. Applying the *'no difference principle'*,
if a fair procedure had been adopted, the employer could still have reasonably
decided to dismiss. This approach was rejected by the House of lords who held
that the employer's decision to dismiss had to be judged by applying the wording
of the test of reasonableness. There was no scope for deciding what the employer
might have done had he adopted a different procedure. Where the employer
fails to observe the code, he will only be acting fairly if the tribunal is satisfied
that *'the employer could reasonably have concluded in the light of circumstances
known at the time of dismissal that consultation or warning would be utterly useless'.*

The House of Lords held in *Polkey* therefore that a failure to follow an agreed procedure in
dismissing an employee is likely to result in a finding of unfair dismissal. This is subject to the
important exception, where it is obvious that use of the proper procedure would be futile. It
seems that in cases of misconduct the decision in *Polkey* indicates that there is a procedural as
well as a substantive element to the band of reasonable responses open to an employer.

In *Perkin v. St. George's Healthcare NHS Trust* 2005 the EAT confirmed that even where
there is a finding of unfair dismissal because of procedural impropriety the tribunal can
apply the principle in *Polkey v. Dayton Services* 1987 and reduce the compensation payable
because of the claimant's contributory fault. Here the tribunal felt that there was a 100%
chance that the claimant's employment would have terminated if a fair procedure had been
adopted and his compensatory award would be reduced accordingly. Now following s.98A[69]
the impact of the *Polkey* principle is diminished.[70]

In *Whitbread plc v. Hall* 2001 the applicant a hotel manager, having received a
final warning about stock irregularities was eventually suspended pending further
investigations. At a disciplinary meeting the applicant admitted the offences

---

69. Statutory Procedural Fairness
70. See earlier in the chapter

and was dismissed for gross misconduct. His appeal against that decision was heard by the operations manager and was unsuccessful. An employment tribunal upheld his complaint of unfair dismissal on the grounds that the disciplinary process was so flawed as to render the dismissal unfair despite the fact that the decision fell within the band of reasonable responses. Flaws which offended the rules of natural justice included the fact that the area manager acted as investigator and judge and that personal circumstances had been ignored. Both the EAT and the Court of Appeal upheld the tribunal's decision that a substantive fair dismissal could be rendered unfair by a disciplinary process that has serious flaws. The court stated *'where misconduct is admitted by the employee the requirement of reasonableness in s.98(4) relates not only to the outcome in terms of the penalty imposed by the employer but also the process that the employer arrived at that decision. Accordingly the employment tribunal should not simply ask whether the dismissal fell within the band of reasonable responses but should also apply that test to the procedure used in reaching the decision'.*

The Court of Appeal in *Hall* above did recognise in the above case that there may be cases of misconduct so serious that even a large employer could take the view that no explanation or plea in mitigation would make any difference to the decision to dismiss.

It is now established that in assessing the fairness of the employers decision to dismiss or otherwise it is necessary to consider whether the disciplinary code was fully adhered to.

In *Cobaj v. Westminster City Council* 1996 following the dismissal of a senior computer programmer for poor attendance, the appeal tribunal which considered his appeal against the decision to dismiss, was attended by the Chief Executive of the council and two members, rather than three members required by the disciplinary code. The EAT disagreed with the tribunal and found that this significant error rendered the dismissal unfair. The EAT stated that *'where an employee has a contractual right to have an appeal against dismissal heard and decided by an appeals panel constituted in a particular way, as a matter of law a defect in the composition of such a body is a significant contractual and jurisdictional failure, not simply a matter of procedural error'.* On further appeal the Court of Appeal agreed that in this case there was a contractual right to an appeal tribunal consisting of three members. However the failure to provide such an appeal was not sufficient to make the decision to dismiss a necessarily unfair one. *'Failure by an employer to observe its own contractually enforceable disciplinary procedure does not inevitably require an industrial tribunal to conclude that a dismissal was unfair. The question which the industrial tribunal has to determine under the legislation is not whether the employer acted reasonably in dismissing the employee, but whether the employer acted reasonably or unreasonably in treating the reason shown as a sufficient reason for dismissal. The relevance to that question of failure to entertain an appeal to which the employee was contractually entitled, as Lord Bridge pointed out in West Midlands Co-operative Society v. Tipton, is whether the employee was 'thereby' denied the opportunity of showing that the real reason for dismissal was not sufficient. As Lord Mackay and Lord Bridge indicated in Polkey v. A. E. Dayton Services Ltd., it is also relevant to consider whether the employer acted reasonably if he actually considered or a reasonable employer would have considered at the time of dismissal that to follow the agreed procedure would in the circumstances of the case be futile.'*

The contemporary view seems to be that even in a case involving a procedural flaw the decision to dismiss an employee may still be regarded as fair and reasonable.

> *Hussain v. Elonex plc* 1999 concerned the dismissal of a computer engineer for allegedly head-butting another employee. Witness statements which had been taken were not disclosed to the complainant at the disciplinary hearing. Both the tribunal and the EAT took the view that the complainant was aware of what he was being accused of and the reasonable investigation and fair procedure adopted made the decision to dismiss a fair one. The Court of Appeal agreed that despite the procedural flaw there was no failure of natural justice because the complainant was aware of the case against him and given a full opportunity to respond to it.

> Support for the view that a less stringent approach to procedural requirements is provided by the decision of the EAT in *Lloyd v. Taylor Woodrow Construction* 1999. Here a redundancy decision had been taken in relation to the applicant which was flawed in the sense that ad hoc selection criterion had been used. On internal appeal however the selection criterion were identified and the applicant was given the chance to contest them and then again on further appeal. Despite the failure in the original decision to consult over selection criterion the tribunal rejected the complaint of unfair dismissal. The tribunal and later the EAT confirmed that the defect in procedure had been corrected at later appeal hearings so that the decision to dismiss was fair. *'The general principle that a procedural defect at the dismissal stage maybe cured at the appeal stage, provided that the appeal represents a rehearing and not merely a review of the original decision applies to a failure to consult in the context of a redundancy dismissal.'* The EAT also said that potential for correcting a procedural defect by means of a rehearing also applies to any of the potentially fair reasons for dismissal under s.98.

> In *Market Force UK Ltd. v. Hunt* 2002 an employee was summarily dismissed after pornographic material was found stored on the hard disc of his computer. The employee claimed that he had intended to delete the material and that he had stored it accidentally but the IT Department took the view that it would be impossible to store the material by mistake. Here however the failure to carry out a proper investigation convinced the tribunal that the decision to dismiss was procedurally unfair. The tribunal also ruled that the compensation should be dramatically reduced applying the legal principle from *Polkey v. Dayton Services*. We will mention this case again in relation to a Polkey reduction in the section on remedies.

Even if the employer invokes the appropriate disciplinary procedure leading to a dismissal it must be implemented fairly and in accordance with the rules of natural justice.

> In *Spink v. Express Foods Group Ltd.* 1990 prior to the dismissal of the complainant sales representative the employer had taken disciplinary proceedings against him which involved holding a disciplinary inquiry. The fact that the employer deliberately decided not to reveal the purpose of the inquiry to the complainant and the allegations against him made the proceedings and the decision to dismiss unfair. The EAT held that *'it is a fundamental part of a fair disciplinary procedure that an employee knows the case against him. Fairness requires that someone accused should know the case to be met; should hear or be told the important parts of the evidence in support of the case; should have an opportunity to criticise or dispute that evidence and adduce his own evidence and argue his case'.*

In cases of misconduct an Employment Tribunal should still be guided by *British Home Stores Ltd. v. Burchell* 1978 which provides that an employer is required to show a genuine belief in the misconduct with reasonable evidence upon which to formulate that belief. This will normally involve adherence to a reasonable investigation and a process which gives the employee an opportunity, in accordance with the rules of natural justice, to put his side of the case. It is only in rare cases, where perhaps the complainant is *'caught red handed'* that there is no need to adhere to procedures.

> In *P v. Nottinghamshire County Council* 1992 the complainant, a school groundsman, was dismissed by the respondents after he had been convicted of an offence of indecent assault against his daughter, a pupil at the school at which he worked. On his dismissal the complainant was paid wages in lieu of twelve weeks notice and told that an attempt would be made to redeploy him in other council work but that proved to be unsuccessful. The tribunal decided that because insufficient time had been spent on investigating the circumstances of his offences and the possibility of alternative work before the decision to dismiss was reached, it was an unfair decision. The EAT and then the Court of Appeal reversed this decision as perverse on appeal. In relation to alternative work the Court of Appeal held that *'in an appropriate case, and where the size and administrative resources of the employer's undertaking permit it may be unfair first considering whether the employee can be offered some other job notwithstanding that it may be clear that he cannot be allowed to continue in his original job. There is nothing in the section to suggest that the question of alternative employment must be investigated before the giving of notice to dismiss'.* As far as investigating the circumstances of the offence is concerned the Court stated that *'when an employee has pleaded guilty to an offence or has been found guilty by the decision of a Court or the verdict of a jury it is reasonable for an employer to believe that the offence has been committed by the employee. Any other conclusion would be ridiculous'.*

The effect of an unjustifiable delay in carrying out disciplinary proceedings could make a decision to dismiss unfair which would otherwise have been held to be fair. This would be the case even where it is shown that the complainant suffered no prejudice as a result of the delay.

> This was the decision of the EAT in *The Royal Society for the Prevent of Cruelty to Animals v. Cruden* 1986. Despite the gravity of the complainant's gross misjudgment and idleness, in this case the protracted delay in implementing disciplinary proceedings against him rendered the decision to dismiss unfair. The Act *'is concerned with whether the employer had acted fairly and not whether the employee had suffered an injustice'.* In an attempt to do justice in the case however the EAT reduced both the basic award and the compensatory award to nil to reflect the complainant's grave neglect and the fact that the employer would be failing in his duty if he failed to dismiss in these circumstances.

Sainsburys Supermarket v. Hitt 2003 is another suspicion of theft scenario. Here a box of razor blades found in the applicant's locker led to an investigatory process followed by a disciplinary hearing. There was a further appeal hearing against the decision to dismiss the employee for gross misconduct. Given the flaws in the investigatory process both the tribunal and the EAT concluded that the dismissal was unfair but for different reasons. The Court of Appeal held that both of the decisions revealed errors of law. Both tribunals succumbed to the temptation to substitute their own opinions of what would constitute a reasonable investigatory process rather than apply the objective standards of the reasonable employer. All aspects of the decision to dismiss, both procedural and substantive are subject to the 'reasonable response test' including the investigatory process. In suggesting that further investigations should have taken place the tribunal was simply substituting its own standard of an adequate investigation rather than the standard of the reasonable employer. *'The purpose of the investigation was not to establish whether or not the applicant was guilty of the alleged theft but whether there were reasonable grounds for the employers' belief that there had been misconduct on his part to which a reasonable response was a decision to dismiss him. The uncontested facts were that a box of razor blades which had gone missing was found in the applicant's locker and that he had had the opportunity to steal it. The employers had investigated the applicant's allegation that someone else had planted the missing razor blades in his locker and were entitled to conclude on the basis of that investigation that the applicant's explanation was improbable.'*

One of the most sensitive of management issues is dealing with allegations concerning an employee's conduct, made by an informant who insists on maintaining anonymity. In *Linfood Cash & Carry Ltd. v. Thomson* 1989 the EAT set out detailed guidance on steps which employers should take to maintain a balance between the desirability of protecting informants who are genuinely in fear and providing a fair hearing for employees accused of misconduct. In *Ramsey v. Walkers Snack Foods Ltd.* 2004 a number of employees were dismissed for alleged theft of money inserted into crisp packets as part of a sales promotion. The dismissals were based on statements by fellow employees who wished to remain anonymous for fear of reprisals. They made statements which were unsigned and did not contain detail which might have revealed who the informants were. The EAT upheld the dismissals as fair despite the fact that the procedure adopted meant that several of the guidelines set out in *Linfood* were not followed. The statements did not have the detail required by the EAT in *Linfood* and the managers involved in the disciplinary process did not personally interview the informants. This made it difficult for the claimants to test the detail of the allegations. Nevertheless the EAT felt that *'what is called for in terms of assessing the fairness of the employers' approach is to look at the reasons they gave for granting the anonymity in the first place, the terms of that anonymity and whether it should extend to being interviewed by other managers, and the subsequent preparation of statements.'*

Automatic Unfair Dismissal

Under the Employment Rights Act 1996 certain reasons for dismissal are classified as inadmissible and automatically unfair and under s.108(3) there is no qualifying period of continuous employment. In recent years there has been a steady increase in the number of categories of automatically unfair dismissal. They are dismissals where the reason is connected with:

- Health and safety s.100(1).
- Leave for family reasons including maternity s.99.
- Trade union activities s.152.[71]
- The assertion of a statutory right s.104(1).
- Making a protected disclosure s.103A.

---

71. TULRA 1992

- Non compliance with the Working Time Regulations s.101A.
- Non compliance with the National Minimum Wage s.104A.
- Non compliance with the Statutory Disciplinary and Grievance Procedure s.34(1).[72]
- Participation in official industrial action s.238A(2).[73]
- For a reason connected with a business transfer TUPE.[74]
- Employers statutory procedural unfairness s.98A.[75]

In each of these cases the onus is on the complainant to establish that the reason for dismissal is with the inadmissible category and is therefore automatically unfair.

Dismissal on the grounds of pregnancy or childbirth

It is automatically unfair to dismiss an employee because she is pregnant or has given birth or has taken maternity leave. This is contained in s.99 of the Employment Rights Act 1996 and it applies regardless of the length of service. A decision to dismiss by reason of pregnancy therefore will also constitute direct discrimination and given that the maximum level of compensation has been removed in sex discrimination cases it could provide a more significant remedy than unfair dismissal. The law relating to pregnancy dismissals is examined in Chapter 7 on Work/Life Balance.

Dismissal in connection with union activities

For dismissals in relation to trade union activities there is no requirement for the complainant to show continuous employment to qualify to present a claim or be within the prescribed age limits.

> Under s.152 of the Trade Union and Labour Relations (Consolidation) Act 1992 a dismissal shall be regarded as unfair if the reason for it was that the employee:
>
> (a) was, or proposed to become, a member of an independent trade union; or
>
> (b) had taken part, or proposed to take part, in the activities of an independent trade union at an appropriate time; or
>
> (c) was not a member of any trade union, or of a particular trade union, or of one of a number of particular trade unions, or had refused or proposed to refuse to become or remain a member.

Previously a dismissal for non-membership of a trade union could, in certain circumstances, be fair if it was to prevent the contravention of a closed shop agreement supported by a ballot. Following the Employment Act 1988, all dismissals for non-membership of a trade union are automatically unfair irrespective of whether there is a closed shop agreement. Section 152 then is concerned with dismissals connected with membership or non-membership of trade union or for taking part in trade union activities. For claims based

---

72. Employment Act 2002
73. TULRA 1992
74. Regulation 8
75. See earlier in the chapter

on membership, the union in question must be independent and so not under the control or domination of an employer or a group of employers. A certificate of independence may have been issued by the Certification Officer.

> In *Overprint Ltd. v. Malcolm* 1992 the complainant employee having joined a trade union was required by his employer to sign a written contract of employment. After taking union advice he refused to do so and was promptly dismissed. He alleged that his dismissal was automatically unfair by virtue of s.152 TULR(C)A 1992. The tribunal found the reason for dismissal was not the complainant's membership of the union but rather the fact that as a consequence of his membership he might make demands on the employer. The tribunal held that the dismissal was automatically unfair under s.152 and ordered his reinstatement. The EAT agreed deciding that there was no requirement for the tribunal to find any substance to the employer's apprehensions about union membership for s.152 to apply. Even if the consequences of membership were nothing more than considerations operating in the mind of the person who decided to dismiss, the reason for dismissal remained union membership.

The EAT in *Dundon v. GPT Ltd.* 1995 made it clear that for s.152 to apply an employer does not have to be motivated by malice or be shown to have deliberately intended to get rid of a trade union activist.

For claims based on 'union activities' carried on at an *'appropriate time'*, further guidance is needed to determine whether a dismissal falls within this category. The Act deals with the question of *'appropriate time'* by limiting it to a time outside working hours or within working hours with the employer's consent.

> In *Marley Tile v. Shaw* 1980, the Court of Appeal confirmed that in a proper case the consent of an employer to trade union activities could be implied. Here however, where a union meeting was held without express permission, causing more than *'a mere trifling inconvenience'*, to the employer's business, it was not carried out at an *'propriate time'*, for it was carried out during working hours and was not in accordance with arrangements made or consent given.

The expression *'union activities'* is not defined in the Act and so we must rely exclusively on case-law to provide us with guidance.

> In *Brennan v. Ellward* 1976 it was held that to determine trade union activities it is necessary to summarise all the acts and facts relied on a constituting *'activities'* including as an element whether any employee involved is a representative or not, and then decide as a matter of common sense whether such acts constitute activities of an independent trade union.

> In *Bass Taverns v. Burgess* 1995 the complainant shop steward was dismissed from the trainer manager part of his job following a presentation he made at an induction course for trainee managers. The employer's contention that the presentation was biased ultimately led to the complainant's resignation and complaint of unfair constructive dismissal. Disagreeing with the tribunal the EAT and subsequently the Court of Appeal held that at the time of dismissal the applicant was taking part in trade union activities at an appropriate time and so under s.152 this meant that the dismissal was automatically unfair. The Court of Appeal made the point that the employer had consented to the meeting being used on a recruitment forum and that consent could not be subject to an implied

limitation that the union recruiter would not criticise the company *'A consent to recruitment must include a consent to underline the services which the union can provide and that may reasonably involve a submission to prospective members that in some respects the union will provide a service which the company does not.'*

It seems that distributing union material, recruiting and advising members and attending meetings are all types of conduct which could be described as trade union *activities*.

The section confers protection on an employee who is proposing to take part in union activities and dismissed as a result.

> In *Fitzpatrick v. British Railways Board* 1991 an employee with a reputation as a union activist was dismissed because it was felt she would be a disruptive influence. This dismissal was unfair as contrary to the section.[76]

Dismissal in connection with health and safety

Under s.100(1) of the Employment Rights Act 1996 all employees, irrespective of hours and service have the right not to be dismissed or subjected to any detriment for engaging in activities such as:

(a) Acting as a safety representative.

(b) Bringing a health and safety matter to the employer's attention where the employee reasonably believed there was potential harm.

(c) Carrying out designated activities in connection with preventing or reducing risks to health and safety.

(d) Leaving or refusing to return to the place of work because of a reasonable belief in a serious or imminent danger.

(e) In circumstances of danger taking steps to protect himself or other persons from danger.

This section emphasises the significance of health and safety at the workplace so that if an employee is dismissed for raising safety issues, or complaining about safety equipment or the working environment the dismissal should be automatically unfair. The limit on the compensatory award for this type of dismissal was removed by the Employment Relations Act 1999. Two contemporary examples of a liberal interpretation of s.100 dismissals are shown below.

> In *Masiak v. City Restaurants (UK) Ltd.* 1999 the complainant chef who had worked for his employers for just over a month, left the premises after refusing to cook food which he considered was a potential hazard to public health. In a complaint of unfair dismissal the chef relied on s.100(1)(e)[77] but this was rejected by the tribunal who felt that the expression *'other persons'* in the section referred exclusively to work colleagues rather than members of the public. On appeal however the EAT disagreed and held the expression 'other persons' in s.100(1)(e) extends to protection of members of the public from danger. The complainant was also entitled to damages for breach of his common law right to reasonable notice an implied term in every contract of employment.

---

76. See Chapter 6
77. See Above

In *Harvest Press Ltd. v. McCaffery* 1999 the complainant was a machine minder who walked out of his workplace after less than three months service because of the abusive behaviour of a work colleague. When he failed to obtain assurance about his safety the complainant claimed unfair dismissal relying on s.100(1)(d).[78] The question faced by the EAT was whether the expression *'in circumstances of danger'* which the employee believed to be imminent, was restricted to dangers generated by the workplace. The EAT held that the word danger was intended to cover any circumstances and would cover abusive behaviour of fellow employees.

Dismissal in connection with statutory rights

Under s.104 of the 1996 Act it is automatically unfair to dismiss an employee for alleging that the employer had infringed a statutory right or for bringing proceedings to enforce such a right. Once again employees are entitled to make a complaint regardless of their length of service.

In *Mennell v. Newell & Wright (Transport Contractors) Ltd.* 1996 the complainant Mr. Mennell an HGV driver, refused to sign a new contract of employment because one of the clauses in the draft contract provided that the employers would recover certain training costs by way of a deduction from payment of final salary due to the employee on termination of employment. He maintained that any such deduction from his wages would amount to a breach of the Wages Act. Eventually Mr. Mennell was dismissed and he claimed that he had been dismissed for asserting a statutory right. The industrial tribunal, accepted the employers argument that because no deduction had in fact been made from Mr. Mennell's wages, there had been no infringement of any right under the Wages Act in respect of which a complaint could be made to an industrial tribunal and, therefore, no infringement of a relevant statutory right. The Employment Appeal Tribunal held that the industrial tribunal had wrongly interpreted the section. *'A threat of dismissal in order to impose a variation of the contract of employment so as to enable the employer to make deductions from wages may amount to an infringement, at the time the threat is made, of the employee's statutory right under the Wages Act not to have deductions made from wages without his freely given written consent.'*

In *Lopez v. Maison Bouquillon Ltd.* 1996 the complainant, a counter assistant in a cake shop, left her workplace and complained to the police that she had been assaulted by the chef who was married to the shop manageress. Subsequently the complainant was told by her employer that she no longer worked for the company. Claiming unfair dismissal she said that the reason she was dismissed was that she left the workplace, but in the circumstances that was perfectly reasonable, given the assault. The tribunal found that the dismissal was unfair. In this type of scenario a complainant who can show that a dismissal is related to the fact that she raised health and safety issues or had taken appropriate steps to protect herself from imminent danger can rely on section 100(1) ERA 1996. A dismissal in these circumstances is automatically unfair and no qualifying period of employment is required.

---

78. See above

A deduction from wages is a breach of a statutory right. Dismissal for asserting such a breach is automatically unfair under s.104 of the Employment Rights Act. In *Elizabeth Claire Care Management Ltd. v. Francis* 2004 the EAT holds that this principle encompasses a case where an employee is dismissed for complaining about the employer's failure to pay her salary on time. On appeal, the employers argued that there is no right to be paid on time, but the EAT did not agree. According to Mr. Justice Silber's decision, a *'deduction from wages'* has a wide meaning. *'It would be strange if an employee could claim that there has been "a deduction from wages"... and that this had infringed "a relevant statutory right" when he was paid all but £1 of his wages but that he could not make such a claim if he was not paid any of his wages.'*

Dismissal for making a protected disclosure

Under s.103A. an employee is protected if dismissed for making a protected disclosure under the Public Interest Disclosure Act 1998.[79] The Employment Relations Act 1999 removed the limit on the compensatory award for this type of dismissal and in July 2000 a successful claimant was awarded £200,000 in compensation.

Dismissal for non compliance with the Working Time Regulations

Section 101A protects employees who are dismissed for refusing to accept a requirement imposed by the employer in contravention of the Working Time Regulations 1998.[80]

Dismissal for non compliance with minimum wage

Section 104A is designed to protect employees who are dismissed in connection with taking action to secure the national minimum wage under the 1998 Act.[81]

Dismissal for participating in official industrial action

A dismissal in these circumstances is considered under the heading Unfair Dismissal and Industrial Action.[82]

Dismissal for a reason connected with a business transfer

Such a dismissal is automatically unfair under the Transfer of Undertaking (Protection of Employment) Regulations 1981 and 2005.[83]

---

79. See Chapter 9
80. See Chapter 7
81. See Chapter 9
82. See below
83. See Chapter 9

Unfair Dismissal and Industrial Action

If an employee is dismissed while taking part in industrial action such as a strike, work to rule, go slow or even an overtime ban which may not be even a breach of contract, the law provides limited protection. Following recommendations in the Fairness at Work White Paper published in May 1998 and the consultation that followed it, the government took the view that employees who are dismissed for taking part in lawfully organised official industrial action should have the right to complain of unfair dismissal to a tribunal. Under the Employment Relations Act 1999[84] it is automatically unfair to dismiss employees for the first eight weeks of their participation in official and 'protected' industrial action and this right is inserted as s.238A of the Trade Union and Labour Relations (Consolidation) Act 1992. Under the Employment Relations Act 2004 for industrial action on or after 6 April 2005 the length of the protected period is extended from 8 weeks to 12 weeks.

This important statutory right must be viewed in the light of existing provision of TULR(C)A 1992 which are still relevant and can still remove tribunal jurisdiction in relation to unfair dismissal during industrial action. An important distinction is drawn between official and unofficial industrial action. Official action must have been lawfully sanctioned by the relevant trade union under s.237(2). Participation in unofficial industrial action effectively removes the tribunal's jurisdiction in relation to unfair dismissal.

It seems therefore that if the action is unofficial then an employer is protected even if he selectively dismisses particular employees, for there is no prospect of unfair dismissal claims.

The right to present a claim for unfair dismissal is also restricted if at the time of dismissal the employee in question was engaged in official industrial action. Under s.238 of the Trade Union and Labour Relations (Consolidation) Act 1992 the jurisdiction of a tribunal to hear a complaint may also be removed.

> *Under s.238(1) this section applies in relation to an employee who has a right to complain of unfair dismissal (the 'complainant') and who claims to have been unfairly dismissed, where at the date of the dismissal:*
>
> *(a) the employer was conducting or instituting a lock-out; or*
>
> *(b) the complainant was taking part in a strike or other industrial action.*
>
> *(2) In such a case an industrial tribunal shall not determine whether the dismissal was fair or unfair unless it is shown:*
>
> *(a) that one or more relevant employees of the same employer have not been dismissed; or*
>
> *(b) that a relevant employee has before the expiry of the period of three months beginning with the date of his dismissal been offered re-engagement and that the complainant has not been offered re-engagement.*

Provided that an employer does not discriminate between those he dismisses and those he re-engages within the minimum periods, the section effectively removes the right to present a claim if an employer decides to dismiss all those workers, who, at a given time, are engaged in a strike or other industrial action. The right to present a claim will arise once

---

84. s.16 and schedule 5

again, however, if the employer re-engages any striking workers within three months of the date of the complainant's dismissal. For this reason the complainant has a time limit of six months from the date of dismissal to present a claim.

For the purposes of the section it can be a difficult question to determine whether an employee is taking part in a strike or other industrial action.

> In *Glenrose (Fish Merchants) v. Chapman* 1990 the EAT said that it is for the employer to prove on the balance of probabilities that employees were participating in industrial action and that either s.238 or s.237 applies. Here some fish filleters had refused to do an extra hour filleting on one day as a protest against the re-introduction by management of compulsory overtime. They were dismissed the following day, at which point the overtime ban had been lifted, so the tribunal did have jurisdiction to hear their complaint.

> In *Coates v. Modern Methods and Materials* 1982 the Court of Appeal held that for the purposes of the section, an employee who stops work when a strike is called, and does not openly disagree with it, while he may be an unwilling participant, he is nevertheless taking part in the industrial action. Here the employee's fear of crossing the picket line and subsequent certified illness during the period of the strike were insufficient reasons to rebut the presumption that she was taking part in industrial action.

'Relevant employees' under s.238(2) are defined as those employees at the establishment who were taking part in the strike at the date of the complainant's dismissal. It does not include, therefore, those employees who have participated in the strike and then returned to work before that date, so the fact that they are not dismissed does not entitle the dismissed employees to present a claim.

> In *Crosville Wales Ltd. v. Tracey and Others* 1993 it was held that the term 'offer of re-engagement' for the purposes of s.238 does not cover the situation where the employer is merely advertising vacancies and subsequently makes job offers to those participating in the industrial action.

In deciding whether a tribunal has jurisdiction to entertain a complaint of unfair dismissal, the time at which it has to be shown that one or more employees who took part in a strike were not dismissed, is the conclusion of the relevant hearing at which the tribunal determines whether it had jurisdiction. So held the Court of Appeal in *P & O European Ferries (Dover) Ltd. v. Byrne* 1989. Consequently if the identities of the strikers who had not been dismissed are revealed during the proceedings, an employer can absolve himself of liability by simply dismissing them. An employer who, by mistake, fails to dismiss all the strikers in these circumstances will still be able to shelter behind the section, therefore, if the mistake is revealed before the conclusion of the proceedings and those strikers employed are summarily dismissed.

There is a difference between the definition of *'relevant employees'* at the date of dismissal where the employer is conducting a lock out as opposed to dismissing during a strike or other industrial action. If an employer dismisses strikers then for the purposes of s.238 *'relevant employees'* exclude those who have returned to work at the date of dismissal. If however at the date of dismissal the employer is operating a lock out *'relevant employees'* are defined in s.238(3)(a) as employees directly interested in the dispute in contemplation or furtherance of which the lock out occurred. This means that an employee who has been locked out, but who had already returned to work at the time of dismissal could still be a relevant employee. In the famous 1993 industrial dispute between the Timex Electronics Corporation and its employees at its Dundee factory, the staff overwhelmingly rejected the company's offer of radically less favourable terms and conditions of employment. The subsequent strike was followed by an attempted return to work under protest and a management lock out. The employers strategy was to recruit a replacement workforce and dismissal notices were issued to existing staff. To retain the protection of s.238 and so removing the threat of unfair dismissal claims the company also dismissed seventeen workers who had returned to work. These workers could still have been classified as *'relevant employees.'*[85]

In *TNT Express (UK) Ltd. v. Downes and others* 1993 following the dismissal of employees who participated in a one-hour long strike, claims for unfair dismissal were presented when within days of the strike there was selective re-engagement of two of the strikers who were long standing employees. Under s.238 the tribunal had jurisdiction to hear the complaint and awarded compensation for unfair dismissal and refused to reduce the amount or account of the employees conduct in participating in the industrial action. The EAT disagreed however and held that all the circumstances should be considered in assessing compensation, including the industrial action. In doing so the EAT departed from its previous decision in *Courtaulds Northern Spinning v. Moosa* 1984.

The legal position in relation to official industrial action and dismissal has been substantially amended by the Employment Relations Act 1999 and the insertion of s.238A into TULR(C) 1992.

> *Under s.238A(2) an employee who is dismissed shall be regarded as unfairly dismissed if:*
>
> (a) *the reason for the dismissal is that the employee took protected industrial action; and*
>
> (b) *subsection (3), (4) or (5) applies to the dismissal.*
>
> (3) *This subsection applies to a dismissal if it takes place within the period of twelve weeks beginning on the day on which the employee started to take protected industrial action.*
>
> (4) *This subsection applies to a dismissal if:*
>
> (a) *it takes place after the end of that period; and*
>
> (b) *the employee had stopped taking protected industrial action before the end of that period.*
>
> (5) *This subsection applies to a dismissal if:*
>
> (a) *it takes place after the end of that period;*
>
> (b) *the employee had not stopped taking protected industrial action before the end of that period; and*
>
> (c) *the employer had not taken such procedural steps as would have been reasonable for the purposed of resolving the dispute to which the protected industrial action relates.*

For the purpose of the section therefore the dismissal must take place within an twelve week period beginning with the day on which the employee started to take the protected industrial action. Alternatively the dismissal took place after the end of the twelve week

---

85. Under s.238

period but the employee had stopped taking protected industrial action before the end of that period. It is also automatically unfair to dismiss after the end of the twelve week period when the employee has continued to take protected industrial action and the employer had not taken *'such procedural steps as would have been reasonable for the purposes of resolving the dispute to which the protected industrial action relates'.* If a collective agreement established a procedure for the resolution of a dispute that will be deemed to be the appropriate procedure for these purposes it would be tempting to presume that the new s.238A would make s.238 redundant however this is not the case. For s.238A to be triggered the industrial action taken must be official and protected which effectively means sanctioned by the relevant trade union and lawfully confirmed through balloting. Section 238 is relevant if the industrial action is official and satisfies s.237(2) but is not protected because of a failure in the balloting process. Also s.238 is relevant where there are selective dismissals outside the eight week period and the employer has nevertheless taken the appropriate procedural steps to bring the dispute to an end.

Remedies for Unfair Dismissal

If a complaint of unfair dismissal is successful, the tribunal has authority to make an order for reinstatement or re-engagement or make an award of compensation. Irrespective of whether he has requested the remedies on his ET1, the tribunal is obliged to explain the remedies of reinstatement and re-engagement to a successful claimant and discover whether he wishes to apply for such an order. Under s.114(1) an order for reinstatement is an order that the employer shall treat the complainant in all respects as if he had not been dismissed, An order for reinstatement requires the employer to treat the complainant in all respects as if he had not been dismissed. By such an order, the employer would be required to make good any arrears of pay or any rights or privileges which would have accrued but for the dismissal. If the employee would have benefited from improvements in terms and conditions but for the dismissal, then the order must reflect the improvement from the date it was agreed. In exercising its discretion to make an order of reinstatement the tribunal must take account of:

- the wishes of the complainant;
- whether it is practicable for an employer to comply with such an order; and
- whether the complainant contributed to the dismissal and whether it would be just to make such an order.

If the tribunal decides not to make an order for reinstatement it must then consider the possibility of re-engagement. Under s.115(1) an order for re-engagement is an order on such terms as the tribunal may decide, that the complainant be re-engaged by the employer.

For re-engagement the tribunal must take account of the following considerations:

- the wishes of the employee;
- whether it is practicable for the employer to comply with an order for re-engagement; and
- where the employee contributed to some extent to the dismissal and whether it would be just to order re-engagement and if so, on what terms.

In *Nairne v. Highland & Islands Fire Brigade* 1989 the complainant was found to be unfairly dismissed because of a procedural irregularity, in that the purpose of a disciplinary interview had not been made clear to him, and he was never warned that he could be dismissed. This was despite the fact that the reason for dismissal was justifiable. The employee in question was a fire officer, who for the second time had been found guilty of a drink/driving offence and as a result had been disqualified from driving for three years. It was a contractual requirement of his job that he was able to drive and it was unreasonable to employ a substitute driver for a three year period. The finding of unfair dismissal was affirmed on appeal and the extent of the employee's contributory fault increased from 25% to 75%. Such a high degree of contributory fault and the fact that there was no suitable alternative job available made this an unsuitable case to order re-engagement.

In *Wood Group Heavy Industrial Tribunal v. Grossan* 1998 despite a finding of unfair dismissal the EAT was convinced that there was a breakdown of trust and confidence given that the employer substantially believed the allegations made against the employee. As a consequence the tribunal felt that re-engagement was an inappropriate remedy for it would be unlikely to repair the breakdown in confidence between the employer and the employee

The EAT in *Stena Houlder Ltd. v. Keenan* 1993 confirmed that when making a re-engagement order the tribunal must set out the terms of employment as specified in the section and an order which left the exact nature of the work and the rate of pay subject to agreement was insufficiently specific. Also in *Rank Xerox (UK) Ltd. v. Stryczeh* 1995 following a finding of unfair dismissal the tribunal ordered that the complainant should be re-engaged in a vacant position which had a higher salary and increased benefit. On appeal against the decision the EAT held that it is generally undesirable for a tribunal to order re-engagement in respect of a specific job rather than identifying the nature of the proposed employment. *'As a matter of law, an industrial tribunal cannot order that an employee be re-engaged on significantly more favourable terms than he would have enjoyed if he had been reinstated in his former job.'*

If a tribunal decides not to make either order it must make an award of compensation. But even if either order is made, a tribunal has no power to ensure that it is complied with. Failure to comply or fully comply with an order of reinstatement or re-engagement can only lead to an award of compensation subject to the maximum limit.

In *Artisan Press v. Strawley and Parker* 1986 after finding that the complainants had been unfairly dismissed from their jobs on security staff because of membership of an independent trade union, the tribunal ordered that they should be reinstated. The employer purported to re-employ them, but in fact their job duties differed significantly and rather than security, the new jobs involved cleaning with minor security functions. A further complaint of non-compliance with the reinstatement order was upheld, the tribunal awarding sums of £18,367 and £20,080 respectively. On an appeal against the amount of the additional awards, the EAT refused to accept the employer's argument that a distinction should be drawn between non-compliance with an order of reinstatement and failing to comply fully with such an order. Here the amount of the awards would not be interfered with.

Regardless of the loss which could include substantial arrears of wages, if the employer refuses to re-employ, the complainant's compensation was limited to the statutory compensation in force at the time, the basic compensatory and additional awards. Now following the Trade Union Reform and Employment Rights Act 1993 there is no longer a limit on the extent of compensation for non compliance with an order.

Compensation

The most common form of redress for unfair dismissal is compensation.

An order for compensation as redress for unfair dismissal may consist of a basic award, a compensatory award, an additional award and where the dismissal related to the membership or non-membership of a trade union, a special award.

Basic award

The basic award is payable in all cases of unfair dismissal irrespective of loss and is calculated under s.119(1) with reference to the complainant's continuous employment and average week's wage. It should be noted however that if it can be shown that the complainant contributed to the dismissal through his own fault, or has unreasonably refused an offer of reinstatement, the amount of the basic award can be reduced by a just and equitable proportion. The computation of the basic award is the same as for a redundancy payment, so the present maximum is £8,700.

The amount of the basic award is calculated by reference to the period the employee has been continuously employed, ending with the effective date of termination. By reckoning backwards from the effective date of termination the number of years employment can be determined allowing:

> *One and a half weeks' pay for each year of employment in which the employee was not below 41 years of age.*

> *One week's pay for each year the employee was not below 22 years of age.*

> *A half week's pay for each year of employment between 18 and 21 years of age.*

To calculate the basic award therefore it is necessary to determine the employee's gross pay up to a maximum of £290,[86] his length of service up to a maximum of 20 years and his age. The maximum award payable therefore is for an employee who is dismissed after 20 years' service, over the age of 41, with a gross wage in excess of £290. He will be entitled to a basic award of 20 x 1½ x £290 = £8,700.

In many cases the employee's period of continuous service will cover more than one age rate barrier. In such circumstances it is necessary to calculate the entitlement at the relevant rate, e.g. for an employee who is made redundant at the age of 44 who, after 15 years' service has a gross wage of £380, is entitled to:

---

86. From February 2006

3 years x 1½ x £290   £1305

plus

12 years x 1 x £290   £3,480

£4,785

A disturbing rule under s.119(4) for employees close to retirement is that on the effective date of termination, for each month that an employee is over the age of sixty four, the amount of the basic award is reduced by one-twelfth for each complete month worked. The justification for this is that the point of the basic award is to compensate the employee for the loss of accrued redundancy rights which, of course, are not payable on retirement. This rule will not apply when the Employment Equality (Age) Regulations come into force in October 2006.

Under s.122(4) of the employee is entitled to a redundancy payment because of an unfair dismissal by reason of redundancy, the basic award is reduced by the amount of the redundancy payment. Since both awards are calculated in the same way, in most cases the redundancy payment will reduce the basic award to nil. In *Bowman v. Allmakes Ltd*. 1995 the Court of Appeal held that the basic award should be reduced by the amount of a statutory redundancy payment only where the true reason for dismissal is redundancy. *'It is not enough that an employer made a payment to an employee which was expressed as being on the ground that the dismissal was by reason of redundancy, even if the employee accepted that description at the time.'* This means that if the tribunal determines that the dismissal in question is not one of redundancy then s.122(4) is irrelevant and the basic award in a finding of unfair dismissal is payable.

Finally under s.120 there is one case where there is a minimum basic award payable regardless of the calculation and that is where the dismissal is connected with redundancy, with trade union representation under s.103 or health and safety under s.100. Even this minimum payment could be reduced because of contributory fault.

Compensatory award

In assessing the amount of the compensatory award, under s.123, a tribunal must have regard to the loss sustained by the complainant in consequence of the dismissal. A significant increase in the maximum compensatory award to £50,000 was introduced by the Employment Relations Act 1999 and it was raised to £58,400 from February 2006.

If there is no loss, then no compensatory award is payable.

> Such was the position in *Isleworth Studios Ltd. v. Richard* 1988 where the complainant was unfairly dismissed when his fixed term contract was prematurely brought to an end. The fact that during the unexpired term of the contract the complainant went on to earn £10,000 in excess of what he would have earned in his former employment meant that he had suffered no loss.

The amount of a compensatory award should under s.123(4) take account of any failure by the employee to mitigate his loss, for instance by refusing an offer of suitable alternative employment. The Court of Appeal held in *Babcock Fata v. Addison* 1987 that any money paid in lieu of notice should be deducted from a compensatory award as should any ex gratia payment made. Heads of compensation that are assessable include the loss of fringe benefits attached to the job, expense incurred in seeking alternative work, net wages lost up to the hearing, estimated future earnings, the termination of continuous employment which necessarily limits future rights and the loss of pension rights.

It should have been stressed that the compensatory award is not equivalent to an award of damages under the common law. Section 123 is a statutory provision constituting its own code for the assessment of compensation and *the 'just and equitable'* criterion confers a degree of flexibility on the industrial tribunal in deciding whether state benefit should be deducted from an award. In *Rubenstein and Roskin v. McGloughlin* 1996 the EAT held that *'In determining whether benefits received by the employee should be deducted from the compensatory award, it is legitimate to have regard to the fact that for a number of social security benefits, including invalidity benefit, there are statutory provisions affecting the damages recoverable for personal injury which mitigate the extremity of the common law by adopting solutions which involve treating employer and employee equally, either by dividing the value of the benefits between them by the device of half deduction or by removing it from both by requiring recoupment.'* The EAT decided that in the case of invalidity benefit to which the claimant had contributed, but which is not in the category of pure 'insurance monies', fully funded by the employee, it was just and equitable to deduct one half of the benefit received by the employee from the compensatory award.

Until recently the compensatory award was limited to financial loss could not extend to hurt feelings. Although unfair dismissal may be traumatic, no damages were available for the distress caused by the employer's action. Lord Hoffman's comments in his leading judgment in *Johnson v. Unisys Ltd.* 2001 are particularly significant. He said that *'I know in the early days of the National Industrial Relations Court it was laid down that only financial loss can be compensated but I think that it is too narrow a construction. The emphasis is on the tribunal awarding such compensation as it thinks just and equitable. So I see no reason why in an appropriate case it should not include compensation for distress, humiliation, damage to reputation in the community or to family life.'*

In *Dunnachie v. Kingston upon Hull City Council 2004* the House of Lords has ruled that the word 'loss' in the compensation provisions of the Employment Rights Act 1996 relate only to pecuniary loss and does not cover injury to feelings, humiliation or distress arising out of the dismissal or it's manner. Ld Steyn confirmed that the statement by Lord Hoffman in *Johnson Unisys* 2001 which seemed to suggest otherwise should not be followed and that the phrase 'just and equitable' does not permit tribunals to award sums other than financial loss. The statutory words from 1971 when they were originally enacted clearly expressed Parliament's intention that awards for injury to feelings should not be made in unfair dismissal cases.

An important issue in relation to injury to feelings caused by the manner of dismissal is that if the compensatory award is not available for this loss could a claim for damages be maintained in the ordinary courts on the basis of a breach of the implied term of trust and confidence In *Eastwood v. Magnox Electric plc/McCabe v. Cornwall County Council* 2004 the House of Lords draws a line between events leading up to dismissal, in respect of which the trust and confidence term applies, and the dismissal itself, for which the employee's only remedy is an unfair dismissal claim subject to the statutory cap. A common law claim will only be allowed where a cause of action has accrued before dismissal. This could include situations where there is financial loss flowing from suspension or from psychiatric or other illness caused by unfair treatment pre-dismissal.[87] The House of Lord felt that the

---

87. See *Gogay v. Hertfordshire County Council* Chapter 4

implied term of trust and confidence could not co-exist satisfactorily with the statutory unfair dismissal code. Lord Steyn regards the current state of the law as unsatisfactory and highlighted the many potential difficulties and anomalies which will now ensue from this demarcation, including duplication of proceedings, and the artificiality of drawing a line between the disciplinary process and dismissal. The answer, according to Lord Nicholls, is to remove the statutory cap so that a tribunal can award full compensation for an employee's financial loss.

There is no doubt of course that dismissal can cause emotional distress so that it is understandable in many unfair dismissal scenarios there are additional claims for unlawful discrimination if appropriate, where injury to feelings may be compensated. Injury to feelings are of course recognised for the purposes of compensation in discrimination legislation[88] so that if a dismissal is proved to be sex or race discrimination then the distress suffered by the applicant can be compensated.

> In *Hilton International Hotels (UK) Ltd. v. Faraji* 1994 it was held that an unfairly dismissed employee was still entitled to a compensatory award for loss of earnings notwithstanding that he was in receipt of invalidity benefit during the relevant period. *'It does not inexorably follow that because invalidity benefit is being paid that a person has no earning potential over the relevant period and so cannot have suffered loss in terms of the section'. Invalidity benefit can properly be characterised as an insurance type of benefit and as such does not fall to be deducted from unfair dismissal compensation.'*

> In *Devine v. Designer Flowers Wholesale Florist Sundries Ltd.* 1993 the EAT found that the complainant, who had been unfairly dismissed was entitled to a compensatory award which reflected the fact that as a result of her dismissal she suffered from anxiety and reactive depression which meant that she was unfit to look for work. *'An employee who has become unfit for work wholly or partly as a result of an unfair dismissal is entitled to a compensation for loss of earnings at least for a reasonable period following the dismissal, until she might reasonably have been expected to find other employment. The industrial tribunal must have regard to the loss sustained by the employee, consider how far it is attributable to action taken by the employer, and arrive at a sum which it considers just and equitable. There is no reason why the personal circumstances of the employee, including the effect of dismissal on her health, should not be taken into account in ascertaining the appropriate amount of compensation.'*

In *Dignity Funerals Ltd. v. Bruce* 2005 the Court of Session considered whether a compensatory award was payable to an employee who had been diagnosed as having depression after disciplinary proceedings were commenced against him for gross misconduct. The employment tribunal had held that no award was payable between the date of dismissal and the date of the tribunal hearing because the applicant was unfit for work. The Court of Session disagreed stating that a tribunal has to consider two main questions in deciding whether to make a compensatory award. Firstly whether the applicant's dismissal was one of the causes of his wage loss and, if it was, secondly what award would be just and equitable in all the circumstances. *'The former question was one of fact...the latter was one of discretion ... any application of the just and equitable test ... must be underpinned by*

---

88. See Chapter 6

findings in fact that the loss was caused to a material extent by the dismissal.' If the dismissal was not a cause of the loss of wages, no award will be due. If it was the sole cause, a full award will normally be appropriate.

Earlier in the chapter we referred to the EAT decision in *Market Forces UK Ltd. v. Hunt* 2002 where a decision to dismiss was found to be procedurally unfair by the Tribunal because of the failure of the employer to carry out a proper investigation. The Tribunal also ruled that if proper investigation had been carried out there was a 25% chance that the applicant's explanation would have been accepted and he would not have been dismissed. On that basis the compensation was reduced by 75%. This is known as a Polkey reduction based on the previously mentioned decision of the House of Lords in *Polkey v. Dayton Services*. In fact the Polkey reduction here was found to be an error of law by the EAT because the Tribunal had offended the elementary principle of law and procedure that each party has the right to be heard and they should have been given the opportunity to address the Tribunal on the issues raised by a proposed Polkey reduction.

In *Gover v. Property Care Ltd.* 2005 the EAT reminded tribunals that they should consider making a Polkey reduction for unfair dismissal in:

1. length of time cases, where dismissal would have occurred in due course;

2. cases where the claimant could have been dismissed on some other ground; and

3. cases where there was a chance of surviving dismissal.

The compensatory award, like the basic award, may also,[89] be reduced because of the claimant's contributory fault.

In *The Post Office v. Ramkisson* 1993 an employee with a long unblemished service record was dismissed for a serious incident of misconduct involving the falsification of a medical certificate in order to obtain a further week's sick pay. Both the tribunal and the EAT felt that given his service record, the decision to dismiss, rather than opt for some other course of action was not open to a reasonable employer applying the proper principles of industrial relations. It was also decided however that as the complainant had contributed to his dismissal by 90%, his compensation should be reduced by this percentage to reflect his contributory fault.

In *Soros and Soros v. Davison and Davison* 1994 the EAT held that in assessing the compensatory award for unfair dismissal it is not permissible to take account of post-dismissal conduct of the employee. Here it was argued that the alleged misconduct of ex employees in selling information about their employer to a national newspaper, after the finding of unfair dismissal, constituted a breach of duty which was relevant to the issue of redress. The EAT said that *'The section is concerned with events which have existed during the contract of employment, not subsequent to it. That is the plain meaning of the language of the subsection. The proposition that any misconduct even if committed after the employee was*

---

89. Under s.123(6)

dismissed should be brought into the scales when assessing compensation was not supported by the decision of the House of Lords in W. Devis & Sons Ltd. v. Atkins 1977.'

In *Voith Turbo Ltd v. Stowe* 2005 the EAT held that a tribunal may, in accordance with good employment relations practice, ignore earnings acquired in new employment during the notice period of the previous employment, when calculating the compensatory award for the purpose of unfair dismissal.

Additional award

The additional award is payable under s.117 where an employer does not comply with an order of reinstatement or re-engagement and fails to establish that it was not reasonably practicable to comply with the order. The amount of the award is not less than 26 nor more than 52 weeks pay. Following the Employment Relations Act 1999 the special award for dismissals relating to trade union membership or the activities of safety representatives was abolished.

Interim relief

If the dismissal is in connection with trade union membership or participating in trade union activities, or health and safety an application may be made for interim relief[90] within seven days of the dismissal, supported by a signed certificate from a trade union official that there are reasonable grounds to believe that this is the true reason for dismissal. A tribunal satisfied that there are reasonable grounds can order that the employment should continue until the final hearing.

> In *Alexander v. Standard Telephones and Cables Ltd. and Wall* 1990 the common law rule that the courts will not grant an injunction which will have the effect of compelling specific performance was re-emphasised, the High Court indicating a solitary exception where it can be shown that the employer has not lost confidence in the employee in question. Since this will rarely be the case in a dismissal situation, the prospect of an injunction to restrain a dismissal must now be highly unlikely.

90. Under s.128(1)

Further Reading

Anderman, S. *The Interpretation of Protective Employment Statutes and Contracts of Employment* (2000) 29 ILJ 223.

Collins, Hugh *Procedural Fairness After Polkey* (1990) 19 ILJ 39.

Collins, Hugh *The Meaning of Job Security* (1991) 20 ILJ 227.

Ewing, K. D. *The Human Rights Act and Labour Law* (1998) 27 ILJ 275.

Freer, Andy *The Range of Reasonable Responses Test – From Guidelines to Statute* (1998) 27 ILJ 335.

Lewis, David *Re Employment as a Remedy for Unfair Dismissal* (1999) 29 ILJ 171.

Pitt, Gwyneth *Justice in Dismissal: A Reply to Hugh Collins* (1993) 22 ILJ 251.

Chapter 12

Redundancy

Redundancy Payments

The concept of redundancy owes part of its complexity to the various contexts in which the term appears.

For the purpose of a redundancy payment, redundancy occurs under the legal definition when an employee is dismissed because an employer has closed his business or the business is closed in the place the employee works. Alternatively there is redundancy if the employer no longer requires or has a reduced requirement for employees to carry out work of a particular kind. In both cases there must be no suitable alternative employment. As far as unfair dismissal is concerned a dismissal by reason of redundancy is a statutory reason for dismissal and provided the employer consults when he need to and adopts rational criterion for selection, such a dismissal may be classified as fair. There is also the layman view of redundancy as a term used by employers and employees whenever a business decides to shed some of its staff. All of these contexts are considered in this chapter.

The right to a redundancy payment for workers dismissed because there is no longer a demand for their services was first introduced in 1965 under the Redundancy Payments Act. The 1965 Act represented a major statutory intervention in the individual employment relationship, for while redundancy/severance payments have always been contractually agreed, the Act made the State redundancy payment a statutory requirement for qualifying employees. It was the first example of any State provision for compensation for workers who lost their jobs through no fault of their own. The complex provisions of the Act are now found in the Employment Rights Act 1996. It should be stressed from the outset that redundancy payments are now dwarfed by potential unfair dismissal compensation so that their significance has greatly diminished over the years.

The object of redundancy provision is to compensate a worker for the loss of a long term stake he has in his job. In the mid 1960s it was thought that the provision of lump sum severance payments to redundant employees would encourage a shake out of underemployed labour in industry generally, with less risk of industrial action. It was also thought that such payments would encourage mobility of labour to accommodate technological advances. Under the original scheme every employer made contributions to the Redundancy Fund and received a rebate of 35% for every payment made. In 1986 the rebate was abolished except for those employers who employ less than ten employees and payments can still be made by the State on an employer's insolvency. Employment tribunals have jurisdiction over disputes relating to entitlement and the amount of any redundancy payment and also where the complaint is one of unfair dismissal due to unfair selection for redundancy.

It should be recognised that between 1965 and 1971 disputes in relation to redundancy provided the main work of industrial tribunals in industrial conflict. When the right not to be unfairly dismissed was introduced in 1971 however, employees were more likely to argue that they had been dismissed unfairly rather than redundant and so entitled to increased compensation. To qualify for the right to a redundancy payment an employee must establish two years service[1] with the same employer. For an unfair dismissal claim of course the qualifying period has been reduced to one year.[2]

Qualifying workers

Originally to qualify for the right to a redundancy payment it was necessary to establish two years continuous employment with the same employer as a full-time employee over the age of eighteen. Now part-time employees regardless of their hours can also qualify for a payment with two years continuous employment. This right is contained in the Employment Protection (Part-time Employees) Regulations 1995. For the moment redundancy payments are only available to employees so that status as a worker or an independent contractor would not qualify.

It is not unusual for controlling shareholders of small companies to claim that as they work under a contract of employment they should be entitled to a payment when the company goes into liquidation. Over the years there have been conflicting decisions as whether controlling shareholders can qualify as employees. The Court of Appeal in *Secretary of State for Trade and Industry v. Bottrill* 1999 considered the position of a managing director of a small UK company who had been engaged under a contract of employment and did not receive directors' fees. He had intended his shareholding to be purchased by an American company but prior to that, his company got into financial difficulties and he was dismissed by the receiver. The Court of Appeal held that there was a genuine employment relationship between the shareholder and his company and he could be classified as an employee.

To qualify the period of employment must be continuous and continuity of employment is examined in Chapter 9. For the purposes of redundancy however s.213(3)(c) is significant for it provides that breaks will not affect continuity:

(a) *if some kind of arrangement was made whereby employment is to be treated as continuing; or*

(b) *established custom and practice dictates that the break does not affect continuity of employment.*

However following *Booth and others v. United States* 1999[3] it seems that if the break in employment is clearly intended by the employer and is designed to defeat the effect of

---

1. Under s.155
2. See Chapter 11
3. See also *Curr v. Marks & Spencer* 2003 Chapter 9

redundancy and/or unfair dismissal then s.213(3) will not apply. The practice of employing staff on a series of fixed term contracts, with breaks in continuity for the purpose of removing statutory rights, has encouraged legislators to implement the provisions of the Directive on Fixed Term Employment in the Fixed Term Employees (Prevention of Less Favourable Treatment) Regulations 2002.[4]

Under s.135(1) An employer shall pay a redundancy payment to any employee of his if the employee:

(a) *is dismissed by the employer by reason of redundancy; or*

(b) *is eligible for a redundancy payment by reason of being laid off or kept on short-time.*

For the purpose of the section therefore it is necessary to consider what would constitute a dismissal, and whether it is attributable to redundancy.

Certain categories of employees are also excluded from making a claim:

- Persons who have attained retirement age which under the Employment Act 1989 is 65 for both men and women. (Subject to the Employment Equality (Age) Regulations 2006.)

- Persons ordinarily employed outside Great Britain unless on the date of dismissal for redundancy they are in Great Britain following the employer's instructions.

- Persons who are covered by a redundancy agreement approved by the Secretary of State.

- 'Office holders' who are not employees.

- Domestic servants in a private household who are close relatives of the employer.

At the time of writing the present age exclusion for redundancy is subject to a challenge in an appeal made to the House of Lords in March 2006.

To qualify to make a claim for a redundancy payment, an employee must have been dismissed by reason of redundancy, laid off or kept on short time. The definition of dismissal for this purpose is set out in s.136(1) of the Employment Rights Act 1996 in broadly similar terms to the definition of dismissal under s.95 for the purposes of unfair dismissal.[5]

Dismissal

Dismissal for the purposes of redundancy will normally be express under s.136(1)(a) but it could also occur on the expiration of a fixed term contract under s.136(1)(b) or even be a constructive dismissal under s.136(1)c).

> In *Bass Leisure Ltd. v. Thomas* 1994[6] the applicant claimed a redundancy payment when she left her job after the employer had tried to move her to an unsuitable job location. As the express or implied terms of the contract did not authorise the move, it was a fundamental breach of contract and constituted a constructive dismissal by reason of redundancy.

---

4. See Chapter 7
5. See Chapter 10
6. See Chapter 1

A decision of the EAT in 1996 in two cases involving part-time lecturing staff, *Pfaffinger v. City of Liverpool College and Muller v. Amersham & Wycombe College*, confirmed that part-time employees employed on a succession of fixed term lecturing contracts are dismissed for redundancy on the expiration of each contract. That is the combined effect of the definition of dismissal and the definition of redundancy under the Employment Rights Act 1996. '*Thus, a college lecturer with three fixed-term contracts during the academic year may be dismissed three times during that year for redundancy. In such a case, the college's need for employees to carry out the function of lecturing ceases or diminishes from the beginning of the vacation until the start of the new term. There is no teaching during that period and therefore no need for teachers. That is a redundancy situation.*'

It should be noted that s.197(3) provided that under a fixed term contract of two years or more an employee could agree to waive his rights to a redundancy payment on its expiration. This provision is now repealed by the Fixed-term Employees (Prevention of Less favourable Treatment) Regulations 2002.

The Act further provides under s.136(5) that there is a deemed dismissal because of the employer's act or some event affecting him, for example the employer's death, dissolution of a partnership, or winding up of a company.

> In *Brown v. Knowsley BC* 1986 the applicant having been employed in a college of further education under a number of fixed term contracts was offered a one year temporary contract from 1 September 1983, stipulated to last as long as funds from the Manpower Services Commission were provided for the course she taught. On 3 August 1984 she was given written notice that as the MSC funding had ceased, her employment terminated on 31 August 1984. The applicant's claim for a redundancy payment was rejected by the tribunal who found there to be no dismissal but rather a discharge of the contract by performance. The EAT agreed that there had been no dismissal, and held that the contract was terminable on the happening or non-happening of a future event, in this case the withdrawal of funding by the MSC.

If an employee leaves prematurely in a redundancy situation without waiting to be dismissed, then this will prejudice the success of a claim.

> In *Morton Sundour Fabrics v. Shaw* 1966 the employee in question, having been warned of the possibility of redundancy, left to take other employment. The court held that as he had not been dismissed, he was therefore not entitled to a redundancy payment.

Even when notice of dismissal by reason of redundancy has been served, if employees subsequently accept an offer of voluntary early retirement, as an alternative to redundancy, they would not be entitled to a redundancy payment.

> This was the controversial decision of the EAT in *Scott v. Coalite Fuels and Chemicals Ltd.* 1988. By reaching an agreement as to a voluntary termination of employment, the nature of an earlier notice of dismissal was consequently changed so that the tribunal was entitled to find that there had been no dismissal for the purpose of redundancy.

> In *Mowlem Northern Ltd. v. Watson* 1990 a foreman employee was given notice that his employment would terminate by reason of redundancy on a given date when his contract came to an end. Without prejudicing his right to a redundancy

payment the employee was offered the chance to work temporarily beyond the date that the redundancy notice expired in the hopes that this would lead to an offer of further permanent employment. The employee took up the offer but after a few months resigned and claimed the redundancy payment. The employer's decision to withhold the payment was upheld by the industrial tribunal who felt that the subsequent termination of employment was not by reason of redundancy. On appeal however the EAT held that *'there is nothing in statute to preclude the employer and employee from postponing the date by mutual agreement until the happening of an agreed event'.* The idea of offering temporary employment in the hope that something permanent might arise was *'a thoroughly sensible arrangement and there was nothing in law preventing it'.* An employee should in such circumstances retain the right to a redundancy payment.

If an employee succumbs to pressure to resign in a redundancy situation, the resignation could still be treated as a dismissal for the purposes of redundancy.

In *Caledonian Mining Co. Ltd. v. Bassett* 1987 a sympathetic approach was taken by the EAT to employees who in a redundancy situation had written to their employer terminating their employment. The men had originally been told that manpower on their site would be reduced, and asked whether they would be interested in alternative employment. Despite an expression of interest by the men, the employer did not respond and failed to offer alternative work. The men did receive an offer from the National Coal Board which they accepted. This led to the letter of termination which the employer argued constituted a resignation, and as there had been no dismissal in law there was no right to a redundancy payment. The EAT agreed with the tribunal however and held that the men had been encouraged to resign and take another job with the intention of avoiding redundancy payments. The true position here was that the employer had caused the men to resign, and in reality the employer was terminating the contract. Accordingly the employees were dismissed in law and entitled to a redundancy payment.

In *Hellyer Brothers Ltd. v. Atkinson and Dickinson* 1993 the Court of Appeal held that despite the fact that two seamen had signed a document showing the reason for contractual termination as 'mutual consent' the tribunal and the EAT were entitled to decide that the true reason for termination was dismissal by reason of redundancy.

The Employment Rights Act recognises that it may be in the employee's interest to leave prematurely in a redundancy situation and still qualify for a payment. If an employee has already received notice of dismissal, he may, during the obligatory period of that notice, serve his own notice to terminate the contract earlier than the employer's notice. Provided the employee's notice is served during the obligatory period which is the minimum period of notice required by statute, basically one week for each year's employment up to twelve, then the employee will not lose his right to a redundancy payment.[7] If the employee's notice is served outside the obligatory period it will be interpreted as a resignation and no redundancy claim can be made. Also, as a response to the employee's notice, the employer can, serve a second notice requiring the employee to withdraw his notice. Failure to comply could lead to an employee losing the right to the whole or part of the payment.

---

7. See s.136(3)

Under s.136(1)(c) a unilateral variation of the contract of employment to which the employee does not assent could constitute a repudiatory breach and entitle an employee to leave and regard himself as constructively dismissed.

> In *Marriott v. Oxford District Coop Society Ltd.* 1969 a foreman supervisor was told by his employer that the position of foreman was no longer required and that his wage would be reduced by £1 per week to reflect his loss of status. The employee continued to work under protest for three weeks before terminating his employment by notice, claiming redundancy. The Court of Appeal held that there had been no true consent to the contractual variation, and the contract of employment had been terminated by reason of redundancy so that the employee was entitled to a redundancy payment.

In Chapter 5 the fluid nature of the contract of employment was discussed, particularly in relation to contractual variation. While the express terms of the contract of employment could provide for a change in contractual duties, there is also a degree of managerial discretion or prerogative to effect changes in work patterns. It could be therefore that a reorganisation of the working day, a requirement to adapt to new working methods or a change in the place of employment, even without express authorisation in the contract of employment, could nevertheless be justified on the grounds of efficiency, and so would not constitute a breach of the contract of employment.

Lay off and short-time

In cases where there is a cessation or diminution in work requirements the employer may respond by laying off staff or putting them on to short-time. In the absence of a contractual right to do so, such action could of course, constitute a breach of contract enabling the employee to regard himself as constructively dismissed and so entitled to claim redundancy or unfair dismissal. For a lay off or short-time of four consecutive weeks or an aggregate of six or more weeks in a period of thirteen weeks, s.148 provides that an employee can serve notice that he intends to make a claim for a payment. For this purpose 'lay off' occurs where no work and no wages are provided and short-time means that an employee earns less than one half his wages in any given week. In such a situation an employee could then serve notice to terminate the contractual relationship altogether and so qualify for a redundancy payment. This is subject to the employer's right to serve a counter notice within the time limits, which will defeat the claim if the employer can show that there is a reasonable prospect of work in not later than four weeks time, for at least thirteen weeks, without the possibility of lay off or short-time working. The onus is on the employer to establish through evidence the likelihood of the period of employment, and failure to do so will mean that the employee is entitled to a redundancy payment.

Redundancy Dismissal

The right to a redundancy payment arises when a qualifying employee has been dismissed by reason of redundancy[8] or is laid off or kept on shot-time.[9] for the purposes of s.148. The reason for dismissal must therefore be redundancy, a presumption of which arises in

---

8. Under s.139
9. Under s.148

favour of the applicant unless the contrary is proved.[10] It is for the employer to rebut the presumption of redundancy on the balance of probabilities by showing that the dismissal was for some reason other than redundancy.

Before we analyse the complex definition of redundancy and the different approaches to its interpretation by the courts you should appreciate that the definition serves different purposes. In the years before the introduction of unfair dismissal in 1971 it is the employee exclusively who would seek to establish a redundancy dismissal in order to qualify for a redundancy payment. Post unfair dismissal the employee may still attempt to establish the right to a payment but a redundancy is a potentially fair reason for dismissal and an employer may have an interest in asserting that redundancy is the reason for dismissal which is potentially fair. An employer alleging a fair redundancy dismissal is more likely today bearing in mind the potential £56,000 compensatory award for unfair dismissal. Using the statutory definition for different purposes has inevitably caused confusion in the approach of the courts and tribunals to its interpretation.

In s.139(1) the Act provides that there is a dismissal by reason of redundancy if it is *attributable wholly or mainly to:*

(a) *the fact that his employer has ceased or intends to cease, (i) to carry on the business for the purposes of which the employee was employed by him, or (ii) to carry on that business in the place where the employee was so employed; or*

(b) *the fact that the requirements of that business (i) for employees to carry out work of a particular kind, or (ii) for employees to carry out work of a particular kind in the place where the employee was employed by his employer, have ceased or diminished or are expected to cease or diminish.*

Business closure

This is the more straightforward part of the definition.

Redundancy could occur[11] because the business is closed or it is intended that it will be. Such a closure could relate to the whole business or just a part of it and be permanent or temporary. In addition redundancy could arise if the business is closed in the place where the employee works. If, however, the employee's contract provides that he could be required to move to a new work location, and the employer attempts to trigger the clause, this could prevent redundancy. Even without an express clause there is an implied term in the contract of employment that the employee may be moved to a new work location within reasonable commuting distance from home. Consider however the following case.

> In *High Table Ltd. v. Horst* 1997 the Court of Appeal considered the position of silver service waitresses who all worked for one particular client in the City of London but who following a reorganisation were no longer required at that place of work. Their contracts of employment contained a mobility clause which authorised the employer to move them to other work locations. Applying s.139(1)(a) the issue was whether the women were redundant because they were no longer required at their usual client or whether the mobility clause extended their place of work to any potential work location. The Court of

10. Under s.163(2)
11. Under s.139(1)

Appeal disagreed with the EAT and rejected the contractual approach to place of work stating that *'if an employee has worked in only one location under his contract of employment for the purposes of the employer's business, it defies common sense to widen the extent of the place where he was employed merely because of the existence of a mobility clause'.* Here the place where the employee worked was the particular client and there was a redundancy situation there which caused their dismissals.

In *High Table* the Court of Appeal is recognising that an employer could easily use the device of a wide mobility clause to defeat a finding of redundancy. In such circumstances the courts should concentrate on the factual circumstances which obtained rather than apply a contractual test to determine redundancy.

Diminution in requirements

There is also a redundancy situation where the requirements of the business for employees to carry out work of a particular kind have ceased or diminished or expected to do so under s.139(b).

There were two different approaches to this definition, both of which have been rejected by the House of Lords. You should nevertheless appreciate that each approach has its supporters. The job function test attempts to identify redundancy in terms of economic requirements of the employer for the work to be done so that if the job function still exists there is no redundancy. The alternative approach called the contracts test is to consider whether the requirements of the business have diminished by reference to all the contractual duties of the employee. An issue of contention is when the definition refers to a diminution for employees to carry out work of a particular kind does that refer to the work of a dismissed employee or is it sufficient that a reduction in work has caused the dismissal.

The term 'bumping' has been used to explain the situation where a reduction in requirements has led to an employee being replaced and dismissed. A good example was used in *Safeway Stores plc v. Burrell* 1997. Where the EAT held that the principle of bumped redundancies is statutorily correct. *'For example, if a fork-lift truck driver, delivering material to six production machines on the shop floor, each with its own operator, is selected for dismissal on the basis of last in first out within the department following the employer's decision that only five machines are needed, and one machine operator with longer service is transferred to driving the fork-lift truck the truck driver is dismissed by reason of redundancy. Although under both the contract and the function test he is employed as a fork-lift truck driver. There is no diminution in the requirements for the fork-lift drivers, nevertheless there is a diminution in the request for employees to carry out the machine operator's work and that has caused the driver's dismissal.'*

The fact that the dismissed employee has been replaced by another employee will not normally lead to a finding of redundancy for it cannot be said that the requirements of the business for an employee have ceased or diminished. There would be a redundancy, however, if it could be shown that the replacement employee was moved because of a reduction in requirements. Here an employee is being dismissed to make way for an employee who would otherwise be surplus to requirements and so the dismissed employee is entitled to a redundancy payment.

If a dismissal has been caused by a reorganisation then the reason for the dismissal may be redundancy if it is attributable to the fact that the requirements of the business for employees to carry out work of a particular kind have ceased or diminished.

In *Robinson v. British Island Airways Ltd.* 1977 the applicant, a Flight Operations Manager found that his duties were absorbed by a new post, an Operations Manager, following a reorganisation of the business. When he unsuccessfully applied for the new post his employer dismissed him by reason of redundancy. The EAT agreed with the tribunal that by analysing the facts against the statutory definition it was possible to conclude that the new post of Operations Manager was an amalgam of duties from different posts including the Flight Operations Manager and this had caused the reduction in requirements for the applicant who was as a consequence redundant.

Would there be a redundancy dismissal under s.139 if a part-time secretary was replaced by a full-time secretary. This was the issue facing the EAT in *Barnes v. Gilmartin Associates* 1998 when the part-time secretary was replaced by a full-time worker and dismissed. Having decided that the secretarial job existed but in a different form, the EAT then concluded that there was no cessation or diminution for employees to carry out work of the particular kind so that the applicant was not redundant. In *Johnson v. Nottingham Combined Police Authority* 1974 the Court of Appeal had held that a change from regular hours to shifts was not redundancy stressing that it was the work not the hours which were relevant for deciding *'work of a particular kind'*. Here the business reorganisation was a substantial reason of the kind to justify a dismissal under s.98(1).[12]

The requirements of the business for employees of a particular kind will have ceased if they are replaced by independent contractors. To replace an employee with a self-employed person will be a dismissal by reason of redundancy and the dismissed employee will be entitled to a payment. This will also be the case where it is the employee himself who is being reinstated on self-employed status. Liability to make redundancy payments could be one of the costs of an employer transferring work from employees to independent contractors, but it may be that there are financial benefits in the long run. Such benefits would include the loss of future rights to redundancy payments and possible unfair dismissal rights and lower National Insurance contributions.

In situations where the employee's skills have become outdated because of changes in working methods to which he cannot or is not prepared to adapt, there have been conflicting views as to whether, if he is dismissed, it is by reason of redundancy or incapability.

In the history of the law of redundancy there are early examples of the courts being called upon to draw a distinction between diminishing requirements for an employee because of a reduction in a particular kind of work carried on, and diminishing requirements for an employee due to his failure to adapt to new working methods.

In *North Riding Garages Ltd. v. Butterwick* 1967 a workshop manager with thirty years experience was dismissed following a take-over and reorganisation of the business. The manager found it difficult to adapt to new methods which had been introduced, in particular coping with costs estimates. The repair side of the workshop for which he had been responsible was deliberately run down and the sales side increased. Following his dismissal a new workshop manager was engaged. The tribunal upheld the employee's claim for a redundancy payment deciding that the presumption of redundancy had not been rebutted. On appeal, however, it was held that there had been no change in the requirements of the business to carry out a particular kind of work, for there was still a need for a

---

12. Employment Rights Act 1996

workshop manager. It was the employee's personal deficiencies which caused the dismissal rather than redundancy. *'An employee remaining in the same kind of work was expected to adapt to new methods and higher standards of efficiency, unless the nature of the work he was required to do was thereby altered so that no requirement remained for employees to do work of the particular kind which was superseded.'*

'Personal deficiencies' was again the reason put forward by the employer for dismissal in *Hindle v. Percival Boats* 1969. The claimant, a highly skilled woodworker with twenty years boat-building experience was dismissed for being *'too good and too slow'* when fibreglass became the main material for boat-building rather than wood. He claimed a redundancy payment on the grounds that his dismissal was attributable wholly or mainly to a reduction in the employer's requirements for woodworkers. A majority of the Court of Appeal held that there was no dismissal by reason of redundancy, for the true reason for dismissal was that the claimant was too slow and his continued employment uneconomical. In the dissenting judgment, however, Lord Denning, MR, placed great emphasis on the statutory presumption of redundancy. *'Redundancy payment is compensation to a man for the loss of the job; and a man should not be deprived of it merely because the employer thinks or believes that he is being dismissed for a reason other than redundancy.'*

The approach to change seemed to be that so long as the job function remains, there is no redundancy. If an employee is given a very wide job function, that is likely to mean where there are technological or social changes in the way that a job is performed, that does not make it a different kind of work for the purposes of redundancy. In cases where an employee has an express flexibility clause in his contract that would not prevent a finding of redundancy where there is a clear reduction in requirements for him to carry out his primary job function.

In *Johnson v. Peabody Trust* 1996 the claimant was employed for a number of years as a roofer by a housing association however a term in his contract provided for flexibility in that if there was no roofing work he could be redeployed on other building operations such as plastering. In 1993 the claimant was, along with others, selected for redundancy due to a down turn in roofing work. The tribunal felt that the claimant was employed as a roofer and the fact that the employers requirements for roofing work had diminished meant that he was redundant. On appeal it was argued that under the contract test, as the claimant could be required to carry out multi trade operations, which had not diminished, he could not be classified as redundant. The EAT rejected this argument and held that here there was a fair dismissal by reason of redundancy despite the flexibility clause in the roofer's contract. The essential nature of the claimant's contract was that of a skilled roofer and the fact that he could be required to do other work did not alter that fact. In applying the contract test the EAT said that *'the contract should not be read in an over-technical or legalistic way but should be looked at in a common-sense manner in order ascertain the basic task which the employee is contracted to perform. Where, as here, an employee is employed to perform a particular, well recognised and well defined category of skilled trade, namely roofing work, in our judgment it is that basic obligation which has to be looked at when deciding whether the employer's requirements for work of a particular kind have or have not ceased or diminished. Were it otherwise an employer could in practice never establish that any skilled tradesman, employed as such, who had accepted a flexibility clause of the kind in this case, had become redundant without establishing that a redundancy situation existed in every single other trade encompassed within the ambit of such a flexibility clause'.*

Earlier we mentioned *Safeway Stores Plc v. Burrell* 1997 where the EAT moved away from the contract and job function test. The EAT held that the correct test for determining a redundancy dismissal involves three stages. Firstly was the employee dismissed? Secondly was this a diminution or cessation in the requirement of the employers business for employees to carry out work of a particular kind, or an expectation of such in the future. Thirdly was the dismissal of the employee caused wholly or mainly by that state of affairs. The EAT confirmed that there maybe a number of underlying causes of a redundancy situation. There could be a need for economies, a reorganisation, a reduction in production requirements or unilateral changes in employment terms. Such factors must be considered in deciding whether they have led to a diminution or cessation in the requirements. If that is the case the question then is whether the dismissal was attributable wholly or mainly to redundancy.

A significant ruling of the House of Lords in 1999 seems to signal a new more simplistic approach to the definition of redundancy.

> In *Murray v. Foyle Meats Ltd.* 1999 the House of Lords considered the statutory definition of redundancy describing it as *'simplicity itself'*. The case involved meat plant operatives who normally worked in the slaughter hall but whose contract of employment provided that they would be required to work anywhere in the factory. When a reorganisation of the factory resulted in a reduction in the need for skilled slaughterers the applicants were selected for redundancy. Both the tribunal and the Northern Ireland Court of Appeal felt that as the requirements of the employer for the employees to carry out work of a particular kind, the slaughtering, had ceased or diminished, the applicants had been made redundant. On appeal to the House of Lords however it was argued that work of a particular kind means contractually engaged work of a particular kind and as all the factory workers were on similar flexible contracts it was wrong to limit the redundancy situation to the slaughtermen. The House of Lords stressed that the key word in the statutory definition was *'attributable'* and both the contract test and the function test miss the point. Irrespective of the terms of an individuals' contract or the function he performs the issue is simply whether there is a diminution in requirements and if so whether the dismissal of the applicant is attributable to it. It is an issue of fact and one for the tribunal whether there is a causal connection between the reduction or needs and the applicant's dismissal.

> The House of Lords by emphasising the word *'attributable'* in s.139 is giving redundancy a wide definition so that there is no reason why the dismissal of an employee should not be attributable to a reduction in requirements irrespective of contractual terms or the job functions he performs. The two questions are *'is there an economic state of affairs involving a diminution of requirements and if so is the dismissal attributable to it'*. Applying the new test a bumped redundancy would certainly be covered by the definition.

As a result of *Foyle* it seems that tribunals should ignore the contract and function tasks the key issue being the link between the diminution in requirements and the dismissal. Certainly the employee's contract is largely irrelevant and it is no longer necessary to show a diminishing need for employees to do the work for which the dismissed employee was employed to do for him to be entitled to a redundancy payment.

Even with a new 'back to basics' interpretation of the definition of redundancy the Court of Appeal in *Shawkat v. Nottingham City Hospital NHS Trust* 2001 still found the determination of a redundancy dismissal a tortuous exercise. The applicant was a thoracic surgeon who was affected by the merger of the employer's thoracic and cardiac departments. He was dismissed after rejecting proposed changes to his contract of employment which would have changed his workload by reducing his thoracic work and taking on some cardiac work. The tribunal rejected his claim that he had been dismissed by reason of redundancy after making a finding of fact that there had been no reduction in the amount of thoracic surgery that needed to be performed or the employee needed to do it. The Court of Appeal agreed Longmore LJ stating that *'the mere fact that an employee with one skill is replaced with an employee of a different skill does not mean that an employment tribunal must necessarily find that the dismissed employee has been dismissed on grounds of redundancy. That is always a question of fact for the tribunal to decide'.* The court stated that the mere fact of a reorganisation of the business where the employees are moved from job to job is not conclusive of redundancy.

To reconcile the decision in *Shawkat* with *Foyle* and cases such as *Murphy v. Epsom College* 1984 the tribunal and the court must have decided that thoracic surgeons and surgeons who perform a mixture of thoracic and cardiac surgery are essentially the same kind of employee. *Foyle* suggests that tribunals should focus on what employees are actually doing rather than their contract or their function but it is still a question of fact for the tribunal to decide whether two employees perform work of the same or a different kind.

While the potential to qualify for redundancy payments are consequently increased as a result of this interpretation of the definition in *Murray* the opportunity for employers to use redundancy as a fair reason for dismissal are also greater.

In cases where the reason for dismissal is redundancy, but the employer was entitled to terminate the contract by reason of the employee's misconduct, the right to a redundancy payment will be lost. Obviously if the reason for dismissal is misconduct then the question of a redundancy payment does not arise. If the employee has already served notice of the 'obligatory period' for redundancy, and the employee is dismissed for gross misconduct during that period, the employee can still apply to the tribunal which can award all or part of the redundancy payment. Furthermore, if the misconduct takes the form of strike action during the 'obligatory period' any dismissal for that form of 'misconduct' will not operate to disqualify the redundancy payment. If, however, the strike takes place before the notice of dismissal for redundancy, and the employee participates, that would be classed as misconduct so as to disqualify a redundancy claim.

> In *Bonner v. H Gilbert Ltd.* 1989 the applicant was given notice that his employment would terminate on 13 February 1987 for redundancy, but in fact he was dismissed on 13 January 1987 for alleged dishonesty. The issue was whether the employer was entitled to terminate the contract because of the employee's conduct. The EAT held that the tribunal was wrong in applying the unfair dismissal test of reasonableness to the employer's decision to dismiss for misconduct. Rather, the contractual approach adopted for the purposes of constructive dismissal should be applied. The employer's burden was 'to show that the employee was guilty of conduct which was a significant breach going to the root of the contract or which showed that the employee no longer intended to be bound by one or more of the essential terms of the contract'.

As we noted earlier, due to the fact that the possible compensation payable for unfair dismissal is well in excess of the State redundancy payment it may be that an applicant is more likely to pursue a claim for unfair dismissal rather than a redundancy payment. Redundancy is of course one of the specific reasons identified as a prima facie fair ground for dismissal. If redundancy proves not to be the true reason relied on for dismissal then a tribunal is entitled to find that the dismissal is unfair.

> In *Timex Corporation v. Thomson* 1981 the applicant, one of three managers, who, after fourteen years of employment with the company, was dismissed when the three management posts were re-organised into two. The two new posts required engineering qualifications which the applicant lacked, but it was also alleged that he was not selected because of his poor job performance. The EAT agreed with the tribunal and held that even though there was a redundancy situation they were not convinced that the reason for the applicant's dismissal was redundancy. Here the evidence of the applicant's incapability seemed to suggest that redundancy was used as a pretext for dismissal. The tribunal were entitled to hold that they were not satisfied as to the employer's true reason for dismissal, which was unfair.

Suitable Alternative Employment

Under s.138 if before the employment terminates, the employer makes the employee an offer either to renew the contract of employment or re-engage the employee under a new contract which constitutes suitable alternative employment, then provided the new contract is to commence within four weeks of the previous one terminating, an unreasonable refusal to accept such an offer will mean that the employee will not be entitled to make a claim for a redundancy payment. Failure to take up an offer of a new contract on identical terms and conditions of employment therefore would normally constitute an unreasonable refusal to accept re-engagement and, as a consequence, an employer will lose the right to make a claim for payment. If the offer is of alternative employment, it is necessary to determine its suitability in relation to the previous employment. For the new employment to be 'suitable' it must be substantially similar to the previous job and not employment of an entirely different nature at the same salary. The question is one of fact and degree and one which the tribunal must examine in the light of the particular circumstances of the case including such matters as the nature of the work, the rates of pay, the place of work, the new status, and fringe benefits. Personal factors affecting the employee may also be considered such as social and family links, accommodation, and the children's education.

> In *Devonald v. J. D. Insulating Company Ltd.* 1972 the applicant was required to move from a factory in Bootle to another in Blackburn. He refused, and on his claim for redundancy the tribunal held that suitable alternative employment had been offered as he was already required under his present employment to do outside contract work.

Additional factors identified in *Thomas Wragg & Sons Ltd. v. Wood* 1976 included the fact that the offer of alternative employment was made late in the redundancy process when the employee had accepted alternative work and the fact that it was a declining industry.

In practice the question as to whether the alternative employment is suitable or not will be considered at the same time as the issue as to whether it is reasonable to refuse it or not.

In *Fuller v. Stephanie Bowman Ltd.* 1977 the applicant typist refused to move from Mayfair to a new office in Soho. She found the move distasteful, particularly as the new office was above a sex shop. The tribunal found that the refusal to move was unreasonable in the circumstances, as it was based on undue sensitivity and the claim for redundancy consequently failed. The headmaster in *Taylor v. Kent County Council* 1969 was not insensitive when he refused to accept work as a supply teacher, given his previous status.

Even if there is an offer of suitable alternative employment it may still be reasonable to refuse it.

In *Cambridge & District Co-operative Society Ltd. v. Ruse* 1993 the complainant and manager of a butcher's shop was transferred to manage a butchery department in a large store when his shop was closed down. Having less responsibility and in his mind status in his new position he gave notice and claimed a redundancy payment. The employer claimed that the transfer was within the terms of a mobility clause in his contract which provided 'you may be required to pursue your employment at any of the establishments comprising the food division'. The EAT agreed with the tribunal and held that there was no unreasonable refusal of an offer of suitable alternative employment. The tribunal was entitled to find that the employee's perceived loss of status in the job offered made it reasonable for him to refuse it, notwithstanding the tribunal's unanimous conclusion that the offer was of suitable alternative employment.

The decision of the EAT in *Gloucestershire County Council v. Spencer* 1985 supports the view that it is for management to set the appropriate standard of work to be achieved. Here the number of cleaners at a school had been reduced from five to four and the hours of work of the remaining employees cut by 45 minutes. The employer recognised that standards would drop, but maintained nevertheless, that the new terms constituted an offer of suitable alternative employment. This offer was rejected by the remaining cleaners on the grounds that they felt they could not continue to do a satisfactory job. The industrial tribunal agreed and found that while the alternative jobs were 'suitable' within the meaning of the section, the employees' refusal to accept the new terms was not unreasonable as they could not do the new jobs adequately in the time allotted. The EAT held that the tribunal was in error, for the standard of work set by the management, cannot be reasonably objected to by employees as a ground for refusing to work. Accordingly the offer of suitable alternative employment had been unreasonably rejected and the applicants were not entitled to redundancy payments.

If an employee accepts an offer of alternative employment on different terms and conditions, he is entitled to a trial period under s.138. The length of the period is four weeks, but if the new job requires retraining, the parties can specify a longer trial period in writing. If, for any reason, during the trial period the employee gives notice to terminate his employment, or the employer terminates for a reason connected with the change to the new job, then the employee is treated as dismissed from the date that the previous contract terminated. To determine his rights to a redundancy payment it is then necessary to examine the original reason for dismissal, whether the offer of alternative work was suitable, and whether the termination by the employer reasonable. In cases where the offer of new employment involves changes in employment terms, which would otherwise constitute a repudiatory breach, then under the common law, an employee who nevertheless accepts the new job for a period could still change his mind and resign claiming constructive dismissal. In such circumstances therefore, there is a common law trial period which on its expiration, can be extended further by the statutory trial period[13] under s.138.

Redundancy on a Business Transfer

To secure the right to a redundancy payment where an employee is dismissed on the transfer of a business undertaking the employee must establish that he is qualified to claim and that he is dismissed by reason of redundancy within the definition. For transfers of a commercial venture covered by the Transfer of Undertakings (Protection of Employment) Regulations 1981[14] an employee's contract is automatically preserved with the transferee employer so that rights in relation to redundancy are preserved with the new employer.

The effect of the Regulations is that where a relevant transfer is made the employee's contract continues with the new employer so that there is no dismissal and consequently no redundancy. Regulation 5(3) of the 1981 Regulations states that a transfer of liability to the transferee employer will only occur where the employee was employed in the undertaking *'immediately before the transfer'*. If an employee is dismissed because of the transfer then liability in relation to him is passed automatically to the new employer. If however an employee is dismissed because of an organisational economic or technical reason under Regulation 8(1) then liability will not pass unless he was still employed at the time of the transfer.

> In *Warner v. Adnet* 1998 a company accountant lost his job when his employer went into receivership and when the staff were re-employed by a new company on a business transfer he was not included. The Court of Appeal held that the dismissal was for a reason connected with the transfer of the undertaking but under Reg 8(1) it was not automatically unfair as it was for an economic reason falling within the ETO defence. Also the normal requirement to consult could be overlooked because it would not have made a difference.

Those employees who are subsequently dismissed by the transferee employer will have the right to a redundancy payment if the dismissal is by reason of redundancy.

Dismissal could even be constructive, as for instance where the transfer employer unilaterally attempts to impose radical changes in terms and conditions of employment on the employee. It is still open to the employer of course to make an offer of suitable alternative employment to the employees which, if unreasonable refused will prejudice his right to a payment.

If an employee is made an offer of alternative employment by the new employer which is suitable but unreasonably refused then under s.141 the employee may lose the right to a payment. Where alternative employment is offered either by the old employer or the new employer then the employee is entitled to have a trial period of four weeks (or longer if agreed) in the new job. The employee has then the option of either accepting the new employment, or terminating the contract in which case he will be regarded as having been dismissed on the date the previous contract came to an end for the reason which applied then. It may then be necessary, for the purpose of redundancy entitlement, to decide whether the new employment was in fact an offer of suitable alternative work.

---

13. Under s.138
14. Now also TUPE 2006

Redundancy Procedure

The Trade Union and Labour Relations (Consolidation) Act 1992 contains a number of rules relating to the procedure to be invoked in a redundancy situation where an independent trade union is recognised in relation to the class of employees involved. In *Commission of the European Communities v. United Kingdom of Great Britain and Northern Ireland* 1994, the European Court of Justice has ruled that by failing to ensure worker representation in the work place where there is no recognised trade union the UK has failed to comply with Community law obligations to ensure that workers representatives are informed and consulted on collective redundancies. It seems that the UK government will respond by providing for worker representation in future legislation. The primary duty imposed on the employer under s.188 is to consult with trade union representatives.

> Under s.188(1) where an employer is proposing to dismiss as redundant 20 or more employees at one establishment within a period of 90 days or less, the employer shall consult about the dismissals all the persons who are appropriate representatives of any of the employees who may be affected by the proposed dismissals.

In *Hardy v. Tourism South East* 2005 the EAT held that a proposal to redeploy 26 employees on the closure of a regional office amounted to a plan to dismiss 20 or more employees and fell within s.188. Despite the proposed redeployment of the majority of the staff the closure of the regional office meant that existing contracts of employment would be terminated. *Hogg v. Dover College* 1990[15] held that the offer of a new contract to replace the existing contract of employment did not prevent there being a dismissal. This meant that the consultation requirements for redundancy were triggered by the proposal.[16]

If the employer is proposing to dismiss 100 or more employees the consultation period is at least 90 days The employer must disclose the reasons for his proposals, the numbers and descriptions of employees whom it is proposed to dismiss, the proposed method of selecting the employees who may be dismissed, and the proposed method of calculating the amount of any redundancy payments to be made

> In *R v. British Coal Corporation and Secretary of State for Trade and Industry ex parte Price and others* 1994 the High Court gave some guidance as to the practicalities of consultation in a redundancy situation stating that:
>
> - a proper opportunity must be given to the union to understand fully the matters about which it is being consulted and to express views on those subjects;
> - the employer must consider those views properly and genuinely;
> - where possible the consultation should take place when the proposals are at a formative stage;
> - adequate information must be given and adequate time to respond.
>
> In *MSF v. GEC Ferranti (Defence Systems) Ltd. No2* 1994 the EAT considered the statutory requirements of an employer to provide information to a recognised trade union over proposed redundancies to enable meaningful consultations to

---

15. See Chapter 10
16. See later in the chapter

take place the tribunal stated that *'whether a union has been provided with information which is adequate to permit meaningful consultation to commence is a question of facts and circumstances. There is no rule that full and specific information under each of the heads listed in s.188(4) must be provided before the consultation period can begin'.* The issue in the case before the EAT was whether sufficient information had been given to the union about *'the number and descriptions of employees who it is proposed to dismiss as redundant'* to trigger the consultation period. The EAT held that here it was insufficient to merely give the total number of redundancies broken down into job categories and more precise details were necessary, in particular relating to the divisions of the company which would be affected by the redundancies.

The redundancy consultation procedures have been amended to bring the UK in line with the EU Collective Redundancies Directive 1998. Under the Directive the information to be given to union representatives when redundancies are proposed is expanded to include the proposed method of calculating payments. The consultation should consider how redundancy dismissals may be avoided and how the consequences of dismissal may be mitigated.

During the group consultation period employers must share information with representatives about the numbers and categories of employees who may be affected by the proposal. It should be a meaningful dialogue about ways of avoiding the dismissals, reducing the number of the dismissals and mitigating the consequences of the dismissal. Employers have always assumed that the notice could be given during the group consultation period counting back from the effective date of termination. It seems that this may have been an overly simplistic view of the requirement of the Directive.

The German case of *Junk v. Kuhnel* 2005 now confirms that allowing notice periods to run concurrently with the consultation exercise is contrary to the principles in the Collective Redundancies Directive 1998. The European Court of Justice ruled that redundancy means *'the declaration by an employer of its intention to terminate the contract of employment rather than the actual cessation of the employment relationship on the expiration of the period of notice'.* Also an employer cannot terminate contracts of employment before he has engaged in the two procedures, consultation and notice. This means that employers will have an obligation to start group consultation in good time with a view to reaching agreement and notifying the relevant public authority[17] of redundancies before the employer takes the decision to terminate any contracts and give notice of termination. Employers cannot therefore give notice before the end of the consultation period, and this will have ramifications in relation to redundancy costs.

Leicestershire County Council v. Unison 2005 is the first EAT case to consider the implications of *Junk v. Kühnel* 2005. The case related to a local authority job evaluation exercise which led to the decision to vary the terms of two groups of employees by dismissing and re-engaging them on new contracts. This was put to a committee of councillors and approved, following which a consultation notice was issued. The EAT agrees with the tribunal's analysis that the council was in breach of its consultation obligations. The EAT confirmed that *Junk* lays down the principle that the consultation process must begin before employees have been given notice of dismissal. Judge McMullen QC said that *'in order to give effect to the purpose of the Directive, which is the avoidance of dismissal for redundancy, consultation*

---

17. The Department of Trade and Industry

should begin before a decision is made as to the implementation of redundancy. By that, we mean prior to the giving of notice of redundancy and, of course, prior to the taking effect of such notice'. Effectively *'proposing to dismiss'*, is the trigger point for consultation under s.188(1). According to the EAT, that requires something less than a decision that dismissals are to be made and something more than a possibility that they might occur. In this case, there was a proposal to give notice of dismissal when the council's officers took a decision to recommend that employees adversely affected by the job evaluation should be given notice. The EAT upheld the tribunal's protective award for the maximum period of 90 days where there had been a total failure to comply with the statutory consultation requirements, even though there had been some consultation with the union before the council officials proposed to dismiss. *'We accept the submission that any 'consultation' prior to the making of the proposal to dismiss cannot be taken into account.'*

If an employer fails to comply with the consultation requirements then the trade union could seek a remedy by presenting a complaint to an employment tribunal. The tribunal can make a declaration as to non-compliance and also make a protective award requiring the employer to pay the specified employees their wages for the 'protected period',[18] specified not to exceed the consultation period to which they were entitled. An employer who fails to comply with a protective award can be required to do so on an individual complaint to a tribunal by an employee.

The duty to consult under s.188 is an obligation that must be complied with even where it is obvious that nothing can be achieved.

> In *Sovereign Distribution Services Ltd. v. Transport & General Workers Union* 1989 the EAT found that the industrial tribunal had rightly made a protective award against an employer who had failed to consult the recognised trade union over redundancies as required by the section. The purpose of the section is to ensure consultation takes place even where the employer thinks that to consult will achieve nothing. *'The statutory duty to consult in many cases provides the only opportunity for employees through their recognised trade unions, to be able to seek to influence the redundancy situation and to put forward other ideas and other considerations, not only as to the overall decision but also as to the individuals who should be made redundant and other material aspects.'*

> In *GMB v. Mann & Bus Ltd.* 2000 the EAT held that where employees are subject to what are regarded as technical dismissals where continuing employment is offered on revised terms this nevertheless falls within the definition of redundancy and the duty to consult arises.

> In *Rowell v. Hubbard Group Services Ltd.* 1995 it was held that consultation must amount to more than a warning of redundancy and be fair and genuine giving those consulted a proper opportunity to appreciate the consequences.

---

18. Which could be 90 days for each employee

Redundancy and Unfair Dismissal

In Chapter 11 we identified redundancy as one of the potentially fair reasons for dismissal.[19] To constitute a fair dismissal the decision to dismiss must satisfy the test of fairness in s.98(4).[20]

> Guidance in relation to the approach to be adopted by employment tribunals in determining the fairness of redundancy selections was provided by the EAT in *Williams v. Compair Maxim Ltd.* 1982. Here the claimants had been dismissed for redundancy, the employer having failed to consult with the recognised trade union. Selection had been left to departmental managers, one of whom gave evidence that he had retained those employees whom he considered would be best to retain in the interests of the company in the long run. Length of service was not a factor taken into account. The employment tribunal's finding of fair dismissal was reversed by the EAT which held the decision to be perverse. Measuring the conduct of the employer in question with that of a reasonable employer, a tribunal taken to be aware of good industrial practice, could not have reached the decision that the dismissals were fair. The employer's decision to dismiss was not within the range of conduct which a reasonable employer could have adopted in these circumstances.[21] While accepting that it was impossible to lay down detailed procedures for a selection process, the EAT felt that reasonable employers would attempt to act in accordance with five basic principles and should depart from them only with good reason.
>
> - As much warning as possible should be given of impending redundancies to enable the union and employees to inform themselves of the facts, seek alternative solutions and find alternative employment.
>
> - The employer will consult with the union as to the best means of achieving the objective as fairly and with as little hardship as possible. Criteria should be agreed to be applied in selection and the selection monitored.
>
> - The criteria agreed should not depend upon subjective opinion of the person selecting but it must be capable of objective scrutiny and include such matters as attendance record, job efficiency, experience or length of service.
>
> - The employer must seek to ensure that the selection is made fairly in accordance with these criteria and consider union representations.
>
> - The employer should examine the possibility of finding suitable alternative employment.
>
> In *Grundy (Teddington) Ltd. v. Plummer* 1983 the EAT held that in deciding to dismiss two managers for redundancy without any warning, adherence to agreed selection criteria, consultation, or seeking alternative employment prospects, the employer had failed to comply with the Compair Maxim[22] principles of good industrial practice and consequently the decisions were unfair. The argument that the EAT in Compair Maxim should not have laid down 'guidelines' as to

---

19. S. 98(2)c
20. See Chapter 11
21. See later the test of fairness
22. See above

what would constitute reasonable conduct was rejected. Equally however, a failure to comply with one of the five principles would not necessarily make a decision to dismiss unfair, for they are dealing with what a reasonable employer would seek to do if circumstances permit.

It is not good industrial practice for an employer to abrogate his decision making in relation to redundancy selection.

> In *Boulton & Paul Ltd. v. Arnold* 1994 the complaint of unfair dismissal arose from the selection of the complainant for dismissal by reason of redundancy. The selection was made by applying a number of criteria one of which was attendance and the complaint of unfairness arose from the fact that in the complainant's case no distinction had been made between authorised and unauthorised absences. When the complainant appealed against her selection for redundancy the employer offered to retain her but on terms that another employee would be dismissed in her place. The complainant rejected the offer and presented a complaint of unfair dismissal. On appeal the EAT upheld the tribunal's finding of unfair dismissal *'An offer to retain an employee under notice at the expense of another employee cannot be held to prevent a finding of unfair dismissal on the basis that the employee has had the opportunity of staying employed. It is unfair to put the onus on an employee to decide whether she or another employee is to be selected for dismissal. That is effectively an abrogation of the employer's responsibility to manage the business.'*

If unfairness in the selection process is alleged then it may be necessary to obtain evidence as to how the selection criteria was applied in other cases to enable comparisons to be drawn. In *FDR v. Holloway* 1995 the claimant alleged that the selection criteria for redundancy had not been applied fairly in his case. He was one of a pool of eight employees who was selected for dismissal by reason of redundancy after applying the selection criteria. Both the tribunal and the EAT agreed that to assist his claim it was right to order discovery of documents and particulars relating to all eight employees so that comparisons could be drawn, and a determination made as to whether the criteria were applied fairly and reasonably in his case.

Certainly the need for consultation in a redundancy situation is one of the fundamentals of fairness and it is only in exceptional cases that a failure to consult can be overlooked.

> So said the EAT in *Holden v. Bradville* 1985. Here the employer had argued that both the need for secrecy in a company take-over and the practical difficulties involved in interviewing and consulting up to thirty three employees selected for redundancy meant that the employer could ignore the need for consultation prior to dismissal. This argument was rejected by the EAT who held that in a redundancy situation you should presume that consultation is a prerequisite to fair selection but it was up to an industrial tribunal to decide whether in the particular circumstances of the case before it, even without consultation, the selection is nevertheless fair. This case was not one where consultation was impracticable and nor was there evidence to support the view that consultation would have made no difference to the result. *'There was at least a chance that an employee could have pointed to her good performance record, her experience and her age and seniority as factors in favour of her retention, with sufficient eloquence and force to persuade the management to take her name off the redundancy list and replace it with that of one of her colleagues.'*

In *Lloyd v. Taylor Woodrow Construction Ltd.* 1999 the EAT held that a defect in the consultation process in a redundancy situation could be corrected at later appeal hearings and as a consequence the decision to dismiss in this case by reason of redundancy was a fair one.

The Court of Session in *King v. Eaton Ltd.* 1996 set out the law in relation to redundancy consultation, both with a recognised trade union and the individual employee selected. Previously the EAT had held that despite the fact that the employer had failed to carry out individual consultation, the fact that there had been extensive consultation with the unions made the decision to dismiss fair. The Court of Session disagreed and felt that the facts revealed no extensive consultation with the trade unions. Any meetings held with the unions were after the employer's proposals had been formulated and insufficient time was given to consider and respond to them. The criterion for fair and proper consultation set out by Lord Justice Glidewell in *R. v. British Coal Corporation ex parte Price* 1994 was approved. '*Fair consultation means:*

- *consultation when the proposals are still at a formative stage;*
- *adequate information on which to respond;*
- *adequate time in which to respond;*
- *conscientious consideration by an authority of a response to consultation.*

Another way of putting the point more shortly is that fair consultation involves giving the body consulted a fair and proper opportunity to understand fully the matters about which it is being consulted, and to express its views on those subjects, with the consulter thereafter considering those views properly and genuinely.'

If there is no consultation between a trade union or relevant employees unless it would be futile consequential dismissals will normally be unfair. The EAT in *Mugford v. Midland Bank Ltd.* 1997 provided further guidance. The EAT stated that '*whether a reasonable employer would or would not consult with an individual employee is essentially a question of fact for the industrial jury directly itself. Individual consultation with the employee before the final decision identifying him as redundant is not a prerequisite for a fair dismissal. On the other hand the obligation to consult is not necessarily discharged if the employer consults with the union where one is recognised. Having regard to the authorities the position is as follows:*

1. *where no consultation about redundancy has taken place... the dismissal will normally be unfair unless... consultation would be futile;*

2. *consultation with the trade union over selection criteria does not of itself release the employer from considering with the employee individually him being identified for redundancy;*

3. *it will be a question whether consultation with the individual and/or his union was so inadequate as to render the dismissal unfair'.*

Quite often employees are selected for redundancy on the basis of a points system based on criteria discussed with their union. In *John Brown Engineering Ltd. v. Brown* 1997 the employer argued that once a fair process for selection has been agreed upon with the union and put into practice without objection then there was no need to consult with individual employees or their representatives about the actual marks scored. Both the tribunal and EAT held that it was an unfair selection for redundancy on the basis of a point system in circumstances which individual employees had not been told of their own marks. '*Obviously individual consultation is the easiest way to assert even-handedness on the part of the employer, but we would not wish to suggest that is necessarily required in every case. On the other hand, a policy decision to withhold all markings in a particular selection process may result in individual unfairness if no opportunity is thereafter given to the individual to know how he has been assessed. We recognise it may be invidious to publish the whole identified 'league tables', but in choosing not to do so the employer must run the risk that he is not acting fairly in respect of individual employees. It also has to be reasserted that it is no part of the industrial tribunal's role, in the context of redundancy, to examine the marking process as a matter of criteria under a microscope; nor to determine whether, intrinsically, it was properly operated. At the end of the day, the only issue is whether or not the employers treated their employees in a fair and even-handed manner.'*

Finally, mention should also be made of the fact that an employee with two years' service who is given notice of dismissal by reason of redundancy has the right, under s.52, during the notice period, to be given reasonable time off during working hours, to look for new employment or make arrangements for future training. The employee is also entitled to be paid at the appropriate rate during the period of absence and can present a claim to a tribunal if his rights are denied.

Redundancy Calculation

If an employee believes that as a qualifying worker he has been dismissed by reason of redundancy, the onus is upon him to make a claim to his employer for a redundancy payment. If the employer denies the claim or simply refuses to make a payment, the remedy of the employee is by way of complaint to an industrial tribunal. If a redundancy payment is made (otherwise than in compliance with an order of the tribunal specifying the amount), then an employer is guilty of an offence if he fails without reasonable excuse to give the employee a written statement indicating how the payment was calculated. The sum is calculated in the same way as a basic award by reference to the age of the claimant, the length of continuous employment and the weekly pay of the claimant.

Amount of the payment

Age (inclusive)	Amount of week's pay for each year of employment
18 – 21	½
22 – 40	1
41 – 65	1½

Another feature of the calculation is the fact that each year the maximum week's pay is adjusted to reflect the current average wage which is £290.[23] Consequently the maximum redundancy payment is 20 years x 1½ (for employment between the ages of 41-65) x £290 = £8,700. For employees on a weekly fixed rate then the contractual rate is the current average wage. In cases where the wage does vary, however, a week's pay is calculated by reference to the average hourly rate of remuneration over the last twelve weeks of employment.

---

23. From February 2006

In a complex decision relating to the calculation of an average week's wage for the purpose of redundancy entitlement, the House of Lords held in *British Coal Corporation v. Cheesebrough* 1990 that in calculating an employee's average rate of remuneration, work in overtime hours must be treated as if they had been done in normal working hours and the remuneration reduced accordingly. Where however an employee's contract provides for bonus payment only for work done during normal working hours, the overtime hours worked should not be treated as if they would attract bonus payments.

While the payment is made by the employer, originally he was entitled to claim a rebate from the Redundancy Fund financed by weekly levies from employers. Under the Employment Act *1988* the Redundancy Fund was abolished.

Further Reading

Hall and Edwards *Reforming Statutory Redundancy Consultation Procedures* (1999) 28ILJ 299.

Index